THE MA[illegible]
DE SADE

A biography and a note of hope

by ROBERT DEL QUIARO

MESSIDOR BOOKS

Messidor Books, P O Box 3625,
London SW12 8TW, England

THE MARQUIS DE SADE
A biography and a note of hope

First published 1994

ISBN: 0 9522614 0 5

Printed and bound in Great Britain by
The Bath Press, Lower Bristol Road, Bath BA2 3BL, England

Set in 12pt times new roman with helvetica headings and footnotes

In memory of

Francisca Yanomami

CONTENTS

pages

Preface i

SECTION A

Chapters

1:	Old name, wrong names	1
2:	Dangerous notions	6
3:	Hard school	12
4:	"Very quick to catch fire"	14
5:	Married, without reassurance	22
6:	"That light head of his"	32
7:	"The least unfavourably as possible"	53
8:	Actor-manager-director-callboy	71
9:	"Wandering and vagabond life"	93
10:	"These items of physical furniture"	103
11:	"Our champion locked up in Paris"	124
12:	Born and raised to follow	131
13:	A beautiful day cut short	135

SECTION B

14:	Figments and flasks	154
15:	"Not done all that I have thought of"	174
16:	The high priestess and the worst enemy	177
17:	"Take that! Take that! Take that!"	193
18:	Badinage and bitterness	204
19:	An errand-wife under suspicion	219
20:	"My way of thinking"	242

21: The Bastille and continued *pressurage* 255
22: "Head-fled-to-hell" 263
23: Rescue, separation and rejection 281
24: "The need to spread myself about" 303
25: Staying close to horrors 322
26: Rhetoric and Robespierre 326
27: Prices, publishing and Provence 362
28: Last arrest and Charenton 380
29: Reduction and demise 397

SECTION C

30: The picnic of free play 417
31: Enlightened in parts 425
32: He *impinges*, therefore he is 434
33: The only safe libertine 451
34: "No passing judgement on me" 454
35: Always on a tether and always on a precipice 462
36: Great structures against the tides 499
37: Jack and José 505
38: A blue flame, burning low 507
39: "Everything scares me" 518
40: "I'll read a little, my dear - don't wait up" 523
41: Like steadfast children 526

Bibliography 533

Main index 536

Index of works by the Marquis de Sade 546

An appeal 549

PREFACE

Millions of people are aware of the name of the Marquis of Sade because it has passed into modern languages as a label for an ill-understood urge to hurt for pleasure. We know the terms *sadism* and *sadistic*. Most of us know little more about him.

I came across references to his works when reading about the Enlightenment, the upheaval in thinking in the 18th century.

Since then, I have travelled and worked in Latin America and Africa. Beyond the equator, the Portuguese say, nothing is forbidden. In other words, down there, away from the restraints of home where your shame would be made plain to you, you can get away with murder, rape, pillage, insult ... You get away with it because you have more power, which is yours because you have more money and education. At work, down there, are not only the relations between rich and poor economies, rich and poor classes, but also the relations between rich men and poor women.

Wherever you go - not just in the tropics - there are women who, not having money or education, cannot avoid being treated as servants or as prey, or as both. Wherever the options for women are few, there are many pairs of eyes with a trapped look, and when you're trapped you're too eager to grab at a way out of hard times. Seeing a likely man's interest, those eyes shine too readily, the child's wish to please having become a desperate need to please. In the poorest societies, hard times can be the hardest - starvation.

It was clear, down there, that the pursuit of life and happiness in liberty, a great ideal of the Enlightenment, has a long way to go. The whole world is supposed to be an Enlightened place now but, looking at the way men still treat women, one doubts it. The urge to dominate, to have, women remains strong and dangerous. Why?

Back to Sade. He is supposed to have been dangerous to women, and he wrote copiously. So let's look at what he wrote, and at how he lived. We might find insights; from those, we might learn better how to pursue happiness in liberty, for women and men, safely and in co-operation, and without loss of excitement.

It turns out that Sade - callous rake and writer of violent sexual fantasies - also knew how to write in the liberal, inquiring spirit of the best of his time. The conflict between the generous man who would respect and liberate all humanity, and the wilful exploiter who would take, use and even destroy any woman - any person, indeed - for his pleasure, that conflict was to be found within the man himself.

In this book, you have a biography of Sade and an attempt to analyse something of what his life and works mean for us now. That conflict is with us still, within men and all about us. We need to resolve it in favour of the better inclination.

*

The book is in three sections, the first two making up the biography, the third has the analysis. I have tried to avoid including more than what I see as a necessary minimum of direct quotation from the bloody mayhem whipped up in Sade's fiction. I wanted to make my points without causing the reader to retch and so that the reader might arrive at the end of my text with an understanding of the original Sadeian works, while still with the option of avoiding their many stretches of revolting description and their great overall length.

This was not a matter of censorship; rather, my concern was to get at the motivation behind these writings and to disarm their power to dismay - and their power to fascinate - by showing the fear in the mind that created them. I hope the reader will become both better informed about Sade and better poised against his badness - and against the like badness in others.

*

Details of the works referred to in the text via their authors' names are given in the bibliography towards the end of the book. I apologise for any lack felt because of the absence of full notes on sources, but money - and therefore space - was very limited in the production of this book. Anyone who wants help in tracing sources of documents may get in touch with me through the publisher, Messidor Books.

Some might wish for more historical context in the biography, but I had to keep Sade centre-stage through much of the action and could not expand the text any further. There are many other books about the period in which Sade lived - the *ancien régime* in France, the French Revolution, the rule of Napoléon and the Restoration - that may be consulted.

There is the matter of titles. With Sade himself, there is no problem for his title of marquis can be spelled the same way in English, and whether you hear the French pronunciation (*mar-kee*) or the English (*mar-kwiss*) in your mind's ear is up to you. However, his wife was, of course, the Marquise de Sade and the English equivalent to the French title of marquise (*mar-keez*) is marchioness. I decided to call her the Marquise de Sade. Also, there is the problem of her mother, whose title in French was Présidente de Montreuil, she having been the wife of a judge, the Président de Montreuil, who presided over high court proceedings. I have followed the usual practice in works on Sade by calling her Madame de Montreuil, reckoning that no English-speaking reader would have any trouble with *Madame*, albeit it means Lady or Milady here, rather than Mrs. I was concerned that two of the three main actors in the story - the Marquise de Sade and her mother - should not seem at all un-French by intrusion of the English - and awkward - word marchioness or by some contrived and distracting English equivalent (not that I could think of one) for *présidente*.

Even so, I have translated every *comte*, *comtesse*, *duc*, *chevalier* and so forth as count, countess, duke, knight... This is inconsistent, but I would not want any reader to be slowed by having to puzzle over such titles which, in the context, serve to do little more than indicate that the persons referred to were noble and apt to be able to live high on the hog - before the Revolution at any rate.

As for the French titles of Monsieur, Madame and Mademoiselle - given respectively to a married gentleman, a married lady and an unmarried lady - I have used where appropriate the usual abbreviations - M, Mme and Mlle. However, I have not bothered with full points after any of these to indicate abbreviation, except where quoting a document in which points were used.

There is the matter of money. I have been as sparing as I could with references to the currencies of France before and after the Revolution, but it might help the reader to note that 24 livres were equivalent to one gold louis (*louis d'or*), a gold coin, and that the livre was superseded by the franc during Sade's time. I hope the text makes clear, where necessary and as far as can be figured out, the financial states of various people at various stages of the story, of Sade especially.

In translating from French texts, I have altered punctuation in a few places, where I thought this necessary in my English versions. I have not tried to provide equivalents of the erratic spelling of some correspondents cited - the Marquise de Sade, for one, would have needed this attention. (We are working on an era when few people in France, or anywhere else, were in full command of their language on paper.) I think such contrivance would have been more distracting than helpful. Otherwise, I have tried to stay as close as may be to the style of the originals, no matter how shaky Sade's grip on coherence here and there. In general, his French was flawless and vigorous.

*

My thanks go to Delma, Andrea, Márcia, Janaine (*muito obrigado, moças*), Eduardo Leão (*muito obrigado, senhor*), Joan Rilje (*merci beaucoup, bergère*), Greg Chamberlain and Laurie Lesser, Pauline Ridel (*merci bien*), and Peck Choo.

The right name of the dedicatee has eluded me, which is as it should be. She was one of the Yanomami people, dwelling in what is regarded as northern Brazil, and was known only to white people as Francisca. The Yanomami keep close their names given at birth, and decline to utter those of their dead lest this expose the speaker to malign magic. The dead are meant to take their bodies and all their other belongings with them through cremation. A name cannot be burned but its place in the beyond should be acknowledged by the living taking care not to speak it. She died on 2 January 1984, aged about 12 years, shot by a man, an outsider, who was working for an organisation meant to help her people. He had demanded sexual relations of her and she had just refused. May her spirit be exalted.

Responsibility for the book is mine.

R del Q - January 1994

SECTION A

CHAPTER 1: OLD NAME, WRONG NAMES

The name of de Sade had been famous long before it became notorious. The instrument of its entry to the languages of the modern world, as the root of *sadism* and *sadistic*, was born in a palace at the centre of European civilisation, on 2 June 1740. He was the only son of an eldest son, in line to inherit land and titles.

He met the first of his many troubles on his second day of life, when he returned from the font christened Donatien Alphonse François. His mother's instructions to the servants who, as representatives of his absent godparents, had taken him to baptism, were misconstrued. She had wanted him named Louis Aldonse Donatien, but the first of those was dropped, the second changed from a form familiar in his father's native Provence to the northern French spelling known in Paris where the birth took place, and the third name placed first. François seems to have arisen from a misunderstanding between the proxies and the priest at the christening. The child and the man became known to family and acquaintances as Louis, and he signed documents as such. The mistake over the Holy Water acquired great significance a half-century later as his income, liberty and life came into hazard through administrative confusion over the full and correct name of the Marquis de Sade.

By any name, he was, in 1740, the latest addition to a noble family which could trace its ancestry back to the 13th century. Earlier documents indicate the existence of de Sades in important positions even before the advent in the mid-13th century of Raimond de Sade, from whom genealogists have established an unbroken succession to the marquis who most concerns us and to scions of the family alive now in the France of the Fifth Republic.

Mediaeval ancestors of the Marquis de Sade had acquired wealth and powerful connections. Paul de Sade, a grandson of Raimond, was one of four officials of the city of Avignon who welcomed a new pope,

John XXII, in October 1316, when he landed from a boat on which he had sailed down the river Rhône from Lyons. Avignon was then a hub of Christendom, being the seat of popes for a century while they were staying away from the city of Rome. It was also papal territory, like the pontiff's states in what was then a fragmented Italy, and so outside the jurisdiction of French kings. Governors and other officials of Avignon, of whom the de Sade family supplied many in the late Middle Ages, were men of influence in what was in effect a small city-state.

The de Sade family's connections with the highest in the Catholic Church were extended by many appointments of members to positions in the hierarchy. It was usual to produce large numbers of children and those born to noble families had a better chance of reaching adulthood. Only the eldest son could inherit the title due to the head of the family - and he tended to be avid for the other secular posts and perquisites that the house might claim - so younger sons would be found benefices as bishops, abbots, deans, papal chaplains and such. Daughters - those not acquired by husbands - often became abbesses, mothers superior, nuns.

Politics and its extension, military campaigns, were also open to the tiny minority of men who were both noble and literate. Various de Sades, from their base in Provence with access southwards to the Mediterranean Sea and northwards to the French royal court in Paris, emerged as counsellors and commanders for popes, kings of Aragon (in north-eastern Spain) and kings of France. Early in the 15th century, a de Sade was made the first president (chief justice) of the new high court at Aix (the administrative capital of France's region Provence), the tribunal which tried his descendant, our marquis, three centuries later.

Such multiplication of influence and advantage does not grow from poverty. A document of 1346 shows a Hugues de Sade in possession of a fortune, with rights to revenue as a manorial lord in Avignon and to tolls levied on traffic passing along the Rhône, a main artery for trade between the Mediterranean and a swathe of territory that had commerce on the rivers of eastern France. This sort of access to income from rents (in cash and as shares of tenants' crops and profits), tolls and taxes was granted by popes, kings and other sovereign rulers to noble liegemen in return for services rendered.

By the 16th century, the family was thriving through various branches, deriving income from various Provençal properties. When the branch of Saumane manor, which had begun in the second half of the 14th century, died out with the demise of a childless lord in the 1530s, this property joined Mazan manor in the hands of a Joachim de Sade. The de Sade patrimony, much of it passing from eldest son to eldest son, was further expanded in 1627 by a marriage to a Diane de Simiane, which brought in more real estate, this being just one of a string of acquisitive nuptial alliances. In the latter part of the 17th century, Gaspard François de Sade was the first of the family to bear the title of marquis, on the way to a colonelcy in the papal forces and the post of Provost of Avignon. By the time he died, in November 1739, he had five sons and five daughters. The eldest son, Jean Baptiste François, born at Avignon in 1702, was the father of the child whose life occupies this book.

This sustained history of wealth amassed and influence exercised also signifies a steady proliferation of links - though marriage and other enterprises - with other noble families of Provence, other parts of France, northern Italy and Aragon, as with thousands of farmers, traders, artisans, shippers, clergy, doctors, lawyers - all of society. The de Sades must have been as well known in that part of Europe, especially in Avignon, as any family. So any notable doings by a de Sade would spread far and wide, carried by a network of interest in the family, itself woven by the interests of the family over the centuries.

When Jean Baptiste François, known later as the Count de Sade, married on 13 November 1733, he spread that network into rare territory for the de Sades, by taking as wife Marie Eléonore de Maillé de Carman, who had been born in 1712 into a family linked to a junior branch of the royal house of Bourbon, which ruled France. All previous brides brought into the de Sade family seem to have been southerners, women of the home ground of Provence and nearby regions, valuable for their connections and properties but without strong links to the brightest lights of the richest court in Europe. The new wife, however, was a cousin to the Condé family, in whose veins royal Bourbon blood flowed, and the young woman had been placed as lady-in-waiting to the Princess Caroline de Condé, a fellow noblewoman to help the queen bee of the Condé court within a court to while away the time with conversation, perhaps confidences, and to be well placed to spot a potential husband.

In this last regard, Marie Eléonore seemed to have done, from a Bourbon viewpoint, no more than moderately for, at the time of her marriage, celebrated in the chapel of the Condé mansion in Paris, the

Count de Sade was a mere lord of a few Provençal manors and the son of a father who was not rich by Condé standards.

That father, Gaspard François, paid 135,000 livres - which was some five or six times his annual income from his estates - just before his death in 1739, to buy for his eldest son the ceremonial office of the lieutenancy-general[1] of the provinces of Bresse, Bugey, Valromey and Gex - all in or near Burgundy in eastern France. The de Sades had a connection with the provinces through the Countess de Sade and the Condé family's sway in Burgundy. The office was worth 10,000 livres a year to the holder in return for little more than a few formal appearances once in a while. Such buying and selling of sinecures - and of public appointments which entailed a job of work - was common in the France of King Louis XV as the royal administration strove to raise revenue and office-holders sought to realise cash from their prestige-laden titles.

Marie Eléonore gave birth in 1737 to her first child, a daughter named Caroline Laure, who lived only two years. (A second daughter, Marie Françoise, was born in 1746 but seems to have lived no more than a fortnight.)

After his son was born in the summer of 1740, the Count de Sade was sent, in the following March, as an ambassador of France to Cologne, at the court of the Elector of Bavaria, one of the most important of the dozens of rulers of the various states then making up what is now Germany. His superiors in the French diplomatic service seem to have formed a low opinion of the count as an envoy to a power with which the government in Paris was trying to improve links. D'Argenson, foreign minister from 1744, reported in his memoirs that, in 1739, the count had revealed infidelities of the Princess de Condé, to whom his wife was lady-in-waiting, to the prince, her husband. This was done, the minister wrote, in order for the count to get himself back into the prince's good books after some estrangement. Having put that piece of gossip against the count's name, the minister summed him up as "a fop, with some intelligence, but little backbone", adding that the elector had complained that the count was too beholden to other interests whose money he had accepted. The count gave up his post.

---

1 This might read oddly in English translation but the de Sades had acquired a title roughly equivalent to the ancient English title of lord-lieutenant of a county, not an army rank.

When, in 1745, the French foreign ministry tried to send the count back to Cologne as a diplomat, the elector refused to accept his appointment "for strong personal reasons," the elector told the king of France. The same year, the count was captured, while travelling in Germany, by Austrian troops, France then being at war with Austria. He was held for some eight months at Antwerp, then under Austrian control, while the elector declined to lift a finger to have him released and the French government did not trouble itself much about him.

"That's what we expose ourselves to when bringing into our affairs people who haven't the first notion, and who aren't capable of the application needed to learn," d'Argenson shrugged.

For all the murky accusations from the Elector of Bavaria, it is worth noting that a foreign ministry briefing in 1747, to a successor envoy about to leave for Cologne, pointed out that the elector was very keen on gaming but "doesn't like to lose, so there's danger in playing with him and winning. This is what most contributed to the chill and the falling-out which the Count de Sade experienced - a falling-out which went too far and which came close to breaking our relations with the elector completely."

The Countess de Sade seems to have accompanied her husband on his diplomatic missions, and so was not then in Paris to look after her son at the Condé palace. When she was on hand, it may well be that she had to give a good deal of her time to the eldest son of the Prince and Princess de Condé. The more attention the countess had to devote to the young Condé, the less she would have had for her own son.

CHAPTER 2: DANGEROUS NOTIONS

Old money and influential connections require care and attention if they are not to dwindle. Anyone who seeks early evidence of the marquis as negligent of what the world saw as his own best interests cannot ignore a piece of testimony - so it appears - from his own pen. In his novel *Aline and Valcour*, written in prison in the 1780s, de Sade has a character tell how he was brought up with a young noble of higher rank, the character's family having done all it could to foster a relationship between the two boys so that, later in life, the social superior would promote the career of the inferior, his boyhood playmate. This, the character goes on, went awry one day when he flew into a rage at the higher-born boy's obstinacy over some dispute during a game. The character - de Sade having him recall the incident in the first person - then struck his companion repeatedly, keeping up a frenzied hail of blows until he was pulled away.

It could be said that, de Sade having been four years younger than Louis Joseph, Prince de Condé (born in August 1736), this passage from *Aline and Valcour* may represent no more than what de Sade wished he had done to defy the young cock of the walk at the Condé palace in the early 1740s, rather than what indeed took place one day in that rambling pile. However, bearing in mind de Sade's propensity for rage when thwarted, demonstrated through much of his adult life, his rapt fury could well have been enough to offset any difference in physical development between the two boys.

There is no more than the fictional indication that such an assault took place. It is scarcely an incident that the house of Condé would want to record or recall, for its princeling seems not to have acquitted himself well, and his termagant playmate became a reviled libertine while Condé himself grew into a loyal stalwart of the French royal family before, during and after the Revolution and the Napoleonic era. However, the account fits what we know of de Sade's hair-trigger temper and points to his disdain, in later life, for the winning and mollification of friends in order to gain influence. Again from his own hand - though this time in a somewhat ill-organised letter of 1760 to his father, while serving in the French army in Germany - he reported himself little involved with the social life of the officer corps:

"I make visits sometimes but only to M de Poyanne[1] or to my former comrades in the Carabineers or in the King's Regiment. I do not stand on ceremony with them; I cannot abide it. If it were not for M de Poyanne, I would not set foot in general headquarters throughout the campaign. I know very well I'm not advancing myself this way. To be successful one has to pay court, but I don't like doing it. It upsets me when I hear someone trying to flatter by saying a lot of things he often does not believe. Anyone who plays such a foolish part has more determination than I ..."

"... To be polite, honest, dignified without being haughty, kind without being vapid; to assert oneself fairly often as long as that harms neither oneself nor anyone else; to live well, to amuse oneself without ruining oneself or losing one's self-control... [I have] few friends, none perhaps for there's not one who's sincere and who hasn't betrayed you twenty thousand times if he has seen the slightest advantage for himself in doing so... [I'm seeking that] evenness of temperament which lets you live on good terms with everyone, without however opening yourself to anyone for no sooner have you done so than you have cause to regret it; to speak very well of, to sing the loudest praises of people who, often without any motive, have said many bad things about you without your suspecting it (for almost always those who have the most attractive surface and who seem to be keenest to seek your friendship, they're the ones who deceive you the most). Those are my virtues; and those are the ones I aspire to ...

"... If I could claim to have a friend, I think I have one in the regiment; though I'm still not quite sure. His name is M---, son of M de ---, and is even, I think, a distant relative of mine through the Simianes we belong to. He's a lad of much worth, very amiable, composes very pretty verses, writes very well, concentrating his efforts in a professional way. I am truly his friend; I have reason to believe that he is mine. As for the rest, what's one to believe? With friends it's like with women: putting them to the test often reveals that the goods are faulty ..."

At some other time, de Sade added in the margin just here: "As I found later with him."

For further clues to the source of the marquis's quick temper and his prideful reluctance to appear amiable for a purpose, one may return to

---

1 Commander of one of the first regiments in which the marquis had served.

Aline and Valcour, a few lines before the account of the assault by the boy on his putative patron. The same character recounts how he was:

" ... linked through my mother to the highest in the kingdom, and through my father to the most distinguished in Languedoc[2], born in Paris in the lap of luxury and plenty. No sooner was I able to think than I made up my mind that nature and luck had combined to shower their gifts upon me. I believed so because people were foolish enough to tell me so, and this stupid presumption made me haughty, domineering and quick-tempered. I believed that everything should give way to me, that the whole universe should accede to my whims and that, as soon as I wanted something, I should be able to have it... How dangerous were the notions which, with complete irresponsibility, people let me fix in my character."

This also, though reaching us via a fictional character, rings true of the marquis, not least in the attempt to evade blame for shortcomings and place it on others. Those others seem to have consisted, in the marquis's hindsight of 30 years later, not only of members of the Condé household during his earliest years, but also of members of the de Sade family who presided over the next stage of his upbringing.

In August 1744, the boy, just four years old, was the recipient of the compliments of the municipality of Saumane, site of one of the Count de Sade's estates, "on the occasion of his happy arrival at Avignon." Officials had journeyed to the papal city to deliver their respects and to wish the child "long life and good fortune as the titular successor of his father." It is not certain that this marks the removal of the young marquis from Paris to Provence, for he might have been only visiting. However, another passage in *Aline and Valcour*, immediately after the description of the child's assault, tells:

"It was about that time my father undertook diplomatic business and my mother travelled to be with him... I was sent to the home of a grandmother of mine in Languedoc and her blind fondness towards me worsened all the shortcomings I have just confessed." His paternal grandmother was Louise Aldonse, *née* d'Astouaud, daughter of a Marquis de Murs, who had married our marquis's grandfather in 1699, borne ten children and been widowed six months before the young arrival from Paris was born.

---

2 Southern France.

Whether or not the greetings of the delegation from Saumane hailed a young lord moved south for good, whether or not he was sent away from Paris because of ructions between him and the junior Condé or because both his parents had decided to spend time abroad, it seems certain that, by the end of 1744, the marquis was established in or near Avignon.

There appears no justification to make out that the child's new life in the family's 15th century mansion at Avignon would have appeared a poor substitute for life in the palatial Condé establishment in Paris. For one thing, there is no hard evidence that the marquis spent much time in the mansion (although he was there from time to time at least). Besides, by moving to Provence, he entered an extensive network of relatives and retainers. He may well have spent periods at various de Sade homes - he had no fewer than five paternal aunts, all in the prime of life and apt to be much interested to see, for the first time perhaps, the heir apparent. Also, when he went south, the boy was no longer in the shadow of the young Condé, his elder and social superior at the Parisian ménage, where the princeling may have enjoyed claims on the attention of the Countess de Sade and her household, ahead of those of her own son. As for physical accommodation, the sheer size of the Hôtel de Condé, sprawling across a vast site in Paris by what is now the Odéon, is no guarantee of its comfort. The boy could well have preferred various homes in the south, with the warmer climate and bluer skies, as well as his new status as the apple of many eyes. After the move south, though, his contact with his parents further diminished.

Whatever affection by his father's relatives touched the young marquis in Provence, it is clear that the main new influence on his development was his uncle, known as the Abbé (Abbot) de Sade. He was Jacques François Paul Aldonse, born in 1705 and the third son of Gaspard François and Louise Aldonse. His older brothers, our Count de Sade and Richard Jean Louis, having survived into adulthood and taken up secular careers, this younger son of a family with old connections to the papacy was an obvious candidate for holy orders.

He capitalised on the family's good lines to the Vatican and to the papal authorities in Avignon, and secured the position - starting several rungs up the ecclesiastical ladder - of Vicar-General of Toulouse, another main city of southern France. His acquaintance, Voltaire, one of the greatest writers of the century, noted the transparent calculation behind this advance and wrote, in 1733, to the prospective cleric: "I hear that you are to be a priest and a vicar-general. What a great deal of holiness all of a sudden in one family! So this is why you tell me you are going to give up making love." In the same letter is a light poem to the effect that the young man would never turn his back on love and, even if he were to become pope, he would continue to take his pleasures - "that is your real ministry". Indeed, the young nobleman had taken the cloth by way of securing a lucrative career which would not greatly intrude on his literary and amorous diversions. By the time his young nephew, the marquis, reached his care in 1744, the Abbé had been Vicar-General of Narbonne, had acquired a regular pension from the Archbishop of Arles and become abbot of the Cistercian monastery at Ebreuil. He spent most of his time at the monastery, and at the château of Saumane, the latter being part of the de Sade family patrimony.

At Saumane, away from the monks for whom he was meant to be administrator and example, the Abbé maintained a succession of mistresses, sometimes more than one at a time. This was the case during the marquis's period there and he probably had some understanding that his uncle was nonchalantly breaking the priestly vow of chastity. So the marquis was exposed, at an impressionable age, to the practice of concubinage, whereby a woman maintains her status and earns her keep only as long as she is worthy of her sexual hire.

Also, apart from the elements of formal education offered him, the boy at Saumane almost certainly received from his uncle his first acquaintance with the figure who was by far the most famed member of the de Sade family until our marquis had grown to maturity and provoked notoriety. This was Laure de Noves who, in January 1325, had married Hugues de Sade **(see chapter 1)**. She produced 11 children before she died of the plague 23 years later. At mid-18th century, it was still generally believed by historians that Laure had been a daughter of Paul de Sade **(see chapter 1)** and it seems to have been the Abbé de Sade who discovered that in fact she was a daughter-in-law, he having found her marriage contract and the wills of her and her husband. He detailed this evidence in a highly esteemed book, which appeared in 1764-67.

The event which determined that she be thrust into a fame that has lasted ever since occurred at the instant when Francis Petrarch, as he noted later, "first set eyes on Laure, renowned for her virtue and long sung in my poems, in the flowering of my youth, in the year of Our

Lord 1327, on the sixth of April, in the morning, at the Church of St Claire at Avignon." Thenceforth, Laure became the theme of a series of sonnets in which Petrarch expressed his emotions about her. Speculation as to whether Laure and the poet were lovers kept gossips, and her husband, exercised at the time and has occupied many researchers ever since. There is no firm evidence that they were.

The poems, works of beauty, excite a response in readers everywhere. This engagement was especially intense in the Provençal and northern Italian region, a rich ground of Romance literature, which bred Laure, Petrarch and the de Sades. Offering a rough parallel from English literature, let's suppose that the identity of Shakespeare's dark lady of the Sonnets was known to her contemporaries and to posterity, and that she was celebrated, especially in her own region and among her descendants, for having been an inspiration to the bard.

Our marquis was well familiar with Petrarch's sonnets and with his uncle's expertise in Laure's history, even before the book by the Abbé was printed. One cannot make out that all members of the de Sade family were interested in or moved by Laure, their ancestor, but any de Sade who considered her significance would be aware that she constituted one part of a great love, as it was perceived, which transcended the vows of marriage and rules of morality, as laid down by the Catholic Church. Talismanic ancestors are prized in many families but, in Laure, the de Sades contemplated a rare spirit - no saint or soldier, artist or actor, but the object of a man's obsession. There is no indication that she had sought Petrarch's attention in any way before 6 April 1327. No amount of evocation of chivalry and courtly love in the Middle Ages, its conventions and trappings, can obscure Laure as target of a passion hatched in another's brain, as an unwitting catalyst going about her business meanwhile - initially, at least. Laure, the flower of the Comtat[3]; Laure, the impinged-upon.

This shade of the de Sade family has beguiled subsequent attention not as a maker of her own life and image, but as flesh that glowed only when a man shone his gaze on it. Women in history books, as in flesh and blood, are often preferred that way. Our boy, at Saumane in the care of a literary historian within his own family, was brought up in the consideration of Laure *l'adorée*, which has been engaging enough to eclipse any Laure *l'amant* for nearly seven centuries.

---

3 Her native region around Avignon.

CHAPTER 3: HARD SCHOOL

Soon after his ninth birthday, in 1749, the young marquis was sent from Provence back to Paris, to enrol in more formal education at Collège Louis le Grand, a school for sons of the élite, run by Jesuits and near the Condé mansion. It seems that the Countess de Sade had withdrawn from her husband's company about a year earlier and gone to live in a convent in Paris - the only recourse for a noblewoman of the era, when there was no divorce, who no longer wished to have anything to do with an uncongenial husband.

Also about 1749, the boy was given a private tutor, another abbot, the Abbé Jaques François Amblet. It is not clear how the marquis was lodged during his five years at the school - perhaps part of the time in his mother's apartment, part of the time with the tutor, or as one of the 500 or so boarders, in dormitories of about 20 beds each, among the school's 3,000 boys. Drawing again on what seems a self-revelatory passage in *Aline and Valcour*, one can take Amblet to be "a man who was both strict and intelligent, very fitting no doubt to shape my education but whom, to my misfortune, I did not keep for long enough."

When not with his tutor, the marquis would have spent his school days under a régime which must have been a contrast to the informal one at Saumane. The pupils were roused at 5.30 a.m., occupied with prayers and study of the scriptures from six and did not have breakfast until 7.45. School work and private study took up their time from 8.15 until lunch at noon, apart from an hour for Mass from 10.30. More school work kept them busy from 1.15 p.m. till 7.15 p.m., including a half-hour break for a snack at 4.30. Dinner and recreation took place from 7.15 till 8.45, when a quarter-hour was allowed for prayers before bed at nine.

The food, so many former pupils of the school in the mid-18th century recalled, was uniformly wretched, relieved only by the fasts required by the Church. The beds in the boarders' dormitories were hard - and so good for the formation of sturdy young spines - and poorly supplied with blankets in the winter.

There is no knowing how intensively the daunting schedule was filled but, given that classes commonly consisted of 100 or more boys, the atmosphere must often have been that of a lecture hall in a large university, rather than that of the more intimate instruction enjoyed by pupils in the fee-taking schools of modern times in Britain and the United States. The pupils were addressed as *vous* (the formal "you" in French), like adults, rather than as *tu* (the "you" used at children and among relatives and friends). This implies a deliberate policy of keeping a certain emotional distance between teachers and boys, so there may have been a reluctance to compensate for an impersonality and superficiality of relationships entailed by the sheer number of pupils. Corporal punishment was part of the discipline at Louis le Grand, although the Jesuit Fathers, alert to stifle any opportunity for sin, were required to expose no more of a boy's body than was necessary to administer a beating. We cannot know for certain whether the marquis was beaten at the school, or whether he saw others being punished.

His name does not appear on the lists of prize-winners at the college during his time there, but his later life shows evidence of impressions made by two items on the curriculum. The school was long on the teaching of rhetoric - Jesuits being always keen that those whom they have swayed shall be equipped to sway others - so the boys learned how to compose and deliver to an audience a well-argued speech, often drawing on the knowledge of the classics, Greek and Latin, which any gentleman of those days was expected to have. This stood the marquis in good stead as a nobleman who had to do more arguing and pleading in his life than any of his peers would have reasonably expected. The school also presented plays - not just on biblical subjects - and thus may have turned the marquis stage-struck, a condition that held him for most of his life, as amateur actor-manager for country house entertainments and as would-be playwright for the professional stage.

Another activity which the marquis may have encountered for the first time at Louis le Grand was sodomy. The Jesuit Fathers in Paris were regarded as having a strong penchant for a sexual practice which de Sade extolled and enjoyed in his later years. There is no evidence that he was buggered at Louis le Grand, although he dropped a lewd hint or two in his letters, years later, about a Father Sanchez. The pubescent marquis - small, blue-eyed, fair-haired, sturdy from his country upbringing - could well have been among the more eye-catching lads of his day at the school.

CHAPTER 4: "VERY QUICK TO CATCH FIRE"

The Marquis de Sade was a few days short of his 14th birthday, in the summer of 1754, when his family secured from an approved genealogist the documents that certified the nobility of the four immediately preceding generations of his family. He was thus able, on leaving Louis le Grand, to enter the training establishment for officer cadets attached to the Light Horse Regiment of the Royal Guards, garrisoned at Versailles to be near the king's residence. King Louis XV often inspected the Light Horse school, which was also kept on its toes by rivalry with an equivalent training corps attached to the Musketeers. In battle, a light cavalry regiment was apt to be used for sudden dashes to surprise an enemy by gaining ground, cutting off a retreat or breaking up an advancing column, the slashing sabre the main weapon. Flexibility and speed in response to orders were required, so the cadets were drilled, on horseback and on foot, in battalion strength and in small detachments. Each budding officer's fee at the school was 3,000 livres a year - probably about a sixth or seventh of the Count de Sade's annual income.

There was nothing remarkable at the time in a boy of barely 14 entering a military career. Even younger lads, noble and common, were thrust into European armies and navies, before, during and after the marquis's day. The officers were continuing a tradition by which their ancestors had become nobles in the first place - as conquerors at their sovereign's side - and were jealously maintaining their scope for military service to the crown. In the 1750s, commoners were allowed to become officers in the French army, albeit not through certain reserved channels, as the marquis's need for certification of nobility suggests.

For anyone in the military, more so the officer, there was the prospect of money - from plunder as well as the regular pay - and glory. Warfare in the 18th century was conducted in fits and starts - winter campaigns were not favoured - but could be relied on as at least a semi-permanent career in continental Europe as French, Austrian, Russian, Swedish, Prussian and other political and territorial ambitions clashed.

Besides, noblemen felt themselves to be fitted only for certain professions. One might show an interest in the farming and husbandry of one's estate but it was beneath one's dignity to engage in trade and manufacture. Younger sons might become priests, or even lawyers, but an eldest son, especially one of such old blue blood as our marquis had, was meant to buckle on an officer's sword, if possible in a regiment with the cachet of closeness to the king. For the Count de Sade, it was right and proper that his son should encounter in adolescence this preparation for institutionalised killing. A failure of the boy to do so might well have reflected badly on his family.

However, in his novel *Aline and Valcour*, more than thirty years later and after many vicissitudes, de Sade reflected that:

"... the essential aim is not to have very young military personnel, but to have good ones; and ... it is quite impossible for such a useful class of citizens [fit, intelligent young men] ever to be brought to its peak as long as the only consideration is to enrol it while young, without finding out whether it has what it takes to serve, and without understanding that it is impossible to possess the necessary qualities since the young hopefuls will not be given the chance to acquire these through a long and fully rounded education..."

The character holding forth in the novel went on to assert:

"There's no doubt that there are few worse schools than the garrison, few where a young man is sooner corrupted in his style and his morals."

In December 1755, after 20 months as a cadet, the marquis was commissioned as a second lieutenant (unpaid for the time being) in the king's own infantry regiment. It is not known why he was not admitted to the cavalry - however, he was in a well-regarded regiment.

Arrayed in blue tunics with gold buttons, white coats with pink facings and a blue lining, and gold-braided hats, the officers of the boy's regiment may have looked, when on parade, better prepared for operetta than for war, but they were in the service of the most belligerent power in Europe. By January 1757, the marquis had been promoted to coronet (standard-bearer) in the Carbine Regiment of the Count of Provence, under the command of the Marquis de Poyanne, and he was in battle against the Prussian army before he had turned 17. If one may call again on the character in *Aline and Valcour*, de Sade remembered in middle age: "I do not doubt that I acquitted myself well. The natural rashness of my character, that fiery spirit given me by nature, did no more than put greater power into an unflinching ferocity which is known as courage and is regarded, no doubt mistakenly, as the only one we must have."

It is impossible to tell whether this was the voice of reminiscence giving himself a late mention in dispatches, as well as looking a little askance at the military ethos, or whether it was a true record of the young officer's plunge into battle, dash and slash closing his mind against reflection and fear. Given his apparent reluctance to curry favour with his superiors, the youth may well have won esteem through his military prowess for he was promoted, in April 1759, to a captaincy in the Burgundian Horse Regiment, superseding a captain who had been taken prisoner. This step up entailed a handsome salary.

From the same month, however, comes the first evidence from the marquis himself of what kind of man was in the making. On his way to Germany to rejoin his regiment, after a leave in Paris, the young captain wrote:

"All the misdemeanours I committed while I was in Paris, my dear Abbé, and the way I have behaved towards the most affectionate father in the world, are making him regret having caused me to enter it. However, my remorse at having upset him and fear that I might lose his affection for ever are punishing me well enough. Now, nothing is left of the pleasures I believed in but the most bitter grief at having enraged the fondest of fathers and best of friends. I rose each day to chase after pleasure, the thought of which made me oblivious to all else. When I found it, I believed I was fortunate, but this seeming delight evaporated with my desires, leaving only regrets. By evening, I was distraught and understood my error - but that was in the evening. My desires returned with each new day and made me fly again to pleasure. I no longer remembered what I had felt the previous evening. I accepted any chance of making love, believed I enjoyed it greatly, then realised I had only been foolish and had not enjoyed it at all... At present, the more I think about my behaviour, the more odd it seems. I can see that my father was very much in the right when he said that three-quarters of my behaviour was just for effect. Oh! If I had stuck to what really pleased me, I would have spared myself much anxiety and upset my father much less often. Was it really possible that I believed the girls I saw would be able to please me? Alas, does one really enjoy purchased delight, and can love-making without tenderness really come from the heart? Now my pride is hurt when I tell myself they loved me just because I paid a bit more generously than other men.

"I have received a letter from my father just now. He wants me to make a full confession to him. I will; and I can promise you it will be sincere. I do not want to keep up deception of such a kind father, particularly because he is altogether ready to forgive me if I confess all my faults to him.

"Goodbye, my dear Abbé, let me have news of you, please, though it will not reach me until I am with the army again because I cannot stop anywhere else on the journey..."

The recipient of this letter was almost certainly the Abbé Amblet, the tutor in Paris, but it survives through a copy that was clearly in the hands of the Count de Sade for he wrote on it that it "has greatly angered me, because I did not want anyone to know what he had done." In the same document, the count's notes identify another copied letter as being from a certain de Castéra, with the marquis on the road to Germany:

"The dear son is in fine fettle - charming, amenable, diverting ... The trip is putting a bit of weight back on him and restoring to his cheeks the colour that the pleasures of Paris had drained rather. We're taking good care in that regard. Teissier[1] is a treasure and I'm urging my companion to see him right. Our two spare horses are giving us trouble: his is eating badly, walking lame (some trouble with a shoe); he claims it's only doing so out of wickedness because, when it can escape, it capers about like a kid. Mine is injured near the withers, but I'm hoping we'll pull through all right. He leaves and carries away regrets at every stopping-place. His little heart - or rather *body* - is very quick to catch fire. Look out, you German girls! I'll do all I can to stop him doing anything daft. He has sworn to me he will not wager more than a louis[2] a day while with the army ..."

(The marquis's pay at his new rank was 10,000 livres a year.)

The count did not like this either: "Think of that! The rapscallion has a louis a day to lose. He promised me he would not gamble a penny, but what he says or doesn't say makes no different to him." The marquis's father put the copies and his notes together and sent them to his brother, the Abbé de Sade, in Provence. News of the apprentice libertine - his father referred to him as a libertine in the notes - was spreading.

For the time being, however, while the marquis's misdeeds could be excused as a sowing of wild oats, it was his father who was more

---

1 De Sade's valet.

2 24 livres.

seriously undermining the standing of the de Sades. Earlier in the 1750s, the count had claimed to be having difficulty paying for his son's education, and had borrowed money from one of his sisters. While he maintained the style that suited his notion of how a man of his breeding and rank should conduct himself - which included both a chilly meticulousness about his dignity and a liberality with his purse - the count failed to take proper care of the sources of his wealth. It seems he did not ensure that the administrators of his estate were forwarding to him as much revenue as he could have received. This was an omission he might have amended by applying himself because there was no disgrace for a nobleman, even in those hierarchical times, in keeping close tabs on his rents, tithes and other income. Also, his diplomatic service for the king does not appear to have brought as much reward as it might have, more likely because the count did not assert himself sufficiently in the courtly hurly-burly of ingratiating oneself with various royal favourites, rather than because the complaint from Cologne had put him under a cloud in the French royal administration.

He often described himself as in poor health, and he suffered from depression, sometimes able to bear only the presence of his valet for days on end at his apartment in the Foreign Missions building in central Paris. There is no evidence of how the count and countess came to live separate lives. She is an ill-defined figure for posterity. Few documents that relate even the simplest outline of her conduct have survived. Her husband described her, some years after her withdrawal to the convent, as "a terrible woman. Her son takes after her." We can be sure he did not mean the libertinage but probably an insistence on not being bent to the will of others.

While his father's abiding improvidence and deepening misanthropy were diminishing the family patrimony, the marquis was eating into it in a much more outgoing fashion.

In 1762, he could have availed himself of the right he had just acquired to display a prized military pennant - a little flag which would mark his presence on ceremonial occasions or in battle, as an admiral flies a personal flag on the ship from which he is commanding a fleet. However, in late-18th century France, such honours went only to those who, having qualified by service to the crown, could afford to pay for them - the marquis did not take his pennant. By then, the French monarchy had long been relying extensively on the sale of honours, including elevation to the nobility, in order to bring in revenue to finance the public administration, the lavish spending of the royal households, and war.

This last was moving to the disadvantage of the marquis and his father. By late in 1762, the Seven Years War was being wound up in peace negotiations, which meant that the French army would discharge most of its officers, the marquis among them. This was no reflection on his soldiering, merely the usual practice in those days of an army seeking to reduce costs by transferring as many officers as possible to an unpaid reserve.

His severance pay would be small, only 600 livres, and that retained to meet debts run up by the officers of his unit. Meanwhile, the count was complaining that his son was not visiting him nearly as often as he might, being caught up in balls, shows and drinking parties. One of his superior officers had been reporting "appalling things" about the young man, the count fumed.

The peace having been signed in February 1763, the cavalry captain was duly discharged from active service and so came to have even more time than before for pleasure - though rather less money to finance it. He was fascinated by actresses and dancers of the Parisian stage, many of whom were using it as the prime way to advertise their availability for bids from rich men for their sexual services. He gambled, he frequented brothels, employed procurers of girls, with little heed for the depth of his purse.

His uncle, the good abbot, continued to set an example in this area. In 1762, Louis XV intervened to release from arrest "Paul Aldonze de Sade, aged fifty[3], priest of the diocese of Avignon, commendatory Abbot of Ebreuil, taken in Paris at the house of a certain Piron, whoremistress, being with a certain Léonore, common prostitute."

All this was regular stuff. Part of the enjoyment for most of the rakes, from teens to dotage, was sharing the roistering among themselves, sustaining the excitement through gossip about each other as well as through sexual encounters, drink and the turn of the cards. The marquis, though, stood out as something a lone operator - police dossiers never show him as having joined in debauches with other skirt-chasers of the Paris of his time. Besides, he was imprudent amid the main broil of noble revellers by disdaining the occasional formalities which, in such a milieu, can greatly mitigate the effect of

3 Rising fifty-seven, in fact.

misdemeanours. He failed to appear, except very rarely, before King Louis XV to pay his respects at the royal court: this needed to be no great chore, just an appearance apparently sober and in proper attire, utterance of a few banalities at the right moment, then away.

In the summer of 1763, the Count de Sade was complaining within his family that it was impossible to have the son and heir "make a reasonable visit or fulfil any duty." A few weeks later, from the court at Fontainebleau, the count lamented: "Alas! I came here to make him be so good as to enter the carriages and to hunt with the King. He was due to come, then he doesn't, when I had arranged everything." Thus was an honour - propinquity to the king during his day in the field, which most of the nobility would have intrigued tirelessly to obtain - spurned by a mere marquis and army captain.

The power of the French monarchy, central administrator and arbiter in the State, had been consolidated early in the century by Louis XIV, the Sun King, through a great shrinkage of the power of the nobles and a gathering of them as satellites to reflect the king's brightness at a populous, opulent court where he could keep an eye on them. Multiplication of their number through sale of titles of nobility made it all the more important for the king and his ministers that this élite continue to acknowledge the monarch to whom it owed its status, and that royal supervision be maintained.

By the time the marquis began to redistribute rents from his father's tenants among gambling houses and brothels of Paris, this supervision reflected the vast resources of the monarchy and the extent of the nobility. Specialist police officers were continuously compiling information about the high-born in the low life, especially in the capital city, not least because Louis XV was keen to know the latest news gleaned in this way from panders, doctors, servants, concierges, coachmen, stagehands and anyone else with a snippet of information to pass on. Thus an instrument of political control also served a compulsion which any reader of modern gossip columns understands.

Still in his rash vein, the marquis was turning his flair for writing an ardent and pithy letter, with no punches pulled, on people with the weight to punch back. The count bemoaned receipt of "a dreadful letter" from a certain "M de Ch", to whom the marquis had written in a very inappropriate manner.

The marquis must have understood that he could have repaired his standing somewhat - and his hell-raising was giving plenty of cause - by circumspection before his king and among his peers, when necessary. His letter of 1760 from the army (cited above) sets out his distaste for flattering and paying court in order to get on in the world, and it seems clear he was determined to continue in that way, whatever his pleasures and the opinion they provoked. It was as though the four-year-old who had lashed out at the young Condé still had not grown up and learned where to draw, and when to toe, the line.

CHAPTER 5: MARRIED, WITHOUT REASSURANCE

Anyone who felt that, what with the marquis's amusements and his family's finances, he was an unlikely candidate for love or marriage reckoned without the passion of the man, and without snobbery harnessed to market forces. Early in 1763, he was concurrently in love with a Provençal noblewoman and the subject of negotiations with a view to his marrying the daughter of a moneyed judge. The love affair shows that the marquis was capable of attachment to a woman whom he did not have to pay and over whom he had no social superiority, although this was not his usual proclivity. Laure Victoire Adeline de Lauris was just a year younger than her lover, born at Avignon, daughter of the Marquis de Lauris and bearing a pedigree matching that of the de Sades. Her ancestor, Hugues de Lauris, the first of that surname whose existence is known to history, was one of the hundred noblemen chosen in 1233 by Charles I of Anjou to fight a hundred more picked by the King of Aragon - a battle bright in the annals of chivalry.

The Marquis de Sade was seeking his father's consent to marry Laure de Lauris when, early in April, the count told him that she had just begged her father not to allow the marriage. The young man immediately wrote to her in Paris, from Avignon, a long and volcanic letter that spurts anger, amazement, pleading, contrition, desire and threat:

"Perjurer! Traitor! What has happened to those sworn promises to love me for life? Who is forcing you into breaking your word? Who is making you break the ties that were to join us forever? Have you decided that my leaving [Paris] meant I had run away? Did you believe I could run from you and go on living? No doubt you judged my feelings by your own. I obtain my parents' consent; with tears in his eyes, my father only asks of me as a favour that I come to Avignon to get married there. I leave; I am assured that every effort will now be put into getting your father to bring you down here. I arrive - God can testify to my speed - in this place which is to witness my good fortune, an enduring good fortune, a good fortune that will never be disturbed again. But ... dear God! Can I go on living through my grief? ... I learn that, inspired by an emotional fit, you're throwing yourself at your father's feet to ask him to give up any idea of this marriage, and that you don't want to be forced into another family. Hollow excuse, dictated by treachery...! You were afraid to be reunited to someone who adored you. The bonds of an eternal link became irksome to you, and your heart, which only responds to inconsistency and flightiness, was not sensitive enough to understand all the attractions [of those bonds]. It was [the idea of] leaving Paris that was frightening you; my love wasn't enough [to reassure you]; I wasn't the man to put things right. Very well then, stay there forever, monster, born to blight my life! May that city, through the deceit of that cheat who will take my place in your heart, become for you one day as vile as your deceits have made it for me.

"But whatever am I saying? Ah, my dear love, oh, my divine love, the only help for my heart, the only delight of my life, where is my despair taking me? Forgive the words of an unhappy man who no longer knows what he is about and for whom death, after the loss of her whom he loves, becomes the only way out. If I lose you, I lose my existence, my life... Let the tears which blind me flow... I cannot live with such disappointment. What are you doing? What has happened to you? What am I to you? Something monstrous? Something you love? Tell me, how do you see me? How can you justify your behaviour? Maybe you find mine unjustifiable. Oh, if you still love me, if you love me as you have always done, as I love you, as I adore you, as I will adore you for the rest of my life, weep over our misfortunes, weep over the deadly blows of fate, write to me, try to give a reason for what you did... I am certain that, if you love me, you have decided to enter a convent. Do you remember how you told me, the last time I saw you, on the day of our disappointments, that you would be delighted if you were put away in a convent? If you want us to be able to meet, you know that is all you can do, for you know that I will not be able to visit your home. When my father told me what you had done, he left it up to me whether I stayed as long as I wanted or joined him right away...

"I couldn't believe you had changed your mind. What could have made you do that? Perhaps this journey [of mine] upset you: but ... you should recognise my motives for what they are. They bamboozled me, made me believe I was running into the arms of happiness, while they were seeking all along to put me far from any such thing...

"Look after your health; I am doing what I can to restore mine. But whatever the state of yours, nothing will stand in the way of my giving you the most tender proofs of my love. Throughout this adventure, I think, you have, and will continue to have, cause for satisfaction with my discretion. But I've done no more than I should and I'm giving myself no points for that... Don't be fickle with me; I don't deserve that. I promise you that I would be furious, and there would be no horror I wouldn't put my hand to. The little matter of the c--- should make you careful how you deal with me. I promise you I shall not conceal that from my rival, and that would not be the last secret I shared with him. On my oath, there would be no kind of horror I wouldn't allow myself. But I am ashamed to contemplate such ways to hold on to you. I don't want to, nor should I, talk to you of anything but your love...

"I insist, I beg you not to see -----[1]; he is not worthy of so much as your glance... Continue to love me, dear one, and let time take care of everything... Perhaps there will come a time, soon, when you will not be so afraid to become part of my family. When I'm head of it, my desires will rule my choice and maybe then I shall find you more convinced. I need to be consoled, reassured, to receive proof of your faithfulness: everything scares me ... I assure you and I give you my word of honour that nothing is more sure than what I'm telling you, that I await only your answer in order to leave here [for Paris]. My father is asking for me again; don't think it's for a marriage [to someone else]; I am quite determined against a marriage ...

"... Do not fail to give the woman who delivers this letter an acknowledgement thus: I can confirm receipt of a letter from the hands of such-and-such... She will be paid only if she brings back this acknowledgement to me ...

"Love me forever; be faithful to me if you don't want to see me die of anguish. Goodbye, my beautiful child, I adore you and I love you a thousand times more than I love my life..."

It is a letter of no fixity but that of passion. No-one reading it could miss the threat, scarcely disguised by the blanks in *little matter of the c---*, to reveal to Laure's other suitor a venereal infection, either suffered by her or, at least, present in the marquis during the affair and so apt to infect his lover. (It is not proven that Laure infected the marquis, despite a hint in that direction by the Count de Sade.) Such a breach of confidence - revelation of a love affair compounded by that of a venereal infection - would be likely to ruin a woman's chances of

1 Sade was using caution that was customary in those days - relatives, servants and police spies might pry into letters.

marriage, much more so in that era than nowadays. However hotly made, amid a letter of much zig-zagging, this was a heavy threat. It is not known whether the marquis carried it out.

The breast-beating of a forsaken swain, the low threats and the chivvying of Laure out of her father's house and towards a nunnery so that the affair might continue, at whatever cost to her credibility as a daughter of her family and as a Christian - all this is of a piece. Even more to be noted is the glimpse of fear in a void behind the pleas and bluster - *I need to be ... reassured ... everything scares me*.

Instead of reassurance, he was given the arranged marriage which he had been resisting. The marquis stayed at Avignon until late-April, trying to revive the relationship with Laure de Lauris, while arrangements were going ahead for him to marry one Renée Pélagie de Montreuil in Paris in May. The collapse of the affair with the *provençale* deprived the marquis of a reciprocated love, so it seems, with an eligible woman, which had been by far his best defence against the marriage his father and his prospective in-laws were negotiating. From a union impelled by love, the marquis was thrust into one created by complementary needs for money and dynastic advancement.

Why did he, wilful pursuer of his pleasures, not turn the scheme down flat? For one thing, parental authority was hard to flout in those times, when parents might bring rebellious offspring into line by having them jailed on the signature of a royal official, readily secured by parents who had enough influence. For another, the young man was chronically short of money, his father's finances being shaky, as we have seen, and he himself being stood down from the army while France was at peace. The Count de Sade wanted to close his purse against the inroads of a roistering son, and the latter may have given some thought, once his hopes of Laure de Lauris had run into difficulty, to the wealth of the de Montreuil family as a source of upkeep for his preferred way of life.

Despite his need to be rid of his son, the count seems to have been slow to market with him, his only commodity in the marriage trade. This may be put down to the count's dislike of company but also perhaps to a commendable reluctance on his part to foist onto others a son who, by the father's admission within his family at about this period, "has not a single redeeming feature".

However, to an outsider who knew the marquis only through the lists of the nobility - in which one might investigate the antecedents of a prospective dinner guest, neighbour or in-law - he was a high-born officer with excellent connections. Even if that outsider had heard of the young man's rakish escapades, these might be rendered as pranks exaggerated in the telling. After all, if every young nobleman who had sown a few wild oats were thus made ineligible for wedlock, many a piece of social climbing through marriage would have been ruled out. Besides, the nobility of France was so numerous by the second half of the 18th century (perhaps as many as 200,000 adults and children, or nearly 1 per cent of the whole population) that it was difficult for any one family to have detailed knowledge of more than a small proportion of its peers. This upper crust had long ceased to be a small military caste of land-owners. Even when it was such, the size of France and the diversity of its regions had worked against cohesiveness of the whole French nobility - witness the very largely local connections of the Provençal de Sades until the 18th century, for instance.

In the stud book, then, the marquis looked a good catch for a family of more recent elevation to the peerage. The Montreuil clan, though by no means one that had bought all its furniture, was not of the ancient military nobility, entwined with popes and kings, which gave the de Sades their cachet. Its bid for a nuptial alliance derived credibility from its wealth.

This appears to have been based on a fortune built up by Jacques René Cordier, treasurer of the war funds of the northern French towns of Berghe and Furnes (both now in Belgium, and the latter now called Veurnes). Such a position, similar to that of thousands of other fiscal offices in France, gave him scope to cream off money for himself, while carrying out his duties. Lacking an extensive salaried body of public administrators, the French kings sold public offices, such as those of tax collectors, to private individuals who then had a broadly free hand to reimburse themselves from traders, travellers, manufacturers, farmers and so on through taxation in their particular part of the country or their reserved area of economic activity. One such individual might have bought the right to levy all taxes in the province of Burgundy, say; another might have purchased the taxing of all traffic on a certain stretch of the Loire river. Some great speculators acquired such extensive rights through this farming out of taxation that they were known as farmers-general. Anyone who has spent much time in the Britain of the 1980s and 1990s will know the spirit behind this kind of ill-supervised privatisation.

We do not know how Cordier behaved in office but any local treasurer who did not divert money to himself during the lavishly funded wars of King Louis XIV would have been exceptional. Aged 27, in 1711, he married Anne Thérèse Croëzer. They produced a son, Claude René Cordier de Launay (the new, last name from a property of the Cordiers) who in turn, in 1740, married Marie Madeleine Masson de Plissay, whose family's nobility was also recent. In the same year, Jacques René bought the estate of Échauffour in Normandy, with a manor called Montreuil-Largillé. The son, Claude René, took the name de Montreuil and, in 1743, reached the zenith of his unremarkable legal career when appointed a president (chief justice) of the Paris taxation court, a position he held until 1754. He and Marie Madeleine, known as Madame de Montreuil, seem to have had about a half-dozen children and so had as many motives for special attention to the potential of the nobility's marriage market for the family's social advancement.

The count wrote calculatingly to his brother, the Abbé de Sade, in Provence early in 1763:

"It is sure that Justice de Montreuil, the father, who gives a hundred thousand livres [a year] to his daughter at present, doesn't give her the half of what will be due to come to her, because he expects more than fifty thousand livres in [annual] income from Mme de Launay, his mother. Mme d'Azy, his sister, has no children at all, so there's another portion which will pass along [to the judge's daughter]. M Masson de Plissay [the judge's father-in-law] has had five children - three married daughters and two lads who aren't wed. The oldest daughter is the widow of M de Chamousset and has no child whatsoever; there's another inheritance..."

In another letter, also to the Abbé at about the same time:

"The more I think about this marriage, the better I like it. Yesterday, I went to see M de Montmarcet who knows what everyone's worth... He told me that Madame de Launay had income of more than a hundred and ten thousand livres, which she would not get through; that Monsieur de Montreuil would have at least eighty thousand livres in income, at his death, taking account of the property he has now; ... and that Monsieur de Montreuil's children would have incomes of twenty to twenty-five thousand livres [each], all being well; that this wasn't a paper fortune subject to ups and downs like those of all these business people; that he thought more of the five years of upkeep [conceded by the Montreuils in favour of the happy couple] than an extra hundred thousand livres..."

The count even primed his brother, the Abbé, to send him a false letter making out that the marquis had fallen ill down in Provence and could not come to Paris until he had recovered. This was in case the bridegroom maintained his stubborn wait in the south (for Laure de Lauris to open her arms to him again) so long that the wedding in Paris would have to be postponed. The Montreuils got wind of Laure, even so, and the count laid down a smoke-screen to the effect that his son was staying so long in Avignon in order to prepare a home there.

The main mover in the Montreuil family's matrimonial campaign was Mme de Montreuil who, in mid-1763, cannot have been older than 43 and was not yet three years past the birth of her last child. Renée Pélagie, born on 3 December 1741, was very likely her eldest child and so the marriage was of special importance to the family.

Mme de Montreuil was taking a gamble. A dissolute, unbiddable son-in-law would be a great trouble and expense, in that scandals would have to be hushed up and loose living paid for. Then again, such a young man, of incontestable quality in his genealogy and in his family's lines to the royal Bourbons, if tamed, would be a golden bough on her branch of the Montreuil family tree. Many who had dealings with her, in connection with the de Sades, testified to her tenacity of purpose, and to her quick adaptability, in guiding the family's progress. She was a drawing-room general of great tactical resource in the battle to keep up appearances and to rise in society. Her husband appears much less often in our story,

His wife did not put all her trust in time and their daughter to bring the marquis to heel. Her other great weapon was money. The marriage contract - the haggling over which befitted a crucial deal in which two parties (the families, not the young couple) sought to have their respective assets (the bride and groom) valued as highly as may be - was drawn up so that no large sum in cash or any easily realisable assets would become available to the couple for some time. For the Montreuils' part, the bride was promised substantial sums as legacies on the deaths of her parents and certain other relatives, and received comparatively little in hand, although the investment and rental income to be provided immediately would have kept all but a few families of the era comfortably. Also, the bride's parents were to provide the young couple and two servants with board and lodging at the parents'

Paris townhouse and country estates for five years after the wedding, or hand over an annual sum in lieu. Once the five years were up, the Montreuil parents were to give the couple 10,000 livres to help set up home.

On the de Sades' side, the count was contracted to give his son his lieutenancy-general of four provinces (Bresse, Bugey, Valromey and Gex), with its annual income of 10,000 livres. There was a complication, however, the count having drawn the income of the years 1761-63. The marriage settlement required that this money be transferred to the marquis, but his father, who probably had nothing like that amount of cash available, declined to do so, insisting that the money ought to be regarded as having been spent on maintaining his son while he was still a bachelor. The count seems to have eased his financial troubles by negotiating a letter of credit for 60,000 livres from the king - in effect borrowing from the royal treasury.

Another clause in the nuptial contract specified that the count turn over to his son ownership of the Provençal estates and manorhouses at la Coste, Mazan, Saumane (where the Abbé was still a tenant, rent-free in effect) and Mas de Cabanes - but the count retained the income from these properties. The Countess de Sade could not be persuaded by her husband to hand over her diamonds to the young couple, as a rich symbol of welcome to the bride and a fitting adornment for a daughter-in-law moving up in the world of the élite. He and the Montreuils were displeased but, viewing the clear evidence of the count's mismanagement and his son's profligacy, the countess's decision looks like a prudent regard for her assets in her old age.

While he and the Montreuils were bargaining over his son and their daughter, the Count de Sade found himself obliged to become unwontedly sociable by way of holding their interest and making up for his wife's lack of application (according to him) in beguiling the prospective in-laws. "I dine and spend every day with one or other of them," he wrote to one of his sisters in Provence. However, he confessed, "I can't stop myself pitying them over the acquisition they're going to make, and I reproach myself for misleading them about the character of the future son-in-law... The only sweet thing about him is his voice. On the least thing as on the most important, it's impossible to make him give way. I think I shall be very keen to leave Paris when he's living here.

"The business with Mme du Vigean[2] is being managed with some difficulty. She's asking that his mother and I be guarantors for our son. Mme de Montreuil talked about this to Mme de Sade to get her to agree to it. She replied: 'But if my son doesn't pay the money back, my pension [provided by income from the family estates] will be seized.' [Mme de Montreuil] said: 'Ah, Madame, what an idea of your son you're giving me! If you think he's capable of that, I am very unhappy about giving my daughter to him. But I have a better opinion of him than you, and we [the Montreuils] will be his guarantors, if you don't want to be, for it's shameful to leave M [the Count] de Sade in the state he is [over this matter]...' "

For all the haggling and misgivings, the great day came. On 1 May 1763, the count accompanied Judge de Montreuil and his wife to the royal court at Versailles, where King Louis XV and his queen gave their formal, ceremonial and highly prized consent to the marriage, supported by the Dauphin (crown prince) and his consort, with various other exalted signatories. The seal was set on the Montreuils' big step up. There was no going back now, not without a loss of face which the families of both contracting parties would not live down for generations.

The count's stratagem for having a sickness report about his son to flourish at the Montreuils was not needed. He fretted greatly, even so, telling the Abbé:

"All this is too much for my poor health; I'm afraid it'll be the end of me... Don't entrust my son with the plate[3], he'll sell it along the way; nothing is sacred to him... Is it possible that the child has misgivings about this marriage, after all he has heard about this girl [Mlle de Montreuil] and about all he has to gain! He must have neither feelings nor honour. I'm not surprised that the journey [from Paris to Avignon] has made his illness worse; he has been scared day and night of being chased by the Lauris family whom he constantly thought he saw at his heels. Give him all the cash you can for the journey..."

The marquis abandoned his wait for Laure de Lauris to embrace him anew, although he was writing to his father in mid-April that he was more in love with her than ever, and that it was not she who had "made him ill," the count reported to one of his sisters in Provence, adding:

2 A noblewoman who was lending the young man 20,000 livres.
3 Valuable heirlooms the count was expecting from Avignon.

"He forgets that he told me he had not seen any other women. Fortunately she doesn't want him."

Hanging the expense as usual, the bridegroom took an express coach for Paris to arrive in time to meet his bride and her family for the first time, and to sign the marriage contract on 15 May at the Montreuils' townhouse in Paris. Society and the market duly satisfied, the pair went two days later to the Church of St Roch in Paris for God also to join them.

The count had borrowed money from the Montreuils in order to kit out the bridegroom and his retinue, and to provide a carriage, so we can believe he looked well enough during the ceremonies. No portrait of the marquis has survived (though researchers retain hopes of finding a miniature that was lost during World War II when German troops pillaged a Condé mansion in France) but various accounts agree on his striking blue eyes, fair hair, rather well-covered figure and fleshy face - in all, quite good-looking. In his prime, he was probably not more than 5 ft 4 ins tall but that would not have made him an especially short man in an era when the average height of Frenchmen was less than the 5 ft 9 ins of our better-fed times.

CHAPTER 6: "THAT LIGHT HEAD OF HIS"

Renée Pélagie de Montreuil acknowledged later, and she could well have done so at her marriage, that her husband was "bound to know the world much better than I do". She had much to learn about him, too. The Marquise de Sade was 21, a practising Catholic, daughter of a precise and calculating mother whose rapid intelligence and ready dismissal of contraries seem to have given members of her family, and others, little scope for assertion. She was daughter also of a distant father. Renée Pélagie reminded her husband 15 years later: "You know my father is not of a loving disposition."

The bridegroom played his part in the nuptials without too much friction. His mother-in-law reported that one could not wish for a "more affable" son-in-law. He and his new wife, according to the count, passed much of the month after their marriage "spending at least a louis a day on going to shows, and they're on the tiles all the time."

The summer of the marriage went well. Mme de Montreuil, greatly taken by her son-in-law's manners and education, supported him in the dispute with his father over the revenue of the lieutenancy-general. The marquis was being regarded as a Montreuil now, to be helped to wax as great as may be for that family's advancement. His coat of arms was altered to incorporate that of the Montreuils. The marquis and his wife spent most of August with her parents at their Échauffour estate. In October, Mme de Montreuil was telling the Abbé de Sade by letter that she sometimes gave the "strange boy" a telling-off, which would lead to a row, but they soon made it up. "He is a scatter-brain but marriage is beginning to sort him out... You will see a difference in him." As for Renée Pélagie, "no matter how much she wants to please and obey us, she will never scold him... He is very fond of her and could not be treating her better."

"He is very good with his wife. As long as that lasts, I'll ignore the rest of it," the count conceded. It was some 18 months later, in February 1765, that de Sade was describing his marriage - for one of his old flames among the nobility - as "an unfortunate bond, made for family advantage", which sowed "only thorns".

The marquis had energy to spare from marital attendance, as well as thirsts which family life could not slake. He rented (and furnished on credit) various pieds-à-terre in and around Paris for debauchery and intensified his trawl among dancers and actresses for courtesans. He also had liaisons with women of polite society. The young man may well have felt better equipped now, with a much bigger purse than his father's to dip into, to return to taking every woman who excited him and who was available. An announced journey to seek a position at the royal court, and arrange for an assembly of notables in Burgundy to acknowledge him as the new lieutenant-general of the four provinces, seems to have been designed to conceal from his wife and her mother a stay in Paris for roistering.

Two days before his mother-in-law wrote about the change marriage had been working on him, the marquis was in Paris, taking delivery, from a procuress called du Rameau, of Jeanne Testard, a 20-year-old woman who needed to supplement her income as a fan-maker. He and a male servant took Testard to a small house where she was put into an upstairs room, which was locked and bolted. In reply to his questions on the matter, Testard said she believed in the Christian faith, to which he proclaimed vehemently that he had proved God did not exist. He added that he had masturbated himself to ejaculate into a chalice when in church. He also told her that he had taken Communion with a girl, kept the two hosts and then put them inside the girl's body before having sexual intercourse with her, saying: "If you are God, take your vengeance."

Testard was taken then into a nearby room where birch rods and whips were on the wall. There were also sacred pictures of Christ and the Virgin Mary, along with pornographic drawings and engravings. The marquis made her look at the objects and told her she would have to beat him before he beat her with whatever birch or whip she selected. She refused. He then trampled a crucifix and masturbated himself to ejaculate onto another. He told her to stamp on that and, when she showed reluctance, threatened her with pistols and a sword until she did as he wanted, the marquis uttering blasphemies meanwhile. She refused his demand to receive an enema so that she might excrete onto the crucifix. Keeping Testard awake and on her feet all night, without food or drink, the marquis read aloud several anti-religious poems. Before the procuress arrived to collect her, he made her promise to meet him the next Sunday so that they might take Communion, after which he would burn one host and penetrate her while the other was inside her.

Testard complained in much precise detail to the police, who arrested the marquis and took him to Fontainebleau for questioning by Louis de Saint Florentin, Minister of the Royal Household. This may well have been the marquis's first encounter face-to-face with Inspector Louis Marais, a police officer who, as a leading member of the vice squad of his day, already knew a great deal about the young man and had written much of what appeared in his police dossier. It was Marais who escorted the marquis to the interview with the minister, who in turn recommended to the king that he should not get off lightly. So, at the end of October, de Sade began his first experience of prison, at the fortress of Vincennes, near Paris. He liked it so little that, within a few days, the erstwhile blasphemer was telling Antoine de Sartine, the Paris chief of police, by letter: "I cannot complain about what has befallen me. I deserve the wrath of God. All I do is lament over my misdeeds and hate my errors. God might have destroyed me without giving me the opportunity to recognise my faults for what they are; I must thank Him for allowing me the chance to put myself to rights." He begged to be allowed to consult a priest, so as to return to the Holy Sacraments through priestly guidance and his own repentance.

On the same day, he asked the governor of the jail to pass on a letter to Mme de Montreuil, requesting that he might see his wife - "the person who is most precious to me and whom by my weakness I have insulted so heinously." Nothing was more sure than such a meeting to put him back on the straight and narrow, he assured the governor. Before he sent these pleas, he had urged the police to keep the incident quiet.

Two weeks after he had encountered the gloomy squalor of Vincennes, which was eased somewhat in the meantime by the arrival of a personal servant (he had asked unsuccessfully for his own valet), the marquis was released. A visit by his father to Fontainebleau, pleading before the king's staff, had helped to do the trick - and the Montreuils had influential lawyers in their ranks - but the royal order to release the marquis stipulated that he stay at the Montreuil country estate of Échauffour, whence Marais escorted him. Operating his by now customary device for damage control in the south, the count wrote to his brother, the Abbé, to have the latter squash any reports of the affair he came across in Provence, with special care to keep their sisters ignorant of what had happened to Jeanne Testard.

The count reflected that his son had played his long scene with her "coolly ... with no consideration restraining him ... quite alone." When he and his younger brother, the Abbé, and other young rips of a generation earlier had gone out and about for pleasure, it was in a party. It seems the count - in his younger days, and even as recently as ten years before - had been more sociable and apt to womanise. Recalling that, he neither understood nor liked this solitary rant-cum-relief by his son with one hired assistant who was not required to assume the horizontal. Looking at his and his son's present circumstances, the count regretted that the young husband had not taken into account his new responsibility to respect the sensibilities of his wife and her family.

Mme de Montreuil and her daughter were greatly shocked but kept their poise. The family stayed on good terms with the rest of the de Sades, and Mme de Montreuil, while acknowledging that the affair had given the marquis pause for thought, was reserving judgement as to whether it and the Montreuils' subsequent help would change his ways for good. In a letter of 21 January 1764 to the Abbé de Sade, Mme de Montreuil devoted rather more space to buttering-up the recipient, and to a slightly cloying report of the supportive and high-minded reaction of her and hers, than to telling how the repentant rake was faring. Renée Pélagie had been mortified by the affair but "has conducted herself just as a lady of virtue ought. It is not my place to compliment her. I leave judgement of her to those to whom she has the honour to belong..." Mme de Montreuil also reported of her daughter that she was three months pregnant (and so must have conceived at about the date her husband was hiring Jeanne Testard). However, by the middle of 1764, she had miscarried or given birth to a child that lived not long enough to be baptised.

The feelings and behaviour of the marquis, cooped up by royal order on the Norman estate of interested and calculating strangers who happened to be his wife and in-laws, can only be imagined. The previous autumn, Mme de Montreuil had reported about the young marquis to the Abbé:

"... I don't know whether the inevitable tranquillity of the country quite satisfies his mind and his likings: they're lively; they lack nourishment. There is fortunately always two sure means: reading and sleeping. You must know his liking for them both.

"There's a Trappist monastery three leagues from here. He has gone there today with M de Montreuil. He was very keen on the trip; not in order to stay there, I think. I hope he'll find it improving ...

"A little deer-hunting in a beautiful forest, horse-riding, a little carriage above all, make for distraction, and the time passes. Each age has its toys ..."

Indeed, the saddle and the study, and lying a-bed, must have provided diversions for a cavalry officer with a taste for literature, and a tiring propensity for differing with whatever company surrounded him. I expect, though, he had to apply large measures of silence and hypocrisy when the company turned to religious topics and when it trooped off to Mass. Whatever tensions and compromises underlay the common courtesies at Échauffour, the rural interlude gave rise to the marquis as actor-manager. Two popular farces of the time were presented in April at Évry, the estate of an uncle of Renée Pélagie, with the marquis, his wife and mother-in-law in the casts. During one play, the marquis sang to his wife some words from his own pen. They included a pledge of fidelity and the sentiment "it takes only one step to pass from bad to good."

At about the same time, the king allowed a request by the Montreuils that the marquis be permitted to spend three months away from Échauffour, not least because he wanted to be formally proclaimed as lieutenant-general of the four provinces in eastern France. The young man seems not to have left until June but his father had been quick to respond to the king's leniency by warning his son in April that, whatever view God in His mercy might be taking of the affair of the previous October, various people here below considered it more serious than the young blasphemer thought. The count added that he had known what he was about when he laid down that his son should remain at Échauffour - "and I cannot understand why M and Mme de Montreuil have gone against this after all my instructions, which in brief were that you must be made to stay there."

At the end of June, the marquis completed the assumption of his title of lieutenant-general when he made a graceful and humble speech to a ceremonial session of the High Court of Burgundy at Dijon.

Three weeks later, during his three-month leave from supervision by the Montreuils, he was introduced in Paris to an actress of the Italian Theatre, name of Colet, who was 18 and already three years into a career as a highly-paid courtesan. The marquis took her home after the performance and, next day, was writing to her of his urgent wish to give all his time, and a share of all he possessed, to her. A woman who had already been through various titled hands, and was becoming accustomed to fees of 500 to 700 livres a month from lovers who knew they were not getting exclusive access to her services, was not so easily contracted. Colet replied that his proposal was quite out of order, at which the young husband wrote again, in unrestrained and passionate terms, to apologise deeply, promise extravagantly and declare that only death would end his love for her. Laure de Lauris would have recognised the style.

Having understood that his fire was stoked high, Colet agreed to add him to her string of benefactors, a liaison facilitated by the king, on 11 September, when he rescinded the order that had confined the marquis to Échauffour, again almost certainly at the request of the Montreuils. Inspector Marais, at the centre of his web of informers, gave the flavour of matters in a report of 7 December:

"The [Marquis] de Sade, whom I took to Vincennes a year ago on the king's orders, as well as on his last journey to Fontainebleau and then to the estate of his father-in-law, where he has had the chance to put by a bit of his income, was given permission to go to Paris in the summer, where he remains and where, to while away his time, he is pleased to give Colet, an actress at the Italian Theatre, 25 louis a month, she being the paid mistress of the Marquis de Lignerac, who ... is aware of the liaison with M de Sade, but the penny has started to drop with the latter that the girl is stringing him along. He went to give vent to his urges this week at Brissault's whore-house and repeatedly asked her whether she knew me, which she denied. I have firmly advised this woman, without explanation, not to supply the marquis with girls to go to private places with him."

Marais was trying to prevent the marquis from taking partners for his blasphemous indulgences, while the latter was trying to counter this by seeking procurers who had not heard the inspector's warning, or were disposed to ignore it.

The marquis's effusions to Colet of the previous summer were sounding hollow by late-December 1764, for de Lignerac had nearly dropped out of the lists for her upkeep, leaving the responsibility to de Sade. Marais was as full of inside information as ever:

"The Marquis de Lignerac, despite his family forbidding it, is still seeing the Colet girl ... and, as his means no longer allow him to maintain her, he is reduced to the position of hanger-on... He contents himself with seeing her in her dressing-room at the theatre, and if he's surprised by someone knocking at the door, so as not to be spotted he immediately stuffs himself under her wash-stand. [The Marquis] de Sade is making every effort to break loose from her. He has slept with her three times again this week, but he is very much concerned to know where she got an enormous sultan[1] which she received on Christmas day." The inspector reported the young man "greatly discomforted because he is not wealthy enough to support an actress by himself." Brissault, known in the trade as *la présidente*, told him that he could not afford Colet, as well the brothel-keeper might for she had rather he continue to spend his money at her place.

The other *présidente* in de Sade's life - this being the formal title of Mme de Montreuil as the wife of a high court judge - was also aware of his ties to Colet and also keen to sever them. She persuaded her son-in-law that the actress had other lovers and, by the turn of the year, he was being edged out of Colet's scheme of things by a duke with much more money. A pair of ear-rings worth 3,000 livres, a Christmas present shown off to all by a delighted Colet, was an unmistakeable clue to the change of orientation. (She died in 1766, aged not quite 21.)

It may have been at Colet's front door that Mme de Montreuil intercepted her son-in-law during her efforts to put him back onto the straight and narrow. She claimed in the following year (1765) that she had brought him away from a courtesan's door a year before and, what's more, that she had "succeeded ... in separating him from Colet and in making him listen to reason, having convinced him that he was being deceived."

Came the spring of that following year and the marquis's fancy turned to another actress. Marais was on the case and reported in April:

"The Beauvoisin girl is deceiving M Douet de la Boulaye every chance she gets, while he showers her with gifts. M de Pienne is still the hanger-on in favour, and [the Marquis] de Sade is picking up the bills for her dresses and outings at the shows, which add up to 20 louis a month."

In May, from the same dossier:

---

1 A piece of bathroom furniture.

"The Beauvoisin girl, for some months, has managed to keep on the string both the Marquis de Louvois and M Douet de la Boulaye, from whom she has extracted more than one might believe possible. This girl, without being absolutely loaded with diamonds, can be seen as very canny in her affairs. She is very elegantly fitted out ... and there are few women who have such a well-stocked wardrobe and who are as well-provided with lace. At home, she is always to be found dressed with seductive propriety, in eye-catching négligées, and no-one is better at dressing to show off the figure... She is even seen as quite faithful to her lovers. However, ... I am persuaded that she denies her urges nothing - and very keen they are, for all her unassuming reserved air, because the Marquis de Louvois left last Wednesday to return to his regiment and, the same night, she slept with the Chevalier de la Tour, who is regarded by all these belles as quite a stud..."

Beauvoisin's origins are not clear but she was probably about 24 years old in 1765, having been a maid in a doctor's house before she was spotted some eight years earlier on behalf of the Count du Barry, through whom she learned about her greater earning power. Bachaumont, a chronicler of the Paris of the day, reckoned Beauvoisin to have "a pretty figure, with some good features, but [to be] ... short and thick-set, which is why she was obliged to leave the Opéra where she had been a dancer." By no means put out, it seems, she became manager of a gambling salon while still in her teens.

Spring was also a good time for long-distance travel, as the roads became firmer. The marquis headed for Provence where the Abbé was to brief him on the condition of the family properties there. The count shrugged to one of his sisters at his son's desire to live in the château at la Coste, the family's main Provençal estate:

"... He'll let it fall down if he wants, sell the furniture if he wants. I used to look after it for his sake; if he abuses it sooner or later, that's his business. I think he's starting to get bored with his father-in-law and his mother-in-law; he doesn't like anything that cramps his style..."

Indeed, so the marquis moved his style south to la Coste, where Beauvoisin spent much of June, all July and the first week of August with him. A private theatre at the château was restored at much expense as the centre-piece of lavish entertainments laid on by the marquis. The Abbé de Sade was among the local quality who enjoyed the balls, banquets and theatricals. He insisted that he was as upset as anyone by the appearance - a surprise to him and to the rest of the

Sade-Montreuil network - on the arm of the young marquis of a courtesan who was presumed by many in and around la Coste to be a relative of the marquise or the lady wife herself, who had not been to the region.

Mme de Montreuil did not allow her son-in-law's removal from Paris to place him beyond her campaign to detach him from his latest fancy. By letter, she urged the Abbé to go to work on his nephew:

"He is in great need of your advice to bring back to earth that light head of his. It ought to be brought under control; all its first impulses being extreme, one remains in dread of them. But his mind is susceptible to reason when he pauses to reflect. All that's needed is time to make him understand, and that no passion have hold of him...

"I know that, at his age, he must be indulged, but he must also behave decently..."

In late-May, before Beauvoisin's arrival, the marquis had visited his uncle and told the abbot of his involvement with the little courtesan. On his way to Provence, he had spent four days at Melun "with the object with whom he is infatuated at present," the Abbé reported to Mme de Montreuil. He went on:

"There's only you and I, Madame, who might have a little influence on him. But what can we do? Not much at the present time. He has to sow his wild oats. He is caught up just now in the fire of passion... It would be dangerous to do what his father has done, to rub him up the wrong way: he would be capable of going very badly haywire. Only by the strength of gentleness, of indulgence and of reason, can one hope to turn him around. You are convinced of that, Madame, and one can't do better. He has a great deal of confidence in you, and a great deal of respect for you; sooner or later, you'll make of him what you want.

"The present fantasy doesn't disturb me greatly: he won't have spent a month in this part of the country before he's not giving any more thought to it. But that would be for him to take up a new fancy. There's the devil of it, and I'm very much afraid that he'll be this way until age has dulled his edge. I've talked to him a great deal about his wife... He's aware of all her worth; he praised her to the skies; he feels friendship for her and much respect; he would be desperate if he displeased her, but he finds her too cold and too pious for his liking, and that's what makes him go and look for amusement elsewhere. Once he has passed the age when the passions are hot, he'll understand the price of the wife you have given him; but one has to pass through this age, which will last longer than we would wish..."

The well-informed recipient of the abbot's letter may have been able to recall, on reading this last phrase, that the writer had been arrested, only three years earlier and at the age of 57, in the company of a certain Léonore, "*fille de prostitution.*" She might be in for a long wait while her son-in-law's edge was dulled.

The emollient old libertine of Saumane concluded to Mme de Montreuil:

"God grant that he does not give us a great deal of sorrow, to you and to me! If we're working together, we'll be able to stave off the blows. He told me that his wife was unaware of his foolish behaviour, and that she would be in despair if she did know: that's something..."

The abbot's prayer was not to be answered. He had sent news of the Beauvoisin affair to one of his sisters, Gabrielle Eléonore, Abbess of St Benoît at Cavaillon in Provence, who in turn gave her nephew a telling-off. From the seat of his pomp, basking in the southern sun and enjoying his new sway as lord at la Coste, the marquis revealed no dull edge in his reply:

"Your reproaches show little consideration, my dear aunt. To be frank, I was not expecting to come across such strong language in the mouth of a holy nun. I do not allow, I do not tolerate nor do I authorise anyone to take the person who is at my home to be my wife; I have told everyone the contrary. 'Never give out that that's what she is,' the Abbé told me, 'but don't bother to stop those who want to say she is, as long as you tell them just the opposite.' It's his advice that I'm following. When one of your sisters, married as I am, used to live here openly with her lover, did you then regard la Coste as a cursed place? I am doing no more harm than she did... As for him from whom you have [the news] you're telling me about, priest though he be, he always has a couple of trollops at his home; excuse me, I'm using your terms; is his château a harem - no, better than that, it's a b[ordello].

"Forgive my contrariness - it runs in the family, and if I have anything to reproach myself for, it's the ill fortune to have been born into it. God keep me from all the foolishness and vices swarming within it...

"Be assured, my dear aunt, of my respect."

This thoroughly disrespectful and reckless response, in which he pointed accusing fingers at his seniors in the family, may well have done him more harm among the de Sades than any incident so far. On one page, he had insulted the abbess, his aunt, referred crudely to his uncle's discreet libertinage and dragged back into the light an extra-marital affair of the previous generation. A year after he wrote the letter, the marquis was blaming its intemperance on Beauvoisin having put him up to it, but this did not convince or mollify his uncle.

His mother-in-law also, receiving word from Provence of what was happening once Beauvoisin and the marquis had got into their merry stride at la Coste, was revising her view of how outrageous he could be. She wrote again to the Abbé in high summer. The letter as sent is not available, and Mme de Montreuil's sentiments survive in what is probably a preliminary draft, including sentences which she crossed out yet left legible, and which may well not have gone into the final text:

"... Prepared though I am by experience to expect anything from M de Sade, I had not wanted to believe him capable of this excess of impropriety, in his silly love affairs. And having often had a suspicion of what is going on, I always banished the idea as insulting to him, yet always feared to have my doubts confirmed... Hidden infidelities wrong his wife and me, but this misbehaviour, in front of his entire home province, insulting for his neighbours, will do him irreparable harm if it becomes known here, and how would it not be? While I am busy using his friends to raise him and his fortune, while it is due to his wife and to us[2] the smoothing-over of an affair which could have ruined him for ever and put him in prison for years[3], look at the recognition we're given for that. And then, in a strident tone, he will wail about his fate, the violence of his passions which seize hold of him, his regret at having made unhappy those who are attached to him. One is not always master of one's heart, but one is always master of one's conduct, and it is on the latter that we are judged. It's on this basis that he will be given the *ranks* [in society and the army] which it's his function to occupy, or be left aside as a bad lot, which would be a humiliating stigma for a man like him. He was starting to be known and regarded more favourably.

"... The visit to Avignon had been mentioned to me as a diversion, a bit of fun. I advised him to include something useful, taking advantage of your goodwill to inform himself about the properties and business which he will have to deal with one day... He wrote a fortnight ago to

2 The other Montreuils and their connections.

3 The blasphemous night with Jeanne Testard.

say he was at la Coste with you, working to learn about everything I was recommending to him, and that, his business over, he would return to join me in Normandy with more pleasure than I had imagined, that he would discover there perhaps a tranquillity which had eluded him for a long time. I don't know whether his Miss Beauvoisin had arrived at that stage. It seems he was expecting her at least. He can well imagine that I am not very eager to see him again. He has abused my indulgence too much, although that has not extended as far as he assures you it has... I was telling myself, on the basis of the picture of his character that had been painted for me and which I thought I recognised, that a little allowance for the fire of his youth, thus winning for me his friendship and his confidence, would keep him away from the great dangers he gives himself to without restraint. His mistresses rule him like tyrants; and what mistresses! If he provided them with less in the way of pleasure and was less generous towards them, he would soon find them dropping him, adored though he thinks he is. Good actor though he might be, the countesses of Saint Pré[4] are better still."

Crossing-out starts here:

"I am amazed, I promise you, sir, that you had the patience to stay six days witnessing the extravagant scene [at la Coste] without completely dispelling the misapprehension, which was given substance no doubt by the servants in their uncomprehending way, that [she] was Madame de Sade. This false impression is just too humiliating for her. Far from hiding her love for her husband, she would make a glory of it if he so deserved. I know your relatives have enough good sense not to be deceived by what happened [at la Coste]..."

Dipping into the letter during a further crossed-out passage:

"... As for his return [to Paris], ... he will come back quite exhausted, to give me worries and torments of every sort, to use all the cunning of which he is capable in order to find the money to pay debts worth 5,000 livres, an account of which he has sent to his wife[5], and then to start on new spending. He can be sure that, although I put my hand to concealing his foolish deeds from his wife or to excusing them so as to prevent any estrangement between them, I shall not hesitate to let her know about them and to make clear to her the depth of her misfortune, just as soon as that becomes necessary in order to avoid the greater

---

4 The actress-courtesans of the Paris theatres.

5 Who was less apt to reproach him over it than was her mother.

misfortunes of leaving her in ignorance; and I shall soon be forced to do this, if he does not stop me through a sincere change on his part, of which he is not capable..."

Mme de Montreuil's second thoughts at the fair-copy stage may have prevented the Abbé learning of her deeper misgivings and harder inclinations regarding his nephew. However, she was much concerned to keep her Provençal sapper up to his task of undermining the liaison at la Coste. On 8 August, at Échauffour, after what seems to have been a second visit by the Abbé to the château at la Coste, she was wielding her far-reaching goad again:

"You've done wonderfully, sir, but I was cross [to learn] that, when you were making progress, you left the party so soon. That girl will have regained the upper hand ...; he [the marquis] can be got round - by working on his pride or his fondness, she will have had their departure delayed and, by using cunning or pleasure, she will have tightened the chain which was ready to be broken. And that's why he won't have arrived at your home on the day fixed. I know[6] she is not expected in Paris before the end of August... This will mean even more expense and be worse all round... I promise you that I am very discouraged. No doubt he'll come back here to find me sooner or later; he will set out wonderful schemes for his behaviour and reasonableness, which he will mean or not mean; at least he will tell himself that he has convinced me. All will be well for two or three months. He will return to Paris. He will start all over again, perhaps going from bad to worse.

"I would much prefer it if you were able to keep him near you. It's three weeks since he wrote to his wife; she is beginning to worry about it and ... I'm afraid I'll be forced to tell [her what has been going on in Provence]. For the time being, she is telling herself that he must be en route, though I don't think so for a minute, but I am not telling her that I have news from you... He must have received a few words from me, very terse at that, sent on the 25th [of July]..."

Like nearly all the other letters between Mme de Montreuil and the marquis before he went to jail in 1777, those pointed words are lost.

Considering the power and influence of the Montreuils, a family of lawyers with contacts at high levels in the police and elsewhere in the royal administration, why did Mme de Montreuil not simply have Beauvoisin taken out of circulation? The thought had crossed the mind

---

6 Mme de Montreuil was a match for Inspector Marais in intelligence-gathering.

of the judge's lady, but it was not that simple. The letter of 8 August had a post-script:

"... Be strict in separating them, on which score I could certainly obtain, without difficulty, all I might ask of the minister; but that would lead to a fuss, damaging to him[7]. So one must not do that. But you must not be afraid of your nephew, much less put up with his aberrations.

"Don't lose sight of him at all because we won't win in this business except by not letting go of him for a moment; that's how I succeeded last year in separating him from Colet and in making him see reason, having convinced him he was being deceived. I doubt that he loves this one with more ardour than he loved the other: that was a frenzy!... On the pretext of business about land, return to la Coste to see what's going on there, whether he's still as smitten [by Beauvoisin]. Roar, put your foot down; you will make [him], out of respect for you, at least show a bit more propriety, keep down the expense, and live somewhere further from the public eye, to receive no guests, which would make for less scandal, for fewer people knowing about the affair and, by ... making less of a brouhaha down there, that will help prevent any at all here. And always try to have private conversations with him, when you will be able to talk sense to him, show you're uncomfortable when you have to be part of a threesome and have to give the appearance of sharing his bad behaviour by seeming to tolerate it[8]. They'll get bored, what with their style being cramped, and the nymph will the sooner make up her mind to leave. If, as I suspect from his last letter ..., he is beginning to get fed up with her, you will take advantage of that, of clouds, of quarrels which can break out and which he will never have the backbone to turn to account on his own. He is easily led; if you bring this to a head, don't let him follow her. Keep him by you for a long time without letting him go; keep him busy, and then we shall see. Given that he'll go on being daft in this way, I prefer that he should be so in Provence rather than here; that won't be known about [here]... His presence here would worry me. He would want, at least for appearance's sake, to live with his wife, and the creditors would be hounding him; ... if he were fed up with his mistress, he would take

7 To Beauvoisin also, but Mme de Montreuil's attitude to irritants from the lower orders never roused her conscience.

8 The Abbé, Mme de Montreuil may have suspected, might have been tolerating it all too well, having been somewhat tickled by Beauvoisin and the revels himself.

another. I prefer that he take one in Provence. It would be quite fortunate perhaps if he were to take up with some [married] woman. They're always less dangerous than expensive courtesans..."

And never mind any broken hearts, down there in the south, which was another country to Mme de Montreuil, concerned with high-society opinion in and around Paris and the royal court. Better tears shed in some household she would only hear about through the post than blocked social climbing for the upwardly mobile Montreuils and their blue-blooded acquisition from his majesty's regiments and the satellites of the royal house of Condé.

The Abbé proved unable to prise his nephew away from Beauvoisin, who was, by strong implication, far from being "too cold and too pious", as the marquis had described his wife. On 26 August, Mme de Montreuil was admitting defeat in her efforts to intervene by proxy at la Coste, but was unable to resist filing to the Abbé a report on his efforts:

"... It seems to me that, in your place, seeing he had made up his mind not to come to visit you, detained no doubt by that girl who was afraid of [the effect of] your advice and of you gaining the upper hand, I would have had the nerve to go to find him at la Coste, not to do the honours at his revels, which would have been to seem to authorise them, but to take him on one side, to talk to him alone, despite that girl and himself, and to talk to him with the reasonableness and firmness which your position with regard to him allows you. Even if he failed to show in writing the respect he owes you, he would surely not have done so in your presence. I know that his valet arrived in Paris, at my townhouse, on the 20th with his luggage. He said that his master had sent him on ahead and that he himself would be arriving in a few days for sure. I am quite convinced he is already in Paris, and that he is staying at the young lady's place. You understand clearly that this will become known and will have a bad effect...

"... If I were in Paris, I would go in person to pick him up at that girl's door, as I did at another's place a year ago, and it succeeded; but I'm not there. Besides, I no longer reckon on having the same credit with his mind and his heart...

"... He owes in effect 5,000 livres, but that's due to tradesmen and workmen, and that sort of person. Of that, only 600 livres ... has to be paid in September... I advanced him 500 which he told me he needed when he left [for Provence]... That girl had offered to lend him [money]. To facilitate the payment of such debts would be to encourage vice...

"... My daughter is still unaware of this adventure; she thinks only that he was amusing himself by putting on plays with his relatives from round about, and that this was the cause of his silence. That's the device I've employed to calm her worries...

"I recall that he had got into murky business in your part of the world in order to raise money; it would be important [for me] to know exactly what that is about: the kind [of undertaking], the sum and the term [for repayment]..."

It seems that the marquis was indeed in Paris on or about 20 August for, on the 21st, Beauvoisin signed a notarised contract to lend the marquis 10,000 livres. This was not done entirely out of love because, in return, Beauvoisin was to receive from the marquis 500 livres a year for life - this commitment to a person in her mid-twenties who, even in the 18th century, might expect at least another 30 years of life. However, Pauvert points out that such contracts were sometimes a convenient fiction concocted by courtesans and their clients so as to place the latters' gifts and other spending under legal protection and thus beyond the reach of clients' relatives. Such a canny woman as Beauvoisin might also have considered, knowing the volatile marquis as she did, that such a watertight deal would protect her in case he were to turn against her and shut his purse.

On 15 September, the marquis reached Échauffour at last and greeted his wife, whom he had not seen since May. He was "well, quite cheery," his mother-in-law told the Abbé, and Mme de Montreuil was glad to find that the summer adventure in Provence had escaped the attention of Parisian society. Even Inspector Marais, seer of the vice squad, reported:

"All summer, [Beauvoisin] stayed shut up at Longchamp, in the little house belonging to the Marquis de Louvois. Only M de la Boulaye had the right to go now and again to the hideaway, and she was making him pay dearly for the kindness she showed by receiving him."

Marais was having the wool pulled over his eyes, or he was doing the same to his superiors in the government. It is sure that Beauvoisin was at la Coste, and unlikely that Marais would have risked throwing suspicion on all his dossiers by filing a report he knew to be false on a few players in the demi-monde. So it seems that de la Boulaye, who was very keen on Beauvoisin, may well have been persuaded to lay a false trail while the resourceful courtesan slipped away to la Coste.

In November, however, the marquis left his in-laws' Norman estate abruptly, on learning that Beauvoisin had suffered in Paris what Mme de Montreuil called "an accident" - probably a miscarriage or some event which endangered her in pregnancy. The judge's lady commented tartly: "The condition she's in, I can't imagine he's finding much scope for his pleasures. If he were to get so bored with her as not to go back to see her again, that would be a very good thing." Saying which, Mme de Montreuil, who generally showed remarkable understanding of the ways of impassioned men, revealed a certain ignorance of the attractiveness of pregnant women, not least those in distress, for some men. A reading of certain of the marquis's works written after 1780 would have enlightened her later - but one must believe she was spared that shock.

By stillbirth or delivery of a live infant, Beauvoisin was relieved of her pregnancy, father unknown - to posterity anyway. She was back among the network of police informers, and Marais was able to report on 13 December:

"... Now that her confinement is over, she is after conquests more brilliant than before and likely to be more to her taste. This week, she appeared at the Italian Theatre like a new star. Giving birth has made her more beautiful and the young M de Saint Contest was eating out of her hand at once, and on account of him she has dismissed M de Louvois and M de la Boulaye. Chevalier Raconis has staved off twenty [of her] creditors for her... All our hangers-on in the swim are scrapping for the chance to put a smile on her face... But the most dangerous of the lot is Chevalier de Choiseul and I noticed yesterday that he was running an eye over her. I greeted him; he replied: 'I've just caught a look of hers which assures me that, in a few days, she'll be mine.' "

So it proved - "and without opening his purse," the inspector noted.

In the first week of the new year, 1766, it seems de Sade treated Beauvoisin to one of his *fin de l'affaire* letters, all spleen and recriminations. Colet would have recognised the style:

"So now you're unmasked, monster! Your wickedness is at its height. The trick is very crude; what was the point of an anonymous letter? You only needed to tell me that you wanted to drop me: I would not have used force to visit you. I could take revenge, pay you back in kind and, by a similar trick [another anonymous letter], take from you that which is raising your hopes, but I would never resort to such low devices. They're worthy of you, vile monster... I shall hate you for the rest of my life... Goodbye, take your new conquest and break with him by the same wickedness that cunning let you use on me. One day, when you are all dried up, when the illusion of pleasure, of ambition, which is eating you, has blown away, you'll not be able to prevent yourself feeling the remorse which is bound to rack a heart like yours. Goodbye for the last time. With what pleasure I expect that, tomorrow at this time, I will be perhaps fifty leagues away from you...! Your unworthy image will be erased from my heart much sooner even than that."

By January 1767, a year later, he was involved with Beauvoisin again. In the interval, according to the police dossiers, he had kept company with various courtesans - for instance, "Miss Dorville, a tall and very amiable girl, recently escaped from la Hecquet's harem," that is, from a brothel run by a woman called Hecquet. The marquis's style in seeking leave to spend his tenants' rents was nothing if not lavish. Here he is in 1766, petitioning one young actress:

"The guards officer Bourneville has spoken to you about me, at least so he tells me... You have someone, I know, who pays dearly for the honour to be loved by you. What a happy man he is! What a shame that I don't have his sort of fortune to offer you! Ah! What am I saying? A fortune! It's a throne you ought to have had; the queen of love should have been queen of the entire universe. So it's only second place I aspire to. Be so good as to confer it on me, I beg you. The vivacity of my love makes me worthy of it. I have less wealth than my rival but more youthfulness[9] and more love."

For all his outpourings in the manner of the worst of the plays which he attended, and in which some of his would-be objects of hire appeared, de Sade's sexual desires continued to find expression further from the footlights. In November, he paid 200 livres to rent for four and a half months a little furnished house at Arcueil, a village near Paris. There he was soon "causing a great deal of scandal, and bringing there day and night persons of both sexes with whom he was engaged in debauchery... What's more, he is known as a very violent man, having insulted and hit various persons," a local police officer stated.

---

9 He had crossed out his first thought: more vigour.

About the day he was receiving the keys of his rural seat of pleasure, the marquis must have been initiating the next generation of de Sades for, in mid-April of the following year, 1767, Mme de Montreuil was telling the Abbé:

"Madame de Sade's pregnancy is moving along; she's about five and a half months gone. I doubt that the birth of this child causes him as much joy as it should and that I was daring to tell myself it would. The father no longer seems to be giving it so much of his attention. He is busy with objects which, to his way of thinking, are more interesting..."

However, before the first of the next generation could come into the world, the head of the previous generation had left it. The Count de Sade, while staying with the Montreuils, died on 24 January after a short illness at the age of 64. With that, the marquis became head of the family and inherited his father's title, which he often used in letters and legal documents, but simplicity and tradition require that he continue to be known here as the Marquis de Sade. Mme de Montreuil told the Abbé: "The way in which his son felt this loss and is affected by it quite reconciles me to him."

Not for long. In her April letter, Mme de Montreuil told the Abbé she was glad to see the back of his nephew:

"He's leaving tomorrow, so he tells me. I promise you that this gives me great satisfaction; at least there'll be a period of calm. What a shame! He has everything one could need to make one happy, in making himself a part of those with whom he has to live. If only he wanted to be reasonable and decent, and not to spoil himself by going with creatures who aren't worth the trouble. Miss B has restored all her influence over him and, since the death of his father, she's using it. He is absolutely blind on this score..."

The journey de Sade was about to start probably took him to Lyons, where Beauvoisin was appearing at a theatre. There is little evidence after that of the two of them remaining linked and it is very likely that the affair ended in the spring of 1767.

In another part of his universe, the marquis and his uncle had been assembling the documents which attested to the young man's nobility having dated back enough generations for him to be qualified for higher ranks in the army. In the French army of the 1760s, what made an officer fit to rise was the blueness of the blood in his veins, however much red blood he might cause to be spilled through his military competence - or lack of it. The genealogical research bore fruit in April when the marquis was promoted to the rank of *capitaine commandant* (roughly equivalent to major) in his cavalry regiment. The young officer sent the news to his uncle, declaring: "... so I now have a foot in the stirrup, as they say, and am sure to make my way..."

Also attending to his dignity, on 21 June he was at la Coste as his father's successor as lord of the manor, to receive the homage of members of the community, on their knees and at his summons, as though the middle ages had never passed away.

On 27 August, the next lord of the manor, if all had stayed as it was, saw the light of day in Paris when the marquise gave birth to her first child to reach baptism, Louis Marie, born Marquis de Sade.

As a lord who rarely appeared on his estates, de Sade was little more concerned to exercise his function of magistrate in the local law court and supervise the collection of dues from his tenants and villagers as he was, when looking up the social scale, to attend the royal court and pay homage to his liege lord, the King of France. In the same way that the royal administration farmed out tax-gathering to private individuals and syndicates, so the de Sades, like many other nobles, delegated the collection of dues on their estates to agents and bailiffs, who paid lump sums to the lord of the manor at certain dates. Such sums were made up not only of cash rents but also the value of proportions of a tenant's crops (a third, say, or a quarter, as with share-croppers in the southern USA and many other parts of the world), of fees for use of the lord's wine press at grape harvest time and for use of his bakery, of payments for the right to fish in streams that cross the estates, of tolls exacted from traders and travellers passing along the roads and rivers through the lord's domain.

About the year 1770, de Sade was receiving some 17,500 livres a year in this way - rather less in real terms than his father had been taking about 20 years before, thanks to the count having failed to give close attention in his later years to extracting the maximum income from the family patrimony. Even so, this was probably an above-average income for the head of a French landed family at that time. As we know, much of it went on above-average expenditure.

No-one knew that better than Inspector Marais. He updated his superiors on 16 October, 1767:

"We won't be waiting long to hear again about the Marquis de Sade's horrors; he is doing more than is humanly possible in order to convince Miss Rivière of the Opéra to live with him, and he has offered her twenty-five louis a month, on condition that she spends the days when she does not have a stage performance with him at his little house at Arcueil. This young lady has refused because she is enjoying the favours of M Hocquart de Coubron, but M de Sade is still after her and, while he awaits her surrender, he has been going all out this week to persuade the Brissault woman to supply him with girls to go and take supper with him at his little house. The woman has been digging in her heels against that, having a pretty good idea of what he can get up to, but he will be trying others who are less scrupulous or who don't know him, and we will certainly hear more about him before long."

Indeed, for in February of 1768 there were reports from police outside Paris of de Sade having taken "four girls" to Arcueil, where they were whipped, given a meal, paid and sent politely on their way.

De Sade was mentioned in the vice squad's jottings for the last time on 18 March: "M de Sade has left Miss Rivière who, since then, has achieved various liaisons, and it is said that the Prince de Conti, touched by the condition of this young person, is having her undergo cures with a view subsequently to take her over... If she was healthy, this is a pretty woman."

CHAPTER 7: "THE LEAST UNFAVOURABLY AS POSSIBLE"

At nine in the morning of Easter Sunday, 3 April 1768, the Marquis de Sade was in the Place des Victoires in Paris when he noticed a woman accept alms from a passer-by. He beckoned her to him and promised her money if she would accompany him. She refused this, believing he was soliciting prostitution. He assured her that, rather, he wanted her to clean his rooms. This she accepted and went with him to a building within walking distance, where he asked her to wait while he attended to another matter before taking her on to his house outside the city, later that morning. Her name was Rose Keller, aged 36, widow of a kitchen worker. She spoke French awkwardly, with a German accent.

An hour later, the marquis came back, with a cab. The two rode away in it, the wooden shutters closed. During the first part of the journey, the marquis said nothing to the woman but, as the cab neared the Barrière d'Enfer (Hell Gate) on the way out of the city, he told her she would be well fed and treated with respect. He said no more after that, seeming to be asleep. After a ride through the countryside, the cab stopped at the village of Arcueil at about half-past twelve. Keller was taken to the first floor of a house, to a closely-shuttered room in which she could just make out two canopied beds. The marquis told her to wait there while he brought a meal, telling her there was nothing for her to worry about. He left, double-locking the door behind him.

She had waited an hour before he returned, with a lighted candle, and gently invited her downstairs. There he escorted her into a small, also dark, room where his manner was suddenly transformed as he ordered her to undress. She asked why and he said it was to have some fun. She protested that she had not come there for any such thing, at which he threatened to kill her and bury her in the garden. He left the room and she, by then very scared, undressed down to her petticoat. He returned and told her to remove that. She said she would die first. He took it off and shoved her into the next room, where he threw her face-down onto a divan, tied her to it and put a bolster and a muff of lynx fur across her shoulders. (There would be no marks on her neck and face if any blows went wide.)

The marquis removed his jacket and shirt, put on a sleeveless waistcoat and tied a cloth around his forehead. He picked up a birch and used it to whip her fiercely. She cried out. He paused in the beating and showed her a knife, promising to kill her if she were not quiet, repeating his threat to bury her himself. He inflicted another five or six bursts of blows, alternating birch and cat-of-nine-tails whip, while she stifled her voice. Having stopped two or three times to rub ointment into her wounds, he resumed the beating. Keller pleaded with him not to kill her, she not having made her Easter confession. He replied that this did not matter for he could hear her confession. She continued her pleas until the beating was intensified and the marquis broke off suddenly, uttering loud and frightening cries. (One assumes he had achieved orgasm.)

He untied the woman and led her back to the room where her clothes were so that she could dress. Having left the room for a few minutes, he returned with a towel and water. She washed and dressed. The towel had become bloodstained and the marquis made Keller rinse it clean. Then he brought a bottle of brandy, getting her to rub some on her wounds so that, in an hour, no trace would remain. The spirit stung but she did as he directed. Next, he gave her boiled beef and a flask of wine, taking her back to the upstairs room and telling her not to go near the window or make any noise. He would let her go in the evening. She begged to be released at once, having no idea where she was and not wanting to have to spend the night on the road as, having very little money, she would be obliged to do. He told her not to fret and left her, locking the door again.

Keller then bolted the door on her side, improvised a rope out of knotted bedclothes, made a hole in the felt packing of the shutters, opened one of them and, having tied her rope to the metal bar of the window, lowered herself into the back garden. She climbed the trellis on the garden wall and dropped into the vacant lot beyond, scraping her left hand and arm, then walked to the street. The marquis's valet, Langlois, came running after her, shouting that his master wanted to talk to her. She kept going. Langlois then took out a purse and offered to pay her. Keller pushed him away and walked on until she met three women of the village, to whom she told what had happened. They sympathised and took her aside into a courtyard to have a look at her injuries.

The above account, except for a couple of interventions of mine in parentheses, follows Keller's statement to the authorities about the incident. Apart from a few mitigating details as to the degree of violence meted out - for instance, de Sade insisted he had not tied the woman to the divan, only told her to lie on it - the marquis conceded that this was more or less what had taken place. However, he also maintained that Keller had understood, from his first approach, that she was being hired for debauchery, not for cleaning. This was important, at least to de Sade, in deciding whether any guilt attached to him from the episode. His view, on which he was still harping years later, was that, if a prostitute had not been paid, a court could and should order the client to pay. If she had been paid and was only making a fuss about ill-treatment, though, she should be warned about bothering law courts with such inappropriate matters and told to change her way of making a living if she did not like what it entailed. In one of his works of fiction, written much later, de Sade created a character amazed at finding judges "moved to pity for the thrashed arse of a street-walker."

A chorus of commentators and biographers has supported de Sade in his shrugging-off of the encounter with Keller as the sort of pleasure a fellow might buy from time to time - bizarre, but no lasting harm done. However, this was not a commonly expressed view of the incident at the time. This is not to say there was a rallying to support Keller, much less beaten women in general. Popular imagination - in the court and the capital city - was much taken by the fact that the flagellation had occurred at Easter. The marquis was already known to some, from the Testard affair, as liking to blaspheme in his lust. Now it was being said that he had deliberately profaned the Christian festival of Easter by whipping a naked woman in denigration of the scourging of Christ before His crucifixion. The marquis's rejection of Keller's plea for her life to be spared because she had not made her Easter confession was also a mark against him, as was his sinful suggestion that he would act as her confessor.

There were precedents in the France of Louis XV for libertines thrashing women in combination with blasphemy, but the marquis was bereft of support which other such outragers might have enjoyed. For one thing, having got into this sort of scrape after his father and protector had died, de Sade felt the lack of goodwill which his consistent neglect of certain formalities before the king, his peers and the Church had occasioned. To the powerful of the land, he was a young rake who not only misbehaved in the *demi-monde* but also disdained to show respect in high society when it was taking itself seriously. De Sade was not so well-connected that so much blasphemy and so little paying court could be overlooked by the arbiters of who should walk free and who should be locked away. He had inherited his father's title, was the head of a family of ancient nobility, and a cavalry offer - but all this and his link to the royal Bourbons was not sufficient antidote to the corrosion that his behaviour was working on the protection about his person.

What's more, there was a sentiment in France that there was too much of this kind of thing going on and that someone should be made an example of. On hearing of de Sade's latest escapade, people would list it with other acts of libertinage by nobles riding roughshod over laws that would have sent those without influence, guilty of similar crimes, to the scaffold. The absolute power vested in Louis XV was declining, not least because the royal administration was allowing more people, and a greater social range of persons, into positions of authority and influence as it struggled to maintain effective government and raise revenue. The king and his ministers felt constrained to pay more attention to public opinion (although this refers to a small proportion of the whole population) as the number of hands in the generation and allocation of wealth was multiplied.

Also, there was a lively and virulent body of unauthorised publications, printed clandestinely in France, or produced in Britain and Holland then smuggled into France. Their writers liked nothing better than to expose low doings in high society. The Keller episode was written up within a month of the event, with colourful additions: de Sade had gagged the woman to stop her cries, had cut her body a number of times with a knife (which a doctor's report showed to be false), had used a wax on her wounds as an experimental curative, the villagers of Arcueil would have lynched him if he had not fled. At least one clandestine newspaper suggested that the wax was an irritant designed to make Keller's injuries smart the more. De Sade had maintained he was trying to soothe her wounds.

The day of the incident, once the villagers of Arcueil had fussed over Keller a little and dressed her wounds, ended with her spending the night in someone's cow-barn on a straw mattress. The marquis, meanwhile, had bidden his gardener at the Arcueil house so-long and returned to Paris at about six in the evening.

The powers that were in the village took statements from Keller and various witnesses. By the following Thursday, Mme de Montreuil had heard of the trouble and sent for the Abbé Amblet, the marquis's former tutor, and a lawyer. They were despatched in haste to Arcueil that day with express instructions to find the woman and buy her silence. She was lodged by this time in the house of a local official, where she told the emissaries that she had been much abused and was now unable to work. After some bluster and haggling on both sides, and a consultation back in Paris because the two men feared Mme de Montreuil would not pay the 2,000 livres Keller wanted, the delegation returned to clinch a withdrawal of complaint in exchange for 2,400 livres, plus medical expenses. Mme de Montreuil had wanted the business done quickly in order to staunch the source of gossip and rumours already spreading in Paris and at the royal court.

However, sealing one mouth was not enough. The next day, Friday after Easter, a royal minister sent a message to the governor of Saumur Castle, a prison on the Loire river nearly 200 miles south-west of Paris, that he was to receive the Marquis de Sade as a permanent prisoner, confined to the building and the grounds. The minister ordered the police to arrest the marquis and take him to the castle. This intervention had been secured by his family, exercising its influence to secure a royal detention order which put him beyond the reach of the ordinary system of justice. The marquis obtained from the royal administration permission to travel to Saumur with the Abbé Amblet, who was made responsible for his arrival, rather than under a police escort which might well have drawn attention to him and stirred further gossip.

Meanwhile, a senior judge who happened to be at his country house, a few yards from de Sade's little place, had taken great exception to the incident. This was one reason for its being pitched into the machinery of the criminal courts, which processed it with remarkable speed. Various officials of these courts, unaware of the even speedier detention of the marquis under a royal order, were soon trying to serve arrest warrants on him. On two dates, the high court of Paris had him cried as "absent and fugitive", a ceremony apt to attract much attention to the errant and his relatives because it involved two trumpeters sounding a fanfare, and the town crier reading a proclamation naming the person sought by the court, at various specified public places in Paris and, in this case, outside the Montreuils' townhouse. Other court officers failed to sequester de Sade's property at the Montreuil mansion because the furniture in his rooms there was deemed to belong to his father-in-law, who was too practised a lawyer to have missed such a trick.

On 26 April, Mme de Montreuil was able to tell the Abbé de Sade:

"The business of your nephew, sir, better clarified by the reports and the investigations of the high court, is seen as an act of madness or of libertinage which cannot be excused, but is stripped of all the horrors which had been loaded onto it.... This affair requires a great deal of prudence, skill and time. That's how to come out of it the least unfavourably as possible..."

As far as her pilotage of her son-in-law was concerned, there is no phrase better to describe Mme de Montreuil's reduced aims, once she had discovered what a trouble he was. Realism dictated a goal no higher than to emerge "*le moins défavorablement possible*."

She went on:

"I do not tell you about Mme de Sade: it is easy to understand how afflicted she is. Her son is doing well: he is teething."

On 10 June, the high court, as it was bound to do, recognised letters of annulment which the king had issued to de Sade. This unusual device in effect wiped out the crime so that, it being declared by the highest authority not to have taken place, no court could proceed with it. This meant that the scandal over the Keller affair might be diminished more readily.

De Sade the amateur actor would have appreciated what the high court was about when it flourished a little hollow authority in the face of the royal prerogative, making him follow the traditional form by appearing bare-headed and on his knees as applicant for ratification of the letters of annulment by the justices. Intensive lobbying by de Sades, Montreuils and their connections among the nobility was instrumental in this.

In the meantime, a royal minster had transferred de Sade from Saumur to the Pierre Encise fortress near Lyons, where he arrived about 10 May, escorted by Marais. The inspector, on arrival at Saumur, had found de Sade enjoying the run of the castle and a place at the governor's table. During the journey across France to Pierre Encise, the marquis complained to his most knowledgeable chronicler yet that he had done no more than give the girl a thrashing, "and that it had never entered his head to scar her, that he can't imagine what can have brought the creature to have made such a complaint, and that he is quite convinced that, if the high court orders an examination by expert doctors, no trace of scars will be found. Nevertheless, he is very much afraid that the information [about the Keller affair] will reopen his past escapades, and he hopes that you will be good enough, sir," Marais reported to a government minister, "out of the regard you would wish to show for his family, to see fit to let no-one know anything of it... He is counting on having, when he leaves Pierre Encise, an order confining him to his estates or to those of his father-in-law, seeing himself as having to spend at least two years without showing his face in Paris.

"In the provinces everybody knows what he has done - at Saumur, at Lyons, at Moulins, at Dijon, he's the topic of the day... If I have well understood M de Sade's drift, he seems repentant only about being detained ... because deep down he is still the same."

The régime for de Sade at the fortress was to be stricter than that at Saumur. He was not to leave his room or have anything to do with the other prisoners, the king had determined. However, a valet used to the task would be allowed to dress a fistula from which de Sade was suffering.

Despite the annulment of his crime, de Sade was not set free. The absolute power of the French monarchy might have been slipping but it was still effective enough to keep the marquis - and thousands of other people around the country - in jail on the king's order alone. "An indecent affair beyond excusing could not have been wound up more decently," remarked Mme de Montreuil succinctly, relieved to have had the affair taken out of the hands of the public courts, and the miscreant in the secret hands of the royal prerogative.

The Dowager Countess de Sade wrote to the relevant royal minister to complain at what she regarded as the harsh treatment of her son in detention. M de Saint Florentin replied:

"I do not think it would be to M de Sade's advantage if I were to put your representations before the king ... because His Majesty could decide to put him back into the hands of the high court..."

Her daughter-in-law, about to complete five years of marriage, showed signs of emerging from the screens of ignorance and the restraints on action created by Mme de Montreuil. Within a week of the Easter whipping, Renée Pélagie was sending the Abbé Amblet to the house at Arcueil to collect some silverware and engravings. The sort of engraving which her husband liked to have on show at his pleasure retreats was not usually the kind to be left where investigating magistrates might see it. Tidying further, after her husband's dissolutions, the marquise gave notice to the landlord of the Arcueil house that the lease was to be cancelled, likewise that of other rented accommodation taken by her husband, at Versailles. Also, she asked the minister for her husband to be allowed to circulate more freely within the château at Pierre Encise - "impossible, above all after what happened in the high court, which would not fail to ask for him back if he were seen to be mixing with people who come and go at the château," de Saint Florentin told her.

The marquise sold some of her diamonds to finance a journey to Lyons - Mme de Montreuil may well have refused to dip into her family's coffers to cover the cost of a trip of which she did not approve - and to pay the pension of her mother-in-law which the marquis was omitting to do, through being unable to reach funds or by neglect. The marquis was committed to the upkeep of his mother, to the extent of 1,200 livres a year in six-monthly instalments.

The minister allowed a series of visits by Renée Pélagie to her husband at the fortress, at least one of which, in late-September, was almost certainly unsupervised for she became pregnant. About 15 November, he ordered the release of the prisoner, who was required by the king to go straight to his estate at la Coste and stay there. The minister told Mme de Montreuil:

"... it is the conduct he is going to maintain which will determine the greater or lesser degree of liberty he will be accorded, and he cannot give too much attention to his moves towards making up for the past..."

Mme de Montreuil told the Abbé, towards whose part of the world the miscreant was being sent:

"I do not doubt that your nephew should have reflected with sufficient seriousness not to give any sorrow to his wife or worries to his family from now on, but I hope that you intend to keep a close eye on him, sir, and to keep nothing from me... M de Sade's health not being good [due to haemorrhoids], he will be urged to rest at his home... Your grand-nephew is doing well and walking unaided; he is very pretty; I take all the care of him that my friendship for his father and his mother arouses in me..."

It is not clear whether the marquise, who seems to have greeted her husband as he emerged from Pierre Encise, accompanied him to la

Coste. In any event, she was in Paris by March of the next year, 1769, and the marquis spent much of the winter at la Coste without her.

While her son-in-law was away from the temptations of Paris, Mme de Montreuil made a reckoning of his financial profligacy and reported on 2 March to the Abbé:

"... At the time of his adventure [with Keller], he was found to be owing 16 to 17,000 livres to various tradesmen through daft spending on his little houses, on his mistresses, on his upkeep - debts which he had carefully hidden from me, always saying he owed nothing, paying for everything cash on the nail... Of 20,000 which had been made over to him from his wife's dowry by the time of his affair [with Keller], 4,000 remained and I have paid off as much again in taking care of those parts of his debts that he told me about and of which I have given him an account... Also, Madame de Sade owes about 3,000 livres regarding her household expenses up to the first of January, which she would have paid at the end of the year '68 if she had not spent the money on her journey to Lyons which Monsieur de Sade desired so ardently... Now, he no longer wants his debts to be reckoned with hers. He is not giving her what she genuinely needs for the current year. On what basis does he see her meeting her expenses? Is this right? Is this proper? Would he regard it as tender, as proper, if she were to reply to him thus: 'I need my money to pay household bills, our staff, my upkeep, so I'll not be going to share your prison, to soothe your troubles'? Far from it: I have found out, although she took care to hide it from me, that she sold the few diamonds she had to pay for her journey and to cover her mother-in-law's pension for six months, the latter being herself in need because of a failure by her son to pay... Every six months it's the same story..."

"What's more," Mme de Montreuil went on, "he still owes 7 thousand 4 hundred-odd livres on an old account from his company at the regiment. The minister and the colonels want the officers who are owed money by the King to be paid out of the funds of those who still owe sums to the same corps; that's being rigorously enforced at present[1]. Must Monsieur de Sade, in his position, make himself cried against on this score as much as on the others and even more so?...

"All this comes to a total of a trifling 20,000 livres, more or less...

---

1 As one might expect, because it was a way for the royal treasury to avoid coughing up back pay and invalidity payments to entitled officers.

"We were thinking, my daughter and I, that one of the most important things for her husband in his position was to hide his past dissolutions, hoping that he was cured of such affairs, and to prevent anyone bringing a complaint against him, even among the common people; so one had to take out a loan of 20,000 livres to sort out his business completely, then he would pay off that loan out of the payment due to him this year from the States[2], he and his wife would live off the remainder of his revenues, and off the increase [in his income] which could come to him through the sale of his property [the Mas de Cabanes] at Arles, if he manages to get rid of it at a good price [and invest the proceeds]. In a word, that would mean a year or eighteen months to turn things around and put them right."

What looked simple, after a little work at the abacus and a mother-daughter council of war in milady's study at the Montreuil townhouse in Paris, did not allow sufficiently for the capacity of the gentleman concerned to make a nuisance of himself. Mme de Montreuil had a lawyer send to la Coste a document which the marquis had only to fill in and sign for his wife to have power of attorney to borrow 12,000 livres of the 20,000 to be sought. Back came a complicated and different proxy document concerning less than the 12,000. The marquis had been told already that this was not on. The document, with observations, travelled again to Provence. The marquis returned it once more to Paris, with a note to say that the lawyers at Apt, the nearest town to the château, "don't know how to do it any other way," Mme de Montreuil reported to the Abbé.

While all this was going on, with each package taking seven or eight days to pass between Paris and the south (perhaps longer, for the to-and-fro was taking place in winter), the creditors were becoming more annoyed and more pressing; some filed legal suits to recover their money. "A certain Corbin, a tapestry-maker who, on Monsieur de Sade's written undertaking, was promised 900 livres on account for last January, is at my house incessantly. He came, the day before yesterday, to tell me that he was going to arrange for a seizure of goods, that he could not wait any longer and have himself put inside in order to oblige me... That might be true; I am so unused to dealing with these grumbles and to deluding people with false promises that all this is

---

2 The notables of the four provinces of which he was lieutenant-general.

unbearable," Mme de Montreuil complained, still in her long letter of 2 March to the Abbé.

The marquise proved to be more adept at stringing along creditors than was her mother, so they were still not having to stand aside for bailiffs when word arrived from the marquis that he would soon be returning to Paris, where he would sort out his finances himself and prove he had done nothing wrong.

"... I have fallen from the heights," Mme de Montreuil went on. "Stop him, sir, by any means whatsoever, from this foolishness of which I believe him to be all too capable. Where has he got permission to return to Paris? Is he to ruin himself utterly, at least to find himself arrested on the way or on arriving here, and to be locked up once and for all? As for that last point, he can be sure that I would no longer be opposed to it..."

Mme de Montreuil added that the marquis was quite wrong if he thought that his behaviour with regard to his finances would hasten his return to Paris:

"... He ought to reckon himself very fortunate if he obtains permission to rejoin his regiment on 1 June; that's as much as I would envisage, because that is essential to his standing, to his rehabilitation in the public mind..."

Meanwhile, her son-in-law's vacillation was making potential lenders think twice and his creditors close in:

"... the name of the Marquis de Sade will be resounding again, and everything that was starting to be forgotten will be brought back to light at the [king's] Palace and among the public. His furniture will be seized and sold for next to nothing. I will be asked to certify as to what there is of his in my house; I will certainly not put my name to any lie and I will let go whatever there is, including his silver service. On the honour of my daughter and the rest of my family, I would not be able to conceal that it was made easy for him to settle his affairs and avoid this trouble, that he has always replied with nonsense and dodged, refused the necessary instruments to his wife... We will see that he is no more sensible after his misfortunes than before. So one has good reason ... to want him to remain for a long time in a good château very peacefully, away from temptations or at least away from the means to give way to them, and one had good reason again to press his wife to separate from him.

"The first of April is coming, the date when they start work on lining up personnel for the regiments; all the officers who are to have troops join up on 1 May[3] ... The minister will get annoyed with M de Sade and, one fine day, without prior notice, will send a letter of thanks for his services and an order for him to pay what he owes; he will appoint him to his company or rather, if he doesn't pay despite that, order him detained because of the money outstanding, and then - God knows. This nephew is too feather-brained to envisage the consequences of what he does and of what he exposes himself to, always drawn along by the desires of the moment... If the power of attorney does not arrive in reply to this letter, it will arrive too late to head off the legal suits [by creditors] and much expense... All the while, the whole business is being talked about and there will be less eagerness to lend because his disorder will be supposed to be even greater than it is in effect.

"Well, sir, there you have your nephew's state of affairs; since his marriage he has gone through 66,000 livres still to be covered: debts incurred by his pleasures, over and above his revenues. However, he has always been stingy regarding his household and his wife, and scrounging from her and from me all that he could.

"He thinks he has everything sorted out, everything laid down when he deluded us with *statements*, with *arrangements* of revenues and of payments for 3 or 4 years in advance which have never taken place because his mad spending has always wiped them out. Two months ago he had sent to me statements *well drawn up, well in order*, by his secretary (an apprentice actor, they say, and who must in that case be very much to his liking), for 1770-71-72, while his head is regulating the accounts for 1769 on the basis of false reckoning...

"I leave him to you, sir; it's for your goodwill towards your nephew to rule you in what you have to do for him. For myself, I wash my hands of him. I am going to let the torrent flow, and concern myself only with my daughter and my unfortunate children[4]. I hope the second arrives safely despite the increasing sorrows that its mother is undergoing, not counting those which her husband is still preparing for her. Our little one [Louis Marie] is doing very well. He is very pretty, grandmother's prejudice aside; he often kisses his father's portrait in his mother's room. I promise you he touches me to the quick..."

---

3 Warfare and manoeuvres in the 18th century were usually conducted in summer.

4 The de Sade offspring.

The lad's father, for all Mme de Montreuil's declaration that she was washing her hands of him, was about to sting her into a further letter to the Abbé. Two days later, on 4 March, she had received news from the south and was deploring:

"Instead of pursuits befitting his situation, the person in whom we have an interest, so I learn publicly, has given a party, a ball, has put on a play, with all that this entails - and what actresses![5] ... I'm assured that you had honoured this with the approval of your presence, which made it excusable as far as I am concerned; but indulgence is not so readily found in everyone and it might do him a great deal of harm, having more serious consequences than he thinks. Things which are innocent in themselves, in ordinary circumstances, change their significance with their situation. It will be felt that a man ... is amusing himself by giving parties instead of working to put his business to rights. I hope that the distraction was slight and brief; the effect is the same, though, and the expense is odious in that it prevents the paying-off of genuine debts and adds to their number. I promise you that I would not have been as indulgent as you; I would have set fire to the hall if I had had no other means to put a stop to it..."

No crossing-out there, so one may be confident that the Abbé received that flea in his complaisant ear.

Two paragraphs later, Mme de Montreuil temporised:

"You will excuse, I hope, my representations, on account of the extreme importance of his conduct for himself and for his children. I do not mention to you his wife's interest in this, it being the least affecting for him, albeit he at least owes her gratitude and a great deal of it. You would be less disapproving, sir, of his return here if you were to consider every bit how useful she is here to her husband. For myself, I promise that, although I have had no part in their agreement over this [his return to Paris], I am the calmer for it. I would be in endless agonies at knowing she was shut up in a lonely château with that head of his."

Through the intervention of not only his wife, but also of his mother the dowager countess, the marquis returned to the Paris area in the spring. De Saint Florentin wrote to the dowager countess on 2 April:

---

5 Brought from Marseilles, the nearest city, no doubt.

"... His Majesty, convinced that you are revealing nothing but the exact truth, is very willing to allow M de Sade to return to the outskirts of Paris at a country house, to undergo there the treatment needed for his health[6] ...; but on condition that he sees very few people there and that he leaves again for his estates as soon as his health permits, His Majesty's intention being that his orders in this respect shall not be revoked..."

About the end of April, de Sade was in Paris and, little heeding the royal order that he stay outside the city, was near at hand when his wife gave birth, on 28 June, to their second child. This son, Donatien Claude Armand, was "big and strong ... much more so than one has the right to expect of such a delicate mother," Mme de Montreuil reported to the Abbé. The father was "fulfilling, since his return, the functions of a good husband by his assiduousness to Madame de Sade, but only time will show if this is calculation or friendship and gratitude..."

By late-August, de Sade was back at la Coste and Mme de Montreuil was refusing to let her daughter join him, despite his insistence, so as not "to expose her to new scenes". The Abbé was sharply advised to let his nephew know "he must not imagine he is going to make us all tremble with his I WANT..."

From mid-September, de Sade may well have been turning his attention to the wants which keep alive his fame and effect as a writer. He left Paris on 19 September - royal permission or no royal permission - heading north. He visited Brussels, staying for five days, then passed via Antwerp, Rotterdam, Delft, the Hague (for the first week of October), Leiden, Haarlem and Amsterdam (from 9-18 October), then started back, arriving in Paris on the 21st. It seems very likely that the marquis - during the tour in the Low Countries and probably at the Hague - sold to a publisher there the manuscript of an erotic work of his. This would then be printed anonymously in Holland and smuggled into France for the market there in arousing literature, which the royal administration and the Church tried to suppress. Writing from prison 13 years later, in 1782, de Sade referred obliquely to a kind of literature in which love was treated as a matter only of enjoyment, and which had "paid for my entertainments over six months in one of the main cities of the realm, and let me travel in Holland for two months without spending a farthing of my own..."

---

6 Perhaps to cure his haemorrhoids so as to get him fit to ride, a necessity for an officer with muster in the offing.

For lack of documents, it is difficult to follow the marquis's activities in the two years between his return to Paris in the autumn of 1769 and the corresponding season of 1771. However, Mme de Montreuil seems to have felt she had good grounds for seeking permission for her son-in-law to reappear at the royal court. This was not to be. The relevant minister told her, on 24 March 1770, that he had cautiously tested the king's attitude to the marquis (perhaps by dropping the miscreant's name into a discussion of another matter), rather than put a direct request to Louis XV. He added:

"... It seemed to me that the bad impressions His Majesty has been able to form of him at different times are still too vivid to be erased, which has decided me not to go too far, because I would have thought that if he were to be refused that would be a great disservice to him, as there is much scope for believing that such a thing would do him even more harm in his regiment. I think that, in this matter, everything must wait while some time passes..."

In the summer of 1770, the marquis and his wife engendered their third and last child. The daughter, Madeleine Laure, was born on the following 17 April.

Whether haemorrhoids had been the cause of his delay in returning to the cavalry, or reluctance to show his face among fellow officers who might rag him or cut him because of his escapades with Testard and Keller, the marquis ended his long absence from the colours. As his family and the king's minister had anticipated, his reception was hostile. He arrived in Poitou in the far west of France early in August, whereupon the officer commanding turned him away and refused to let the more junior officers have anything to do with him. De Sade - whose propensity for protesting at such insults in the most vigorous terms would hardly have deserted him - was then put under arrest. It appears that the O.C. had been on shaky ground because the War Ministry intervened, no doubt at the behest of de Sade and/or his family, writing to de Saignes, lieutenant-colonel of the regiment, to brush aside his adjutant's objections, order that de Sade be allowed to take up his duties, and hint pointedly that the colonel himself should have told the ministry what was going on before the ministry had been informed by sources outside the army. The subsequent atmosphere in the officers' mess must be left to speculation.

The marquis seems not have remained for long with his regiment. On 13 March next year, 1771, he formally asked the War Minister for a commission roughly equivalent to the one he already held, but without salary. This was granted, but the accompanying official notification made clear that de Sade was no longer attached to his company in the cavalry regiment, and that the new rank, although gazetted, was a dead letter. No active service at the rank would be offered to the marquis. It may well be that senior officers in the army had lobbied the king and his minister for the blaspheming bounder, with a military record of little substance since the peace of 1763, to be quietly moved out of the army's career structure, whereby other officers would not have to serve alongside him. This kind of pressure, within the government of a bellicose European Great Power, would be apt to outweigh that of the Montreuils' agitation for upward mobility through further promotion of their son-in-law.

On 1 June, the eclipse of the marquis's military career, and of the Montreuils' attendant hopes, was clearly signalled when de Sade was given official permission to withdraw from the War Ministry 10,000 livres deposited there by a Count d'Osmont, who thus bought the commodity which was the marquis's active service rank of major.

The 10,000 realised from the sale of his majority may well have helped the marquis stave off his creditors. Early in 1771, he had been writing of an "extreme need to get hold of 60,000 livres to pay pressing debts" - roughly £120,000 or $180,000 in 1994 values. (This was three times the sum which Mme de Montreuil had been trying to raise only two years before in order to regularise his affairs.) This necessitated the sale of an estate or borrowing the said sum, he told his unknown correspondent. This was why he had put his estate at Mazan up for sale at about 150,000 livres - but there were no takers and time was short. He was prepared to borrow the 60,000 livres at interest of five per cent a year - a little high, but he was in no position to haggle for long - and with a promise to pay back 70,000 or even 80,000 at his death.

He went on:

"But this sale and the 60 thou must be done very much on the quiet ... because of Mme de Sade's general mortgage..."

It seems that the marquis was trying to sell one of his principal estates without telling his wife, who had loaned money to her husband on the strength of his estate at Mazan and perhaps his other properties in Provence. De Sade was seeking, on the quiet, to bring off a big property deal which would have entailed complicated repercussions for his wife's finances and, by extension, those of his in-laws. Renée

Pélagie, kept in ignorance of a sale of Mazan, would have been unaware that at least part of the security for her loan had left her husband's hands, while he would be making exclusive use of the proceeds of the sale. That is, he was hatching a reckless and quite disrespectful fraud. There is no indication as to how the marquis intended to keep Renée Pélagie and her relatives in ignorance of the disposal of Mazan if they visited Provence and found another landlord presiding at the estate, or how he thought he might keep the Abbé de Sade from reporting such a sale, which would have taken place under his nose, to the Montreuils. Perhaps these consequences had not occurred to him. The Marquis de Sade was not strong on the ramifications of an impulse of the moment or of a selfish improvisation.

One way or another, the marquis reckoned by 20 May to have matters in hand - well, nearly. He wrote to his main tenant-farmer at Mazan, François Ripert:

"... I am quite pleased, sir, to have come to arrangements with nearly all my creditors and, by means of a considerable sum that I am paying them in interest, I have got them to wait until the first of July next year. Don't think that, as for the rest, everything's wrapped up, but at least I have much reduced the sum which I can't do without..."

That sum was 26,000 livres - including 13,400 owed to tradesmen who were refusing to be held off until July 1771 by interest payments, 5,000 to "the Jew Beaucaire" and 3,000 loaned through Ripert himself, perhaps from some other source. The tenant, who would no longer be such if the lord and master were able to sell the Mazan estate, as he was trying to do, was asked to seek out three creditors and "offer them what security and what guarantee they want with reasonable interest payments", which suggests they must all have been in Provence. However, there was no getting around the need for the 13,400 livres.

The hard-pessed debtor also wrote to the lawyer Antoine Fage, his agent at Apt:

"You will be telling me unequivocally that you can find in yourself at present very little desire to oblige me, if you do not join in making the three creditors I am mentioning wait, and in finding for me a sum of 13,400 livres.

"You'll be asking me now what firm ground I have for setting July '72 for such heavy payments; I will reply that I have four bases instead of one: the first is my income from the States of Burgundy [the four provinces] which I am due to receive then; the second is the reimbursement from my [regimental] company which will certainly be made to me then[7]; the third is a considerable sum to which I will have access from my wife's dowry; the fourth eventually will be from the sale of my estate which I will be sure to clinch when I am down there... But I beg of you, you should busy yourself with nothing but the 13,400 livres I must have sent to me in June, considering that, if I don't make this payment that's due on 1 July, everything's gone to the devil, no-one will give me any more time...

"Imagine the importance of this, and it's absolutely essential that it be done, if not I am ruined in my wife's eyes..."

Having got to grips - albeit rather shaky ones - with his creditors, de Sade was planning to install himself and his family at la Coste for some time, as the royal minister would require. The marquis intended to do so in some style, and sent instructions to Ripert accordingly:

"... I don't see why you have put back until my arrival in Provence the items for the menagerie and the garden; it seems to me that I had told you very firmly to get the work under way at once, above all the garden, because I'm wanting to enjoy the fruit next summer, which won't happen if you have neglected the planting in the winter...

"I beg you to overlook nothing in all that I have instructed you regarding my plan to spend time at la Coste, which will start sooner and last longer than you imagine perhaps: garden, farmyard, cheese, wood, etc. - get all that under way so that, on arrival this autumn, I find everything ready for me to live with the greatest economy..."

For all his intentions to tighten his belt, in his own way, and for all his nimble footwork in staying ahead of his creditors, they were breathing hard enough on de Sade's neck for him to find himself in the debtors' prison in Paris during the first few days of September. He got himself out by paying 3,000 livres on account to the creditor who had petitioned for his imprisonment, and by signing an IOU for the rest of the sum (total unknown to posterity). The IOU was good for only five weeks - to be paid off by 15 October. It seems that, by then, he had done a flit.

---

7 The proceeds of the sale of his rank, which in fact amounted to 10,000 livres in the summer of 1771.

CHAPTER 8: ACTOR-MANAGER-DIRECTOR-CALLBOY

By the start of November, de Sade had moved his ménage to la Coste, to the 42-room château at the highest point of an escarpment in the Lubéron uplands, its fortified village grouped below the manor. It was rocky country, not yielding a living easily to cultivators. He arrived with wife, all three children, their governess and - a new character on the Sadeian scene - his wife's sister, Anne Prospère de Launay.

She was almost certainly the second of three daughters delivered of Mme de Montreuil, and she bore a surname available to her family through the estate of Launay which treasurer Cordier, probable founder of the family fortune, had held. It is almost sure that she was born in the period 1743-45, but there is no surviving evidence of her existence before May 1763, when she was one of the witnesses who signed de Sade's marriage contract. By the time she reached la Coste, in the autumn of 1771, she was a canoness, someone who spent at least part of her time in a community of religious women but who had taken no vow of chastity, or other pledges, that would make her into a nun.

For Renée Pélagie to be "shut up in a lonely château with that head of his" would cause her mother "endless agonies," so she had said, yet here was another Montreuil daughter being allowed into his southern lair. The only sliver of a clue as to why Anne Prospère joined her sister and her brother-in-law comes in a sworn deposition by Renée Pélagie in Paris three years later, in 1774, when explaining events which had occurred in the interim. In the third person, the marquise stated of herself:

"... she was joined [at la Coste] by Miss de Launay her sister, on the pretext of keeping her company and of breathing clearer air there..."

A few weeks later, the marquise added to a correspondent that "the point in my statement which concerns my sister" was not understood by the judges who had to deal with her statement, so her lawyer in Paris "had to explain it to them... He saw right away what it was about and the reasons for drawing a veil over this item."

Was the "pretext" that Anne Prospère may have used - accompanying her sister so that the latter would not be alone with "that head" and so that the younger woman would pass the winter in a better climate - employed to obtain permission from her mother to travel south? This "pretext" could have covered any number of real reasons why Anne Prospère wanted to travel, and there are no firm grounds for speculation that she was already the lover of her brother-in-law. She might have been keen to get away from something - an uncongenial convent or a boring home life, perhaps the consequences of some *faux pas* of hers which had nothing to do with the de Sades - rather than wanting to move to la Coste in particular. Likewise, the marquise's later reference to a need to conceal information about her sister's presence at la Coste does not conclusively point to an involvement with the marquis. Even so, Renée Pélagie's need to draw "a veil" stirs suspicion.

To judge by the documentary evidence, though, the party brought together in Provence - the handful of nobles and the two-dozen or so staff in the houses and on the estates - was enjoying only unobjectionable pastimes, at first. Soon after their arrival, Anne Prospère and the children's governess, Mlle Langevin, undertook an inventory of the master's linen and lace.

However, the marquis having been banished by king and creditors from enjoyment of theatre in Paris, he moved to set up his own dramatic company in his stretch of Provence, thereby putting his sister-in-law onto the boards. In reactivating the theatre in the manor at la Coste and constructing another such at his château on the Mazan estate (still unsold, clearly), he was reviving his favourite role of master of the revels and actor-manager, as enjoyed with Beauvoisin as his consort in the summer of 1765.

In January 1772, the marquis was sending out elaborate and flattering invitations to local notables on the occasion of a production of one of his own plays at la Coste. The next month, perhaps having been dissatisfied with the amateur playing of family and staff, he was contracting professional actors, probably from Marseilles. The actor Bourdais and his wife were to "perform in my château, and wherever else I see fit, all the roles I shall assign to them in comedy and tragedy, undertaking to meet all their expenses incurred in the way of lodging, food and travel, and to pay them the sum of eight hundred livres over and above." Stagehands and a supporting company of players were also hired.

A play of de Sade's, *The Marriage of the Century (Le Mariage du Siècle),* was to be presented, it seems, with an all-professional cast except for the participation of the marquis, and on other occasions with a cast including more amateurs from above-stairs, not least Anne Prospère as the heroine Pauline, de Sade as the young hero and the marquise as Sophie, a minor role. It is not clear whether either cast in fact went before an audience. However, from 3 May if not before, the Sadeian company began to shuttle between la Coste and Mazan, putting on a programme of plays which was to have included works by about a dozen French playwrights, most of them contemporary, but nothing by the actor-manager himself.

It seems that the audiences at the two châteaux were all guests, admitted free, so de Sade's theatrical enterprise was an expensive hobby. His relatives were, of course, much quicker to comment on this than he was. The Abbé de Sade wrote to lawyer Fage:

"I think as you do about my nephew's passion for the theatre, which ... is pushed to extremes and would soon have ruined him if it had lasted.[1] I have said nothing to him about this up to now because I felt the uselessness of my representations; but I notice with pleasure that the difficulties of getting the actors to agree among themselves and of sorting out their endless double-dealing, the difficulty of finding money to cover the expense, the obstacles that arise at every turn in the way of satisfying this passion, are starting to put him off it, and I await only a favourable moment to land my great blow, which would have already been done if his wife wanted to act in concert with me and if she were less willing to go along with her husband's fancies." There is no knowing what great blow the abbot had up his sleeve - perhaps to inform Mme de Montreuil of just how elaborate and expensive the style of 1772 at la Coste and Mazan was proving.

She was worried, back in Paris, at the lack of direct news from her daughters and the rest of the party in Provence. Other sources were telling her that "plays and amusements" were making "my children ... move about a great deal," she wrote to the Abbé on 27 May, adding sniffily:

"... These shows, being quite inconsequential in themselves, when one gets involved in them within one's own society and with one's equals, are very ridiculous indeed, not to put it any more strongly, when one gives oneself over to them without restraint, when one presents oneself in a show to an entire province (which is shocked thereby), with

---

1 Why it did not will become clear.

people whose profession is to amuse those of Monsieur de Sade's kind and station in life, when the pay suits them, but not to be put on a par together in front of the public. If this sort of thing has remained his overriding passion, not to say his madness, he is the master of his own person and actions up to a certain point; but he ought not, and he shall certainly not, thereby further compromise his wife and his sister-in-law. This is an indignity which I shall rectify, if he does not take care of the matter himself by getting back on the right path. What is all this moving-about for? These parties? To achieve the obliteration of his wealth, which has already been much reduced by every possible extravagance. Does he think this might be a device which will draw me, as he has been pressing me for a long time, into putting my hand to the re-ordering of his business? I could do so, no doubt, but only on condition and with firm guarantees. I am tired of being duped; one makes sacrifices for decent and reasonable things, but not to maintain extravagances. When he were to have frittered away everything, he would send back to me the wife and children for whom he cares hardly at all and whom I would certainly take in - and he would have gone on suffering the fate which plunges him into misfortune and misery, and which he was not meant for!"

The last remark can be taken as Mme de Montreuil's sarcasm regarding her son-in-law's capacity for lamenting when painful consequences of his vagaries had caught up with him.

* * *

For a moment, however, let's turn away from de Sade's troubles with getting his strolling players to rehearsals on time and with paying - among many other items - for the vast poundage of candles needed to illuminate their performances. The abiding struggle by de Sade against the limits of reality, which theatre let him believe he could shift, at least for a while, is becoming familiar to the reader. How did he fare, though, in his impingement on the canoness? For we can be confident that the marquis, responsibilities as actor-manager and lord of the manors notwithstanding, found time to work on his sister-in-law.

He was not only a libertine by practice but also had the intellectual equipment to suit his theoretical and proselytising bent. From his disdain for paying court, even to the king, in order to advance in society, and from his blasphemies when closeted with Testard and

Keller, one has indications of his contempt for bowing the knee to mortals, to their beliefs and to God. Besides, he was aware of the challenge being set out by writers of the time to established respect for the hierarchies of church and state based on traditional obedience and traditional domination. He was finding in such critical arguments support for his attitudes to anyone and any corporation that claimed to regulate his life, or the life of anyone else on whom he turned his iconoclasm.

He was full of arguments against chastity, religion and the keeping-up of certain appearances. Those arguments offered escape from priestly admonition and Hellfire - and pleasure withal, as did the revels of wine and theatre (albeit kept bubbling by precarious credit and promises to pay), of which the marquis was master at la Coste. We do not know how Anne Prospère was conducting herself before she travelled south, how seriously she had been taking the religious life, how attached she already was to her brother-in-law. However, a long stay under the same roofs with de Sade, in the ambience of Provençal countryhouses at play, must have represented a departure from her previous ways. All but a little of her earlier life would have been spent in the household of her parents - not a frolicsome or various ménage, it seems - and even if she had undertaken her attachment to the religious life only out of boredom or cynicism, by way of escaping from home or investigating with reservations the only career open to unmarried women of her class, she would have had to spend *some* time at religious observations and study. As an unmarried woman with an inclination - however involuntary - towards the religious life, she can have had little experience of social life in the capital beyond polite salons and closely chaperoned outings to approved entertainments.

Lacking other options beyond a return to family or to convent, to an arranged marriage as a bride of a nobleman or a Bride of Christ, Anne Prospère stayed in Provence beyond the end of winter. The marquis claimed later, in a passage which is probably about her:

"What discoveries [she] made...! She saw very clearly that her understanding was being insulted, her wit was being dulled, by an effort to have her regard as crimes the most delightful emotions of her spirit, likewise the most delightful inclinations of nature. What happened? Perceiving clearly that there was a wish to change her heart, [she] let it speak, and that heart soon drove the outrage from her. Through how many charms this pretty wit, guided by the heart, showed itself! The blindfold having fallen, every object appeared new to [her], and all the powers of her spirit took on a new degree of strength. Everything about her, even her figure, benefited by it. [She] became the prettier for it. What frost spread itself over her former pleasures! And what heat over her new ways of thinking!..."

For all that, we have only his word for it. I like to think that the canoness, who was almost certainly seeing Provence for the first time, appreciated the clearer southern light as it was reflected from the sharper landscape of stone, olive and mulberry, at low winter angles and in high summer, different to the more rainy greens of the meadows and orchards of her parents' estates in Normandy and the Île de France. Even that notion is speculative, though, and no more than a glimpse of Anne Prospère in her own right emerges when we turn to the Abbé de Sade's role in her stay in Provence.

The Abbé - 66 years old at the time but well preserved by a life of unhurried libertinage and *belle-lettrisme*, supported by regular stipends from a complaisant Church - was also much pleased by her. In a letter written to Anne Prospère after the winter and spring of 1771-2, when she had returned north, the Abbé assured her he would never refuse her anything he could provide, so he promised an affection for her untainted by any impurity. However, "I know of nothing as delightful as you are and I am a child of a warm clime; out of such a combination arises a very warm affection, which is what I feel for you. You wish me *to give up this* and *put calmer feelings in its place*. I am firmly decided to do whatever you want; the question remains as to whether I can do so.

"You want a man of Provence to love like a man of the Auvergne... The sun excites the blood of a man of Provence, the snows calm that of a man of the Auvergne....

"I would like to spend my entire life with you: but I will not see you at all. I am aching to go to Clermont: I will not go. If I were to obey my heart, I would write to you every day, letters full of fondness and warmth: to please you, I will write, infrequently, cold letters... I think I can say that such a disguise will protect your honour and your life...."

She was, he added, to take care to keep her communications also restrained, or "I shall not be able to control myself: I shall make a bundle of all my warmth and come to melt your snows and make a torrent that would carry you away..."

The style inclines to the mooning of a forsaken Mediterranean macho, familiar to many northern European women opening their mail back home after excessive hopes had been built on their smiles in the southern sun. More important, though, is the evidence that Anne Prospère had been asking the Abbé to modify his letters, whose intemperate declarations were causing her trouble and embarrassment through their being intercepted and read by authorities, probably her superiors at a convent and/or members of her family. Instead of that, the old libertine made a self-indulgent repetition of this dangerous nuisance, in the shape of a letter promising to do as he had been asked. Sexual molestation takes many forms.

It was to be expected - though not by the usually alert and suspicious Mme de Montreuil, it seems - that de Sade would find his sister-in-law exciting as a *religieuse* to be diverted from obeying her confessor. The degree to which he diverted her is much more difficult to fathom. We do know, however, that his taste for excitement ran beyond women of the convent.

* * *

Forsaking the pleasures at his country estates, de Sade left in late-June for Marseilles, the main French port on the Mediterranean Sea, to pick up some money belonging to him, so he said. He took with him his valet, known as Latour, who was sent out to arrange for prostitutes to make up a group of "really young" girls to have fun with his employer. In the morning of 27 June, with Latour, he arrived at a second-floor flat, resplendent in breeches of marigold-coloured silk, a feather in his hat, sword at his hip and gold-topped cane in his hand.

Again, as with the Testard and Keller incidents, the episode is recorded in detail through subsequent statements made to investigating officials by the women concerned - four this time, aged 18, 20, 20 and 23. The marquis began by sending three of the women out of the room and locking the door. When he had the valet and Marianne Laverne, the 18-year-old, lying on the bed, he whipped the woman with one hand while manipulating his servant sexually with the other, calling Latour "*monsieur le marquis*" (my lord marquis). The valet called de Sade "Lafleur". Having sent Latour out of the room also, de Sade showed Laverne a little cut-glass box with gold edges, containing aniseed sweets. She was invited to eat as many as she could - to make her break wind, she was told - and she swallowed seven or eight. His next move was to ask her to allow him or Latour to penetrate her anally, for which he would pay her 20 livres. She refused.

(Five of the six prostitutes of the city who gave statements in the case said that they had turned down a similar request from de Sade. The evening before the episode in the flat with Latour and the foursome, de Sade had called on two other prostitutes in the area, one of whom stated that he had told them he wanted "to bring them next day some aniseed to make them fart and for him to receive their wind in his mouth." Only one of the two was at home when Latour arrived next morning to pursue the invitation and she declined to be of service.)

Next, de Sade took a cat-of-nine-tails, improvised out of parchment and studded with bent pins, from his pocket and got Laverne to whip him with it. She gave him three blows but then decided this was not for her, so the maid was sent out to buy a broom. Laverne whacked de Sade's backside with the broom until her stomach turned queasy and she went to the kitchen for water.

Mariette Borelly, aged 23, took her place, stripped and bent over the bed for de Sade to beat her with the broom. Then she beat him, while he made cuts with his penknife on the mantelpiece, perhaps to keep count of the blows. (The police later found a set of figures written there - 215, 179, 225, 240.) This done, de Sade had Borelly lie on the bed, on her back, while he penetrated her, Latour buggering him meanwhile.

The order of appearance by the four women, established by de Sade after he had drawn lots, required that Rose Coste be brought in next. The valet caressed her and penetrated her vaginally before de Sade whipped her while masturbating Latour. The last of the four women, Mariannette Laugier, was summoned for the marquis to caress her, after which he prepared to lash her, saying he still wanted to land 25 more blows. By then, the cat-of-nine-tails was bloodstained and Laugier tried to escape. The marquis made her stay and sent for Laverne, who had been seeking coffee to settle her stomach. Then de Sade offered more sweets to the women. Laverne, who had already eaten some, refused; Laugier took some but spat them out.

Laverne was made to proffer her backside for de Sade to sniff at her anus for wind. Laugier turned away to the window, rather than go on watching this. Laverne refused the marquis's request that she allow Latour to sodomise her and was trying to leave, amid some tears and disaffection among the women, when de Sade wound up what must have been a sweaty encounter in the noonday heat of high summer, giving them six livres each and promising ten more if they would take a boat trip with him later.

In the afternoon, when Latour arrived back at Borelly's flat to pick them up for the boating, this was turned down. By the evening, Latour had arranged with a Marguerite Coste, aged 25, to do business with the marquis, already a client of hers. He had been consulting his tailor after siesta, then dining with a prominent actor, before he visited the woman, whom he persuaded to eat a lot of the aniseed sweets. The marquis then asked whether she felt any movement in her stomach, and said he wanted to take her anally. She would not allow this - only sexual intercourse "in the way God has ordained," she stated later. (Either partner in an act of sodomy, in France at that time, was guilty of a capital offence.) However, he was allowed to put his tongue to her anus in the hope of feeling - tasting, perhaps - her wind.

Rather than follow other authors in speculation over whether any of the prostitutes allowed herself to be buggered or not - there was the temptation of a louis apiece to do so, then the risk of a capital charge if she admitted she had - let's look into what de Sade was seeking throughout the June morning in Marseilles.

Notice that the valet Latour, whose responsibilities and talents clearly extended the role of body servant more than somewhat, was sent to trawl for "really young" girls. Staying with the marquis's penchant for sodomy, one can discern here a wish for tight anuses which would enhance the physical excitement for the sodomiser as his penis penetrated them. This would be particularly valuable for a man who had difficulty in achieving ejaculation. (A letter from de Sade, in jail a dozen years later, refers to his troubles in this area - **see chapter 22**.) A snug, young anus might also be helpful to a man whose penis was small. We know de Sade was not tall - not nearly as tall as Latour, the women stated - but no comment on his penile dimension has reached posterity.

Apart from a wish to avoid hiring older prostitutes because their anal orifices might well have been slackened by much use, de Sade would also have been concerned to steer clear of such women because they would have seen it all and done it all in their trade more often than the youthful quartet in Borelly's flat. Younger prostitutes would be much less likely to be able to maintain their professional detachment as de Sade and his man went into action.

It was important to him also that the action be not only closely directed by himself, but also that it allow no slackening of pace as the episode continued. Once he had drawn lots to decide the order of appearance of the female members of the cast in the Marseilles matinée, the director was always chivvying at them, giving them something different to deal with, keeping them aware of his presence and his actions. They were urged to eat aniseed sweets, which meant they had to decide what that was all about and whether they would take them. It was supposed to be to loosen their stomachs and make them fart - if they felt queasy and passed wind, that would be holding their attention, upsetting any inclination to turn a mere sufficiency of regard towards the client while their intimate thoughts dwelt on their own concerns. The upset in their bowels would be a product of de Sade's action, hence his desire to bring his face close to their arses and enjoy the winds *he* had stirred up. Before any of the four had a chance to get used to that, out came the cat-of-nine-tails for beatings, always the marquis deciding how many strokes and on whom they should fall, keeping the structure of the event under control through a little score-board on the mantelpiece. The cat-of-nine-tails was objected to - no problem, send for a besom, then use that. Meantime, ring the multiplicity of changes afforded by the presence of four vaginas, four female anuses, two penises, two male anuses, twelve hands, and by an exchange of stations and identities by the two men; and agitate to have the penises put into the young, female anuses - not only to feel the grip of the tight tissues but also to hear the women gasp and to see them squirm at the uncomfortable penetration.

No woman drifts into reverie when she's with the Marquis de Sade - he always holds his audience throughout the show, even if that means using anise, sodomy and the lash.

To let the refusal of any one initiative stop the action - the sodomy, say, if it was indeed refused - was above all to be avoided. De Sade tried hard not to suspend the pell-mell tilting at the women's poise by insisting on what he was being denied, by getting angry and so driving the women into a sullen stubbornness, gazing out of the window, chewing the ends of their sweaty and dishevelled hair, suggesting a coffee break, drifting back into themselves and out of the seethe which had stemmed from and revolved around *him*. The incessant sequence of shocks, varied for piquancy under the direction of him who pays, was essential to keep the tension high. If it were to drop, engagement would be dissipated, attention would wander off. For the young master and focus of the revels, anything but that.

Agreed that, during most of the episode *chez* Borelly, rarely were more than two of the hired foursome being acted on by de Sade and Latour at any one time. For all the nimbleness of his improvisations and the extent of his stamina - the marquis used to pride himself on what he called "the de Sade energy" - and for all the support by Latour, two perspiring men with a crystal box of sweets, however moving all three might be, were insufficient, he might well have felt, to maintain the desired level of engagement in all four women. Much as de Sade might have wished otherwise, from time to time various of the women were able to sit out a scene or two. Even so, any of them was apt to be summoned back on stage at any moment by the actor-manager-callboy who was also the author of the piece, making up the action as he went along, and director of this production - your hand there, his up here, your skirt off now, your legs wider, now I'm going to sniff...

Besides, with all his crazy wants and notions, and all the cash he was throwing around, what else would the soubrettes be talking about during their breaks in the wings but this gent "Lafleur". The Marquis de Sade had the attention of Marianne, Mariette, Rose and Mariannette sure enough. There were even tears! Delightful confirmation of one's effect!

The effects of his activities were still engaging two of the Marseilles prostitutes whom he had enjoyed that summer Saturday when, next morning early, the marquis and his man were heading north out of the city on the road to Aix, en route back to wife, family and sister-in-law. The Sadeian players were due to present a double-bill of plays - *Fortunately* and *The Married Philosopher* - to their guests at Mazan on the 29th, the Monday. Marianne Laverne had been bringing up blood and black matter since later in the day on Saturday and, by Sunday morning, was feeling very poorly and keeping to her bed. So was Marguerite Coste, similarly afflicted. These were the two women who had swallowed a substantial amount of their client's aniseed sweets. As soon as she was well enough - after a priest had tried to give her the last rites but found she could not stomach the Host - Marguerite Coste complained to the authorities that she had been made ill by sweets a client had given her. Various prostitutes in the district knew who "Lafleur" really was. An investigation, including analysis of the vomited matter, was begun and prostitutes were interviewed.

The theatre-goers of la Coste and Mazan may have attended another performance or two, but news of the hue and cry down in the port made its way up into the Lubéron hills within a few days. On 10 July, de Sade paid off his player-king, Bourdais, not with the full 800 livres of his contract but with 352, having disbanded his troupe of actors and stagehands. Next day, when officers arrived at la Coste to execute an arrest warrant from Marseilles, they were told by the marquis's lawyer, Fage, that the master and the valet had left the château a week ago and had sent no word since of their whereabouts.

The marquise was also absent. One of her first moves, on hearing of the trouble brewing in the wake of her husband's outing to the coast, was to consult her sister. According to Renée Pélagie's third-person legal deposition of 1774:

" ... she [the marquise] casts about to deal with her doubts, to calm her alarm; she addresses herself to her sister, but the trouble she discerns in the latter's spirit, the unsteadiness of that one's replies, do no more than add to [the marquise's] agitation; she hastens to Marseilles with [her] sister; although she finds, although she is convinced, that nothing more than a little sexual adventure has given rise to the legal proceedings, she also understands that the most excessive prejudice has seized everyone's mind [in the city], that this was not the right time to dispel it. She would have wanted to expose this prejudice, but her sister's dejection was draining the strength that she thought to find within herself; she returns..."

To one of her husband's estates, it seems. The reaction of Anne Prospère to the incident has suggested to some commentators that she was cast down at news of a lover's infidelity, and with women of the street at that. This might be so. However, an unmarried young woman with religious affiliations might well feel depressed at learning of such behaviour in her brother-in-law - and at realising that the party in Provence was over thereby - without having taken him as a lover. Again, no close liaison between the canoness and the marquis should be construed - not from this glimpse provided by the marquise of her sister's feelings.

If she had happened to read the scandal sheets, which were battening onto the new Sadeian brouhaha by the end of July, and to hear the lurid gossip, Mlle de Launay would have been even more upset. At least one chronicler in Paris had word from Marseilles that de Sade (whose exploits of 1768 with Keller the correspondent also recalled):

"... gave a ball, to which he had invited a lot of people, and had slipped chocolate pastilles into the dessert, which were so good that many people ate them ... But he had mixed in ... cantharides. The effect of this medicine is known: it was so potent that all those who had eaten it, burning with a shameless ardour, gave themselves up to every excess inspired by the most amorous rapture. The ball degenerated into one of those licentious gatherings known among the Romans; the most well-behaved of women could not resist the uterine fury that was working on them... Several people have died of the excesses to which they surrendered themselves in their appalling priapism, and others are still very unwell."

It is clear the tale had been greatly improved along the way, purple vocabulary and all, to the *Secret Memoirs* of Bachaumont, in a passage dated 25 July 1772. Mlle Borelly would have been amazed that so much action could have taken place in her little apartment.

The machinery of the law followed its course, again with remarkable speed. The property of the fugitive men was inventoried and declared to be impounded. When they had not surrendered to the authorities within a fortnight, they were publicly cried as wanted men outside the château at la Coste and at crossroads in the village nearby. Even after Marguerite Coste and Marianne Laverne, the two women who had become ill after eating de Sade's sweets, had signed notarised withdrawals of their complaints against him, in mid-August at Marseilles, the process continued, with the file passed to a royal prosecutor who ordered further interviews of witnesses.

It was Fage, no doubt better provided with cash than the Montreuil sisters on their visit to Marseilles, who had gone to the city and approached various parties. Hence the prostitutes' withdrawal of their complaints, hence also much pressure from Fage on de Sade's main tenant farmers for money. Fage and the Commander de Sade - the marquis's eldest surviving uncle, who had returned from his travels as a Knight of Malta - made joint visits to judges at Aix, seat of the High Court of Provence. An even heavier gun was brought to bear: M de Montreuil, the judge and father-in-law himself, arrived in Provence during August - the gravity of the matter driving him to risk his uncertain health through a long journey in the heat of summer - when he visited la Coste, the Abbé's château at Saumane, and Marseilles.

Yet all this lobbying failed to put a brake on the proceedings, which continued at a great pace, especially for the dog days of the legal calendar. (Then, as now, in France as elsewhere, tribunals and attorneys tended to leave actions aside in August, as they enjoyed their long vacation.) This suggests that powerful interests were at work - enemies of the Montreuils in the upper levels of the legal establishment perhaps - to fell de Sade and fell him quickly.

The marquis and his valet still being fugitive, their case was heard at Aix in their absence and was concluded on 3 September with death sentences for sodomy and poisoning. The verdict carried the style of centuries of dread-striking. The two were to be brought to the forecourt of the cathedral at Aix:

"... on their knees, barefoot and bareheaded, in shirtsleeves, each with a rope about his neck and holding in his hand a burning candle of yellow wax, of one pound in weight, where they are to ask for pardon of God and the king ..."

Then, in full view of the public:

"... the aforementioned Lord de Sade [is] to have his head cut off on a scaffold, and the aforementioned Latour to be hanged by the neck and throttled on a gallows until natural death shall ensue, after which the corpses of the aforementioned Lord de Sade and of the aforementioned Latour are to be burned and the ashes scattered to the winds."

The sentences having been confirmed on 11 September by the High Court of Provence, and the two convicted men still being absent, next day effigies of de Sade and Latour were solemnly burned, after a dummy execution, in a public square at Aix. This show, of course, was merely part of the putting of the fear of God into the susceptible; it did not mean that de Sade and Latour were to escape their sentences in person, once apprehended. Note also that de Sade, being a nobleman, was in for a quick death (decapitation by an axe), while Latour, a commoner, was to have his life slowly and painfully squeezed away by a rope around his throat while he twisted above the crowd. This was a standard discrimination. However, once in ashes, they would be united in the ignominy of being dispersed on the air, the remains of convicted buggers not being deemed fit for burial in consecrated ground.

Although sodomy was a capital offence, it rarely led to the death sentence in 18th century France; such a sentence for a nobleman who had committed the deed in an orgy with prostitutes was unheard of. Even the addition of a conviction for poisoning, and even if that were construed as attempted murder, would be unlikely to draw a death sentence, given the respective social ranks of the perpetrator and the victims.

However, the proceedings and sentence were within the law. Agreed, the chemical analysis of the material brought up by Marguerite Coste showed no trace of arsenic or any corrosive, but she and Marianne Laverne were ill at the material time - the former, at least, more so than would have been consistent with a straightforward bout of stomach trouble in a crowded city during high summer. Agreed, the prostitutes withdrew their complaints before the court verdict but, in most legal codes around the world, then as now, this did not preclude the authorities from pursuing a prosecution if they believed a crime had taken place, whether the victims wished this or not. There was no civil suit by Coste and Laverne, which would have lapsed on their say-so, but a criminal case brought by the State in the name of the king and the public interest. The evidence of the two women, like that of other witnesses, remained material to this criminal prosecution, regardless of their withdrawal of complaint. Agreed, it seems that the marquis may have intended no more than to make the women fart, for his pleasure, and not to try to injure or kill them, but he pressed the sweets on them (as he did his lash and broom) with regard only for his own desires and none for their well-being. He behaved, customarily, as though payment of money wiped away his reckless disrespect and made all well.

While his effigy was undergoing the full rigour of the law, the marquis may well have been spending the remainder of the summer beyond the reach of French judges, travelling in Italy, calling himself the "Count de Mazan". The Bachaumont journal, which made out de Sade's morning in Marseilles to have been a Caligulan orgy, went on to claim:

"... It was thus that M de Sade enjoyed his sister-in-law, with whom he has fled, to distance himself from the torture he deserves..."

This story, that Anne Prospère went with de Sade into exile after the Marseilles affair, has been accepted by just about every writer who has taken up the marquis ever since. It is a spicy addition to the pudding, but the documentary evidence for it is debatable. There is even very little to confirm that de Sade did spend time in Italy immediately after his death sentence.

The marquis, looking back on the events of 1772 from his middle age 18 years later, then newly released from detention and concerned to cleanse his reputation, went so far as to claim, about the Montreuils and their cohorts:

"I am more than convinced that it was they who gave rise to my Marseilles affair, they who bribed the girls to make statements about such horrors - which had never entered my head. Ah! don't imagine that what I'm telling you about this is so fantastical: People without number are telling me so now, and that, not knowing what to do in order to separate me from my wife's sister, with whom I was living then, ... they invented that outrage so as to have their way."

Considering de Sade's capacity for telling whatever lies suited him, one might accept none of the above. The notion that the episode at Marseilles was a complete fabrication certainly has to be discarded. However, does the assertion from this unreliable source, that de Sade and Anne Prospère were parted by the Marseilles scandal, snuff out the possibility that the two of them subsequently spent time together, in Italy or elsewhere? The nature of their relationship is left obscure by de Sade's claim of 1790. The key phrase in the original French is *avec laquelle je vivais* (with whom I was living), which carries the same ambiguity as the English translation. Was de Sade working on his sister-in-law's body as well as her mind?

Governor de la Tour of Savoy, under whose administration de Sade was a prisoner on 17 March 1773, stated categorically to a senior colleague, in a report of that date, that the marquis had undertaken "the abduction of Mlle de Launay, his sister-in-law, whom he took to Venice and a part of Italy as his wife, and with all the liberties due to a spouse."

The governor's informant regarding the alleged flight into Italy was a certain Albaret, a Montreuil retainer. Why would he see fit to tell someone outside the Montreuil family of the dishonour of one of its daughters, a nubile virgin, so one ought to suppose, whose prospects of a good marriage would decline as news of any affair with her brother-in-law spread in society? Albaret would have expected that such remarks to such a high-ranking and well-connected figure as Governor de la Tour, administrator of a province of the Kingdom of Sardinia[2], then France's south-eastern neighbour, would be passed to other officials in the kingdom and very likely to Mme de Montreuil herself, the source of his livelihood. That was a powerful motivation for him to

2 The province of Savoy was, in those days, part of the Kingdom of Sardinia, whose capital was Turin and whose royal house provided the kings under whom Italy was unified in the 19th century.

tell, not necessarily the truth but whatever best suited his employer. On the face of it, that would *not* have been a story which illuminated degradation of Anne Prospère, one of her mother's assets in the game of dynastic advancement. Consider, however, that it was in the interest of the Montreuils that their rogue in-law, in the spring of 1773, remain in de la Tour's custody. In the same report as that which conveys Albaret's views, the governor added:

"... his [de Sade's] relatives ... are working without respite to procure a pardon for him [at Aix], or at least a commutation of sentence, [but] they are concerned, until this has been obtained, that he should not reappear in France where he would be apprehended and perhaps subjected to the ignominious execution which has been set for him..."

The governor concluded, for his colleague's instruction, that the marquis's behaviour in France and his unruly conduct in Savoy "justify the bad opinion of him and show that he has a powerful intelligence, is without religion and morals, and is apt to go to any kind of extreme..."

The Savoyard conclusion was that such a bad lot ought to be closely confined while in Savoy, which was just what the Montreuils wanted. Hence it would make sense, from the point of view of Albaret's employer, for him to cast aside the inclination to hide Mlle de Launay's dishonour and let de la Tour hear about it, provided the Montreuils were confident that the governor would not spread the news any further than was necessary. What's more, if Albaret had decided to *invent* some lurid account of de Sade's recent past in order to convince de la Tour that the marquis should stay locked up, he would hardly have concocted a tale which cast the gravest aspersions on a marriageable Montreuil maid.

Now let's look at two undated letters by Sade's agent Fage, and let's allow, as is probable, that they are from 1772, in the summer of which year de Sade sweated for his pleasure at Marseilles. The first says:

"Mme de Sade and her sister have left for Paris. Only the little ones are still at the château, and I will send them off as soon as I get the word. It will be decided as soon as possible who will be given the administration of the family's properties. I think this will pass to Mme de Sade. Meanwhile, she has given me a general power of attorney to represent her in Provence..."

Hence Fage could not have been writing after 18 December 1772, the date of a family meeting which indeed conferred administration of the properties on the marquise, her husband being legally barred from doing so since his conviction at Aix in September.

From the lawyer's other letter:

"Madame de Sade left for Paris on the 16th of last month; she will not be back before about the end of this month... the harvest is pressing ... I've been at full stretch to arrange the journey, having been obliged to send the children on their way and all the rest of it, there being no-one at the château..."

The mention of the harvest makes the last possible date of Fage's letters October - if he meant the grape harvest, in which case the marquise, having left "on the 16th of last month", would have quit la Coste in mid-September. She went *with her sister*, according to the first letter. There remains the possibility that Fage meant the harvest of the region's other crops, which had to be gathered earlier in those times than did the fruit of the vine. In that case, Renée Pélagie would have started for Paris on 16 July - the first 16th after the marquis's busy day at Marseilles.

However, the possibility that Fage was referring to the *later* harvest means that the Montreuil sisters might not have quit Provence before 16 September. That would have left plenty of time for Anne Prospère to flee with de Sade in the second week of July, when the motive for him to make himself scarce became clear, reach Italy, think better of what she was doing, return alone to Provence and her sister, then depart with her for Paris.

It may be - supposing the canoness and the actor-manager did decamp together - that she found the company of de Sade, unalloyed and in a foreign country where they knew few people and had to budget carefully (always a pain for the marquis), much less congenial than it had been at la Coste and Mazan, where her sister, her nephews, niece, the Abbé, the players, staff and a variety of visitors offered more society. One can imagine that the marquis could be a stimulating companion, especially on his own ground and when sexual congress and his theatrical productions were among the ties that bound, but can also imagine that his insistence on his peculiar world view, focussed through his perceived right to untrammelled pleasure, could become wearing after a while, even a short while.

There was certainly a great and sustained effort, after the summer of 1772, by the Montreuils to gather any correspondence which might relate to the marquis's activities. Count de la Tour, writing to a minister in his capital, Turin, on 21 July of the next year, had no doubts why this was:

"... For some time now, sir, I am being pressed by Mme de Montreuil ... to procure for her all the letters which she and her daughter had written to [the marquis]... She promises me that it is for her a most pressing requirement that their content be kept from the public, because mention is made in them of her younger daughter who had been seduced by the same [Marquis] de Sade, her brother-in-law..."

Given Mme de Montreuil's resources of money and diligence in suppressing documentary evidence, it is no surprise that there is a dearth of such papers to corroborate the governor's statement. Even so, I am inclined to believe de la Tour, who seems to have had his head screwed on properly and who is shown by other matters even to have had that rare poise in public office, the willingness to admit in writing that he had been wrong. There seems to be no trace of his having retracted his reports of Mlle de Launay's affair. Besides, the Sadeian pathology points unwaveringly to the marquis having taken his sister-in-law, given any kind of chance. What a delight! To seduce a canoness away from the Church that he reviled. To spoil by his penetration and his seed a maiden among the stock that would raise the Montreuils in society by dynastic marriages, into one of which his father had sold him nine years before. Such a deed would stick in the vitals of the all-directing *présidente* for as long as she lived. However tightly she might pull her purse-strings when he tried to dip inside, however sharply she scolded him over his deviations, she would never be able to undo the undoing of Anne Prospère. His episodes with Testard, Colet, Beauvoisin and Keller were expensive nuisances to the Montreuils - especially in that they scuppered his prospects at the royal court and in the army - but they did no more than offer his in-laws a negative demonstration that he was not the vehicle of advancement they wanted him to be, and was nothing like sufficiently interested in becoming. Reckless frolicking among commoners - courtesans, prostitutes, actors, servants - was one thing; forbidden knowledge of a blue-blooded woman - of one whose blood and coat of arms had been mingled with his own - was another. *First* knowledge, what's worse, of a woman who could not be more closely akin to his mother-in-law and his wife. What a coup for the cock of the walk at la Coste! What an explosive impingement! What an enduring engagement of attention!

Mind you, the cock was not feeling so cocky in March 1773, nine months after a pair of stomachs he upset in Marseilles had thrown his theatrical Provençal idyll up into the air. By then, he was detained in the Kingdom of Sardinia and was in the humble and self-pitying vein he found at times when under lock and key. Part of the relevant letter is missing, but he was referring to pressure on himself regarding certain aspects of his contact with the outside world when he wrote to Governor de la Tour:

"... I give way as willingly as may be, neither having nor wanting to have in the future any correspondence that the whole world could not read, and renouncing quite sincerely that [correspondence] which has put me in here, which I was weak enough to keep up at the beginning, and all of which I greatly regret.

"I have been of age for some years, sir; I have lost my father, to my misfortune, for I would not be here if I had him still; my mother is very old and very infirm, and is finishing her days peacefully in a convent, involving herself in nothing whatsoever; my uncles and the rest of my family have certified to me in writing that they are having nothing to do with my detention; I have not offended the Court of France, much less that of Sardinia; my wife is asking to have me back, I am dependent on no-one; so who can hold me, and who can dare to do so without being grossly vexatious and doing the greatest injustice?..

"If, however, those who are doing this [to me] put forward as their sole justification the desire to crush an inappropriate and regrettable affair[3], they are pressing their disgruntlement beyond necessity, because I have declared with the utmost seriousness that I was renouncing, I keep declaring just that every day and continue to do so in the most explicit terms in the attached letter for Paris...[4]

"What must I do, sir, to be believed?... I break off all contact, I offer to hand over all the letters, I swear to go no nearer to Paris than a hundred leagues away and for as long as so required, to stop all harmful statements, pleas, proposals that could damage or obstruct a resolution which they are afraid I won't allow, which I want perhaps more than they do..."

In other words, de Sade was claiming that the was ready to give up an affair, nature unspecified, and to surrender all the letters related to it,

3 The original French is *intrigue*.

4 Not available.

as well as to acquiesce to whatever terms "they" - one supposes the Montreuils - might lay down in order to wind up the episode. Also, one makes a reasonable guess that the *intrigue* meant an affair with Anne Prospère.

Mme de Montreuil had indeed kept up a great ferreting after her son-in-law's documents, especially those which might be in "a little box or casket thought to be red and bound with copper". Sardinian officials were urged, in December 1772:

"... If he has brought it with him to the jail, you are begged to try to get it back, without his knowing in advance, and to take out of it any papers it contains. As for the key, if it's not there, you'll have to manage without it.[5] All the said letters being of interest only to him and his family, one would wish that you might be good enough to have them sent, without examination, to the Sardinian ambassador [in Paris], who will have the kindness to pass them on to his family..."

Mme de Montreuil was also greatly concerned to prevent de Sade sending statements of justification to French and Sardinian ministers, other persons of quality with whom he was connected and - much more dangerous for the family's good name - to publishers in Turin and in nearby Switzerland, where French censorship had no weight. Such statements might mention Sadeian escapades new and old. Also, de Sade being de Sade, they would surely shift any blame from himself onto others, most likely his in-laws.

There was even an inquiry, to what must have been an already hard-pressed Savoyard bureaucracy, by the *présidente* about a medical consultation the marquis had had in November with a doctor in Savoy. "The family has a great concern to know just what this report is all about." Indeed, for if de Sade were suffering a venereal infection, he might have passed it to his sister-in-law.

However, like much else about de Sade in the second half of 1772, the nature of his health trouble is not clear. Likewise, the later fate of the canoness. It seems that her family did manage to line up at least one prospective husband for her. In July 1774, however, Renée Pélagie was writing of how the man and his family "will not agree to the marriage unless he [de Sade] is jailed for life, and they want the word of the minister [of the French royal household] to that effect." Nothing

5 Incitement to break and enter - and this from the wife of a high court judge. However, reputation overrode statute for Mme de Montreuil.

came of this venture, it seems, and there is no record of Anne Prospère having married.

In November 1774, so it appears, she was writing to the Abbé de Sade - only one sad and weary part of the letter has survived:

"... One has nothing worse than one's own (you know as well as I, sir, that those close to us are often not our best friends).

"You are very fortunate, uncle, to be left to yourself in your solitude. As for myself, I would wish for nothing else. Paris bores me, society exasperates me, I have happy moments only when I am in my rooms, to which I withdraw as often as possible, and study is all that distracts me from the troubles of my life. One must wait for time to bring a change in it; that's what is generally required and no-one must neglect that in any way ..."

Anne Prospère died before she was 40, after a short illness, in May of - almost certainly - 1779. By then, she had faded from the life of her brother-in-law - her role in which remains out of focus for us - but not from his memory. When he died at Charenton, 35 years after her demise, among the few portraits in his room was one of her.

CHAPTER 9: "WANDERING AND VAGABOND LIFE"

Whatever he was about after he left Marseilles on the morning of 28 June 1772, de Sade comes back into our clear view as of 27 October, when he arrived at Chambéry, in Savoy, accompanied only by male servants - probably Latour and a certain Carteron, also known as La Jeunesse.

Within a few days of his arrival at Chambéry, the marquis had taken a six-month lease on a house near the town. However, he had little time to settle into what he was trying to make an unobtrusive life. He was outside the reach of the King of France, but not outside that of his mother-in-law. On 8 December, his house was surrounded by police. Their officer, as soon as he had taken the marquis's sword and pistols, searched him and the house for papers. He was taken next morning to the fortress of Miolans, under a detention order of the King of Sardinia. His cell was called Great Expectation and situated on the south side of the 12th century prison, which had superb views of the Alps and of the valley of the Isère river. Despite that, the marquis was soon fretting and trying to whittle away at the conditions of his imprisonment. He wanted Latour allowed to come and go, and himself allowed to receive and send letters. These concessions were made, as long as all correspondence pass via the governor of the fortress.

While more senior officials were trying to have papers taken from de Sade's effects, sealed and sent to his family, the governor of Miolans was finding his new prisoner ill-tempered and apt to bribe his way to an escape. Hearing that de Sade was writing memorandums to support his past conduct, to be sent to Sardinian and French ministers, and to others who might help him, Mme de Montreuil asked her Savoyard contacts to intercept these, "if they contain any lies or harmful material about his wife's family, from whom he has had only kindness..."

The early months of 1773 were taken up by much correspondence and unease among all parties - wary, on their dignity, pleading, plotting. De Sade was sending petitions and apologies to whomever he thought might speed his release, with intervals of foul-mouthed raging at the governor and at an unstable card-sharper of a fellow inmate, one Baron de l'Allée, who further worsened the spiteful atmosphere in the jail. The governor - called de Launay but no relation to the Montreuils - opined of the marquis: "I find nothing solid in him." However, help was at hand, from early March, when Renée Pélagie arrived near Chambéry from Paris, disguised in men's clothes and accompanied by Albaret. They registered, as the Dumont brothers, at a village inn. The marquise sent her associate to Miolans with a letter in which she begged the governor for the messenger to be allowed a quarter-hour unsupervised with de Sade, to give him some news. The governor had been warned by his superiors to expect her and allow no contact, so Albaret was sent away. During the next few days, various Savoyard officials politely rebuffed other such approaches by the marquise but a certain Lieutenant Duclos, on the prison staff and suspected by the governor of being too thick with the prisoners, visited the village where she was lodged.

By 18 March, Renée Pélagie had arrived at la Coste, having decided she could achieve no more in the Chambéry area, and wrote to the King of Sardinia: "My husband should not be numbered among the miscreants who deserve to be swept out of creation. It was an excessively active imagination, Your Majesty, that led to a certain misdemeanour; prejudice against him has inflated that into a crime whereupon the storm of justice broke over him - and why? Just because of a young man's foolishness that imperilled no-one's life or honour or any person's good standing..." This was not consistent with her mother's line, and her journey in travesty to Savoy cannot have been in step with family thinking.

Easter fell late in 1773, in mid-April, at which juncture the marquis suddenly made his peace with fellow inmates and the governor, distributing apologies to all wronged parties, and carried out his Christian duties appropriate to the festival. The governor was delighted and reported a complete change of heart and behaviour, due to "the grace of the sacrament". Anyone who knew more of de Sade's blasphemous ways might have suggested that he was up to something.

He and de l'Allée arranged about this date to take their meals together, then complained that the food was usually cold by the time it reached de Sade's room. They were then allowed to eat in a room next to the canteen and near a lavatory whose window had no bars. The drop from this window to the hillside was no more than about 13 feet. At 7 p.m. on 30 April, de Sade and de l'Allée began their dinner, served by Latour who, when the kitchen staff were having their own meal, stole the key of the unbarred room. Then he went upstairs to the marquis's cell, lit candles and put two letters to the governor on the table. At 8.30, the three men climbed out through the unbarred window, helped from outside by Joseph Violon, a local man who had been running errands for de Sade and who knew the area well. They set off on foot westwards towards the French border.

As luck would have it, they got a good start. Returning to duty at about nine, the guard noticed a light in de Sade's room, decided that he must be playing draughts with de l'Allée and that this could go on a bit longer, before the latter would be sent to his cell for the night. The guard lay down, just for a few minutes. The next thing he knew it was 3 a.m. and light was still burning in de Sade's room. He called the governor, who forced the locked door and found a letter from each of his noble ex-prisoners. The one by the marquis was an elegant mixture of gentlemanly regrets: "If there is one thing that spoils the joy with which I cast away my fetters[1], it is my fear that you may have to take responsibility for my escape. Regarding all your plain dealing and good manners, I cannot conceal the fact that this consideration troubles me"; of baseless bluster: "fifteen well-horsed and well-armed men are waiting for me under the wall of the fortress ... all set to lay down their lives rather than allow me to be retaken... I have a wife and children who would pursue you even unto your last breath in order to avenge my death"; of goodwill: "I will be grateful to you as long as I live and lack only the chance to demonstrate this. I trust that there will come a day when I might be able to give public recognition of the gratitude you have inspired in me ..."; and of meticulous attention to his effects. He left a list of these and asked that they be sent to the marquise at la Coste, particularly the six maps which decorated his cell, "a brand-new blue frock coat ... and two little china dogs, one all black, the other black with white patches, of which I am very fond." De Sade knew how to travel light, when pressed, but he was used to the sort of reliable porterage a gentleman traveller needs.

He also had the cheek to ask de Launay to arrange for him to be excused paying the last six months' rent for his house at Chambéry, the lease of which he left with his farewell letter.

Mme de Montreuil was greatly displeased, but not so put out of her stride that she failed to chivvy Savoyard officials to take care of de Sade's trunks at Miolans and have them sent to her.

---

1 These were entirely figurative.

The marquis made his way to la Coste and Renée Pélagie, who was soon claiming that he had spent no more than 24 hours there before he left to lie low elsewhere until "his persecutors ... have changed their way of thinking."

While the marquise busied herself with running the château and estate at la Coste, discussing with Fage and other retainers the eternal staving-off of the eternal creditors, her husband came and went. He was by no means harried from ditch to dyke by officials and policemen eager to return him to the custody of the king of Sardinia or to have him meet his Maker via the scaffold at Aix. Communications were slower in those days, various local administrations less apt to co-operate. De Sade was under sentence of death, but this had been handed down by a criminal court at Aix whose writ would not readily run outside Provence. He had lately escaped from jail, but that was in another country. The Savoyard administration, although its soldiers gave chase in the early hours of 1 May, did not concern itself greatly about its departed detainee once it had grounds to believe he had crossed the frontier into France. Considering what a termagant he had been during most of his time at Miolans, and what a great deal of extra work Mme de Montreuil and others interested in him had occasioned for the Savoyard bureaucracy, the little province's officials were probably very glad to have got rid of him.

Besides, no-one should imagine that the Sade-Montreuil dynasts were resigned to their errant being executed as the high court of Provence had laid down. That would have cemented the dishonour which the sentence had brought on the family. De Sade was based in Provence, and he continued to spend much of his time there after his escape from Miolans, but any official on his home ground would have been aware of pressure from the various branches of the de Sade family in the region, from their connections in and near the royal family, and from the Montreuils and their network at the royal court and among the judiciary. This pressure would stay the hand of anyone who lacked similar weighty and coutervailing support as he thought of moving to arrest de Sade on behalf of the high court at Aix.

The marquis continued to pursue his established interests. In the summer of 1773, he was probably at Bordeaux to involve himself with, perhaps even appear in, a production of one of his plays. Writing from prison a dozen years later, he claimed to have spotted at Bordeaux "two spies" tracking him for the Montreuils. He added that he had given the pair a thrashing, and "whipped a whore to teach her what to say and what to do." He complained to his mother-in-law, four years after the event, that he had wanted to travel on to Spain from Bordeaux and had written to her for the money to make the journey, but she had refused.

The marquis appears to have been back at la Coste in the autumn, showing himself very little, leaving at least the paperwork in the running of the household and estate to his wife, which also helped to conceal his presence. The marquise seems to have got rid of all the staff of the previous year who would have been aware of the Marseilles fracas and the death sentence, except for the faithful and trusted maid Gothon Duffé. When asking the tenant-farmer Ripert to recruit a watchman, Renée Pélagie stipulated someone who would "say nothing in the house, and would be as discreet outdoors as inside. That is, he shouldn't talk about the affair in the house, seeing that those who live there don't know about it, and away from the house he shouldn't talk about what he sees and what goes on inside ... Come and see us, my dear Ripert, without telling anyone where you're going..."

The incoherence of the judiciaries and the public administrations of the day, and the comings and goings of the marquis, were merely delaying Mme de Montreuil's grand design, however, not overturning it. She wanted to have the marquis back behind bars - but not in a condemned cell at Aix, waiting for an axe to seal the dishonour of him and his. Rather, the aim was for him to be detained under an order from the king of France which would not be rescinded until his conviction and sentence had been annulled by the high court of Provence and thus wiped from the escutcheon of the de Sades and the Montreuils. With this aim in view, the need for intelligence reports on de Sade's movements and whereabouts, and for the complicated preparation of an expeditionary force, would have played a large part in explaining why it was not until 6 January of the new year, 1774, that Inspector Goupil of the Paris police, backed by four archers brought from the capital and a local squad of horsemen, scaled the walls of la Coste with ladders and burst into the château. According to the marquise's colourful notarised complaint later in the year:

"... The rage inspired by their action painted on their faces, [the police detachment] asks her, with the most frightful oaths on their lips and with the most indecent remarks, where is M de Sade, her husband, whom they have to take dead or alive... She sees barbarity before her eyes; horror and terror seize her one after the other; she sees, she cannot hide from herself, her mother's hand in this... She replies that her husband is away. This is the signal for the most frightful outburst of rage..."

Goupil and his men turn the place upside down, seizing and burning documents, breaking open doors and cabinets, tearing pictures, before uttering a few parting threats - "spewing out that they had orders to fire three pistol shots each at the Marquis de Sade and then to take his body to Lady de Montreuil" - and going on their way.

The inspector's notes of the undertaking show that he had 10 meetings with Mme de Montreuil, before and after the rampage, and that she was closely involved in the details of the raid, even approving the purchase of "two peasant outfits", probably as disguises for officers or informers who had been keeping any eye on la Coste. If she had to pay for the whole operation, which seems more than likely, then it set her back 8,235 livres (perhaps £16,500 or $25,000 nowadays), according to Goupil's detailed expenses claims. However, Mme de Montreuil met at least part of this payment, as she did others connected with her son-in-law's deviations, by drawing on Renée Pélagie's dowry, which would otherwise have gone to the marquis.

Goupil was also helped by the Abbé de Sade and by lawyer Fage. Within a month of the invasion of the château, the marquise was taking her business away from Fage, with whom she had "very serious causes for dissatisfaction," she told Ripert, being no more specific. Her husband had no business with anyone, according to the law, because his property had been impounded since the arrest warrant against him in the summer of 1772. Renée Pélagie transferred her affairs to Gaspard François Xavier Gaufridy, also based at Apt, who was a contemporary and childhood playmate of her husband, and long since an adviser and general factotum to the de Sade family in its Provençal business. He was referred to as a lawyer, although he may well have lacked formal qualifications as such. Gaufridy appears often in the rest of this story, not least because most of the many letters he received from various de Sades and Mme de Montreuil have survived.

In spring and early summer of 1774, Renée Pélagie was struggling to pay the bills at la Coste, not only having to maintain the household but also to cope with the consequences of mismanagement dating back many years. The debts of her husband and of her late father-in-law, the Count de Sade, were eating into what income came her way from the family estates. Much of that was being diverted, as usual, by her husband, this time to support him during another journey in Italy.

The marquis left Provence in mid-March, probably disguised as a priest, having borrowed the appropriate clothes from Ripert, whose brother was in holy orders. On 19 March, the marquise reported to her tenant-farmer at Mazan:

"I am returning to you, my dear Ripert, the portmanteau and the hat... Sir priest began his journey in fine style, according to the carter, except that the rope controlling the ferry across the Durance [river] broke when he was on it, going to Marseilles to take ship [for Italy]. The ferry passengers wanted to make their confessions."

It is not recorded as to whether the militant atheist in priest's clothing improvised a confessional box in the middle of the river and heard of the sins of distressed fellow-passengers as the ferry-men struggled to prevent the Durance turning into the Styx. He would have enjoyed doing so, the danger having galvanised the emotions of the faithful and made him, sacrilegiously impersonating a man of God, the focus of their whole attention.

His wife up-dated Ripert on 12 May: "... After having arrived in good order at his destination, having paid in advance the rent, hire of furniture, etc., for you get nothing when you're abroad unless you pay cash on the nail, he was recognised by someone. Not having much confidence in the person's discretion, he stole away in the night for another place, all of which cost him a ridiculous amount of money..."

On the same date, de Sade was also writing to Ripert: "I have made a big mistake in my reckoning [of how much money I would need]... I had forgotten a small matter which adds up to more than a little, that of food..."

More than a little indeed, for de Sade, who would not have put aside his gourmet tastes just because he was on the run and far from home. Being unable to travel in style, to renew revelry and luxury about him everywhere he went, the marquis fretted in exile, his purse too thin, his status as fugitive precarious. This could not go on. In the early summer of 1774, he wrote to Gaufridy: "I feel that I am not cut out to be an adventurer, and the need to play the part is one of the great tortures of my circumstances..."

De Sade decided to call on the judiciary, which was his scourge, to step between him and his greater scourge, Mme de Montreuil, so as to protect him from her. As a wanted man, he could not risk appearing before any court, so his main associate had to leave her role as mistress of estates and take up that of wronged petitioner at the bar of a Paris court. At least this relieved the marquise of the fraught financial improvising at la Coste. In the spring, she was writing to Ripert:

"You ask me what guarantees I'm going to give for the 1,500 livres [owed to a creditor]; I'll tell you that I have a silver gilt porringer, a silver coffee pot; if that won't do, a jewel case or a silver medal..." The pawnbrokers and assayers of Provence must have been very familiar with the name of the marquise. On 3 June, "the jew Beaucaire" came to the château at la Coste and made "a terrible fuss". Later, there appeared "a man who's owed money from when the plays were on..."

The marquis wrote to his wife from Italy to brief her on what was required of her in Paris. The creditors would have to wait, as usual. Then he unburdened himself to Gaufridy:

"The prompt resolution of [my] affairs demands it. How can one proceed without that? You see what lengths we're having to go to!... Madame de Montreuil's mania for settling nothing is extraordinary. After all, what does she gain by this? Perpetuating the dishonour in this unfortunate affair, that of her daughter and her grandchildren, putting the properties into an appalling disorder[2], and making me ... follow the most sad and unfortunate life, for you can well understand that one is never at ease in a country when one has to conceal oneself all the time and play all sorts of parts so as not to be recognised..."

Which was fine for de Sade when play-acting was part of his dispelling reality, but very distressing when it was part of reality pressing upon him.

The great aim for the marquis was to show himself in what he regarded as his true colours, to change the poor view of him among his in-laws by publicising himself as hard done by and a good chap really. He never lost this estimation of his own actions and worth, and quite failed to understand that his mother-in-law, having assessed abundant evidence, saw him very differently. He explained - none too coherently - to Gaufridy:

"... After all, it is quite clear that I'm being made to seem more culpable than I was regarded as being; if that's so, [by asserting myself] I'll be doing no more than presenting myself as a more genuine and more worthwhile fellow. But it seems to me that the very kind of

---

2 Because de Sade could not attend to them in person, I suppose, though some would say that his close attention was even worse than his distant neglect.

mistake that I admit to is not at all serious and nothing to be condemned for. Is one punished for what one thinks? God alone has that right because He alone knows one's thoughts, but the law can do no such thing, above all when (like the ones I admit to in my statement) they are regretted at once. Besides, it is not even claimed that I ever had such thoughts. It is claimed that I was given bad advice which I did not reject, but which [in fact] I never took up, and the story of the cantharides given in order to simulate what I was recommended [to try], that seems to me not to be, as my lord Abbot makes out, such a great crime. The high court [of Provence] for one did not decide it was. For, if you have the court record in front of you, it being recognised that nothing more [noxious] than cantharides was involved, this element is no longer mentioned in the judgement; the withdrawal [of complaints] by the girls, for one thing, proves it..."

There is no knowing what de Sade had been recommended to try, but which he left aside in favour of cantharides administered to the Marseilles prostitutes. It seems that whatever it was - which he might have thought about but did not put into practice - was something a good deal more dangerous than aniseed sweets with cantharides. A powerful laxative which would have loosened a girl's bowels sufficiently for her to excrete over her client, into his face, into his mouth? It is clear, from his works written in prison during the 1780s, that de Sade was much fascinated by coprophilia, especially in the form of men eating turds from hired or captive persons. As it was, according to the prostitutes' statements to the Marseilles authorities, he gave them sweets with the intention of having them fart while he had his face close to their arses, perhaps also with the aim of the cantharides having their traditional supposed effect of arousing the girls sexually. The episode of 27 June 1772 carries the ring of a thin alternative to the beshitted outrages of de Sade's imagination, as written up in *The Hundred and Twenty Days of Sodom.* In any event, notice in the above paragraph de Sade's whine - resorted to time and again, when he found it in himself to mount some sort of confrontation with his accusers - to the effect that what he was supposed to have done wasn't so bad really, and that there was a misleading hand of someone else behind it. The marquis was rising 34 when he wrote to Gaufridy to this effect.

The letter went on:

"... For pity's sake, give madame [de Sade] lots of encouragement, give her good advice, and may she achieve the impossible by settling the whole thing in the four months I'm giving her to do so. But, in God's name, may she sort things out so that I don't have to lead the wandering and vagabond life I'm leading now..."

Once in Paris in July, seeking to help her husband by securing a judgement that her mother-in-law was harassing him, Renée Pélagie was soon telling Gaufridy to write to her only care of a tailor whom she trusted, rather than to her hotel where the staff were police informers. She could hardly stay at her parents' townhouse, since she was in litigation against her mother.

She might as well have litigated against the Pyramids. The marquise was soon reporting to Gaufridy that the royal attorney "has taken care to tell everyone that I'm mad. I've been greeted by this compliment, and will be again, so I'm assured." She kept her spirits up, penning chirpy letters to Gaufridy about how this or that shard of her husband's case could be glued to some other so as to bring him nearer to a recast innocence, and expressing a general optimism. Renée Pélagie was struggling, though, in a labyrinth of petitions, deferrals, reservations and adjournments for further information, in which her parents were well versed and well connected. What's more, King Louis XV had died on 10 May and much of the royal administration, including that of justice, was still feeling the effects of a consequent upheaval of personnel and policy.

The Abbé de Sade, also writing to Gaufridy, summed up:

"... I wish with all my heart that she may get the judgement[3] set aside; but I fear she is greatly deceiving herself on the basis of flimsy indications... What would be needed is a lot of special consideration which I do not see her being given, especially if her mother doesn't lend a hand... Nothing is more necessary for her than to reconcile herself with a mother who is very bitter towards her, and with reason. Mme de Sade has little capacity for dealing with matters of this kind... This makes me fear that she will get little advantage out of her journey..."

In November, at the end of the four months her husband had allowed for her tilt in the judicial lists of Paris to unhorse her mother, the marquise left the capital and joined her husband at Lyons. Mme de Montreuil's attitude to her son-in-law and his wife was about to be confirmed yet again.

---

3 The death sentence passed at Aix.

CHAPTER 10: "THESE ITEMS OF PHYSICAL FURNITURE"

A less wilful individual than de Sade - approaching middle age, hugely in debt, under sentence of death in one country and a detention order in another - might have seen this as a good time to mend his ways, at least until he had firm decisions from the authorities in France that he was to be allowed his liberty. In fact, he adjusted very little, even worsened his predicament through new exploits. He had the walls of the manor house at la Coste repaired and extended, perhaps with the thought that this would make it harder for any further police raiding parties to force an entry.

On her return to la Coste, the marquise wrote to Gaufridy on 20 November, full of good intentions:

"... I am neither visiting nor receiving anyone, wishing only to occupy myself in putting my affairs in order, and keeping only Jean of my former servants. All my affairs are close to being settled; what's needed is order and economy: that's my plan for the whole winter..."

Anyone less resilient and more apt to learn from experience than Renée Pélagie would have reckoned that, with her husband back from his travels, such a plan was doomed. Harbingers of its undoing had already gathered by the time she was writing her promise of austerity for, while at Lyons that month, she and the marquis, in effect the latter, had engaged servants to take the place of those with whose services she had dispensed. There were seven new recruits, six of them female - comprising a woman known as Nanon, five "really young" girls (an echo of another recruiting expedition, two years earlier, at Marseilles) and a lad of a secretary.

Over Renée Pélagie's signature, but in her husband's style, a letter went to Gaufridy from Lyons regarding a need to reassure connections of the lad as to what sort of ménage he would be joining at la Coste:

"You are going to receive a letter in which you will be asked whether the Count de Mazan[1], presently at Lyons, is the same man as the Marquis de Sade of the Aix case. You will see fit, I beg of you, to reply to this with a little fib in the Jesuit way which, without

1 So the old alias still had mileage in it.

compromising you, confirms nevertheless that this is not the same man; as, for instance, by pointing out that there are several de Sade families - the Sades d'Eyguières, and those of Mazan, of Saumane, of Tarascon - but that for sure the Sade of the story, having to be abroad according to your estimation, assuredly cannot be the one who is now at Lyons. Your letter can only fall into the hands of people who don't amount to much; it's nothing more than a question of some information to do with a young man whom M de Sade wants to take with him. We will see your letter; it has to be shown to us, so I hope you will want to put it together in the way I'm asking you for; you will oblige me inestimably..."

Whether or not the agent at Apt was so drawn into aiding and abetting his master's acquisition of staff, the young secretary joined the aforementioned Jean and the valet La Jeunesse at la Coste. Gothon Duffé was transferred to Mazan. Latour, also still under sentence of death, had thought better of his Sadeian connection and disappeared, probably to America.

The seven recruits from Lyons, and nearby Vienne, may well have been delighted at having been picked for jobs at a country house in the south where there would be regular food and wages, so they were promised. (We are talking of a France of hard times, where many of the poor, rural and urban, were desperate for employment.) Such a stylish couple, on their way from Paris to one of their Provençal estates for the winter and wanting staff - what luck!

For all their knack of raising easy credit and their access to cheap labour, de Sade and his wife were scratching about for money. Following Renée Pélagie's embrace of order and economy, there were no shows or parties, and the main meal of the day was at three in the afternoon before the manor was closely shuttered at sunset. Of an evening, the master would read in his study and, in a nearby room, the lady and her maids would busy themselves about the mending and spinning. "As night falls," the marquis told Gaufridy, describing the new austerity, "the château becomes irremissibly closed, fires out, no more cooking and often no more provisions."

Even before he was drumming up new staff at Lyons, the marquis had given his mother-in-law new cause for ire, and cause for reopening her lines to the Abbé de Sade. On 22 November, she was reminding the abbot by letter of her motives for having dropped him from her network of confidants and supporters:

"I assure you, sir, that the philosophical indolence which you and my lord the Commander [de Sade] had taken up at critical moments, which called for the most intense activity, caused my silence, allowing me to hope for no further intervention on your part..."

However, the marquis's recent behaviour, which was being discussed in society, was "destroying the impression, which we had been trying to put about, *that he had left for Italy, not because he was guilty as people were saying, but that he was afraid of his family.* All the Provençales are spreading the word in Paris that he is down there, and off the bridle...

"Is it possible that, among a family of his *Name*, so numerous, with two respectable uncles, no-one has had the backbone to talk sense to him forcefully and to make him follow a path befitting the situation; or to take hold of him, in a word, and watch him in such a way that any trouble be avoided. I promise you that, in their place, I would have done it, on the quiet, until circumstances had been changed for the better, and would have calmed that head and restrained it... His family ... is quite put to one side and every kind of charge arising has fallen on me again, like his anger: calumnies, satires, nothing has been left out in attacking me and everything connected with me... He holds his unhappy wife captive, forced to be the aide to his infamous manoeuvres, or he dazzles her eyes and her reason by the same means. You say so yourself, sir, and that she only writes at his dictation.

"You are not even 4 leagues away [from la Coste]! and yet you cannot go, accompanied by someone reliable and apt like yourself to be respected (and so you would be!), to take a stand and put the whole thing to rights! and speak firmly! You would be listened to..."

In the same letter, Mme de Montreuil indicated that she had felt it necessary to make a payment of 1,265 livres to head off some unspecified trouble connected with her son-in-law, perhaps by buying the silence of a complainant.

From him came the first hint that the declared end to the unbuttoned life was not being made good behind the shutters at la Coste. On 27 January of the new year, 1775, de Sade wrote to Gaufridy:

"I am preparing for you a well-ordered refutation of all that the child said, especially the personal accusations by the Abbot..."

About the same date, the marquise must have been warning her mother that something was amiss for, on 11 February, the *présidente* wrote directly to Gaufridy, whom she had never met. She knew of him through her daughter and through the Abbé, and now she was enlisting his aid in a matter about which the marquise had just consulted her and which:

"... it is important, very important, to stop without delay... I have told her: 'hand over everything at once, but with precaution so as to avoid being open to trouble later.' She tells me she has taken these precautions, in part, and that she is provided with all the certificates of good condition... I would have no worries on this point if the persons in question had only been alone with her, occupied with spinning and servant duties... If that were the case - nothing to fear, and nothing to be done other than to send them to you as the most reliable person to whom she could entrust them ..., to take them back to their relatives, to get from the latter valid and adequate receipts so as never to be bothered by this matter; to hand them [the persons] back to them [the relatives] in the presence of the Royal attorney with whom the relatives filed complaints such as abduction done without their knowledge or by enticement, in front of the same priests who wrote to the lady [the marquise] to ask for them back. Have signed and sealed in front of them [the relatives, attorney and priests] the withdrawal of legal proceedings which have been started, in that what they were asking for has been restored to them and in that no-one has ever claimed to be holding back against their wishes. Yesterday we wrote from here to the [royal] attorney at Lyons ..., saying that the lady was firmly resolved not to keep, against their parents' wishes, these children whom she had taken for charity's sake, rather that she wanted only to give them back to them [the relatives] safely and with a proper receipt for herself...

"Well, that all makes good sense, but action is needed. Set off. Take them yourself. It's a delicate job, not to be given to anyone but you, and [take] with you just one person on whom you can rely, to keep these children close at hand and in a safe place, until you have made your arrangements with each of the relatives who have complained. It's up to you, sir, to put all this prudently to rights, in line with your own knowledge...

"I was looking, the day before yesterday, at some news from Lyons... This story is much talked about there. They know there about the departure of the little girl who is at the Abbé's place. It's being recounted more or less as it is. That has managed to alarm the parents who were asking for restoration and who had filed complaints. They are making a lot of fuss and sticking to their legal proceedings.

The lady has compromised herself by the replies she has given to the Royal attorney and to the priests. She shilly-shallied, talked about the convent[2], said they would not be handed over until she had been reimbursed for the cost of their upkeep [while at la Coste]... All that has soured people, appeared more suspect and had a very bad effect...

"... Go find her right away, sir; read her my letter... Get busy without delay. There's not a moment to lose. Seeing where this affair has got, it can't be dealt with in writing. Go to Vienne and to Lyons, and do business..."

Mme de Montreuil, all too well practised in such damage-control operations, had no need to mention in her letter the name of the source of the problem. If only "the persons in question" had had no more to cope with than their duties spinning thread, cleaning the grate, mending the linen and tending the flocks - and had no other company but that of the marquise. As it was, though, they had spent the period from late-November, the probable date of their arrival at la Coste, until mid-January, when news of the upset began to surface, in a strong and remote place with the Marquis de Sade. In the 200 years between the late-18th century and the late-20th, the manor house fell into ruin, not least through neglect in the marquis's time, and there is no plan of how it was then. However, we know the château had 42 rooms, as well as cellars, and the village jail was part of the structure, with the marquis holding a set of keys.

The five girls and the young secretary brought to la Coste from Lyons and Vienne would have been very much out of their depth when confronted by the marquis, on his own ground and with all his resources to hand, in pursuit of his pleasure. He might have modified somewhat his persuasive arguments for libertinage to suit a handful of youngsters from the lower orders. Drawing on his library and collections of amusing objects, he could have spiced his persuasion with lubricious readings, examinations of drawings, carvings, engravings and tapestries which depicted erotic scenes. The cellar was well-stocked and so alcohol was available to loosen the attitudes of the budding acolytes - no need to offer them the best wines, of course.

The marquise might have been keeping the household functioning on a succession of loans - including some from the canny old Commander de Sade in exchange for pledges of her silver - but her husband always

---

2 For the servant-girls or for herself?

managed to find a little cash when it was a matter of buying some fun. A little cash might have been enough for green kids whose pay may well have amounted to not much more than their board and lodging, and a promise of a sum of money every quarter if they keep their noses clean. We are thinking about a man whose custom, when seeking relief among commoners, was to buy it.

During the winter at la Coste, though, the marquis might not even have bothered to dip into his purse for a putative harem whose members probably had little notion of just where they were and little scope for summoning help. The *droit de seigneur* must have seemed very much in being, although it was supposed to be a dead letter by the 18th century. It could easily be enforced by violence, threatened or enacted, on the part of the lord and master. Servants in those days who stole anything - or were accused of theft by a master frustrated in his demands of them - might not only find themselves out of a job but dangling from the end of a rope.

What's more, there is no certainty that any servant-girl, cowering and trembling in the corner of a gloomy room in a great gloomy house, her employer bearing down on her with candelabra in one hand and whip in the other, could have any hope of the lady of the manor interposing herself between the maid and imminent assault. It seems that, during certain episodes at least that winter, Renée Pélagie made herself scarce or was pulled into the whirl whipped up by her husband. The girls told investigators later that the marquise had been "the first victim of a frenzy that can only be called madness."

No-one who is familiar with de Sade, life and works, can resist drawing a comparison between the winter of 1774-75 at la Coste and the much more elaborate - because much better financed - fictional winter at Silling Castle in his novel *The Hundred and Twenty Days of Sodom* (*Les Cent Vingt Journées de Sodome*) written in prison ten years later. In each season, a specially picked group of youngsters is put at the sexual service of a directing master-libertine (well, four of same at Silling). The fictional recruits are kidnapped into service and all perish under the mayhem of the masters. I like to recall that, in *The Hundred and Twenty Days,* de Sade shone, just for a moment, a light into the void behind the consuming libertine and his ravenous appetite for attention. After a description of one of his libertine lords - so rich and influential that the law of the land can shield few people from his desires - de Sade allows a peek behind the powerhouse: "Yet, for all that, ... a steadfast child might have thrown this monster into a panic; ... whenever [he] found that he was unable to use his treachery or his trickery to overcome an enemy, he would come over fearful and cowardly; the least idea of any kind of fight on equal terms would have made him hide himself in the remotest region of the world."

We do not know how effectively the young servants of la Coste stood their ground against the nearest thing the château had to a monster, but the ménage was broken up before one would have expected the marquis to have tired of his quasi-captive playthings. La Coste, unlike the fictional fastness of Silling, was not cut off by snow and deliberate destruction of bridges on mountain roads.

Mme de Montreuil, regarding from Paris the consequences of the winter, commented: "In his château with her [the marquise], he thinks himself too strong, too secure, and allows himself everything." Not quite - the servants in Provence got away with their lives, unlike the fictional victims in the Black Forest. Even the small-scale indulgence at la Coste, however, relied on funds other than the master's own. Mme de Montreuil's remarks continued: "And even there, if she were not on hand, he would lack the means to satisfy his deviations and so they would not be the dangerous kind..." That is, he was drawing on his wife's money, available to him as her husband through her dowry, to elaborate his entertainments to a dangerous degree.

The *présidente* continued, to Gaufridy:

"... Wouldn't you be able to confer with Saumane [the Abbé] about ways to be able to arrange some security, some alleviation, at least for that poor prisoner, for it's said that [the manor] is all locked up and that she is not allowed out. One is greatly fearful about him..."

Mme de Montreuil, of course, was fretting only about how her daughter ("that poor prisoner") was faring at la Coste. The condition of any servant-girl there, or anywhere else, would not have so moved her.

At Saumane, the Abbé would have liked very much to have handed on "the little girl" who had left his nephew's place and found refuge at his house. The old roué - having heard what the girl had to say about what had happened to her at la Coste, and she seems to have been highly articulate - prepared accusations against the marquis accordingly and became all the more determined to involve himself in the affairs of M and Mme de Sade as little as possible. However, there were complications for the abbot. Renée Pélagie was concerned, as her mother knew and approved, to secure certificates of good health from a doctor for all the servants from la Coste before they were returned to their families. She explained this to the Abbé in February, but added a plea that he prevent the girl in his care being seen, by a doctor or by anyone else. The obvious interpretation is that, after her stay at la Coste, the girl was in a condition which no doctor could certify as that of good health.

All the more reason for the disgruntled abbot to get shot of her? Well, no. Nephew and uncle had more in common than the latter, at least, liked to be reminded of - but reminded he was. Still in February, the Abbé received from the marquise a letter that bears the hectoring, fluent style of her husband at his most self-serving, rather than her own manner:

"When, last year, Provence was resounding with talk of a girl whom you were harbouring in your château at Saumane - a creature, so they said, stolen from her relatives, whose search [for her] your secretary blocked, pistol in hand, on your instructions; when, more recently, I was at Lyons and two local women came to me to complain about very bad treatment received, they said, at the château of Saumane, I calmed everyone down, kept everyone quiet, and did all I could to root out these vile calumnies. I hope that you might see your way clear to do the same in this new case, to stifle the talk of this girl [arrived from la Coste], above all to stop her returning to Vienne - as it seems to be your intention to have her taken there, which would be dangerous, because she is telling all kinds of horrors everywhere - and to keep her at your place where she will be happier because she will have her liberty, which I was obliged to refuse her at my place for reasons of policy that make my house into a kind of prison - but these are reasons very different to those which you appear to be supposing and in which that nephew whom you are pleased to rail at so much, to treat as a madman, has no hand..."

In the next paragraph, someone has seen fit to cross out certain words with a heavy pen:

"This story, albeit it is occasioning such gratuitous abuse, gives cause for you to be reminded that it was eight years ago that it turned out ---- that girl called Rose ------ to which you owe the silence of that girl who was saying about you ---- much stronger things, and who was very determined to add that statement to that of her pregnancy.

"Forgive me if I raise matters from long ago, but how can one not be made desperate by the fierceness which you always seem to bring to bear on your nephew, even though he could not be more innocent? I have nothing to fear from this girl who escaped from my place; everything she says is lies and calumny. I could offer the strongest proof that she left my house intact: she only has to be seen... What dreadful things can this creature say about me! And how could you give credence to what you are reporting to me? You are treating me very sweetly in your letter and, to take your word for it, I would be thought the director of my husband's pleasures. No, sir, that neither is nor has ever been the case and, in this instance, how would it be so, since it is quite certain that my husband has not set foot in la Coste for a year? They can come and carry out all the searches they want: they won't find him or any trace of what you see fit to talk about. I have nothing to fear on that score.

"Boredom is the only thing behind the escape of this little girl; she preferred to look after the flocks than to spin in her room. She will be very content at Saumane, if you want to give me the satisfaction of looking after her there. In case she might have ... come out with a complaint about some attack or about some remarks by my servants, that's something, in spite of my care, I have perhaps not been able to stop. But to say that M de Sade might be involved, and that I might have taken part in these outrages, now that's a calumny, firstly because I am incapable of such a thing, which you must be fair enough towards me to believe, and secondly because my husband is not and cannot be here...

"As of the day after this creature's escape, I have sent her colleagues away and I no longer have any of them at my place. It is quite true that they were here; but it seems to me that no-one has anything to tell me about taking servant-girls to serve me, and feminine domestic servants are, it seems to me, always more natural in a woman's house than in a man's.

"... Be very careful, I beg you, in all this, my dear uncle, that this girl who talks with so much *frankness* and *ingenuousness* is not snuffed out by some secret enemy..."

The Abbé would have known that much of this was bluster and misrepresentation - for one thing, he knew very well the marquis was at la Coste - but the blackmail must have been an accurate enough dip into his own licentious past to keep him in line regarding the servant-girl from la Coste. She remained at Saumane, uninspected by a doctor or anyone else, as far as we know.

Mme de Montreuil's intervention continued to be conducted through Gaufridy, likely to her best agent in Provence now that Renée Pélagie was taking her husband's part (and mixed up in his bizarre conduct) and the Abbé was wishing himself shot of the whole business. With her unwavering concentration on achieving her strategic goals for her family, and her disregard for fair dealing (especially towards the lower orders of society), she told the lawyer on 9 March:

"... the person who is at Saumane, it's she who worries me the most because of the chattering. To move her elsewhere is dangerous and would have very grave consequences. To leave her where she is would lead to other problems. A convent, provided one could put her there safely once everything has calmed down, seems best to me. A selected convent or a reliable individual to supervise her in some remote place, and to treat her properly if she doesn't spread any gossip, persuading her that she has a greater motive than anyone to say nothing because what she was saying would be to her own detriment and would get her into a lot of trouble as a result...

"There is too much friction between those belonging to M de Sade and my daughter for one to hope that they will ever march in step. The abbot more so than any. Besides, they go along with nothing of that which I have had the honour to ask of them, notwithstanding well ordered and well considered steps, the motives for which it was not appropriate to set out in writing. They do us the honour of taking us for imbeciles, apparently..."

Also grumbling to Gaufridy, on 28 April, the Abbé reported that all his relatives were in agreement with him in regarding Mme de Montreuil as a great nuisance - "this lady who treats us like wind-up dolls made to move according to her will..."

He begged Gaufridy "to do all that you can to rid me of this little girl whom I am looking after at my place out of an excess of indulgence towards people who deserve nothing of the sort from me, and with whom I want to have no dealings. When I next have the pleasure of seeing you, I will tell you many things which I cannot entrust to paper..."

There lies the problem for us in trying to discern what happened to the servants at la Coste. Something nasty, one can be sure, but the subsequent efforts by the blue-bloods in the case to hide the truth from their contemporaries also obscure it from posterity. Whatever the Abbé told Gaufridy when they next shared a bottle and a few confidences, it probably included an account of what was behind the servant-girl's chattering - but may well have glossed over the ruthless blackmail from la Coste which was making the old priest lodge the escapee.

Gaufridy's efforts to bury the affair out of sight of high society were approved by Mme de Montreuil, as she read the documents sent to her from his office at Apt, not least the witnessed statements from relatives that their offspring, lately *chez* de Sade, had been returned to them. She had taken counsel in Paris, regarding one particular complainant, and decided, she told Gaufridy on 8 April: "... I think we can rest easy on this point. Making statements isn't everything; they need proof..."

However, returning requested parties isn't everything; they need to be in a sound condition. Mme de Montreuil continued: "To tell the truth, they're claiming that the proof [of what the relatives said had happened to the young servants] exists on the bodies, the arms, and that it accords with the children's statements..."

Gaufridy was told to find out, on behalf of the *présidente*, what the truth of this was, for "only the truth can determine the way in which we put the truth to use. If the statement is found to be well-based, we must calm things down rather than stir them up... If it's no more than a cunning yarn based on old stories, in order to make one buy silence, then one must openly turn to face the storm and, the lie being proven as such, seek justice against the calumny..." Having made clear that she was not disposed to pay complainants to keep quiet unless she was sure there were unavoidable grounds for doing so, she indicated that she still had cause for much disquiet about events at la Coste, especially her daughter's part in them: "... The children have no grievance at all against her, on the contrary. They are talking about her as being in jeopardy herself, the first victim of a frenzy that can only be called madness. But they vehemently charge the other..." In French, *l'autre* (the other) could refer to a masculine or a feminine person - Mme de Montreuil may well have intended the obscuring ambiguity. It is probable she meant her son-in-law, but one must not lose sight of the adult woman, Antoinette Sablonnière, known as Nanon, who was also recruited at Lyons the previous November for duty at la Coste. The *présidente* might have been referring to her.

However, her letter went on to indicate a deep unease which can only be her abiding nervousness about the marquis:

"... Can a mother stay calm, knowing her daughter is shut up under the same roof, and living in the uncertainty, at least, as to whether what she is told about the fate of that daughter is correct or falsified? If they were not together, at least then I would be less worried. Each letter I open makes me tremble... To write to her about this would be useless. I know all too well that everything that arrives for her, or that goes from her, passes through milord's hands or perhaps is turned over to him by his faithful Carteron, the one they call La Jeunesse, before reaching her..."

It seems that, by early April, Gaufridy had not interviewed the girl at Saumane - more than likely through the pressure from the marquis on his uncle keeping her from Mme de Montreuil's go-between - because the *présidente* went on to urge him to pass on to her what the girl was saying. Mme de Montreuil may well have understood that Gaufridy was in contact with the lord and lady at la Coste, and that he could relay to them these next sentiments of hers:

"... Don't think that, whatever might be done [by the marquis and/or his wife], he will avoid legal proceedings against him forever. She would let herself be cut into little bits before she would consent to anything that would do him harm..."

This was not the most tasteful hyperbole (if hyperbole it was), given some of the marquis's propensities.

However much those were being exercised, once the maids had left la Coste, de Sade continued the quiet life, as far as those few locals who encountered him were aware, of a country squire more inclined to the study than to the field or to magistracy over his vassals. Improvement of the protective walls was advanced at the château. There was a scheme, with one of the local worthies, to mine for gold near the village. If it had stuck pay-dirt, de Sade might have had the finance to become the grand libertine of his most expansive and sanguinary fantasies, but it never came to anything. He read a great deal, as ever, and gave desultory attention to drawing up a statement of his debts, another matter that was always with him, but not so pressingly as to divert him from the prospect of an exciting purchase when that arose. "They say," he wrote to Gaufridy one spring day, "that there's a sale at the Sablières place. If there's a harpsichord to be had there, big or small, you would oblige me infinitely by holding on to it for me; I would pick it up right away. Likewise if there are any books..."

Even so, the loss of the servant-girls had not left the master entirely bereft of extra-marital sexual diversion in the spring of 1775. Towards the end of June, a girl called Rosette, who had been living clandestinely at the château (not difficult in a manor of 42 rooms with outbuildings), went on her way. Another young female guest of the marquis at about this time was a dancer called du Plan, through whom he subsequently explained the later discovery of human bones in the grounds of the manor house. Writing to his wife from prison in 1781, he claimed that the bones:

"... were brought by that one among the girls who calls herself Du Plan; she is very much alive, she can be questioned; a cupboard was festooned with them as a joke - good or bad, I leave that to you - which is truly what they were used for, and they were disposed of in the garden once the joke, or rather the boring bit of palaver, was done with. Have the bones found counted, check the result with the account which I have, in Du Plan's writing, of the number and the kind of bones she herself brought from Marseilles, and you'll see whether there is one unaccounted for..."

Be that as it may, the story of the human bones excited further the already eager appetite for news and rumour about de Sade, and it was widely believed that his sexual violence at la Coste had gone as far as murder, with subsequent macabre use of human remains. It had not been forgotten that, in order to have his way with Rose Keller seven years before, he had threatened to kill her and bury her in the garden of the house at Arcueil.

By the end of April, mainly due to Mme de Montreuil's well-directed and diligent pressure, the trouble over the abuse of staff at the manor was nearly snuffed out. There was still some tidying, however. On 11 May, Nanon, aged 24, gave birth to a daughter, whose baptismal papers deemed Nanon's husband to be the father although popular opinion reckoned de Sade responsible. The Abbé also stirred the pot by appealing to the royal court for the marquis to be shut away, his mental incapacity making him a threat to society and chronic nuisance to his family. In mid-June, Gaufridy was walking in the grounds of la Coste with Renée Pélagie so as to inform her, by handing her a letter from Mme de Montreuil, that her mother had secured a royal order for Nanon to be detained without trial, so that she could not go to Lyons and re-open the affair with more complaints. The notary had been instructed by Mme de Montreuil to deliver the letter in this way because to have told the marquise inside the house, even if he thought himself alone with the her, would have risked discovery by the marquis, who was known for eavesdropping, Mme de Montreuil maintained.

About this time, Nanon stormed out of la Coste after a final row with Renée Pélagie, who then suggested that the woman had stolen silver from the house. However, Nanon reached the convent of Jumiège, asked sanctuary of the prior and told him of recent events. He turned away three of de Sade's estate workers, who had come to apprehend her, and wrote to the Abbé de Sade that the marquis would have to be locked up for life. The prior believed that the marquise was no better than her husband, for no-one at la Coste had made Easter confession and the marquise "lets her maids mix with a married Lutheran woman" - this last no doubt being the maid Gothon Duffé, who was Swiss.

At the end of June, the marquise was at Aix to hand over to his mother, who had suddenly turned up at Lyons making a fuss before the magistrates, the young secretary, whose knowledge of the world may well have been broadened since he was engaged by the marquis seven months or so before. The marquise later told Gaufridy: "When I learn ... that little Malatié has arrived at Bordeaux, my mind will be still more at ease. His tears upset me... What's more, he struck me as so stupid!"

A little while before he left Provence, Malatié had written to Gaufridy to ask for help in getting a job. The weak grasp of literacy betrayed by the drab little letter confirms the suspicion that the marquis had not picked up the lad for his secretarial skills.

On 5 July, a royal minister told Mme de Montreuil that he had formulated the order for Nanon to be held in a religious house at Arles, in the Rhône estuary, the very place Mme de Montreuil had proposed. Nanon had been installed there only a few days when her baby daughter, still at la Coste, died. The wet-nurse to whom it had been entrusted had run out of milk, being pregnant. She insisted later she had not known she was pregnant when she took on Nanon's child, but thought her milk had stopped temporarily because she had to work hard tending silk-works. (The production of silk thread was one of the village industries.) The marquise reported that various hostile parties had tried unsuccessfully to have the wet-nurse admit that she and those who had passed the infant to her knew she was pregnant at the time and so, by implication, were arranging for the child to die.

Nanon was not told of the infant's death until nearly a year later, during one of Gaufridy's visits to check on her behaviour and her disposition to keep her mouth shut. In July of 1777, the woman's father, Annet Sablonnière, was petitioning government offices in Paris for his daughter to be set free. Mme de Montreuil reported to Gaufridy that "the Minister, who has some consideration for me, is keeping me informed of proceedings and tells me he has no wish to take a decision without having my opinion. I feel it can be dangerous to resist excessively because, for one thing, a father has to be given reasons when he perseveres, and that can lead to dangerous clarifications."

So, if Gaufridy's next bulletin on Nanon's state of mind were to "give grounds for presuming her changed and more sensible, I agree, if she wants to get out, to undertake to obtain the consent of Madame de Sade. But you are aware of all the conditions which you must put to her, and only by complying with these will she deserve our kindness. No change of attitude - not by her father, not by her friends, not by her family - in order to make a grab for money, for there won't be a penny piece given; and if she deviates an inch from the straight and narrow, she'll be locked up again in an instant and punished according to the law as she deserved..."

The law mentioned by Mme de Montreuil would not be that which she had been taking into her own hands with regard to Nanon and others who might ruin her family's good name.

In August, Gaufridy having visited Nanon to sound her out, the *présidente* was prepared to be specific on the conditions that would attend the young woman's release. She told the lawyer:

"... the first move is to have her father undertake to keep her from going to rejoin him in the areas where it is not at all acceptable that she should appear, and which would certainly be placed out of bounds to her as a condition of the favour[3] that would be granted to her... I have heard some stories which she will do well not to put me in the position of having to reveal, for her own sake... So she will do well, whoever questions her, not to let anything slip, saying *every time* and to *every* question: *'I know nothing about it!'* ..."

Sablonnière, perhaps expressing himself through a literate helper, owned a pithy way with a letter. He addressed one lawyer acting for the *présidente:*

---

3 The release from detention.

"... You are apparently authorised by Madame de Montreuil to continue to keep Antoinette Sablonnière, my daughter, in slavery, and this without legitimate cause... If you have some good motives, attack her through due process; if not, I am determined to use this means on behalf of my child, over whom I have more authority than anyone. I hope to succeed in that, or the powers in the land are sleeping... If such acts of violence are allowed, we are no longer in France where no-one is kept like a slave... I am poor, but I will find the resources to deny iniquity its triumph..."

For all that, iniquity, if that is what Mme de Montreuil was, achieved its usual conditional triumph in such cases. Nanon was released early in the following February, 1778, having been forbidden to come within three leagues of Lyons and Vienne, likely to have been the only towns she knew. She signed - with a cross, for she could not read or write - a receipt for 328 livres in lieu of wages owed, and swore to speak not of what she knew. The marquise spent 24 livres on linen for Nanon, later congratulating herself on not having provided good quality material.

Iniquity usually has good contacts. Mme de Montreuil was soon asking the royal minister concerned, a dinner guest of hers at the time, to arrange for Nanon to continue to be kept under surveillance by his police and other agents.

* * *

Back in 1775, it was not until 10 November that the Abbé de Sade told Gaufridy that the girl lodged with him at Saumane since early in the year was fully recovered. He was about to remove her from a hospital, where he had put her three weeks before, and hand her over to Ripert, the marquis's tenant-farmer at Mazan, well off the beaten track and where she would be unlikely to meet strangers who would make something out of what she might have to tell.

One has to allow for the keen interest by many influential parties - not least the Abbé, under pressure from blackmail - in keeping this girl out of circulation. So it may be that she had been more kept under wraps than under medication. However, there are persuasive indications that she had been badly hurt during the previous winter at la Coste, which de Sade had turned into a keep of his pleasure where no help could reach, however loud the screams. Whatever doubt might remain as to whether she was ill-used at the château, there is none that she was considered, after she left, only to the degree that her co-operation or lack of it affected the de Sade/Montreuil manoeuvres to prevent the latest exploitation by the marquis turning into a greater scandal, a deeper stain on the escutcheon. Once patched up, she was marooned on a remote farm of which she had never heard, no worse fed and sheltered than she was used to perhaps, but certainly not restored to her former surroundings and not properly treated for her trouble.

We do know she had got away from Ripert's farm by the summer of the next year, 1776, and made her way back to Vienne, but we do not know whether she limped for the rest of her life, whether she had been robbed of the capacity to make love or to conceive, whether she was subject to recurrent nightmares - but we can doubt that she was ever quite the same again. At this juncture, she sinks back into history's indistinct legion of sexual prey, without our having found out her name.

In 1775, among those with options and to spare, Mme de Montreuil's efforts to re-open the Aix case were being frustrated by various jurists who, however keen they might be to oblige, were keener to make no move without clear instructions from the royal court, where ministers were reluctant to put the case before the new king, aged 21, lest he be revolted by the details and thus set his mind against the marquis. Louis XVI, unlike his predecessor, had not developed a penchant for snippets of scandal. Mme de Montreuil acknowledged that the ministers had a point and persevered with caring for de Sade's children.

The marquis, who had remained undetected in July during another police raid on la Coste, by hiding in a niche under the roof, decided to bring the Count de Mazan back into being. As such, he left again for Italy, telling Gaufridy to "let it be believed that I will not reappear for a very long time." Once abroad, he fretted over not being able to make himself understood (not over being able to understand, you may note) because hardly anyone spoke French and his Italian was not good. He was advised that he would never become fluent "without an Italian mistress, and I assure ... you," he wrote to Gaufridy, "that there's a means which I shall certainly not use." He sent to the marquise for shirts - "above all, impress on them to take care with the cut of the neck" - and raged to Gaufridy for money, adding that, on his return to la Coste, he would have "with me six *Bohemian deserters* whom I have engaged here and who'll know how to defend me against the *valiant and brave horsemen of Provence...*" Gaufridy must have known better than anyone what a joke that was, for how would such a squad be paid?

More to the point, while in Italy, de Sade's aversion to religion kept him from entering churches but this gave him more time to admire many works of art, especially erotic ones. Examination of a statue of a hermaphrodite caused him to remark: "the intemperance of the Romans dared to seek pleasure even in these kinds of monsters", and the Venus de Medici was "the most beautiful piece I have seen in my life. One feels penetrated by a gentle and sacred emotion on admiring it... The proportions of this sublime statue, the grace of the figure, the divine contours of each limb, the graceful swellings of the breast and of the buttocks make up a masterpiece which could rival nature in our days..."

For all that, his mind was never far from home. There, so he had grumbled to Gaufridy before he left, "I'm regarded as the werewolf." From Italy, he returned to the theme, for the benefit of the same recipient:

"... Put yourself in my place, I entreat you, and feel all the horror of my position; I'm ruining myself here, it's costing me a terrible amount to live very badly. There's no doubt Mme de Montreuil intends to ruin me and my children, and it is very unfortunate for me that I've found no-one with enough backbone to get her to see this. I was counting on you to manage that but, using charm (which she has from the devil, to whom she has bequeathed her soul, I'm sure), charm which I neither understand nor ever will understand, [she] captures all she touches and, as soon as her hocus-pocus has lighted on someone's eyes, I'm cast aside as no better than dog-meat. They see it, they bemoan all that she does to me, yet they approve of it and no-one dares take sides with the powerless oppressed... If, a year ago, you had written more forcefully to this shrew, I would not be so upset today...

"I can hear you saying to me: 'Sir, your new misdeeds have prolonged your troubles.' But hear me reply to that: 'Sir, my troubles, my loss of credibility, my position, prolong my misdeeds and, while I am not rehabilitated, there won't be a cat beaten in the entire province without their saying: 'It's that Marquis de Sade again.' "

In other words, it's not that my badness is extending my difficulties, rather that my difficulties are making me go on being bad, which is all scurrilous tittle-tattle anyway. The marquis was a dab hand at inverting cause and effect when it came to dodging blame, and this letter was one of his most succinct essays in the genre.

Even more interesting was de Sade's synthesis of his art appreciation in Italy and his attitude to the uses of servants and the lower orders in general. Responding to Titian's portrait of his serving-woman, the traveller noted:

"They say that she was useful to him in more than one way: these kinds of items of physical furniture are difficult for an artist and a man of letters to do without. It's good to have them here and there at one's orders; nature is satisfied and the head does not go haywire! Love is not right for a man who works. If his desires catch light and he doesn't have immediately at hand the means to extinguish them, the fire of the senses takes the place of the fire of composition and the work suffers accordingly...

"If I were king, not only would I allow this licence to people who live the creative life, but the desire to have great men would even bring me to order them to provide themselves with it! It's the same with caring for a household. A philosopher or an artist is obliged to turn these responsibilities over to other people. These chores which cannot but cramp one's genius are capable in themselves of bringing down a great man..."

Well, that's all right then. The servant-girls sent back to their families, with the marks of the master's attentions at la Coste, had been facilitating the bloom of his creative genius by acting as convenient drains for his lust, so that his essential work in the study would suffer minimal deflection. Intellectual snobbery takes many forms.

As for the household chores, no-one should think de Sade was referring to floor-polishing and pot-scouring. It would no more occur to milord marquis to do that than to fly to the moon - rather, he meant the distracting and tedious business of ordering provisions, settling with tradesmen and reckoning debts. He was keen enough on the details of hiring staff, though, especially when looking for some that were "really young", and on the enlargement of the walls for his château, for that might keep the Inspector Goupils of this world from carrying him off to a royal fortress.

While he was abroad, Renée Pélagie travelled to Aix about the sodomy/poisoning verdict, taking with her a manservant of her husband's, for whom she had a peach-coloured suit tailored, set off by a grey ratteen frock coat and black breeches. One would not have thought there were bare pantries at home, or that she had been advised not to go to Aix - let alone go there attended by an eye-catching servant

- lest she be pointed out as her husband's fellow orgiast. No, the marquise had to be accompanied by a servant in impressive rig. *Bella figura* above all.

Her husband, soon after this, was obliged to show himself off against his better judgement. When he was in Naples, about the end of January of the next year, 1776, a French diplomat suspected he was a certain Tessier, who had taken advantage of his position as cashier at a salt warehouse at Lyons to run away with 80,000 livres. Suspicion was deepened by a French officer in Naples, who declared that there was no colonel in the French army by the name of the Count de Mazan, de Sade having been unwise enough to give his adopted persona the military rank to which he had aspired. Under pressure from the diplomat, who had put the Neapolitan police on his tail, de Sade agreed to be presented at the court of the King of Naples, in his colonel's uniform. He was more afraid of being recognised and insulted because of his personal notoriety than of being arrested as Tessier - but there is no record of any presentation at court and he got out of this scrape somehow.

By March, the marquis was writing to Renée Pélagie of his homesickness for la Coste. She immediately sent a servant to Naples to tell him that return would be folly. Even so, on 4 May, having shipped to France two chests full of antiques and curios, and a dictionary of rhymes, the marquis set out by land for home. His interest in art, architecture and the erotic had led him, while in Italy, to various fellow connoisseurs, including Dr Ménil, a French physician at Florence in Tuscany, and Giuseppe Iberti, a doctor in Rome. These and others kept up correspondence with de Sade for years afterwards, helping especially to extend his archive of material on sexual behaviour. At one point, a letter from de Sade to Iberti on this topic was intercepted by the Inquisition of the Catholic Church and, when the papal police (all Rome being then ruled by the pope) raided the doctor's apartment, they caught him in the act of writing up an account of a sexual adventure for his French correspondent. Iberti spent four months in jail.

In one castle, de Sade noticed "a sort of bow, very small and of a peculiar construction, which used to belong to a Spaniard whose only pleasure was to fire from this bow (with no intention but that of random destruction) lots of poisoned pins into streets and crowds." In 1990, New York City was excited about a man who had taken it into his head to blow darts at the lower quarters of women passers-by. The Marquis de Sade would have recognised the urge to hurt, to have an effect, in the New Yorker of the darts, as he had in the Spaniard of the pins. Whether he would have recognised the immaturity and social inadequacy at the root of that urge is another matter.

Back in Provence, there were flurries of anxiety as various ex-servants fled the various coops where they had been stowed for silence's sake - most notably the girl who had been at Saumane, then been lodged with farmer Ripert. She seems to have been helped to get away from Mazan by a former valet at la Coste whom Renée Pélagie had sacked for "not holding his tongue". He brought the girl before a lower-court judge in the Provençal town of Orange, to whom she made a statement. The marquise dispatched Ripert, on 30 July, to find out what was being stirred up by "this little girl whom you have let escape, by stupidity or by bad luck, this not being the moment to clarify the point." Mme de Montreuil, very suspicious as to what the real motives behind the development might be, also wrote to Ripert for news. However, it seems nothing came of these last twitches of the servant-girls affair. A threat from the judge's lady, via Ripert, to the ex-valet may well have done the trick:

"You will do well, I think, to keep an eye on and restrain this [fellow], and to tell him that he can count on protection only so long as he behaves himself properly, and that, if he lets slip wrongful remarks about masters whom he says he respects, he will be put into a secure place, like Nanon..."

Whatever the girl told the judge at Orange could not have strained his credulity more than another item of word-of-mouth from the summer of 1776 must have strained the belief of any hearer who had followed the career of the marquis at all attentively. Renée Pélagie to Gaufridy:

"... There's a piece of news circulating in the district, which we're not denying, that Monsieur de Sade has embraced religion. We'll be telling you why - but I'm letting you know about it now so that you shouldn't be taken by surprise - I'm telling people that he has seen the pope..."

CHAPTER 11: "OUR CHAMPION LOCKED UP IN PARIS"

Lacking the benefit of a papal blessing, in fact, the marquis reached Grenoble, in the Alpine south-east of France, at the end of June and arrived at la Coste in late-July. By mid-October, he had gone to Montpellier, on the far, western side of the Rhône river in southern France, and taken up with the Rosette who was at la Coste, on the quiet, in the previous year. She in turn was induced to recruit a certain Adélaïde for service at la Coste, telling her there was not much company at the château but that she would manage well enough as long as she went along with all the master's requirements. The same month, still at Montpellier, a friar name of Father Durand was promising an illiterate weaver called Trillet that his daughter Catherine, aged 22, would be as safe as could be while working at la Coste, where the moral order matched that of any convent. The marquis had asked the monk to find a cook for the house. On meeting Catherine Trillet, de Sade offered her 25 per cent more than the wage she was getting at Montpellier. She accepted and set off across the Rhône in a wagon with the friar, to be received at la Coste by Renée Pélagie.

The marquis arrived in the first week of November to find there was little for his new cook to put in the pot. With winter coming on, the marquise was also short of warm clothes and of wood for burning, and there were panes missing from the windows in her bedroom. The frames that more concerned the marquis were the ones he was ordering for pictures recently acquired, along with book-bindings. Laid low by a cold, Renée Pélagie took to her bed and sent to her mother for money, emphasising that times at the manor had never been harder. Mme de Montreuil sent 1,200 livres - but to Gaufridy, with instructions that this money was only to be made available piecemeal for household necessities.

De Sade's idea of domestic needs was different. He wrote to Father Durand for more staff and, one afternoon in the second week of December, the friar arrived with four new servants. After dinner, each of the four was locked in a separate room. During the night, de Sade tried to have sexual relations with them, for extra pay. Next morning, three of the four left with the monk in the wagon by which they had come. Back at Montpellier, they told their story to weaver Trillet, who promptly told Father Durand what he thought of the monk's recommendation of la Coste as a fit place for his daughter. Durand made out he believed the marquis to have done with his wild behaviour of past years. Even so, Trillet made Durand write to de Sade about sending the young cook home. Then, being unable to read the letter, he took it to Durand's superior to verify that it said what he wanted. It did not. The superior told Durand to write in the terms Trillet required, then expelled the friar from his monastery.

The marquis was at la Coste on 17 January of the new year, 1777, when Trillet arrived just after noon to demand the return of his daughter. He got into a row with de Sade and tried to fire a pistol at him at close range, but it mis-fired and Trillet ran off. During the afternoon, he was airing his grievance to all and sundry in the nearby village. Catherine sent a messenger from the manor to tell her father to calm down, but he walked back to the house, accompanied by four men of the village, and fired a shot into the courtyard when he thought he saw the marquis. His four-man escort abandoned him and Trillet stormed off to a local inn for a drink.

Three days later, finding that some residents of the area were inclining to treat the affair as an attempted murder of the lord of the manor, Trillet left the village, having talked of his "most sincere friendship" for the marquis. However, he soon dropped that when he filed a complaint at Aix to the effect that de Sade had refused to hand over his daughter - omitting from the statement any reference to his pistol shots. The marquis, on learning of this, told Gaufridy that Catherine had signed a paper to confirm that she had no grievances. He was vexed that Gaufridy had been slow to head off any official investigation arising from Trillet's complaint, which could put him into more hot water, whereas the public prosecutor at Aix ought to be told that Trillet *fille* was in good health and that Trillet *père* had tried to do away with him.

Furthermore, de Sade told his agent, what matter if it were believed he was having sexual relations with Catherine - whom he later described as "stupid and malleable" - because she was past the age of consent and under no restraint or abuse? On another occasion, he cited what he called her ugliness as cause for discounting an affair with the cook. (Her father had said she was pretty.) Besides, the marquis exclaimed, there could have been no carnal knowledge by force of a woman "as strong and as tall as I am". The villagers of la Coste were "villains who deserved to be broken on the wheel" (still a judicial punishment at that time) and he would "heap on the wood without a second thought" if they were sentenced to burn on a pyre. What's more, Gaufridy had joined the ranks of those who believed the worst of him at every turn, having decided in this instance that he was in the wrong again and so having failed to represent him. The marquis had few equals when it came to portraying oneself as hard done by all the world.

By way of response to Trillet's hot-headed visit to la Coste, de Sade, who habitually spurned notions of respect for the law in its role of protector of the poor and susceptible, showed signs of panic at a relative of one of his "items of physical furniture" having counter-attacked. The marquis babbled for the shelter of the law and the State to be extended over him. He complained to the local lower-court judge and sought an audience for Gaufridy with the royal attorney at Aix. He frothed to his agent:

"Today, a stranger comes to ask for his daughter at the point of a pistol; tomorrow, a labourer will come to ask for his day's pay at the point of a rifle..."

What's more, during his trouble-making down in the village, Trillet "said he had been told that *he could kill me with complete confidence that nothing would happen to him* ... I am convinced that, if that man *had* killed me, people would still have said that *I was in the wrong*...

"I am convinced that I have done very well and that I'll be congratulated for it in Paris, where I have written to even better effect, whatever you were saying about that, because there's nothing to disturb good order in having a cook, but to come looking for her at the point of a pistol is something which very much disturbs good order..."

The marquis even went so far as to call on his greatest tormentor, as he saw her, to protect him:

"... If I get no justice here, at least I surely will in Paris, and most certainly Mme de Montreuil will have this man arrested on his return to Montpellier..."

The royal prosecutor at Aix delivered a sharp opinion, via a third party, that:

"... he could not conceive how a man as intelligent and reasonable as you [Gaufridy] should be caught up in the reflections and threats of M de Sade. Even if it were true that this lord had been as indifferent as he has told you towards this girl he is concerned about, and that she were as vestal as her ugliness makes you think she is, the motive which brought the father to come to reclaim her alone required that she be handed over to him at once... No engagement to do a job can be regarded as standing in the way of a father who is reclaiming his daughter; he alone has legitimate rights over her; the master frustrated in the retention of a servant can claim no more than compensation; but when the reclaim is based on such strong motive as that of the corruption of his daughter by her own master, all [other] claims must fall, and the father is within his rights to take his daughter wherever she is, even by force.

"There is not even need for a conviction for corruption to have been established, the mere fear of same suffices and, there having been very strong reason for this with regard to M de Sade, suspicions and fears of this kind about him would not be misplaced..."

Quite so. The prosecutor must have had a fat file on the marquis, and he remarked later in his opinion that de Sade and his connections would have done much better to have kept the Trillet business as quiet as possible, for it was causing a great stir, rather than publicise it further through calls to the authorities for action against the angry weaver.

Catherine Trillet, however, when she left la Coste, did not go to Montpellier to rejoin her pistol-packing papa, but went to Paris, travelling with the marquise while the master and his valet La Jeunesse took a separate coach for the capital.

Why did the core of the ménage at la Coste suddenly undertake a journey over the best part of 500 miles - in the mud, rain and cold of mid-winter - to a city where dwelled de Sade's main creditors and his mother-in-law? Where he was apt to be spotted by agents of the country's most efficient police force, not least those veteran Sade-trackers the inspectors Marais and Goupil, and locked away, perhaps to be delivered to the authorities in Provence who had axe and fire awaiting the convicted sodomist?

The answer probably lies in a mixture of motives. For one thing, news had reached la Coste in late-January that the marquis's mother, the dowager countess, then aged 64, was gravely ill. De Sade's standard reaction, later in life and when at liberty, to news of illness in an elderly relative was to rush to the bedside, as well as to the lawyers and agents, of the sickly individual, to find out how he stood to benefit by the will. He had shown scant interest in his mother all his adult life and there is no reason to think he was moved to undertake the difficult journey to

Paris out of filial regard. An inheritance from his mother, though, might help him mend his finances.

Also in January, as the dourness of a frugal winter was weighing on de Sade's spirit, relations with Mme de Montreuil shifted. The marquis may well have decided - even while his wrath at her boiled - to try, in his way, to force his mother-in-law onto the defensive. He had tried something of the kind in 1774, when he sent Renée Pélagie to Paris to seek a legal judgement against the *présidente* that she was harassing him. Since that ploy had failed, his finances and his estimation in society had become even worse. Who was there to be the target of an outburst of Sadeian rage at this but she who could open his way to unlimited libertine predation among the lower orders, if only she chose to smile indulgently at a hot-blooded chap's little preferences and - the crucial part - to give him a free hand with her purse. She who could do all this, but never would.

For whatever reason, or lack of reason, Mme de Montreuil received in mid-January, by her own account of 21 January to Gaufridy, "... ten big pages of threats and invectives ..., which you could have no idea of unless you read them..." This moved her to declare:

"... too exasperated by the injustices and infamies I am suffering from them, I absolutely renounce my involvement in anything that concerns them. If I am attacked in the way that I am being threatened, I have the means to respond and have no fear in the world on that score. Too bad for those who will force me into all the clarifications and *proofs* which would arise from this... If I wanted to avenge myself or to punish them [for the invectives], I would take these to the ministers, who can appreciate better than I can their conduct and mine, and the justice of their complaints and their reproaches. Whether she [the marquise signed the letter] is the author or only the clerk, she is not to be excused in my eyes..."

Word of this combination of anathema and counter-threat having reached la Coste, it might well have been that de Sade and his wife decided to travel to Paris in order to berate Mme de Montreuil in person and/or to try to win her over. The shock of Trillet's clumsy assault may have jolted him into horror and fear at having found that some unlettered workman could come within an ace of killing him, that members of the victim classes could bite back and might even be deemed in the right for having done so. Such a turn for the worse, such a shock to the certainties he lived by and needed, was apt to provoke in the marquis a desire to flee, even towards the power who could have hired any number of Bohemian deserters to protect him against the spoil-sport - worse, the dangerous - Trillets.

Then again, the motivation for the journey to the capital, as it related to Mme de Montreuil, might have been different. It seems there was another letter from the *présidente*, sent within a day or two of the fierce one quoted above. In March, de Sade referred to a "better letter". Also, the lawyer Reinaud, one of the marquis's representatives in Provence, was writing to Gaufridy in February, while de Sade was still travelling:

"Here's the conclusion of your troubles, no doubt about it, my dear Gaufridy. I would stake my life that Madame de Montreuil's letter is a trap... The marquis is falling into its jaws like a simpleton... On my honour, before the month is out, our champion will be locked up in Paris..."

One could hardly have read Mme de Montreuil's counter-blast and renunciation quoted above as a trap, so there must have been a much kinder letter between that and the departure, probably on 30 January, of the quartet from la Coste. Muddy roads notwithstanding, there was just about enough time for a second letter to have reached la Coste from Paris between the 21st and the 30th.

I am inclined to think Reinaud was referring to another letter having been what he saw as prison bait. Yet the first letter - with its dire prospect of Mme de Montreuil quitting her role as money dispenser of last resort, as well-connected protector against complaining relatives of wronged servants, as best hope of having his conviction and sentence at Aix overturned - was *also* liable to have galvanised the marquis and his wife into heading north.

In any event, perhaps de Sade, in the winter of 1776-77, did not need a great deal of prodding to set him on the road to the city of light. Unable to circulate beyond a few towns and villages of the hinterland of Provence, his cramped financial resources shrinking the heights of his libertine fancies to the depths of fragmented adventures as he tried to coerce assorted unsatisfactory servants into sexual co-operation, the erstwhile consort of such luxurious courtesans as Colet and Beauvoisin must have hankered greatly after the capital of all the pleasures, where he had not been and indulged himself since he beat a retreat from his creditors at the end of summer in 1771, nearly five and a half years earlier.

On arrival in Paris, on the evening of 8 February, the marquis discovered that his mother had died on 14 January, the news having eluded him for three weeks. Two days after they had reached the capital, the marquise reported to Gaufridy that her husband was very much affected by his mother's passing. Or so he seemed, for he was writing, also within a few days of his arrival in Paris, to an unknown friend with sentiments somewhat removed from an only son's mourning (and from a son-in-law's attention to a powerful mother-in-law):

"My mother's death ... has brought me here, no doubt at the moment you were least expecting me because I was writing to you a few days ago to renew my urgings that you come to Provence. The circumstances of this death, and those of my other parents [the in-laws] with whom I am not yet entirely reconciled, force me to remain incognito for a while yet. Also, I beg you not to tell anyone that I'm here. Even so, I'm burning to see you, to tell you about my deeds of daring, to hear about yours, and to do a few together. The services I was asking of you for Provence can now be performed here... Besides, I will promise you that, for myself, I have the greatest need of these services, never having found anyone who laid them on for me the way you did; but I'll do the same for you in return if you insist, so you'll have nothing to reproach me for. Fix a rendez-vous in a spot where there aren't too many people, or at your place, and that had better be in the evening; I'll be there on the dot, and we'll go do a little hunting. You can send your reply to the man who will deliver my letter, without asking him anything, nor going into any details about me, for reasons that I'll give you..."

The marquis and the marquise decided not to tell Mme de Montreuil of the former's arrival in Paris until, so the marquise wrote to Gaufridy, Lent had begun and the *présidente* therefore was seeing fewer people, and thus was less apt to be near "bad advice". So she was probably not told until 12 February, Ash Wednesday. On the evening of the next day, in his wife's room at the Danemark Hotel, de Sade renewed old acquaintance with the Paris police and - fulfulling Reinaud's prophecy with 15 days to spare - was taken under a royal arrest warrant to the fortress of Vincennes.

CHAPTER 12: BORN AND RAISED TO FOLLOW

The wonder at this juncture may not be that the marquis was arrested but that, after all the havoc of the 14 years since she married him, Renée Pélagie was still with him. Remember that she had few other options - no more than to return to her parents or to enter a convent (as her mother-in-law had done). A professional career was out of the question for a noblewoman. She could not a run a shop or a factory - trade was beneath her, the commoner's pursuit which her ancestors had struggled to leave behind, and which her husband and her parents would never have allowed her. In those days, women were not trained in the law or medicine, and to this day the Catholic Church does not admit them to the priesthood. Even to establish herself as a figure in Parisian society who might gain a reputation as a writer or salon hostess, she would need a husband of good standing as well as sufficient money to keep abreast of the social whirl. She was far from having either.

Renée Pélagie had been brought up a dutiful Catholic in a family which prized its daughters most while they restricted their ambition to marriage or the religious life. All of a sudden, she was married to a man she hardly knew, and she saw little of him during the first years of their wedded life. Although her mother succeeded for a time in keeping from her the extent of her husband's sexual adventures, she learned while still a young wife that she was tied to a libertine. She may never have found out many details of his escapades, in the way that investigators of the time did through access to witnesses, correspondence and police dossiers - and in the way that a modern reader may via historical research.

Even if she did know about every expensive courtesan, every haggling pander, every birch stoke, every human bone in a secret room, she was also subject to her husband's counter-arguments. He would remind her that theirs was an arranged marriage for dynastic advantage - no love-match - before which he had promised her nothing beyond what could be entered in an accountant's ledger. Besides, his troubles arose from the world censuring the sexual activities he found necessary, and which hurt no-one who had not been paid for services, rather than from the activities themselves, he would claim. The marquis was a fluent and indefatigable self-justifier in his letters and there is no reason to think he was any less articulate when face-to-face with his wife or anyone else he chose to try to persuade.

He was no morose, taciturn exploiter but a charming, even spell-binding one - when in the mood. Someone as showered with choice among men as Beauvoisin would hardly have spent so much time with him otherwise, especially as other would-be lovers would have added more to her store of material wealth.

There is little doubt that, in his involvement with his sister-in-law Anne Prospère, he was delighted at being able to work on her mind. While taking similar pleasure at re-shaping the attitudes of his wife, he would also be moulding her into becoming a more congenial and tractable companion, as well as a reliable ally in combat against relatives and the authorities. Further, if his wife were with him, the marquis would be better placed to extract money from his mother-in-law, who might let Renée Pélagie live on short commons but, if only for appearance's sake, would send some cash now and again to stave off the sort of destitution that would provoke more tut-tutting in society.

Renée Pélagie went to the altar schooled in obedience to her mother and to Mother Church, never having encountered such a phenomenon as de Sade. Dull he was not. His range of interests was broad - as a connoisseur of fine art and literature he showed no great depths but knew more than enough to impress a young woman with a fragmentary convent education (as well as her mother, at first). His affinity for the theatre was genuine. He must have cut a fair dash in conversation at his father-in-law's table, a cavalry officer with many a tale to tell of battles fought for his sovereign, a young seigneur of estates, a glamorous hub of country-house theatricals and revels, an expounder and elaborator of new ideas current in books and in the talk of the day, a dapper dresser with fine blue eyes, a *bon viveur* who always found the money to stay at the table. There had been no-one like him *chez* Montreuil. He dazzled.

It seems certain that de Sade took Renée Pélagie's virginity. However good or bad their sexual life - at one time, at least, he found her "too cold and too pious" - she achieved a *modus vivendi,* it seems. She may have shrunk away from him sometimes, often perhaps, but by no means all his sexual encounters involved violence of the kind used on Keller, for instance. Renée Pélagie probably knew no male sexuality but his, had three children by him and was the recipient of his most tender and erotic letters. Granted that most of these, if not all, were written in prison, when his scope for writing to other women whom he might have desired sexually was closely limited, but at least some of the sentiments in them may be construed as true yearning for her, rather than an unfocussed expression of a prisoner's masturbatory fantasies.

There may well have been times - at la Coste, perhaps, in spring, with the Midi in bloom, the creditors at bay for a while and Renée Pélagie lady of all she surveyed - when she felt as well, whole and at ease as she ever did in her adult life. Let's say she was more apt to be so when the marquis was away. She and he spent no more than short episodes of their long married life in each other's company so his presence did not stale by continuation, I suggest, as much as it might have, and she was given the mercy of relief from his more trying behaviour - albeit undergoing, even in his absence, unsettling reminders of its consequences, through police raids, prosecutors' interrogations, creditors' threats, servants' complaints and her mother's censorious overview.

The transfer from her main adherence to the Montreuils, to main loyalty to de Sade, did not come suddenly and was not unshakeable. When the brouhaha about the maids at la Coste was in full swing and the cupboard near bare, early in 1775, Renée Pélagie showed signs of loss of nerve, as well one might. She told a royal prosecutor first one story, then another. She might even have said she would abandon the whole mess and retreat to a convent. She gave out that, if her maids were to be taken away, she would have payment first for their keep - this when her best interests required that she send the girls back to their homes with the minimum of demurral. She wrote for help to her mother, against whom she had been directing a legal action in Paris a few weeks earlier. Yet, when she emerged from this trauma, she was again her husband's companion and agent in adversity - as, on 17 May 1763, she had taken an oath before God to remain, come what may.

Was she sufficiently bedazzled and sworn to become head of the harem - "first victim of a frenzy that can only be called madness," as the maids are reported to have said - behind the shutters and under the lash at la Coste? We have the denial, over her signature but in her husband's style, in a letter stuffed with lies, that she was ever any kind of "director of my husband's pleasures". If the maids had been bending the truth, in pursuit of an interest in reporting la Coste as a dangerous and sinful place, they might well have portrayed the marquise with a whip in her hand and fire in her eyes, rather than among the prey. All we can say for certain is that she was prevailed upon to condone her husband's exploitations that hungry winter, as she condoned his others at other times.

In her essay on de Sade (*Must One Burn Sade?*), Simone de Beauvoir calls the marquis's relationship with the marquise "that ambiguous friendship which every despot brings to that which is unreservedly his." Just so. Did she need it? Admitted that here comes a quotation from a dozen or so years later, after Renée Pélagie had been through even more turmoil; however, it is a key to an understanding of her. During the first upheavals of the French Revolution, in 1789 in Paris, she wrote to Gaufridy of the break-down of social order: "Everybody wants to be top dog... I would much rather be a galley slave; then at least you would know what you were meant to do."

When with her Louis de Sade, she always knew what she was meant to do - to listen and to serve faithfully. Renée Pélagie had been born and raised to follow.

CHAPTER 13: A BEAUTIFUL DAY CUT SHORT

The marquise could not follow her husband into the fortress at Vincennes. She did not even know where he was until June 1777, four months after the arrest. In the first days after the police had taken him away, she hung about outside the Bastille fortress, near the centre of Paris, hoping for a clue as to whether he was being held there, but the guards moved on anyone who stopped to look at the building. Her pleas to royal ministers met the minimal assurance that her husband was well. Mme de Montreuil coolly denied to her daughter that she had been instrumental in having the marquis locked up again. When writing to Gaufridy, the *présidente* referred to the arrest as "that which the minister has done." However, she was by no means a neutral observer. On 4 March, she told Gaufridy:

"... Everything is going as well as could be wished and altogether securely: it was time!... This has attracted no attention here and it is the intention of the ministers that ... not a word be said about it in public... He is in a secure place - that's all there is to be said to those who might ask. Where is he? We know nothing (neither his wife nor I ...) but he is well."

The marquis could hardly have disagreed more. He was behind walls 16 feet thick in one of the most massive jails in existence. Each cell had a triple door, the innermost part sheathed in iron. Elaborate arrangements of iron bars in the small, high windows allowed at most a wan shaft of light into each cell. At least two men were needed to open and close the three gates in the only passage through the outer walls, the gates having been inside two deep moats that surrounded the whole edifice. The fortress had been built in the 14th century through the 16th to keep attackers out - now it was very effective at keeping prisoners in. The regime of social isolation inside the jail was also a means to prevent inmates suborning staff. By mid-April, the marquis was writing to his wife that, in the 65 days since arrival at Vincennes, he had been allowed out of his cell for only five walks of an hour each, "in a kind of tomb about 40 feet square, enclosed by walls more than 40 feet high", escorted by a guard who had to remain silent.

This was especially irksome to de Sade, who was used to riding and walking, and who was inclined to corpulence if he neglected his exercise. Worse than the close confinement, and the lack of baths, was the sudden loss of society. De Sade complained of having company for a total of only about 10 minutes each day, when the two meals were brought at 11 a.m. and 5 p.m. (During the rest of the time, prisoners had to fall back on their daily pound of bread and bottle of wine, and their four apples a week.) From a life as lord of estates and student of the modern world, amid retainers and many books, a life lit by the sunlight of Provence, he had been snatched away to dank twilight, to near-solitude and to much-reduced importance in his new milieu of irritating petty rules. What's more, no sooner had he been raising the glass of Parisian pleasure to his mouth, after so long without a taste, than it was knocked from his hand and he was left with nothing but that hand to attend to his sexual urges. He complained to his wife of "solitude, which is lethal to me... This frightful solitude in which my spirit withers away..."

What little company there was did not please him. He told the marquise of constant "taunts and mockery" directed at him in the fortress. A prisoner who had been so concerned when at liberty to make his mark on all he encountered might have taken more philosophically the traditional reaction by members of the lower orders when put in a position of power over a member of the aristocracy. He took up his pen to Renée Pélagie in deep self-pity:

"I am swamped by despair. There are times when I am utterly frantic... I intend to turn my fury on myself. If I am not at liberty in four days, I will definitely smash my skull against the wall... Oh, my dearest one, when will this vile situation end? Nothing is worse than the dreadfulness of what has happened to me. There is no adequate way to recount all I am going through... For comfort I have only my tears and my protests, but no-one can hear them... Where are those times shared with my precious loved one? Now I have nobody; it is as though all of nature had died for me!"

He also threatened suicide to Mme de Montreuil:

"From the depths of her tomb, my unhappy mother is calling me: I seem to see her open her breast and draw me to return there, as to the only refuge that remains to me. It satisfies me to follow so closely after her, and I ask of you, Madame, as a last favour, to have me laid beside her."

Whether or not his wife and his mother-in-law understood that the marquis would never commit suicide - not least because he would not be present to witness the effect on others - Renée Pélagie at least offered her sympathy, by letter, for she was not allowed to visit her husband at Vincennes. Her mother had approved the government order which forbade that. Insomnia, attacks of nervous tension and chest pain bothered him. The marquise sent written balm:

"What sort of night did you have, my tender husband? I am very concerned, although they're telling me that you were well. My mind won't be at rest until I've seen you. Calm yourself, I entreat you... I know how your poor head goes haywire and sees only the worst... Don't worry about me at all; I will manage perfectly, caring only about you... Count on me as on your best friend whom nothing can shake. Don't get it into your head that people are working to distance me from you; it's clear that's not possible and would not succeed..."

In another letter, Renée Pélagie reported, as best she could, on her children:

"... I see them rarely, being occupied exclusively with you. I leave them altogether in the care of their grandmother. That doesn't prevent their being worthy of your affection and of mine.

"About your daughter, who is in a convent [education], we still can't be definite about how she will look or how she will behave. She is still too young. She is a terror when she wants something.

"Regarding your [elder] son, he is as gentle as a lamb and of such a lively character that he can't be kept quiet except by giving him something to do, which is easy enough because he wants to know everything and would spend entire days with books. I think he will turn into a good-looking lad.

"The knight[1] is always chirpy and good-tempered, with less aptitude for study. It looks as though that will come... He is more of a cuddler and will be better at making his way with people. I always give him a second hug because of the resemblance [to his father]. My tenderness towards them brings me naturally back to you, whom I love with all my soul..."

The grandparents seem to have been very fond of their Sade grandchildren. "The extraordinary thing is that my father loves them,

---

1 The younger son's courtesy title as the second son of a count.

and you know that he is not the loving kind," the marquise told her husband.

In April 1777, two months after his arrest, de Sade was replying:

"What you tell me about your children delights me. You can have no doubt how charmed I shall be to hold them in my arms, albeit I can have no illusion - for all my tenderness - about the fact that it is for their sake that I am suffering at present." That is, he was being kept out of circulation so that he should not further dishonour the name which his children would have to bear when they took their place in adult society.

Two months later, the father was waxing a good deal less fond when, after an outburst to his wife to the effect that each of his spells in prison had driven him to "a thousand new extravagances", he added:

"... Oh! the handsome profit we've drawn from all my prisons! You know what took place after the stretch at Lyons [in Pierre Encise], what was done after the one in Savoy [at Miolans], so ... this present spell inside would only serve to teach you to repeat three or four times what your bloody mother says is for my own good...

"... Away with you, her and your children - you'll repent over what you are making me suffer in here for those damned brats whom I loathe as much as you and everything belonging to you..."

De Sade's shock at his imprisonment and his lack of books and papers kept him from dealing adequately with letters from his Italian contacts, Dr Iberti and others. The marquis tried to reply in such a way that they would not suspect that he was incarcerated. However, these letters "are terribly difficult to put together - talking about a work which perhaps I will never finish ... brings back memories and causes me much heartache..." The work may have been a book about Italy, but it is also possible that he had been trying to put into coherent shape his research and insights on erotic art and behaviour.

The main anxiety of the new prisoner of Vincennes was to know how long he was to stay there. In March, a month after he had arrived at the fortress, the lachrymose self-pitier of the first few weeks was thrust aside, for his wife's benefit, by the more familiar, raging de Sade:

"As long as I can see you sticking to the unbelievable stubbornness you're using in denying me the only thing I'm asking for, which is to know the length of my term, you will allow me, my dear friend, to take all your fine expressions of tenderness as no more than heartless mockery of my situation..."

This was a recurrent theme, and a recurrent tone, in his letters. No-one could say when a prisoner under royal warrant might be released. Renée Pélagie, who should have known better but was anxious to soothe the inmate, wrote to him:

"You know that I have never lied to you. I give you my word of honour that your case will come to an end and that you will soon be out..."

The marquis, casting about fretfully for clues about a set term, complained when his wife sent him a large package of provisions, because that was for him "a more than sufficient indication of the enormous length of time which no doubt I'll have to stay here." (He also complained when the provisions were too scanty.) He would examine her letters for signs - in one there were certain marks after 36 lines. Did that mean his term was 36 weeks? But this was November 1777 and he had already been at Vincennes longer than that, so was he to stay inside for 36 months? The marquise, being in ignorance, could no more enlighten her husband through their correspondence in invisible ink - a trick the prison censors tumbled to that November.

In the meantime, the prisoner appealed to Jean Charles Le Noir - the police chief of Paris, Sartine having moved on in 1774 - in his highest rhetorical style:

"... I have the greatest apprehension that this moment when I have no strength to exercise on my own behalf might be abused by way of some attempt on my goods or my wife. I love this companion in my adversity with a full heart, and I would sooner renounce the former than the latter. It would be base to take advantage of present circumstances to remove from me the only friend left to me in the world.

"Allow me to take you as a confessor: your soul is so fine, your equity so well recognised, that one of the great consolations that an unfortunate can have is the permission to throw himself into your arms. I beg you, therefore, to range yourself against any disposition contrary to my interests that could be devised during my detention, and above all against any that could be conceived in order to take my wife from me. If that's what is under way, let them also take my life from me, for I firmly swear I shall not exist for a moment after having lost her. To this plea, sir, allow me to join another - that you grant me that liberty, the loss of which is becoming, for the kind of constitution I have received from nature, the most horrible torture that could be inflicted on me..."

There was no relief to be had from the king's officials, however. The marquise could have told her husband as much. "Happy are they who have no acquaintance with the ministries or the offices," she lamented to Gaufridy. "If my husband wasn't dependent on all those monsters, I would have taken my vengeance long since" for their stone-wall reply to her petitions: "the King's will is otherwise".

The marquise went on:

"It's all one to Madame de Montreuil. She has the patience of an angel and, as long as she is gazing at her beautiful dulcinea, she is content. Once I'm out of her clutches, I'll rather plough the soil than fall back into them..."

The "dulcinea" in whom Mme de Montreuil was supposed to take such delight may well have been Françoise Pélagie, aged 17 at the time and the marquise's youngest sister. The two older Montreuil daughters having both fallen, in their different ways, into the hands of the Marquis de Sade, no-one should be surprised at the *présidente* treasuring the remaining, unsullied and therefore still marriageable daughter. (It is not sure that there were only three daughters in the family but it seems likely that, if there were others, they did not live beyond childhood.)

All the petitions and requests in this matter so far were in ink. On 5 January 1778, though, the marquis let enough of his blood in which to dip a quill and write, from his cell at Vincennes, a plea to his mother-in-law for a date to be set for the end of his jail term. He went on:

"... Oh! you whom I used to call mother with so much pleasure, you whom I have come to claim as such, and who has given me only shackles[2] instead of the consolation I was waiting for, let yourself be softened by these tears and by these bloody characters with which I have sought to pen this letter. Imagine that this blood is your own, since it now gives life to creatures whom you cherish, whom you hold so close, and in whose name I implore you..."

De Sade the playwright would never have failed to squeeze such a rhetorical effect out of such a melodramatic device. Dipping again into his little reservoir of red, he continued:

"... Alas, good God, you see me at your feet, melting in tears, begging you to grant me at the same time the renewal of your kindness and of your commiseration. Forget everything, forget everything, forgive me, help me...

---

2 Figurative ones for de Sade at Vincennes.

"... Take me from the terrible state of uncertainty where I find myself, and you will no longer see in me anything but an unfortunate astounded by your kindnesses, ashamed at having so little deserved them, who will no longer draw breath but for you, so as to wipe away the wrongs which his deviations have caused you, and to pay, if that's possible, with this blood ..., for all the tears which he has made you shed and for which you are all too well avenged by his remorse..."

Mme de Montreuil might not have had this in blood from de Sade before, but she had had much the same over-inflated remorse and promise to be a good boy from now on, if only she would forget and forgive. She ignored the letter.

In other letters of the first half of 1778, while still at Vincennes, de Sade referred several times to Mme de Montreuil working out a vengeance, even "her personal vengeance", against him. He wrote also to his wife of her mother avenging herself for "an old wrong *which belongs more to you than to me.*" This might be a recurrent allusion to his relationship with Anne Prospère, his sister-in-law, but the reader of these letters has to grope in a mist of deliberate imprecision, for de Sade knew that his letters had to pass the prison censors before they left the fortress. De Sade was also concerned that his mother-in-law might find papers left at the hotel in Paris where he had been arrested. These would strike her as "indecent".

Mme de Montreuil, however, was more exercised to stifle possible sources of further scandal in Provence. She had pumped Catherine Trillet, the cook from la Coste who had come to Paris with the marquise, for information. Trillet soon became disappointed with the capital. The marquise became disappointed with the young woman's "schemes to get hold of money", and her plea to be returned to Montpellier was heeded. Once there, she and her father, who had taken a shot at the marquis, were warned by the royal prosecutor at Aix that, if they made further fuss about their encounters with the de Sades, all that had happened at la Coste would come into question. After that hint from on high, the Trillets dropped from view.

Also, the *présidente* was urging Gaufridy to obliterate all traces of debauchery at la Coste, and she was all the more anxious through not having clear information as to what these traces were, perhaps because the notary was being slow to act and/or reluctant to describe in detail what had been found. Manuscripts or "mechanical devices"? she wanted to know. She referred, in connection with the affair of the servant girls from Lyons and Vienne, to "a certain room which it would be good to destroy... I must know everything in order to deal with everything."

In August 1777, de Sade's woes at Vincennes worsened with the recurrence of haemorrhoids, his wife wrote to Gaufridy, asking that he pass the news to the Abbé de Sade, "to cheer him up". The abbot had greeted the first news of his nephew's arrest, in February, by saying "everyone will be satisfied". He did not enjoy the satisfaction for long, but died on the last day of the year, leaving his property much encumbered by debts and a complicated arrangement with a Spanish woman and her daughter who were staying with him at his house when he died.

The main thrust of Mme de Montreuil's efforts regarding her son-in-law was to have his conviction at Aix overturned, now that she could be sure he was not at large and apt to cause new trouble before she could finish burying the old. She tried to have him sign over management of his affairs to her, but he was having none of that. He also fulminated from his cell against her next gambit - to have him declared insane and so unable to appear in court at Aix, and herself made his proxy at any appeal hearing.

During the first half of 1778, Mme de Montreuil completed her preparation of the ground for the re-opening of the sodomy and poisoning case. The valet Latour was not to be found, but Gaufridy was being briefed closely on how to make the Marseilles prostitutes stick to their withdrawal of complaint, how to challenge elements in their initial statements that were unfavourable to the marquis, and on how to coach them in what to tell the court at the appeal hearing. For an even firmer guarantee of a successful appeal, she reached an understanding with two senior judges of the Aix high court. Just in case one of them needed reminding, Mme de Montreuil told him:

"Remember, I beg you, sir, how essential it is for me and those who belong to me, that in no way should it emerge, not to anyone whatsoever, that I have any part at all in your knowledge [of the case] or in what might ensue..."

After this and much more lobbying in high places by the *présidente*, on 27 May, King Louis XVI signed a permit for the marquis to appeal against the verdict and sentence of the Provençal high court, he having insisted on appearing in person. Even so, he had some qualms about placing himself in the hands of a court which had handed down a capital sentence against him. "Isn't it always very dangerous to go and offer one's head when one has been condemned to lose it?" he asked. He insisted on seeing his wife before he would agree to go, but this was refused.

Yet de Sade hated the gloom and stagnation he was undergoing at Vincennes. "Spring is here; I sense it keenly in all that my blood is making me suffer here," he wrote to the marquise in March 1778. "I'm already feeling in here well enough deprived of nature, without being even more frustrated by this little gift which it makes to us every year and in which even the most wretched of beings take part." Through the mails came a whiff of spring from the south to make him champ at the bit of incarceration even harder. Gothon Duffé reported from la Coste that the estate was in fair order: "Everything here heralds the spring - the blossom is about to give way to the fruit... Yes, sir, it's a pleasure to be at la Coste in this beautiful season, but the most precious part is lacking - he who turns it all to brightness."

The longed-for seigneur, thus flattered by one of his few loyal retainers, was disposed to travel when, on 14 June, his old acquaintance Inspector Marais of the Parisian force collected him at Vincennes and they set off for Aix, where they arrived on the 20th. The marquis spent lavishly in the canteen of the local jail, where he was held pending the court appearance, by way of impressing other prisoners, especially a young woman among them. He did not have to rely on the prison catering for all his food, or on his mother-in-law's lawyers for all his moral support. Gothon wrote to him on 27 June in blithe and uplifting terms, albeit after a little help with the vocabulary and spelling, it seems:

"Since the moment that I learned of your proximity from [Mr Gaufridy], I have felt an inexpressible joy. It makes me hope that I shall have the honour and the pleasure of seeing you again soon... Your absence, at such a distance, and the uncertainty that your affairs leave me in, cast me into the greatest despondency. I assure you, sir, that I am very sad and that I cry very often when thinking about your situation... If there's anything, sir, in the region that might give you pleasure, you only have to send for it. By day and by night, you can make use of me in any way I might be able to manage. [Mr Gaufridy] is seeing with pleasure to sending you some fresh flowers from your terrace, some apricots ..."

Gothon also made sure the agent from Apt took the master some jam and clean clothes, and she suggested she might go shooting on the estate for a hare which Gaufridy could also bring for the marquis to enjoy, via the prison kitchen at Aix.

This seems the place to recall, in part, de Sade's obituary tribute to Gothon, written in April 1782:

"... She had faults, no doubt, but she made up for them with virtues and qualities... Gothon liked men. But ... aren't men made for women and women for men?... Gothon, as Mme de Sade so amusingly puts it, *got married because she was pregnant*. Well! ... a little philosophy! What's terrible about that? For myself I see only virtue there. That's a wish to give her child a father, that's a wish to make sure it gets its daily bread, that's a wish to take it out of that abject class which can fall only into poverty or crime. But she was unfaithful to her husband a number of times... Ah! that's what I cannot excuse!...

"For all her faults, Gothon was a faithful servant. She gave agreeable and prompt service with a light touch. This was a good brood mare who liked her master's stables. That unlucky girl down there, with only the help of MM Paulet, Payan, Sambuc and company [other staff members and villagers at la Coste], would have made up, over twelve or fifteen years, a complete household for me. Indeed, I feel the loss of her. Besides, it has to be said - yes, now that we've spoken of her virtues, we can concern ourselves with her qualities - Gothon had, so they used to claim, the most beautiful - Ah to hell with it! what's to be done here? The dictionary has no synonym for this word and decency does not allow one to write it in full, although it only has two letters. Well now, yes! Indeed ... it was the most beautiful a.[3] that has escaped the Swiss mountains in more than a century - her name is made. *Milord Justice de Montreuil*, although brought to Provence, ten years ago, by matters of the greatest importance (and which he carried out wonderfully, no doubt about it) could not refuse to give one of his moments of leisure over to the delightful contemplation of that celebrated star..."

(The marquis's father-in-law, in 1772, was in the south for a rare intervention in what was mainly his wife's province, as he did his bit to quell the consequences of his son-in-law's weekend at Marseilles. **See chapter 8.**)

On 30 June 1778, however, de Sade was being taken from the prison at Aix in a sedan chair with the curtains closed, which prevented a

---

3 a. for arse, de Sade having written *c.* for *cu*.

crowd of onlookers from seeing him. After brief addresses in his favour by a barrister engaged to represent him, and by a royal prosecutor, the judges, as agreed in advance with Mme de Montreuil, declared the previous trial, death sentence and all, null and void, there being no evidence of poisoning. There were formal complaints of debauchery and sodomy still on the files so the judges felt it necessary to order a new inquiry into them, but this was of no substance.

The Commander de Sade, with all the convoluted formality of his 75 years, had weighed in from his status as the marquis's only surviving uncle, sending a letter to one of the judges at Aix on 25 June:

"Sir, there was placed in your hands the restoration, to a family which you love, because it loves you, of the good name whose removal had been unjustly sought, and I feel a double joy on learning that the libertine, about whom we have so many grounds for complaint, will be no longer, through your equity, regarded as the most criminal among all men."

Keen to make doubly sure of the right result for her dynasty, Mme de Montreuil was writing on 8 July to the Aix judges to urge that the appeal verdict leave to no stain on the honour of the marquis, and hence none on those with whom he was inevitably connected.

The witnesses did their rehearsed stuff in court and, on 14 July in public, the judges declared the marquis not guilty of sodomy, only of debauchery. He was sentenced to be warned as to his future conduct, banned from Marseilles for three years, and required to pay a fine of 50 livres. (The commander did not like the sound of the fine. Gentlemen of his rank were not fined in criminal courts.) It was a much lesser sentence than that of death and one's ashes surrendered to the winds. The dressing-down was delivered immediately, in chambers. Then de Sade was returned to the city jail.

At 3 a.m. on the 15th, Marais woke him to start a journey back to Vincennes. He was still held at his majesty's pleasure, under the order which had authorised his arrest on his arrival in Paris in February 1777. Decisions of the law courts did not affect such orders. Mme de Montreuil had wanted him cleared of sodomy and poisoning - as well as removed from beneath the sentence of the axe, the fire and no Christian burial - for the sake of family honour. Also for the best interests of the family, she wanted him to stay incarcerated so that he could not besmirch it again. She had won on both counts. Early in June, the *présidente* had made clear to Gaufridy that the marquis could not expect to walk free after being cleared at Aix:

"... He is too intelligent not to anticipate that, after all *that has happened* since the affair [at Marseilles], and about which the minister is all too well informed by all the complaints which have been brought, he must not count on his successful appeal being followed by his liberty..."

The commander concurred. He wrote to court officials at Aix on 28 June:

"The family has punished the libertine as far as it has been able. He will not trouble society further. The King and the government are party to the arrangements which will need to be undertaken so as to conserve the honour of a family which has never had anything to reproach itself for... My confidence, my gratitude and my respect are tributes I owe to you, and which I delight in extending to you..."

As the summer sun rose on their right over Provence, on the morning of 15 July, the marquis and Inspector Marais, the inspector's brother Antoine Thomas and two other guards, were heading north. By the evening of the second day on the road, in a special coach, the party had reached the town of Valence, where the five put up at an inn called The Louvre. De Sade, who was looking out of a window of his room on the upper floor, told the others he had no appetite and strode up and down while the Marais brothers began dinner in the same room. During the meal, the marquis said he wanted to go to the lavatory. While he was in the toilet off the corridor on the upper floor, Antoine Thomas stood guard at the head of the stairs, the only way to the ground floor. The marquis emerged from the toilet and moved towards the guard, then seemed to stumble and fall. The guard moved to help him to his feet but tripped over something. Like a shot, de Sade ducked under the man's arm and hurtled down the stone steps towards the street door in the yard below. Marais and his men decided quickly that their quarry could not have left the inn, so they combed the main building, its stables, stores, cellars and roof - not a trace of him. A search of neighbouring houses and gardens also drew a blank. The inspector asked the landlord of The Louvre to alert the local police but this was impossible because the inn was on the edge of Valence, outside the town walls and gates, which were closed each night.

In the morning, 17 July, at first light, Marais was at the gates as they opened. He hurried to the town police, who soon put together a patrol of a dozen men to scour the town and its outskirts, meanwhile sending a posse of riders to check roads that led to bridges over the river Rhône, which de Sade might try to cross if he were heading south to la Coste or the Savoyard frontier - but their man was clean away.

The marquis's first dash from the inn had ended in a hut just outside the town. Then he got two farmers to guide him to the river. One of the countrymen went into a nearby village where a boat and a boatman were found, at a stiff price, and de Sade was off downstream for Avignon. He disembarked outside the city in early evening, had a meal at a house and hired a carriage for an overnight journey to la Coste, where he arrived, "expiring of fatigue and hunger", next morning, giving Gothon "a terrible fright". His first act was to send a note to Gaufridy to ask for "some lemons and all the keys, right away".

The marquis embraced his new liberty - and Gothon, no doubt - with delight. He chortled and tut-tutted over the gossip of the estate and the village, renewed happy acquaintance with the parish priest and sent closely argued and assertive letters about his situation to royal ministers, Mme de Montreuil, other relatives and his wife. He was much impressed by Marie Dorothée de Rousset, an educated unmarried woman who had taken over as housekeeper at la Coste since the marquise went to Paris, and he was keen to visit Saumane to attend to any inheritance likely to be due to him from his late uncle's property.

About a week after de Sade had arrived at the manor, Renée Pélagie was told at last by her mother of the appeal hearings at Aix, the success in having the verdict and death sentence overturned and the fact that, even so, her husband was still incarcerated. (Word of his escape had not reached the capital yet.) There was a clash. The marquise reported to Gaufridy:

"... I have had a terrible scene with my mother on the day she told me about the end of the affair. Regarding his detention, she informed me of her intentions with a revolting haughtiness and tyranny which made me fly off the handle... And ... she was telling me that the *families* will never allow him to come out. What upsets her the most is to see that my ideas and aims come from me and not from M. de S., who she thought was making me imitate him parrot-fashion."

On learning of his arrival at la Coste, the marquise was all for rushing to the side of her "adored darling", which Mme de Montreuil fiercely forbade on pain of Renée Pélagie being locked up herself if she tried it. The *présidente* was unequivocal to Gaufridy:

"... Regarding Mme de Sade, I will tell you frankly that her family, to whom her honour is bound, ... will never let her expose herself to be degraded and compromised again, as she had been, by rejoining her husband, at least not until a *long* period of good conduct [on his part] has shown that she would be safe. If her affection or her blindness draws her to him, the government will lend us every assistance for such a right and proper cause. If she helps him, so be it. But she is to stay in Paris. Her expenses are not great and her husband's family, under its administrators, will be able to cover them... In her sorrow, a mother's pity, a mother's instinct, has always drawn me towards her to ease her plight, without deflecting me from all that has made me keep my distance..."

Earlier in the same letter, of 1 August, Mme de Montreuil commented on her son-in-law:

"... I hope that the good resolutions being aired will be maintained, but only time can confirm them. One cannot place too much blame on someone who takes back his freedom when the opportunity presents itself. Everything depends on how it's used. His family will decide perhaps that it must act to stop depredation continuing and to prevent total ruin, by conserving funds and ensuring the payment of remaining creditors in Provence out of revenues, as well as a decent upkeep for husband and wife from the rest of the income. Access to borrowing [by the marquis] must be blocked in order to prevent the alienation of capital and of revenue yet to accrue, which has always been his way. If there is really an intention to behave well, there must be no resistance to sensible precautions based on a lack of trust [of the marquis] which past experience makes all too appropriate. He has gone through more than one hundred and sixty thousand livres ... since his marriage. That's a fact that can easily be proved..."

Pegged down in Paris, the marquise started making the rounds again of royal ministries to try to have the royal order against her husband withdrawn.

As far as her mother was concerned, the marquis was subject to a royal order of imprisonment - it was just a matter of time before he was caught and returned to jail. Meanwhile, she was putting aside all letters from him without breaking the seals lest there be any suspicion that she had colluded in his escape or in his continued liberty. Also, she instructed Gaufridy to supply her with weekly reports on her son-in-law's activities.

The marquis seems to have been far too careless about preserving his liberty, given that he had plenty of time to flee abroad or to establish himself in a part of France where he was not known and to lie low there. In fact, he stayed at la Coste, the first place anyone would have looked for him, glad-handing locals, enjoying the fuss in the village over his sudden reappearance, sending letters and making plans.

Gaufridy remained an important conduit in all this, although Nanon may have turned up briefly at about this time and told the marquis of attempts by the notary, when she was in detention, to have her help machinations which would get de Sade put away for life. Whatever the marquis may have thought about this, he could well have felt it was better to have Gaufridy at least partly on his side, so that he could have some supervision of what the notary was doing, rather than sever all links with him, which would have put him entirely in Mme de Montreuil's camp. After all, Gaufridy was a family retainer in service to an aristocrat who valued such relationships. De Sade was relaxed enough about their link to tease the notary, in August 1778 from la Coste, after Gaufridy had taken some remark amiss:

"I assure you, my dear lawyer, that you have very much misunderstood my phrase, if you found in it some mistrust, and that I know of nothing which could be closer to telling you *that I have always recognised in you the greatest scrupulousness in keeping me informed about your correspondence with Mme de Montreuil.*

"Isn't that so? Haven't you done just that? More recently, haven't you let me see one of her letters? So I have good cause to extend my confidence to you and I could not conceive what there was in that expression that could shock you..."

Gaufridy's true loyalty is hard to discern - perhaps he himself was not clear where it lay. From Mme de Montreuil's frequent assurances to him that his letters to her would not be allowed to pass before any eyes but hers we can construe that they contained material that the notary did not want the marquis to read. However, at one point in about 1775, the *présidente* had been warning the royal prosecutor at Aix that Gaufridy would never reveal how an invader might reach the innermost rooms at la Coste, "albeit he knows in his heart of hearts that he ought to do so. But he won't, and it would even be unwise to let him think that such an operation was being considered." I believe he would not completely abandon his contemporary, the marquis, whose company and gossip Gaufridy enjoyed, and a portion of whose rents and tithes he was able to keep for himself. However, it was Mme de Montreuil who could best be relied on to pay the bills. Besides, he must have known as well as anyone that the marquise, because of her husband's callous profligacy, was living much less well than she could have done. Hence, the agent at Apt was inclined to help her.

In any event, de Sade, buoyant on the strength of his escape and on congratulations from relatives over the result of his appeal in court at Aix, could not have seen Gaufridy's attitude as more than a detail in August 1778. He was lining up personal visits to embrace his Provençal relatives and celebrate his relief. The marquis, childishly eager to embrace his success at Aix as a new beginning which washed all past stains from his record, chose to declare his exculpation in court as a genuine decision by "enlightened judges, enemies of treachery and lies", rather than a ruling achieved through relentless lobbying and arm-twisting by his mother-in-law, his uncle the commander and others among the high and mighty. His long epistles to his relatives and other parties played lengthily on this theme, without so much as a demisemiquaver about his treatment of the prostitutes at Marseilles or the servant-girls behind the shutters of his château. Cleansed anew, he stood "in need of no fetter but my own heart. I find there all that can dispel that respectable mother's[4] fears, all that can restore calm to the breast of my relatives, all that must prove to my judges that I have always been more unfortunate than culpable, and all that can at last bring home to myself that breaking dawn of a beautiful day, so desirable after so many storms."

"I have suffered enough - for six years, it seems to me, which is quite enough," he wrote to Gaufridy in mid-August, asking the notary, who was about to set off for Aix, whether he could sound out the royal prosecutor there, "without seeming to, and find out from him what he thinks of my escape and whether I could expect a bit of peace and quiet here... Besides, my presence is essential for my affairs, you can tell that authority about them yourself and, while telling him how I am conducting myself, very easily acquaint him of the necessity and the justice there is in leaving me be..."

Various parties, unspecified in his notes to Gaufridy urging the notary to ferret out what was really going on, were warning de Sade in the second half of August that another raid on the château was in

---

4 Mme de Montreuil's.

preparation. All the more reason to run for it and lie low - but he detested that. He had soon become fed up with travel in Italy, where he could not lord it as he was wont to do in Provence or Paris. There was a language problem for him in Italy, but he was also ill at ease in Savoy and France at other times when he was constrained to live circumspectly. He was happiest when in place as lord of the manor at la Coste or Mazan, or cutting a dash in the *demi-monde* of Paris - either of which required a deep purse. When on his estates, at least he was close to his sources of income, mainly rents from his tenant farmers. While wintering at la Coste, with money running very low, and under especially pressing need to avoid reminding the world of his existence and his sexual proclivities, he had still been able to keep himself amused by arranging a much reduced version of countryhouse high life *à la maison* - at the cost of damage to members of the staff.

In August 1778 at la Coste, the marquis tried to brush off the warnings that his newly acquired liberty might be cut short. He told Gaufridy that no-one was any more interested in locking him away again than he was in drowning himself. However:

"... On 19 August, I was feeling very relaxed while walking in the park [of the château] with the priest and Missy Rousset, in the evening, when we heard such a noise of agitated footsteps in the little wood that it gave me a sharp fright. I called out a number of times to ask who was there; there was no reply. I moved forward and saw Sambuc the estate guard, the older one, a bit the worse for wine, who told me, with a considerable air of worry and fear, to slip away very smartly because the inn [down in the village] was beginning to fill up with people who looked very suspect. Missy Rousset went down to find out, and returned after an hour, ... to assure me she would bet her life that these people were what they said they were - silk traders, that is - and that there was absolutely nothing to fear... Not much reassured by what I had heard, I left the same night to take refuge with the canon..."

This was a certain Vidal at the nearby village of Oppède. The news, sent twice daily from la Coste by Rousset, continued to be disquieting. On the 23rd, still by his own account, de Sade, "as though pushed by a hand stronger than I," fell into "a kind of agitation so violent that no-one at all familiar with my situation could have done other than see in that cruel condition the collapse of my unhappy liberty." The canon's maidservant summoned her master, to whom de Sade insisted that he wanted to go home. The canon's arguments against this foolhardy action were resisted and the marquis returned to la Coste. There, "so as not to deprive me of the ability to take a little rest, no-one dared to point out my imprudence too emphatically to me. Next day, I was urged to go back to my hiding-place. I continued to insist on staying..."

I think de Sade had become distressed and bored at the lack of people to listen to his talk, to lift his spirits, to tickle his sexual fancy. Besides, at the little house outside Oppède, he had again been without the books, *objets d'art*, curiosities, good cellar and retainers he had sorely missed while imprisoned at Vincennes and Aix. He loathed being under restraint, whether through lack of money, prison bars or a prudent seclusion that was tantamount to admitting he was under the domination of others. He wanted to underestimate the implacable purpose of Mme de Montreuil and of the police.

The marquis's security was enhanced, so he believed, on 25 August when he received letters which told him that his mother-in-law had sold his title of lieutenant-general of four Burgundian provinces, which had belonged to his father **(see chapter 1)**. Having been cleared at Aix in July, de Sade was no longer deceased in the eyes of the law and so might be deemed as back in possession of the title for the first time since his death sentence and execution in effigy in 1772 after the Marseilles affair. However, he was a fugitive from a royal order of detention and under a heavy cloud in high society because of his various escapades. The government was disposed to strip him of the lieutenancy-general, which would have been a reminder of him if he had been allowed to keep it. The *présidente*, always acute at perceiving the least unfavourable step to take, decided to turn the honour, which would not serve by then as so much as a fig-leaf to put in front of her son-in-law's bad reputation, into money which would help to reduce his debts. The title was bought by the Count de Sade d'Eyguières, head of another branch of the family.

On learning of the sale, from Mme de Montreuil via Gaufridy, the marquis concluded illogically that no-one who was about to have him re-arrested would have sent him such a blow to his pride. He was further confirmed in his confidence by letters from his wife, which also arrived on the 25th. One of them said: "The surge of persecution is done with, no-one discusses it any longer; rather, everyone finds the marquis's preoccupation with his properties right and proper after such a long time away."

Renée Pélagie's opinion was not shared by Inspector Marais. At four the next morning, the 26th, he was storming into the manorhouse with nine other officers. Gothon, "naked and all het up," according to de Sade, burst into his room, yelling for him to run. There was no hiding-place ready under the roof this time and the marquis, in a nightshirt, could only lock himself in a nearby room. The raiding party broke open the door and brandished swords and pistols at their quarry. Marais made the most of his revenge on the man who had caused him much inconvenience at Valence and much embarrassment before his superiors. Shouting insults about de Sade being locked up and the key thrown away, for having carried out sexual perversions "in a blacked-out room with corpses", the police tied him up and bundled him out of the house. All the while addressing him as *tu* (the familiar form of "you", so a calculated insult to someone of de Sade's age and rank), Marais and his men put him on show, sometimes bound and gagged, in towns of Provence where he was known, as the party travelled north. There was no curtained sedan chair at Avignon this time, rather mockery in front of a crowd of more than 300 people. He told his wife: "They have too much humiliated a man whom you love."

On 7 September, the inspector delivered his prisoner to the fortress of Vincennes, where he was locked into Cell No. 6.

SECTION B

CHAPTER 14: FIGMENTS AND FLASKS

The Marquis de Sade was rudely plucked from the light, air and comforts of a Provençal summer *en château* and thrust into the gloom and stuffiness of Cell No. 6 at Vincennes. The ventilation was poor, the floor dusty, the walls damp, the stench from the gutter in the corner that served as a toilet only to be tolerated as it gradually became part of the prisoner's everyday ambience. The natural illumination never amounted to more than thin fingers of light via the tiny, heavily barred windows. Candles were needed at five o'clock of even a summer afternoon. Rats and mice abounded, especially when the prisoner relaxed his vigilance against them and tried to settle down for the night. De Sade asked for a cat to be allowed into the next room to keep down the vermin, but was told that animals were not allowed under the regulations. "If animals are forbidden, the rats and mice should be too," the marquis fumed at the jailers. "That's different," he was told.

In being returned to the fortress, de Sade was not only deprived of the warmth and light of outdoors in the south, he was also removed from his study at la Coste. There he had been able to read his books and manuscripts - a prized adjunct of his ideas and tastes - and to write letters. After his arrival at Vincennes on 7 September 1778, however, he received some books on the 22nd but had no right to letters from his wife for a fortnight, did not see his luggage until 19 October, and had no regular supply of writing materials until 7 December. At least he was waiting only nine days for a barber to shave him - even if prison regulations had allowed him anything as dangerous as a razor, it is doubtful whether de Sade would have used it to shave. A gentleman of his stamp left such a job to his valet or, when in jail, to a warder. Such a gentleman also regarded regular baths as a necessity, but "these have never been known here," he reported to his wife, so his own stale smell complemented that of the accommodation. He reported himself "immersed in grime and muck, eaten alive by insects, lice, mice and spiders..."

He missed even Cell No. 11 at Vincennes, which he had occupied before he was taken to Aix for his court appearance. From there, he had been able to enjoy, albeit only as a spectator, something of the local life, including a summer *fête*, and No. 11 had been more airy than No. 6. Life in the latter was made worse by lack of a proper chimney, having instead a faulty flue which leaked smoke from the fire into the room. The marquis offered to have what he saw as the simple necessary repair done at his own expense, but the administration was not interested. The trouble with the flue prevented a fire being made in the room on many a winter day.

By his own reckoning, de Sade had company in his cell for about seven minutes in all each day, made up of four visits by a warder - at dawn to wake him with a perfunctory question as to whether he had slept well, then twice to bring him meals, once to shave him and sweep the floor. Even when a warder did wait while de Sade was eating, "as entertainment, there is a man (and this is a great concession) who habitually, without a word of exaggeration, takes ten pieces of snuff, burps six times, blows his nose ten times and coughs up good thick phlegm from his throat at least fourteen times - and all that inside half an hour... Most appropriate and stimulating, particularly when I am downwind of the whole show..."

De Sade was allowed out of his cell and the stretch of corridor immediately adjacent to it for no more than controlled exercise periods of an hour each, twice weekly, in a small, high-walled yard. These were a pleasure only by comparison with the dank days and nights in the cell. The prisoner walked with a guard, whose conversation was not much diversion even when he bothered to talk at all. De Sade's walks were increased to three per week on 29 March of the next year, 1779, nearly seven months after his arrival from la Coste, to four on 19 May and on 15 July to five (each day but Tuesday and Friday). These outings were not enough for de Sade. He complained of "violent attacks of nerves, irritation and tension which allow me no more than one peaceful night in a week... Baths and fresh air every day, that's what I need to calm me, but it's not in *the rules*..."

The royal government, modernising some of its practices while leaving its principles rooted in absolutism, was becoming increasingly assertive over bureaucratic details. As an arm of the government, the administration at the fortress of Vincennes was very keen on its regulations. The marquis found that certain topics, not always easy to predict, were not allowed to be raised in discussions between prisoners and staff. He reported ironically: "The dullness of my intelligence not letting me perceive the boundaries, ... I thought I might have had my head bitten off twice, once for having asked *the names of the dauphin's godparents,* the other for having asked *whether the* [prison] *surgeon had many people to dinner on the holiday.* You see clearly from this that I need to be sent a little list of topics which I can talk about, so that I shan't risk any more blurting out topics of such import as those."

Much of the cheerless and pettifogging atmosphere at Vincennes emanated from the governor, Charles de Rougemont, a vain stickler for precedent who, like many another administrator in the France of his day, had bought his appointment by bribing a royal minister's mistress. He was more than reimbursing himself for his investment by supplementing his salary through profiteering from the food and other supplies for the jail. He was widely loathed among the inmates of Vincennes during his tenure - including de Sade, never one to suffer readily any restraint, much less that administered by someone whom he regarded as slow-witted, uncultured and a bully. The marquis, however, took his criticism of the governor beyond the latter's qualities of character, seizing on de Rougemont's illegitimacy, which had been publicly declared by a court of law, to sneer from his position of blue-blooded birth in wedlock at the bastardy of the man set over him. Note, too, that de Sade's period at Vincennes from 1778 was by no means the first time he had been unable to establish good relations with a prison governor, even with a genial one as when he was at Miolans in 1773.

Legitimate nobleman or not, de Sade lost his name and title at Vincennes. The staff referred to each prisoner by his cell number, so the marquis was "Mister 6". This was a matter of discretion - so that no-one should overhear the true name, and hence know the dishonour, of any inmate - rather than a calculated insult. Even so, someone as touchy in his pride as de Sade might well have felt there was a slight in this practice, which contributed to what he called, from his considerable experience of incarceration, "a vertigo" the like of which did not exist outside prisons.

The marquis recognised, in his better moments, that much of this disorientation, this loss of perspective, was due to a prisoner taking everything personally. Even when at liberty, de Sade was apt to perceive events as pertaining only to him. In jail - at any rate, in a jail where inmates are held one to a cell - a prisoner's long periods of solitude are interrupted by brief contacts with staff. De Sade was all too ready to forget how banal and inconsequential these were for the staff members and to draw from them a great plug of resentments on which to chew. "They upset me and they thwart me at every turn," he fumed by letter to Renée Pélagie.

Much of the trouble that befell de Sade at Vincennes - where the cavalry officer, actor-manager and seigneur of estates was no longer cock of the walk - occurred when he went beyond writing complaints to his wife. One day in the spring of 1780, "the warder was rude to me in a quite unmistakeable way, very much calculated to make me lose my temper. I reacted; there was a scene..." The marquis denied it afterwards, but it seems he struck the warder. The administration decided at once to withdraw de Sade's exercise periods and the governor sent an officer to inform him, which provoked a scene and a half. De Rougemont reported:

"There is no insult, horror or filth that he did not let himself utter against him [the officer] and against me, whom he dared to call a pr[ick], and threatened to make mincemeat of [the officer] as soon as he [the marquis] had got out of prison... M de Sade, ... having created a frightful noise, with which the fortress and dungeon alike resounded, having called to the other prisoners that they should bear witness to the terrible treatment which he was being made to undergo, ... having stirred them after a fashion to rebel by urging them to stand up for each other[1], and having told them several times that *it was the Marquis de Sade, cavalry commander, who was being treated so* - after, I say, a speech of the most loathsome kind, in which he respected no-one, not even the most respectable in the realm, M de Sade ... concluded this scandalous scene by insulting M de Mirabeau..."

The Count de Mirabeau, a prominent figure later during the French Revolution, was then another prisoner at Vincennes. The governor asked him for his version of de Sade's outburst. Mirabeau complied: "A prisoner who had stated several times that he was the Marquis de Sade and who was making a frightful noise, came to a window which overlooks the ... garden where I walk and, in the most foul and odious terms, called me the f[ucking] s[od] who was the cause of his being

---

1 Not a common notion with de Sade

deprived of walks, that ... I must go and kiss the a[rse] of my protector [de Rougemont] for this latest favour... He said to me finally: 'Now, you f[ucking] s[od], speak up, tell me your name if you dare, so that I'll be able to cut off your ears as soon as I'm outside.' At that, my patience snapped: 'My name ... is that of a man of honour, who never dissected or poisoned women, who will gladly inscribe that name on your back with his sword, if you have not been broken on the wheel before he can do so, and who can find nothing to fear from you except that you might put him into mourning..." (Mirabeau and de Sade were distantly related so etiquette would have required either to acknowledge publicly the death of the other.)

The governor, having stopped de Sade's walks, also decided to make his confinement to quarters even less agreeable. His room was no longer swept by the staff, and the warder who brought his food had taken to serving him, as he put it, "like a pig, because the speed with which they flee my room ... never gives me the opportunity or the time to ask for whatever else I need, and mine host's three scullery boys are always ready to open fire whenever my door is opened..."

The marquis complained bitterly about the loss of his exercise in the open air - "the gift enjoyed by even the lowest of the animals" - but his petty pride let him spurn, the following 17 September, a decision to restore his walks. A senior member of the prison administration, a retired major, visited de Sade to announce the fact, for which the latter thanked him. Then, however, scarcely had the major managed to utter the first phrases of the rider to the good news - "but, sir, that's not all; the fact is that you have no right whatsoever ..." - than the prisoner cut him short: "What now, sir? A little sermon? I beg you to spare me that; I know all there is to know about morals." The major tried again to deliver the dressing-down but de Sade butted in again: "Sir, as long as the man of whom you speak [the warder] behaves himself, he will find me peaceable; when he ceases to do so, he will find someone quite ready to put him straight, one not being the kind to put up with rudeness from anyone, certainly not with that from a rascal of a warder..."

The major gave up and went away. The marquis was left with his arrogance well exercised, his body still not so. In the letter where he reported the incident in detail to his wife, de Sade prated on: "In that I could tell from the first sentence of the oration by the dry stick of an individual whom they chucked at me this morning, it seemed to me that the piece would have to rattle on about the moral and physical essentials of the miserable atom known by the name of *warder*. I saw that the orator was going to be chilly and boring, that he would talk catachresistically,[2] without metaphor but with pleonasm[3], that his text would be badly chosen and his epitaph inappropriate, that each element would be uniform, graceless and stripped of that saltiness and those nuances so necessary for the soul of a speech and so well recommended by Cicero; what's more, that the subject matter, altogether dry, was intrinsically quite alien to my existence and to the sort of art which I cultivate. Instead of all that, I dismissed the orator..."

This shows de Sade in one of his least edifying veins, that of the posturing know-all who, when faced with a telling-off by authority, tries to discredit it by searching for flaws in the manner of whoever has to administer it. Such behaviour in a man in his late thirties, albeit upset at being in jail, indicates immaturity. The parade of terms from the rules and forms of classical rhetoric is no more than the prisoner showing off his arcane knowledge - gained at Collège Louis le Grand a quarter-century earlier - in an effort to puff himself up into a superiority over the officer who, by conspiracy of his mother-in-law and the royal authorities, as de Sade would have it, had been given the upper hand over him. That sort of effort to make oneself seem more than one's circumstances allow requires an audience to acknowledge the ploy and so validate it - for de Sade, his wife beyond the walls and reading his letters.

The marquis's concern to allow the major - as representative of the prison administration and of the king's government and of everyone else who was cramping his style and abridging his liberty - no scope to express his authority over him was so great that he interrupted the officer after the first breath of admonition. According to the code by which de Sade lived, or so he used to pride himself when it suited him to do so, one may see that an officer and a gentleman does not behave in that manner to another such. Besides, here was de Sade so bothered about his scrabbling for petty status, and to prevent anyone impinging on his scope and pride, that he hazarded the restoration of the walks which he had held so precious rather than forgo a moment of strut and pout, rather even than keep quiet and then shrivel the lecturing major later in the privacy of his own fantasies. Nor could he resist the

2 catachresis - incorrect use of words

3 pleonasm - excessive use of words

posturing report - to his wife, in a letter which he knew would be read by the police and could be passed to the administrators of the fortress, like all his letters - of how the gold-star pupil of the rhetoric class had seized his little triumph, or rather could not be polite or patient enough to find out whether the major might be engaged in a ciceronian joust of metaphors and epitaphs, but instead must settle the encounter in a bully's way, by barking at the other chap until he walked away. De Sade was then able to savour his lazy victory - a pyrrhic victory - before the all too uncritical regard of his wife but, essentially, alone.

The marquis did not have his walks restored until March 1781 - 36 weeks after they were first suspended. This deprivation did not teach him enough circumspection to avoid a similar incident two years after the first big rumpus with a warder. At the end of July 1782, another exchange of harsh words between the marquis and a warder led to the prisoner striking the jailer in the face. This time, not only did de Sade lose his walks, he was no longer even allowed beyond the door of his room into the adjacent stretch of corridor - this in high, sweaty summer in the dank fortress. It was not until 15 December that he was so much as allowed to keep his door open for a while, and the walks were not restored until the new year, 1783. In the meantime, de Sade complained of being fed "through a trapdoor, like the madmen", and no-one came to sweep.

Walks or no walks, de Sade suffered from time to time with haemorrhoids, one of his old troubles, chest pain, dizziness and nose bleeds. The lack of attention to his hair, and the general debilitation of prison life, made it start to fall out, he complained, but with some irony: "It is past repair and I am past vanity... When I get out, I will wear a wig." In July 1780, a month beyond his 40th birthday, he wrote that he had passed "forty delightful years" and it was time for him to take on "somewhat of a coffin hue". He was ready for death, "awaiting it without desire or trepidation."

His door being kept closed night and day made the problem of the smoky flue in his cell worse, and this in turn aggravated trouble with one of his eyes, which was difficult to treat in a choleric inmate confined to one damp room where he read a great deal by candlelight. The inflammation and pain were considerable - "half my head is on fire" - and de Sade rediscovered his fear of extreme illness and death. The trouble seems to have subsided without attention by an oculist from

Paris, which the marquis was demanding of the governor without success, but it returned to bother him later.

His various ailments waxed and waned, but his condition as a prisoner, as a creature reduced and in tutelage, was constant. "What am I here if not a child?" he complained to Marie Dorothée de Rousset and, in another letter, recalled that, before being put into the fortress, "I was free ..., I was a man, and now I'm *an animal in the Vincennes menagerie.*" Elsewhere, he wrote: "I'm behaving like a dog, and when I see all that pack of runts and curs barking behind me, I lift my leg and I piss on them." De Sade's turning of his new-found animality into defiance also took a more high-flown form, as in his letter to Rousset which begins: "The eagle, Mademoiselle, is sometimes obliged to leave the seventh region of the air in order to lower itself onto the summit of Mount Olympus, onto the ancient pines of the Caucasus, onto the cold larches of the Jura, onto the snow-clad rump of the Taurus, and sometimes even near the quarries of Montmartre..." He liked sometimes to present himself as a special being brought low by "eleven years of misfortune, six of them kept in a dog kennel, [which] still are not enough for that greedy beast, [the] hyena" - meaning Mme de Montreuil. He was, like prisoners throughout the ages, a social being afflicted by loneliness. He was moved to ask the administration of the fortress whether he could have with him "a little puppy dog, so that I might have the pleasure of raising it" - which was refused. Prison life for de Sade was lonely and monotonous, even for such a busy mind as his. At one point in 1783, asking yet again to be let out, he cited his desire "to be released from the necessity I have now to spend twelve hours at a stretch reading or writing, having nothing better to do."

Indeed, de Sade was driven to the classic distractions and consolations of the prisoner - literature and masturbation. Not that either was a discovery for him in jail. He had long been a keen reader of the works of the Enlightenment, which reached him at Vincennes as and when the prison administration, inconsistent in its censoriousness, allowed. Rousseau's *Confessions* was stopped, works of Voltaire were passed. Holbach's *System of Nature,* from which de Sade drew more inspiration than the Baron d'Holbach would have expected, was not allowed into Cell No. 6, nor were the newspapers. Also forbidden, in a long list of books which the marquise was not permitted to send her husband after his request, was a *History of Vampires.* He enjoyed lighter reading - fiction of the day - for the evening and, at one point in

1783, was asking his wife for "some rather racy novels, a bit ---, you know very well what I mean. The sort of thing to bring me charming thoughts in my solitude..."

The marquis's prison reading did not always bring him charming thoughts. One night in February 1779, having been delighting again in Petrarch's sonnets about his ancestor Laure de Noves **(see chapter 2)**, he put aside his uncle's book about the poet, fell asleep and "suddenly ... I could see her!... Her eyes were still as fiery as when Petrarch sang of them. She was covered in drapes of black muslin, her beautiful fair hair cascading over it... 'Why do you languish on Earth?' she asked me. 'Come, be with me. No more ailments, no more troubles, no more woes in the boundless space I inhabit. Be brave and follow me.' When she said that I threw myself at her feet and spoke to her, calling her 'my mother', and I was shaking with sobs. She reached out to me and I covered her hand with my tears. She wept also: 'When I used to live in the world you hate, I enjoyed foreseeing the multitudes of my descendants, even as far as you, *but I did not expect you to be so unfortunate.*' At that, I was swallowed by my despair and fondness, and threw my arms about her neck, so as to have her stay with me or to go with her and refresh her with my tears. But the ghost vanished. Only my anguish remained..." Even in his dreams, then, de Sade would fall into his recurring self-pity.

De Sade seems to have been slow to take up his pen for any purpose but that of writing letters. The shock of being returned to jail, the initial lack of writing materials and his belief that he would not be held for long all contributed to his apparent lack of application to any literary work. However, there is more to writing than sitting with pen in hand and marking characters on paper. There is also preparation - and we know that de Sade, quick though he was when he had decided what to write, believed in notes, plans and rough drafts, not only on paper but also in the mind. Besides, it is clear that much of his writing - letters, notes, finished literary pieces - has been lost through destruction by relatives and others eager to diminish what they regarded as the stain which he had left on the family honour, or through the usual obliterations by the passage of time.

Examining the period in question here - from 1777 at Vincennes - the one Sadeian "notebook of notes or reflections" known to have survived is entitled by de Sade the fourth of the series and covers only 12 June to 21 August 1780. It offers, though, a pointer to Sadeian literary work still to take shape for one of its 16 notes suggests a "*project for a remarkable debauch by a Poitou count.* William IX, Count of Poitou [in western France], born in 1071 and died in 1122, had devised at Niort a house of debauchery in the form of a monastery where there was to be an abbess, a prioress, etc., and where, making use of the monastic life, one would spice with impiety all the pleasures of prostitution (History of the Troubadours, volume I, page 4)."

Another note, also indicative of complete works to come, deals with two societies far from France, "... the peoples most given to all kinds of vice and crime. Among them, incest, adultery, theft and murder are not only tolerated, but even seen ... as virtues, and their talk is all of the very great number of these sorts of crimes that they have committed. On the other hand, these are the most handsome people and the best endowed by nature in the world... (See the *Travels* of Chardin.)"

The marquis had long been a collector of snippets of history and anthropology, especially those with sexual elements, and one can reasonably speculate that such material, expanded by de Sade's comments and fictions, made up at least part of the documents which Mme de Montreuil was much concerned to remove from view on her son-in-law's trail on the road to Vincennes.

While his pot of surprises yet to come was fermenting - he swore to his wife in May 1780 that he would re-write from memory those manuscripts of his which he had last seen when locking them away in his study at la Coste - de Sade also applied his pen to historical essays derived from his reading and his travels, and to drama. He sent dialogues and whole plays to his wife, asking eagerly for her comments and telling her that she was to let only Rousset and the Abbé Amblet, his former tutor, read them, aside from herself. La Jeunesse, by then the marquise's servant, went to work willingly at making fair copies, remarking that de Sade's closely-packed manuscripts made it look as though a swarm of bees had landed on the paper. The marquis would have liked nothing better, apart from liberty, to have his plays put on the stage in Paris. He confided to Amblet in 1784 that acceptance as a playwright "might obliterate the mishaps of my younger days and bring about a kind of change for the better in me, taking all my attention and making me drop everything else."

At Vincennes, in the early 1780s, his facility for drama was even readier than it had been at his father-in-law's country estates 20 years before. He began work, for instance, on *The Man of Whim* (*Le*

Capricieux) on 24 December 1780; "the outline was done on 8 January 1781 and the play completed on the evening of the 24th of the same month. It was revised and corrected from 24 January to 8 April of that year; from 5 to 19 April inclusive it was written up in fair copy, all of which entailed 16 weeks of work. It contained 1,824 verses then", de Sade noted with the structured precision he never tired of bringing to what engaged his interest, and which would have untangled many of his troubles if he had applied it to his financial affairs, as his mother-in-law often used to tell him.

So keen was de Sade to have his plays taken up beyond the walls of the fortress that he was unwontedly prepared to acknowledge, even bend to the will of, the police censors in this regard. They took the view that, while he was writing plays, de Sade was not making trouble for the prison administration or his family, so he might as well be allowed to continue, and to send them to the outside world. However, the censors retained suspicion that he might be working smut and subversion, in disguise, into his plays. The marquis saw fit to write to Le Noir, the police chief: "I repeat to you my same protestations that I have sought to insert no innuendo or double-meaning whatsoever into these plays, and that I will have not the least difficulty in altering anything to which one might take exception."

This uncharacteristic willingness to be flexible did not last in the face of criticisms from the recipients of his plays, once they had passed the police censors. De Sade recognised, in 1782 after five years in jail, that *The Man of Whim*, for example, might not have "the feeling of the times, which would be a miracle [if it did] for how would it not be marred by this outdated style so closely linked to my situation?" The Abbé Amblet, the recipient of this rare admission by the author that a play of his might lack a certain something, replied via the marquise that he could find nothing good about it at all, "that if this sort of work amuses you, then you can carry on with it as amusement, but as for putting it on the public stage, he says that is impossible. You want him to be frank and there you have what he frankly told me..."

De Sade was piqued by this sort of sting, whether from his old mentor or from his wife. When, in the spring of 1784, Renée Pélagie seemed to him to have "turned a deaf ear" to the script of his tragedy *Jeanne Laisné or the Siege of Beauvais* (*Jeanne Laisné ou le Siège de Beauvais*), he warned her: "While I am occupying myself with good things, it is absurd of your guide-donkeys to want to prevent me doing so. Alas! my God, they shouldn't get upset, I won't be in this vein [writing plays] for long; once the gates are opened, then you'll see whether it's to that job I'll be applying my talent." Likewise, when in 1782, the marquis found his wife tardy in sending material to help him in the innocent study of natural history, he complained: "When you don't encourage my decent tastes, then all the more reason for me to turn to other kinds." (In other words: It's your fault, you on the outside, if I turn from acceptable pursuits to naughty ones, through your lack of help and encouragement.) "The more people vex me, then the more my brain is bound to go astray," he dodged again, in another letter of 1782.

The marquis's capacity for finding a way to pass the buck, whatever form the buck might be taking, may be familiar to readers by now. As usual, he should not be taken at face value. Concurrent with his dramatic and historical writing at Vincennes, Mr 6 was indeeed showing signs of impatience with producing examples of literary genres which he could show to the Abbé Amblet or to the police censors. This restlessness stemmed from earlier days than those when critiques of his prison plays arrived from beyond prison walls.

He persevered with writing them - de Sade told Amblet in 1784 that he was "drawn towards that career despite myself... I have in my folder more plays than a great proportion of the much-vaunted authors of the day has turned out, and have outlines ready for more than twice as many as I have completed. If I had been left in peace, I would have fifteen comedies ready on leaving jail." Yet - then in prison as earlier among women and men in the world at large - barriers in the field of morality bothered him. "Metaphysics, in my view, is the dullest and grossest thing, and I am put off when I have to sprinkle it on my works as dramatic art demands."

He went on to refer to "the rather less irksome test I will give my talents in this regard as soon as I am free... And it will be with a very keen satisfaction that [I'll give] myself over to my only genre ..." - by which he meant works to which an author is reluctant to put his name in an era of censored literature. Remember that, when he was at liberty **(see chapter 7)**, the marquis had met, so he claimed, the costs of "my entertainments over six months in one of the main cities of the realm, and [of my travels] in Holland for two months without spending a farthing of my own", thanks to certain works he had written. Writing for the theatre, "on the other hand, [has] been worth to me no more than a breeze in the capital of Guyane... What a difference!" De Sade already knew very well that it could be lucrative for an author to yield to the temptation to write titillation for a quick sale, rather than stick to more seemly literature.

He claimed that he never wrote to titillate, but always with a deeper purpose even when the intention of a work of his was to arouse the reader sexually. When he took up the quills in the candlelight of Cell No. 6, and mingled their scratching with the rustling and squeaking of the rats and mice in order to write his *Dialogue between a Priest and a Dying Man,* de Sade was drawing on a concern which had been with him at least since, in the year of his marriage 1763, he demonstrated to Jeanne Testard in no uncertain terms his militant atheism and his sexual expression thereof. This work, finished about the middle of 1782, offers a priest visiting a dying man to administer the last rites of the Church, but the moribund, who is allowed the lion's share of the conversation, argues the case for atheism:

"We are pawns in the power of an irresistible force and have not the least scope to do other than deal with whatever comes our way and follow the trail laid down for us. Every virtue and every crime is embraced by nature and its mighty science consists of the perfect equilibrium it keeps between virtue and vice... Why should I be rewarded for virtues which I have through no action of mine, or punished for crimes for which I am not ultimately responsible?... Nature generates and regenerates eternally... Nothing perishes, nothing is lost; man today, worm tomorrow..." The dialogue ends with the dying man summoning six beautiful women, who have been waiting in the next room to furnish his last orgy, in which the priest joins at the atheist's invitation.

This short, one-sided polemic would excite little condemnation in our disbelieving age but, in the France of de Sade's time, known advocates of atheism went to jail. Everything the marquis wrote in prison was liable to be inspected by the authorities but the *Dialogue* seems to have been kept away from them. It - like various other writings from Vincennes, such as the project for the monastic house of debauchery and the anthropological interest in crimes rated as virtues - indicates the shape of things to come, already incubating in the brain of the Marquis de Sade.

They might have hatched more quickly if he had not given so much time and energy to that pastime of prisoners which is even older and more widespread than immersion in the written word. We have it from de Sade's notes that he masturbated on each of the two days - 24 and 25 August 1778 - before his seizure at la Coste in the small hours of the 26th by Inspector Marais. There is no sure evidence that, once he was re-installed at Vincennes on 7 September, the marquis greatly increased the rate of self-stimulation he had employed when he was at liberty and without access to human sexual partners. On 7 September 1784, the sixth anniversary of his arrival in Cell No. 6, he drew up an account of the past six years, drawing on copious notes he had made, sometimes in the margins and blank spaces of letters received, sometimes on sheets of his own paper. He reckoned to have effected, during the 2,192 days of those six years, 2,568 "introductions".

It is not easy to interpret de Sade's chronicle of how and when he took himself in hand. Much of it is written in abbreviations and symbols not intended for anyone else to read. For one thing, it would be as well for the authorities to be baffled by it if they ever got hold of it; for another, he was concerned to be sparing with his supplies of paper. Even where complete words are used, the prisoner referred to episodes "with prestiges" or "without prestiges", "prestiges of which twelve big and six enormous", "of 8½", "of 9 inches", "prestiges with the sterc.", "viperishly" (*vipériquement*).

It seems certain that the "prestiges" (the same word appears in the French original) were dildoes which de Sade used for anal penetration, necessarily self-administered. (Remember the role of the valet Latour in the encounter with the prostitutes at Marseilles, and de Sade's concern to recruit a young male secretary for the closeted winter at la Coste.) The "sterc." (*le sterc.* in the original) remains obscure, even when what appears to be an abbreviation is qualified as "the whole sterc." However, given his classical education, de Sade would have known that, in Latin, *stercus* means dung. (Many years later, he referred to one of his enemies as a "vile stercus".) It may be that the marquis was recording here his success in provoking excretion by his anal penetrations. As for the term "*vipériquement*", I hazard a guess, knowing de Sade's preference, that it described two fingers inserted into the anus and then parted into a V, stretching the passage.

The oddity here is neither the frequency of masturbation by a middle-aged man, in jail or out, nor the enjoyment of buggery by objects, but the "extravagant and meticulous accounting", as de Sade himself described it, of the events. I come, therefore I am - that's the motivation behind many a lonely wank - but de Sade needed to write it down every time for further reassurance.

Another abbreviation which occurs many times in the marquis's summing-up ("*pr. Hél.*") is likely to signify "*pour Hélène*" ("for Hélène"), this being a name of the marquise in the code between her and her husband. It is probable that her ladyship never knew of the extent of his dedications to her in this regard, but she was well aware of his special sexual wants while at Vincennes for she was called on to supply the dildoes, which are called "flasks", "holsters" or "cases" in the letters between husband and wife. Who else could have been entrusted with this delicate job, or even have been expected to understand what was required?

There was the subtle difficulty of conveying what was wanted to Renée Pélagie, and thence to the craftsman, without being so obvious that anyone in the prison administration reading the correspondence would easily understand what was going on. Even so, the more experienced hands among the police censors and fortress staff would have figured out, I think, what de Sade was arranging, and they would have turned a blind eye, masturbation by prisoners being a reliable adjunct to the keeping of order in any jail. The marquis tried a little camouflage, however: "This case (for one must explain everything with our overseers) is to hold the maps, engravings and several little landscape drawings which I have done in red ink." Was de Sade also trying to provide a plausible explanation for bloodstains left on the "case" after deep anal penetrations? In any event, the censors disliked the next sentence - making reference to a nun - of this letter of July 1783 so much that they applied the heavy obliterating ink for which they sometimes reached when they caught Mr 6 in his scatological vein.

Renée Pélagie herself seems to have missed the point for a while, having reported in June 1781: "Your flask is on order. I can't conceive how you would be able to put in your pocket a flask six inches in circumference..." De Sade, apparently taking at face value this indication that the marquise had not understood what the flask was really for, wrote in the margin of her letter: "I am not going to put it in my pocket, but somewhere else, where it will turn out to be far too small..."

However, one might allow the marquise, who could show more wit than her husband or her mother often gave her credit for, the benefit of the doubt and suggest that, in the one sentence, she was deftly evading the censor's eraser and poking a little fun at her husband's penchant for large invasions of the back passage (as long as he was in control of same).

The marquis was very exacting in his orders for penetrative objects: "I have taken the exact measurement on the hole, and that's definitely right. But it must be at least three inches longer, although the circumference is the essential thing... [My] present prestige is like that. So that's how Abraham [the manufacturer] should make it, or send a ready-made if there is one..." Abraham knew quite well what his "flasks" were for, it seems: "He assured me that he had supplied one of the same size to his lordship the Archbishop of Lyons; tell him he ought to remember that..."

On another occasion, de Sade was demanding a "nine-inch holster by eight and a half in circumference, with a screw three inches high, in ebony or rosewood..." for their smoothness.

Striving to satisfy such an acute need, de Sade drew on his wide vocabulary - which had been formed in the bordello and in the study of *beaux arts* - to get his point through any censorship and across to the marquise. "You have to say to your tradesman that it's a case for holding culs - de lampe - yes, culs-de-lampe and other little drawings that I have amused myself by doing..." (The word *cul* in French means "arse"; *cul-de-lampe* is a French term, used in English also, for an ornamental support of inverted conical form, in architecture, as well as a printing and design term for an ornament used to fill a space at the bottom of a page, as at the end of a chapter in a book.)

The marquis, erstwhile traveller and what we would now call sexual tourist, could also become nostalgic and lyrical about his anal longing, as when acknowledging the receipt from his wife of a new novel: "You sent me *Le Beau Garçon*[4], *sweet turtledove. Le Beau Garçon*: how that word pleases my slightly Italian ear! *Un bel giovanetto, signor*, they would say to me if I was in Naples, and I would say: *Si, si, signor, mandatelo lo voglio bene.*[5] You have treated me like a cardinal, *my little mother*... but unfortunately it's only in a picture... The case, then, at least the case, since you reduce me to illusions..."

In another letter: "Send it, I beg you, because for lack of it I am obliged to use something else, which spoils, tears and crushes my *culs*

---

4 *The Handsome Boy.*

5 A handsome lad, sir ... Yes, indeed, sir, send him along, I like him a lot.

--- *de lampe*, and that's most unpleasant. It's *out of decency* and so as not to frighten you that one contents oneself by asking for a case 8½ [inches] in circumference, for strictly speaking one needs 9, measurement taken on my *culs-de-lampe*..."

Frightened or not, it was Renée Pélagie who had to face the tradesmen and place the orders for the flasks and cases. At one point in 1783, she reported to her husband: "As for the case, I don't know where to go to order it, for the workmen take me for a madwoman when I talk to them about a case as big as that: they laugh in my face and they don't take the job. They want the money in advance, afraid that they'll be left with the thing on their hands, and afterwards, however it turns out, you have to take it because you won't get your money back."

The marquis replied: "Joy of Mahomet, you said that the case I am asking you for has given you trouble. I can well understand that it would if it had been made, but when it's just a question of getting it made, I do not find in the limited capacity of my cerebellum that the mere act of placing the order could irritate in you the nerves which alert the soul to the feeling of distress. They take you, so you say, for a madwoman; that's what I don't understand; and I cannot admit that the request for a *thick* case by a *little* woman could provoke any disturbance in the pineal gland where we others, atheist philosophers, establish the seat of reasoning..."

The main disturbance for de Sade at Vincennes was the perpetual uncertainty over when he would be released. The prison log of 7 September 1778 recorded that, "at half-past eight o'clock of the evening, his lordship the Marquis de Sade entered the Dungeon of the Fortress of Vincennes, escorted by Mr Marais, Inspector of Police, and remains there confined until further order from His Majesty..." In those circumstances, held under royal *lettre de cachet,* the prisoner lacked a calendar on which he might mark each day that passed and brought him closer to liberty. De Sade, who loathed being in the hands of a force on which he could not act, ferreted frantically for such a structure amid this disorientation. He examined every communication and phenomenon that might carry an indication, however disguised or coded, of when he would be returned to full daylight and fresh air.

Numbers provide structure for societies that live by commerce and by rent. De Sade counted obsessively. The number of syllables in a letter from his wife was construed as the number of weeks he would remain in jail; a date on another letter showed that Renée Pélagie had known when his appeal at Aix was to be heard, so how could she make out that she did not know the date of release from Vincennes; the number of items he had just received through trade in the jail's main commodity - candles and nightlights - suggested his total term in months.

"It's solved, your odious enigma. The day I will get out is *7 Feb* of 82 or 84 (the difference is considerable, so you see that I am not much further forward); the vile and lunatic word game is the name of the saint for that day, which turns out to be St Amand," De Sade wrote to his wife in the autumn of 1781. In April that year, though, he had divined: "It's in December 83 that I'll be able to glimpse my freedom, and there's the significance of your three pheasants sent last December. Of course, it was quite clear; I was foolish not to understand it right away..."

Probing again: "On Thursday 6 January, at the end of 9 months after the candles were borrowed, the very same day, I was given 25 in place of the 10 I had loaned, which seemed to lay down quite firmly 9 more months in prison making 25 in all..."

The marquis also applied his figuring to the problem of when his exercise periods would be restored:

"Note to be cut out and kept and which indicates the future:

"There is something about walks in 12 and in 3. When I lost them six weeks after a 2, which makes 12, they gave them back to me on 3 May.

"Hélène a 12 talks about the stockings of 3 (Troyes) in *Champagne*, which provides the notion of walks..."

The prisoner's urgent, recurrent absorption with numerical clues makes for baffling, albeit disturbing, reading. Perhaps only those who have been held at the caprice of some unaccountable authority can appreciate it fully. However, it arose from the unquiet nerves of a longing to glimpse light at the end of the tunnel - or lights along the way, when he turned his juggling of numbers to his longing for walks or for Renée Pélagie to be allowed to visit him.

As Pauvert points out, no-one should think that de Sade was incapacitated intellectually by this flicking away at the abacus of his hopes and fears, however incomprehensible his outbursts appear to us now. Even the most intensive stretches of frantic hunting for signs were concurrent with lucid literary output and letter-writing. Besides, the latter half of the 18th century was a time, among the numerate and literate minority which had the leisure for such pursuits, of much interest in divination by examination of sequences of numbers, this being consistent with involvement in the general scientific ferment of the era.

De Sade himself was not so rapt with figures and signs that he could not distance himself from them: "So what do you want me to do in here, if it's not calculations and giving birth to figments of the imagination?" he wrote to his wife. On another occasion, he asked Rousset: "Well what kind of reasoning can you expect from a man who's treated as though he hadn't any?"

"As far as the signs are concerned, once and for all, I never make any," Renée Pélagie protested in January 1781, to little avail. Still, the numerical extrapolations took up less of his letters and notes as the years passed in Cell No. 6, but they would break out now and again, five years and more into his captivity, not least when his mother-in-law resumed her familiar place at the front of his attention to his catalogue of demons, as when the prisoner told his wife in February 1784:

"Your mother must be totally *drunk*, or *mad enough to be tied*, to have risked her daughter's neck by making a *19 and 4*, or *16 and 9*, and not to have tired of it for twelve years. Oh! what an indigestion of figures she had, this nasty woman! I am of the opinion that if she had died before the raid[6], and she had been opened, millions of figures would have come out of her guts..."

More accessible to the modern reader, in a world that could not manage without lists, are de Sade's tottings-up. For instance, at one point he wrote to Renée Pélagie: "Today, Thursday 14 December 1780, *the 1,400th day, the 200th week and the expiry of the 46th month* of our separation, having received from you sixty-eight fortnightly deliveries of provisions and a hundred letters, and this one from me being the 114th ..."

Thus he stacked numbers in what might otherwise have been a void through which he could have tumbled into madness. His yearning for a terminal date was very much part of a desire for structure, for banishment of uncertainty.

The rest of his time at the fortress was taken up by eating (too much), play-acting with costumes, communicating with other prisoners (forbidden by regulations) in fragmented and unsatisfactory ways,

6 By the police to arrest him in Paris in February 1777.

arranging and sniffing flowers sent from outside, and dreaming (by night and day).

Throughout all abided the gloom and dirt of Cell No. 6 with its smoky flue, the lack of opportunities for exercise outside it, the mean-spirited administration of the prison and the prisoner's propensity for rows with its members, as well as his physical decline, unwashed in the damp, dark confinement, notably in terms of eye trouble. Yet he read voraciously and wrote letters, plays and notes - by no means all acceptable to the censors. He masturbated and was "shoving all sorts of things into my arse". He picked over any action or object from without so as to pluck the numerical sign which would uncover the date of his release or any fixed moment which would provide a rock to cling to in the brackish pool where he floated unwillingly and inescapably.

Now, before we go on to events outside Cell No. 6, but related to its inmate, let's consider whether he should have gone there at all.

CHAPTER 15: "NOT DONE ALL THAT I HAVE THOUGHT OF"

The royal administration - acting via Marais and his men bursting open the doors of la Coste on a summer night, and via Governor de Rougemont and his men keeping shut the doors of Vincennes year in and year out - had no doubts that the Marquis de Sade was where he ought to be. His relatives had requested a royal detention order; those relatives were noble and influential; the fellow was a notorious reprobate - enough said.

Not as far as de Sade himself was concerned. He returned now and again to his argument for the defence. This was his typical style:

"Yes, I'm a libertine, I admit to it; I have thought of all that can be thought of in that line, but I have certainly not done all that I have thought of and I certainly never will. I'm a libertine, but I am neither *a criminal* nor *a murderer* ..."

"But I affirm - and will prove in the most genuine way, when required - that I am incapable of anything serious and that there is in all this a sequence of events which I alone can disentangle and which I will make clear when required. Fateful coincidences, indiscretions, too much weakness and too much confidence in people who didn't deserve it, some letters that were too sharp, *big and dangerous aims* (you know what I mean) could, and I acknowledge them, make it look as though I had done some wrongs. My enemies have taken advantage of that, and there's the only basis for the view taken which, no doubt, ensures that I am being treated as I am," he wrote to his wife.

Not only "the enemies" were behind his fall from grace; there was also his own "too fiery imagination ... always chasing after happiness without finding it in anything." Yet, at another moment, he offered a different insight into himself, his favourite topic: "It's not an over-lively imagination which leads to my sort of errors, it's being a burnt-out case." (Note that this latter remark - and he very rarely played such a harsh light on himself before his old age - was made to Police Chief Le Noir, in whom an opinion that de Sade had no more oil in his lamp might have led to his release from jail. So there might have been calculation here by Mr 6.)

More typical of his line on the police chief was this excuse by placing his guilt in the shade of a greater crime: "I've slapped some arses, I admit; and he has put a million souls in danger of starving to death." (This was probably a reference to supposed mismanagement by Le Noir, in one of his government jobs, of food supplies to French cities.) Besides, the marquis, by his own account, had indulged in nothing more "than parties with girls such as occur eighty times a day in Paris." "I am guilty only of what everyone does."

Would the prosecution like to move from the general to the particular? Very well: The bones at la Coste, which led to much report of the marquis having killed and dissected women in his château, had been brought by the dancer du Plan who used them as a joke, to decorate a cabinet, after which they were disposed of in the garden. How much credence would a jury give to one of the de Sade's hired dancing girls, especially as represented by a statement in the possession of the self-confessed libertine *châtelain* himself? Still, tomfoolery in bad taste with dry bones was not an offence, and there is no firm evidence of any crime connected with them. Live flesh and bones are a different matter, but the man in the dock is not to have his defence pierced. How could anyone suppose he had raped Catherine Trillet, the cook from Montpellier whom her gun-toting father tried to rescue from la Coste, considering that she was "a girl as strong and as tall as I am, and nearly my age..."

As for the little servant girls from Lyons and Vienne, said to have been their lord and master's prey at the shuttered château in the winter of 1774-75, "I swear and I protest that I have been guilty these five years [up to September 1778] of no more than a little too much confidence in a strumpet who needs hanging rather than being set free... At Lyons, I went along to a well-established p[rocuress], and I told her: I want to take to my establishment three or four servant girls; I like them young and pretty; provide me with that sort. That p[rocuress], who was Nanon, for [she] was a well-established p[rocuress] at Lyons - I will prove that when it's necessary - promises me these girls and gives them to me. I take them, I make use of them. At the end of six months, parents come to ask for these girls back, maintaining that they are their children. I hand them over; then all of a sudden there's a case against me for abduction and rape!..."

De Sade has kept his argument on the narrow ground of the supply, as he makes it out to be, of girls by a known procuress. The boy "secretary" is left out of the picture; so is the evidence, still strong even for examiners coming onto the case 200 years after the event, that some of the maids left the marquis's employment injured. In the next sentences, he seems to cook his own goose when he admits that some of the servant girls were virgins when they reached him. Then:

"But here's the greatest of all the injustices. The law on this is as follows, and I have this from Mr de Sartine [former police chief of Paris], who had the goodness to explain it to me himself one day, as he would remember: It is expressly forbidden in France for any p[rocuress] to supply virgin girls, and if the girl supplied is a virgin and she files a complaint, in no way is the man to be arrested, it's the p[rocuress] who is to be punished rigorously and at once."

This defence, relying on a fine point of law and careful selection among the facts of the matter, stands only if it can be established beyond reasonable doubt that Nanon was an established procuress at Lyons, and acting as such on the material occasion towards the end of 1774. Gilbert Lely, an author all too ready to let de Sade's glamour dazzle him out of objectivity, takes the view in this matter that Nanon, far from being an established procuress at Lyons, was a chambermaid in the de Sade household who had agreed to visit the city to "choose objects of lust for him". That is, Nanon was acting at the instigation of a person who was employing her in another capacity, rather than having been a professional procuress, so one may conclude that, if she committed an offence, it was that of having aided and abetted de Sade in his offence of debauching virgins.

The marquis, let's remember, is on record as having been convinced that "nothing is less respectable than a whore, and the way you use that has to be no different to the way you pass your motions"[1]. The best he could hope for is that verdict allowed in Scottish jurisprudence, "not proven", which seems to suggest that the court reckons the accused did whatever it was, but can't quite pin it on him. If more documents had survived, we might well have a clearer line on whether a court of law ought to have locked away the Marquis de Sade, given the chance, which it was not.

---

1 The French original is *on pousse sa selle*, so de Sade was making a pun, *selle* meaning not only *motion of the bowels* but also *saddle*. This was hightly appropriate from an ex-cavalryman with a tase for excretory images and fascinations, not least when expressing contempt and/or about his lust. So one phrase served to put across the idea that one could use a prostitute as one might pass a turd, or might ride a saddle when on horseback.

CHAPTER 16: THE HIGH PRIESTESS AND THE WORST ENEMY

In fact, expediency locked him away. The Présidente de Montreuil, writing to Gaufridy in December 1778, called her son-in-law's current imprisonment "a wise *precaution* against the *lapses which have compromised him* so often." She was "not going into details with anyone, except with you, who know everything, which must not be divulged..." Six months earlier, she had been telling the Provençal lawyer that de Sade "has too much intelligence not to anticipate that, after all that has happened since the affair [of the prostitutes at Marseilles] and of which the minister is only too well informed through all the complaints which have been brought, he must not count on his successful appeal in court being followed by his being set free..."

This was not at all clear to de Sade, any insights he might have had into the motives for his incarceration having been blunted both by the secretive workings of the royal administration and his obsessive belief that he would be at liberty but for the machinations of his mother-in-law. Even after Marie Dorothée de Rousset had arrived in Paris from la Coste, in November 1778, to join Renée Pélagie's efforts on the marquis's behalf, it was more than a year before the seconded housekeeper was able to tell Gaufridy that she had been allowed to see, either in ministerial files or in a copy of same, "the grounds for detention. This wasn't easy; the audacious person who managed it ran the risk of being sent to the galleys or to jail for life... We have learned by this piece of daring that the dear *présid*[*ente*] was not so much to blame as we used to think. He has even more powerful enemies." Rousset did not specify.

The dear *présidente* herself would have concurred. In mid-September 1778, eight days after Marais had installed de Sade at Vincennes, Mme de Montreuil was at pains to let Gaufridy know: "People have tried to persuade Mme de Sade that I was *the force behind this latest event, in concert with milord the Commander*[1] ... That woman has to be clearly informed so as to disabuse her, bringing

1 The marquis's only surviving uncle.

to bear the certainties to which she can have no reply whatsoever, so that at least her mind be set at rest..."

There was little rest, in mind or body, for Renée Pélagie while her husband was at Vincennes. On receiving the news that he had been recaptured at la Coste, the marquise swore loathing and vengeance without end on her mother if she did not arrange for her to rejoin her husband within three days and wherever Mme de Montreuil had caused him to be taken. The marquise's mother sent a message to say that, on her word of honour, she did not know what her daughter was talking about. Royal ministers were likewise "just blank walls," Renée Pélagie lamented.

She told Rousset: "My God, what a blow for me! What a chasm of grief you see me thrown into again! How can I get out, whom can I trust, what can I believe? It is absolutely impossible for me to make a judgement, or find a solution, from all that I've been told and all that's been done. The vexations, the duplicities, the plausible air of straight dealing in some people as though it could never hide deceit, all that transfixes me..." No wonder the marquise appealed to the housekeeper at la Coste: "I am in great need of your advice and your wisdom to extricate me from the frightful chaos I am in..." Rousset, full of intelligence and a lawyer's daughter, arrived in Paris and moved in with the marquise at the latter's little apartment in the Carmelite convent in the rue de l'Enfer (Hell Street).

Mme de Montreuil, although bearing misgivings at the advent of a person who might well upset Renée Pélagie further with messages from de Sade, delivered as he was bundled away from la Coste by Marais and his men, was soon at home to the transplanted *provençale*. The latter reported to Gaufridy: "She received me with all possible courtesy, decency and trust. Our conversation was long and entirely about M. de S. There was nothing about you. She started by telling me that Marais had been punished, having to meet his travel expenses himself, 'and I think,' she told me, 'that he has lost his job because on receiving your letter I went to file my complaint; I have followed this closely enough to think that he has been sacked.' I replied that this was no more than he deserved..."

Rousset and others of the household at the manor, as well as Mme de Montreuil when she heard of it, had complained to high authority about the way de Sade was treated by the police raiding party. However, it is by no means clear that Inspector Marais - a valuable collector of information where Parisian high society met Parisian low life - did lose his position over what seems to have been a rare excess on his part.

The report from the confrontation with the *présidente* continued: "Picture to yourself, sir, two individuals who have some hankering to get to know each other, or rather two cats who want to go into combat, the aggressor sheathing its claws but using them now and again to stir up its adversary. Once the battle was joined, without either party giving any indication that combat was under way, we skirmished until the moment when I wanted to go on the attack. Then, through the confusion and the heat of the fight, I understood with complete clarity that M. de S. was well-loved, and that it was paining her heart to know he is where he is...

"After a resumé of all the obligations M. de S. has to her - and she's right about that because there are many - came the wrongs.

'He recognises them,' I say to her, 'but he won't make amends for them where he is.'

" 'Ah, if you knew, Miss de Rousset, all that he used to promise me in the old days! Look, in this room where we are now, what pledges has he not taken!'

" 'I believe it; he intended to carry out his promises. Man is weak, madame, as you know; the passage of time and his misfortunes have worked much alteration.'

" 'I hope so! But tell me, Miss de Rousset, *would you take total responsibility for him?*'

"Well, Mr Gaufridy, it was as well that I had expected the question. Avoiding over-eagerness but without hesitation, I replied modestly: 'Yes, madame. His family is, however, is against him, *not one of them having lifted a finger to ask for him to be returned to them.*'

"... I told her that I had seen Lady de Villeneuve and Lady de Saint Laurent[2], that they wished him released, and that I presumed the same attitude was held by milord the Commander and the Cavaillon aunts..." - his two paternal aunts in holy orders at Cavaillon in Provence.

For the further benefit of the lawyer at Apt, who had never seen the faraway *grande dame* with whom he shared many secrets about de Sade, Rousset concluded:

---

2 These were respectively the marquis's youngest paternal aunt and another noblewoman expected to have sympathy for him.

"Madame de Montreuil is a charming woman, delightful in conversation, still well preserved[3], short rather than tall, with a neat figure, a disarming laugh and winning glance, an impish intelligence, the sagacity and directness of an angel, albeit astute as a fox, but kind and attractive in her way...

"... Like milord Marquis, she has bowled me over..."

To the said marquis, Rousset reported: "I have visited the high priestess and will do so again; I am not disappointed but if I were to hurry this matter it would be disaster; too many minds are made up. We will succeed if we tread carefully and prepare a sound argument. Our imprisonment will not continue beyond next spring."

This was a very unfortunate prediction. Before the spring of 1779 - by the end of January, in fact - Rousset had sounded a wider range of opinion about the marquis. His in-laws for instance, would keep him locked up for much longer than a few months. Marie Dorothée exclaimed to Gaufridy that the marquise's "entire family is truly amazing. One of her maternal uncles wrote to her: 'Your opposition to your family is wrong. You are at fault for being so crazy about your husband. You should have kept in mind your brothers and sisters who have to be given a chance in the world...' If all that bunch has to be matched and married before he can be let out, that will be too cruel..."

The youngest child of M and Mme de Montreuil, a daughter called Françoise Pélagie, aged 18 at this juncture, was still unmarried. Her wedding took place four years later, in January 1783, when she became the Marquise de Wavrin, but this did not diminish the importance for the Montreuils in keeping de Sade out of circulation. Alliance of more Montreuil children to high-born families multiplied the number of people with an interest in hearing no more of the reprobate marquis, whose behaviour had brought shame and ridicule on certain noble names, and could do so again if he were given the chance.

Through Renée Pélagie, Mme de Montreuil already had the prospect of her family's name becoming entwined with future branches of the family tree of the de Sades, for their old blue blood flowed in the veins of her two de Sade grandsons, whose upbringing was under her supervision. By the end of October 1778, less than two months after their father had been put back into Vincennes, she was packing off Louis Marie and Donatien Claude Armand from Paris to the village of

---

3 Aged about 58 then.

Vallery, where the Montreuils had a house, south-east of the capital and near Sens. There they started school under the instruction of the parish priest - no Jesuits or boisterous crowd of lads at Louis le Grand in wicked Paris for them - and still in the care of their nanny, a Montreuil appointee name of Langevin, who was also looking after Madeleine Laure, their little sister. Their father having deposited his seed where a noble sire should - three effective times - his essential job with regard to the almanach of the nobility was done. Besides, given that he was apt to be such a nuisance, why let him out now?

It is small wonder that Mme de Montreuil, her profligate son-in-law all the more evidently part of a passing generation in her dynastic scheme of things as his incarceration was prolonged, took the view of a matriarch whose main attention was elsewhere. She reported to Gaufridy in December 1778 that she had told Rousset: "My daughter has no better advocate before me than my own heart. The causes for ... complaint I have had from M. de S. are of no account in the *present situation*, about which I am very cross, but which I cannot rectify at present. I *am preventing no-one's moves.* I do not because I very readily understand the uselessness of doing so...

"... There are those trying to make her [the marquise] believe that this is an unjust piece of tyranny visited on her by the family, or by the government. For myself, I would tell you frankly that, if it's correct that they think that way (and I beg you to tell them this), in no way do I place myself in the path of this desired liberty, and that they can ask for it. The only thing that I want to avoid, in not asking for it myself, is that, if they find it turns out badly, at least they will not aim at me the same reproaches that they offered to me twice before for having brought about his freedom..."

From his cell, in May 1779, the marquis berated Rousset for what he saw as her having intentionally misled him into having set his hopes on being released that spring. The trouble was that it had taken her some months to perceive the strength and extent of distaste for him in society. "One cannot mention his name without the very paving stones starting to raise themselves against one... Things that happened a dozen years ago, of next to no importance in themselves but since inflated by people's ill-will, are seen as though they had taken place only yesterday," she wrote.

That did not stop her working for the cause. In July 1780, after patient preparation through lobbying among de Sade's connections,

Rousset was petitioning royal ministers to have the prisoner freed or show sound cause for his continued captivity. Princesses of the royal family had raised the matter with de Maurepas, the most influential minister, who was looking at the relevant documents, she told Gaufridy. Marie Dorothée was rightly apprehensive that, if officials were to examine closely the prisoner's recent conduct and correspondence, "we're done for, because he's behaving very badly and he's raining on us by letter horrors and stupidities. I'm being called a wh[ore]; there are worse names for other people..." Some of them were not encouraged, to say the least, in their contributions towards his prospective release, by having received foul, insulting letters from him.

The dogged housekeeper was not deflected by this biting of the hand that would enlarge. However, the responses she was receiving from the powers in the land were not uplifting. Those enemies "even more powerful" than Mme de Montreuil matched de Sade's deserts all too well, she reported to Provence in October 1780. "Some of them will have to die and others to forget for us to have any hope..."

In the same month, she added to Gaufridy: "Serious, very serious, considerations are causing me to fear a long imprisonment. Whether these are true or false, they are nevertheless the minister's battle horses for shutting the mouths of all right-thinking people[4]. Lord and Lady de Maurepas, two princesses and various others have said, after reading this material: 'He is in the right place; to dare to ask for his release, his wife must be a fool or as guilty as he is. We do not wish to see her...'

"The various police detachments who have been to the château have filed abominable reports. They are very vulgar types. M. de S's whole history is written up in a dossier... Certain details that I had believed to be known to only a handful of people are out in the open and many other matters - Heaven bless us! - which should never be spoken of at all also make me believe he will be locked up for a long time..."

De Rousset and the marquise were ranged against not only the obduracy of those in the royal administration and in high society who based their opposition to de Sade's release on his case history, but also against counter-lobbying by those prepared to head off any ministerial wavering of resolve in the matter of the marquis's continued detention. Gaufridy was told by de Rousset: "A Provençal whose name we haven't been given, but whom we would know (from Aix, I suspect),

---

4 Miss de Rousset sometimes lacked the deft touch with a metaphor.

had dealt a cruel blow to M de Sade. 'What are you thinking about,' he told the minister, 'setting free a man who has done this, that and the other, etc.?... I knew the details of the affair better than anyone, etc.' The release order was not made, to the great astonishment of him who was waiting for it; he found out the reasons for the change. It was not concealed from him that it was a Provençal who had taken it upon himself to nudge the powers that be."

De Sade grumbled, in June 1781, that he was being ill-treated, not only with regard to his own deserts but also by comparison: "People of my rank and my birth, for deliberate and well-proven crimes, proven in a much more convincing way than these dismal and stale devices which slander has dared to invent in order to ruin me, have nevertheless been allowed to wipe their slate clean on much better terms. I would mention only two: the Duke d'Olonne, completely at liberty after a prison term of eight years spent in the arms of a very pretty woman and the company of the most agreeable of men, in the most comfortable and stylish apartment and at the best table in Lyons; and the Chevalier de Bezons, back in Paris more dazzling than ever, despite a widely known murder, and this at the end of a year at Vincennes and three of lesser confinement or in exile..."

Yet, when a lesser confinement was offered to him, de Sade did not grasp it with both hands. On 31 March 1781, the marquise told Gaufridy that he "should not say a word [about] my good news. I have just obtained the royal order for M. de Sade to be transferred to the fort at Montélimar so as to be closer to his affairs..." Montélimar is on the lower Rhône between Lyons and Avignon, much nearer his Provençal estates. "They've told me I have to pay the costs and everything. I have said I will, without knowing where I'll get the means," the marquise added. She had prevailed upon the Marquise de Sorans, a lady-in-waiting to a sister of the king, to arrange for Louis XVI to let de Sade be moved to Montélimar.

Renée Pélagie also took a little filial delight in having scored a rare success in the great world beyond her mother's shadow: "My mother is piqued, very piqued, by what I have managed without her; I could tell by her manner..."

Mr 6, reminded yet again that his movements beyond the cell were entirely in the control of others, was also very piqued. On the evening of the day after his wife was writing so cheerily to Provence, the marquis poured the rhetorical bile: "Although it might be the simplest, easiest and least glorious thing to trick a prisoner, although this might be a very dull diversion, and which must point to a very low and vile spirit, although in a word this can only be the stupid and ridiculous pastime of a very old drivelling woman, and of a quite imbecilic creature, you have even so no victory by it, and I have been fooled by the story for no longer than a half-hour or so, it has to be said.

"Always proceeding from the gentility in the noble pleasures of the most high and mighty Lady de Montreuil! The lackeys and bootblacks catch each other out on April the First, so let's catch out her son-in-law. My God, what gentility of character, what height of spirit, what grandeur of feeling! Ah! never, never does the true font become tainted. By just one glimpse of gallantry in the entire army does one pick out a bastard of the great Turenne! We always hold to the purity of our origins and the thoroughbred never lets you down!"

After these lumbering insults and this leaden sarcasm - worth only a low mark in rhetoric class at Louis le Grand, for sure - directed at his mother-in-law's alleged stupidity in deceit and her supposed lack of noble blood and manners, both recurrent themes with de Sade, he got down to cases:

"What the devil are you about with this Montélimar fort business of yours? There has never been a fort at Montélimar. If there had been, the general staff would have put it in the *Army Almanach*; under *Montélimar*, there's only the *Marquis de Chabrillant*, who certainly has no prison under his command. I have gone through my three almanachs: in each one, Montélimar is mentioned once, and by all the other towns where there are forts or citadels, there is alongside *such-and-such a town and fort, or such-and-such a town and citadel*. Besides, I know Montélimar and all the surrounding area rather well (having spent an entire month at the Marquis de Chabrillant's place, where the château is by the gates of the town), so I am quite certain there has never been a fort at Montélimar. Perhaps there's some old tower inhabited by barn owls or screech owls, but as for a royal establishment for prisoners, there is most certainly no such thing there. I'll put my hand in the fire if there is...

"But let's take this seriously for a moment. There is near Montélimar a castle for prisoners called *Crest Tower*, so perhaps you misunderstood, and this is what you're talking about. On that supposition you will allow me, I beg of you, to dispense with writing that handsome letter of thanks to Mme de Sorans, of which the style, which you do me the honour of wishing to point out to me, is nothing more or less than that her valet would use if she had thrown him out and he wanted to get back in her good books.

"Crest Tower is a prison decidedly more frightful than Vincennes and, what's more, extremely unhealthy; where they only put prisoners whom they want to be rid of in a hurry. It's an abominable cesspit, where one gets hardly a glimpse of daylight, and in the middle of fever-breeding swamps..."

De Sade may have had a point about the insalubriousness of the tower; even so, it was by no means clear that this place was what Renée Pélagie meant by Montélimar, and it was plain that an influential courtier, Mme de Sorans, was trying to help during a time when his friends in high places were very few. A more graceful, reflective prisoner than the marquis would have mentioned to his wife the uncertainty over just which location was intended for him, asked for clarification, pointed out that Crest, if that were the case, seemed unlikely to be suitable and - apart from sending a note to de Sorans thanking her for her efforts to date - left it at that, pending further information. Not so Mr 6, with his propensity for countering initiatives from outside at the charge, all spurs and sabre, nostrils flaring - all very well if only the prisoner's touchy pride were at issue, but altogether misplaced from a disgraced libertine detained under *lettre de cachet*.

He had given up, late in 1778, attending to management of his estates, about which he was sending instructions in the first few weeks after his arrival at Vincennes in September that year. The lord of la Coste, Saumane and other properties decided that he would deal with no questions of leases, rents, powers of attorney and so forth while he was still in jail - all the more reason for his family to have him released, he may well have calculated, so that the estates would not deteriorate for lack of decisions about their management. The marquise found herself having to ask farmer Ripert: "Wait patiently for the return of M. de Sade to the district." Her husband went so far as to forbid mention of the matter to him, and Renée Pélagie pleaded in April 1779: "If it were not for your having forbidden me to do so, I would talk business to you. Believe me, for your own good, you should drop this barrier."

It may be clear to the reader by now that the marquis was rarely disposed to heed his wife or anyone else on the topic of discarding his stubbornness for his own good. In being so quick and hot about spurning the prospect of a move to the south, he might have thought that there was no point in a transfer to the lower Rhône to be closer to his lands because he was not going to give them his attention while a prisoner, even if the jail had been among the mulberry bushes of la Coste itself. However, de Sade did hanker, while at Vincennes, for his role as landlord and wrote more than once of his wish to be out so as to mend his health and oversee his business affairs. It may be that, back in the south, he would have ended his deafness to requests for his signature on contracts and proxies.

This was not the heart of the matter, though. It had its dwelling, as often with de Sade, more deeply in his character. Having continued his letter of All Fools' Day by elaborately wrapping his point to the marquise that Lady de Sorans could whistle for thanks from him, he added: "Believe you me, we have put on enough shows in the Dauphiné and in Provence." That is, the police's treatment of him after the arrest at la Coste, as he was paraded through the local region, as well as the widespread scandal around his name and person in his paternal ancestors' provinces, made him shrink from further attention being drawn to him there. He invoked "the honour of your children" in urging Renée Pélagie to have her mother desist from reviving any distressing scenes, but he harped so insistently on this motive for avoiding a transfer that one can only suspect it was his own dignity that he was seeking to shield from further hurt. De Sade summed up at the end of his letter of 1 April:

"1 - I beg that I be given no sort of transfer at all, above all no escort by a [police] detachment. I would hand over ten thousand livres to avoid that...

"2 - I agree to remain here, and prefer to do so, throughout the time the punishment has still to run, however long that might be, ... however frightful this time here might be, ... always excepting my preference for my own lands where I am ready to go whenever required, even as an exile, whatever trouble that might cause me, but without escort..."

This self-absorbed outpouring - without so much as a word of acknowledgement of, let alone gratitude for, his wife's achievement in prising a transfer out of the royal administration - brought Renée Pélagie two days later to write in reply a letter remarkable for its sharp admonition and, as such, all too rare in her letters to her husband:

"Write a letter of thanks at once to Mme de Sorans, ... telling her ... that the behaviour which you are going to maintain will prove to her that you will deserve her kindness more and more, by fulfilling your duties as a father and as a good citizen, in restraining the disorder that reigns in your affairs. If the citadel of Montélimar is a rat-hole, as you say in your letter, that's too bad, but much less weighty than the sad perspective where we have been plunged up to today.

"So, stop, I beg of you, without further comment. What good are your useless writings? For delaying the pleasure of seeing you, blocking all the good I'm offering by this transfer. I tell you again, your schemes and your figurings have always been wrong, doubly wrong and more than absurd... For once in your life have confidence in those to whom you owe just that and get ready to leave. I have nothing more to say to you."

Excellente, madame la marquise!

The marquis, of course, found a way to mock the wagging finger. In the margins of his wife's admonitory letter, like a sulky schoolboy scribbling over his teacher's rebuke on his translation from a passage of Virgil, by "the sad perspective where we have been plunged", de Sade wrote, in his worst clever-dick of the Upper Fifth manner: "I would very much like someone to inform me how one is placed when one is plunged into a perspective. They have a lot of intelligence and they speak fine French, those who put together these letters!" The officer at Vincennes who tried to tell off Mr 6 had provoked a similar response.

The implication accompanying the protective pedantry was that Renée Pélagie was merely the clerk and signatory of a letter composed by someone else, and de Sade might have had a point for the letter represents a very rare and very considerable departure from her usual clement and appeasing style when writing to her husband. Remembering that the marquise still had as her guest in Paris Marie Dorothée de Rousset, I suggest that she, who had a brisk way with a pen at times, might have been behind it, especially in that, over her own signature, she added her terse two-penn'orth to the pro-Montélimar argument, also in the first week of April: "Your interest, your happiness, will depend on the way you behave at Montélimar... I think you will do well not to give out your name during your journey. The escort who will take you is, they say, a sensible and honest man. He will conduct himself with appropriate reserve... This is how it is and has to be, do you understand?..."

Under this sharp instruction, de Sade conceded ground, albeit with typical pleading that he was labouring against the foolishness of others and that circumstances were serving him badly. He told Renée Pélagie:

"When I re-read your last letter, I really believe you are made to imagine that I refuse. If you had a little reason and humanity, wouldn't you sense that I am like a blind man here, that I neither see nor understand anything, that being used for ten years to being deceived in everything by a monster who makes sport of all the most disgusting and lowest vices, such as lying, treachery, fraud, etc., etc., etc., etc., etc., etc., etc., I have to tremble at everything?

"If what you are doing is for my happiness, do you need to consult me or to believe what I say? Does one ask a sick man for his opinion about blood-letting, when it is necessary for his recuperation?... Get on with it and don't listen to me... That's my last word. I hand myself over..."

Fat chance. During the next few weeks, de Sade shilly-shallied elaborately in trying to modify or resist the transfer. He wanted ten days or a fortnight to finish making a fair copy of one of his plays. Then he remembered that an acquaintance of his had "a little country place near Montélimar. Arrange with him, so that I would not be a nuisance to him, for me to be locked up there, either on my own or with him when he might want to keep me company. There I would wait for you... At least no brouhaha here, no uproar... As for the journey, I would be on my word of honour about the date and the very minute laid down for me, on pain of ten years at Vincennes, and I swear to arrive via a route that would take me no nearer to Lyons than twenty leagues, if required..."

But he remained anxious to avoid the harassment and embarrassment of an escort. He drew up a memorandum to suggest a man on such a journey as his should be subject to, instead of an escort, the issue of a series of certificates by local authorities as he passed through their respective areas, this augmented, if required, by a supervising "spy" who would proceed at some distance behind the traveller. The "spy ... never speaks to him, and never gives the impression of knowing him or of being in his company."

This kind of quibbling might have seemed reasonable, from a proud nobleman who had a sore recollection of his treatment the last time he had moved across France in the hands of the authorities. However, much less likely to win concessions were his next offerings on the matter of the transfer. De Sade wrote to Gaufridy promising a hot reception if the latter were "insolent enough" to come to visit him at Montélimar. He complained to Le Noir, the police chief, that the whole business was a trap set by Mme de Montreuil and he made two requests - another "last word" on the matter - which were "to spend two weeks locked up at my wife's home in Paris to fit myself out with some clothes, to see about my health which is very bad, ... and to see my children[5]; to leave there with my wife and on my word of honour, ... for my lands, for as long as may be required.

"In return for this clause, if it is granted to me, I give to you, sir, and to all those who might wish to have it, my word of honour ... to be for the rest of my life toeing the line so closely, on the best of behaviour, ... the most exemplary in every way, matching even the angels. [I would] no long concern myself with anything but the happiness of my wife and my children, with putting right everything which depends on me, being my misfortunes and the breach made in my finances..."

What's more, he promised Le Noir "to sign and hand over to you an instrument whereby I would cede to Mme de Montreuil all rights to act on behalf of my children in whatever way she might deem appropriate, without my introducing the least obstacle, and even making over to her, so as to assist her in this regard, whatever portion of my goods she may find necessary, approving everything - education, employment, travels, marriage, etc., and making provision for all of this, even beyond the extent to which I might be contracted. To erase the past completely, without the least reminder of it escaping me, and agreeing to all that you may be pleased to add [that may be] necessary to secure the full satisfaction of all."

If de Sade had ended his latest "last word" there, he would not have done badly towards the police chief, but he was not one to know when to let well alone. There was a "second clause. If, instead of the above, the Montélimar idea is persisted with, ... I would go, I am ready to leave... But I would escape from there as soon as I could, whatever precautions were taken; I would get away to a foreign country. I have a prince ready to put me under his protection, make no mistake about that, sir; a monarch who does not have his subjects put away at the behest of who[res], and who does not put them into hands of pro[curesses], and from there I would drive a hole - and in the cruellest way - through all the schemes of Mme de Montreuil. I would bring her low through the public prints... I will reveal how and why some people are given credit in France, and that if I'm without it, that's through not

5 The apparent order of priorities is noteworthy.

having had a hundred thousand livres a year to buy off the fawners after righteousness, as did those to whom the State has sacrificed me, the State which in my misfortune has to serve as father to me, since I had used up my youth in serving it, the State which has paid me only in chains, and which has fed me only my tears.

"I would not leave it at that. For all the fine precautions taken, I would still have a sure way to remove all *standing* in society from my children ... and I would use it. I would leave them no more than the breath they had *from their mother*, and I would leave them with no recourse but to curse the execrable creature who had forced them to have a father no longer."

Then, as though he could not place himself at the disposition of Le Noir, even on the basis of two gentlemen negotiating, without having puffed himself up like a frightened frog into a position of assumed strength, de Sade turned on the smarm, to an extraordinary degree, even for him:

"Be so good as to reflect on all this, sir. When one is certain of achieving with a man all one wants by good means, why wish to use bad ones?... And are we in this world, sir, the one and the other, I to serve as fodder for a [moral] bankrupt discredited in the eyes of every thinking being, and you to offer me to her in this way? Make my happiness, sir; I put myself in your hands. Think about the internal satisfaction of a man full of virtues, such as yourself, in having wiped away the tears of an unfortunate man, in having put him where his duty and his family lie, in being sure that that entire family loves you, cherishes you, that it regards you as its father, that it appreciates, even more than the happiness it has rediscovered on earth, the delight of having it from you alone. It is the very person of God therefore that you will be representing in this world. Consider, sir, consider that, if the eternal Being should bestow on you by chance one of his functions, it is for you to imitate not his lightning-bolt but his kindnesses."

If the threats to escape were not enough to convince the police chief that de Sade should be held in nothing less than close confinement, then that final treacly evocation of the Almighty, from a man whom Le Noir knew to be a god-spurning libertine, ought to have done so.

De Sade maintained the uncertainty over the transfer - sometimes accepting and rejecting it in the space of one letter - over the next few weeks, notwithstanding a visit to him by Le Noir, which was supposed to clarify matters. One constant throughout the zig-zagging was his desire to turn himself from shuttlecock into battledore, to act upon the authorities instead of their continuing to act upon him. He reached again for Le Noir's heartstrings in order that Renée Pélagie be allowed to accompany him to any place on his own lands - for one thing, because only the marquise could mange his business affairs; for another, and more important: "*What if I were to have the misfortune to lose her, without having made any amends!* And that cruel idea plunged me ... into the deepest distractions of grief..." There was much more in the same vein. Even in an era given to self-dramatising purple prose on paper, de Sade took the genre to excess.

In the latter of half of April, the marquis summed up a letter to Rousset, written once he had his play complete, in this venomous way:

"... I ask with the most urgent insistence to have no escort whatsoever. If that is absolutely required, I shall leave, because I cannot resist force, but I will never pay for the escort and *I will take my revenge for this procedure in the worst ways I can imagine.*

"... I ask to go to my lands and not to Montélimar, and if they persist with the boring and ridiculous Montélimar project, I will stay in a room there all the time and never come out, and therefore no-one will ever have the sweet pleasure *of passing judgement on me*, and I swear I won't attend to my business for a moment, and will let Gaufridy know not to think of coming to see me because he would certainly be badly received..."

Heed the point about his denying anyone "the sweet pleasure *of passing judgement*" on him - come what may, no magistrate or ribald crowd was going to bring to bear on him, in an encounter he had not sought, sentences of a tribunal or epithets of the vulgar mob. He made no more revealing remark about himself.

In the letter to Rousset, he wound up with more flourishing of his "word of honour" that, if his requests were met, there was nothing he would not do "to give every kind of contentment and satisfaction; I end at last by swearing to you ... that they will have every reason ... *to regret it* if they refuse..."

By 1 May, the notion of a transfer to Montélimar had been dropped, de Sade having proved himself yet again his own worst enemy. Far from having any inkling of that, he fell to petty crowing and strutting: "What pleases me at least is that you will not have had the glory of congratulating yourselves on having made me your dupe, not for a single moment. Tell Lady de Montreuil from me that, when she wants to catch someone like me, she'll have to use a finer mesh, and that she should above all choose better than the perfect imbeciles who make up her advisers. It's not a job for ragamuffins of that calibre to try to pull the wool over my eyes and, locked up though I am, I'll run circles around them when I'm in the mood... It is false and doubly false that you had ever got Montélimar..."

"What's more," he added, in a letter to the marquise later in May, the supposed police chief who had visited him at Vincenees was "not Le Noir at all; it was someone hired by your mother... If he comes back, he'll see what sort of reception he'll get from me..."

CHAPTER 17: "TAKE THAT! TAKE THAT! TAKE THAT!"

The signature of the King of France was the only instrument which could let de Sade, prisoner until the royal administration decided otherwise, out of jail. Towards the end of 1783, the government, responding to an impetus among influential thinkers of the day that arbitrary imprisonment ought to be curbed, began a review of the list of prisoners held under *lettre de cachet.* Baron de Breteuil, newly appointed Minister of the Royal Household, divided them into three kinds. The first was of those too mentally deranged to be let out safely. The second - those "who, without having disturbed public order by offences, without having done anything which might expose them to the punishments prescribed by Law, are given to excesses of libertinage, debauchery and dissipation. One or two years of deprivation of liberty is a very heavy corrective: it must suffice to inspire sensible reflections and to bring about a return to good conduct in any soul not completely corrupted."

The minister suggested that, in such cases, it was not always necessary to go along with the wishes of the prisoners' families, which "sometimes exaggerate the wrongs of the subjects whose detention they have sought..." The third kind was "those who have committed acts of violence, of excess, of offences or crimes which impinge on public order and safety, and which Justice ... shall have punished..."

The baron, in a memorandum of March 1784 to the government's provincial representatives and to the police chief in Paris, went on: "For all these prisoners, ... it is fitting to have regard to their behaviour since they were detained; and, independently of other considerations which can ... put back or bring forward their freedom, it is correct to make that depend above all on the way in which they are behaving, on the greater or lesser change which is taking place in them, and on that which one would have to fear or to hope of them, once they were free again." The minister also stated that henceforth no-one's detention under royal order should be of unspecified duration.

He had visited Vincennes in December 1783, while the memorandum of the following March was in the making, to interview de Sade. There is no record of what took place. Even if the marquis were sweet as apple pie to the minister - on which we cannot rely - the latter had much evidence of the sour de Sade. Breteuil must have been aware of the ministerial dossier on the prisoner, which gave Rousset much disquiet when she secured access to it and which contained reports from Inspector Marais and other police officers long acquainted with the marquis and his predatory libertinage.

The minister and his advisers also had to give new weight, in considering the detention of Mr 6, to his conduct at Vincennes. We have seen what de Rougemont, the governor of the fortress, and the Count de Mirabeau thought of it. We have seen samples of the marquis's letters, forming official opinion of him as they passed through the hands of the police censors and these officers passed entire letters or summaries on to the ministry.

Renée Pélagie, ready as ever to grab at a straw of hope and make a brick of optimism out of it, reported to Rousset in February 1783 that, in a letter to her, her husband had spoken well of Le Noir and of the prison surgeon. "You can't imagine how much that commonplace remark has counted in his favour, so much so that I reckon that, if he kept that up in his writing, they would change the way they think about him." By September of that year, though, the marquise was telling her husband, regarding the police: "They've told me that you had just written another letter whose sentiments would prolong your detention as long as you were not changing your ways."

De Sade, in his letters from Vicennes, gave the absolutist government of a Catholic king a variety of material to take exception to. One favourite topic, touching his own condition closely, was that of crime and punishment:

"... the laws punish an infinity of crimes which carry no more than very slight consequences and which are no more ... than very slight impediments to the happiness of societies. On this side are for the most part those crimes which attack accepted morality, whereas, on the other hand, the laws lay down nothing against much more genuine crimes which have terrible consequences, such as greed, perfidy, ingratitude, deceit, etc. A man rapes a maiden: he is lost. Yes, here's a wrong, no doubt, but one whose consequences ... are no more than to have put that girl in a condition that she's bound to be in sooner or later. But a miser allows a numerous family to perish alongside him ... what a succession of horrors, what a complexity of crimes arises from that miser having refused to help! Yet what's done to him? *Nothing* ..."

The marquis pushed his critique further in the area of private and public morality:

"It's not the opinions or the vices of private individuals which damage the State; it's only the morals of men in public life which have an influence on general administration. Whether a private individual believes in God or not, whether he respects a whore or gives her a hundred kicks in the belly, each mode of behaviour neither upholds nor weakens the constitution of a State. But when the official who has to supervise the provisioning of a capital city doubles the price of foodstuffs because the suppliers have paid him off, ... when the superintendent of a full royal hospice allows the unfortunate servicemen whom the king installs there to die of hunger because he wants the feast day before Lent to be richly celebrated by his family, then from one end of the State to the other, the disturbance of that misappropriation is felt... While the embezzler triumphs, the other [the private individual] rots in a solitary cell. *A State turns its hand to its own ruin,* Chancellor Olivier used to say at the courts of justice under Henri II, *when it shall punish only the weak, and the wrongdoer enriched by his crimes shall find impunity through his gold.*

"Let the king correct the vices of government, let him put right its abuses, let him have the ministers who deceive him or rob him hung, before he curbs the opinions or tastes of his subjects! Once more, those tastes or opinions will not shake his throne, ... the falls from grace of those close to it will topple it sooner or later..."

This kind of sentiment from Cell No. 6 at Vincennes was all the more apt to cement the royal administration's view that de Sade was in the right place because the censors who read such stuff, passing between the marquis and his few correspondents, were also coming across a great deal of similar material from anonymous subversive pamphleteers writing and distributing in Paris and throughout France.

The marquis went further: "Let those who ought to set us an example do so, then we'll have no need of laws; let those whom chance ... raises to the highest jobs adopt irreproachable behaviour, then they'll assume the right to demand that ours be the same.

"It's the multiple abuses of the government which multiply the vices of private individuals. By what effrontery do those who are at the head of this government dare to punish such vices, dare to demand virtue, when they themselves are offering the example of every kind of depravity?

"By what right does that crowd of bloodsuckers, which quenches its thirst through the adversities of the people, which, through its vile monopolies, plunges that unfortunate class - whose only fault is to be weak and poor - into the cruel necessity of losing its honour or its life, further confining it in the latter case whereby it loses its life to its miserable condition or on a scaffold; by what right, I say, do such monsters demand virtue? What! as they're satisfying their greed, their avarice, their ambition, their pride, their rapacity and their lust, [as] I see them sacrificing without remorse millions of their king's subjects, [why] couldn't I, if that was to my taste, sacrifice just as they do?..."

Elsewhere in his letters from Vincennes, de Sade showed a lighter touch when putting his quill to a personal interpretation of public policy, especially the penal kind, albeit still recklessly skewering his old foes the police, in whose hands his fate partly lay. Take this, sent to his wife:

"They let everything go by, the police; it's only damage done to whores that they don't pass by. You can steep yourself in guilt through every possible abuse and infamy, as long as you respect whores' arses: that's what matters, and it's quite simple; whores pay and we don't pay, not us. Now I'll have to try, when I've got out, to get myself a little police protection; I've an arse just as a whore does, and I would be really glad to line up a bit of respect for it. I would let *Mr Fouloiseau*[1] see it - even kiss it, if he likes - and I am quite sure that, *warmed* by such a sight, he'll put my name right away into the list of the protected.

"They've told me that, on arriving in Paris, when you had me arrested [in February 1777], that's how you were taken so they could be *reassured* about you. First it was a matter of finding out if the said arse had been outraged at all - because the Présidente claimed that *I was an outrager of arses.* Therefore, she wanted *an expert examination.* They say she was on hand to point out thus: *Gentlemen, look here, he's a little devil and full of vices; he could well have --- who knows? He had so much libertinage in his head!...* So then you had your skirts hoisted. Magistrate Le Noir put on his glasses, Albaret held the candle, Le Noir's coppers took the notes. And a formal report was drawn up in these terms:

" '*Item,* we reported to the said Danemark Hotel, at the behest of *Marie-Magdeleine Cordier, wife to Montreuil,* we hoisted the skirts of

---

1 One of de Sade's names for his father-in-law, M de Montreuil, by which the marquis implied that the judge's title of nobility was more recent and less splendid than his own.

the said *Pélagie du Chauffour,* her daughter and, having carried out an examination with the requisite care, we recognised the said *du Chauffour* as being well and duly provided with two fine white buttocks, quite splendid and quite intact. We drew near - and had our clerks draw as near - to the said member. They, at risk and danger to themselves, effected an entry, parted, sniffed, probed - then, like ourselves, having observed nothing but healthy parts, we have delivered this present act to stand in proper form, setting forth, by reason of the said display, that the said *Pélagie du Chauffour* be taken into the hands of the Court and held henceforth under our puissant protection.

" '*Signed:* Jean Baptiste Le Noir, Paris nightowl, and born-protector of the brothels of the capital and its surroundings...'

"... I give your buttocks a big kiss and I'm going - the devil take me if I don't - to give myself one off the wrist in their honour! Don't go and tell the Présidente ... for she's a good Jansenist who doesn't like a woman to be *given a bit of Greek*[2]. She claims that M Cordier[3] has never pinned her down except by *the vessel of procreation,* and that whoever strays *from the vessel* must go and burn in hell. And I who was brought up by the Jesuits[4], I whom Father Sanchez taught that one ought to *swim in the void* as little as one could because, according to Descartes, *nature abhors a void,* I cannot agree with *mother* Cordier. But you are a philosopher; you have a very good knack when it comes to *taking it the wrong way,* knowing the drill, with a squeeze when taking it the wrong way and with heat in the *rectum,* which makes me agree very strongly with you.

"I am very much yours, and that's the truth..."

This inventive and satirical letter carries a frolicsome lewdness such as can pass between husband and wife where he, at least, feels free to write or speak it, whether or not she feels free to read or hear it. There is no indication that the marquise penned or voiced such sentiments to the marquis or anyone else. However, Pauvert believes this letter did not reach Renée Pélagie. The police, and government officials, who are likely to have read it, might have taken it as cause for nothing more than a guffaw or two as it was passed around the office, although one

---

2 De Sade wrote: *qui n'aime pas qu'on molinise une femme*. Pauvert identifies *molinise* as of de Sade's coinage, referring to a certain Molina of whom we know little. I am offering a rough English equivalent, too modern perhaps but comprehensible in much of the anglophone world.

3 One of M de Montreuil's surnames.

4 Jesuit fathers, in the France of de Sade's time, were reputed to be inclined to sodomy.

should never take the sense of humour of the police for granted, especially when one of its own is being guyed. Be that as it may, it is unlikely that the following, unleavened by the knockabout comic vein that de Sade sometimes found, went down well:

"It does not befit the Présidente de Montreuil - cousin, niece, parent, goddaughter ... to every dirty little bankrupt from Cádiz to Paris; the Présidente de Montreuil, niece of a rogue thrown out of the Invalides ... because of his thefts and frauds; the Présidente de Montreuil, who has in her husband's family a grand-father hung in the Place de Grève; the Présidente de Montreuil, who has given her husband seven or eight bastards and who has put all her daughters to whoring; it does not befit her to seek to vex, punish or quell the defects of temperament which one cannot control and which have never done harm to anyone. It does not befit *Dom Sartinos*[5], found one fine morning in Paris with no sign of where he came from, ... a bit like those poisoned toadstools that you find all of a sudden in the corner of a wood; Dom S[arti]nos, who was found at last to be the issue, on the wrong side of the blanket, of the Reverend Father Torquemada and of a Jewess seduced by the former in the jails of the Inquisition in Madrid which he used to run; Dom S[arti]nos, who has built up his fortune in France only by sacrificing people as cannibals do...

"It's not ... for that little bastard Rougemont, for that execration of vice personified, for that scum in doublet and hose who, on the one hand, prostitutes his wife so as to get prisoners and, on the other, makes them die of hunger so as to have a bit more money to pay the disgraceful lackeys in his debauchery; for a clown who, all said, without the whims of Luck and the pleasure she takes in casting down those who ought to be raised and in raising those who are made only to grovel, who without that, I say, perhaps would be more than happy to be my scullery boy if we were all in the places for which heaven marked us at birth; it's not for a beggar of this calibre to seek to set himself up as censor of vices, and of the very vices which he has to an even more odious degree, because ... one becomes all the more contemptible and all the more ridiculous when one seeks in others to interfere with that which one has oneself only a thousand times more so; it is not for the halt to mock the lame, nor for the blind to seek to lead the one-eyed..."

---

5 A transparent iberianisation of the name of Sartine, police chief in Paris before Le Noir.

At his most furious, on the topic of his mother-in-law, de Sade clouded his bile to rare depths, as in February 1783: "... here's the one hundred and eleventh torture that I am inventing for her. This morning, in my suffering, I watched her skinned alive, dragged over spikes and then thrown into a vat of vinegar. And I was telling her:

" 'Execrable creature, take that, for having sold your son-in-law to hangmen!

" 'Take that, for having acted as procuress for your two daughters!

" 'Take that, for having ruined and dishonoured your son-in-law!

" 'Take that, for having made him hate the children for whose sake you're sacrificing him!

" 'Take that, for having made him lose the best years of his life, when he was looking to you only to save him after his hearing in court!

" 'Take that, for having preferred to him your daughter's vile and detestable embryos!

" 'Take that, for all the words you have been piling onto him for thirteen years, so as to make him pay for your stupidities!'

"And I was increasing her torments, and I was insulting her in her pain, and I was forgetting my own..."

In assessing the marquis's behaviour at Vincennes, and what they might have to hope or fear from him if he were released, Louis XVI's officials would have been aware of his views, not only on his own misdemeanours, public administration, the police and his mother-in-law, but also on religion. Remember we are in France in the 1780s, and public professions of atheism are quite unacceptable.

De Sade, in November 1783, was writing thus on the topic of d'Holbach's *System of Nature,* "the basis of my philosophy, and I'm a devotee of it even if that meant *martyrdom*":

"... a golden book ..., a book which ought to be in all the libraries, a book which undermines and destroys for ever the most dangerous and the most odious of all idle fancies, those which above all have made blood pour onto the ground and which the entire universe ought to unite to overthrow and to crush all life from, if the individuals who make up this universe had the least conception of their [potential] happiness and tranquillity. For myself, I swear that I am a world away from being able to understand what possesses those people who still hold to them [the idle fancies], and I am very much of the opinion that they cannot really believe in them. These people for whom the slightest application of intelligence is impossible, they're imbeciles and they don't want, or can't take the trouble, to look deeply into anything. For it's quite certain that theism cannot stand up for a moment to any examination, and one would need to have omitted to study even the simplest operation of nature not to recognise that it acts alone and without any guiding hand, and that this guiding hand, which explains nothing and rather itself requires explanation, is just the *nec plus ultra* of ignorance."

Two months earlier, the atheist in No. 6 had made his views even clearer: "By all that I hold most sacred, I will never believe the teachings of the devotees of a god who think they are allowed to offend the created in order to honour the creator. Build your impious chapels, worship your idols, detestable pagans... with all that, you are breaking the most sacred laws of nature ... Remember that you are forcing me only into hatred and contempt for you..."

The recipient of the bulk of de Sade's letters, on religion as on all other topics, was his wife, who was used to his godlessness and did not let it deflect her from making clear, in her letters to him, her adherence to the Catholic Church. However, her customary joyful reference to Easter evoked from Vincennes, in the spring of 1783, this pithy combination of the marquis's atheism, loathing for his in-laws and penchant for masturbation:

"Go and take a big bite out of your footling Good Lord and murder your parents. Me, I'm going to w[ank] my c[ock], and I would say, I assure you, that afterwards I'll have done a lot less harm than you have."

What harm - or good - might he do if let out of prison? All the traits of the Marquis de Sade might yet not trouble the authorities if he were back on his estates in Provence, especially if he were kept short of cash. After all, the railing against God, the king's government, accepted morality and his relatives was confined to private correspondence, read only by a few of his close associates and by a few policemen and ministerial officials, all of whom were not unfamiliar with such sentiments, certainly not after they had been on the receiving end of de Sade's letters for a few months.

However, there were indications from Cell No. 6 that the occupant would not limit himself to letters within his own circle. For instance, from January 1783: "I swear to [Mme de Montreuil] ... that I would have poisoned myself three years ago, if I didn't have as my sole consolation the prospect of proving to her, *by doing a thousand times worse than I have done already*, that her means of trying to correct me are as daft as she and her advisers are monstrous."

Governments are on the alert for private disaffection spilling into public ferment. In the France of the day, this meant a ceaseless hunt for clandestinely published and circulated books and pamphlets. As far back as 1773, when de Sade was held at Miolans in Savoy, the Paris police were concerned, on behalf of Mme de Montreuil and the French administration, lest he gain access to a printer through whom he might publish scandalous and scurrilous material. More than once, the marquis noted in letters and manuscripts remarks on the lines of: "Hold on to that sentence against the day that I can have it published."

In the spring of 1781, while the Montélimar affair was under way, the marquis spelled out to Le Noir that he would be a danger to his mother-in-law: "I will bring her down via the public prints, which will contain such patent truths that no-one will be able to cast doubt on them..." The police and the royal ministers would have needed little imagination to decide that there was a clear and present danger that de Sade, fluent and persuasive to a fault, would also use publishers to call down fire on a much larger target than the Présidente de Montreuil, drawing on such drafts as this part of a letter of May 1779:

"During the time that's wasting, I divert myself in here by making plans. I have some rare ones... Paper, ink and a few rascals in my pay - that's all I need. I won't need any police or ministry ... A few memories, a little money, and the printers of the Hague. Oh! what delights! The pleasure that I promise myself from that sweetens all my bitter troubles. I feel not a moment's more sorrow once I start thinking of taking my revenge..."

Then, in December that year: "Oh! I'll lay them bare, all the horrors, all the foul webs woven, all the conspiracies driven by greed and rapacity. I know them all now, I've learned them at my own expense: All France must know about them too."

By October 1781, de Sade's pride had led him to decide that his special troubles entitled him to a double dispensation: "If I were undergoing an ordinary punishment, then my character and my conduct could be subjected to examination, but what is being done to me has never been done to anyone. No punishment meted out to any of the guilty men of our time has come anywhere near mine. So I must be allowed to complain and to avenge myself in any way I can..."

"... These tyrants at least should have the art of better choosing their victims. It's not on those who know them deeply, it's not on those whose penetrating insights are going to bore as far as their secret thoughts, that they ought to be splattering their poison. Such hands, as soon as they are released from their fetters, are going to tear off the blindfold of illusion, and the idol, once laid bare by those hands, will offer the gaze of the enlightened multitude only the bestial and disgusting matter that comprises it..."

This strong hint - that an aristocrat who had turned against at least some elements in the social hierarchy of the time in France would be especially dangerous to them because he was an insider who knew secrets not available lower in the social order - would hardly have been missed by the censors.

De Sade, in a letter of 1783, saved Breteuil's civil servants at the Ministry of the Royal Household the trouble of devising a summing-up sentence on Mr 6: "... as for my vices: imperious, choleric, quick-tempered - extreme in all things - of such an unbuttoned imagination regarding morality that it has had no equal, atheist to the point of fanaticism; in a few words there you have me, and what's more you must kill me or take me as I am, for I'm not going to change."

Pauvert emphasises his view that de Sade wanted to think that his term in prison was fixed and so his conduct there could change nothing, while those outside concerned with him were waiting for him to mend his ways before he could be released.

This makes sense, but it is also important to emphasise how intensively de Sade's mind squirmed under the limitations of circumstances whereby he was much more impinged upon than impinging. The reckless letters were essential to him as an expression of his need to continue, despite the confines of Cell No. 6 and the pettifoggery of the prison regime, to have an impact - somewhere, somehow, even by savouring fantasies of what he might do. While the marquise, Rousset and a few others were still prepared to correspond with him, he could still believe he was having an effect - on someone. He would even prefer, by his letters and other kicking against the pricks, to lower official opinion of him than to desist and admit that he was being moulded by another will.

As Pauvert points out, de Sade referred in his letters from Vincennes to his view that his term in jail must be fixed, but he also acknowledged the repeated warnings from Renée Pélagie and Marie Dorothée that his unbridled letters and violent behaviour were serving him badly. Towards the end of one epistle in 1783, he banged his stubborn head fretfully and frankly against the plain fact of his life as a prisoner under royal order: "Well, there you have a letter which, I have no doubt, is going to *prolong* my detention still further, eh? So you will have to tell these *prolongers* that their prolongation is an utter waste of effort, for if they leave me here ten years, they will not fetch me away any better than I am, believe me..."

The marquise preferred to believe him when, now and again, "he says that, if he were let out, he would behave well. The great sorrow is that they don't want to put him to the test..."

Indeed not - when visiting officials in the summer of 1781, Renée Pélagie tried, three years after her husband's arrival at Vincennes, "to tell them that incarceration was warping his personality; they replied that, when a [prisoner's] personality was going to be warped, that becomes evident in the first two years; besides, the rest of his letters were full of intelligence, of discrimination, and that his was a case of pure maliciousness."

Or, as Miss de Rousset, the recipient of that letter, had reported, back in 1778, the official line on the Marquis de Sade was: "He says stupid things; if he were at liberty, he would do them."

CHAPTER 18: BADINAGE AND BITTERNESS

Marie Dorothée de Rousset, as reported above, gave of her best efforts in the campaign to have de Sade released from Vincennes. These included simple and direct advice to the prisoner that he should use much more circumspection with regard to where the power to shape his future lay, and should be a great deal readier to adapt his writings and behaviour accordingly. Towards the end of 1778 - when she was newly arrived in Paris, visiting Mme de Montreuil and generally familiarising herself with the Sadeian situation - Rousset wrote to the marquis:

"You have been too abrasive with Mr Boucher, first assistant to the police chief [1]... He is still so upset about it that, during a first visit I made to him, he made clear to me his annoyance on this score. I think he's very straightforward; and even if he weren't, the knowledge that you need him ought to be enough to make you handle him carefully... Don't forget that it's necessary for you to weigh your words in your letters and your talk, keeping them on the straight and narrow of the most sane and sensible thinking."

One can imagine the hollow laughter from Mr Boucher's clerks on comparing that wise paragraph with the intemperate bile in fact pouring out of Cell No. 6. For the time being, though, Rousset kept her hopes bright, and mixed cool advice with warm encouragement. In November 1778, she told the prisoner:

"Don't let this despair ever get anywhere near your heart, understand?... Swear this to me on all that's most sacred. If you refuse me that, you are my friend no more and I abandon you. I very much want to know about your moments of discouragement and boredom. Be sure that we have ours too. The hope of forgetting them - you in a conjugal embrace, I in the charm of sympathy and friendship - sustains me and gives me courage..."

Rousset's sympathy and advice for de Sade had no more than a marginal and temporary effect on him. Her intelligence saw to the core

---

1 The officer whose department supervised prisoners' correspondence.

of the difficulty. In May 1779, for the benefit of Gothon Duffé, holding the château back at la Coste, the transplanted housekeeper reported:

"If matters are not going any faster, mademoiselle, it really isn't my fault. Unfortunately, the person[2] is wrong-headed, so wrong-headed. I could sweat myself clean away to nothing without seeing an end to it all. The person who is most concerned, far from supporting me, spoils everything by one rash move after another. Having written to me with a heap of fooleries (not to mention the ones sent to his wife - those are commonplace), he has tried to compromise me badly by revealing to the royal ministers that I was writing to him and that I was giving him confidential advice. I have received reproaches [from official quarters] about it. I haven't been able to deny it. They have excused me and let me off because of the honesty and motives of my heart. 'You see,' they've told me, 'how wrong-headed he is; you ... only write to him pleasant, helpful and diverting things, which he nearly always takes the wrong way. Oh! he is in the right place; to give him his freedom, that's to seek to expose him to new upsets. If there has to be a time in his life when he can't help making a nuisance of himself, it's just as well that this is happening now, when we're keeping a close eye on him; ... besides, you've written to him on the quiet, we know that. What good does it do him? None.' "

It was possible to smuggle letters in and out of Vincennes, hidden in consignments of food, books and clothing, for instance. It was not beyond the police, having discovered and read them, to put them back in their hiding place to see whether the clandestine correspondence might develop into a conspiracy much more worth pouncing on than the transparent innocence of Rousset's aid and comfort to the marquis.

How had she become involved? It is not clear whether de Sade and Rousset had met before the summer of 1778, when he arrived at La Coste out of the blue on the morning after his escape from the custody of Inspector Marais at Valence. In any event, she and Gothon Duffé were running the château during the lord and master's brief spell at liberty in the sun. In May 1779, the marquis recalled in prison, in a letter to her, one of their last conversations during the previous August in Provence. They had sat on "our bench" in the grounds of the manor and he had spoken of himself to his sympathetic housekeeper. When she had got back there, de Sade went on in his letter, she was to "go

2 In Cell No. 6, of course.

into the little green salon and say: 'My table was there, where I wrote all the letters ... and he sat in that chair dictating...' You will imagine that you can see me but it will be no more than your shadow, you will imagine that you can hear me but it will be no more than the speaking of your heart." About the time he was writing that piece of casting of more spells that bind, he received a portrait of himself drawn by Rousset - or "the saint", as he called her from Vincennes when well-disposed towards her:

"This portrait the saint has done is special... She can do anything with those five fingers of hers. At la Coste there was only one thing I wanted her to do with those very fingers, but she would not... Tell her ... I will keep the portrait as long as I live..."

From the remark about how Rousset insisted on not using her five fingers at la Coste, one can deduce that she was not available to de Sade for any sexual service. Even so, de Sade, wanting as ever to be making a sexual impression, especially after more than a year incarcerated at Vincennes and Aix, could have been expected to try to engage Rousset in this way. By her own acknowledgement, she was thin and plain. There is no evidence of a lover in her life - albeit there are few documents about her apart from those concerned also with de Sade - and abundant indications of her capacity to give her tender heart and perceptive mind to a cause. She recognised that trying to have the marquis removed from imprisonment under royal order was a large and complicated task, though the degree of difficulty therein rocked her back on her heels once she had grappled with the job for a few months.

We do not know just what de Sade told his housekeeper on "our bench". What the marquis seems to have regarded as full and fearless revelation of himself might well have added up to nothing more than another self-serving, blame-dodging justification, in which a dash of unwillingness to give material to someone who might bear witness against him one day was mixed with a full measure of flamboyant promises, on his oft-proffered word of honour, that he had done little more by way of libertinage than tan a few arses - the whole being as wordy as it was worthless. Whatever Rousset heard at la Coste, no doubt her flexible intelligence overcame any feeling of shock she might have felt, and no doubt she made an impression on de Sade as a valuable *confidante*. De Sade's forty days of liberty at la Coste in high-summer of 1778 were not enough for his housekeeper to do more than start to learn what went on in his mind, before Inspector Marais and his men put an end to their face-to-face conversations. Rousset and the marquis never saw each other again.

Later, when he was back at Vincennes, there followed indications of what Rousset might have become for de Sade. There was not only her diligent effort to lobby on his behalf in high places, not only her pointed advice and sympathetic rallying of his spirits, but also the sort of deft and deflationary needling and teasing that one's most perceptive and witty friends provide. In the sun and air of Provence, Rousset might have worked some alteration in him; through the walls of a prison, her chances of doing so were much reduced.

For one thing, Mr 6 was alone, chewing angrily on the discomforts and irritations of prison life, fretting bitterly at the uncertainty over the length of his incarceration - this was no ground in which to grow a friendship to dispel such bile as his. For another, the prisoner came to believe, by the spring of 1779. that he had been wantonly misled by his wife and by Rousset who, in their optimism of the previous autumn, had been writing to him of their confidence that he would spend no more than one winter at Vincennes. Their remarks in this regard were not well-founded and de Sade had a point when he complained that he should not have been offered such cause for hope, which he had seized as avidly as any prisoner held *sine die*, until there were firm grounds. Then again, de Sade might have reflected that his small team of supporters, inexperienced in the ways of lobbying in the offices and salons of the royal administration and of those close to it, could be forgiven for letting their wish for his release distort their reports to him about his prospects. However, forgiveness was no forte of the self-absorbed and choleric marquis, in jail or out.

Rousset's teasing of him was light and simple, as in early December 1778: "A pleasure, Sir, to have your news. In between our sweethearts and the pleasure of good company, we do you the honour of thinking about you from time to time..." And, all in the one letter, she could sharpen her tone just a little in order to administer an oblique and singular telling-off: "... There are no more kisses for you, since you've refused them. Another fellow is learning to accept them and he says: I'm getting to like them! Goodbye, goodbye, I might write on someone's wormy head that I love you. One can confess that to you without peril, am I right?"

No, she was not. Marie Dorothée did not understand the danger in this sort of banter with de Sade. It suggested, albeit in fun, that Mr 6 might not have the total attention of the two women in the convent apartment. Such news about his main supporters is apt to perturb any prisoner; for de Sade, who lived by the rapt responses of others to his actions and his very existence, it would cut deeply. He grumbled suspiciously in letters to his wife and ignored, it seems, Rousset in his correspondence. She complained: "For what reason are you not on speaking terms with me, Sir... You know that one has nothing to hide from one's friends... Vincennes is souring you in a cruel way. Our lessons, our resolutions, are going to the devil. It is always worth recalling them, when all the vivacity of friendship is entreating you and is sighing - for what? For the honour of receiving your news..."

On 26 December, she was sharper: "You're enough to destroy the patience of a Capuchin monk made of wood with your whims and your bad temper! Women must be daft to attach themselves to a sourpuss like you. We fly into action at the first sign of whatever might please you. Everything we do is with the best of intentions. The gentleman is never content."

Next day, though, Renée Pélagie received a bleak letter from the marquis, which Marie Dorothée acknowledged as having dispelled badinage: "Your wretched letter has brought home to me all your sadness. If I wanted to be down in the dumps, perhaps I would be even further down than you. My sensitivity and my heart are being put under too heavy a load..."

On 29 December, Rousset had recovered her broader view of the marquis and herself: "Two days of rest have taken away my bile and my bad temper... In general, our sex is more humane, more generous: one must love you and pity you, despite what comes of it...

"... You have always given me credit for a great deal of sensitivity; for sure you will never plumb the depth of it. My vivacity would be as silly as yours if I didn't rein it in but, as I have told myself once and for all that reason must prevail above everything, I care little about being pretty or plain... You who always want to be the pretty boy, you fling your fire all around you. From time to time, we see that some get singed. As for me, who keeps it close, I am very much afraid that it might stifle me..."

There we have, in the contrasted pair of observations, an insight into her own character and a valuable one into that of de Sade. Rousset's letters offer some of the most perceptive views of the marquis available. One wishes she could have remained for longer as observer and recorder beside the Sadeian way, but there were overwhelming reasons why she could not. It is easy to understand that his continued incarceration, and the abiding unwillingness of the royal administration to end it, combined to wear away hope of progress in both master and housekeeper. Less apparent, but apt to burn out their relationship, was the touch of sexual fever in it. This by no means overwhelmed reason, which Marie Dorothée set above all else, but it arose in part from deprivation and solitude - either side of the fortress walls - rather than wholly from a sociable generosity. Here is Rousset, still in the closing days of 1778:

"My jokes haven't pleased you! You don't reply to them. But do me the honour of telling me, Mr Thorny Branch, if the reservation is applied to my letter as a whole... Ah! you want seriousness! You touch on my strong point... It's good to learn your preference, you not having expressed it sooner!... Quite seriously, you need have no cause for jealousy over the guitar teacher. This is a proper sort of chap, with sensible attitudes, full of virtues, more good-hearted than quick-witted, a good friend, amusing; we don't see him often because his commitments don't let him visit. I asked him to give a few lessons[3] to pass the time. While busy with writing or something else, I have the pleasure of hearing Madame at her scales; I know that at least she isn't getting bored... I wanted to test to see whether you were the jealous kind. Since you are, I'll keep myself well in check as far as that's concerned..."

She kept her word to steer clear of remarks that might arouse his jealousy of his wife, but she regarded her own relations with the prisoner as out of those bounds. In the same letter:

"But may Heaven keep you from ever having the least little hankering after me! I would throw you to every devil there is. You would be in no danger, eh? You would be pleased with yourself over it? Well now, you would be deceiving yourself. I warn you to keep your guard up. Plain is cleverer that pretty. You have always known me as a grumbler, endlessly moralising, only laughing when you're not near. Now, on the other side of the picture, you'll find a sweeter countenance by no means entirely ill-favoured, and a certain cheeky style which just slays the men before they know it. You'll fall for it, right into my traps!..."

3 To the marquise only, it seems.

Plain may be cleverer, but pretty may not need to be. Marie Dorothée knew that too. A few days later, in the second week of 1779, she commented on her efforts to have de Sade released from prison: "If I had been a pretty and obliging Parisian woman, I would have succeeded with time in hand! I'm plain, I have only good reasons to offer. Ha, that's not worth a damn!"

Even so, a week later, she was prepared to be remain thoughtful, reporting to Vincennes on her encounter with a French translation of *Clarissa*, the English novel by Samuel Richardson:

"I would have detested men, if I had gone on reading. Clarissa's tender and amicable character delighted me enormously. It was the first time in my life that I have congratulated myself on being a woman. We have the advantage of being more pleasant, more honest. We are often your dupes... If women had the courage to answer with total contempt ... and to learn from that, you would be very much the dupes in your turn... Women in general are straightforward. Should each of you men have one? Which one of you would complain about that?... Huh! I'm deceiving myself; you're consistent. 'I've found out enough about women, I've had every kind,' you say, 'so I don't want them any more...' Think about whether, considering that attitude, you want to hazard yourself in a game with me. Be sure that you will end up sorrowing...

"... Yes, we all have a weak point, but you have one too. Which will be the more skilful so as to overcome the other?... Don't flatter yourself that you have all the talent in this field. The women you've had loved and cherished your passions and your money. With Saint Rousset, there's nothing to bite on! So what will you take hold of her for?... Believe you me, stay out of the lists, there's still time! I seem to see Tantalus by the river; you aren't going to drink from it, I promise you! What confusion for a man who would like *frotittouneo*..." (I admit defeat in trying to find an English equivalent for this item of Provençal slang - as it seems to be, and something lewd at that - which Rousset, who was fluent in the dialect of her home region, inserted into her challenge to de Sade, who had a certain competence in the tongue, though he excused his errors in it by claiming that he "had never spoken it except with the peasants.")

In French and in Provençal, the courtly epistles to Vincennes continued, as on 24 April:

"Do you want me for your lover; it's necessary to find out whether your wife would allow it. What good would it do me if you were smiling on me while she was scowling at me. Get her promise in advance so that this won't upset her, and then we will arrange matters quite well by ourselves... But let me have a word or two as to what use to me such a lover would be, you being far away. Look, when I have a lover, I want him with me all the time because he has to be the focus of all my soul's resources. I watch him, I admire him, I give him thousands of big kisses every day and, even after my tenderness has laid these baubles before him, I believe I've done nothing. This is but a tiny sample of what is going on in my thoughts; I don't want to tell you everything. What's the point of stirring up the head of a poor prisoner who has no-one to console him or to scratch his itch?... I feel very sorry for you, but there it is. You'll not be young much longer..."

Rousset did not end her letter without putting some ointment on the wound left by that barb, which must have seemed in Cell No. 6 to be too true to be funny. She added, about her future letters:

"... in patois I'll be telling you: 'My dear de Sade, delight of my soul, I'm dying for lack of seeing you. When will I be able to sit on your knee, put my arm around your neck, to embrace you just as I like, to say lots of sweet nothings into your ear' - and if you pretend not to hear, my heart against yours will be enough to let you feel that I have a tender and refined soul which will surely make yours open. I think that little declaration is every bit as good as the kindnesses you tell me about. Indeed, I have felt it keenly. The title of good friend is due to me; I will never renounce it..."

The letter ends: "Goodbye, pretty face and better heart, I embrace you in the fashion and in the way you'll like best. You make me quite angry sometimes, but even so I love you in a fashion that can't be put in words..."

On 7 May, Rousset was responding to some point in a letter from de Sade, since lost, and letting the teasing run hotter: "I was far from intending to make you have a disturbed night. I was intending to make you laugh, not imagining that a prisoner might be so inflammable by nature. Let me just try to put right the wrong I have done you. I protest strongly that I have not committed, nor caused you to commit, a venial sin...

"... It is possible that I might have provoked in you what's goading you. All that was needed was to come and find me, I would have made a little space for you alongside me, you would have found that I know how to cure the ills of your kind; I would first have checked to see whether the fever was high; if I had reckoned that you needed to sweat, then I would have put it [*sic*] in a narrow and hot little place which assuredly would not have done any harm..."

After the hot place, the cooling hand: "... My goodness, your head is aching... I would like to touch it to know whether it's very hot. Listen: perhaps you put too many things into it, that might well be why it feels so heavy to you; your situation has something to do with that, but your daydreams make it worse..."

Marie Dorothée was bright, educated, a commoner, short of money, without position in society beyond the very low one of friend and companion to the wife of a disgraced marquis. She was in Paris with only one task, the discouraging and ill-rewarded one of pressing for the *lettre de cachet* against the marquis to be revoked. She was not desired and, having reached her mid-thirties, was unlikely to be. In view of all this, she was apt to be unable to find a role except in service. When her duties as housekeeper at la Coste were changed all of a sudden into those of supporter and fellow lobbyist with Renée Pélagie in Paris, Rousset was still, albeit informally, in the service of her master and mistress, although such terms do not seem to have been used among the three of them. It is no surprise, then, that she spent many hours at the writing desk, and that her pen ran to badinage of an amatory, even sexual, kind directed at the object of her engagement in Paris.

It is no surprise that this badinage became feverish at times. De Sade may well have been the only person outside her family to use an unrestrained vocabulary to address Rousset about the life of the emotions; her intelligence told her that failure to respond would be foolish weakness and her excitement at this novelty bursting into her experience further directed her to answer him in kind - and perhaps to excess.

In the circumstances, it became all the more probable as time passed that Rousset's teasing and banter would never be challenged to move from pen and paper to looks and touches. She was the prime promoter of his release and therefore well placed to understand that she was trying to move a great mountain of opposition. Hence she might have played at pushing the banter and sexual allusions further, in the knowledge, perhaps hazily perceived, that the walls of Vincennes were going to protect her from ever having to face a reckoning in the shape of the object himself. Also, it is likely that Marie Dorothée took pleasure in needling the high and mighty marquis, lord of estates, rake and man of letters; that she enjoyed duelling with him on equal terms - quills at a distance specified by royal order. How else would the country spinster get a chance to give her supple wit and well-digested learning such an outing? For all that, the correspondence and the feelings that both parties were putting into it carried more than a hint of the masturbatory - one hand on the pen, the other straying beneath the desk - as is often the case with de Sade. In a letter of the summer of 1779, he was as clear as could be about the relief he would seek from various stimuli arriving in Cell No. 6:

"Now, tell me, sweetheart, so you want to know what was the second effect?[4] Listen carefully to me: when a cannon is over-loaded, what must be done to free it - there has to be a discharge... Right, you have read it, the second effect... When I am here all alone, I get irritated when I feel myself burning like the devil in hell with nothing to soothe me a little. Ah! there it is, goodbye my beauty, it's time for me to go to bed... Ah, away with you, those two thousand kisses of yours are all very well; what do you think I'm going to do with all those when I can't give back even one? Good night, get along, there's going to be the devil to pay for having talked a bit more silly nonsense with you. I can't do any more of that now, what's the use?... Look, my angel, you know what the Carthusians do, well I'm going to do the same and it'll be on your account. Goodbye."

About the same date, de Sade had been in his more usual, nastier, vein to his wife: "Your Saint is mad, tell her so from me. I don't know how anyone can manage to have a temperament as chirpy and as mad as that all the time..."

This was one item in such an acrimonious flurry of correspondence about this time that Marie Dorothée called a halt: "Now, Sir, let's not write to each other any more. It is not worthwhile our writing harsh words to each other - that embitters the heart too much; I don't want to hate anyone. You'll forget me easily, won't you, without much trouble? For my part, I'm going to arrange to outdo you in that..."

After that, no more badinage, no more fever heat.

* * *

4 Of a letter from her to him.

Whether or not Marie Dorothée could see more clearly for having cleared her head of "love in a fashion that can't be put into words", by October 1780 she was reporting to Gaufridy: "Our man is still behaving more or less in the same way - badly, that is. This amends the sensitivity of my heart towards him and towards his situation which, although sad, is better for him perhaps than any other..."

Besides, the two women in the little apartment were not as one, after they had spent some months living together and working towards the same goal. In October, Rousset told the lawyer at Apt: "The person in question here is still deluding herself... She has seen and understood; I have given her, and gone though with her, the most precise and sensible thoughts on the matter. Then she closes her mind to it all so tightly that she says to me every day and with complete *reasonableness*: 'When M de Sade is out we'll do this, we'll say that, etc.' Every plan more crazy than the next! I laugh or I shrug my shoulders; sometimes I sing; she looks at me and falls asleep out of vexation... Later, we work at our bits of clothes, we eat, go to bed..."

Besides, while there was heat and wit flowing between Marie Dorothée and the marquis, Renée Pélagie had not been altogether indifferent. She wrote to her husband:

"They're quite something the little outbursts that the Saint sends you.[5] This language[6] drives me mad because I feel that I will never get near what you can do. But what do you think of her sanctity? She's struggling to break its bonds and is telling you a pretty thing or two! Isn't she trying to pull the rug from under me? Careful now, my good little folk, I am against this with all my being; I'll put obstacles in your way so that you go no further than I allow. I read your letter easily enough [although it was in Provençal], but for a few words. It's well put together to make one laugh. Go on amusing yourselves like this, you two, as long as you never go too far."

The various frustrations and difficulties brought Marie Dorothée, in October 1780, to tell Gaufridy that the marquise had caused her "a thousand-and-one million vexations which she could have spared me if she had had better manners, more loftiness of spirit or, to put it briefly, those natural and refined feelings which breeding provides and which virtue and a sense of justice sustain throughout one's life.

---

5 The marquise had not been above riffling through her guest's letters to her husband when she thought Rousset was not looking, so the housekeeper told de Sade.

6 The passages in Provençal.

"All in all, my dear friend, there are individuals so weird in the way they carry on that they inspire more pity than anger. This one[7] is among them; I have closely examined and dissected the subject. I am no longer surprised that the unfortunate fellow [the marquis] has done so many foolish things; he lacked a person with a bit of backbone; she herself has no more than ... threads ... spun by spiders..."

By January next, 1781, Marie Dorothée was opining to Gaufridy: "My friend, those two heads taken together aren't worth that of a twelve-year-old schoolboy."

Also, being a housekeeper and from a home which would not have been greatly prosperous, Rousset brought insight to the financial costs of maintaining the demanding prisoner in Cell No. 6. She informed Gaufridy:

"The wild notions of M. de S. are going beyond anything. The other day we reckoned roughly, very roughly, that his personal requisites, sweets, candles, medical bills, come to more than two thousand livres a year. He has a mania for buying and hiring books; the three hundred livres that you were told to charge to Chauvin will be for a subscription to the works of Voltaire which are going to be coming out forever..."

Pauvert points out that Renée Pélagie, having moved in September 1781 to lodgings in the Convent of St Aure in Paris, was paying 200 livres a year in rent and 300 livres a year for food, with her servants La Jeunesse and a maid having a room included. He notes also that the upkeep of the marquise and her two people together cost about half that of de Sade at Vincennes.

Rousset had been contemplating her return to Provence since the previous autumn when she told Gaufridy, early in 1781:

"I see clearly that I'm going to be forced to travel again for my sins. If anything makes up for that, it will be the pleasure of embracing you, of no longer having before my eyes this abominable mess; it'll take ten years off me. I have arranged my departure for ... spring, if nothing goes wrong. I have dropped a hint about this to my companion[8] who made a face as though she didn't believe it at all. This is the only proper way I can devise for us to part like reasonable people, and it means I'll

7 The marquise.

8 Renée Pélagie.

bring together what I want to do and what I need to do. At her place, I have to spend too much and I'm not well looked after..."

In May 1781, probably having spent some of the winter staying with friends in Paris other than the marquise, her declining health also demanding a return to her native south, Marie Dorothée indeed left Paris for Provence. She had told the marquis:

"Let's occupy ourselves with more solid matters... I'll be writing to you about everything that could affect your affairs, not too often though, for my health doesn't let me write for very long. If it improves, I will still be at your service, at that of Madame de Sade too. That's the only way to show that we won't have fallen out with each other."

Back at la Coste, Rousset declined to occupy the château, which was not in good repair, though she busied herself in the grounds and the building. She took possession, at de Sade's behest, of all the keys, even those Gaufridy was not allowed to have, such as the key to the study, "including the hiding-place", and the key of a casket which de Sade, once out of prison, was much concerned to find.

Gothon Duffé, who had become pregnant and got married, gave birth in October 1781 and died soon afterwards.

The following 22 March, Rousset reported to the lord of la Coste:

"Your park looks pretty, the trees have made the most of your absence... Three days ago, twenty-nine fruit trees were cut down to their roots, each with the same malice..."

This news shook de Sade out of his resolve to have nothing to do with his properties. For the first time in years, he wrote to his agent Gaufridy, exclaiming:

"*Trees cut down, and fruit trees at that!*" and issuing orders to pursue "the rogues who did it." Two months later, at de Sade's insistence via his wife, Rousset resumed her occupation of the château at la Coste, when she reported to the master: "Your saucepans, and all your kitchen utensils in general, are in a filthy state fit to make thirty-six cats throw up..."

The marquis, ever the squire, indicated to Renée Pélagie he was much less interested in below-stairs than in the park:

"I shall most definitely not reply to the tedious chatter from Milli[9] Rousset. How is it possible to use one's intelligence on such foolishness? I can conceive, and I even find pleasing, the idea that one might misuse one's intelligence for exciting things ... but I cannot conceive of one using it to talk *saucepans, rotting rooms, pox, kitchen utensils* and all the other foolishness, the planning of which must have taken the *présidente* de Montreuil six weeks, and for poor Rousset to have copied it out... So her divine letter ... is going to be buried in the most perfect oblivion. I shall lower myself sufficiently to deal with these petty details when I am on the estates: until then, I do not want even to think about them..."

The prisoner tried a few more times to amuse Rousset with a lewd phrase or two from his lonely cell, but seems to have received no reply. One of his last letters to her, probably in 1783, ended: "Goodbye, handsome angel. Think of me sometimes when you are between the sheets, your thighs parted and your right hand busy - looking for fleas. Remember that, when you're like that, the other hand has to be doing so-and-so, for without that you have half the pleasure..." (De Sade was an indefatigable proselytiser for anal penetration.)

Rousset, who admitted she was "truly tired of many things", was finding that her health was still in decline, as was the château. The marquise told Gaufridy in October 1782: "Miss de Rousset, sir, has just let me know of the disaster overtaking the château of la Coste; the ceilings, the beams, fallen, worms in the beds, etc..."

The same autumn, the strong wind did not help. Rousset reported to Gaufridy:

"There's a terrible storm; the collapse spreads every quarter of an hour; the tiles, the rubble which falls like a peal of bells, make me more and more frightened. I can see cracks in every corner." The chimney in her bedroom collapsed; the wind tore out windows and tossed her about in her bed "like a feather". In the following January, 1783, Marie Dorothée retreated during another gale to sleep on a mattress in the kitchen, "which is hardly in any better shape" than the rest of the house. Renée Pélagie expressed her sympathy to Gaufridy, who was passing on to Paris the news from la Coste, but the demands from Cell No. 6 kept her in the capital.

---

9 Provençal equivalent to Mademoiselle.

The housekeeper, on the ridge above the village, was also bothered by disorder in the countryside. On 1 January 1782, she had reported to the agent at Apt: "If we had a police force and if the troopers had stayed, the poor warden's house would not have been burned down. We are among mad wolves. Everybody's complaining about M. de Sade and lawyer Gaufridy. It's supposed to be their fault, if the police don't do their job..."

In February of the next year, Rousset was telling Gaufridy:

"All winter they've been cutting timber quite flagrantly[10]. The townspeople are in favour of it because they buy the wood... The unreliability of this blasted locksmith puts me in a terrible predicament [being with little company in the château]... The first madman to come along could cut my throat while I sleep. Not being about to keep watch nor to look after the surroundings, and seeing that the main door is jammed in a way that defeats my strength, all the grapes have been taken and the vine branches above the château devastated and uprooted. The hunters from Ménerbes and Bonnieux have almost reached as far as la Coste..." So they were close to trespassing on the marquis's exclusive rights to hunt on his own land.

The housekeeper died at her post, of tuberculosis most likely, on 25 January 1784, three weeks past her 40th birthday.

---

10 On the lord's lands, which was an infringement of his rights.

CHAPTER 19: AN ERRAND-WIFE UNDER SUSPICION

The Marquise de Sade felt she had no option but to remain in Paris as her husband's errand-wife. This perseverance was maintained although the prisoner had begun the longest of their many separations by prison walls raging at her - in the first week of October 1778, when he had been back at Vincennes for less than a month - that he would curse her "as the lowest of women" if she were not to reveal how much longer he was to be kept in jail. A few months later, another letter accused her of "a bout of deafness on one side when you are asked to do something. That's all the go, I know, very fashionable, quite the thing! The trouble is that it is tedious. The self-conscious posture is affected too often..."

He fretted at disappointment, as he did with Rousset, believing that his hopes had been built up only to be toppled, irresponsibly so. Renée Pélagie was told off for having fed him "vile lies... It is no use excusing yourself by saying you had been misled. You should have told me nothing until you were certain. In brief, you are an idiot who allowed herself to be bamboozled, and those who bamboozled you are villains who deserve to be strung up and left to hang while the crows eat the flesh from their bones... May you and your abominable family and its pack of lackeys be tied up in a sack and thrown into the water. When that has happened, let me know right away for I promise Heaven that will be the happiest day of my life..."

In another letter, he frothed on: "I used to hide my true opinion, for I have been taught deceit, but I have always believed you to be a heartless woman who bends before every breeze and is felled by the least blow. You are a blob of wax and anyone can change your shape." This last quality might be seen as the one which most commended Renée Pélagie to her husband.

On another occasion, in September 1780, de Sade blew his top at the marquise over some failure he had found in her service to Cell No 6: "What drivel, good God! it's only right that I've written on the folder that holds your letters: *Triumph of Stupid Inaction*. How true that is of a woman who never in her life has had to apply herself to anything but a few pins, a hairstyle, and to undertake any job but to moon for half the day over an almanach..."

The marquise kept her poise under the bombardment and replied gracefully: "I am afraid you are mixing me up with the people who have harmed you. I keep your letters carefully in order to show them to you on your release and prove how wrong are your ideas of what we are trying to achieve, and how full of wind you are. I can just see you start away in disgust but that won't wash; I will hang on to you. I will lock you in my room and you will not get out before you have read them all, compared them with what really happened and told me: 'My dear, I admit you were in the right'..."

For the time being, he was far from admitting any such thing, sweet though Renée Pélagie often was to him by letter. "You are my sole purpose," she told him on 24 July 1781 and, a fortnight earlier: "I see very few, really very few, in the full meaning of the word, who have the heart and soul that you have. If your poor head didn't go astray sometimes to write unseemly things, you would be the perfect being."

The marquise - apart from uttering one of the bigger ifs in the history of human assessment - undertook a great deal of scurrying, poring and noting for her husband. Early in 1779, de Sade had recovered sufficiently from the shock of being thrust back into Vincennes to resume work on his Italian Journey (*Voyage d'Italie*), about his travels and observations in that country. La Jeunesse, in a corner of the marquise's apartment, "has started to copy the notes for your book," she reported, and "I'll do for you all the research that you want," she assured the prisoner. In that connection, and perhaps regarding de Sade's more arcane research, "I've written to the doctor to ask him to give me news of the little doctor in Rome" - that is, she had written to one of de Sade's best contacts in Italy, the court physician Dr Ménil in Florence, for word of Dr Iberti in Rome.

De Sade did not have to rely on his wife for anything like all the research needed for his reminiscences of Italy, at least some of the books he was drawing on having been with him in the fortress. Even so, the full range of his demands on his wife as quarter-mistress was little less than he had been accustomed to make on his entire staff when at large as a man of letters and bon viveur. Pauvert has neatly drawn together a series of phrases from the marquise's letters in this regard:

"My good friend", "My tender friend", "My good little fellow", "My little chum": "I've searched nearly all Paris to find six red towels;

there's none to be found ..." "I've searched all the bookshops, one after the other ..." "All the stationers say the same thing, that they can't cut twelve sheets to the size you've indicated to me, nor can they gild them ..." "... the chocolate cake (you are quite right to complain about it, because it's bad, but here's another one) ..." "... the canvas curtain, I haven't found one in a darker grey ..." "I've been, my friend, to a number of crockery places, without finding the kind of earthenware you're asking for ..." "*The Druids*, Leblanc's tragedy, is not in print ..." "We're doing a great deal of research for your plays ..."

Everything had to be just so for the author and master in the miniature study/château of Cell No. 6. Once de Sade had his teeth into a project, no expense - of his family's money and his wife's time and energy - was to be spared. In the summer of 1782, he took a notion to design a House of the Arts. By 6 July, Renée Pélagie was reporting to him: "Here, my friend, is the reply from the man to whom your plan was entrusted. I've taken back your plan, promising that, if he'll draw full-scale, we'll use him to simplify the job. His fee is six louis..." The expert's commentary refers to "a vast idea, ingenious and well conceived, which can only do honour to its author..." Well, the chap wanted the six louis.

At least de Sade had the grace to admit - some of the time - that the project was no more than "a merry piece of pie in the sky... One can very easily be mistaken when one has only oneself to judge a work of this kind..." However: "Now, I affirm before the whole universe that the idea in my plan is splendid... I know enough about architecture and I have given enough study to all the finest examples of this art in Italy, where I spent all my time with people of that profession[1], to be able to decide whether an idea is splendid or not, and I say to you again that my idea is superb, and so sublime that it is beyond any realisation. There would be no State, nor any sovereign in Europe, rich enough to realise it..."

There was no space among the grand dreams in Cell No. 6 for a thought as to whether the six louis might be better spent on food and comfort for his wife. On the other hand, there was never a complaint from Renée Pélagie at her being sent hither and yon as her husband's finder and fetcher. She seems never to have entertained the idea that all this - or anything else that her husband visited on her - might be beneath

1 Give or take *un bel giovannetto* or *due*.

her dignity. Late in 1778, she wrote to him at Vincennes: "If you haven't lost your memory, you must know that there's nothing less of a duchess than I am."

Also, she would try to smooth her husband's relations with her colleagues in his service. Miss de Rousset told him, at the end of 1778: "Madame tells me: 'Don't scold him, I beg you, he's unhappy; tell him something to make him laugh, racy jokes, silly nonsense, whatever you like...' "

At one point, in December 1780, the correspondence between husband and wife reminds one which of their signatures was the more potent. The marquise asked him for an authorisation to allow her to draw on arrears of her dowry, due from her mother under the terms of the couple's marriage contract of 1763. (The de Sades lived long before legislation which granted married women the right to own property which was not subject to their husbands' aegis.) The marquis replied with a lewd verse, and it is not clear whether he signed the authorisation, though it seems he did.

De Sade could be tender in his correspondence to his wife. A few snatches from his Vincennes letters speak of a conjugal relationship much warmer and more diverse than many arranged marriages. According to de Sade, one of his mother-in-law's greatest crimes was to have kept him from "you, my dear friend, ... you whom I would love in spite of everything as the best and dearest friend of mine who could ever have existed in the whole world... I am crazy with delight at seeing copies in your writing; that gives me a pleasure that you wouldn't believe. I would still remember that, while I was in Italy, you began to copy out *The Bachelor* (*Le Célibataire*) because it had some parts that you thought I would like; and that thoughtfulness of yours has come to my mind a hundred times..."

"... I ask your pardon for having fallen from grace by putting you in the way of boredom[2]. I would like to have Voltaire's talent, so that my productions might manage to interest you and, even if I did have, I wouldn't use it except from my heart with one aim in view, which would be to offer them to you..."

In December 1780, he asked for a little piece of one of his wife's dresses, provided it was one she had worn. Then, giving a racy twist to

---

2 By having sent her his plays, which he had decided were not to her liking.

a response to a request from his wife that he send his laundry in the usual way:

"Charming creature, you want my dirty underwear, my old underwear? Do you know that's a refined taste? You see how I sniff out the price of things. Listen, *my angel*, there's nothing in the world I would rather do than satisfy you on that score, for you know that I respect *the tastes, the fantasies*; however weird they may be, I regard them all as respectable ... One is not in control of them and ... the oddest and most bizarre of them all, well analysed, always comes back at root to a matter of refinement. I undertake to prove it as required: you know that no-one analyses like I do..."

"... Since we're on the subject, I would like to tell you, *fresh pork of my thoughts* (that's because I love pigmeat and I get to eat very little of it here), that I have been working at the job of giving you a plan of the cushion demanded by the infirmity of *my backside*. I would like you to get *a close acquaintance* with it, and I have, therefore, prepared with all the skill at my command a sheet of paper on which I have traced an exact plan of action on the item in question; the sheet takes the exact form that the cushion ought to have; you'll make it with feathers and horsehair (they're just the thing for that) and cover it with an ordinary, strong material. The sheet is the right size, but you ought to make it a bit bigger rather than a bit smaller, nicely soft and nicely padded..."

Even when he was being sweet, the errands were never far away; nor were nasty barbs, even when traffic between the prisoner and his wife was moving smoothly. In 1783, when Renée Pélagie was busily, and with some embarrassment, supplying disguised dildoes, she sent Mr 6 a note: "Your case is ready; I'll send it to you, now you'll be able to put something else beside your flask .."

"... And the lot in your arse," the recipient wrote in the margin, "all too easily, unfortunately..." This suggestion that his wife's rectum was too commodious to afford him best pleasure was of a kind with the embedding of this undermining insult in apparent affection and solicitude - in February 1784, when very cold weather descended on Paris, he wrote that he would be most vexed if Renée Pélagie did not wrap up her "ugly little pallid bosom".

For all that, there were indications from de Sade in jail that he regretted some of his wilder treatment of his wife when at liberty. In 1783, he revealed that "I have the strongest desire to make good with her many of the thoughtless acts of my younger days - because in fact *one's own wife is not meant for that kind of thing*, that's a truth which I felt and which I talked about to her, more than six months before coming here" - during 1776, therefore, or earlier. This resolution - if that is what it was - would not be inconsistent with a keen lust in Cell No. 6 for the prisoner's main hope and comfort. He told her in November 1783:

"... Don't see in the depths of my heart anything but the wholly sincere wish to prove to you that I love you and will love you all my life in spite of what they're making you do, in which you have no hand whatsoever, I'm always quite sure...

"... on my oath I have great longing to see you. As we're going to regard each other as a pair again, we'll need to size each other up after such a long separation. But the devilish thing is that we still won't be able to *make a snug fit*. Why not indeed? The bailiff?[3] Well now! the bailiff, what's he going to do? He'll hold the candle; that's just his mark. Me, I'm *doing some snug fitting* in advance, I warn you... Don't you know that a chap turns into a randy devil, being like this so long without getting a *snug fit*..."

Much of the traffic from the marquise's lodgings to her husband's room, as I have indicated, was intended to persuade him to purge his writings of material which further hardened the opinion of the royal administration against him. On the last day of 1781, Renée Pélagie could not have put the case more simply: "They tell me that they can only judge you by what you write, and that, for as much as you go on writing in this way, they'll go on thinking very badly of you."

On 10 November, 1783: "It's very true what they've told me that you would have been out long since if you hadn't always written things which reveal a way of thinking that can't be accepted and that brings about your misfortune."

After a while, this was mostly water off the back of the duck in Cell No. 6, who did not use much ink in refutation. However, when he felt his dignity pricked by his wife's finger-wagging at his insults to Mme de Montreuil, Governor de Rougemont *et al.*, he could be fierce in reply. She had told him, on 6 May 1782: "One musn't say anything malicious of people if you're depending on them." Four days later, the blue-blood rumbled back:

---

3 The governor of the fortress.

"You are certainly mistaken in your letter. It was La Jeunesse you thought you were talking to when you used that sentence about *dependence*. That style is more applicable to your servant than to your husband! I depend only on the king, know no master but the king, am ready to give him a thousand lives and my blood a thousand times, if he wishes, but beneath him I acknowledge no dependence because, between him and his princes and me, I see only inferiors. I advise you to change your *slavish* and *grovelling* style. If misfortune has degraded you, so much the worse for your soul; don't tar me with the same brush at least, for that would reflect badly on you. If La Jeunesse has said something bad about those on whom he depends, he's in the wrong. But if the Marquis de Sade, by some sarcasm as well deserved as it is cutting, has made the troupe of rogues which is bothering him feel its stupidity and its inferiority, then he's right..."

Apart from nudging him towards mending his ways for his own sake, there were times when the marquise rebuked him on her own behalf, as on 18 May 1782: "My God! why don't you want to give my heart its due - for it's utterly devoted to you... Let me tell you that you're writing in there things which you don't really think and, when you come out, not before then, I am going to take my revenge for your abuses. And here's how I'll avenge myself for that: I'll give you cast-iron proofs in writing, and accounts of all that I'm doing for you, and that in front of a witness, so that you shan't be able to turn on your heel..."

De Sade's intransigence in speaking his mind from Vincennes by letter was destroying his prospects *and* diminishing his chances of a visit from his wife. Renée Pélagie was quite plain on the matter, on 13 December 1781: "They say you're writing things that prevent their letting me see you."

Eighteen months later, nothing had changed: "I am always asking to see you. You are always creating obstacles by your ways."

True - although the question of Renée Pélagie visiting him was a little more complicated. For one thing, his well-wishers outside had to consider whether it would do more harm than good, as Rousset put it on 29 May 1779: "It would be very easy for Madame to see him - for me too. But what good would it do us? I fear that he might be four times the devil after than before. He'll pour a stream of filth at both of us, and I'll wash my hands of him, as I've already done several times..."

There was another obstacle to a wifely visit. De Sade, sifting all about him for clues as to when he might be released, took it into his head that, if Renée Pélagie were to visit him, that would mean he was in for a long incarceration because if, on the other hand, he were soon to be released, he would rather be spared the alloyed pleasure of meeting her in a place he loathed. In a letter of February 1779, he explained to her: "If I have to be here for a long time, and no question about it, ask to see me, however irksome it might be; that can only be a great consolation for me. If I don't have to be here for a long time, don't ask for it, because the pleasure I would get from seeing you here would be bound to be mixed with a limitless amount of sorrow for me. Do you see that's how it is, just now?..."

Besides, de Sade, as ever, wanted the business arranged on his own terms, demanding that any visit be unsupervised. This was against prison regulations, however, so there was to be no complaisant governor lighting the way of Renée Pélagie and her Louis to renewed conjugal congress, rather a police officer whose brief was to insist that every world be audible to him, during a meeting in the council chamber of the fortress. For all that, as the couple moved into a fifth year without having seen each other since the marquis had been arrested in Paris in February 1777, de Sade came to accept a third pair of eyes and ears at the reunion. That would still be a nuisance, but he was planning a way for her to let him know, without the supervisor catching on, how much longer he was to remain in jail. On a letter from his wife, May 1781, he jotted:

"I'm going to put my hand in yours; press it as many times as there are still months or weeks to go; press hard if you mean months, press softly if it's weeks. I swear to you by my God and by my life that I'll keep the secret; don't refuse me, I beg of you."

One does not know whether Renée Pélagie had been alerted to this ploy by the date of her first visit. In any event, she had no idea when her husband might be released; if she had, and been aware of the arrangement for signals, she would have needed to squeeze his hand black and blue when, on 13 July 1781, they came face to face at last.

Whatever took place in the council chamber at Vincennes, the immediate aftermath was disturbing. During the rest of July, through August and into September, the police were allowing none of de Sade's letters to his wife to reach her. The chronology of letters and events after the marquise's first visit to Vincennes is difficult to plot, but it appears that Renée Pélagie managed to secure an interview with Le

Noir, the police chief, in the second half of October, after which she reported to the marquis:

"I went yesterday, my sweet friend, to Mr Le Noir's office to find out whether he had spoken to Mr de Rougemont so that I might see you. Imagine my surprise when he indicated to me that if I were to persist in trying to see you, it would be necessary for him to get orders in advance from the minister and to tell the minister of your behaviour and about your threats, so that in the event of an incident there would be no possibility of his being blamed for not having given due warning. That has cast me down..."

There is no sure trace of what had put the police chief so much on his guard against trouble from Mr 6, though since Le Noir and his staff were well aware by this time how much of a blustering and fulminating nuisance he could be, no doubt some conduct even worse than the usual was in train. About this juncture, de Sade again lost his temper with a warder and struck him. However, the main concern of the police officers reading de Sade's letters of that autumn might well have been the tone and content of his remarks to his wife.

Replying to Renée Pélagie's news of her visit to Le Noir, de Sade was fulsome:

"I'm not losing a minute in replying to your letter, my dear friend. The disquiet it aroused in me is too upsetting for me to wait even a moment. In the name of God, don't attack me any more with blows like that, they're too sharp. Me, making threats against you! May Heaven strike me down on the spot, and may I never see daylight, if I have ever made so much as one. Ah! good God, threats against the one creature I adore... I say to you, I think it and I repeat it here, that I shall see you with a dagger in your hand, that I shall throw myself at your feet and that I shall adore your vengeance... My threats and my so-called misbehaviour have been directed at the man who acts as my servant. What connection has that with you? In the name of God, come to see me, and try in the meantime to get Amblet in to see me. If you persist in believing that I have let slip the slightest word against you, I'm going to snuff out my life and that's flat."

Next day, he was marshalling evidence, still to his wife:

"The staff of this establishment, called and questioned right away by myself after my letter of yesterday evening, have assured me most firmly that they have never been aware of any wrongful intent of mine towards you; and how could they have done - they themselves went on to assure me further - because they have never heard any such thing? I urged them to clarify the matter with Mr de Rougemont, and the preposterous reply that they brought me this morning ... cleared it up for me and set my mind at rest. The dear fellow is getting his own back, which must be enough to persuade you completely that everything he has been able to say is nothing but slander in retaliation for what he's no doubt calling my slander; and insofar as we have seen through all that, I know you to be straightforward and fair-minded enough to think no more of it. I offer you again my most sterling word of honour that I have undertaken neither notion nor act of threat, and that I love you and adore you to such a degree, my dear friend, that I would rather tear myself apart than say about you, or to your face, the least thing that might upset you."

This has the familiar ring of the Marquis de Sade protesting too much, the "word of honour", drooping from too much excited flourishing, and the melodramatic gesture towards a centre-stage suicide being regular props in his long-running show, in which our hero always shifts the blame onto someone else before the final curtain - in this case, Governor de Rougemont, the handy villain at Vincennes.

Bear in mind that de Sade, although he would not admit it in anything like these terms, had great need of the continued emotional and material support of his errand-wife. If she were to abandon him, who would take her place as writer of gentle and would-be uplifting replies to the surly and self-absorbed rants, as hunter throughout Paris for just the right book on Florentine art and just the right size and texture of dildo, as loyal spouse keeping the marital vows she swore some 20 years before? Others among his Montreuil and de Sade relatives would have kept up the payment of his keep in prison, but there would have been no more extras - no more attempts to supply him with books a good Catholic would find dangerous to one's immortal soul, no more chocolate cakes and fine liqueurs, and no more lobbying of officials for his release. Apart from the Sadeian reflex, when accused of naughtiness, to protest all too floridly that he had done no such thing and, well, if he had, then it was all someone else's fault, there might well have been calculation in his elaborate disclaimer of any threats to Renée Pélagie - calculation stemming from fear of losing his one true believer.

The visit of 13 July 1781 was the reappearance in the marquis's life, for the first time in more than four years, of his succour and sounding-board as flesh and blood, a woman whom he would enjoy if he could, yet could not. The jailed husband sees his wife, under inhibiting supervision, and is left, once she has gone away, to chew on the fact that she spends all but that sliver of her time beyond his range of sight and hearing, beyond his control. That sort of chewing, to the Marquis de Sade, was apt to lead to frothing at the mouth.

On 26 July, the marquise reported to Miss de Rousset at la Coste: "Since I saw him, he has been depressing me with a heap of fantasies he has dreamed up; finding nothing better to do, he is jealous. Even at this distance I can see you laugh. 'Well, of what?' you ask me. Of Lefèvre (he flatters me enormously, wouldn't you say?), because I happened to say that Lefèvre had bought me some books for him. Also, he is jealous of Lady de Villette because I wrote to tell him that she was offering that I go to live with her... Please let me know, I beg you, where he digs up all this stuff..."

Lefèvre was a young man from the Provençal village of Mazan, where the de Sade family had an estate, who had left his family's farm to be valet to the Abbé de Sade. The abbot taught him to read and write, which fitted him to be the marquis's secretary for a time in 1771 and 1772. Being a commoner of no personal fortune, he would have been considered in society as not at all suitable a lover for a noblewoman such as the Marquise de Sade, hence her ironical aside in the letter to Rousset about flattery in the notion of Lefèvre as a cause of her husband's jealousy. At the time of Renée Pélagie's first visit to the marquis at Vincennes, Lefèvre was still connected with the de Sades sufficiently for the marquis, given the provocation outlined, to work himself up into a mighty lather over him.

De Sade went so far as to have his wife copy out and put in a letter an oath of fidelity which he had dictated to her:

"I give you my word of honour on all that I hold most sacred in the world that I have never stayed at Mme de Villette's house, that I am not staying there now and that I will never stay there; that I will never consider setting up in Paris any household, neither for myself nor for two people, and that I will never live with anyone but you and live nowhere other than in your lands in Provence as of the moment that you are given permission to go there, desiring to dwell and live my life with no-one but you for the rest of my days. I add to this promise a pledge to leave right away the place where I am now living to go and dwell inside a convent, and to see there no-one whatsoever but people who are connected with matters related to you, and to hold fast to this until you are set free, when I will rejoin you forever.

"Montreuil de Sade"

The Marquise de Villette, the other object of de Sade's jealousy mentioned in his wife's letter, was a 24-year-old beauty married to a rich homosexual 20 years her senior. She was a patroness of Voltaire in his last years, and was esteemed for her generous and pleasant character. "*Belle et bonne*,"[4] Voltaire had called her. Also, she was hostess, at the Villette mansion in Paris, to many parties and dinners where, de Sade feared in his isolation, Renée Pélagie was meeting brilliant company which might distract her from attachment to him. Near the end of 1778, the marquise had written to her husband of Mme de Villette: "She does me a thousand kindnesses. I cannot find words to tell you how generously [the Marquis and Marquise de Villette] behave. The twice I have dined at their house, I saw some outstanding people there: *Lalande*[5] etc... They move in very smart circles..."

In the summer of 1782, a year after the height of the furious jealousy which followed his wife's first visit to Vincennes, de Sade reminded her: "Remember that you gave me your word not to go to the country, above all not to the home of your beautiful Villette, who I suppose is a keen fu[cker] and perhaps even a bit of a lesbian."

In a letter almost certainly of 5 August the previous summer, Renée Pélagie had tried to calm her husband's remonstrations about how she was dressed for her visit - altogether too gaily, in his estimation. He made disbelieving notes on the letter, these being given here in italics and parentheses:

"... I've tried to ensure that what I wear does not get me noticed (*Put your modesty somewhere else*), and if you were to see the other women (*Whores like you*) you would acknowledge its simplicity... Yes, my tender friend (*Fèvre*), I love you, I have never stopped adoring you for a moment. Calm yourself, go to sleep (*'While I'm f[ucking]'*), be sure that I'll come to see you and, if the time depended on me, that would be before this could reach you...

---

4 Beautiful and good.

5 A famous astronomer.

"So as to move the furniture out of my apartment, I'll have to pay 9 months rent that's owing (*Oh! I get it, your nine, now, likewise your pregnancy*), and I have to pay a quarter in advance on moving into the convent[6] (*How can anyone tell lies with such cheek!*) ... one way or another, I should be at the convent in a few days. I'm getting information about the Anglaises or the Ladies of Saint-Aure (*There's absolutely no convent of that name*); these are the most secluded of the better convents (*Montigny's would suit you better!*)[7] as far as I can tell. But I want to be sure so that I wouldn't have to move again.

"Dated this 5 August (*Now there's the figure that marks him, this fine gentleman out there; that and the 7, which apparently is his measurement*)."

De Sade seems to have been weaving a fantasy in which five and seven signified Lefèvre, the latter figure representing the length of his penis - in inches, one supposes.

Also about this time, as nearly as one can judge, de Sade vented his anger on a portrait of Lefèvre, done by Rousset while she was in Paris helping the marquis's cause and sent to Cell No. 6 by her. He stabbed it with a sharp instrument, spilled on it what could well be blood, and wrote on it: "This is how a blood-sucker of that kind, a rogue of that type, a little peasant of such low birth deserves to be treated when he takes it upon himself to forget the respect that he owes to his master, and this is what I hope the original will get one day from me, or from someone else ... from d'Olonne,[8] even if it has to cost me a thousand louis...

"... The woman who, with the sole aim either of a despicable revenge or, what's perhaps even worse, out of the crude and animal desire to satisfy her lust, gives herself shamelessly to a valet, to a peasant of the lowest kind whose father received charity from her husband, that woman, I say, no longer has so much as the right to the name of wife, she is no more than a shameless she-wolf open to universal ridicule, she is no more than a creature a thousand times more contemptible than those women whose need to live legitimatises such horrors ... a monster

---

6 Renée Pélagie was moving out of a small apartment in the old Marais quarter of Paris, which she had occupied for rather less than a year, for rooms in a convent - not the Carmelite one where she was before. De Sade's note seems to suggest that he jumped to the conclusion, in the heat of his jealousy, that his wife was pregnant, the "9 months" having set him off.

7 Montigny was a procuress of the day.

8 The Duke d'Olonne was reputed as a murderer.

who dishonours all at once her children, her husband and herself, and who can claim nothing more than to sink down like the sows in the mire where she went to pick up the despicable instrument of her crime."

It is unlikely that the portrait, with holes and comments, was sent to Renée Pélagie.

Despite this revulsion at the idea of his wife taking a lover, de Sade reserved, as ever, to himself the right to philander, not only to the extent of having affairs with noblewomen, but also to countless liaisons with prostitutes and to the enjoyment of penetration of his own body (during the Marseilles episode, for instance, by Latour, the very kind of low-born servant whom he put outside his wife's sexual bounds). Later in his imprisonment, in the spring of 1782, de Sade was writing to Rousset in Provence about the recent death of Gothon Duffé, faithful servant at la Coste, who had died soon after giving birth:

"... Gothon liked men. But, mademoiselle, aren't men made for women and women for men? Isn't that nature's design? Gothon ... got married because she was pregnant... What's so bad about that?... That's wanting to give a father to her child, that's wanting to make sure it gets fed, that's wanting to take it out of that abject class that has the options only of poverty or of crime. But she was unfaithful to her husband... Ah! that's where I see no excuse! Women's adultery can lead to such ghastly troubles, carries such harmful and deadly ramifications, that I have never been able to accept it. Weigh my principles, sift through the story of my debauches, and you'll find that I have hardly ever cut across this marital tie ...; and for every dozen maidens, so-called, whom I set out to seduce, you won't find as many as three married women. On this matter, then, Gothon was in the wrong..."

De Sade thanked Renée Pélagie, in August 1781, for having copied out and signed the dictated promise of good, circumscribed behaviour:

"I could not be more obliged to you, my dear friend, for the attention which you have been so kind as to extend to me by sending the note which I was asking for, written out word for word. It has certainly calmed me, but the hidden horrors, the twisted vileness which I've found in the abominable letters that your odious mother has made you write ... have put into my soul a dose of sorrow and unease much stronger than the calmness which your note was able to lay on me..."

He could not resist reaching out from his cell into his wife's wardrobe and dressing-room. His letter went on:

"... I tell you again on my word of honour that if ... you're dressed like a wh[ore] again, like the last time [you visited me] - I won't come down to see you. This will be my first question when they come to fetch me: 'Is she dressed the way she was the last time?' If the answer's affirmative, I won't come down. If negative, well perhaps they would be tricking me; anyway, I'll come down, but as soon as I spot ... the white dress and your hair done so that it can be seen, I'll be off back upstairs like a shot, I swear by my God and my honour, and would wish to be known as the lowest of men if I give way."

At that, de Sade wrote his signature as though he had made his point and the letter was ended. However, his agitation then spawned a long and revealing post-script:

"What's the good of this excuse: *If you were to see the other women?* Other women don't have husbands in jail or, if they have and they carry on like that, they are sluts who deserve nothing but insults and contempt. Now, would you attend Easter Communion got up like a tarty actress in some travelling show or a woman hawking quack remedies at a fair? No - am I right? Well then, the reverence offered ought to be the same; grief and sadness ought to yield, in this case, what piety and respect for God ought to bring to the other..."

One has to smile at the evocation by de Sade, in whom the self-aggrandiser seems to have been gaining ground here over the militant atheist, of himself as a rightful object of his pious wife's devotions, on a par with those she offered at the most exalted festival of the Church. From the tomb of Cell No. 6, pending the rolling away of the stone, Sade Crucified by Marie Madeleine de Montreuil continued:

"... However extreme fashions have become, you will not persuade me there is no style for a woman of sixty years. Adopt that, however far from that age you might be.[9] Remember that my misfortune puts us near that age and, even if we are not that old yet, we have no option but to follow an appropriate behaviour and dress. If you are to remain a respectable woman, you must only please me, and you will certainly never please me except by the style and *the substance* of the greatest propriety and the most perfect modesty...

9 The marquise was 39 at the time.

"... So I'm insisting ... that you come here wearing what you ... women call a *housedress*[10] and in a big, a very big, bonnet with no elaborate hair-style underneath, your hair only combed. Not the least hint of false curls, just a bun and no braids at all; your figure in no way emphasised, your bust very much covered and not scandalously half on show as it was the other day, and that the colour of your dress should be as dark as can be. I swear to you on all that I hold most sacred in the world that there will be a tremendous scene if you deviate in the least from what I am laying down for you here. You ought to be ashamed at not understanding that the people who dressed you up, as you were the other day, were laughing at you in their hearts. Oh! how they must have been saying to themselves: 'The pretty little puppet! How easy it is for us to do what we like with her!' Be your own woman for once in your life..."

This last remark may be recognised as masculine code for: "Do as *I* tell you." The marquis went on:

"... I understand that there are things to which you are forced by circumstances to lend yourself; but these are so indecent or so ridiculous, perhaps even so outrageous, ... that come what may I profess myself satisfied that you have not consented to them! But ... you must not meet these proposals with anything but refusal and with threats to take your own life rather than hear them spoken. I say this because I know very well in what abominable hands you are! ... I know all too well that you are in the home of your dreadful mother... Yes, I do not hesitate to say to you, I would rather you were with Mme Gourdan[11]: at least you would be on your guard against that woman's machinations, instead of which nothing can arm you against the cunning traps that will catch you when you're with the other one[12]. Do you think that I'll be able to forget for as long as I live the remark: 'I would give fifty louis to the man who would arrange to take the virtue of that silly little goose of a girl'? No, no, I will never forget it and, if you would like to compare all the circumstances, to recall clearly to mind the times, the places, the situations, then my greatest mistakes will be immediately explained to you!..."

Quite a claim, though it would take more than the construing of one remark for anyone to lay bare the roots of the Marquis de Sade's

10 A loose, enveloping garment.

11 Another procuress.

12 Mme de Montreuil.

greatest mistakes. Be that as it may, are we meant to understand that de Sade was claiming also that Mme de Montreuil had once suggested, however flippantly, that she would give a bounty to whoever breached the maidenhead of Renée Pélagie, her eldest daughter? From what we know of the poised and correct Présidente de Montreuil, via her letters and those of others, such a remark was beyond her. No ambitious dynast of her kind would trade her daughter's hymen for mere cash. One must suspect de Sade - not a reliable reporter on the subject of his mother-in-law, as on many another - of outright invention or at least of a very free paraphrase. Perhaps de Sade was alluding to a coarse outburst - whether out of character or not one cannot tell - by that much less well defined figure, his father-in-law, the Président de Montreuil.

De Sade was not content to leave his mother-in-law's supposed role in the matter at that. He wrote to her directly, on 2 September 1781, it seems:

"I bother you very seldom, Madame, and you have to believe that, when I do so, I must have a burning need to address you. Of all the blows that you brought upon me since I got here, I have felt none more keenly than the one with which you have just torn my heart. You are putting your hand, Madame, to that which is persuading me that my wife is dishonouring herself. Is it possible, good God, that a mother either tolerates such infamies or works to persuade her son-in-law that they are real. Your schemes are frightful but they are being figured out, Madame. You would wish that I were to separate from my wife and, once out of here, not want to take her back again. How badly you have understood my feelings for her if you have been able to believe that anything in the world could produce such an effect..."

No reply from Mme de Montreuil has come to light. To find one would be a surprise.

Back at the quill in the stuffy and humid Cell No. 6, in August 1781, the postscript to Renée Pélagie was still growing:

"... My dear friend, remember this, the respect given to virtue by those women who have always looked up to it is the despair of those women who have always scorned it; these latter, wretches that they are, are like those sham unbelievers who want others to cast down the god which their hearts really fear to name. Hold on to it, hold on to it, this virtue! That's what will make me ashamed of my misdeeds, it's only that which will make me loathe them. The natural trait of man is to imitate; that of the thinking man is to become like that which he loves. My misfortunes have always been due to my having been shown the example of vice - do not prolong them for all eternity by the worst act[13] that could be put before me. I would not live through that; or if my attachment to life were to overcome my resolve to kill myself (which I doubt), that would only throw me into such a turmoil that would soon end my life in some way or other. Inconstancy or infidelity [in a woman] arouses a lover or a husband, they say: true, in a poor specimen of a man. You should never regard me as such. I will never forget that sort of infamy and will never seek to get back a piece of goods that would no longer be mine. I have always been disgusted by the thought that a woman who is in my arms might have her mind on another man, and I have always dropped immediately any woman whom I suspected of having cheated me in that way..."

Beauvoisin, for one, and Colet, for another, might have laughed at that claim; so might have Laure de Lauris for, even if de Sade, applying his usual distinction between courtesans and the rest of womankind, was thinking only of women whom he had not paid for sexual relations, his pursuit of the *provençale* noblewoman after he believed she had another suitor also gives the lie to his assertion that he had brooked no infidelity.

The afterthoughts in the letter continued:

"... I do not believe this of you, but you have stirred up the suspicion and now it is fixed in my mind.[14] They have advised you very subtly. I will probe into the matter, I will search for proof: I will find nothing (at least, I hope not), but the suspicion will have grown and, in a character such as mine, it is a slow poison whose abiding effects increase the damage with nothing in the world being able to halt its progress...

"... It used to be so pleasant for me to glimpse at least a happy old age in the company of a loyal friend who could never have let me down. This was - alas! - my only consolation, all that could blunt the spears which are piercing me now. And you have pushed horror so far as to begrudge me this sweet hope of my declining years!...

"... Oh, my dear friend, I will no longer be able to look up to you! Is it true? Tell me, have you deceived me so cruelly? What a dreadful future, if so! O great God, may the gates of my prison never be

---

13 Her adultery.

14 Remember that Renée Pélagie's supposed adultery had been hatched entirely in his own head.

opened! May I die here rather than come out to know my degradation, as well as yours and that of the trolls who advise you! May I die rather than come out to meet my degradation, to wallow in the ultimate excesses of the vilest crimes, which I will seek again with delight so as to benumb myself and ruin myself! There would be nothing beyond my devising. Goodbye, you see how calm I am and how much I am in need of seeing you alone. Arrange that, then, I urge you."

In his long postscript, de Sade was pleading to his wife that she eschew adultery so as to remain a good example to him, the beacon that might guide him away from misdeeds. Leaving aside his failure to take any desires of hers into account - such consideration by the marquis having been long past praying for - note that this view of her sexuality seems to have appeared late in his life. There was no sign of it while he remained a libertine at liberty - then he was calling Renée Pélagie too frigid and too pious for his taste, before he brought her into his pleasures. His beacons then were the debaucheries of his own choosing. He passed, in the letter, from the pleading to a preening of himself as too fine and proud to chase after an errant woman, then to blaming his jealousy on his wife and the people behind her, and last to a bathetic pre-emptive pinning of any future return of his to libertinage, after release from jail, on those same others who had snuffed out the one good example that might have kept him on the straight and narrow. Even for the Marquis de Sade, this was vintage tosh.

To Renée Pélagie, it may well be that all this was not much more than the latest extravagance from a husband she well knew to be wilful and explosive. Her answers were not enough to turn away wrath for long, but they were soft: "I am not satisfied with my clear conscience - I need you to be happy. It is better that you tell me of your suspicions, your disquiet, than keep them bottled up because I can readily prove my innocence..."

The rage and suspicion hurt her, even so: "This attitude you have towards me at present weighs on me, suffocates me, humiliates me, because I live only to see you and I think of nothing else... I say nothing but you are slicing into my heart. It will never heal. I have nothing to answer for. My behaviour is an open book. No, it cannot be that you, when you know me as I am sure you do, truly mean what you write...

"My heart is constant: it adores you and it always will..."

The marquise remained a woman of the nobility, with a couple of servants, but her life as the wife of a disgraced outcast was not easy. On 18 August 1781, she reported her plan to move into a convent to Marie Dorothée de Rousset in Provence: "I'm not telling anyone at all what I'm about. When I do, I'll find a reason to give people and to give my family; in all conscience I can't give the real reason, that would do too much harm to M. de Sade. I have been to spend a week in the country at Madame de Villette's place as a dutiful friend. I had written to tell him that she offered for me to go and live with her. He flew off the handle and wrote the most racy things about [the Marquis de] Villette who, if he knew, would cut him into little bits... I'm keeping quiet about all this..."

In the autumn, once installed at the Convent of Saint-Aure, the Marquise de Sade, not yet 40 years old, connected with the royal blood of France, wife to the head of a great family of Provence, reported again to Miss Rousset:

"... I am established here with the rest of the worn-out old things...

"... I am finding myself a little ill at ease in this house. Mother Esprit-de-Jésus is no longer the prioress; she is in the infirmary dying of a chest ailment as one does.

"I have the apartment on the first floor, beside the bakery. It's the best in the house: a big room, a little side room and toilet.

"For company, in which I do not confide, I have a merchant's widow three years older than I, who has spent her life in convents, ... with a lot to say for herself, shrewd and friendly. The other [lodger] is a lawyer's daughter, twenty years old and a good child, but not at all suited for convent life and as apt to pick up good ways as bad ones.

"There's no shortage of bread, but the food is just enough to prevent one starving to death. The lodgers in their rooms have no contact with the nuns; the administrator, the prioress, the servant, that's all [we see]... There's an assistant on the staff, name of Miss Martin, ... who knows the world, who used to know ... my mother-in-law, and who gave my husband a slap when he was little because he was annoying her. This one, I think, is the house spy..." Spy or no spy, Renée Pélagie might have taken a leaf out of Miss Martin's book, in response to the husbandly despotism emanating from Cell No. 6, on the next wifely visit to Vincennes.

The marquise was paying annually 200 livres for accommodation and 300 for food at the convent, for herself and two servants (La Jeunesse and a maid). This little establishment was costing a good deal less than half as much to maintain as was the marquis at Vincennes, especially if one puts a monetary value on the marquise's work as researcher, finder, despatcher and such for the detainee.

It is difficult to be sure of the sequence of events, but it seems that, although these seizures declined over time, there was at least one more outburst of jealousy by de Sade against his wife while he remained at Vincennes. Towards the end of 1781, having battened onto an innocent remark of Renée Pélagie's in a letter - "I'm getting so chubby that I'm scared to death of becoming like a fat sow" - the prisoner noted by her words: "through having been tumbled by my understudy! Fat! what does that word mean?" (In French, *grosse* can mean both "fat woman" and "pregnant". Renée Pélagie incautiously used the word, which allowed her husband - on his usual hair-trigger as far as such openings for suspicion were concerned - to jump to the wrong conclusion.)

The marquise lamented to Miss Rousset on 1 November 1781: "... It is impossible, whatever he might do, that my attachment should diminish. But this attachment doesn't prevent me feeling his behaviour acutely. He's saying now that I'm pregnant, and that he's sure of it..."

Renée Pélagie persisted in patient denials of this fancy, and went on asking the police chief to restore her access to Vincennes: "He might be liable to outbursts because of his despair, but a bit of kindness and patience would quieten him and make a new man of him," she told the officer, who could have been forgiven for failing to concede the point.

By 13 January of the next year, 1782, Renée Pélagie was telling Gaufridy: "Regarding his lands or his transfer, he is as sour as the day he went in... This puts me in a black mood, a melancholy beyond words. If I didn't get a hold on myself, I would cry all day long...

"The death of M de Maurepas[15] has brought about no change... The mind of you-know-who swings from good to bad. However, while he's having a visit from me, he always stays well-behaved; it's afterwards that thoughts upset his mind and make him write things which are really not good at all..."

By June, de Sade seemed to have passed through the worst of his jealousy, after a succession of visits, although these seem to have been suspended for four months from about the end of the previous year, 1781, almost certainly because of bad conduct by Mr 6. On 23 June,

---

15 A senior government minister.

the prisoner conceded to his wife, regarding her supposed infidelity: "You are not capable of it. Six visits were enough for me to get over my fancies. These were insulting you, which is enough for me never to entertain such notions. I am better equipped to value what I love."

He may have decided that Renée Pélagie might still be a ball of wax, but had set the way he moulded her.

Even so, there was another outbreak of fantastical attitudinising when another member of his family gave him what might have seemed an unexceptionable piece of information. At the end of 1783, de Sade learned that Louis Marie, his elder son, aged 16, was in line for a posting as an officer in an infantry regiment by way of starting his military career. De Sade was incensed that the lad was not going to join the carabineers. He declared that he had promised himself, when Louis Marie was born, that the boy would serve in the same regiment as he. One recalls that, near the time of the birth, in the summer of 1767, de Sade was sneaking off to Lyons to join the actress Beauvoisin, rather than his regiment (a cavalry one, at that juncture, by the way, not the carabineers - however, de Sade was in the carabineers when, also at the age of 16, he came under Prussian fire, and it may have been recollection of that period which stirred him).

In January 1784, he kept up a great hullabaloo about his son's first steps under arms. He told his wife and the prison governor - and would "tell the whole of Europe, if need be" - that he was entirely against the infantry for his son and would spend whatever sums were required to put him under the right banner. If that meant mortgages and borrowing (he did not say more mortgages and more borrowing, though that would have been nearer the mark), so be it. Mme de Montreuil had no business meddling in what was a father's prerogative, nor did he need her or her family in order to have Louis Marie placed in the officer corps.

What's more, he had long insisted that neither of his sons (he did not say how little attention he had paid to them, whether he was at liberty or not) was to leave home without having been under his personal instruction for a year, and without having been assigned a servant by his father. While he was on the subject, he reminded Mme de Montreuil, via his wife, in case his mother-in-law had an advantageous marriage in mind for Louis Marie, that he would not let the boy marry until he was 25, that only a wedding at Lyons or Avignon would be appropriate, and that the young husband would not be allowed to set up home in Paris, but only in Provence near his father. De Sade reckoned, it is clear, to be out of prison by the time his son was eligible to marry.

In case his wife failed to pass the former carabineer officer's strictures to the young man in question, he adopted the role of heavy father and wrote thus to his elder son:

"I have just learned, Sir, that your mother's parents intend you for a second-lieutenancy in one of France's finest infantry regiments. I forbid you, Sir, to accept this posting; you are not fitted for a second-lieutenancy in the infantry, and I will not endure it. Either you shall not enter the service at all or you shall do so under the orders of M. de Chabrillant, who is related to you, in the corps of carabineers.

"If, despite the express order which I am giving you, Sir, to refuse this posting, I learn that you have been weak enough to obey relatives to whom you owe no obedience whatsoever while your father is alive, you shall bid me goodbye forever, for I shall not see you as long as I live.

"Any who may conceal this order of mine from you shall answer in their own soul and conscience for the misfortunes which your disobedience shall bring down on their head, and I lay on them in advance my every curse if, within two months, I have not received from you confirmation in writing that you will carry out my will.

"THE COUNT DE SADE, YOUR FATHER"

This bolt from the paternal Olympus, temporarily headquartered in Cell No. 6, was expressed in the formal *vous* (you) form for extra impressiveness, rather than the *tu* which a father might use when writing to his son. However, we are dealing with nobles keen on the formalities, within the family as elsewhere, so one should not be greatly surprised by de Sade's use of the formal style when addressing his wife and other relatives. (He would switch sometimes from *vous* to *tu* and back again, within the space of one letter.)

De Sade's combination of belated paternal attention and unwonted rallying to the standard soon slid from the forefront of his concerns as Louis Marie joined the Rohan Soubise infantry regiment. His father had no more power to direct his children's lives than he had to walk out of Vincennes.

CHAPTER 20: "MY WAY OF THINKING"

The Marquis de Sade, of course, was firmly of the opinion that his incarceration was doing no good whatsoever. When he turned his pen to this matter, as he often did, he examined it exclusively in the light of whether his being confined under royal order was any good for him, ignoring almost all consideration of whether this might be keeping others out of the way of any harm he would otherwise be able to do them. Looking back at one point over some of the jails which had held him, he railed to his wife:

"What good did Pierre Encise do me? Miolans? The first time I was at Vincennes? All this had dulled my intelligence and my spirit, made me bitter, reinforced my old habits. Given my perverse temperament, restrictions can only make me worse." He had been the same since he was a child - "Amblet raised me and he could tell you" - and would not change now.

In July 1783, he accused the marquise:

"... You thought you were going to work a miracle, I bet, by imposing on me a terrible abstinence from *the sin of the flesh*. Well, you are mistaken: you have stoked up my brain, you have caused me to summon phantoms which I will have to give substance. That had begun to fade away, but now it will begin again with a vengeance. When you overheat the pot, you understand, it's going to boil over..."

His pot was not to be cooled by him or anyone else, he insisted. As early in his detention at Vincennes as March 1777, a few weeks after he had been arrested at the Danemark Hotel, he was writing to Mme de Montreuil:

"Do you think you are going to make me behave myself by punishing me like a little boy? A quite useless move, Madame... You have enough intelligence to understand that a fault whose origin lies in the effervescence of the blood is not to be corrected by souring that blood even more, by inflaming the brain through isolation and irritating the imagination through solitude..."

De Sade was still insisting, after his appeal hearing at Aix and his return to Vincennes via an escaper's interval at la Coste, that no-one could be held responsible for actions that welled out of internal forces:

"It is just to punish wrong-doing that a man committed in spite of having been able to stay his hand. But if he could not, if all his actions stem from an initial impulse, an absolute necessity arising from his own organs, from the movement of his liquors, if they are so linked to his physicality that no choice is available to him (as many thinkers have claimed), the law, in such a case, is quite despotic because it is odious to punish a man for wrong-doing which he could not avoid."

The prisoner was drawing on what were, in his era, recent discoveries in medical science which were neither as well understood as they are today nor had they been given the terms which describe them nowadays. Like other well-informed people of his time, de Sade was groping towards comprehension of observations such as those of doctors who had noted the spasms of the body which could occur involuntarily in humans and other animals, even after decapitation. Related to this was the understanding which was emerging from study of changes of mood and behaviour occurring in humans according to different stimuli and circumstances, these latter seeming to affect the subjects through certain systems of communication in the body. In our times, we would talk of the nerves, of epilepsy, of changes caused by disease of the brain, of psychological disorders arising from aspects of the subject's social environment, and so forth.

For thinkers in the second half of the 18th century, especially such a convinced atheist as de Sade, acceptance of physical phenomena as causes of behavioural changes in individuals facilitated the challenge, also under way in that era, to traditional religious beliefs. The Catholic Church held that, although individuals might commit sins, every action, every phenomenon, was an Act of God. By study of the medical science of the age, however, one might come to the conclusion that every human and animal act was governed by nature, and was the culmination of a succession of consequential events whose last conduit was "his own organs, ... the movement of his liquors".

From all this, de Sade was able to find confirmation for his rejection of God and religion, and able to embrace a replacement author of his misdeeds. De Sade the despiser of another's domination of himself had to spurn any directing divinity, yet de Sade the dodger of responsibility had to be sure of some force to which he could ascribe his wrong-doings. Nature filled the bill. The notion that a person of maturity, respectful of human society and the whole environment, could strive to overcome the maleficent effects of outside irritants was also very much current among enlightened thinkers of his time, but was not convenient to de Sade. He rarely entertained it.

"The ways we act do not depend on us," he told his wife in 1782, "they relate to the way we are made, the way we are organised..."

In another letter: "Ideas are linked with matter, for sensations are nothing other than the different forms or accidents of matter - no hand, no sensation of touching and therefore no idea derived from that; no eye, no sensation of seeing."

Another questioned rhetorically the responsibility of any sexual libertine "if excessive swelling in tiny vessels [of the body] can disturb a brain in a moment and make a villain out of the most honest of men in the space of one day..."

For all that, de Sade did not rely exclusively on ill-understood scientific observations and his self-serving interpretation thereof, when seeking to justify his stubborn adherence to his beliefs and behaviour. In November 1783, he replied to another fruitless wigging from the marquise:

"My way of thinking, you say, can only encounter disapproval. What's that to me? Anyone who adopts any way of thinking for the sake of other people must be crazy! My way of thinking is the fruit of my reflections: it is linked with my very being, the way in which I am put together. I am not the helmsman who can steer it differently; I could be, but I won't do it. This way of thinking that you find wrong is the only solace I know; it eases all my woes in prison, it makes up all my pleasure in this world and I hold on to it more fervently than to life itself. It is not at all my way of thinking that has led to my unhappiness, but that of other people. The reasonable man who holds in contempt the prejudices of fatheads necessarily becomes the enemy of the fatheads... A traveller takes the high road. Traps are laid along the way. He falls in one. Are you saying this is the fault of the traveller or of the rogue who laid the traps? Now, if as you say my freedom is available at the cost of sacrificing my principles or my tastes, then we can bid each other goodbye for ever, for I would rather sacrifice a thousand lives and a thousand freedoms, if I had them. I push these principles and these tastes to a fanatical extent, which itself is the work of the persecutions of those who tyrannise over me. The more they continue their harassment, the more they root these principles in my heart, and I declare openly that there is no need to talk to me about liberty if that is offered to me only at the price of destroying them. I am telling you this. I would tell M Le Noir.[1] I would tell all the world..."

While rating his own principles and preferences highly, de Sade admitted the existence of no principles among those whom he regarded as his oppressors. They were rotted by corruption and expediency, he maintained. Writing in a lighter vein to La Jeunesse, his copyist and his wife's servant, in 1779 or 1780, it seems, the master waxed as bawdily as he could, bearing in mind the censors, in making mock of prison and its administrators. His nickname for La Jeunesse was Señor Quiros; by any name he seems to have been someone ready to concur with de Sade's sentiment when the latter wrote to him: "The creator of nature produced vines and cunts, so you can be certain he meant us to enjoy them both." The letter, in part, went thus:

"... You're being cheeky, my lad! If I were there, I would give you a good hiding... I would rip off your poxy false hairpiece that you repair every year with the arse hairs from the bidets on the way from Courtheson[2] to Paris... What are you going to do, you cunning dog, to mend it?... You'll go at it like a country bumpkin shaking down nuts, tugging right and left at all the old black things that line the shops of an evening all along the rue Saint-Honoré, and then next day with a bit of strong glue you'll arrange all the bits on your scaly old forehead so that it'll look like nothing more or less than crabs on a wh[ore's] 'pothole', right, my lad?

"Now then, ... try to shut up for a minute, I beg of you, because I'm fed up with being insulted for so long by the riff-raff. It's true that I do what dogs do when I see all that pack of yapping lap-dogs and scruffy pups barking behind me, I lift my leg and I piss in their faces.

"F[uck], you're carrying on like some clever old chap in a book! Where did you pick up such fancy stuff?... These elephants which kill Caesar, this Brutus who steals cattle, this Hercules, this battle of Prunelles, and this Varius!... You filched all that one night on the way back from taking your mistress to sup...

---

1 No need, for his officers would have read this letter and noted its defiance.

2 Pun on *courtisane*, French for courtesan.

"What's all this you're telling me about a fat woman?[3] I gave you my little trick for full women;[4] yes I did... Is it you who's full; is it Mme Patulos? Or maybe it's Missy PRINTEMPS? Tell me ... who is it that's full out of your lot ... you remember my song: *He's a lucky one who can [fuck] himself.* Well I sing it here six times a day and whistle it four times.

"Hey, old monkey-c[ock]! Old worry-chops covered in blackberry juice,[5] prop for Noah's vine, backbone of Jonah's whale, old matchstick for lighting a br[othel], rancid candle at two-dozen to the pound, rotten girth of my wife's donkey, you haven't discovered islands for me?... You haven't been to discover islands for me and you haven't found seven of them for me in a morning. Ah! old pumpkin steeped in bug juice, third horn on the head of the devil, cod's body on a slab like the two ears of an oyster, whore-keeper's reject, dirty linen from the *red things* belonging to Missy PRINTEMPS! If I had hold of you, how I would wallop you, with your ugly old cooked-apple face that looks like a roast chestnut, to teach you not to lie that way..."

De Sade's knockabout monologue to his erstwhile valet and travelling companion in Italy, although muffled by translation from one language to another, and from one era to another, is worth including here for the rare glimpse it provides of the marquis letting his hair down when in contact with a person whom he did not want to impress or overwhelm in argument. One can imagine the two of them - the sleek and fair little lord and the lean, tall and dark retainer - lurching out of a Neapolitan bordello in the hour before dawn, the one having enjoyed the best *bel giovannetto* of the house and a fine wine upstairs, the other having taken a cheaper *ragazza* and a rough *vino rosso* in quarters below. Perhaps, from what we know of the marquis with his valets, La Jeunesse and a woman or two might have been brought into play with the lord and master in order to multiply his effect. Studded though the letter is with allusions which escape us now, it represents a relief from de Sade flourishing his "most authentic word of honour" amid a welter of abstractions which do little to illuminate the roisterer in him.

---

3 *femme grosse.*

4 De Sade had a recipe for causing pregnant women to abort - a criminal offence in the France of his time. He kept it in writing, which did not help his cause for this seems to have been found in his papers after his arrest in February 1777 in Paris. He claimed to have kept it as a curiosity and never to have used it on any woman.

5 La Jeunesse was very swarthy.

However, like most of de Sade's correspondents, La Jeunesse came in for his share of the prisoner's railing against injustice, albeit adapted to the particular reader:

"As you know, Señor Quiros, in France there is plenty of 'respectable' respect for whores. A man may slander the government, the King, religion - none of that matters a jot. But a whore, Señor Quiros, by the devil's fly-buttons, a whore! One has to very careful not to offend a whore lest, like a shot, the Sartines, ... Montreuils and all the other bordello clerks arrive with hard-handed soldiers to back up the whore and lock away a nobleman for twelve or fifteen years because of one whore. Now, there is no more valiant body of men than the French police. If you have a sister, a niece or a daughter, Señor Quiros, advise her to take up whoring, for she cannot join a more exalted profession. How else can a girl rely on as much support, as much credulity, as much shelter as a respectable woman of wealth can enjoy, besides living in the lap of luxury and an endless ecstasy of debauchery? Now this is truly the way to promote morality, my dear friend, the very means to ensure that a pure girl learns to hate the low life. By heaven above, how neatly plotted! Señor Quiros, what understanding is abroad in our days! For my part, Señor Quiros, I solemnly promise you that, if heaven had not given me a position in life that will let me support my daughter, I swear by all I hold most sacred that I would make a whore of her without hesitation... Ask Lady Montreuil, go and ask her, if there is any better maker of virtues than the lock. I know all too well that there are animals - such as yourself, Señor Quiros, I'm sure you will forgive me - who try to maintain that, if a man is jailed once and it has no effect, then it is very dangerous to put him inside again. However, that is a foolish misapprehension, Señor Quiros. This is the correct argument: prison is the only cure known in France, therefore prison must be good and, being good, is to be applied in every instance. But it did not succeed - not the first, not the second, not the third time... Very well, they reply, all the more reason for a fourth try! Prison was not at fault because we have - well, not proved conclusively but set out that prison is good, therefore the object of the remedy is at fault and should be imprisoned again. Bleeding is good for a fever - in France we know nothing better, therefore bleeding is the best cure... But [one] may have delicate nerves or be short of blood, so bleeding does no good and some other therapy should be found. Not a bit of it, one's doctor will say, bleeding is just the thing for fever, therefore one should be bled... What's more, as a doctor he makes money by bleeding you, such-and-such a fee every time the lancet cuts, so you have to be bled. And Sartine earns by having you jailed, pockets so much for each inmate, so you have to be locked up..."

So, if jail was not the right medicine, then what? The marquise was the recipient in June 1783 of one fanciful prescription from her husband:

"If I had been given *Mr 6* to cure, I would have done the job in quite another way for, rather than lock him away with cannibals, I would have cloistered him with girls; I would have supplied him with so many that I'm damned if, over the seven years he has been inside, all the oil in his lamp hadn't been burned! When you have a horse that's too spirited, you gallop it over heavy going; you don't lock it up in the stable. That way, you would have put your man on the *right way*, on what one calls the *honourable* path. Away with these *sophistries* [of mine], these researches spurned by nature (as though nature took any notice of all that), these *dangerous* departures of an over-fiery imagination which, always running after happiness without ever finding it in anything, end by putting ghosts in place of reality and *unseemly deviations* in place of a straightforward enjoyment. *Mr 6*, in the middle of a harem, would have become *the friend of women*; he would have recognised and *felt* that nothing is more beautiful, nothing greater, than real sexual contact, and that without it there is no way back to health. Being entirely occupied in serving the ladies and satisfying their exquisite desires, *Mr 6* would have given up all of his. The habit of no longer experiencing any but proper encounters would have got his mind used to overcoming those tendencies that could prevent him giving pleasure. All that would have ended by pacifying him, so you see how, in the bosom of vice, I would have been returned to virtue..."

The rare breath of a Sadeian acknowledgement that he had strayed from "the right way", and that he ought to return to the path by conquering those preoccupations which prevented him giving pleasure, offers a zephyr of hope. However, readers might recall that, when Mr 6 was at liberty and had paid harems of various kinds from time to time, it was the women who found the going heavy as he concentrated on his own exquisite desires. The recipe for breaking the unruly stallion of Vincennes by exhaustion in a seraglio was far from realistic, and was another variation on de Sade's theme of fretting about his incarceration, rather than offering means to end it.

He would have all France, all Christendom, change before he would alter his views to those which his captors and his relatives wanted him to embrace. Attitudes and rules were not immutable - they were varied over time and differed according to where in the world one stood - so why should everyone in France toe one line. To his wife, the marquis was eloquent in his recalcitrance:

"Because of failure to give due honour to a whore's arse, a father is exposed to the possibility that he will lose his children's love irretrievably through being kept away from them, he is plucked from his wife's embrace and from the properties he manages, ... he is stopped from giving his children their place in society and from ever taking his own position therein, he is the butt and victim of a mob of jailers, he has to waste his time and money, and let his health be ruined, as well as be caged like a lunatic these seven years!... What could have led to such monstrous consequences? Did he plot treason? Did he conspire to cut short the life of his wife, of his children, of his king? Not a bit of it - not a hint of any such thing. He has had the misfortune to believe firmly that nothing is less respectable than a whore, and that the way you use that has to be no different to the way you pass your motions...

"If one were to go and tell the King of Achem, who has himself attended by seven hundred wenches on whom three or four hundred lashes fall daily on account of the least misdemeanour, and who tests his military sabre on their necks, or tell the Emperor of Golconda, who never goes out and about except on twelve women making up the shape of an elephant, and who makes a sacrifice out of a dozen of them by his own hand whenever a prince of the royal blood dies; if, I say, one were to go and tell those lords that there is a little patch of land in Europe where a man in black[6] has constantly in his pay three thousand rogues searching out for him the ways in which the citizens of this little patch (people who regard themselves as *very free*) spurt their spermatic matter, and that there are dungeons all ready, scaffolds in good order, for any of these *very free* people who still have not been able to understand that it was a very great crime to open the sluices in one way rather than the other, and that the least agitation in the head at such a moment, when nature requires one to lose all restraint but the man in black requires one to keep control, was punished by death or by twelve to fifteen years in jail; if, I say, one went to relay all this to the

6 Police chief Le Noir, whose name means *the black*.

monarchs I have just cited, there is no denying that they would be quite justified in putting away the bearer of the tidings as a lunatic. But those people over there are not at all subject to policing, they lack the happiness of illumination by the light of Christianity, they are slaves, while we, on the other hand, are *very Christian, very policed and very free*.

"O maker of this vicious little round ball, you who might have wafted into place with just one breath ten thousand million balls like ours in the vastness of space, you who would not spare even one sigh over the loss of those ten thousand millions, how you must be amused by all the foolishness of the little ants which it has pleased you to sow across your globes, how you must laugh about the King of Achem who lashes seven hundred women, about the Emperor of Golconda who turns them into post-horses, and about the man in black who requires one to keep control as one spurts one's s[punk]. Good night, my little wife."

For all the long flights into unreality as to how he might be made more amenable while in prison, and for all his rejection of the motives for his having been put there in the first place, de Sade indicated that he might be approachable. In the spring of 1779, he wrote to Rousset:

"Indifferent as I am to misfortunes, I have little fear of new blows dealt by fate, and the scaffold makes me neither deceitful, nor treacherous, nor humble. Yet, despite this unshakeable firmness, this solid character on which I pride myself, the merest thing, a token of *real* friendship, a proof of confidence, would have made me into all you would wish, would have made me scour mountains with my emotion and break my head open with my discipline..."

The trouble was that the decision as to what was *real* friendship would have lain with de Sade, who was excessively ready to detect an insult and was a stickler for his place in the social hierarchy. He neither gave nor attracted friendship readily. Much the most promising of his rare indications that some way might be found to work on him, while in prison, was a passing remark to his wife in November 1781:

"It would have been more worthwhile sending me once a fortnight an intelligent man who would have worked alternately on my heart and on my head, and who would have put them back together..."

As near as may be, he was offering himself for psychotherapy, but the society of his time, and the royal administration, would have allowed no more in this area than the visits of a priest, whose calling Mr 6 would not have respected.

In a similar spirit, the prisoner told his wife in another letter: "You cannot expect to have a man come away from the chasm in one leap... Settle for inculcating in him a desire for delights that are less violent but are in the same region as those to which he was addicted. That way, you will bring him step by step away from the mire... A person's digestion has to take to a diet gradually - an abrupt and total fast ruins it..."

Just so (forgiving the mixed metaphors), but no-one in the Sadeian milieu apart from himself and his wife understood the efficacy of such a graduated therapy, and the man himself was far from being able to keep a consistent grip on the idea.

When giving his attention to how his condition might be altered to his advantage, de Sade did not limit himself to ideas about prison régimes. He also thought about how he might be allowed to live at liberty, without too great a compromise on his part. In a letter of summer 1782, he was at the familiar Sadeian hymnal - that he was beyond reform: "The beast is too old .... ten thousand years of imprisonment and five hundred pounds of chain would only fix my habits more securely... We cannot shape our behaviour, it stems from the way we have been influenced, the way we have been put together..."

Then he suddenly made what for him was a subtle and extraordinary distinction between private behaviour and social conduct:

"What we can do is to refrain from spreading our poison, not only so that those around us do not suffer by it but could not even be aware of it. Behaviour towards one's children and one's wife so clean that, even when she compares her situation with those of other wives, she cannot have any suspicion of her husband's bad behaviour; that's what we can do, and that's what a decent man must manage, for one is not labelled a villain if one only has a little oddness in one's pleasures. Keep this from public knowledge, especially from one's children, and so that one's wife never has the slightest inkling of it, and let one's duties to her all be carried out in *every way*. That's what matters, and that's what I promise..." He went on to swear he would never so much as come near giving his children "bad principles - between killing them and turning them to the bad, I would not hesitate for a minute, and I would almost believe the first to be the lesser evil..."

The departure in the letter just quoted adds up to no more than a promise of efficient deceit in his infidelities - no more flaunting the debauchery. Many relationships have stood on just such a watertight deception. What would the marquis be doing in the intervals between his acts of clandestine libertinage? In February 1784, he suggested to Renée Pélagie that he might "live in such part of the world as I would desire, there to give myself entirely to the arts and the sciences, to be surrounded by my wife and my children - there are all my wishes in a few words."

In another letter, of August 1782, to his wife, he was specific about where in the world he might be placed, fruitfully and out of harm's way:

"I want to make an odd bet with you and your team - that, over the last ten years, one hundred thousand livres have been wasted on making me one hundred thousand times worse than I was at the start, and on bringing the honour and esteem of my children down by more than one hundred pegs...

"I used to be put up at the doctor's[7]. One servant and I had bed and board - very good they were - for 800 livres [a year]. Reckon another 1,200 for my other expenses and so on, then work out what would have been left over from [the real expenses of] the last ten years. I would have come away with an extra hundred thousand in my purse, a good book to put before the world and a load of information ready in my head. A glance at what has really happened leads you to understand the contrasting result of that. However, you will claim that you had to impose silence and isolation.

"Well, you see, that could have been achieved the other way. France has an ambassador in Florence... Barbantane, who is a canny fellow and a relative of mine, would have supervised me and, to encourage me to stay within the boundaries of Florence, could have had ready a French royal order which, once he decided to use it, would have sent me back to prison [in France] before a week was out. [While I stayed in Florence,] he would have kept an eye on my correspondence, my expenses and so forth. I would assume a foreign name and that bunch of villains which is forever clamouring for me to be locked away would be told that I was as good as a prisoner of the Grand Duke [of Tuscany], which the rascals could well believe because they did not see

7 The home of the physician Dr Ménil in Florence.

me any longer or hear any news of me. That is how intelligent people manage things.

"Now, compare the procedure of complete idiots who hand over the protection of their affairs to bowers and scrapers, rather than seek the best way towards the happiness and well-being of their family."

This outline moved no-one to shift him from Vincennes to supervised scholarship in a Tuscan exile, in the congenial, learned and unbuttoned company of his old acquaintance Dr Ménil.

The urgent tone and absence of sarcasm in de Sade's letter of September 1781 to Mme de Montreuil, cited above in connection with his declaration that no machinations of hers could prise him away from his wife, suggest he had hopes that his plea therein would be heeded. Coming from the stubborn marquis, and going to his arch-enemy, the latter part of the letter makes for very strange reading:

"Do not leave me to die without having had a chance to remove from [my wife's] memory all my misdeeds... Bring us together again, under any supervision you choose, in any country... Then if I behave badly towards her in any way, may I never see her again, may I be imprisoned again and, if it is so deemed, may I be put to death... If you had wished to see me at the deepest humiliation, despair and wretchedness that one can reach, celebrate, Madame, for you have your desire. Religion and nature require that you shall not exact your revenge as far as the tomb, and that you shall not frustrate my wish to make amends. To this heartfelt prayer I join the supplication that you shall not set me at liberty except to be reunited with my wife... Be so good as to allow me to see her - alone - as soon as may be, I beg of you...

"... Can you believe that such a long detention has not made me reflect? Can you suppose that it has not awakened some remorse? I ask only one favour of you, Madame, and that is for you to put me to the test... Be so good as to have a little pity for my condition, I beseech you! It is dreadful. I know that I am handing you your triumph over me... Allow me ... to throw myself at your feet to ask your pardon for laying before you the horror of my condition. You should see in this only ... the true feelings of my heart... I implore you shamelessly and I must blush before you, madame, only on account of my faults..."

His mother-in-law's position was the same as it had been in 1777 when he was arrested in Paris - she believed that hers and his were better off with him in jail, and she would leave the matter to the proper authorities in any event. There is no record of a reaction from Mme de Montreuil to the marquis's letter.

These departures into concession, into retreat, by de Sade were always succeeded, sometimes in the next sentence of the one letter, by a reassertion of his need to regain the indomitable mode. In August 1782, the prisoner told his wife, from the sweltering and humid Cell No. 6:

"In 1777, I was still fairly young[8]; the heap of trouble in which I found myself could have prepared the ground[9]; my heart was not hardened and closed against kind feelings then in the way that you have since taken care that it should become. A quite opposite approach on your part could have worked great things. You did not want that... I thank you for it; I greatly prefer having only to sweep your numbers out of my head, rather than having had to drive away a universe of things and details, very delightful in my estimation, which know so well how to soothe my unhappiness when I let my imagination wander. One could say that you have been very badly advised; but, in all conscience, I am very glad that it all went as it did."

A quite opposite approach, as he put it, by Renée Pélagie might well have meant her replying to his rage and insults in kind, or abandoning him. As things stood, he found a way, as ever, to blame someone else for his situation, even for the hardness of his own heart. The last sentences cited above represent a chilling acknowledgement of his own closure against the warmth and amity that the world might yet offer him, in favour of fantasy enjoyed in solitude. He was using his practised bluster to make out that he did not care whether or not he was lost, with no way back from the pen and masturbation.

He did get out of Vincennes, early in 1784, but only to travel under close escort the few miles across Paris to another fortress-prison, that of the Bastille, closer to the centre of the capital. The government had decided that Vincennes was no longer to be a jail. The first de Sade knew of this was on the evening of 29 February, when police came to his cell to take him, right away and without luggage, to his new quarters.

---

8 Aged 36, at the date of his arrest.

9 For a suggestion that he modify his conduct in exchange for his liberty.

CHAPTER 21: THE BASTILLE AND CONTINUED *PRESSURAGE*

After his wheezy lungs had enjoyed rare breaths of fresh air, during the few hours of winter night it took to transfer him by coach from Vincennes, de Sade resumed undergoing, at the Bastille, his *pressurage*. This was the word he applied to his incarceration, and an apt one from a lord of estates in the south of France where grapes were subjected to *pressurage* in order to squeeze out their juice for making wine. The king and his ministers having given their prisoner the time and, by and large, the absence of distractions to write extensively, de Sade filled his vats in Cell No. 6 at Vincennes, and then on the second floor of the Liberty Tower at the Bastille, with words. He had little option but to write, having been already much inclined to literature since before he had seen the inside of a prison, and that being a main means by which he could conduct a semblance of his former life beyond the walls and guards. While at Vincennes, de Sade had complained at one point that, if he was to be locked away, at least he might be allowed the means "to live according to my fancies". The closest the authorities came to fulfilling that wish was to let him have pen, ink and paper, out of which he pressed an astounding vintage, never to be forgotten once tasted.

In February 1781, he had written to the marquise: "Yes, I'm a libertine, I admit to it; I have thought of all that can be thought of in that line, but I have certainly not done all that I have thought of and I certainly never will. I'm a libertine, but I am neither *a criminal* nor *a murderer*..." Two years later, he had declared that he was being squeezed into summoning "phantoms which I will have to give substance..." Within the confines of the alphabet, he did so, writing fancies far beyond the horizons of the debauches of his earlier days. The difference, remember, was one of *degree*, not of kind. De Sade, when at the work which has put his name into the dictionaries, was making a wine alien and disgusting to most palates, but using the old grapes of human experience and familiar methods. He just pressed much harder than most - *was* pressed much harder, he maintained.

He started work on the novel *The Hundred and Twenty Days of Sodom* in the summer of 1783, while still at Vincennes, and the early notes for it probably caught up with him at the Bastille on 29 April 1784 when his luggage arrived from Vincennes. One can imagine his relief and pleasure at finding, as he unpacked, that the police had missed the embryonic version of a tale of "beings of a deep criminality which they acknowledge in themselves, whose only deity is their lubricity, only rule is their depravity, only taste is for debauchery; profligates without god, without principle, without creed, the least criminal of whom is befouled by more outrages than you could count, and in whose estimation the life of a woman - what am I saying? the life of one woman? - the lives of all the women who inhabit the Earth mean no more than that of a squashed fly."

So much for his pledge to Renée Pélagie, by a letter of mid-summer 1782 (**see chapter 20**), "to refrain from spreading our poison". For the time being, however, as of Leap Year day 1784, the poison was confined to an octagonal cell on the second floor of the Liberty Tower of the Bastille fortress, smaller than No. 6 at Vincennes but having a window, albeit with three sets of bars, that gave more light. Each of the eight named towers contained one room on each of four, five or six floors. The freedom alluded to by the name of the Liberty Tower was strictly relative to the fortress, arising from that part of the Bastille having been reserved formerly for prisoners who had the freedom of the courtyard below. The food was generally reckoned to be better and more plentiful than that at Vincennes - no Governor de Rougemont trimming the supplies to line his own pocket - but de Sade was allowed, at first, no knife to cut up his meals, nor scissors for his stationery and fingernails. The marquis, his ready propensity for complaint now meshing with a range of petty regulations new to him, told the marquise: "I enjoyed seven years at Vincennes with knife and scissors, without any harm coming of it. I have not improved in those seven years, I know very well, but nor have I got any worse. Will you not make this clear to them, and so obtain for me unrestricted use of these two items?"

From 14 April, the gentleman in the Second Liberty was allowed "at dinner a knife, the which he shall return each day when his utensils are cleared away," according to the fortress log.

The prisoner was ironic to his wife when reporting the servant problem: "... they say I have to make my own bed and sweep my room. The first is done in good time, because it was being done very badly and besides I rather like doing it. But the second, unfortunately I have no idea how to go about it; this is my parents' fault for not having included that particular skill in my education. The thing is that they did not foresee - well, *many things*. If they had foreseen them, there would be no tavern servant who could keep up with me. Lacking that, however, I beg you to arrange for me to have some lessons. Now, if the manservant here sweeps only once a week for four or five years, I'll watch how he does it, and you'll see that after that I'll be doing it quite as well as he..."

De Sade was much sharper - and rightly so, as any flat-dweller below a top floor will testify - about the noise from upstairs, from the inmate of the Third Liberty: "It was even necessary to take from me the only consolation of the unfortunate, the only balm which soothes their sores, *sleep*, and so, three feet from my pillow, they've lodged a man who sleeps all day and who, on the stroke of midnight, and until eight o'clock in the morning, charges about, smashes things, breaks things, bellows and does other such favours."

This nuisance seems not to have lasted - at any rate, de Sade did not keep up his grumbles about it - and the marquis himself had a little more scope for exercise than had been the case at Vincennes. Prisoners at the Bastille were allowed to walk not only in the deep courtyard in the centre of the fortress - reputed to have been icy in winter, a furnace in summer - but also high above the city of Paris on the battlements between the towers. Even so, each prisoner took his walk alone: the administration of each royal jail was concerned to prevent conspiracy among prisoners, as well as to protect the family of any of them from the gossip that might arise from news of his incarceration reaching the world at large.

Walks were agreeable, but de Sade was asking the administration, within a few weeks of his arrival at the Bastille, for his exercise periods to be arranged so as to facilitate a more important activity, his literary work: "It's impossible for someone who is busy to break off from his work today at such-and-such a time, tomorrow at some other time. So I am asking with some urgency to be given a fixed time ... and that this time be exactly the same every day, even if that means my not taking the air on those days when there is some impediment at the set times..."

What the marquis did not tell the administration, although it may well have been large in his motives for asking for a firm timetable for his walks, was that such a reliable régime meant that he could be sure of when a turnkey would come to his door. (The meal times were already fixed.) Knowing when he was to be interrupted, de Sade could avoid being taken by surprise, not only when in the midst of an elaborate masturbation with self-penetration by his painstakingly acquired dildoes, but also when writing notes and works which he did not want to lose to seizure by the authorities, and when hiding such material in his cell. Also important for a prisoner who wanted to write without interruption or inspection was the option of staying late at his quill, when the rest of the fortress (except him upstairs perhaps) was at rest, so de Sade complained about the rule which required lights out at 2200 hours. He seems to have been able to circumvent this regulation later in his time at the Bastille.

These grievances aroused his customary eloquence - "persecutions" and "stupidities" they became in letters to the police - but should not obscure the fact that he lived higher on the hog than many another prisoner, before or since. When he entered the fortress, his board and lodging were being charged to the Montreuil family at 2,400 livres a year. Pauvert reckons that, what with further sums spent on personal expenses and titbits supplied by the marquise, the occupant of the Second Liberty was soon costing 4,000 livres or so a year. Pauvert points out that this sum was five or six times the pay of a warder at the fortress, and he compares it with the annual salary of the Marquis de Launay[1], governor of the fortress (6,000 livres), and of de Losme-Salbray, one of his senior officers (1,500).

When de Sade entered the Bastille, few of its rooms were occupied by noblemen regarded as too dangerous to let out - only two apart from the marquis. Various other such prisoners in France had their royal orders rescinded early in 1784. Unaware of this, de Sade himself remained as imperious as ever in setting terms and conditions for his release. In a letter which he called "the product of a meditation as long as it was calm and cool-headed", ending in an "unshakeable resolution" which, if defied by others, would entail "a terrible succession of misfortunes", he thundered to his wife:

"I want to spend a year, no matter where, with you and my children before any scheme or any party may take them away from me, and I will stop at nothing *to block whatever you may have arranged contrary to this one plan*... I will be opposed to their being separated from me before I shall have had time to get to know them and to make them love

---

[1] That name de Launay yet again - but the governor of the Bastille was no relation to his counterpart at Miolans or to Anne Prospère.

me thereby. This consideration is too important with regard to the remainder of their lives, and of mine, for me to give it up... I would choose a thousand times more readily to have no children at all than to have children who did not know me, or knew me only in so far as they wished me dead..."

In the meantime, while still locked up, de Sade evoked a wonderful new form of transport, demonstrated by the Montgolfier brothers in the France of his time, in expressing to the marquise his fear that her family was plotting "to lift me out of here like a *balloon* in order to take me to Valeri[2]. Don't you try it, heed me now... I would throw myself under the coach[3], at the risk of being crushed under the wheels, if I could not save myself in any other way, rather that let myself be taken to any place belonging to your infamous mother... The vile woman, delighted to have me before I had had the time to see or get to know anyone, would no sooner have hold of me than she would have me thrown into a dungeon and then give out that I'm dead..."

There was much more imagination than reality in those projections of himself beyond the prison walls. De Sade's expression of his imagination on paper achieved more substance in the plays which he continued to write and revise in the Second Liberty, discussing them through the mail with his old mentor the Abbé Amblet. Also, that imagination distilled a mighty poison during the hours between the predictable interruptions by the prison's daily round. Drawing on the notes of sexual behaviour he had been collecting at least for two decades, on 22 October 1785, de Sade began the draft of *The Hundred and Twenty Days* that survives to this day. He worked only in the evenings, when he could be confident of proceeding without an interruption which could have scuppered the whole project if an officer of the fortress had seen what he was about and seized the manuscript as an outrage to God and good government. With tiny handwriting, he covered one side and part of the other of what became, when he had joined all the bits together, a piece of paper 39ft 8 ins long and 4½ ins wide. Once he had completed the draft 37 evenings later, on 28 November, the paper could be tightly rolled for easy concealment. Pauvert speculates that de Sade hid the manuscript inside one of his smooth wooden dildoes - if so, an entirely appropriate niche for a

---

2 A Montreuil country estate, far from the eyes of any city. Its correct name was Vallery.

3 The hot-air balloons of the Montgolfiers indeed were not reliable for long-distance travel.

stunning celebration of sodomy, among other activities. Four months earlier, the marquise had been lamenting to Gaufridy that her husband was still unable to "curb his pen and this does him untold damage."

The details of the span of time de Sade devoted to this extraordinary act of concentrated creation, all the more remarkable from a writer with bad eyesight working by candlelight, we have from the author himself, by way of a note on the manuscript itself. As far as we know, he never added to the version of *The Hundred and Twenty Days* which survives, and which includes specific indications that it was not fully developed. However, many Sadeian works have not reached us, those who took care to destroy them having left no more than flimsy hints that they ever existed, so de Sade might well have produced another version of the terrible tale, of which there is now no trace whatsoever. Any further draft of the manuscript might have been carried off in the pillage of the Bastille in July 1789. The one that survived was missed by the insurgents and is amazing enough. I will return to it in the last section of this book.

One reason for de Sade not having worked again on *The Hundred and Twenty Days* was his abiding attention to theatrical output. During his first months at the Bastille he was asking the marquise for "the new comedies or tragedies of the season... I've an even greater need of them this year... I've done a lot of work in both genres so I can't do without what's coming out, so I can learn, and check what I've done..." In a long letter to his former tutor, the Abbé Amblet, painstaking and unrelenting critic of his plays, de Sade wrote, also in 1784, a measured counter to the old cleric's reaction to his play *Tancrède*. The prisoner went on:

"... It would give me great pleasure, no doubt about it, to see my works performed in Paris and, if I managed a success, the reputation I would get might make the indiscretions of my youth forgotten and rehabilitate me in some way. This would occupy a lot of my time and put everything else completely on one side. I even dare to say that this is the only means [to bring me away from bad behaviour], and the reason for that is physical: a superior force is needed to combat a strong force. Milady de Montreuil doesn't see it like that, for the great good reason that she makes it her business to take everything the wrong way. She's always afraid I'll put her in a play; well she can set her mind at rest: we should leave the *Calibans* to Shakespeare, they don't go down well in our [French] theatre...

"... You advise me to write history? I've tried, ... but I don't have the same feeling for it. Besides, the best work of history often reaches not even two hundred readers, while the feeblest play always pulls in three or four thousand to the theatre..."

With that, de Sade placed a large clue as to why he worked so intensively on plays. The history book would not only reach a mere handful of readers, as the marquis pointed out, but also would affect them severally, in libraries or at home where the author would not witness their engagement with his work. By contrast, a play staged in a theatre-going city such as Paris would excite immediate reactions from hundreds of spectators every night, while the author, in the wings or the auditorium, could savour every shift of their attention to his piece.

The work bottled up on the 40-foot roll of paper might evoke, in any reader able to stomach even half of it, a gasping and fascinated engagement. A passage towards the end of the introduction - in which the author addresses the "dear reader" and promises him that at least some of the contents "will get you so het up as to cost you your spunk" - is unequivocally that of an author moulding the reader's response, and pleased to be doing so. Yet the writer would not be able to witness the reader's shudder of disgust, or yelp of ejaculation; nor would he - although I think de Sade was reckoning to get *The Hundred and Twenty Days* published by one of the Dutch printers with whom he had links - be able to put his name on the book, which any government he had known at the time of writing would confine to a semi-clandestine circulation and fame, at most, the author remaining anonymous to all but a few trusted cronies.

No, the theatre offered the only bright promise, for such as de Sade, of refurbishment to his reputation, of celebrity among the most glamorous people of the most glamorous city in the world, of instant response from the multitude in a great room where all eyes and ears were turned to the most engaging presentation of his work that the finest actors and designers could produce - in his very presence, if he so wished, and he would, he would. The schoolboy theatricals at Louis le Grand, the country-house amateur dramatics with his new wife and in-laws, the revels of which he was master at la Coste with Beauvoisin, the strolling troupe with the marquise, her sister Anne Prospère and sundry professionals in Provence before the unfortunate business at Marseilles - the spirit of all those manifestations of de Sade the thespian would be revived in a capital milieu which alone could furnish a success to exceed them all most gloriously.

Well, at least the hope thereof, and the labour thereunto, kept the wheezy gentleman in the Second Liberty from being a whit less of a nuisance than he otherwise might have been.

CHAPTER 22: "HEAD-FLED-TO-HELL"

While fashionable Paris was having to do without theatrical diversions by the Marquis de Sade, it was titillated by a nine-days wonder which may well have brought to some of the longer-memoried a recollection of the libertine reputation he was concerned to cover with a lacquer of new acceptability. In November 1784, the actress and courtesan who had once passed for the Marquise de Sade, died at about the age of 43. The subsequent sale of her astounding array of jewellery, clothes and furniture took a week to complete. While the capital was goggling at the late Beauvoisin's fruit of love (or love's lucrative substitute), her erstwhile patron, host and debtor, the inmate of the Second Liberty, was managing with the substitute familiar to prisoners. For a man who gave so much attention to seeking his own sexual pleasure, an unbroken régime of masturbation might have been expected to trouble him less than it seems to have done.

From the Bastille, probably in the latter half of 1784, having been in jail for seven years, de Sade wrote to his wife an extraordinary letter about his sexual episodes. It is hard to interpret, not only because he used code words, metaphors and euphemisms, no doubt in order to get the letter past the censors, but also because the marquis was groping for an understanding of his condition, for once, rather than declaiming his certainties. The key to the letter is the word *manille*, which de Sade underlined and which, since it had a special meaning for the writer and his correspondent, cannot be given an English equivalent. Various writers have offered opinions as to what it meant for the Marquis and Marquise de Sade but, before I add to the pile, here is the first part of the letter, in which the prisoner seems to be replying to a warning from his wife to be careful about his use of the mysterious *manille*:

"I know very well ... the *manille* has to be used with moderation. But what do you want! When that's all one has ... The best I can do is to manage without anything extraordinary. A good hour in the morning, for five *manilles*, deftly stepped up from 6 to 9, a good half-hour in the evening it's three, with lesser proportions... There's nothing there to get upset about, I think, for it's quite reasonable. Besides, when one's used to something it doesn't cause any bother - in fact, it's a good thing. I just don't see how it could be better. Don't let anyone come and tell me after this that I haven't gained anything from the Vincennes dungeon ... if one loses a little on [one] side, one gains a lot on the other; it's like a man who is burning down his house on one side and rebuilding it on the other. Because on the side that's not burning, there's truly exemplary behaviour - sometimes three months in fact. It's not that the bow is not being drawn - oh! don't fret about that ... - but it's that the arrow doesn't want to fly, and that's what kills me. One wants it to fly - without the result; the mind takes off instead, and that doesn't sort things out..."

The probability is that *manille* stands for self-sodomy - de Sade using one of the custom-made, smooth dildoes which caused his wife so much embarrassment and trouble when he was ordering them from Cell No. 6 at Vincennes. De Sade's concern with the dimensions of his dildoes, with a view to maximum satisfaction from depth and breadth of penetration of his anus, seems to recur in this letter when he mentions figures and proportions, likely to be numbers of insertions, inches of depth plumbed and width of instrument used.

What may be an excess of literal-mindedness prompts me to note, in passing, that *manille* could be interpreted as a shackle or a fetter, which is one of the meanings of the French word *manille*. From that, one could suggest that de Sade was referring to a device by which he was curbing tumescence, a penis hobble of some kind, physical or even mental. However, he was clearly complaining of difficulty in achieving ejaculation - the side of the house that did not burn represented lack of ejaculation, sometimes having lasted three months, though this was not for the want of trying, in that the bow had been drawn, which is to say he had been manipulating his penis. The failure to find relief in this way had caused mental disturbance - that is, the mind had taken off instead of the arrow of his semen.

The letter went on: "... But I have quite made up my mind about the stubbornness of this arrow in not wanting to fly, especially as, when it does cleave the breeze, there's a veritable attack of epilepsy. But for having taken bothersome precautions, I'm sure they would hear it in the Faubourg Saint Antoine[1]. The convulsions, the spasms and the pains - you've seen examples at la Coste. Now, though, you would reckon

---

1 The district of Paris bordering the walls of the Liberty Tower.

they're at least twice as bad. So ... I am taking to the *manille*, which is gentle and which entails nothing of all that..."

That passage leaves intact the notion that *manille* means self-sodomy, also without demolishing the tentative theory that it might refer to a curb, which de Sade could have regarded as "gentle" and an acceptable resort in that it did not entail the turmoil of his difficult ejaculations. However, self-sodomy could have provided relief through sexual activity without ejaculation, in that the dildo-wielding subject can transfer, with practice and habituation, his sexual sensitivity from his genitals to his anus, especially if the dildo and its operator make great demand of the anus, the intensity of his feelings allowing him no scope for his concentration to stray elsewhere.

All in all, taking account also of de Sade's propensity for sodomy, active and passive, and his aversion to curbs in general, I put aside the suggestion that *manille* was a penile hobble and proceed on the basis that it was self-sodomy. That leaves the question of why the marquis had such trouble with ejaculation. Note that Rose Keller, at the end of the flagellation on Easter Day, 1768, heard "loud and frightening cries" from de Sade, that the maids at la Coste in the winter of 1774-75 reported "a frenzy that can only be called madness", and that various male libertines in de Sade's fiction reach orgasm - often with difficulty and after unusual stimulation - in an outburst of writhing and yelling.

Back to the letter from the Bastille: "... I have tried to analyse the cause of this attack, and I think I've found it in the *extreme thickness*[2]. It's as though one were trying to make cream come out of the very narrow neck of a bottle. This thickness expands the ducts and lacerates them. In that case one says: the arrow has to fly more often. I know that very well, but it does not want to, and to force it when it doesn't want to, that kills me with fits. If I were also to have the means - other than the *manille* (for the *manille* no longer fires the arrow at all) - if I had *those other means* that I use when I'm at liberty, the arrow becoming less sluggish and flying more often, the crisis in shooting it would no longer be so violent, nor as dangerous... [There are] *terrible episodes, violent efforts,* if the arrow, too thickened by too much rest, has to tear the quiver as it passes through..."

---

2 Of his semen, one must suppose.

One does not fire an arrow from a quiver, so here the marquis's archery metaphor was mishandled. However, he was a cavalryman. So, of course, he called the fusiliers to his aid:

"... Think of a rifle loaded with a bullet, a bullet that swells while it remains in the barrel; if you fire the rifle after two days, the explosion will be slight; if you allow the bullet to get thick, when it's shot it will burst the barrel...

"... I would like you, if you have a reliable doctor, to discuss with him everything I'm telling you here, for I'm quite convinced that there is nobody in the world who goes through what I go through in this crisis... I must have a deformation which other men certainly do not have, a deformation which was less apparent in my youth and which is going, as I grow older, to show itself with ever increasing effect, and that prospect casts me down..."

All this was affecting his mental equilibrium, he maintained. When the arrow flew, he experienced "head-fled-to-hell" during a long subsequent crisis.

"... Far from agitation of the mind causing this, quite the reverse - for the more the mind is agitated, the less the arrow will fly. There again, you have seen this and you cannot but remember this well. The less it flies, the more the mind becomes agitated... If the arrow doesn't fly at all and one tries to force it: *horrible faintness*; if one succeeds, *terrible crisis*. And if one doesn't succeed, *head-fled-to-hell*. Decide whether I need to see a doctor and, above all, to take baths which, I am quite sure, must be good for this condition. If you can, tell me something about this, and be certain of all my tenderness."

The Bastille was little more congenial than Vincennes in the matter of baths for the inmates - a cause of annoyance to de Sade. Even less likely to be available to assuage his sexual problem were "*those other means* that I use when I'm at liberty". We cannot be sure what he meant by that, but I suggest he ejaculated much more readily when others were present, responding to him and to his impingement on them.

Let's note that only de Sade was giving evidence in this letter, having brooded for seven years in jail and hatched who knows what obsessions and exaggerations, albeit presented to his wife in a rational form. He might have been under a misapprehension arising from an obsession with the quality and/or quantity of his semen, this being not uncommon, especially among inmates of institutions for whom their semen is an important element in their retention of self-esteem as sexual beings and effective beings. I come, therefore I am; I come copiously, therefore I very much am. In his novel *Juliette*, written about a decade later than his letter of 1784, a character declares: "for us libertines, the quality and quantity of our semen is most important." Also, consider that every male sexual orgasm is a derangement, a spell of the vapours, to some degree, varying from individual to individual and from occasion to occasion. However, de Sade, the orgiast, may well have had more opportunities than most of us to observe other men at orgasm and may have had substantial indications that, as he claimed, his ejaculations involved more turmoil than other men undergo in such episodes.

All things considered, the letter rings true - it is clear of Sadeian bluster and the symptoms described are consistent with the writer having suffered from consequences of an old venereal infection, benign but badly treated, as Pauvert points out. The semen can become thick and somewhat granular, making each ejaculation painful. Also, the urethral channel can shrink.

This disorder might well be one cause of his irritable behaviour, and of his fascination with sexual stimulation which postponed, or eschewed altogether, ejaculation by himself. Also, his collision with delirium, with derangement, with sexual climax as a destructive phenomenon, could hardly fail to engage his curiosity, even his fear. Even so, the case file on the patient in the Second Liberty has many other data in it, and I shall look into it more deeply in the last section of this book.

There is no trace of any reply by the marquise to the letter.

* * *

Whatever his solitary sexual difficulties and adventures, it is hard for a long-term prisoner to avoid sinking into a routine. For de Sade, author in a cell, "the days follow one another," he lamented to Renée Pélagie in October 1787. "I go to bed at midnight with my mind on fire and tired from work; the result is that I can't get to sleep before four in the morning," he wrote to a Bastille officer in January that year. The colourful drapes and cut flowers in his room helped to brighten the scene, his books were a solace, but his mother-in-law and her retainers remained the cause of his incarceration, he was sure, and their numerical riddles would buzz about in his head from time to time, as they had done at Vincennes. At one point, probably in 1785, he wrote to his wife: "You see, my daughter, milady number-juggler will say, that one must, this time as at others, reach a 37. And, full of respect for a reply as stupid as it is insolent and banal, you will bow submissively and you will tell me *that you have asked,*[3] *but that still cannot come about, that my writings,* etc., and a thousand other such turpitudes with which you have stuffed your letters since you started writing to me in prison..."

In June 1785, as *The Hundred and Twenty Days* was nearing the end of its preparation, de Sade passed the age of 45. He was living in one room, spending a great deal of his time writing and, although his regular meals do not seem to have been large, he was a great consumer of wine, liqueurs, cakes, chocolates, jams, crystallised fruit. By 25 May 1787, Renée Pélagie was reporting to Gaufridy: "I thank you for the news you give me from the country; I'll pass them on to M de Sade whom I see every fortnight precisely. He's keeping fairly well, but he is getting very fat..."

One of the prisoner's many commissions to his wife ordered "enough ... of this cloth to make a frock-coat for the fattest man in Paris... You'll bring, I beg of you, ... a pair of very warm and very broad fur-lined boots: the fattest leg in Paris has to go about in soft boots..."

In October 1788, the marquise was asking that the governor of the Bastille see to it that a certain manservant-cum-warder be restored to her husband because, "being as fat as he is, it is impossible for him to change his shirt on his own. When he gets hot, he runs the risk of catching pneumonia..."

De Sade did not catch pneumonia, although he continued to be troubled, as at Vincennes, by headaches, "nervous pains", coughing of blood and faintness, and by difficulty with his eyes. One oculist prescribed that the patient "occupy yourself with making a wide-mesh net or with knitting, so as to occupy yourself in a way that would distract you without tiring you, for fear that your eyes find the six hours [spent writing from six p.m till midnight] you tell me about a little too much ..." The author of *The Hundred and Twenty Days of Sodom* replied that the oculist "would do well to suggest to the patient some occupation more worthy of a man of letters than that of knitting."

*　　　　　　　　*　　　　　　　　*

---

3 For a date for his release, no doubt.

De Sade kept up unworthy and familiar occupations of his own devising. At the Bastille, he had much time - and much motivation, in his view - to continue intermittent railing against officials high and low. Early in 1785, for the eyes of his wife and careless of the police censors, the marquis complained scurrilously of the police chief: "... Ought Mr Le Noir not to have come here, in the time I have been asking to see him? Isn't the first duty of his job to accede to the wishes of a prisoner, when one is expressing them daily? But Madame Jeanne's arse has knocked all that on the head, am I right? He sets much greater store by paying court to a whore's c[unt] - than to looking after a suffering unfortunate. So the public isn't to know about all this one day! I'm the most cowardly cur on Earth if my first and sweetest undertaking, as soon as I'm able, isn't to tell them about it. There are printers and liberty in Holland! I'll take advantage of that, be sure of it..."

De Sade the would-be subversive propagandist was also de Sade the blue-blooded snob, for his threats to undermine members of the fabric of royal and Catholic France were matters of petty and personal vengeance rather than of an ideological commitment against the government and society of the day. The Marquis de Launay, governor of the Bastille, was described by his charge in the Second Liberty as a "so-called marquis whose grandfather was a valet and his great-uncle a groom at the Vandeuil Academy..." The better class of marquis on the second floor could not resist a sneer, soon after he came to the Bastille, at the senior officer de Losme-Salbray, who seems to have been much excited at the arrival there of the notorious libertine: "... he was all over me, confessing to me about systems which would make me tremble, me who believed he had thought of everything that could be thought of..."

A few months later, the prisoner was reporting de Losme-Salbray as "an atrocious rouge [who was] thrown out of the king's guards for swindling and cowardice, son of a gardener *at Vitry, near Paris*, and whose exploits have been to stand guard in front of some commodes at Versailles and to give, so it's claimed, the first twist of the tongs to Damiens[4] when he was brought into the room where this blighter was on duty..." Several other inmates of the Bastille regarded de Losme-Salbray as an understanding and pleasant jailer of a rare quality.

It was not until December 1785 that de Sade found a kindred spirit at the Bastille - perhaps the only one during his various stretches in jail.

4 A prisoner under torture after he had attacked King Louis XV.

One Pierre-François de Rivière du Puget joined the staff of the fortresss. He was a year older than the prisoner and had in common with de Sade a Provençal background (the Chevalier du Puget was born at Aix), a career in the cavalry (he had served in the royal dragoons) and a record of combat against France's enemies east of the Rhine. De Sade would read his manuscripts - those he could acknowledge as his own - to the officer and they would discuss them. The marquis wrote verses comparing du Puget to a sun which had lit the gloomy fortress. He sent him coy and flattering invitations to hear the author read his plays. The officer's opinion "would be altogether special for the author, but the request is inopportune, clearly... To give up a delightful day for boredom! I cannot imagine how such things get proposed, and I remember better than anyone that I used to regard these invitations like ambushes..." This kind of thing might seem a little cloying and precious between two middle-aged *sabreurs*, but it was not out of the way for literary gentlemen of the era, letting off a little esteem.

Du Puget might have had a calming influence on de Sade, but a prison administrative report of October 1787 referred to a typical incident: the marquis received word from the governor that his walks were being stopped because his obstructiveness towards certain minor changes had been expressed "with the greatest impropriety, heaping insults on [the governor] and uttering the most outrageous stupidities..." On an occasion in the next June, the inmate tried to leave the Second Liberty in defiance of another order to stop his walks, at which a warder stationed by his door in expectation of this reaction had to keep him back at gunpoint, and got a stream of insults for his pains.

* * *

For all his termagancy, de Sade retained one faithful supporter. Renée Pélagie was allowed to visit de Sade once a fortnight from mid-March 1784. The marquis had never enjoyed the attention of a large band of people and, by the time he entered the Bastille at the end of February 1784, even the few who were prepared to lift a finger on his behalf had dwindled. He knew that Gothon Duffé, maid and sometimes housekeeper at la Coste, had died in 1781. He probably learned, about the time of his transfer from Vincennes, of the death of Marie Dorothée de Rousset, also at la Coste, although there seems to be no evidence of his having acknowledged her passing.

It is almost certain that he was not informed, while incarcerated, of the death of his sister-in-law Anne Prospère de Launay, who might not have been counted among his supporters but was an important element in his emotional life. She died **(see chapter 8)** on 13 May 1779, or perhaps 1781 for the letter from Rousset giving the news to Gaufridy is hard to date exactly. For sure, though, she had been dead for some time when, in a secret letter of 18 April 1787, the marquise deftly avoided revealing her sister's death while replying to questions from her husband which we do not have:

"The silence which I was making myself keep, so as not to speak to you, my gentle friend, of my sister, was quite reasonable, in that to have broken it in order to satisfy you, would only make you draw wrong conclusions and would worry you. You're demanding that I reply to these questions before me, swearing to me that you'll never again open your mouth to me about this and that you'll calm down? Well, it's to calm you that I'm going to answer.

"What made her leave my mother's home? - Nothing that concerns you or dishonours her.

"Is she my enemy? - No.

"What sort of place is she living in, without specifying the street or district? - Whatever it is, it can do you no harm. There's no use in carrying on with this reply..."

This letter was probably passed to de Sade during one of his wife's visits and while the supervising officer was not looking. The Bastille was near enough to her lodgings for Renée Pélagie to avoid carriage hire eating into her meagre resources and to walk to and from the fortress. The recipient of her visits was not aware of this until the first summer of his spell in the Bastille but, when he found out, he unleashed an instructive admonition:

"So it's revealed, the cause of that excessive flush and of that frightful state you're in, each time you come to see me: it's because you come on foot, like a *shopkeeper*, like a *street trollop*... And your relatives let you do it, and your rascally servants don't prevent it! How common! what a scandal!... If you really had any friendship for me, would you not look after yourself, would you not understand that my only happiness, my only hope is to get back together with you in good health, one day? Why do you want to undermine this one dear hope of my life by risking death as you're doing? A woman on her own, on foot, in the streets? Just one drunkard... Just one stone thrown by a ragamuffin... One tile falling... One shaft from a coach... One brouhaha... Apart from all that: arriving all of a sweat in a damp room, and staying there two hours without a change of clothes, and to go back home thus repeating the operation... No doubt about it, you must be mad, mad beyond all description, to take such risks ... and do you consider the worry this causes me? It's no good saying 'my lodging is only a step away'... I forbid you to walk."

Whatever the sincerity of this outburst, there still remained the large requirement, hinted at in the letter, that his wife continue as his supplier, shopper, lobbyist, sounding-board and target for venom in the outside world. Also, without Renée Pélagie, no-one - not free of charge, at any rate - would have acted as researcher for his literary efforts. In December 1786, the penman of the Second Liberty was irritably pressing his wife:

"... In what language do you have to be told that all I need about *Lisbon* is the name of an inn, the name of the keeper of that inn, of the street where it's situated and of the buildings next door; that I need the same thing and the same details for *Toledo* and for *Madrid*, and that all I need otherwise, for Toledo, is the name of two or three fashionable streets and of two or three others in the courtesan district, with those of the main places where one goes for a stroll in the three said cities, *Lisbon*, *Toledo* and *Madrid*; also some details of the Spanish coinage, and whether the forms of torture among the nobility are the same in Spain as ours, or what they are, if they differ..."

Spain and Portugal figure in his novel *Aline and Valcour* so it is more than likely he was working on this at the time.

Among his literary support, too, de Sade was losing personnel. La Jeunesse, the marquis's theatrical copyist and erstwhile valet and travelling companion, died in May 1785 after six weeks of agonising illness (the marquise sold some of her clothes so as to raise 36 livres to send to his wife and children) and the Abbé Amblet, whom de Sade had known since he was about nine years old, faded from the scene. There survives no Sadeian correspondence with the old cleric after December 1786. No word of his death remains.

A month after La Jeunesse had died, the marquise was ill and feeling the lack of him to write letters at her dictation. She reported Madeleine Laure, her daughter, aged 14, as "a great layabout", not being disposed to act as her mother's secretary even if her level of literacy was up to it, which seems doubtful. The marquise had a better opinion of Madeleine

Laure since the latter had come to live with her (from the care of Mme de Montreuil's servants) but was not sanguine about finishing the girl's upbringing, she being "very slow in everything".

Her father, though, remained far too quick in anger. Officers at the Bastille added to the complaints against him which had been logged by their counterparts at Vincennes. The marquise told Gaufridy, in July 1785, that her husband "can't restrain his pen", that this was doing him no good and that it also meant her being prevented from visiting him and from having his letters passed on to her. The same month, Governor de Launay of the fortress reported to de Crosne, the new police chief, a request from the marquise for her visits to be restarted. He went on:

"... the prisoner, who is extremely difficult and violent, was creating scene after scene in front of her, especially one day when he didn't want to conform to the custom of speaking up[5]. He flared up very violently at Mr de Losme. The police offices are full of letters stuffed with horrors about his wife, his family and ourselves. While taking his walks, he insults the guards for no reason at all. It is because of his spitefulness, which seemed to increase when he was receiving visits by his wife, that Mr Le Noir felt it right to deprive him of them, at least for a while ... his wife and his family would be well served if one were to allow a visit only once a month. If he does not abuse that privilege, one might then allow more frequent visits. Since he has been seeing no-one, he is better behaved. The kindness and decency of milady the Marquise de Sade makes her ask to see him, but almost every time she received nothing but torrents of insults and stupidities. The truth is that she fears for her life, if he were to be set free one day..."

The fortnightly visits by the marquise seem to have been restored in February 1787, but there were other interruptions because of her husband's intemperate behaviour. He did not save all his insults towards her for her appearances at the Bastille. After his transfer to the fortress, he wrote fewer letters, to her and in general, and addressed her in writing - we do not know about the visits - almost invariably in the formal *vous* form, meaning "you", rather than the intimate *tu*. Besides becoming colder in this way, the letters from husband to wife became more consistently nasty and hectoring. In March 1784, barely a week after his arrival at the Bastille, de Sade had coldly promised his wife no

---

5 So that the supervising officer could hear what was being said by prisoner and visitor.

further communications but "lists ... of requests and commissions". He could not manage to be so austere towards Renée Pélagie with the quill, but many of his rancid outbursts must have made her wish he had. De Sade was more bitter than ever over his continued imprisonment, and over the lack of firm information and reliable promises about his release: "Well, my very dear and very amiable and above all very frank spouse, were you deceiving me neatly when you promised me, on one of your visits, that it would be you who'll come to seek me out, that I'll go free and see my children! Was it possible to be lower and more unworthy in treachery and lying..."

Yet, tempering the prevailing bitter wind, he wafted on 24 August 1787 a caressing breeze from the Second Liberty, responding to the receipt from Renée Pélagie of a portrait of her:

"There are things which make for such pleasure that words fall short of feeling; the soul is too moved so that it needs to withdraw into itself for a moment in order to enjoy what it is going through. One would be breaking one's delight in forcing the soul to describe it. That's what is happening to him who thanks you[6] for the delightful present that you have just given him - a dear and divine present whose inspiration, always multiplied, will make blossom, despite evil-doers, until the last moment of its existence, a thousand flowers always fresh on the thorns of life.[7]

"He embraces you, and will thank you much better yet when he'll be able to take you in his arms.

"PS: The portrait, ... everything is fine, everything pleases, everything makes for an incredible pleasure, and be sure that you'll take away my life before you'll take back an item that will not leave me until death."

Staying with family portraits, however, and returning to the prisoner's more usual mood, note that he seems to have sent back to his wife, in May 1784, pictures of his three children and another that showed her with him. In any event, there is a record of the marquise having asked an officer of the Bastille to hand over such portraits to one of her servants whom she was sending there for the purpose. This was later in the year in which de Sade had waxed furious about his elder son Louis Marie entering a regiment of which his father did not approve

---

6 Still *vous*.

7 The original French is every bit as lumbering.

(**see chapter 19**), then his younger son Donatien Claude Armand was commissioned in a regiment where a Montreuil, one of the lad's maternal uncles, was a major. "I have no children at all," the former cavalry commander fumed to his wife in October.

Also in 1784, he sent back, with a sour note telling her to bother him no more with such "prattle about business", a document which, if he had signed it, would have authorised the marquise to draw on an inheritance of 25,000 livres left by an aunt of hers. The inheritance had been frozen since 1781 for lack of de Sade's permission, as Renée Pélagie's husband and so the regulator of her access to property. She was not the only potential beneficiary thus frustrated for it seems that the aunt had willed a house which had to be sold for the marquise and others to realise their various shares of the proceeds. De Sade consistently refused to see a lawyer whom his wife sent to him a number of times about the matter, and he was still blocking the procedure in 1787.

The marquise, between slipping into and struggling out of troughs of illness, wrestled with the affairs of the de Sade properties in Provence, her hands tied by her husband's refusal to peruse or sign any papers. Some of the old creditors had written off their chances of seeing their bills met, but others were more stubborn and litigations dragged on. Renée Pélagie lamented to Ripert, the tenant farmer at Mazan, in September 1785: "... The business of the estate of the Abbé[8], the land rights at Saumane, *the debts*... My uncle[9], with whom still nothing is sorted out, also has rights. All this ... is a hydra..."

However, various family members met a number of times to slice off the hydra's heads by appointing the commander, aged 83 in 1786, as administrator of his imprisoned nephew's goods. In October, two lawyers visited the marquis to go through the legal formality of asking him - in vain - to sign an authorisation for his uncle to take the reins. The family then took the consequent step allowed by the law and petitioned the courts, in view of the wilful neglect of affairs by the head of the family, to override his objections and allow administration to the commander. This was granted on 21 June 1787, with Renée Pélagie having access to revenues from the Provençal estates, mainly under the aegis of the commander but also of her father. One might have

8 The Abbé de Sade, who had died in 1777.

9 The old Commander de Sade, uncle to the marquis.

expected the de Sades and the Montreuils to have completed such an out-flanking of the marquis long before 1787, but his wife, unwilling to join manoeuvres against his fixed position lest this constitute a betrayal of her husband, had not agreed to co-operate in the initiative until she was convinced that the neglect of the estates' administration was doing his interests great damage.

The marquise was no less devout before her God than she was loyal to her god-spurning husband. In her letter of April 1787, where she answered his questions about her late sister, Renée Pélagie then responded to what seems to have been an objection from him about her observance of Lent:

"Lent, far from harming my health, is a time of diet, and I am never ill during this time. My gentle friend, believe me that for me to see you thinking as you do distresses my spirit. Your fate is certainly not a matter of indifference to me, for I would shed my blood to secure your happiness in this world and the next.

"You fall into another error in believing devotion to be sad. True devotion is not at all remote or sombre, you'll see. For I will not give up my religious duties when you are freed, one of the essential duties being to help to make happy everyone around us. As you see my duty combining with the leanings of your heart[10], you have nothing to fear.

"I will not persecute you in the least to make you take up my way of thinking[11], although I neither cease nor shall cease to offer my wishes that this change take place, because a forced respect ... cannot please God..."

On her visits to the Bastille, the marquise would carry with her tender, secret notes to be passed to her husband out of sight of the supervising officer - nothing subversive, just a message which would belong only to her Louis, having evaded the police censors. In July 1785: "There's only one true happiness for me in this world, and that's to be reunited with you, and that you shall be contented and happy. We shall live and die together. I always have this on me so that, if I get a chance to give it to you, I won't miss it."

Then, in August 1786: "Would you doubt my love, my tender friendship? All my feelings are for you, all my wishes are that your

---

10 A strong indication that Renée Pélagie had not read the manuscript of *The Hundred and Twenty Days of Sodom.*

11 Is this a mischievous use of the marquis's totemic phrase by which he described his personal creed?

freedom shall unite us soon. I feel all the consideration of what you write to me. My heart returns it a hundredfold, be sure of it... I love only you in the world. I think of you always. I build a thousand castles in Spain for the day of your release, for what we'll be doing, for all that will be able to contribute to your happiness..."

Renée Pélagie's castles were built in the air. Her mother, as ever, was more realistic. She reported to Gaufridy in March 1785: "The position is still the same. I cannot foresee when it will change. I have heard that the effervescence of character is not changing at all, and that it was feared that setting him free would lead to the same consequences as it did previously. This is a case in which I no longer have to concern myself, having taken a role so many times and secured his liberty as a gesture to his wife, who has had all too much cause to regret it. You know what you know, sir, and there is no more to be said..."

* * *

Her son-in-law, contrary to *la présidente* as usual, had much more to say, mainly in his role as man of letters. On 1 October 1788, de Sade drew up a catalogue of his literary works completed so far. This was apt to be examined by the prison authorities so it did not include *Dialogue between a Priest and a Dying Man* or *The Hundred and Twenty Days of Sodom*. However, it listed ten plays, eight volumes of novels and tales (of which *Aline and Valcour* was by far the longest and most ambitious), 16 short stories, 90 historical tracts, 62 thoughts, and two volumes making up *The Portfolio of a Man of Letters*. Pauvert reckons the whole, including the clandestine manuscripts, would have made five large books of the kind we know now, material adding up to one having been produced at Vincennes, the rest in the Bastille.

I have neither the space nor the inclination to analyse, or even mention, every item in de Sade's literary work. Most of them are of little concern nowadays beyond specialised historico-literary research. When he lifted his pen to impress the world, rather than the recipient of a letter, he rarely wrote well. His fictional characters are instruments in the promotion of an idea or a point of view, their flimsiness becoming most apparent whenever the author settled into a long polemic of which one or other of them is the mouthpiece. The physical appearance of persons and places is presented perfunctorily. The author seems to have had minimal interest in human communication that did not involve the spoken or written word, often in hectoring tone, or the sexual organs. He was writing in prison, with little human company and not having seen a landscape or a room, other than a cell and the council chambers where prisoners received visitors, for years. However, de Sade drew his literary material from within himself. His quality of description altered little once he was writing outside jail.

The Portfolio is built around the notion that two sisters, one flighty and the other *sérieuse*, have left Paris for the provinces, having told a man friend still in the capital to send them letters while they are away. This loose framework left the author plenty of scope to string together various items from his notebooks, ranging across the human condition - there is an essay on the death penalty (de Sade was against it; his wife, by the way, in favour) and a scheme for putting criminals efficiently to work for the State. At the time of his catalogue, the marquis had completed two volumes, the others having been prepared in outline. He noted his intention not to finish the work until public reaction to the first two volumes had been tested.

Various works of de Sade, mentioned in such catalogues or hinted at elsewhere, have disappeared. Also lost are the diaries he wrote, some of them in code, during his time at Vincennes and the Bastille. (These may have been the basis of *Confessions* he wrote after release from jail, also vanished.)

In the margin of his 1788 catalogue, de Sade added another novel:

"... *Les Malheurs de la Vertu* - 1 vol. - work of an entirely new kind. From beginning to end vice triumphs, and virtue is seen humiliated; only the dénouement gives virtue all the lustre due to it, and there is no being who, having read it, would not abhor crime's false triumph and cherish the humiliations and misfortunes which put virtue to the test."

This, *The Hardships of Virtue*, became *Justine* in its later versions. It is the first manifestation of what is probably the most famous of de Sade's works, which follows a well-meaning girl through a series of episodes in which her virtuous efforts fail to keep her out of the grip of exploitative criminals, most of whom are libertine men. The marquis referred in the margin of the last page of the manuscript to the recurrent difficulty he had with his eyes when writing it.

The other important item from the period 1778-89, and included in the Bastille catalogue, is *Aline and Valcour,* which follows the style of other famous 18th-century novels - *Les Liaisons Dangereuses* by Laclos, *Clarissa* by Richardson - in being made up of characters' letters to each other. It elaborates a broad, implicit criticism of the France of de Sade's time through social and political comparisons with various fictional communities, as Swift did more effectively for England through *Gulliver's Travels.*

The start of October 1788 was a good time for the marquis to take stock of his copious literary output because he was changing residences, moving at his own request from the second floor of the Liberty Tower to the sixth, where the room was probably better ventilated and a bit larger. Soon, he was enjoying other new benefits - a hour of walking every day on top of the towers, whether or not he was having any exercise that day down in the courtyard, and newspapers (at the request of his wife). The marquis decided that the Sixth Liberty needed a Sadeian touch, spending money on curtains, a stronger bed, a locksmith to install a bookcase with doors. The marquise, writing to Gaufridy, worried that, because her parents would not meet what they would regard as "useless expenses" of their son-in-law at the Bastille, she would have to economise in her own household in order to cover the bills, unless the Commander de Sade were to authorise a payment from the Provençal revenues. He did allow this. All in all, Renée Pélagie was rather better placed financially now that she could have access to revenues from the de Sade estates, and in that she had been able to circumvent her husband's intransigence and draw on the inheritance from her aunt.

The marquise was struggling more often in those days with her health, frequently tired, sometimes unable to walk, subject to rigorous diets. In unwonted reflection on her poor health and his demands, her husband wrote to her in October 1788:

"It bothers me very much, my dear friend, to be costing you so much, especially at a time when you are ill; but, when I started on this expense, I did not know of your indisposition: I would certainly not have done it if I had known...

"... If you[12] desire my well-being in the unhappy state I'm in, don't worry about it, for at least I'll fare as well as one can in prison... I embrace you and beg you to look after yourself properly. You would not believe how much your condition worries me and how upset I am to be causing you, on this occasion, so much expense and trouble..."

---

12 A rare switch to *tu*.

In general, though, his mood was more sombre and introverted. On 29 December 1788, the marquise replied to a secret letter of his, handed over during a recent visit:

"... It struck the sharpest distress into my heart. I was so overcome that I could not even think. The next day ..., if M de Villedeuil[13] had given me an interview, it would have been impossible for me to utter a word... I, refuse to see you and to listen to you! Can you believe that I am refusing to see you, to listen to all you have to say...

"I have taken all the secret papers and packets; those that you told me to open, I've opened; those that you wanted me to keep hidden, they're awaiting your release. At that time, you'll do me more justice, I'm sure of that..."

Her husband was in his twelfth year of fretting over the lack of a date for that release. Renée Pélagie's letter went on:

"... If I knew the date, I would tell it to you, for you know very well that I can hide nothing from you, and it's this condition of mine perhaps that makes them keep the information from me so carefully.

"I carry out my duties with all my heart, and I always will. Do not distress yourself and above all take care of yourself. I am going to make every effort regarding M de Villedeuil ... and when you are let out, you'll very much regret having suspected me of being among your enemies..."

Now the marquise was using the *vous* form of "you" consistently to her husband.

The winter of 1788-89 was very cold in Paris. The marquise wrote to the governor of the Bastille on 31 December:

"Monsieur de Sade, sir, makes me fully aware of your kindness and attentiveness to him; it's this which emboldens me to implore you most urgently to do all you can to continue in this vein and to let him have all the alleviations and amenities one can.

"The excessive cold must be even worse in his tower. I want you to keep a careful eye on him so that he does not succumb, and even to move him to another room, if there is a warmer one..."

In another letter to a different correspondent, the marquise reported her husband "sad, melancholic. I fear the length of his detention may be leading him into despair, and I worry that some misfortune might befall him in that tower where he's all alone..."

---

13 The new minister concerned with de Sade's case.

CHAPTER 23: RESCUE, SEPARATION AND REJECTION

Chilly and lonely though it may have been, the Sixth Liberty overlooked the street. It was from the street that rescue, and an end to de Sade's solitude, came. The harvest of 1788 was a bad one and a hard winter followed. By the spring of 1789, the price of bread was high in the main cities of France, especially Paris. This was not only due to the shortage of grain but also to hoarding of food stocks by merchants who were trying to push prices, and their profits, even higher. Chronic neglect of agriculture was another abiding cause of the shortages and the price inflation. A multiplicity of tithes and taxes, as well as rents in cash and crop shares, had been leeching wealth out of agriculture and into the hands of landlords and tax-gatherers for generations. Many of these recipients failed to invest more than a sliver of their incomes into food production. (We have seen what de Sade did with much of his.) Also, tolls levied on goods moving within France made distribution of food from the fields to the towns far more expensive than it would have been otherwise - each toll imposed on a boatload of wheat passing along a river, or on a wagonload of corn moving along a highway, added to the price of the loaves in the cities.

Attempts by royal ministers to reform the French economy in the 1780s had been headed off by the influential body of people whose wealth depended on the system as it was. This group was still growing as the royal administration continued to sell titles and farm out the gathering of revenue in order to maintain the machinery of government. Meanwhile, argumentative, arousing pamphlets and orators were offering radical criticisms and solutions.

King Louis XVI had felt obliged to summon a meeting of the Estates-General, an advisory assembly that had not sat since 1614 and consisted of representatives of the clergy, the nobility and well-to-do commoners (the Third Estate, many of them lawyers), brought together in their respective strata. In the spring of 1789, as this all-male meeting was being prepared, its procedure was a prime issue. In order to reflect its much greater numerousness in the population as a whole, the Third Estate was to be allowed more representatives than the First and Second (clergy and nobility) put together - but this would have no decisive effect if any votes were to be by estate (that is, the clergy and nobility able to out-vote the Third Estate by 2:1) rather than by head (the third able to carry the day through its greater numbers).

Stirred by all this, much of the population of Paris was translating its hunger and anger into action. Mobs broke into food stores and carried away the stocks, attacked the homes of employers and of suspected hoarders. Weapons were seized during raids on police and military posts. Conscripted men deserted the army to join the mobs. Reaction by the authorities was often hard-handed, troops firing into closely packed crowds and killing hundreds of poor Parisians.

The Marquise de Sade, in a tone reminiscent of her regrets about her husband's loose tongue and pen, reported to Gaufridy on 3 April 1789: "The great mistake is that heads have been allowed to get over-heated. There have been too many writings on both sides. There's been too much slackness. Can the slide to the bad be stopped? God alone knows..."

At the end of that month, Renée Pélagie, lady of property and of devotion, sent a vivid report of the mass pillage of a house belonging to a certain Réveillon, who was believed to have told the Third Estate of the Estates-General that a working man could keep himself and his family, "despite the high price of essentials", on 15 sous a day (very little) "and still afford to keep a watch in his waistcoat..."

The marquise told her agent at Apt, "the Saint-Antoine district, and that of Saint-Marceau where I live, were the scene of the revolt...

"A bunch of ne'er-do-wells without jacket or shoes, among whom many carried whip marks or brandings[1], forced the workshops to let out the workers... They [gathered] here, in this district, armed with big sticks, tools and even with planks. The first day, they charged into the Saint-Antoine district, into the house of this Réveillon, who had run away, and ... smashed everything, drank the wine and the liqueurs, even ingredients for paint which poisoned some of them. [They were] claiming that they weren't thieves. But, on the following days, after they had pillaged ... houses, attacking and overturning carriages, [they were] making people hand over all the money they had on them.

"To make them leave you be, you had to say that you were in the Third[2] and to accept the stick they were handing you. Their number

---

1 So they were convicted criminals.

2 In the Third Estate, which the marquise was not, but her self-confessed lack of noble airs may well have stood her in good stead for once.

grew to eight thousand. That looked quite a handful to me, and troops [those in the capital], the city watchmen and the mounted police were not up to the job; two regiments of cavalry had to come.

"They fired on them and killed many of them, hanged others and put many into jail. More innocents than wrong-doers perished, what with crowds of on-lookers and residents watching from their windows. Trouble-makers on the roofs started tearing them apart, throwing down the tiles, stones, on the soldiers; the infantry stuck close to the walls and fired back. Bad luck on those on the receiving end. There was nothing else to be done. [The trouble-makers] haven't appeared in the city again. There are still many of them outside Paris, but everything is guarded in such a way that they're no longer to be feared..."

Meanwhile, above all this, the main concern in the Sixth Liberty was to complete the décor. The prisoner, via his wife, asked Gaufridy on 11 May for "the two little vases of painted metal which are on my bureau... They will have to be packed in wool or cotton, and put in a little box."

While the mob was taking over his house, Réveillon found his way to the Bastille, where he was lodged for his own protection and where "the frequent visits he receives," according to the marquis on 29 May, meant that the latter's hour of courtyard exercise had to be spent in the tiny office where prisoners were quickly put out of sight of passing visitors. "While waiting for Mr Réveillon to return to his shop," the snobby marquis went on about the inconvenience the tradesman was causing, "I'm asking ... that my hour in the courtyard be exchanged for one on the towers..." He added a few insulting sentences about Governor de Launay. His walks were stopped on 5 June, the written order to this effect having to be supported by a rifle pointed at his chest when de Sade tried to leave his tower in defiance of the instruction.

The marquise made what proved to be her last attempt to have her husband curb his pen: "Leave saying to them things which they dislike; you see where that ends ... it's not by annoying people that one brings them to do what you want..."

She continued her weekly visits, making one on 15 June, but was ill on her next date, the 22nd. In the meantime, she had sent a long commentary of hers on the manuscript of *Aline and Valcour*.

On 23 June, King Louis XVI, trying to keep in step with changing attitudes, asked the Estates-General to examine ways to abolish the *lettres de cachet*, consistent with maintaining public safety, the honour of families in certain cases, and vigilance against sedition and espionage.

However, one long-serving prisoner under *lettre de cachet* was moving more quickly than the king, the assembly or even the common people of Paris. At noon on 2 July, de Sade poked through his barred window a metal pipe he had for pouring urine and dirty water out into the moat beside the street (standard practice in those days). He then bellowed through his primitive amplifier that he and other prisoners in the fortress were being murdered and that they must be rescued. This was nonsense. The marquis had just been told that, the cannon on the towers now being kept permanently loaded in view of the disturbances in the city, he would no longer be allowed to exercise up there. There was no danger of the prisoners so much as missing a meal, let along being put to death.

The governor decided that the performance with the pipe was the last straw. Next day, he wrote to the minister, de Villedeuil, describing the incident and recommending that, "this being a time when it would be very dangerous to keep this man here", it was necessary to transfer de Sade to the asylum at Charenton, near Paris, or to some such place where "he would not be able to cause disorder, which he does here unceasingly". De Launay went on: "this would be just the time to relieve ourselves of this being whom nothing can quell..." The minister agreed, and acted quickly. At 1 a.m. on 4 July, de Sade suffered an experience familiar to him. A party of armed police, led by Inspector Quidor (Marais had died in 1780), took him from his bed and transported him through the night to Charenton - "naked as a maggot, pistol at my throat," according to him. The Sixth Liberty was sealed behind him by an official so that his effects would be safe.

The asylum, run by a religious order, was situated by the River Seine, in a large and handsome park, but de Sade complained fiercely about the "false pretext" by which he had been transferred to "a house of madmen, with whom I have been ignominiously mixed with no distinct treatment, although my reason, thanks be to heaven, has suffered no alteration. And in the state of discomfort and rigour that I am, it's ... absolutely impossible to sleep, to eat and take the air..."

De Sade, very much used to his own company as a long-term prisoner, had raged at disruptions to his snug routine at the Bastille. For him to have been thrust suddenly into a house full of the mentally ill - mercurial, noisy, unbiddable - must have been a great shock to someone who had often fretted while in jail about how much he desired to be left in peace until he was released. In fact, as various contemporary commentators and inmates made clear, the régime at Charenton was much more pleasant than that of the Bastille, and was regulated only by the bells which signalled breakfast, lunch, dinner (all served in the asylee's room) and time to retire. There was a number of common rooms where one could play billiards and cards - not quite the thing, even so, for a middle-aged curmudgeon of a writer. He complained to the authorities with the full weight of his vocabulary of vexation about the way he had been treated by the police in the small hours of 4 July, and signed his deposition as having been "drawn up in a lodge of madmen, surrounded by madmen, at Charenton this 9 July 1789..."

Also on 9 July, he sent, via his wife, an authorisation for the official who had sealed the Sixth Liberty, a certain Chenon, to break the seals and open the room in the presence of the marquise, who was to check that his effects were all present. She was also, de Sade wrote, "required to burn one of them, which there is no point in describing..." Perhaps this was whatever contained the roll of paper that was the manuscript of *The Hundred and Twenty Days of Sodom*, hence his wife might burn the container without learning of the work's existence.

In any event, the matter was not put to the test. The five days which had passed before de Sade could write his authorisation for the opening of his room at the Bastille turned out to have been a crucial delay. For one thing - apart from any trouble finding space, time and materials at Charenton - de Sade was replying to a request from Chenon for the authorisation. This note from the official in Paris had to travel to Charenton after de Sade had been taken away in the night, then the reply from the marquis took a normal four days to reach his wife in the capital. Pauvert has found, in the papers of Le Noir, the former police chief in Paris, clear information that the authorisation reached the marquise on 13 July. Next morning, she took the document to Chenon and they decided to set out together for the Bastille, where the hand-over of de Sade's effects could be made. However, the official decided to record his receipt of the authorisation before they left for the fortress and, while he was doing so, there arose near his office the turmoil in the streets which, later that day, led to the mob storming the Bastille, killing the governor and two of his senior officers, putting the rest of the staff to flight, and grabbing whatever they could find inside that they believed worth taking.

One cannot say whether the crowd would have burst into the Sixth Liberty while Chenon and Renée Pélagie were there - it may well be that the marquise would have stayed only to take formal administration of the contents, leaving their removal for another day when she had had time to arrange for a vehicle and removal men. Even so, 14 July was no day for a public official and a countess to be on the streets near the Bastille and one cannot contradict Le Noir's view that Chenon's punctilious attention to keeping his minute books up to date as he went along "saved him, and perhaps Mme de Sade..."

She made her way home and, later that day or the next, sent to Chenon an authorisation for him to go to the Bastille without her. The marquise might or might not have known what had happened at the fortress, but was trying in any event to save what still could be saved of her husband's 600 or so books, clothes, curtains, furniture, drink, sweets and manuscripts. Her syntax showing understandable signs of stress, she told Chenon: "Here, sir, is the authorisation you asked for. Considering the circumstances, I empower you by this note to do what you think is best and to try again for these effects, so that it [*sic*] in no way shall be exposed to pillage and to public view..."

There was a post-script: "I'm leaving for the country until there is an intervention which restores calm." The rampage through the Bastille lasted two days, spreading de Sade's library and other goods through pawnshops, second-hand dealers and various poor homes across Paris. De Sade was furious. He raged to Gaufridy later: "... I had fifteen volumes ready for the printer; [now] barely a quarter of those manuscripts remains with me. Madame de Sade, by unforgiveable slackness, had let some be lost, has caused others to be seized, and there's thirteen years down the drain! Three quarters of these works were still in my room at the Bastille..." He bewailed the loss of "six hundred volumes, two thousand livres worth of furniture and effects, valuable portraits, all ripped apart, burned, carried off, pillaged, with no chance that I could ever recover a shred of it; and all that due to the negligence of Madame de Sade... I am weeping tears of blood over the loss of my manuscripts!... One can get new beds, tables, chests, but one doesn't bring back ideas..."

The marquis maintained that this wife had had plenty of time to arrange for his manuscripts and other belongings to be removed from the Second Liberty, once he had been removed in the small hours of 4 July and the room sealed. "Madame de Sade *dined, went to the toilet, said her prayers and went to bed.* At last, on the morning of the fourteenth of July, she made up her mind that it was time to have the seals broken, and to send me my belongings, to me who was still naked (fortunately the weather was warm) and still stagnating among the madmen. Unfortunately, the day she had chosen to wake from her lethargy was the one on which the people formed a mob and went to the Bastille..."

Indeed, the marquise might have moved before the bureaucratic processes described above had taken their course, and might have nudged the relevant official to break the seals. However, her husband was showing his customary unfairness, for the ten-day delay would have been normal in such a case while the relevant authorisation was sought, signed and returned. What's more, Renée Pélagie had no reason to suspect that the Bastille - a fact and symbol of royal authority, foursquare in the French capital - could be stormed by the mob, much less that it would be within a fortnight of her husband having been removed from it. The event, still regarded and celebrated as the main action in signalling a revolution in France, astounded Paris and the rest of the country. However, the marquis, as usual, took the narrow and personal view.

It is not clear how many of his lost works he re-wrote, or even felt he needed to re-write, once he had settled into life outside prison and was busy with society and literature in Paris, not least the large task of correcting and revising his novel *Aline and Valcour* for publication. We do know that, in the autumn of 1790, he formally reported the loss of his manuscripts to the police. At the end of a description of his notebooks, he referred to "a work written on long strips of lightweight paper... This handwriting will be the best guide in the search. One will be most obliged to those who will be so good as to take the time to make it." It seems that a certain Arnoux took from the Bastille the manuscript of *The Hundred and Twenty Days,* which then found its way by unknown means to a family called Villeneuve-Trans before it surfaced and found a publisher early in the 20th century.

In the summer of 1789, de Sade, outside the city at Charenton and protected by the asylum's status, was not suffering his wife's anxieties. She had returned to Paris on 20 July, for a few days at least, and was there again on 5 October when she felt the need to head for the country once more, along with many others of the better-heeled. The marquise reported to Gaufridy on 8 October: "I fled Paris with my daughter

[and] a servant woman, without manservants, following the general flood in a delivery wagon, so as not to be dragged along by the women of the common people who were taking all the women out of their houses by force to go and fetch the king at Versailles, making them march through the rain, the mud, etc." The women's walk, the 15 miles to the royal court at Versailles and back, was to call for lower bread prices and for the troops stationed in Paris to be removed. The non-participating Renée Pélagie went on: "I arrived safe and sound; I slipped through by the back-roads..."

Louis XVI arrived safe and sound in Paris, which was delighted to have him in the city because it was believed that his presence would guarantee a supply of affordable bread.

The king and his ministers were refusing to approve initiatives being passed in the National Assembly, into which the Third Estate had transformed itself - abolition of the nobility's privileges to exact tithes and taxes, for instance - and they moved more troops from the provinces to the capital.

Renée Pélagie complained to Gaufridy on 26 November: "Every day we are threatened with massacre ... one goes to bed with no confidence of a safe tomorrow. Two days ago, at the Palais Royal and at the food market [in central Paris], they were stealing shoe buckles and ear-rings, and making people turn out their pockets, ostensibly to give everything to the public treasury... History will never believe what is happening..." The marquise also worried about "the freedom in writing and talk and information that's pouring out... One won't dare speak, or even think aloud, until the decent people have the upper hand. We have twelve thousand rogues in the Bois de Boulogne..." - then on the fringe of Paris.

Further away from the hurly-burly of the capital, the marquis was not proving a model detainee at Charenton. On 12 January 1790, the prior of the establishment asked the chairman of the Constituent Assembly (which the National Assembly had become because it was writing France's first constitution) either to remove de Sade or allow the prior to lock him up, "so as to protect this house against the misfortunes which threaten it..." The prior was not specific about what de Sade had been doing to upset the asylum.

His wife would have been glad of asylum herself. On 11 March, she told Gaufridy: "The shopkeepers are refusing to sell because people go to buy in order to change paper money[3]. There's constant fear of an upheaval. There has been a terrible massacre at Meaux; the mayor has been hanged, so they say, and the bishop has fled... The password for wrong-doing is to say: 'This one's an aristocrat - he wants to take away the king', and all of a sudden he's hanged without due process..."

As someone whom the royal administration had given no due process, de Sade was apt to secure renewed liberty out of the crumbling of the old order. The Assembly had appointed, on 24 October 1789, a committee to look into the matter of *lettres de cachet*. Mirabeau, who had clashed with de Sade at Vincennes, was on it. It was the general pressure of business on the Assembly members, rather than any foot-dragging by Mirabeau, which meant that it was not until March 1790 that they voted to abolish the arbitrary royal warrants of detention. The king confirmed the decision on 26 March. A few days before, Mme de Montreuil, her eye for any hope in adversity as sharp as ever, wrote to Gaufridy to point out that the Assembly's decree "is written in such a way that it could allow exceptions" to a general release of prisoners held under *lettres de cachet*. The judge's lady went on: "It's a question of finding out whether, in certain circumstances, the families concerned ought to instigate [the exceptions]." Those properly convicted and sentenced, legally under arrest, the subject of formal legal suit, or certified insane, might remain under lock and key. However, de Sade's conviction for poisoning and sodomy, and his death sentence, had been quashed, mainly thanks to Mme de Montreuil's efforts and money, and he had successfully resisted any formal declarations of insanity.

His mother-in-law did not wonder for long whether her family might still have enough influence to keep the marquis locked away. She told Gaufridy that the families "ought to remain neutral" and let the administration decide. France was changing rapidly and it might well be dangerous for any aristocratic family, with members who had held high office before 1789, to try to press the new political heavyweights for incarceration of its reprobates as it had the old. Mme de Montreuil seems to have acknowledged this cause for caution when she added to Gaufridy: "That's the only way to have nothing to reproach oneself for, nor anything to clear up, however things turn out..." Who could tell

---

3 The new paper money was not trusted and was losing its value rapidly - there was more confidence in the old coins.

which would be the powers tomorrow, and who might be accountable to them?

In the meantime, Mme de Montreuil wished that the new turn of events would make her son-in-law happy, "though I doubt very much that he knows how to be," she added, allowing two members of the younger generation of the family, much less aware of his faults, to set off for Charenton on 18 March to let him know what the Assembly had resolved. Louis Marie and Donatien Claude Armand, aged 22 and 20 respectively, walked in the grounds of the asylum with the father they had not seen for nearly 15 years and dined with him. De Sade reported later to the lawyer Reinaud, in Provence:

"At last, after nine months, my children came to see me[4]; one of them found the nerve to ask the prior by what right and in what name he was holding me. The fellow, not daring to cite the orders of the king, which were no longer valid, fell back on the wishes of the family. 'Oh,' I said then to this jailer, 'those orders, sir, are even less regarded today than those of the minister, I no longer recognise them! *I require you to open the door for me*. The jackanapes dares not resist; the two halves of the door are parted, and I bid him goodnight..."

It is not clear which day was the last of the marquis's long detention - he said it was 2 April, Good Friday, and hailed it as "a good day for a good deed". On that date, he was two months short of his 50th birthday and was ending 13 years of incarceration broken only by 40 days of snatched liberty in the summer of 1778. He seems to have been well enough informed of the changing ways to pass through the gates of the asylum in full-length trousers, rather than breeches (*culottes*) that came to just below the knee with the lower part of the leg clad in a stocking. Breeches were worn by noblemen, or by any man who wished to show that he did no demeaning work that could damage stockings, and were out of favour in the new egalitarian atmosphere in France. (Hence the term *sans-culottes* - without breeches - for the common men of France who supported the changes of the era.)

The marquis had no money but managed to cover the five miles into the city where a lawyer who had acted for him gave him a little cash and a meal, and lodged him for the night. Next morning, he visited the St Aure convent to see his wife - his faithful correspondent, supporter, supplier, visitor, researcher and punchball of the last dozen years - who

4 He often referred to his sons as his children, as though his daughter did not exist.

refused to have anything to do with him except to send a message to say that she was going to seek a formal separation from him. The marquise told Gaufridy that this was the result of "mature and well-considered reflection over a long period of time. M. de Sade, in his heart of hearts, must allow the justice of the motivation which brings me to this resolution and must understand that there can be no other way. As for whether there'll be a commotion over this, that's up to him... I shall reveal no more than he forces me to, in order to justify what I'm doing. *But I will reveal it if he forces me to.* Now that politics are preoccupying everybody, society is not at all bothered about him or about me..."

One can only speculate as to why Renée Pélagie decided to withdraw "body and goods" from her husband, for there is no record of her having explained herself. However, it is clear that she could find much cause for not wanting to renew embraces with the owner of "the fattest leg in Paris". For one thing, the vigorous lord of the manor who had been snatched from her hotel room in 1777, had become even less easy to persuade against his will during his detention. His letters from prison, and his behaviour during her visits to him, bore witness to a bitter ill-humour against her, her family, their children and the world at large. His virulent atheism had turned no less intransigent with the years, while the marquise seems to have become more inclined to heed priestly counsel.

If her husband were as intent as he had threatened on publishing attacks on the Montreuils and others who he believed had done him wrong - albeit his targets were being toppled by the upheaval in France even as he moved into a position to draw a bead on them at last - then the marquise would have found such an alignment with the common pamphleteers of the time demeaning and politically unsound. (We have seen her complaining of "the freedom in writing and talk" which was fermenting trouble.) Besides, during her husband's time at Vincennes and in the Bastille, the marquise had received from Cell No. 6 and the Liberty Tower manuscripts into which the writer had stirred too much, for her taste, of his insight into the sanguinary and exploitative in human behaviour. She never saw *The Hundred and Twenty Days of Sodom*, of course, but other writings, offered for her valued opinion, aroused a certain poised disquiet. One work, probably one which has since been lost, drew the comment in 1781: "... these sorts of characters are too strong and ..., in things written for the public, one must, for the good of all, do everything one can to avoid upsetting the nerves of personalities who are not as strong ..." - as the marquis and his conjugal sounding-board, I suppose.

Then, in 1788, reacting to part of the novel *Aline and Valcour*, by no means a scurrilous work and one which de Sade was to have published under his own name, Renée Pélagie commented that it was "regrettable for humanity that there should be characters of a certain kind [malevolent ones]. One must, you tell me, make them known so that one may protect oneself against them and so as to make them detested. That's true but, when it's only to that end that one is working, there's a certain point where one has to stop, so as to keep from depraved minds the means to sink into worse corruption..."

Hardly the firm intention of the author of *The Hundred and Twenty Days of Sodom*.

The Marquise de Sade, as amateur literary critic feeling her misgivings grow as she read, could not have felt any better about the way her correspondent was tending when she found, secreted in the part-manuscript of *Aline and Valcour* in order to dodge the prison censors, a hot note promising that, at his first opportunity, she would be "well screwed, yes, in every way." No small ambition this, in a middle-aged prison inmate rendered obese by too little exercise and too many liqueurs and sweets, and suffering intense and chronic difficulties with attaining ejaculation by a regime of masturbation and self-sodomy - especially when the female in the case was also, by her own admission, no longer a sylph. Yet, knowing her husband as she did, the marquise might well have decided apprehensively that lust would find a way - a way along which, being often ill and settled into what one must believe was a sedentary celibacy, she would no longer have wanted to caper, with him or with anyone else.

The prospect of being buffeted again, in her 49th year, by the turbulence of life with her intractable and godless Louis, after more than a decade of knowing where he was and that he was being prevented from doing anything like his worst, must have made her recoil further into a resolve which the other Montreuils had long been recommending to her.

The marquis was not altogether surprised although, in his letter to Gaufridy in early May, he launched into a sarcastic grumble:

"The emotional Madame de Sade, as eloquent as she is caring, will not even see me. Any other woman would have said: 'He is upset; I have to dab the tears from his cheeks', but she is not familiar with that cause-and-effect of the emotions. I could be made to lose more yet - she wants my complete ruin and so she is seeking a separation. She will, by this incredible initiative, make credible all the defamation that has been splattered over me, heap unhappiness and notoriety on her children and on me - or she will retreat definitively into a nunnery in order to decay in tranquillity, as she would say, and where some father confessor will bring her consolation, making easy her way into crime, the way into the vileness and infamy by which she will drown us all..."

That is, de Sade had soon understood that a formal separation entailed an awkward monetary settlement with his wife and her family, taking into account the hard-nosed marriage contract of 1763 between the house of de Sade and the house of de Montreuil, pursuing their respective dynastic and financial interests. He told Gaufridy he had seen a change in Renée Pélagie's attitude towards him, when she was visiting him during his last years at the Bastille, which had worried him. However, "my need of her made me conceal my feelings..." It seems Renée Pélagie had no direct communication with her husband while he was at Charenton.

The pocket money provided by his Parisian lawyer was not going far, especially in a city of high prices, so the marquis's first letters on his release from Charenton were pleas to Gaufridy for money, right away. Mme de Montreuil loaned her son-in-law a little cash, via her lawyer, but only on the understanding that he press the Provençal agent for money to repay this debt promptly and to provide the means for him to avoid further borrowing.

On 17 April, a court in Paris dissolved the arrangement of June 1787 by which the marquis's business affairs had been placed under the administration of his uncle, the Commander de Sade, returning full control to the newly released head of the family. Eleven days later, though, his wife received from the same court formal leave to proceed with suit for a separation order. Having been notified by the court of the contents of the plaint, the respondent lamented to Gaufridy:

"All the slanders which have been uttered about me in taverns, in the corps of guards, written up in the almanachs, in the gutter press, form the basis of this pretty memorandum; the most vile obscenities are scandalously invented in it... In brief, it's a monument of horrors, lies and hamfistedness, as crude, as vague, as it is dully and stupidly written. And has no-one parried the blow, you ask? Is no-one opposing it? Not a soul, my deal lawyer! Three or four opinions concur in advising me to forget this monument of impudence and not to reply to it. I have followed this advice..."

By lying low in this way, de Sade avoided provoking his wife into recounting his misdeeds in court. The marquise, in her formal suit, had done no more than present copies of legal documents related to the Keller affair of 1768 and to the judgements at Aix in 1772 and 1778, by which her husband was first sentenced to death for poisoning and sodomy, and then had conviction and sentence overturned. Even so, the distorting lens through which de Sade habitually viewed his misdeeds and his need, in mid-1790, to re-establish himself in Parisian society and literary life both contributed to his pique at finding a tribunal in the city being reminded of such old troubles.

On 9 June, having received no response from the husband in the case, the court granted the marquise a separation. Also, it ordered the marquis to repay to her 160,842 livres received by him between mid-1766 and mid-1777 from the Montreuil family under the terms of the matrimonial contract. The marquis had nothing like that amount of money so, after haggling through lawyers, it was agreed on 23 September before the court that de Sade would not contest the separation order or challenge the debt of 160,842 livres, while the marquise, for her part, undertook not to sue for the money while her husband was alive, as long as she continued to receive annual interest on the sum, fixed at 4,000 livres.

This interest was less than Renée Pélagie might have received through a sum such as 160,842 livres invested in a reliable market, and the settlement of 23 September explicitly recorded that the low income stemming from de Sade's properties had been taken into account in determining the annual interest. The main factor in persuading the marquise and her legal advisers to settle for bi-annual payments of 2,000 livres may well have been a reluctance of the marquis to sell his Provençal estates, which would have been his only hope of realising the full sum owed and which he would probably have resisted tooth and nail, scandal over the separation or no scandal, because he would have lost thereby the only source of income which did not entail his working for a living - working beyond his study, that is. Also, Renée Pélagie was confronted daily in Paris by evidence that reliable markets for investment were being disrupted by social, economic and political turmoil. Better, perhaps, income from the run-down de Sade estates (through agent Gaufridy, who was on her side) than the uncertainty of a messy separation case (perhaps contested by the marquis in his rhetorical, self-excusing element), beyond which there might or might not be secured from a profligate husband a capital sum that might have to be hazarded on a volatile market.

Although the settlement before the Châtelet court notaries stipulated that de Sade was to instruct his agents to begin interest payments to his wife, and that all litigation was thereby wound up, the marquis was still fretting over the arithmetic. On 18 December, he unilaterally declared to the marquise, via Gaufridy, that she would be receiving from his properties no more than any excess, up to the 4,000 livres stipulated, after he had taken the 10,000 livres a year which was the minimum he needed for survival. He justified this by asserting that her family had misled him as to the income from his estates while he was in jail, and that his wife had not subtracted, from the reckoning of monies he had received from the Montreuils in respect of her, the sums she had received from his late mother's estate, also while he had been incarcerated. What's more, Renée Pélagie was obliged to pay to him what she had inherited from his mother, so he claimed.

The marquise's reaction, when writing to Gaufridy on 15 March next year, 1791, was that the settlement of 23 September had to stand as a contractual obligation. Besides, her husband was fortunate to be called on to pay interest of only 4,000 livres on such a large debt, and it was none of her doing that his properties were not yielding enough to keep him. Indeed, had she not disencumbered his estates to a great extent, and so made them more lucrative than they would otherwise have been, by paying off various of his debts over the years? Also, their children were dependent on her, as they had been nearly all their lives. All in all, she was not retreating in the least from the accord of the previous September.

After further skirmishes in court, one of which led to Renée Pélagie paying the marquis 4,800 livres in respect of his counter-claims, it was not until January 1792 that a settlement close to the terms of September 1790 was secured. It is clear that de Sade had driven a hard bargain as culmination of nearly 30 years of draining money out of the Montreuils and giving back no more than he was forced to do. The family had bought its alliance to old blue blood at a huge price in treasure and embarrassment. The marquis, court settlement notwithstanding, turned out to be by no means a regular payer of the agreed interest to his estranged wife.

During his first weeks of liberty, de Sade was becoming better acquainted with the next generation of his blood. His youngest child, Madeleine Laure, whose 19th birthday fell on 17 April 1790, was seen by her father for the first time since infancy. He reported in August: "My daughter is every bit as plain as I was telling you. I have seen her three or four times since; I have observed her very carefully and I promise you that, in mind and body, she's just a good fat lump of a country lass. She stays close to her mother who, to tell the truth, shows her the example of neither grace nor wit. That's just as well, considering what she will have to become..."

The detached father meant that, with noble airs and graces falling out of esteem in a changing France, his daughter's lack of same would suit the levelling tendency. His sons, though, were "most amenable, decent, intelligent, but distant. They won't go to la Coste, like me, to the poorhouse, to find out about its powers, its resources, its family, and so won't make themselves loved. It pains me to see this, but they have a touch of the Montreuil haughtiness, and I would be better pleased to see in them the Sade energy."

The marquis had not been near the poor of his domain for at least a dozen years, but he would have blamed that omission on the work of others.

He was as alert as ever for signs of demise in propertied members of the older generation. This seems to have been a family trait. In late-July 1789, while de Sade was fuming at Charenton, his only surviving paternal uncle, Richard Jean Louis, Grand Prior of the Order of the Knights of Malta, lately promoted from commander, aged 86, was felled by a stroke at his house in the southern French city of Toulouse. News of this reached his youngest sister, the Marquise de Villeneuve, at Avignon on the evening of 2 August. The septuagenarian noblewoman, reckoning that her brother must be near death, set out that same night for the grand prior's château of St Louis, near Carpentras, with two carts which, on arrival, she had filled with the most valuable furniture and taken to the de Sade manor at Mazan, before anyone else could beat her to the booty. The old man died on 20 September.

Lady de Villeneuve was the object of a rude snatch herself in May 1791, when political radicals took her off briefly to jail in Provence. The marquis was outraged at this "abomination" and offered her lodging at la Coste as a safer place, he judged from Paris, to live. In October that year, Lady de Raousset, eldest daughter of the Marquise de Villeneuve and so de Sade's cousin, died suddenly in Provence. Writing about this from Paris to Gaufridy, the marquis spent a few sentimental words about the playmate of his youth at their grandmother's mansion in Avignon, but then got down "to business". This was a timely occasion to arrange that Lady de Villeneuve's will should include a plum legacy for him, her nephew, now that the old marquise's property would be augmented by an inheritance from her daughter. It was up to Gaufridy to "strain every sinew to make sure that this money does not disappear. The whole crowd of them[5] will be fussing around her... Get her away from them, talk to her and have others go on and on about her nephew ... and his heartfelt devotion." Gaufridy was also charged with sending to Donatien Claude Armand, de Sade's second son, the cross worth 6,000 livres that Lady de Raousset had promised the young man. "I have told him about this. The lad earned it by the service of his loins. Now there is an affair of Lady de Raousset you might not know about, but we can joke about it now - she was the one who took his virginity. So, I beg of you, the cross!"

In March 1792, de Sade came to suspect that Donatien, a second lieutenant in the army, had gone on leave to visit Lady de Villeneuve and he fretted from fear that the young man - also anticipating her demise - had been on an out-flanking manoeuvre planned by the Montreuils to snaffle the old woman's wealth before the marquis could get his hands on it. "His brother would never have been capable of such an outrage," said the lads' father. However, he received assurances from his wife and from Gaufridy that nothing of the kind was afoot.

The lord of the manor very much wanted to visit Provence himself, soon after his release in 1790. However, he was deterred by news of mayhem in the provinces of France, including the south-east where he would be travelling. There were "theatres of horrors, where cannibals are carrying out every day dramas in the English style[6] which make the hair stand on end..." He regretted to Gaufridy: "Matters which have to

5 Other relatives and retainers.

6 De Sade was well-read in Jacobean tragedies.

be finished here, and the fear of being hanged in Provence from a *democratic gallows*, will detain me until next spring..."

What bound him most firmly to the capital was his opinion of himself, brought to full flower in the dank rooms of Vincennes and the Bastille, as a man of letters, not least a playwright. The ferment of Revolutionary Paris, where censorship had withered and theatres were opening at a great rate, seemed to offer a long-desired opportunity for de Sade to see his plays take the boards. On 2 May 1790, a month after he had walked out of Charenton, he was calling on Molé, a famous actor whom the aspiring author had known twenty years before, to promote his plays. The marquis made other such visits to actors and directors who had been prominent when he was a young patron of the stage, and he started to send scripts to managements. On 3 August, the Italian Theatre, where de Sade had panted after Mlle Colet 26 years before, received *The Seducer* (*Le Suborneur*), a dire play trussed up in eight-foot lines of verse. A fortnight later, de Sade presented himself at the Comédie Française and read to the committee there his short, free-verse play *The Boudoir or the Credulous Husband* (*Le Boudoir ou le Mari Crédule*), which was rejected by a margin of only one vote. The committee promised to look at it again after certain amendments had been made by the author, whose habitual reluctance to accept correction melted into ready accommodation at the prospect of getting a play produced.

His luck turned at the Comédie Française on 16 September when *He Who Was Soured by Love or Sophie and Desfrancs* (*Le Misanthrope par Amour ou Sophie et Desfrancs*), a long free-verse play, was accepted by the whole committee, after which the theatre never took the script out of its archive for long enough to mount a production.

On the basis of his eager distribution of various scripts, the marquis wrote to Reinaud on 6 March 1791 with a list of five of his plays "received and ready to be staged" at various named theatres. One supposes that the country lawyer, unfitted to spot the difference between an author's estimation of the readiness of his script and a theatre management's readiness to put it on the stage, was as impressed as he was meant to be by de Sade's wishful thinking and passed the news of the master's success among his Provençal connections.

The wish for acclaim in the artistic capital of the world - as Parisians would regard their city - became infected by frustration in liberty having been added to bitterness distilled while *hors de milieu* in jail. At large for thirteen months and still no actors proclaiming his lines, still no applause to drown memories of the bad Marquis de Sade - so he wrote on 2 May 1791 to the Theatre of the Nation, as the Comédie Française had renamed itself in the meantime, to remind the company of the esteem and affection in which he had long held the theatre. He went on: "In return for my loyalty, you have refused the last work I read to you, which, I dare to mention, was not of a kind to be treated so severely.

"Whatever disappointment that this blunt, formal and unexplained rejection has made me feel[7], I won't be laying before you in the future any less of what remains in my drawer or what will refill it in due course.[8] But, sirs, allow me, so bluntly treated by you on the occasion I have just mentioned, to try your indulgence and your fairness with regard to two other aims.

"You have had for a long time a play of mine, unanimously accepted by you[9]... I ask you most urgently, sirs, to put it on as soon as possible; give me this encouragement, I beg you; this will be easy for you if it's true what they say that several authors, not wanting to adopt your arrangements, have withdrawn their plays; for myself, I go along with all of it, sirs, and ask only that you don't keep me waiting...

"The other favour I beg of you [is for you to hear] as soon as possible readings of three or four works quite ready to be put to you and which I wouldn't want to place anywhere else..."

A classic letter, deviating from its modern equivalents only in that it indicates the custom of authors having to read their plays to theatre committees before the age of the photo-copier or even of carbon paper. At least the author, sore though his throat might be at the end of a long reading, having played all the parts, knew that any wait for a decision was not due to the committee passing a script among scattered members.

All de Sade got out of his reading and his pleading to the Theatre of the Nation was free admission for five years.

However, on 22 October that year, 1791, a play of de Sade's was performed for the first time before paying customers, when the Molière

---

7 Could the company have sent its old green room hanger-on a mere standard rejection slip?

8 Was the Theatre of the Nation afraid of just that?

9 *He Who Was Soured by Love.*

Theatre staged *Count Oxtiern or the Effects of Libertinage* (*Comte Oxtiern ou Les Effets du Libertinage*), a dramatisation of the novel *Ernestine* which he had written at the Bastille. It was not a happy opening night. The author was trying to stay sanguine when he told Gaufridy: "I have been staged in public at last, my dear lawyer ... the success, thanks to cliques, to claques, to women about whom I had said something rude, is *very much in the balance*. It'll be performed again on Saturday the twenty-ninth with changes; pray for me, we'll see..."

In fact, *Oxtiern* did not take the boards again until 4 November. Two days later, a theatre critic of *The Monitor* (*Le Moniteur*), deftly saving his Sunday punch till last, gave a po-faced summary of the plot, which was all passion and treachery, then opined: "This play is of interest and has vigour, though the character of Oxtiern is a revolting atrocity...

"An intervention tried to disrupt the second performance... At the start of the second act, a disgruntled or mischievous member of the audience ... shouted: 'Bring down the curtain!'... A stagehand was mistaken enough to obey this lone call and lowered the curtain more than halfway. Then a large number of the audience, having got it raised again, yelled: 'Throw that fellow out!'... This led to a certain difference of opinion among the assembly. A very small minority launched a little half-hearted whistling for which the author was more than compensated by the strong applause of the majority. He was given a curtain-call at the end: it was M. de Sade."

A few weeks later, the playwright was feeling far from compensated. He reported to Gaufridy: "The dreadful rumpus [*Oxtiern*] has caused meant it not being put on again under that name and my postponing further performances. People were cutting each other's throats over it. The police and the management had to be on their toes every time it was staged... We're going to bring it back during the winter."

They didn't, however. The winter brought rejection of more plays at other theatres, then the Italian Theatre's production of *The Seducer*. It went into rehearsal on 24 January 1792 and the opening night was 5 March - a far rowdier occasion than the second night of *Oxtiern*. There was so much noise from the audience that the actors were taken off the stage during the fourth scene. Political radicals in the audience put on distinctive red hats and let it be known that, from now on, such hats would be a signal for "patriots" to rally together in public places, especially at shows, where "the aristocracy would be relentlessly opposed by the friends of liberty," the *Theatre Journal* (*Journal des Théâtres*) reported on 10 March.

By then, de Sade was disclaiming nobility and insisting he was no more, and no less, than a man of letters, but the radical commoners were not impressed. He was terse to Gaufridy on 7 April: "The Jacobin faction ruined a play of mine last month at the Italian Theatre, only because it was by a former aristocrat. They appeared in red wool hats. It was the first time anyone had seen such a thing... I was singled out to be the first victim. I'm fated for these things..."

Despite this pressure on managements from the ultra-radical Jacobin Club's roving disruption squads in their Phrygian caps, the Louvois Theatre in Paris, on 2 May, enthusiastically accepted de Sade's play *The Unequal Man* (*L'Homme Inégal*), a prison work under a new title evocative of the political concerns of the day. He was invited to bring his script to the theatre on the 4th at 11 a.m. "to agree with the actors whom you chose certain little changes which have seemed necessary, and then to produce copies of the script..."

This, however, turned out to be another false prospect, for the night of the red caps proved to be the winding-up of de Sade's career as a writer for the Parisian stage, though he never gave up hope of its revival.

For those who could read, or who picked up information from them, there were opportunities, thanks to two publications of 1790, to be reminded not only that the aspiring author de Sade was a marquis, but also that he had an unusual record. *The Bastille Revealed* (*La Bastille Dévoillée*) by Pierre Manuel described him as having been "detained ... for inhuman experiments he is accused of having conducted in Provence on living individuals..." A much stronger line was taken by the *Collection of the List of Former Aristocrats* (*Collection de la Liste des ci-devants*) by Jacques Antoine Dulaure, which came out in parts, number XXVIII being entirely devoted to de Sade:

"To all [the] rogues in their castles, in their coaches, their red spurs, their red or blue ribbons, one must add the Marquis de *Sade*, whose infamies surpass, perhaps, all the infamies of the nobles of his time...

"... And this man, whom prison saved from the scaffold, for whom fetters were a favour, has been confused, one does not understand how, with the unfortunate victims whom the ministerial tyranny was unjustly holding. This execrable rogue lives among civilised men, dares with impunity to reckon himself in the ranks of the citizenry; he has, they say, just produced a tragedy already accepted at the Comédie Française...

"... This monster, when trying to win the goodwill of the actors rebelling against the public and the municipality, has been seen defending them heatedly, mixing on the floor of the theatre with the vile agents of these rebel players, and striking the patriots who were calling for police regulations to be carried out."

There seems to be no other account of de Sade landing blows on behalf of what must have been the royalist side of the monarchist-democratic division at the Comédie Française. However, some of the actors there with whom de Sade was in contact in 1790 were aligned with conservative monarchists, and we know, as did the warders at Vincennes and the Bastille, that de Sade could be rough when he felt himself opposed by those whom he saw as his social inferiors.

It might seem that the evil aristocrats of de Sade's drama should have pleased Parisian theatre-goers eager to witness representations of the wickedness of the crumbling upper crust. De Sade, probably anticipating this trend, had revised the ending of the novel *Ernestine* into a comeuppance for the predatory protagonist Count Oxtiern in the play that bears his name. However, a trouble for de Sade as playwright, apart from his enraging status as a former aristocrat, was that he tried to bring to the stage characters who, like the four masterful libertines of *The Hundred and Twenty Days of Sodom*, showed a convinced and potent wickedness, and had no other need but their own pleasure in order to indulge in violence. This evoked a corruption of human nature which was not susceptible to reform through argument and education, and so defied the enlightened philosophy of the age. Besides, to read of the crimes of evil aristocrats in denunciatory publications perused at home was one thing; to see and hear such crimes simulated before you as a member of a crowd in a theatre was another, altogether more apt to be affecting.

CHAPTER 24: "THE NEED TO SPREAD MYSELF ABOUT"

Although his plays came to grief, another fruit of Vincennes and the Bastille got the Marquis de Sade published for the first time. *Justine or the Hardships of Virtue* (*Justine ou Les Malheurs de la Vertu*) came off the press in late-1791. The author told Reinaud that it was a work "too immoral to be sent to such a moderate, pious and decent man as yourself. I was short of money, my publisher [Girouard] was asking for it to be well *peppered* and for him I have made it fit to stink out the devil... Burn it without reading it if it happens to fall into your hands. I'm disowning it..."

Indeed, he left his name off the devil-daunting novel but this would not have prevented his receiving the proceeds of the sale to Girouard of what the publisher turned into a high-priced first edition. Pauvert has discovered that the regular summaries of recently published books, which used to appear in France at the time, gave an unusual amount of attention to *Justine*, mainly to denounce it as a hideous tale apt to corrupt the young - excellent publicity. No wonder other editions of the book soon followed, most carrying salacious engravings to illustrate episodes in the story. Most of these were pirated and so would have brought de Sade no fees - he was an author in an age of minimal regulation of copyright.

However, Paris and the rest of France, not least the literate minority, was much distracted by political, social and economic upheaval, which also meant that publishers and readers were giving most of their attention to works on the re-forging of France. Whatever money de Sade realised from the debut of *Justine*, it was not enough to support a man who was not disposed to live frugally. Most of his letters to his agent Gaufridy were taken up, wholly or partly, by pleas for him to send money from the southern properties so as to maintain the newly liberated man of letters, who needed subsidies for his sputtering literary career and his return to polite society. He had adapted well to life outside jail, after an understandable initial inability to engage the city in which he had long been boxed away. A month after his emergence from Charenton, the marquis was telling Gaufridy:

"My eyes went in there, and my chest; in there I developed, for lack of exercise, such an enormous corpulence that I can hardly move about... All my capacity for enjoyment was snuffed out in there; I no longer take a fancy to anything, there's nothing I like; the world that I was foolish enough to miss so much now seems boring to me - even sad! At times the notion takes me to become a Trappist monk, and I cannot guarantee that I won't disappear altogether without letting anyone know what has become of me. I have never been so misanthropic as I am since I returned to human society and, if I seem strange to other people, ... they can be quite certain that they have the same effect on me."

He soon had his chins up a bit, however, and was agreeing with Gaufridy "when you say that *the most important thing is to live independent of other people!* Nevertheless, society is necessary, as I felt during my long retreat and, my misanthropy ebbing away from me a little, I feel the need to spread myself about. The despair at not having been able to get my ideas across for twelve years has dammed up such a great quantity of them in my head that I'll have to give birth, and I still talk [to myself] sometimes when I'm alone... There's a real need to talk ... and, because of that, I can see that the Trappist life would not suit me too well..."

De Sade's tolerance of Gaufridy's less than wholehearted espousal of his interests still held good in 1790. Despite the notary's collusion with Mme de Montreuil at times against the marquis, Gaufridy's long association with the de Sades meant that, in the marquis's view, there was still no-one better able to extract money from the southern estates, although the notary was dilatory in this, and to keep him informed about his relatives' doings in Provence. Gaufridy was a senior retainer, de Sade a feudal lord - such relationships are not readily severed. When reviving the link by his first letters of the spring of 1790, having written to the notary hardly at all while in prison, the marquis unwontedly shouldered some blame: "My arrest at la Coste was not your fault but mine. I believed I was out of reach, not having reckoned how vile the family I had to cope with could be. I trust you understand that I am only talking about the Montreuils. You cannot begin to imagine what devilish and man-eating schemes that bunch directed at me. Even if I were the scum of the Earth, I would not have deserved the ferocious treatment I have undergone at their instigation..."

Still in the spring of 1790, the marquis was writing in forward-looking style to Reinaud: "I shall carry out [my plans], if God and the enemies of the nobility let me live. Regarding which, don't go taking me, despite that remark, for a [reactionary] hot-head. I protest to you that I am nothing but a neutral, cast down at having lost a great deal, even more so to see my sovereign in irons, distressed ... at the impossibility of the monarch's supervision of government being achieved and sustained while thirty thousand armed layabouts and twenty pieces of artillery interfere with it; but lamenting very little, all the while, the passing of the old order, which decidedly caused me too much misery for me to shed any tears over it. There's my profession of faith, and I make it without fear... But that's enough of that; one has to watch what one says in one's letters, for never did despotism break their seals as much as liberty does..."

At the end of May, Gaufridy was reading that de Sade had spread himself sufficiently to be "lodging in a charming lady's home - she has been unhappy herself and knows how to take pity on those who have been likewise..." To be more precise, he was living in a small flat across the way from Mme de Fleurieu, another *présidente* in that, like his mother-in-law, she was the wife of a high court judge, but estranged from same. "She covers me with kindnesses: sometimes I visit her country place for a little distraction, and I go so far as to say, although there is decidedly no other feeling between us but that of friendship, I always forget my troubles when I am with her ... she is forty years old. I add that last bit of information so you can see that, taken with me who is fifty, we have a combined age of ninety and so you know there can be no danger in this..."

Indeed, he continued to Gaufridy: "... No more unseemly pleasures ... all that disgusts me at present, as much as it used to set me ablaze in times past... My physical strength is barely enough to sustain me against all the illnesses afflicting me. There's coughing, eye trouble, headaches; there's rheumatisms, I don't know what; with all this exhausting me, thank God, I have no chance to think of anything else, and I deem myself four times the happier for it..."

Perhaps Mme de Montreuil's long, rigorous cure for Mr 6 had indeed burned all the oil in his lamp more effectively than the harem that the inmate had prescribed for himself would have done.

He was pleased with the welcome given him by various relatives, including Mme de Sorans, about whose offer of help he had been very rude during the manoeuvres over a prospective transfer for him from Vincennes to Montélimar in 1781. He had "looked up some acquaintances, some friends. I receive their respect and I cultivate them, all this revolving around a still, tranquil centre where I exercise the most stoical philosophy."

De Sade broke with Mme de Fleurieu about the date - 25 August 1790 - he met Marie Constance Quesnet, an actress who seems to have had no great success on the stage, aged about 30 and bringing up her young son after her husband had left her and gone to the Americas. Being an actress and the daughter of a tailor, she was a commoner and so an unlikely match for a count always much conscious of his lineage, although the Assembly had abolished titles of nobility in June. The head of one of the great blue-blooded families of Provence became Citizen Sade - the prefixes of *de, du, de la* and *des* having also been removed from family names by the levelling legislators. More to the point as regards the new relationship, Sade was still married, despite the legal separation, to a woman whose devotion to the Catholic Church would never have allowed her to countenance divorce, although the new government was legalising it.

In September, a servant stole 1,500 livres from Sade but Audibert, a tenant farmer in Provence, loaned his landlord 15,000 livres. Shorn of his title he might be, shorn of his property he was not. Writing to thank Audibert in November, Sade advised him not to heed "the pernicious talk of those ... who corrupt the people while falsely persuading them that they're putting them on the right path". The allusion was to those radicals who would extend the Revolution to a nationalisation of private property. The thrifty tenant should bear in mind that "our wise legislators[1] truly intend that each should keep his properties..."

Also in November, Sade was well enough funded to start setting up home at 20 rue Neuve des Mathurins, near the Opéra and the site of the Condé palace where he was born. (The palace had been demolished in 1773 to make way for streets and houses.) Gaufridy was sent to the manorhouse at la Coste for furniture to be forwarded to Paris, where it would furnish "my *last refuge*, a rather nice little shack which I declare shall feel eventually my dying breath! Yes, lawyer, there's a garden and I shall be buried in this garden..." To picture the scene, Gaufridy was invited to "visualise a good stout country priest in his presbytery." It

1 Most of them propertied men themselves.

was staffed by "a good housekeeper who, just now, is making a mighty fuss ... because someone has mislaid the key of her cellar, a cook and a manservant; that's my entire staff, my entire retinue; am I overdoing it?"

Sade was still asking Gaufridy in late-1791 for furniture from la Coste, much of which seems not to have been available, probably due to the ravages of time and thieves. The landlord placed the blame elsewhere: "I do not see how Madame de Sade did not give instructions for the château to be completely stripped of furniture once she anticipated that many years were going to pass without anyone going there. I used to take this precaution in the past when it was a matter of a year or two, so why not do so when one's talking about twelve or fifteen years? But the good lady would say her Our Father and that was much more important than taking care of my concerns..."

All of which ignores the fact that the marquise could have had no more idea than anyone else of how long her husband, held at the whim of the royal administration, would be out of circulation, and it leaves out of account his own wilful neglect of his affairs while he was in jail. One letter from him to Gaufridy would have arranged for his furniture to go into store, safe from the depredations of the mistral, and other forces.

Whether or not Marie Constance was the housekeeper turning No. 20 upside-down to find the cellar key in November, she was the one presiding in January of the next year, 1791. In June, Sade was replying to Reinaud, who seems to have been warning him against the perils of hanging around the theatre: "What the devil do you mean by attacking me? Mistrusting the skirts of the theatre - me? Ah! I tell you that I do just that! You only have to know that crowd in order to learn to mistrust it as it has to be. Oh! no, no, we [I and Marie Constance] are far from the theatrical set and there's nothing so virtuous as my little ménage! For a start, not a whiff of love; she's entirely a good and decent home-maker, amiable, sweet-natured, thoughtful, who ... has seen fit to take over the running of my little house. She and I draw on the modest allowance her husband provides for her; I provide her board and lodging..."

Then a touch of calculation for his old age: "If she stays with me, in order to give her a motive for prolonging my life, every *five years* I shall purchase for her a little annuity, a neat way for me to give her an interest in my staying alive and, by that, just by looking out for herself, she'll turn into my preserver..." Thus, Marie Constance's income from interest-bearing bonds would grow as another one was bought for her every fifth year while Sade lived.

Back to the letter: "... but of *hanky-panky* not a whiff. Could I live alone, surrounded by two or three valets who would have *robbed me blind*, perhaps *killed* me? Wasn't it essential to put a *reliable* individual between such rogues and me? Could I skim my pot, check the butcher's bill, when I'm stuck in my study amid Molière, Destouches, Marivaux, Boissy, Regnard,[2] whom I look upon, think about, admire, and whom I never emulate? Besides, don't I need someone to whom I could read [what I'm writing] *while it's hot*? Well, my companion fulfils all those needs; may God keep her by me, despite the breathtaking plotters who are working morning, noon and night to take her from me! My one fear is that, fed up with so many secret *Montreuillesque* manoeuvres, the poor creature might become disgusted, tired of it all and abandon me..."

Sade remained convinced that the Montreuils were behind most of his troubles. In May 1790, he had been telling Reinaud: "Nothing matches the infamous activities of the Montreuils toward me... Furious at seeing me free, there's nothing they're not making up now to give the world a low opinion of me. Do they see me set up, at anchor, somewhere? Then they send around as soon as may be some of their emissaries to tell a hundred rotten tales about me. They forced my wife to separate from me. She didn't want to... They take their vileness as far as to paying journalists to tear me apart in their papers..."

Whatever tittle-tattle about the wheezy libertine was being planted among the ex-nobles, bankers and professionals who also lived along the rue Neuve des Mathurins, Marie Constance lived up to her name and stayed with Sade. He did not only repay her with board, lodging and annuities, he also dedicated *Justine* to her. He may well have read the novel to her, bit by bit, as the second version took shape on his desk. He made notes of her comments and suggestions, which he valued highly. He called her Sensitive (*Sensible*). Reading *Justine* - a sustained, obsessive denial of women's access to independent thought and action - one finds it hard to appreciate any sensitivity that did not tell him to burn the thing and take a careful look within himself before he took up his pen again. In the dedication, Sade calls Marie Constance "the example and honour of your sex, combining the most sensitive soul with the most discerning and the most enlightened intelligence", and

---

2 Playwrights.

pours on much more awkward effusion, leading one to think that Marie Constance's qualities extended beyond the cellar keys and the butcher's bill to refraining from criticising the author and answering him back.

She remains an ill-defined figure. Little writing in her own hand, few documents from public archives, testify to her existence. She was a poor female commoner in an age when such a person had even less scope than she would now. One perceives her almost exclusively through her much better documented companion, who had found the latest in a succession of useful women who facilitated his insistence on living his life in his own way.

At the start of 1792, the gross gentleman who had walked out of Charenton 21 months earlier with hardly a penny in his pocket, reported himself to Gaufridy as a common citizen and aspiring man of letters, "having eight complete outfits of brand-new clothes, pretty good linen, a small but charming house, attractive enough to be admired - in Paris where people have had enough of looking at luxury - three or four good houses where I can go to dine or sup whenever I choose, free admission to all the shows, a certain literary esteem, a decent companion full of care for me and pretty good wine in my cellar; you'll clearly perceive, I say, dear lawyer, that it was impossible for me to move from the situation I was in twenty-one months ago to that where I am now without much expenditure, circumspection, work, strain and courage. Now, all that brings in its wake some debts..."

Which was where, as usual, that Gaufridy came in, trying to match his rent-collecting to the master's needs. This time, he was exhorted to sell anything to raise cash to be sent to Paris. Sade's pleas to Provence for money were the more urgent because of the price inflation in the capital, as the distraction of the royal administration and the attendant uncertainty inhibited the supply of food to the city and made traders reluctant to accept paper money. Amid the neat linen in their snug home, Sade and Marie Constance sometimes went to bed hungry for lack of cash to buy food.

Fearing those who were better used to this condition, King Louis XVI and his family escaped on 21 June 1791 from the Tuileries palace in Paris, where he had been held under the supervision of the National Assembly. The Assembly ordered his arrest and he was captured at Varennes, on his way to the frontier and an escape abroad, where many French nobles had already fled. The king was brought back to Paris, which had been ordered to receive him in silence, on pain of a flogging for anyone who cheered, hanging for anyone who insulted him. Sade, perhaps having decided it would be prudent to show himself as part of the democratic surge, wrote and had published a pamphlet in the form of an *Address of a Citizen of Paris to the King of the French*. Many such political pamphlets were in circulation in the city. Sade claimed later that he had caused a copy of his to be thrown into the king's coach as Louis XVI was passing through a dumbstruck Paris on his way back from Varennes, but it seems most unlikely that such an act took place during the decreed aloofness. Even if someone had thrown a paper into the king's coach on that occasion, it could hardly have gone unnoticed, lacking the cover of tumult, and gone unrecorded by everyone but the author.

On the day of his escape, the king had left at the Tuileries a document addressed to the French people, in which he complained of how he had been treated recently during the upheavals in Paris. His former cavalry officer replied in the pamphlet:

"You, the strongest [among us], you who used to command us, you who used to govern us by that invincible attraction of love and the unity of all, you have employed the subterfuges that stem from weakness; and the soul of a French knight, where we ought to have found only virtues, has offered us no more than the vices of slavery and of servitude.

"Ah! Sire, how wrongly you have perceived your true interests, how badly you have understood the people which used to raise you above itself! This people ..., rightly furious at the abuse of government by your former ministers, was beginning to reconsider its view of you; it was separating the wrongs done by your flatterers from the virtues which it used to like to see in you, and it was saying: *The good is the work of his heart; the bad is that of his ministers.* Happy and mild humours these, which, with a little patience and good conduct, would have yielded you much more than you have lost - for, Sire, you had only respect at Versailles; you would have won hearts in Paris.

"You complain about your circumstances; you groan, you say, in irons... Well, what sovereign of pure and decent heart, what sovereign enlightened enough to prefer the happiness of his peoples to the empty trappings of despotism, will not agree to give up his physical comforts for a few months to [await] spiritual comforts such as those being prepared for you through the consummation of the work by the nation's representatives! Besides, is life so unhappy in the most beautiful palace of the most beautiful city in the world, above all in that this situation is but momentary and in that it is the sure way to arrive at the perfection of happiness of twenty-five million men? While you are finding yourself unhappy in this position which would delight many others, deign for a moment to reflect on that of those who were victims of your despotism, on that of those sad persons whom one signature of yours, fruit of conniving or of a mental aberration, snatched from the bosom of their family in tears to be thrust forever into the dungeons of those dreadful Bastilles with which your realm used to bristle ...

"... Were you intending to go and stagnate privately in some obscure corner of Europe? Supposing that is so, what weakness! Were you wanting to return to France in arms and retake Versailles on heaps of the dead? If that is so, what cruelty! What blood your hand would have spilled! For, have no doubt, sire, there is not one Frenchman ... who would not prefer death to the rebirth of the abuses of your former tyranny ...

"If you want to reign, do so over a free nation; ... that's what appoints you as its chief, that's what places you on your throne, and not the God of the universe as people used to be weak enough to believe ... Your grandeur is therefore entirely our work; make yourself worthy of it and you will keep it forever."

The king, who could be excused because his flight was "the work of your priests and of your courtiers", should separate from his wife, Queen Marie Antoinette, Sade wrote, touching a popular antipathy to the Austrian consort. She was widely, and rightly, believed to be intriguing with France's enemies abroad with a view to rolling back the changes in her adopted country: "She is no longer necessary to you; send her back to her own land, which parted with her only in order to spread ... upon France the destructive, hateful poisons which it has always had for this nation...

"You take me perhaps, by my words, for an enemy of the monarchy and of the monarch - no, Sire, ... no-one in the world is more deeply convinced than I that the French empire can only be governed by a monarch; but this monarch, chosen by a free nation, must be faithfully submissive to the law - to the law made by the representatives of this nation ..."

Sade did not mention that, in the era of royal warrants for arrest, there had been different motives for locking up different people. However, his pamphlet should not be seen as altogether insincere and opportunistic, albeit not setting out all his political views of the time.

He was concurrently a registered elector of the Place Vendôme section, in central Paris, the city's government having been reorganised into 48 sections, and an associate of fellow nobles who favoured reforms in the administration of France but would keep the king at the head of it. Gaufridy wrote to ask, as the welter of opinions confused him in Provence, what Sade's true line was so that the notary could adopt it also. The master replied, on 5 December, that this was a very difficult request for him to deal with:

"First, as a man of letters, my obligation to work now for one party, now in favour of another, sets up a shuttling in my opinions which is felt in my private thinking. Do I really want to plumb it? It lies with none of the parties, to tell the truth, and is made up of [elements from] all of them. I am against the Jacobins, I hate them like poison; I revere the king but I cannot abide the old wrongs; I embrace a great many of the articles in the [new French] Constitution while others repel me; I want the nobility given back its brilliance because there's no progress in its having been taken away; I want the king to be at the head of the nation; I do not want a national Assembly at all, but two houses [of Parliament] as in England, which gives the king a diluted authority balanced by the involvement of a nation necessarily divided into two orders - the third is superfluous, I have no place for it. There you have my profession of faith. What am I, just now? Aristocrat or democrat? You tell me, please, ... for I have not the least notion..."

For the atheist Sade, the two necessary orders of society were the nobility and the commonalty (the French second and third estates). The order he would jettison was the clergy. In this, Sade was at one with the most radical cutting edge in France, in so far as it was slicing into the esteem and power of the Catholic Church. The Assembly had abolished the clergy's special status in November 1790, declaring all priests and nuns to be no more or less than any other French person. In May 1791, Pope Pius VI was burned in effigy in the streets of Paris after he had condemned the alteration of the clergy's situation. Nuns were whipped and priests beaten by anti-religious zealots. On 3 July, the ashes of Voltaire, a great sceptical author of the Enlightenment, were carried across Paris in an elaborate procession. It gave a prominent role to Citizenness Villette - the former Marquise de Villette, with whom Sade the jealous prisoner had once forbidden his wife to lodge - riding on a carnival float as the goddess of Reason, an abstract quality which good revolutionaries could revere in lieu of the Holy

Trinity and its mysteries. We do not know whether Sade watched the "beautiful and good" *citoyenne* Villette personifying the downfall of the Christian religion which he abhorred, as she and the rest of the Reasonable pageant passed in front of the Tuileries where his anointed sovereign had been re-installed by the Assembly's troops after being captured on his abortive bid for exile. If Sade was a witness to all this, any resultant turmoil in his mind may have preoccupied him less than the rumbling of his large, irregularly fed stomach.

* * *

Louis Marie, Sade's elder son, resigned in July 1791 the commission in the infantry which his father had raged against from jail and, some four months later, left France for exile, or so it seemed. Sade, perhaps exercising caution in his letters, did not put this down to a desire by the young man to flee the egalitarian upsurge in the country. Rather, he appeared to be "nursing a private grievance. He is unsettled, wants to travel to the furthest parts of the world; he hates his fatherland..."

By contrast, Sade *père* was meeting the new military obligations of male citizens in Paris by paying, as was allowed, small sums of money in lieu of service in person in the civilian militia, the National Guard. He had been enrolled as active citizen number 596 of his municipal section, that of the Place Vendôme, on 1 July 1790. This category of active citizenship was reserved for men aged over 25 who paid taxes above a certain level, which excluded the majority of adult men in Paris (and all the women) from the franchise and from decision-making in each section. The Revolution in France was a middle-class, male democracy indoors, with a ragged, poor majority in the street.

In October, Sade was appointed by his section to take charge of its cavalry - a fitting job for the former captain of horse. It was not that the Vendôme section often had to put a large body of cavalry into action, rather that it was reckoned useful to have a reserve of horses and riders which could operate in the event of civil disturbance or if France's enemies came near to the capital. Sade would have been expected to have a good idea of where in the section good mounts and reliable horsemen could be mustered.

It was during 1791 that the influence of the constitutional monarchists - who would keep the king as a directing head of government, much as Sade had advocated in his royal pamphlet and his letter to Gaufridy - declined as the more radical elements in the city became less inclined to tolerate their organised activities. Various of Sade's relatives and associates were prominent constitutional monarchists and he had been busy among them. However, perhaps trimming his sails to the prevailing political wind, Sade became more involved in the work of his section meanwhile.

It was not until after Sade's winter of theatrical discontent that he saw his other son, Donatien Claude Armand, who was still in the army and stationed far from the capital. The young man turned up at the house in the rue Neuve des Mathurins - "all of a sudden he was walking into the room and embracing me" - in late-March 1792. He was in Paris for half a day as courier for his commanding officer and "we had barely four or five hours together," his father reported. (Donatien deserted the army in May.)

Another surprise from a distance was less welcome. The Revolutionary spirit had reached la Coste, whence the new local administration had written to ask the lord of the manor, no longer publicly recognised as such, to affirm his loyalty to the Revolution and the new national constitution. Citizen Sade exercised his rhetoric in a long, democratic affirmation that would have amazed, by its purpose, the Jesuit fathers who had taught him at Collège Louis le Grand forty years earlier. Next day, 19 April 1792, Sade heard that the Constitutional Club at la Coste, whose decisions were likely to be implemented by municipal officials, had resolved that the highest brickwork of the manorhouse, which made it semi-fortified against attack, should be demolished. The former marquis's pen was immediately busy in defence:

"Mister Chairman, I trust you will allow that it would seem the oddest thing to find, within the mere passage of three lustres[3], my ill-starred house at la Coste successively sullied by the low lackeys of ministerial despotism and degraded by the enemies of those same lackeys. Such a train of events would entail confusion ... in the man who has more reason than any to execrate, to abhor, the previous government, as to what he should think, in that he might be forced to regret the passing of that government in spite of everything, if he were

3 Fifteen years.

unable to discover defenders and friends even among those who should share the loathing of the past administration... Do you not consider that those who would have served me badly in this way would be accused of an unjust act?...

"If so much as one stone of the house that I own in your district is taken down, I'll present myself to your brothers among the Jacobins in Paris with the request that this be chiselled onto it: 'A stone from the house of the man who made topple the stones of the Bastille and which the friends of the Constitution ripped from the home of the most unfortunate among the victims of monarchical tyranny. Passers-by, enter this infamy in the annals of human inconstancy!'

"Do not touch my old walls, Mister Chairman. Look into my heart, pore over my writing, read the letters printed and circulated throughout Paris when the fine ladies of France were leaving and the king was fleeing - you will find there whether the author of such writings should suffer harassment through his property... Have I gone to live abroad, sir? Have I not consistently deplored such a retreat? Am I not an active citizen of my section?... Is not the only title I claim that of man of letters?

"However, you do not approve of my fortifications. Very good, gentlemen, rest easy. I am now addressing the whole community. I ask no more than the privilege of being the one who lays them low, the next time I am in your county. With the Constitution in one hand, a hammer in the other, I would have all of us turn the demolition into a *civic event*. Until then, gentlemen, we should hold back and *respect property*. I take these words from the Constitution itself; you will share my regard for them. As I wrote yesterday to your esteemed municipal councillors, Brutus and his colleagues had neither breakers of stones nor burners of houses in their ranks when they gave Rome the dear liberty which tyrants had stolen from it."

The democrats of that corner of Provence were bowled over by this stirring stuff, above the plain signature "Louis Sade", when it was read to the next meeting of the Constitutional Club of la Coste. On 3 May, it acknowledged a letter "full of the fire of patriotism". The friend of their childhood need feel no apprehension for his property would be under the protection of the community. The council wrote on 11 May to express itself "profoundly moved by the sentiments and constitutional principles" that permeated Mr Sade's letter. They wholly accepted its sincerity and assured him that his properties were under perpetual protection. They added that the erstwhile lord had the "affection and the fraternal and inalienable friendship of all the citizens of la Coste".

The young maid who had been taken injured to Saumane from the shuttered manor in 1775, after little respect had been shown to her there, was thus pushed even further from local memory by the flourishes of the literary citizen's plea for preservation of the stones that had rung with her screams. The cause of her distress was well and fondly remembered locally in 1792 by the first men of la Coste, whose council assured the faraway master:

"Our hearts are truly afflicted to discover that the troubles in this district, much less frightful than you thought, have deprived us of the sweet pleasure of seeing you among us. Indeed, there have been some troubles in the spots where aristocracy and fanaticism[4] thought they could master and overturn the superb edifice of our Constitution. The expedition sent against the town of Apt ... by the patriots from round about has restored calm... It entailed an infringement of the law, but that seemed to be a matter of necessity."

In other words, there was some rough stuff before the enemies of the Constitution saw the error of their ways, it seems. The club gushed on: "It is enough to be aware, sir, of your talents and your understanding, which so well equip you to assess the benefits and advantages for all, which our sublime Constitution gives us, for you to be counted among its true friends... Your letter ... was read to the last meeting of our Society... It received applause beyond measure, so much so that it was resolved to make mention of it in the minutes...

"Come, sir, share the benefits of the Constitution among us..."

There was nothing to fear in "the societies of so-called *Friends of Order and of Peace* ... in which there is no end to the directing of blows (on the quiet) at the Constitution so as to delude good countryfolk, most of all idiots and women, the weak and credulous sex, into thinking that it embodies an attack on religion..."

Sade was delighted, enthusing to Gaufridy: "I have received the *fraternal* letter from the gentlemen of la Coste. It's very good; there's sensitivity, affection, a lot of Jacobinism and the promise to put *my properties under their protection*, a promise which pleases me greatly, considering that in doing so they won't be able to *set light* to [my château]."

---

4 The religious kind.

Meanwhile, in case his flourishing of the Constitution and examples from classical antiquity at the rustic would-be Jacobins did not work, on the day after he had spreadeagled his rhetoric between the municipality and his bricks, Sade again urged the dilatory Gaufridy to send from la Coste a fourth load of effects, originally asked for the previous December. This was to include items from a natural history cabinet, "gold and copper coins, and Roman medals, ... that splendid Priapus mounted on a ring", letters of his father's and - most important - a little box of manuscripts. "Send all this without fail, I beg of you, because I worry about it being still in a house menaced by Jacobin stone-breakers and fire-raisers..."

Also in the spring of 1792, Sade's fancy was turning again to thoughts of a visit to Provence - with Marie Constance. Gaufridy was chivvied from Paris:

"Nothing, my dear lawyer, is more certain now than my journey... Where shall I stay?... Where shall I establish my general headquarters? I'll be in Provence for a short time only, three months or so, and during those three months we shall scurry about, you and I, a great deal... However, a residence is necessary, a meeting place; where shall I have it? Mazan, uninhabitable; Saumane, I'm afraid of that place; la Coste, a bit upsetting, the château I mean, and I would be inclined to take a house in the village - but does such a choice smack of fear ...? It's to be preferred for its evocation of equality, goodwill, democracy, is it not, but would it be condemned by my equals, and the thinking behind it *maliciously exposed* by my inferiors?"

In other words, the aristocrats (no longer of title) thereabouts would sneer at Sade for setting up residence in the village among the commoners, while the latter would see through, and spread the word about, his attempt to appear one of them by living among them.

Still, it would be a modest sojourn: "Our party will be very small. We will either stay as paying guests ... in a decent house or we will hire a cook, and the two of us will have only one servant. No parties, no dinners, no open-house, no fuss and show..." The merry and extravagant days of Beauvoisin in Provence were long gone indeed.

Before the end of March, though, Sade had been told from the south that Gaufridy and his son were on the run from Apt. They were probably involved in a royalist movement which had fallen foul of the sort of men who were running the council at la Coste. On 7 April, Sade tried to test the waters, through Gaufridy, who seems not to have been greatly deflected from his usual rounds:

"Let me know ... who ... took themselves off from la Coste to Apt with so much fury. What's the general attitude of the la Coste people? Who are the Jacobins there?... In a word, how do you think I'll be received at la Coste, if it's there that I take a house...? Is the resentment of all the people there directed only at the priests who don't want to take the oath of loyalty [to the Constitution], or is it also somewhat against the *owners of capital*?..."

A succession of letters arrived from various people in Provence, most of them perturbing Sade further as to what his reception might be there. He made light of all this to Gaufridy on 28 April: "Devil take me if you haven't all gone mad in Provence!... As for you, if you get into a second bit of trouble, lawyer, don't go anywhere for a cure but Paris, rue des Mathurins, No. 20, where I'll put you right ... in a week. *Six doses of Palais Royal* will set you up right away, I'll answer for it..." That is, if Gaufridy had to leg it on account of radicals after his blood again, he could come to Paris to wait till the heat was off. There, Sade would offer him a few visits to the Palais Royal district, where prostitution was busy.

Gaufridy no more took up the offer to go north than Sade visited his lands in the south. By June 1792, Sade was trying to arrange a spell in Provence from April to October the next year - the state of the roads meant that spring was the best season for long-distance travel and that one would do well to return before winter. A prime motive for Sade to spend time in Provence was to preside over the sale of at least one of his properties in order to finance purchase of a home in Paris - for preference, his snug "last refuge" at No. 20. In September, though, his chances of exchanging tenancy for ownership receded when a courtesan bought the house for 77,000 livres - at least Sade would not have to wonder how such a woman came by so much money. There was no visit to Provence in 1793 either, for various pressing reasons which will become apparent.

Meanwhile, in June 1792, more news of the would-be levellers in Provence indicated that the Priory of the Célestins at Avignon might well be demolished soon. This would disturb the tomb of Laure de Noves, object of Petrarch's sonnets and thus a famous figure in the history of the de Sade family, into which she married **(see chapter 2)**. Sade wanted to offer a new grave that would not be disturbed, perhaps at a church on one of his estates, but was worried that such a move would be seen as an aristocratic fancy, out of tune with the democratic times.

In July, it became clear that the stirring in the south would no longer be kept in its place and deflected from Sade by sonorous letters. A Mlle Soton reached Paris, having ridden all the way from la Coste on horseback, to lay before the Assembly a written statement about Gaufridy, the local priest (no longer allowed to officiate under the new, anti-clerical administration) and a few other residents of the area.

Sade heard of this and reported to Gaufridy that the young horsewoman's grievance was over the way her mother had lost a position teaching at, or supervising, schools in the area of la Coste. He and Marie Constance were soon trying, with hospitality and kindness, mainly supplied by the latter, to keep Soton from talking around the capital and to dissuade her from continuing to demand "Mr Gaufridy's head," as Sade told his agent, no doubt laying on a bit of exaggeration for the amusement of knowing he might be making Gaufridy tremble and, more important, perhaps to prod him into greater urgency over sending money to the landlord. Turning up the heat further under the Provençal notary, Sade told him: "Soton vigorously accuses you of being in league with the Montreuils. I don't believe it, and have only one thing to say so that you understand I don't believe it: *you are my friend, and the Montreuils are my biggest enemies*..."

He hinted that he was in a position, in the democratic capital, to make an end of the Montreuils through one word in the right place, but he was taking pity on them. The implication was that Gaufridy, an associate of the Montreuils as Sade well knew, might also be lost, especially now that a Provençal after his blood was making a fuss in Paris, if active citizen 596 of the Vendôme Section were so to decide. After that nudge in the ribs, Sade closed his letter of 10 July with an old refrain: "Goodbye, dear lawyer; in the name of heaven, money, money, money..."

Mlle Soton visited Sade's house later in July, cried more than somewhat and made remarks which shocked him out of teasing when he next updated Gaufridy: "That nuisance of a wench strikes me as very dangerous; she's always up to something, and now she's saying that she can't prevent herself involving me too in the petition of complaint she's handing over. She has had a memorandum drawn up; she has asked her lawyer if she may let me see it but he refused, which shows they want to push me into all this tomfoolery. She goes to see Mme de Sade who, so she claims, gives her advice which makes you and me look very bad. Right now, this girl is at my door with a soldier, whom she brings without wanting to say what he's doing here. I'm having them sent on their way and I'm going to make sure she's not let in here again; all she does here is to attack one or other of us, so she'll see what I have to say about it..."

Early in August, Sade was feeling even less ironical: "Every misfortune is hounding me all at once. I'm ill ... and we're so loaded with work at our section that I don't even have time to take a proper cure. I'm both on guard duty at the Tuileries and on watch in the section, sick as a beast and stony broke.

"... Soton ... presses on; the day before yesterday, she had delivered to me a letter from her mother, full of threats and horrors. This letter, as unreadable because of its style as because of its handwriting, leaves one to understand that the matter of it is confidences she claims to have had from Gothon[5] and which she wants to reveal. Now these confidences ... are related to all the slanders invented about me... So send me as soon as possible the certificate I'm asking you for. Also, try to have it signed for me by as many people as you can and, if required, that will knock down all [these accusations]..."

Sade may well have been referring to an authorised copy of the court decision, at Aix in 1778, by which his conviction and sentence for poisoning and sodomy were quashed. The more witnesses who signed such a paper, to support its authenticity, the better.

In the first week of September, a crowd of nearly 100 people from la Coste village broke into the manorhouse and pillaged it, then came back two days afterwards for another go. They did much damage to those fixtures and fittings they declined to steal, and drank the cellar dry. The local authorities, who in May had offered Sade handsome assurances about the inviolability of his château, at first shrank from tackling so many rampaging, drunken people, but rallied in time to save the floorboards and roof, then walled up all the doorways for protection. They recommended to higher authority, the administration of the Rhône Estuary Department, that a fellow la Coste councillor, who had joined in the ransacking of the manorhouse, be dismissed. However, the departmental administration soon sent wagons to remove, under

5 The late servant at la Coste.

requisition, furniture and other goods saved from the manor by the council of la Coste. After an argument, in which departmental officials adopted a high-handed tone to overcome the locals' misgivings, the furniture was taken off to Apt. Two days after that, locals managed to chase off a man who was breaking up the great front door of the manorhouse in order to take its ironwork.

In Paris, Sade had received news of some of these events by 10 October, when he was begging Gaufridy for the full details of the damage and losses. He also knew of confusion at his Saumane and Mazan estates. Ripert, the tenant who had helped to keep the injured maid out of circulation in late-1775, had been obliged to give up running the main farm at Mazan and turn it over to a hard-line Jacobin from the village, who "takes the job, affects a diligence made up of slapstick and cheek, shakes up everything, won't let go of anything, deals on the side with the local administration, doesn't send a penny" to the owner, according to that owner, who declared himself distracted to the point of suicide by these reverses. Sade wondered whether all this meant he had won back his liberty only to starve to death. Would he come to wish himself back in the Bastille?

Then details of the pillage at la Coste arrived from Reinaud. Sade told Gaufridy: "So la Coste is done for as far as I am concerned?... I cannot express what this loss means! The house had enough furniture for six houses!... I am in despair! If you had not been so slow about sending stuff on, everything in there might have been saved..." As for the departmental requisition of furniture and effects, "if they carry on like that, those villains will make their rule despised." He had heard that officials at la Coste had done their best and he would send his thanks.... "Goodbye, goodbye! My heart is pierced."

In the autumn, Sade heard from the south that most of the manorhouses of his area of Provence had been similarly maltreated, most of the pillagers having been simple looters rather than political zealots or grudge-bearers.

CHAPTER 25: STAYING CLOSE TO HORRORS

Sade's status in Paris as a citizen in good standing was being jeopardised, as he saw it, by his relatives - his two sons in that they had quit the army to go abroad, and the Montreuils as the mentors of the two young emigrants. Feeling and action against the king and aristocrats had been rising during the summer of that year, 1792, as France went to war with Austria, a conservative power that wished to restore the full sway of the French monarchy, and shortages and looting disrupted food supplies. On 20 June, some of the National Guard, with their families, marched to the Assembly, where they sang a radical song to the members, and went on to the Tuileries, where they found their way to the royal family's apartments. They surrounded the king, put a Jacobin red hat on his head and chanted political slogans at him. He showed no fear and the boisterous crowd left after it had had its fun and showed it could treat the king as it liked. There was ferment in the city from radicals who told the Assembly that, if the king were still being recognised as such on 9 August, there would be an armed insurrection to overthrow it. On the morning of the 10th, the king having neither abdicated nor been deposed, a mob broke into the Tuileries where, this time, the royal guards fired on them. The crowd - armed mainly with pikes, axes and knives - massacred 600 guards.

It is hard to tell what was the role of Sade, and even that of the entire Vendôme section, in the events of 10 August. There are indications that some residents of the sections near the Tuileries, which would include the Vendôme, fought alongside the king's guards to defend the palace. Then again, it is entirely possible that the section, at that juncture known for moderation among its rather well-to-do population, stood aside aghast. Much later, when under arrest by a radical government, Sade claimed he had fought with the radicals on the 10th, his "blood boiling with rage" at "the tyrant and his shameful wife" - but he was casting about then for any scrap of anti-monarchical credentials he could clasp to his status as a former aristocrat, apt to be sentenced to the guillotine. I am inclined to think that Sade - distracted by his faltering literary career and his difficulties with Provence, near-disqualified from street-fighting by his obesity and his various ailments -

raised a pike for neither side on the day which did more than any other in the 18th century to undermine the French monarchy .

Citizen Sade told Gaufridy on 6 September: "The horror of the massacres carried out - albeit with justification[1] - is unparalleled. The former Princess de Lamballe was among the victims. Her head, fixed on a pike, was shown to the king and queen, and her wretched corpse was dragged about the street for eight hours after it had been the object of the most ferocious debauchery. The throats of the obstinate priests[2] were cut in the churches where they had been locked up, among them the Archbishop of Arles, a most virtuous and worthy man..."

Fear in Paris of army regiments seizing power to crush the Revolution was further inflamed when a fortress on the eastern frontier was handed over to foreign enemies by soldiers who no longer wanted to fight for the new France. Hundreds of priests, suspected plotters and people found with false identity documents were being put in jail without trial, while due process before the Assembly's new court to hear prosecutions for subversion was being undermined by panic. On 1 September, as Sade, still in the third quarter of the year, was begging Gaufridy for an advance on fourth-quarter income from Provence, a batch of prisoners passing through the streets on the way to jail was butchered by a crowd of Parisians, and more than a thousand other such persons - aristocrats, clerics and common criminals - were likewise murdered in the city that week.

On 21 September, the Assembly turned itself into a new body, the National Convention, which voted next day to do away with the monarchy.

A week after the guards had fallen before the mob at the Tuileries, Sade moved to establish more documents to keep himself afloat amid the turmoil. He wrote three letters - one to Montreuil, his father-in-law, another to his wife, the third to his sons - and had copies witnessed by upright citizens as true records of what he had written. The Assembly had declared that parents were responsible for their children's behaviour, and had been taking a tough line with parents of emigrants who did not return. Sade spelled out to Montreuil that emigration without official permission was against the law, so the "mad behaviour" by the Montreuils in encouraging his sons to flee abroad had brought

---

1 He may well have inserted this phrase in case his letter were pried into.

2 Those still refusing to take the oath of loyalty to the Constitution.

embarrassment upon him. "Were you demonstrating your *high nobility* by insisting that your children ... take the side of the *nobles*?" he asked Montreuil. "As for me, sir, I have never been afflicted by that laughable form of madness, have never wanted my family to feel other than patriotism and honesty...

"Mme de Montreuil, your ambitious other half, throws away everything, betrays everything, in trying to breathe life back into the rotted skeleton of that vile government by lawyers and into the stinking claws of the ministers who used to brandish royal detention orders ...; but I, sir, who have written, published, declared to all those who have wished to read or hear me, that I was ready to lose the very last drop of my blood before I would put my hand to anything which could re-establish in France the detestable régime under which I suffered so much, I, sir, furious at the adherence which you forced my sons to take, I will have to denounce at once your house as the centre of the idiot aristocracy, where all these frightful schemes, and many others perhaps, were hatched and carried out. I have very much wished to refrain from doing so, out of what remains of my consideration for you, but now I declare to you that if, within a fortnight, you have not caused my sons to return to their duties (for myself, I cannot, because their address is being kept from me), then I repeat to you, sir, that if, within a fortnight, they are not in Paris and, like their father, in arms for the defence of the fatherland, no consideration will prevent me and I shall denounce you right away to the national assembly and to all France as the instigator of their criminal emigration..."

He told his sons that they had aligned themselves with an unworthy cause "at the instigation of your mother's family." Louis XVI was "a rogue and a traitor whom only madmen would follow. Besides, I am telling you that I am in my section's service and so the present circumstances could set us against each other; it is not fitting that you should be armed against your father... A decree of the national assembly makes parents responsible for the conduct of their children and puts the former under the sword of justice if the latter do not return [from emigration] as soon as may be. I ask you whether you ought to remain any longer in a situation which points a blade at the breast of those who gave you life... In brief, my sons, I order you to come back at once and threaten you with my hatred and my curse if you delay for even one day in obeying me."

It seems certain that the letters were not sent to the addressees. However, they constituted, with the similar letter written to his wife, a useful outburst to have at hand, ready to flourish at any het-up radicals who wanted to throw Sade into jail because of his relationships with emigrant nobles. As such, while saving the writer's skin, they might well have sent his parents-in-law, his wife and his sons to the scaffold. The letters might have done as much if they had been found by outsiders during a search of Sade's property. He may well have stored them carefully, only to be offered to the authorities *in extremis*. Even so, there seems no question which neck he preferred to keep from under the revolution's blade if it turned out to be a choice between his and those of his closest relatives.

Sade stayed in France throughout the Revolutionary upheaval because exile would have been highly uncongenial to him. Having fled abroad, he would have been likely to find himself among other emigrant French aristocrats. They would have been apt to snub him as a libertine who had been imprisoned under the legitimate royal régime and let out by its enemies. Besides, exile would have been unremunerated, at least until he had found a publisher who would pay for manuscripts in French, which would have been problematical while by far the biggest market for books in that language, that of educated people in France, was being thinned and made less accessible by inflation, war and political change. By staying in France, Sade kept his best chance of receiving the sort of income he was used to - revenue from Provence. He had much trouble getting this out of Gaufridy and other agents in the south while he was chivying them from Paris; trying to direct them from abroad, however, would have been even more difficult, not least because it was a serious offence to send funds from Revolutionary France to emigrant nobles. Another strong motive for his staying put was to be near the Parisian theatres which, at any moment, so he believed, might have made a success of one or more of his plays and transformed his reputation.

CHAPTER 26: RHETORIC AND ROBESPIERRE

This man of letters - in an era when literacy was far from a general accomplishment and at a time when depredation and flight among the social élite were making it even less so in France - was a valuable asset in the Piques (Pikes) Section of Paris in the last quarter of 1792 and later. The Place Vendôme Section had been given its new and sharper name in September. On 25 October, Sade, one of the section's secretaries, was named one of its two representatives, to meet their counterparts from the other wards of the capital, in a municipal initiative to improve the city's hospitals. Three days later, he had ready - on what advice we do not know - five recommendations which he put before the capital's hospital management board. These are expressed in general terms but show abiding concerns of hospital managers - the need to extract funds from central government, as well as inefficiency and conservatism among existing administrators. Sade's section voted that his five proposals be published and distributed to the other 47 sections of the city. One can only speculate as to whether this was because the recommendations (or their author) had made a special impression, or because the Piques activists wanted to be seen by their comrades across the city as diligent in reform.

In any event, Sade stayed busy on this matter, being named with two other citizens on 17 January next (1793) to inspect five hospitals and report to the board. The report, dated 26 February, bore five lines in Sade's writing to testify that it arose wholly from inspection and notes by the three men. It may well be that the findings of Sade and his colleagues were instrumental in securing for each patient his or her own bed - no small advance in a city where those who could not afford to set up private treatment rooms at home often spent their time in hospital two or three to a bed. For a patient to lie against a body slowly cooling and stiffening in death from disease was commonplace.

Sade the hospital inspector was also Sade the property administrator. The sections of Paris had sealed against any looters or squatters many townhouses that were empty since their owners had left the city (the country, in many cases) to avoid the re-making of public life that was going on. The Montreuils, perhaps trying to establish that they had not fled France, asked for their mansion to be re-opened. It stood in the Piques Section and Sade, so he told Gaufridy on 30 October 1792, was about to be appointed the official who supervised the removal of that district's seals. As such, he might well get a chance to ferret about in his arch-enemies' townhouse. "If I find anything that marks them as aristocrats, as I am sure to do, I will show them no mercy," he promised Gaufridy. "Did you chuckle, Mr Notary?"

It is not clear as to whether Sade did get the job of breaking the seals on the Montreuil townhouse. Even if he had, it would not have been certain that he could have searched the house for what would have been his quarry anywhere his mother-in-law had lived - documents of his, letters and literary manuscripts, which she had had removed from la Coste and other places during his incarceration. Such an incursion to a family's house would be a municipal duty, during which the corpulent administrator Sade might find it awkward to convince any zealous, and much more nimble, *sans-culottes* in his party rummaging through the mansion that certain papers they had found should pass into the personal control of Citizen Sade, rather than to an assessment by the public authorities. In such circumstances, Sade might even find his new status as a democrat, which he was building through much rhetoric and work so as to distance himself from his aristocratic past and his aristocratic relatives, hard to keep bright as the egalitarians of the Piques realised that the author of certain sanguinary-erotic musings brought from the Montreuil mansion, and the author of the section's recommendations on hospital management, were one and the same, give or take a *de*.

From whatever second thoughts on his part, or re-allocation of responsibilities by the section, Sade did not search the Montreuil mansion, it seems. If he had, there was one set of items he would have been particularly keen to find. The last load of effects sent from la Coste by Gaufridy, before the manor there was pillaged in September, had contained a little box which Sade put high on the list of material his agent was to send. It did not appear to have been forced but, when Sade looked inside, it was empty. He suspected that the Montreuils had found a way to have the lock picked during their search for letters that had passed between him and Anne Prospère, his sister-in-law.

However, perhaps Sade felt - being at liberty to recreate and improve his lost literary works, and being esteemed as a citizen of a self-transforming France - he no longer had an overwhelming need to find documents from his past. He drew Gaufridy's attention to how much of a linch-pin he was becoming in the Piques Section, witness a copy, enclosed with the letter, of one of his municipal memorandums. This may have been the hospital management recommendations or, more likely, an essay *On the Way to Approve Laws*, which the section had printed and circulated among the other 47 divisions of the capital in the first week of November. This paper was concerned with the political heart of the matter - control of the Revolution. It tackled the question of who among the people (that is, who among certain adult males) shall make basic law. Sade read it aloud to the Piques Section's General Assembly twice in late-October 1792. There is no better example of his rhetoric - all the finer for being applied to a cause other than his own self-esteem:

"CITIZENS:

"The most important question of all is in hand, and nothing is more remarkable than your apparent slowness in responding to it ...

"Let's reason together for a moment on how to keep [this power won by your exploits in wrenching sovereignty from tyranny]. I will ask you first how you regard those whom you have charged with making laws for you... Never lose sight of the extreme difference between the envoy of the subjects of Louis XVI and the representatives of a people which has just reconquered all at once its rights, its power and its liberty. The former, having only favours to ask ..., was able ... to maintain in you that tongue-tied attitude to despotism ... None of all that exists today; straightforward, free men, your equals, to whom you delegate only momentarily a portion of the sovereignty which belongs only to you, cannot ... have any higher claim to this sovereignty than you do. Sovereignty is *single, indivisible, inalienable* - you destroy it by dividing it; you lose it by transferring it.

"The enlightened men whom you have called to the honour of making a new Constitution for you have no other rights whatsoever than those of submitting ideas to you; to you alone belongs the refusal or the acceptance of these ideas; ... you are the beam of light[1] ..., your deputies are the burning glass who possess no more than what they

---

1 In the original, the phrase "beam of light" is *faisceau de lumière*, which evokes not only the image as Sade developed it but also a more menacing allusion, for *faisceau* also means a bundle of weapons (pikes in this case, no doubt) and a stack of faggots. One can imagine Sade allowing a momentary pause in his actorly address immediately after "*faisceau*", to let the bellicose and the kindling images spring into the minds of his listeners, before completing the metaphor with a lighter touch.

have received from you, and shall not light up the land except by the fires which you shall have passed on to them. People, you can do anything without them; they can do nothing without you. No-one imagines how essential it is to establish these basic ideas; the aristocracy is not as far away as one thinks, the smell of it still wafts through the atmosphere it was darkening such a short time ago - this will not be a matter, you may say, of the same men being corrupted by its putrid fumes, but all the same they will rot those who come to breathe them ...

"Oh, my compatriots, let a necessary mistrust never leave you therefore, never cease to think about the means to preserve this freedom, which is not acquired except through torrents of blood, and which a mere moment can snatch away ...

"Citizens, ... you have already been told that your approval was not needed for the laws which are going to emanate from the national Convention; you have been told that your representatives, assuming your power, have acquired, by this act of delegation alone, both the power to create laws and the power to approve them; ... they have become judges of their own cause. You have been told this and you have given way to it. Yes, no doubt about it, you have given way to it, because no objection has been heard ...

" ... If your representatives can pass you by as they make laws, if your approval seems to them unnecessary, from this moment they show themselves as despots; from this moment you are slaves... How can they believe that the portion of sovereignty that you entrust to them could ever give them the right to make an attempt on the other [portion]? The greatest misfortunes await you if they carry on regardless ...; you are lost if they hand down to you laws which you have not approved for ... they will soon eclipse the authority which must never leave your hands.

"Without diminishing in any way the legitimate confidence which we have placed in our representatives, even so let us demand of them that they look on themselves as no more than individuals charged with presenting ideas to us - we alone must lay down our laws; their only task is to propose them to us...

" ... Let [the laws we have] do their job for us temporarily, and let you work [meanwhile] with rule and balance on this Constitution which must make our happiness and which - if it is sound, if it is given mature meditation - will become perhaps the law of the universe. If, on the contrary, you act with precipitation ... on such essential objects, if you do not obtain in the end, for each of your laws, this approval by the people ..., then your enemies ... will soon succeed, not in conquering you - you are Frenchmen - but in dividing you."

The orator went on to propose local assemblies throughout France to pass judgement on draft laws which would be read to them for their discussion, the decision of the majority to carry the day. However, if a proposed law receives only minority support - "your representatives revise it, scrap it or recast it; if they manage to improve it, it is presented a second time to all of France in assembly, just as before, in all the districts of all the departments."

Sade seemed much concerned to allay any fears that the people (the men, that is) would find such meetings a chore, or would not be up to the job: " ... for a festival, for a procession, the enslaved farmer used to travel great distances in the old days; do you imagine that today the free cultivator would be reluctant to cover a few leagues when called to the honour of approving a law, ... to that of exercising his sovereignty in the most majestic way...

"But, perhaps someone here will object, would the ... assemblies be able to pronounce on a law? In part made up of enlightened people, but in the main made up of those who are not, how will this *motley* collection set forth its will on such a grave matter? Would a careful selection of persons not be much more suitable? Let's be wary of believing any such thing; although one must have a selection of men to propose laws, never imagine that one must have such to approve them. It is the will of the people alone which is to approve or not the laws made to bind it; so it must do the job en masse, without election - [that] would put the adoption or rejection of a law in the hands of those who unfortunately are most likely to have the knack of evading it ..., and it is just that stumbling block which must be most carefully avoided."

Which was all very democratic, but would be cumbersome in practice as thousands of couriers travelled between the capital and every other part of the biggest and most populous country in western Europe, with draft legislation in various stages of submission, approval, rejection, revision and re-submission. Sade did point out that he was dealing only with the making of the articles of the new constitution - "the ordinary laws have to be put into effect too quickly, and besides are of too little consequence, to require approval by the people." However, this modification - quite against the tone of his main argument - appears only in a footnote to the published text and may well represent a retreat by Sade after he had spoken to his section's assembly and certain practicalities of what he was proposing had been pointed out to him.

For all that, the author's heart, for once, seems to have been in the right place - on the side of the downtrodden. The main text goes on: "Solon said that *the laws were like spider's webs, through which big flies passed while little flies were caught.* This ... leads us to recognise the need to bring into the approving of laws, perhaps even before anyone else, that part of the people worst treated by fate and, since it is they whom the law *strikes* most often, so it is for them to choose the law by which they agree to be *struck.*

" ... I have no suspicion towards anyone, I mistrust no-one; no individual in the world perhaps has more confidence in our representatives than I do, but I know how far abuse of power goes, I see to the bottom of all the tricks of despotism, I have studied men and I know them; I know that they give up with great reluctance power which is *entrusted* to them and that there is nothing so difficult as setting limits to *delegated* authority. I love the people; my works prove that I was setting out the present system long before the cannons which overthrew the Bastille were to announce them to the universe. The finest day of my life was that when I believed I saw the benign equality of the golden age reborn, when I saw the tree of liberty shelter with its benevolent branches the remains of the sceptre and the throne. This inadequate paper is only the result of my fears - if I arouse them in you also, you will soon oppose that which has caused them to be born, and we shall all be happy; if I am mistaken, my fault is that of my heart, I will find myself excused in yours; let me have your understanding of this, I shall revise my scheme accordingly. My only pride here is in my openness; I might be a worse speaker than anyone else, but I would not want to love you any the less."

One might look askance at Sade's claim - made in passing but full of arrogance - that the overthrow of the Bastille had laid his democratising works before the universe. It had, in fact, opened the way for *Justine* to get into print (and *The Hundred and Twenty Days of Sodom* to disappear - just as well for his standing as a Revolutionary). Still, *Aline and Valcour* was on the way, and it contained enlightened views of the past and blueprints for the future.

In his paper, Sade had been telling the section - and through print all the other sections of Paris - that the advances during 1792 by the *sans-*

culottes had given them much additional power, but that this must be consolidated in the autumn. They should seize their time by an assertion of grassroots strength, in the face of the Convention, the elected national assembly, so that the latter should become no more than a proposer of laws which would not take effect without the approval of sectional and cantonal (rural district) assemblies. If that sort of legislative mechanism had been established in France, much control of the Revolution would have passed from the central body to thousands of groups across the country. In fact, at the National Convention in late-1792, power was being concentrated in fewer hands as small committees were given authority to deal rapidly with the mercurial events in and around a France at civil and foreign war, rather than wait for full debate by the members as a whole. A scattering far and wide of legislative authority would have been regarded by most members as a backward step, making for great delays in decision-making - and a great dimming of their own power and prestige.

Sade, the ex-marquis, was revealing himself as an eloquent adherent to the sort of fundamentalist democracy which had befitted the small bodies politic of classical Greece and Rome, familiar to him through his reading, and which might have seemed reborn in the masculine gatherings of the activists of the French capital's sections - citizens who were confident of their hold on the city's streets, who had seen off an anointed king and were becoming suspicious of the other potentate in the Revolution besides themselves, the Convention.

* * *

Even such an active citizen as Sade was not able to avoid his turn at regular guard duty, alert against any conspirators who might attack public officials or property. Payment in lieu of such service was no longer allowed - anyone who failed to do his bit without good reason was jailed for a day - and so Soldier Sade was called on 4 November to report outside the Convention at 9 a.m. on the 6th.

Given all his commitment to the new ways, Sade found it incredible that Gaufridy, being closely connected to the portly citizen, was not proof against the troubles that the notary was suffering from radicals in the south. Gaufridy was the representative of a man whose patriotism was beyond reproach, in that its foundation was "ten years in the Bastille", and who was part of "the Revolution, body and soul". Sade's purse, though, being chronically thin, tied him to the past. In early December, he was again fretting over whether he could travel to

Provence. The Marquise de Villeneuve, his acquisitive aunt, had said she would like to see him, so he had been told, and he was keen to determine whether she might die and leave him some of her wealth before long. Also, he wanted to judge for himself the condition of his properties at la Coste, Saumane and Mazan. However, there remained the difficulty of predicting his reception in the south. If "old enemies", perhaps allied to the new radicals, were feeling sufficiently confident to act against him, they might insult him publicly, or even murder him, especially if some of them had been convicted as pillagers of la Coste, he having filed a complaint with the authorities.

Reinaud, the lawyer at Aix, and others in the south advised that such a visit would not be safe for an ex-noble, but various other Provençal people, newly arrived in Paris, said he would be able to circulate in the province. While Gaufridy was seeking a consensus on this with Reinaud and others, Sade asked the agent to send money enough for the Piques activist to redeem his silver from pawn, asked him to swear he would not resign his position as Sade's agent before the spring of 1794 (Gaufridy had told how he had been privately warned to cease representing Sade), and to send 11,010 livres in three equal tranches from May 1793 through May 1794.

At the end of December 1792, Parisian money-lenders were charging Sade, and many other individuals, interest of 7 per cent *a week*.

Also that month, in the south, he was added to the Rhône Estuary Department's list of emigrants, the local administration probably having concluded that his absence from his Provençal estates indicated that he had gone abroad, like other southern nobles. This setback was compounded by a departmental official entering his name as Louis Alphonse Donatien Sade - almost the combination of Christian names his mother had intended for him more than a half-century earlier when he went to the font, but not his registered baptismal names of Donatien Alphonse François.

On 21 January 1793, the guillotine removed the head of "Louis Capet; age: thirty-nine; profession: last king of the French". The revolutionaries had decided that King Louis XVI was a Citizen Capet, the monarchy having been abolished the previous September, and the Convention had unanimously found him guilty of crimes against the people. By a majority of 53 votes in 721 cast, the Convention then condemned him to death.

The prices of food, and the popular propensity to hunt down suspected hoarders and counter-revolutionaries, rose in Paris. By way of response to the radical developments in France, particularly to the execution of a monarch, royal governments elsewhere in Europe pushed harder to defeat Revolutionary France and restore the royal house and the nobles there to their previous ascendancy. By March, the Austrian army had taken the northern French city of Liège (now in Belgium) and people in western France, far from the ferment and enthusiasm in the capital, were organising a revolt to prevent any more of their young men being pressed into the army. These threats inspired the administration in Paris to set up a court with power to hear summary trials of anyone prosecuted for crimes against the new republic. Vigilante committees were to be established throughout France to intern foreigners and suspected citizens.

The elected representatives of the people, in Paris, reacted to such dangerous and changing times by handing over the day-to-day administration of France to a Committee of Public Safety - 14 members of the Convention.

With the impaired sense of incongruity that befits a dedicated playwright in the middle of a bloody revolution, Sade wrote again, on 1 March, to the Theatre of the Nation to say that he had amended the script of his one-act comedy *The Boudoir or the Credulous Husband*, along the lines of the actors' suggestions of the summer of 1790. He submitted the amended version of the piece and, hard-up though he was, offered to waive his fee as an author if the theatre would stage the play right away. He must have decided to eschew an author's payment in the hope of having a play staged so as to bring his dramatic work to the attention of other theatres and hence lead to more of it going onto the boards. Free-lance writers know well this surrender of remuneration in hope of exposure. It did Sade no good. On 15 March, having received no reply, he told the Theatre of the Nation that he wanted the script back, if the play was not going to be accepted for production. "It didn't occur to me that that which one *gives* had to be subject to the same delays as did that which one *sells*."

He was soon regretting this haughty tone, once he had learned that the theatre company, miffed at his attitude, was preparing to send back the script with a sharp note to the effect that it always paid authors for plays to be produced and that it was too busy to read the script just then. Realising that his customary spleen was alienating one of the city's best theatres, Sade grovelled. He told the company's secretary on 12 April it would be a shame to fall out over the matter. He had admired the theatre since he was a young man, as the great actor Molé would remember. He asked the secretary to smooth any ruffled feathers, begging as only a desperate author can. Well, the secretary informed him, as luck would have it the script was just about to reach the head of the queue for the reading committee's attention, which it would have soon. Whether it did or not, this was to no avail.

Although his reputation as a playwright would not spring to life, his clout in the Piques Section was sufficient to bring to its assembly the unlikely figure of Citizen Montreuil, Sade's father-in-law, in the late afternoon of 6 April. Sade lived less than a half-mile from the Montreuil mansion. The former judge (probably in his late 70s and perhaps as old as 81) and the former marquis had probably not seen each other for more than 20 years. They chatted for an hour as the light faded over Paris. "The whole thing was as relaxed as one could wish," Sade reported. The most likely motive for the head of the Montreuil family to seek out its rogue son-in-law was a need for protection against the hunt, often capricious in its choice of targets and rapid in its execution of them, for aristocrats who might be working against the Revolution. The Montreuils, as we have seen, could put the survival and progress of their dynasty before embarrassment over the means they used to that end.

Two days after this re-union, Sade himself became a judge, being named to a local tribunal. The next letter to Gaufridy was ebullient. First, Sade broke the news that Montreuil had visited him. "Guess the other surprise! You would not get it in a hundred tries! I'm a *judge*, yes, a *judge*!... Who would have told you that fifteen years ago, lawyer, who would have told you that? You see clearly that my head is growing up and I am beginning to turn sensible. Send me your congratulations and above all send some money to his worship the judge or, devil take me ... if I don't *sentence you to death*!"

Sade was never one for good taste in his jesting. He went on: "Make the news known round and about so that at last they'll understand down there that I'm a patriot, for I swear to you in earnest that I am such, heart and soul."

The next cry to Gaufridy for money, on 5 May, was much less cheery:

"As, unfortunately, these delays [in sending money] are putting a dagger into my heart, as *bereft of letter of credit, of goods to pawn* and *of any means to raise a loan*, it has to be, since you are leaving me in want, that *I shall absolutely die of hunger*; so, I'm saying, I can neither forgive you nor find grounds of any sort whatsoever for these vile delays, which are having me turn to *beggary...* Yes, that's what I'm come to!... I am indeed! For four days now, I have been without servants in my house, no longer having anything to feed them with, and I subsist only by going hither and yon to dine. In a week, three promises [of mine] to pay are going to land on my head - four hundred[2] for my rent and two hundred for personal debts, and my furniture is going to be seized if I don't pay. It is so, my friend, yes, it is so that, on the receipt of your letter, received on the fifth day since I was without means, and in which you consult me *coldly* about the ways to send me money, yes, believe me, I give you my word of honour on this, it is so that I leapt to my pistols and, but for a friend, *I would have blown my brains out!...*

"What I'm asking you for *is money*, what I want *is money*, what I must have *is money*. I have some five hundred thousand francs in property under the sun; sell at once a patch of ground for the *thirteen thousand ... that I must have through next May*, so as to avoid the cruel agonies that you use to tear my heart when every quarter comes around. My health, changed by long misfortune, is no longer in a state to stand up to such blows...

"Now! Get on with it... In the name of God, do whatever you like, with Saumane, with Mazan, with Arles, with la Coste! Cut, squeeze, borrow, sell up, do any damned thing but send me some money."

"You're wrong to say that you can do nothing on your own account; your powers as agent and my trust give you the right to take anything on yourself ... except to keep me waiting..."

It is hard to identify such a long period - four days - at any other stage of his life when Sade had no-one to do for him. Even during this hiatus of mid-1793, though, Marie Constance almost certainly rallied round in the kitchen and with the laundry. These were desperate straits, however. It is easier to be an egalitarian when one's stomach is full and there is a skivvy to fill it.

---

2 Francs, the livre having been superseded.

Although he could not eat it, or pay his debts with it, Sade was glad to receive, on 13 May, a certificate from the Piques Section to the effect that François Aldonze Sade (yet another scrambling of his name), man of letters and former colonel of cavalry, was a resident of the section. In other words, he was officially designated as not an emigrant. Further to establishing that he was still in France, Sade was in touch with the Rhône Estuary Department, which resolved on 26 May that Louis Sade (*sic*) was indeed resident in the country, accordingly took his name off its list of emigrants and recognised his undiminished right to hold his properties in that department. This happy restoration lasted only a month for, when a re-organisation of local government in June created a new department in Provence, that of Vaucluse, papers transferred from Rhône Estuary still showed Louis Sade on the list of un-person emigrants and it was as such that the Vaucluse clerks stowed that name in their files.

The recurring confusion over his Christian names may have arisen from his having been called Louis in intimate matters and various combinations of his baptismal names in formal dealings. Sade might well have been so used to being known by relatives and others as Louis, which his mother had wanted as his first name, that he had trouble recalling his three baptismal names in their right order and spelling, when required to put them in full on legal documents.

In June, the sections of Paris, still pursuing their efforts to increase grassroots political clout and curb the power of the Convention, were much concerned to head off a proposed decree by the latter to set up and maintain a professional army of 6,000 men in the capital. Being aware that political power grows out of the barrel of a gun, or the point of a pike, the sections urged the Convention to defend the city, not with a paid standing army but with a popular militia which would arise from the sections at need, bearing the weapons which would be held by those sections rather than by a central government arsenal. Sade was secretary of an assembly of all 48 sections on 15 June, and was one of four delegates from this gathering who were to present the sections' argument on the matter to the Convention next day. He drew up the address and was the delegate who read it to the assembly:

"Legislators, we must tell you, and we are going to prove to you, this decree is ... *impolitic, unjust, dangerous*...

"We consider this decree *impolitic*... because it would strip the workshops [of workmen to serve in the new army]...

"Your decree seems *unjust* because, rather than favouring the class down on its luck, the high pay proposed for the revolutionary soldiers would be seized on by idlers and by schemers, [and] because it offers to those who have done nothing twice as much as to those who risk their lives in the defence of the fatherland..."

(A day's pay in the Parisian army was to be double that in the armies fighting foreign enemies and insurrectionists in the French provinces.)

"Your decree is *dangerous* because a revolutionary army in Paris would be no more than a praetorean guard, of which the ambitious or the usurpers would soon take advantage to clap us in irons...

"To the citizen of Paris alone belongs the right to defend his city; and the city which, at the first beat of the drum, ... makes a hundred and fifty thousand men ready for action, can take care of its own defence.

"But ..., they say, ... it is for other motives that this [new] army is being raised. Legislators, tell us these motives - to disguise them is to render them suspect. We no longer live in the barbarous ages when the government wrapped inself in mysterious shadows only so as to hide its outrages from us... No, the French people have not made so many sacrifices for liberty in order to topple back into slavery, and we ask you for the withdrawal of a decree which would soon topple us into it..."

After this pledge-cum-warning to the Convention, on 11 July Sade was back in his administrative role, presiding over a meeting of the section's hospital commission, which resolved that each section forward to a Parisian commission for the improvement of hospitals the names of all its in-patients, whose condition and treatment would then be investigated. Twelve days later, the busy Citizen Sade had become the chairman of the Piques Section and, about then, Montreuil attended a section meeting.

Prominence, however, was no guarantee of continued success or safety among the new rulers of France. In April, extreme Jacobins had been calling for the arrest of "treacherous" members of the Convention and, by June, the sections had organised detachments of the National Guard and an *ad hoc* militia of *sans-culottes* to surround the Convention and force it to accept the arrest of two ministers and 29 members. This strengthened the hand of the Jacobins in the administration. The Committee of Public Safety was changed on 10 July from a 14-man body into a unit of only nine members, dominated by the radical Maximilien Robespierre.

On a date in late-September, Sade stood in the Place des Piques (as the Place Vendôme was then known) to speak a high-flown public eulogy of Jean-Paul Marat, the influential radical whom the young provincial Charlotte Corday had assassinated on 13 July, and of the reforming jurist and educator Louis Le Peletier de Saint-Fargeau, who had been murdered earlier in the year. The assembled citizens in the great square were told by the rotund orator that "the sweetest duty of truly republican hearts is to give due recognition to great men; from the effusion of this sacred act are born all the virtues necessary to the upholding and the glory of the State..." Marat and Le Peletier were "sublime martyrs of liberty, already placed in Memory's temple", from where, "always revered by humankind", they would soar above those of us here below, "like beneficent stars ... useful to men ... as the model of all the virtues..."

First the smile, then the snarl - for Corday, who had gained entry to Marat's house on the pretext that she had information for him, then stabbed him in the bath to which a skin disorder used to confine him for much of his time:

"Shy and gentle sex, how can it be that your delicate hands should have seized the dagger...? Ah! your eagerness to come to throw flowers [now] on the tomb of this true friend of the people [Marat] makes us forget that the crime was able to find an instrument among you. The barbarous assassin of Marat, like those mixed beings whom one can place among neither sex, spewed forth by the Inferno to the despair of both, belongs rightly to neither... Let there be ... no further offerings to us, as some are daring to make, of her effigy under the beguiling badge of beauty. You over-credulous artists, break, turn inside-out, spoil the features of this monster, or present her to our gaze only amid the Furies of Tartary..."

Still with feminity, but onto a higher plane: "Sole goddess of the French people, holy and divine LIBERTY, allow us to shed again at the foot of your altars some tears for the loss of your two faithful friends, let us wind cypress boughs [of mourning] into the oak garlands with which we surround you..."

The Piques Section's assembly voted, on 29 September, to have the speech - by no means exceptional for the era in its purple style - printed and distributed, too.

Sade's chairmanship of the section did not last long. Some of the extremists in Paris were pressing for more and more categories of crime to carry the death penalty - hoarding of food had recently been made a capital offence - and for more intensive sniffing after backsliders and malcontents. Sade - overweight, overworked and over-fifty - was entitled to find the ferment at assembly meetings too much to handle. On 2 August, he exchanged posts with the vice-chairman. For one thing, he had been coughing blood and felt exhausted; for another, some citizens of the section had proposed something "appalling ... quite inhuman". Whatever it was, Sade declined to put it to the vote and gave up the chair.

It was during his chairmanship of the Piques Section that Sade used his position to put his mother-in-law and father-in-law, the Montreuils, on a list of section residents who were exempt from prosecution for opposing the Revolution, in that they were deemed to be cleared of any suspicion. How could the prisoner of Vincennes and the Bastille - who had then imagined Mme de Montreuil "flayed alive, dragged through thistles and then dropped into a vat of vinegar" - have resisted the opportunity to send to their deaths the heads of the family which had seen to it, so he believed, that he spent years of his prime behind bars? Was this official, who sheltered the Montreuils from the Revolutionary Terror, the prisoner under royal warrant who had wished the "vile family ... stuffed into a sack and thrown into the sea", which would give him "the happiest day" of his life?

Sade himself acknowledged the paradox. He told Gaufridy on 3 August 1793: "I only had to say one word and they would have been destroyed. I kept quiet; you see how I take my revenge." In another letter: "I pity them, I repay with contempt and indifference all the wrong they have done me..."

Why this act of mercy to his arch-enemies? The Sade at liberty in Paris in 1793 was not the de Sade of the jail years. After he left the asylum at Charenton in 1790, he had built up a social life, as well as a cosy (albeit indebted) domestic ménage with Marie Constance. He was also engaged in his career of a man of letters, of which he had great hopes. As the old order came under challenge, he added to his activities in politics and administration. The more one committed one's pen and one's voice to the shaping of the new mould, the less time one had to hark back to the gloomy cells where fantasies of torture were distilled out of rage and frustration. During one letter of vengeful fantasy about Mme de Montreuil, de Sade wrote from Cell No. 6: "I multiplied her tortures and insulted her in her agony, and forgot mine."

In Revolutionary Paris, there were other involvements to drive away Sade's woes.

Besides, to Sade vengeance was personal, a matter of seeing the pain and fear in the eyes of the victim, of knowing that he was the cause of the screams, the wounds, the immolation. But could he not have stood at the foot of the scaffold as his mother-in-law bowed her head beneath the blade of the guillotine, in the knowledge that his signature had put her there, and then gone home and masturbated over his seal on his revenge? He could have - but the executions of criminals, so deemed, in pursuit of an unnatural ideal (adult male tax-payers equal in their citizenship but different in their property) would not have pleased the arch-debauchees of Sade's writings and did not please their creator. His taste was not for a legalistic apparatus to come between the libertine and his debauch.

Sade delighted in the outrage of virtue and beauty (or of a passable substitute) by the libertine himself or by an accomplice with whom he could identify. In trying, in 1772, to bugger the Marseilles prostitutes, and to disturb their digestions or sexual responses with his sweets, he was seeking to have an effect upon them that would exceed the usual, startle them, engage their attention to him. The role of the valet Latour in the orgy with the prostitutes was to multiply his master's effect during the episode - in that the marquis could manipulate and direct the valet, and be penetrated by him. Hence Latour was another participant who was impinged upon by de Sade, whose engagement was brought about by de Sade. The cold and distancing procedures of tribunal and guillotine would not be so.

Also, Sade may have felt that the moment when he knew his vengeance over the Montreuils had come when his father-in-law visited the Piques Section and re-opened relations. As the old man talked, no doubt concerned to avoid the scaffold for himself and his family, Sade must have understood he had the Montreuils in his power, understood their impotence before him. After that encounter eye-to-eye, there may have been no more need in him to strike any blow. It was with a light touch, and clearly describing his decision not to take an opportunity to fire a shot, that Sade, referring to the former judge's attendance at a section meeting in late-July, told Gaufridy, "I had him in range of my culverin[3]."

3 A long cannon.

*   *   *

Sade was asked, in autumn 1793, to propose new names for streets in the section that were to be divested of names redolent of the old régime. References to religious orders, saints, kings, queens, bishops and such were dropped in favour of evocations of liberty, the citizen, democrats of classical antiquity, aspirations to tranquillity and the like. Sade offered, for instance, as a new identity for the street where he was living, rue Neuve des Mathurins, the name rue de Caton, thus evoking a member (known as Cato in English) of the conspiracy which felled Julius Caesar. Sade was given another outlet for his long-standing rejection of religion as Revolutionary France, spurning the Catholic Church, continued to promote Reason as the new Holy Ghost. The national administration, as part of its effort to alienate the country from religion and break other habits of thought, tossed out the Gregorian calendar in favour of a new and irreligious cycle of recorded time, the first day of Year One being what had been known as 22 September 1792, the day the monarchy had ended. The new months had names that can be translated as Foggy, Rainy, Fruitful, Snowy and so on. "Death is a sleep forever," said a slogan displayed, by order, on the buildings that had been Catholic churches. The Cathedral of Notre Dame, in Paris, was transformed into a Temple of Reason. On 15 November, Sade was before the National Convention again, among a delegation from the Piques Section with a petition for reason and other abstract qualities to be worshipped in the former churches, with familiar trappings of hymns, incense, processions, all adapted to the new philosophical ways. Readers will not need two guesses as to who wrote the petition and read it to the legislators. It was placed in the record and forwarded to the government's education committee for consideration:

"The reign of philosophy is destroying at last that of deception; at last man is moving into the light and, destroying with one hand the frivolous toys of an absurd religion, he uses the other to raise an altar to the divinity dearest to his heart. Reason displaces Mary in our temples, and the incense that used to burn at the knees of an adulterous woman will be lit anew only at the feet of the goddess who broke our bonds.

" ... For many years, the philosopher used to laugh behind his hand at the monkey tricks of catholicism; but, if he dared to speak out, it was into the dungeons of the Bastille with him, where ministerial tyranny knew ... how to keep him quiet. Ah! how could tyranny not have supported superstition? Both having been raised in the same cradle, both having been daughters of fanaticism, both served by these useless beings known as priests of the temple and monarchs on the throne, they could only have the same foundations and could only shelter one another.

"The one true republican government was able, in breaking the sceptre [of the king], to destroy with the same blow a sanguinary religion which, with its holy daggers, so often cut the throats of men, in the name of ... God... For sure, in the light of new ways, we had to adopt a new cult, that of a Jewish slave of the Romans not being appropriate [to the newly enlightened French].

"Legislators, the way is laid out, let us tread it with a firm step and, above all, let us be of one mind in sending the whore of Galilee into retirement from the trouble she used to take in order to have us believe, during eighteen centuries, that a woman can give birth without ceasing to be a virgin!...

"Let [our] prized monuments, soiled by lies, be dedicated as soon as may be to the most majestic purposes - let us worship the Virtues, where we used to revere phantoms; let the emblem of a moral virtue be placed, in each church, on the same altars where vain pledges used to be offered to ghosts; let this expressive emblem, in setting our hearts ablaze, make us pass unfailingly from idolatry to wisdom; let filial piety, grandeur of spirit, courage, equality, good faith, love of the fatherland, beneficence, etc., let all these virtues, I say, each one erected in one of our former temples, become the sole objects of our homages - by adoring them, we learn to follow them, to imitate them..."

"... Thus man will purify himself; thus his spirit, open to truth, will be fed by virtues [in the new temples - the places] where it used to go to draw only on the vices with which religious charlatanism poisoned it in times gone by.

"Then general prosperity, sure result of the happiness of the individual, will be extended to the most distant regions of the universe and everywhere the terrible hydra of reactionary superstition, pursued by the combined torches of Reason and of Virtue, having no other refuge but the vile haunts of the expiring aristocracy, will perish beside it of despair at philosophy's triumph on earth at last."

So Sade declared, his oratory not entirely at one accord with his personal beliefs for he had misgivings about the promotion of reason, or anything else, as worthy of worship, especially when wrapped in ceremony and hocus-pocus reminiscent of the Mass.

Apart from these public applications of his talents, Sade was showing in private some of the lesser-known skills of the free-lance writer. A month before he came to the bar of the Convention as advocate of the virtues, he had sent Gaufridy a statement of income and expenditure, to be certified as correct by the public authorities in whose areas his Provençal estates lay, no doubt in connection with an assessment of his worth for taxation purposes. He made out that his net income was only 100 francs a year. Among the deductions for expenditure, he entered 4,000 francs due to his wife each year under their settlement of January 1792, but which he had not been giving her, as well as the purchase for 1,000 francs of an interest-bearing investment for Marie Constance, whom he listed as Citizenness Quesnet, his "daughter".

* * *

On the face of it, there was a great alteration between the Marquis de Sade who had tried to take advantage of the discontent of the summer of 1789 for his own ends and the Citizen Sade who was striving, in the autumn of 1793, to serve his section, his city, and his republic. Better to say, though, that there had been a great alteration in the man's circumstances, transformed from the solitary masturbatory confinement of the Sixth Liberty to the agreeable companionship of the rented "shack" in the rue Neuve des Mathurins (or Cato Street), amid the involving seethe of the Section des Piques. Sade was still trying to save his own neck, and he was still the energetic impinger - whether cooped up in the Bastille and applying his quills to his plays, or trying to bring the hammer of argument and administration to bear on the white-hot metal of a France at the Revolution's forge.

Having emerged from Charenton in 1790, and having felt an initial "misanthropy ebbing away from me a little", Sade felt "the need to spread myself about. The despair at not having been able to get my ideas across for twelve years has dammed up such a great quantity of them in my head that I'll have to give birth... There's a real need to talk... " And to act.

There was the theatre, but he had no success in it as a writer and was little more than an outdated hanger-on. There was his association with constitutional monarchists who would take the Revolution no further than a moderate reform of government without toppling the king, but they lost ground as the majority of activists in the capital strove for a more profound political and social change. The massacre at the Tuileries on 10 August the previous year (1792) had arisen from a great assertion of the informal political strength of the *sans-culottes* in Paris. From then on, they advanced even more rapidly in the general assemblies of the capital's sections, rising in numbers and effectiveness in sectional politics and decision-making, pressing for an embrace of more radical policies.

Meanwhile, though, could Sade not have avoided the political fray? Could he not have stayed upstairs at No. 20, "stuck in my study"?

Yes, but there were strong motivations for him to haul his obese body down the stairs and into the streets and meeting halls where France was being re-made and whence a call was being sent for the whole world to do likewise. For one thing, even if he had tried to stay in his literary nest, he might well have been sniffed out by the Revolutionary administration's hunt for former aristocrats, indeed sometimes just for the seeming well-to-do. Adherence by such persons to an apolitical quiet life could be no defence against accusations of being opposed to the Revolution. Some of Sade's former associates among the constitutional monarchists had lost more than ground - they had lost their heads - which was a powerful incentive for any adaptable survivor among them to abandon moderation and run with the hunters. If Sade, an ex-noble, could keep in the good esteem of the radicals, he might keep himself out of their voracious prisons and off their much-trodden scaffolds.

Besides, not only was he an ex-noble but one with an especially odious record and reputation, which exposers of aristocratic rascality had been delighted to recall in print once the censorship was swept away with the royal government which had maintained it. Sade could not realistically expect that his infamous past would be forgotten - his misdeeds had made too great an impression on too many memories and left too many documents in too many files. His outstanding contribution at the section, though, while he could maintain it, was apt to keep that past, if not always out of the mind of every one of his colleagues, at least out of their public remarks - and apt to keep his name off the lists of the suspect. What's more, in case any of his fellow activists at the Piques ward did take him on one side and tax him with reports of his debauchery pre-1777, Sade would have been ready with the blame-dodging which he had polished with much practice when younger and would have modified since to suit the new style: Family intrigues against me, citizen ... Slanders concocted by relatives of my estranged wife for their own wicked purposes, my dear fellow ... Gross exaggerations by pamphleteers of the day confusing me with other Sades down there in the south - now they *were* a dissolute rabble of aristocrats while *my* family was in trade and farming, decent common folk, and I am but a man of letters...

There's no evidence that any such exchanges took place - why bother? Look how useful the fat old boy is; listen to his way with words as he shows how keen he is on the Revolution.

Furthermore, once a man was mixed up in the hurly-burly of the Revolution, living cheek by jowl with his colleagues in a densely populated city, it would have been very difficult to bow out, unless he were to have been pepared to feign illness and stay at home all the time - no sort of life for such as Sade. No, once on the boards, the only way was to go on playing your part in the Revolutionary drama of high seethe.

For all that, might Sade not have lain low in Provence, rather than stay at the dangerous hub of France in ferment? He might, but the south, too, was perilous for former aristocrats, as he knew from his tentative and abortive attempts to visit his estates since his emergence from detention in 1790, having drawn back for fear of democratic gibbets. Also on that score, there was considerable doubt as to whether any of his houses there was then habitable by such as he and Marie Constance. In any event, Provence was ruled out for Sade by his need, as an ever-aspiring man of letters, to remain in Paris, near the theatres and publishing houses which might yet transform his reputation and his finances.

Sade's late housekeeper at la Coste, Marie Dorothée de Rousset, had provided a sharp insight: "you who always want to be the likely lad, you throw all your fire round about you." There was plenty of scope for the man who liked to be busy, to be asserting himself, in the turmoil of Paris in 1792-93. Sade used to pride himself on "the Sade energy", which he poured into political thinking and argument, administration of hospitals, public oratory.

He was well equipped for all this, not only by an education of high quality from his uncle and his Jesuit school, his military training and his extensive reading, but also by the persuasive devices of rhetoric and theatre, expressed through a fine voice. Sade was displaying, by his own account in 1790, "such an enormous corpulence that I can hardly move about". There is every reason to think he was similarly covered three years later, but he would also have kept a knack for the telling pause, the arresting change of tone or volume, the deftly developed summing-up of points at issue - all in a well-crafted speech from an imposingly stationed figure. Pauvert reminds his readers that the general assemblies of the Piques Section were held in a local Capuchin church, and that Sade might have followed the custom of the day, among such orators, of speaking from the pulpit. If so, a double satisfaction - an opportunity both to exercise the actor's eye for seizing the focal position on any stage *and* to grasp to his purposes an instrument of the religion he spurned.

Also, Sade would have been able, during what were often long and heated meetings of Piques activists, to draw on theatrical technique whereby passion may be simulated, repeatedly and without strain, on the voice especially. The notary or upholsterer alongside him might have spoiled an effect in assembly by diffident fumbling of the clinching phrase, by a constricted throat, but Sade would not only have created out of the air another sentence of shape and impact, but also have retained the means to project it clearly, winningly. The Piques assembly is on record as having acknowledged both the "principles and the energy" of the discourse of active citizen 596.

Sade, through his way with words on the page and on the platform, was articulating perceptions and attitudes which many of his readers and his hearers were forming in their own minds but were needing the intervention of such as he to bring them into focus and to relate them to other facts and impressions in the mercurial political milieu. Sade would have been careful to keep his rhetoric in touch with the general will of the section, in so far as he could estimate it. For instance, I suspect that his opposition to the Convention's initiative to create a standing army in Paris, paid and therefore controlled by the central government, reflected the rejection by the *sans-culottes* in the section of such a force, which could be used to quell the armed militias of the capital's various districts if they were to rise against the Convention and ministers. Yes, Sade also might have believed that the creation of such a professional army in Paris would have been wrong, as a restriction on the scope of the sections, but he would not have unlimbered his intellectual equipment on the matter until he had seen which way the sectional wind was blowing.

His ability to wind the stem of popular seethe around the staff of his reaching rhetoric suited the radical thrust of the section. Given the constraints of the place and the times, however, this quality of his could not be allowed to drive from his mind his role of servant of the renovating republic. Whatever heights and heat his discourse reached, Sade had to be sure, when beyond his house and garden, never to forget his lines in this part.

One might think he would be in greater danger of that through a failure to find and sustain the common touch convincingly. His letters show, on occasion, a disagreeable snobbish contempt for those with newer blue blood than his own - the Montreuils and Governor de Launay of the Bastille, for instance - and for anyone with social pretensions above one's station, such as the valet Lefèvre whom Sade imagined, while in Vincennes fortress, to be his wife's lover. Remember also his haughty refusal to send his thanks to Mme de Sorans, when she was trying to help him to a transfer from Vincennes to Montélimar, because he would not put his name to what he felt to be a demeaning letter for a man of his rank.

Yet there is evidence that Sade was comfortable, when at liberty, with people whom he out-ranked, in the social order before the Revolution at any rate. He seems to have frequented, in the old days on and around his estates, the notaries, doctors, clerks and artisans of his acquaintance, rather more than he did the local nobility. Among such people, he could easily hold sway through his learning and gift of the gab, as well as through his undeniable social position as lord of manors, but he must have tempered his primacy with enough attention to others' concerns and enough good humour. We know, from his prison letter to his valet La Jeunesse, that he could let loose an inventive stream of ribald joshing to the right sort of recipient. Also, Sade's letters from jail to Rousset, when he was feeling well disposed towards the lawyer's daughter, would have made lucid, various and diverting conversation, leaving her without any feeling that she had been talked down to.

One can imagine that, at the Section des Piques twenty years on, Sade was able to offer a fitting modification of the sort of conversation enjoyed by the people who had been invited in 1772 to performances at la Coste and Mazan by the Sadeian strolling players. There would have been all the more motivation in this regard, in 1792, from the fact that any aristocratic *ton* could have been fatal. Even so, the section, like most of the other 47 wards of Paris, was by no means a crowd of illiterate labourers. The middle class that had been growing in western Europe and North America during much of the 18th century was seizing political power, and Sade was again among skilled craftsmen, self-employed traders, notaries, medical practitioners - people who would have been thrilled by the import and transport of Sade's speeches without having been confused by their elaboration of correct subjunctives and proliferation of dependent clauses. Oh, the rapt faces! Oh, the rolling applause! Oh, the approving votes to have his words printed and sent to the other sections, sometimes to all the departments of France and to the armed forces! Much better than scribbling at home all day, every day, till the Revolution had blown over.

The old world was being demolished, never to return if everyone made enough effort. This was easier to believe at the hub of a section at the hub of the Revolution, where one could lose sight of the strength of the reaction, especially in distant provinces and among those cowed into silence, against the demolition of established traditions and practices. In the vortex, it was easier also to let the demands and distractions banish reflection on whether or not one believed in democratic and egalitarian ideals, easier to banish any revulsion at the ways in which these were being perverted daily.

Sade may well have been regretting still, in private, the passing of some elements of the previous régime, not least that of the sovereign to whom he had been doubly sworn in loyalty, as noble vassal and commissioned officer. Yet there was renewal in the air - a logical system of weights and measures (the metric one) for the whole country, advancement of scientific study, a calendar arisen from nature rather than old superstition, schemes and plans galore. Some of these projects - whose designs were put on public display in Paris - bore a close resemblance to Sade's grandiose plan, conceived under incarceration at Vincennes in 1782, for a House of the Arts. The ones matched the other not least in that lack of funds - in the Revolutionary administration of the 1790s as in the house of de Sade ten years earlier - prevented their moving beyond the drawing-board. "Merry piece[s] of pie in the sky" indeed, but they helped to promote a break with the past and an embrace of a different future.

Best of all, the old religion was being abolished - true Sadeian work! To sweep away error, superstition and a hierarchy wielding a body of laws and punishments that was preventing all within its reach from attaining their full potential through the untrammelled exercise of their energy and intelligence. To sweep away a God whom each believer could engage only by humble prayer, with no certainty of a response, and who alone could smite each and every element of creation. Sade, who was insisting as long ago as a night in October 1763 that he had proved God did not exist, but restricting the news to the prostitute Jeanne Testard on that occasion, was hurling his best thunderbolts 30 years later at the same enemy, but this time before France and all the world.

Why did Sade not spread himself further, beyond the Pikes Section, taking his administrative and oratorical skills onto the Revolution's broader and higher stages? He appeared at meetings where all the Paris sections were represented, mainly in connection with his hospital work, and to speak on behalf of his section at the Convention. By and large, though, he stayed among those who were raising the radical heat at the section, at the smaller forge where he had a large say in how hard the bellows were pumped. He might have found similar scope in the Convention or at a ministry, but there he would have had to establish all over again, and for a much larger body of people and their connections, that he was a genuine Revolutionary. Such politicians and administrators might well have used their access to ministerial and police files to unearth evidence of Sade's past and use it to fell him. In those suspicious and violent times, better the devils he knew, and who knew him as one of them. Also, Sade was already at full stretch to cope with the demands put on him by the need to maintain his home, to keep his various ailments at bay, to fulfil his sectional duties and to try to find time for his literary work - enough to occupy each day without any attempt to cut a greater dash in the Revolution.

He might even - an astonishing suggestion, made by Pauvert - have been experiencing "the feeling of thinking communally, of detecting his mental solitude shake a little." If so, he might even have liked it, at last giving the lie to his mother-in-law, who, on his release from Charenton in 1790, had doubted very much whether he knew how to be happy. I suggest only that Sade - with a more or less secure home and a stimulating range of demands on his intellect - in 1793 was as close to living a fulfilling, healthy life as he had been since he was a child.

*　　　　　*　　　　　*

To protect that life, he was still adding to his file of documents which, in the event of his loyalty to the Revolution coming into question, might stand him in good stead. In the first week of December 1793, the Interior Ministry sent him a copy of a letter, written by the governor of the Bastille to a royal minister on 3 July 1789, which reported the then marquis's harangues through the window of his cell to incite the crowd in the street below. For Sade to have asked for this document was risky, in that the governor's letter constituted a clear reminder that Sade had indeed been noble. He might well have decided, though, that he would take the chance in order to get his hands on documentary evidence that he was a nuisance to the royal régime at the Bastille in July 1789. It might also have been that Sade had an inkling that his opposition to the new standing army and to the old religion was not being as well received beyond his section as within it, was attracting the attention of powerful men with different views.

For sure, Sade was not the only one interested in the files of the monarchy. On the morning of 8 December, a Citizen Juspel, bearing a warrant issued by the Paris police, arrived at the Piques Section offices where he asked a local activist to go with him to arrest Citizen Sade. An official, combing through archives from 1791, had discovered that Sade applied that year, on behalf of himself and his sons, for posts in the king's Constitutional Guards, under the command of the Duke de Cossé-Brissac. Members of this force had become discredited as the Revolution proceeded through the abolition of the monarchy, to the execution of the king and to rule, in effect, by the Committee of Public Safety. By late-1793, when Sade was arrested, anyone authoritatively believed to have been a member of that regiment was almost certain to be arrested. The warrant against Sade, based on letters found among de Cossé-Brissac's papers, named him as a suspected person.

Although the stated reason for Sade's arrest was sufficient ground for detaining him, given the concerns of the administration of the time, it was almost certainly a pretext, disguising deeper motives. For one thing, remember that Sade was a prominent opponent of the scheme by the Convention to establish in Paris a standing army - a powerful counterweight, if necessary, for the assembly and the ministries to use against the city's sections if they were to mount an armed challenge to the elected representatives. The Convention could hardly have failed to notice the main adherents, Sade among them, of the contrary desire, for unpaid popular militias with their own arsenals in the capital.

Robespierre, the rising force in the Convention and much concerned to break the strength of the sections, was a prime mover in the drive to set up the professional army.

What's more, Sade was also prominent through his eloquence in the clamour against the Christian religion and in favour of its displacement by a new cult of reason and the virtues. Here, too, he was at odds with Robespierre and his allies in the Convention. Robespierre was preparing to urge on the assembly - as he did a few months later, in May 1794 - a national recognition of "the Supreme Being and the immortality of the soul" (no "sleep forever" for him), as well as the sort of virtues which Sade had extolled to the assembly in his speech of the previous November.

On the face of it, viewing the debate from our unfaithful times, there might seem little between Sade and Robespierre in this regard. Whether the incense were swirling around rites of Reason or of the Supreme Being, it would be embellishing an object on which people might focus their longing to worship, while steering them away from the old Christianity that had been hand in glove with the discredited monarchy. Either way, there would be music, liturgy and uplifting discourse - and awe would strike. However, Robespierre was much exercised not only to lift up virtue but also to strike down vice. He told the Convention that "vice and virtue ... are the two spirits that dispute the earth. Each has its source in the passions of man. In accordance with the direction given to his passions, man is raised towards the heavens or is cast down into the murky abysses... Immorality is the basis of despotism, as virtue is the essence of the Republic..."

Robespierre was choosing to retain the mystery and inaccessibility of a godhead, which Sade was burning to sweep away, and the representative was zealous to block any path to immorality, which Sade, in private necessarily, was always keen to open, if only for himself and a chosen few.

The essential difference between the two was a matter of social and political control. Reason and liberty were subject to human definition and, if set above all else, might be taken by their adherents as licences to any libertinage, any road to ecstasy. Robespierre's purposes, on the other hand, required that the adaptable abstract qualities be placed below an unalterable Supreme Being apt to become a means to keep its adherents in line. Robespierre, the northern lawyer of little property, seems not to have been a man for ecstasy, not beyond that of the solitary thinker hugging the intense and close-kept delight arisen from his knowledge that he has made others follow his design. Sade knew this pleasure, too, but with him, the southern lord of lands and manors, there was a wish not only for liberty - *his* liberty - to revise and extend anything and everything, but also an urge for the flesh which could not be declaimed to any National Convention or allowed space on Robespierre's narrow stairway to the heavens.

Furthermore, the politician and administrator in Robespierre was coming to understand that, if rural insurrection against the Revolution, especially in the west of France, were to be quelled, it would be prudent to stop offending Catholics in the more conservative provinces. Also, a disarming of the Revolution's militant de-Christianisation might help to mollify France's enemies abroad and thus bring a truce to the draining foreign wars. On 6 December, two days before Sade was arrested, the Convention, under Robespierre's prompting, decreed freedom of religious observance in France.

For all Sade's awareness that he had to keep quiet about his preferred routes to ecstasy, it is likely that Robespierre, who was careful to maintain a network of informers, and other members of the Convention knew, before Sade's arrest, of his exploits pre-1777 and of his authorship of *Justine*. If so, whatever the differences over Revolutionary theology and policy, they would have been hard put to believe in Sade as an advocate of virtue, however silver-tongued he was on its behalf, at sectional and national assemblies. Investigators for the Convention's Committee of Public Safety, where Robespierre was main mover, probably knew before 2 January 1794, when the printer and publisher Jean-Joseph Girouard was arrested in Paris, that he was not only a publisher of royalist propaganda but also of *Justine*. On the day of his arrest, Girouard confessed to his questioners that he had printed certain anti-Revolutionary material and *Justine*. The record continues:

"Q: Who is the author?

"A: I don't know who's the author of it, but it's the former marquis de Sade who sold it to me.

"Q: Why do your presses seem to be dedicated entirely to works from counter-revolutionary aristocracy and to obscenities, which indicate a man [yourself] without morals, without shame, which characterise a true counter-revolutionary, for one cannot be republican with such morals?

"A: I was printing anything, with no discrimination, as there was a living to be made and I had a numerous family."

With that classic shrug of the inky-handed journeyman by Girouard (already talking of his life in the past tense - he was guillotined six days later), the investigation seems to have been broken off, without further pursuit of the bigger quarry. The committee soon spotted this and, on 4 January, prompted its chief investigator to ask where "the former marquis de Sade" was living. (Within a mile of Robespierre, in fact, for they were both Piques residents - all the more reason for the representative to have been well aware of the man of letters and his activities.)

Next day, Girouard was asked this question, to which he replied, the investigator noted, "that he doesn't know where he lives at present, but at the time when he [Sade] handed over the work to him [Girouard] in manuscript ..., he was living in the rue Neuve des Mathurins ..., not recalling the number, which he thinks was 19 or 20.

"... Asked if he had seen the said de Sade again since the sale of the manuscript and if he had given him others to be printed, ... replied that he had seen him several more times and had bought from him another manuscript entitled *the Philosophical Novel*[4], a work written in the Bastille, ... and that he had stopped seeing this former marquis about three months ago..."

By then, the first week of 1794, Sade had been gone from No. 20 for a month, into the Revolution's jails.

With all these clouds having gathered over Sade, no wonder his record of Revolutionary zeal at the Piques Section had not been sufficient, on the previous 8 December, to keep Juspel and Sade's colleague from making their way to the rue Neuve des Mathurins, where they found the ex-marquis and Marie Constance at home, searched the house and put Sade under arrest. Juspel left Sade's part of the house closed under official seals. Sade's attachment to the literary life did not desert him, even during this shock. He asked Juspel to send corrected galleys of *Aline and Valcour* to Girouard, as he was taken away to imprisonment at the Madelonnettes, a former convent in central Paris which had been more recently a reformatory for women, including prostitutes. On arrival, Sade wrote for help to his colleagues of the Piques Section, who responded to the abrupt change in the fortunes of

---

4 *Aline and Valcour*, of which Girouard was printer and publisher.

their esteemed vice-chairman - he whose memorandums and speeches had kept their hands applauding and their printers at the stick until a few days before - by shying away from him, no doubt lest suspicion fall on them also. The section's new chairman seems to have been very much a Robespierre man - another sign that the main force at the Convention was bending the sections to his will. The section's Watch Committee confirmed the connection between Sade and the king's guards - something it had only just discovered, it seems - and added some allegations of its own.

Sade kept wriggling vigorously to avoid the guillotine. From the lavatories of the Madelonnettes, where he was lodged in those days of stuffed jails, Sade wrote to tell the Committee of Public Safety that some error had put "a loyal citizen, ... a true patriot" in prison. On 12 January 1794, Sade was brought from the jail to his house so that he would be present, as the law required, when the seals were removed and a thorough search made. Fourteen letters from the provinces were impounded and sent to the police department.

Next day, Sade was transferred to a former Carmelite convent, also an *ad hoc* jail in central Paris, where he spent an infernal week sharing a cell with six prisoners who had malignant fevers. Two of them died a few feet away from him. On 22 January, he was moved to the St Lazare hostel, a former home for lepers which had not been such for some years and which was pressed into service as a jail four days before Sade arrived.

On 8 March, the Piques Watch Committee filled in a questionnaire about Sade from the Committee of Public Safety:

" ... *Profession before and after the Revolution:* Former Count.

" ... *Income before and after the Revolution:* stated by himself to be 8,000 livres.

" ... *Relations, connections:* With Brissac, Commander of Capet's Guards, so as to secure posts [in it] for him and his; letters deposited at city hall show that this man was corresponding with enemies of the Republic. In order to make his patriotism seem genuine, he brags about having been imprisoned in the Bastille during the old regime, although he would have undergone a different and well-deserved punishment if he had not been of the noble cast. All in all, by every indication, a most immoral man, profoundly suspect and unworthy of society...

" ... *Character and political views which he showed in May, June, July and October 1789, on 10 August [1792]; and when the despot fled and when he was executed; ... and during the worst of the war; whether he signed petitions and decisions fatal to liberty?:* Since he appeared at this section, he has constantly, since 10 August, pretended to be a patriot, but those here were not fooled. He showed what he was really made of ... in a petition against revolutionary principles and against the establishment of the Revolutionary army, decreed into existence by the Convention."

The Watch Committee referred to one instance, in 1792, when Sade had been slow to condemn, for lack of proof, a leading Revolutionary figure who was falling from grace. Then it recalled Sade "making continual comparisons in his private talk to Greek and Roman history, by way of proving it was impossible to set up a democratic and republican government in France." Over 12 signatures, this erratic piece of hindsight was sent to the Committee of Public Safety.

About the same time, Sade was unlimbering a rebuttal. Very well, as a former officer in de Cossé-Brissac's regiment, he had written to the duke in 1791. (He could hardly deny it, given that there were documents which proved the point beyond doubt.) However, "I was wrong about him, as were many others who thought he was a friend of the Revolution." De Cossé-Brissac had said, before witnesses, that he did not want Sade's services because he declined to take recruits who had as much cause as Sade did to have a grievance against the king. Sade reiterated his record of solidarity with the Revolution, including his exhortations down his metal pipe from a cell in the Bastille, his joy at the execution of the "outrageous tyrant" of a king, the positions and tasks given him at the Piques. He did not know where his children were - if they were illegal emigrants, let their names be reviled before everyone. As for the child in his care - the son of his housekeeper, Citizenness Quesnet - he was bringing up the boy to be a patriot. His home would always live by "the greatest alertness to a citizen's duty." It was quite wrong to make out that he had been a noble - his ancestors had been in trade or farming. On his release, he would seek a divorce from his wife and then marry "the daughter of a tailor, one of the best of women patriots to be found in Paris [Marie Constance]." A further rhetorical flourish had him cautioning himself, for the eyes of the Committee of Public Safety: "Sade, remember the fetters that the tyrants made you wear, and die a thousand deaths rather than exist under any government that sought to bring them back." This camouflaged flash of criticism is the only departure from respectful advocacy in his submission to the committee.

Also while in the Revolution's jails, Sade continued to take care of his mundane duties as a citizen, paying his taxes and contributing to the financial levies for the upkeep of France's armies combatting foreign enemies on its frontiers and civil unrest in the Vendée. He wrote to Gaufridy, disguising his detention thus: "Although [I'm] still in the country for a spell, you'll receive my letter postmarked Paris." He also remained concerned with the details of his relations with, and revenues from, Provence:

"I am very upset that this little absence[5] is denying me the pleasure of paying my respects to the person to whom you gave my address... It seems to me that, having declared in writing that la Coste was yielding me no more than two thousand, I would not be very far wrong in presenting documents which prove that I'm drawing from there no more than two thousand two hundred and ninety-six... Mazan has done what I was wanting... Arles hasn't tried to get going... Saumane's refusal is incomprehensible... The actor Bourdais[6] is a cantharides fly from the Montreuils... If I wanted to cause a lot of trouble for the municipality at la Coste, I would file a complaint about its slackness in attending to the patriotic speeches [of mine] I have sent it, but I have too much contempt for the ringleaders down there..."

Sade's nose for legacies from his well-heeled relatives was not impaired by the stink of the lavatories at the Madelonnettes for, still in January, he told Gaufridy that a new law on the division of inheritances put him in line to benefit by a will in the family of his paternal grandmother. This turned out to be another vain hope, as did his attempts to have the administration at Apt release nine cases of effects taken to Gaufridy's house after the sack of the manor at la Coste, then impounded by the local authority once the lawyer had been found mixed up in separatist politics: "It is clear, citizens, that you have been too hasty... No-one respects the law as I do; were it to demand my blood, I myself would open my veins to offer it; but no law whatsoever takes effect until it has been promulgated, and this one has not been... Until then, I ask you most insistently to lift [the seals]..."

---

5 Already of 34 days, when Sade was writing this from the Madelonnettes on 11 January.

6 Hired by de Sade for the theatricals *en châteaux* in 1772, still not paid in full, and now suing for his money, without success in the end.

On 27 March, Sade was moved again, this time because he was deemed to be unwell, to Picpus sanatorium, still in central Paris. He was not really any more ill than usual, but had become one of the thousands of detainees of the Revolution who got themselves transferred from the ordinary, crowded jails and the threat of execution to much better-appointed and much safer *maisons de santé* in various parts of the country, usually in and around Paris. This almost invariably required a large bribe to whichever official arranged the transfer, and inmates had to be regular with very high payments for their board and lodging. No pay, no stay - there were instances of nobles who, no longer able to meet the costs, were sent back to common prisons, thence to the guillotine.

It is not clear how Sade managed to find the money to secure and keep a place at Picpus, but there seems to have been no funds arriving from Provence since his arrest the previous December, when the sanatorium had begun its lucrative service. However much Sade paid, a sojourn at Picpus was well worth having. He described it later to Gaufridy as "a paradise on earth." The ample building was a "beautiful house," with a "superb garden, select company, nice women..." (The company included, though Sade did not record the fact, Choderlos de Laclos, author of the epistolatory novel *Les Liaisons Dangereuses*.)

Historians of the Revolution refer to a devil-may-care atmosphere at the various sanatoriums where rich nobles and commoners were paying through the nose to keep their heads on their shoulders and enjoying, in some comfort, what might be their last opportunity for pleasure and congenial company before an official change of attitude to their asylums sent them to the scaffold. There is no evidence of Sade indulging in unbuttoned behaviour at Picpus, though he did have access to writing materials. He used these, so he said, at least in part to exercise "the unfortunate habit" which jail had instilled in him of "drawing up petitions - as much for myself as for my comrades in adversity, who all usually brought their requirements to me."

During the spring and summer, the Revolution ate more and more of its own, and many bewildered by-standers. The rapt flight from due process was expressed before the Convention on 10 June when Couthon, a member of the Committee of Public Safety, derided the notion of conviction before a tribunal requiring proof of guilt, established through testimony and evidence. This excessive concern for the rights of the individual before the law had inhibited "the people's justice from attaining that awesome sway and energy which was its proper mode... It used to be thought splendid to put justice for the individual before justice for the Republic... Now any such compromises or superfluous procedures are a danger to the people as a whole... Indulgence towards the enemies of the fatherland is an outrage, clemency is parricide."

Couthon then read a new decree to the Convention. Among its fierce clauses was a stipulation that the Revolutionary tribunal could hand down no sentence but that of death. Also, the definition of suspects was further broadened to include all who "tried to confuse the view of the people, *to corrupt morals*, to divert the consciousness of the people or weaken the energy and adulterate the integrity of revolutionary and republican principles" (my emphasis). These swingeing and catch-all initiatives were swept past misgivings in the Convention by a speech from Robespierre.

A fortnight later, Sade was still arguing against the tide. His written statement of 24 June to the Convention detailed his political record, with attached copies of documents he had been collecting with just such a struggle in mind, such as the letter of complaint against him by the governor of the Bastille and his eulogy of Marat. He also pointed out that the police officers who dealt with his arrest the previous December had since been jailed or executed.

As Sade waited at Picpus for his petitions to have an effect, an intrusion by the Revolutionary inferno reinforced his understanding that he was fighting for his life. On the night of 14-15 June, a gang of workmen broke a wide gap in the garden wall and started to dig a huge ditch. So many pople were being guillotined that a new cemetery was needed. During the next six weeks, 1,306 bodies and their heads were brought by cart and tipped into ditches (the one had soon become three) at Picpus, which also received daily the contents of the zinc containers that caught the blood from the scaffolds. However, the soil in the Picpus garden was a heavy clay. It resisted the human remains. Putrefaction bubbled on the surface of the ground. The ditches were covered with planks, the bodies and heads thrown in through trapdoors. Lime was applied in great quantities, but with floods of water which, also staying above the clay, spread the putrefaction further in the garden. All the while, the stench, during one of the hottest summers in Paris that century, was abominable. For connections of the prisoners at Picpus, then, it may have been just as well that visits by outsiders were forbidden from late-June, when the régime at the sanatorium began to turn harsher, with a tighter supervsion of letters passing in and out.

While the prisoners at Picpus were suffering all this, Sade's file reached the desk of a Revolutionary tribunal's prosecutor, Fouquier-Tinville. Perhaps Sade or his connections had been unable to keep up payments for his stay at the sanatorium or, more likely, the intensification of the Terror was overcoming considerations in the public administration of the money being made from the inmates of the *maisons de santé*. On 26 July, the official completed formal charges against 28 citizens, the 11th of whom was "Aldonze Sade", described as "former count, captain in Capet's guards in 1792, correspondent with enemies of the Republic. He has consistently struggled against the republican government, asserting at his section that such a government cannot function... It appears that the testimony to his patriotism, which he has offered, has been no more than a device to avoid investigation of his role in the tyrant's conspiracy, to which he was basely committed."

Next day, a court bailiff made a tour of various prisons to round up the 28 people on the prosecutor's charge sheet and bring them before the tribunal. He managed to find only 23 of them - among the five missing was the said Aldonze Sade. It is clear that the bailiff did include Picpus in his tour because at least one of the 23 was collected from there. As was its custom, the tribunal spent little time in handing down its verdicts of guilty and sentences of death, 21 of the 23 being so condemned, while one fell ill in court and the other was acquitted. The 21 were put into carts, with other condemned prisoners, to be taken through the streets of Paris to execution that same day.

However, their journey was unusual in that no zealous radicals shouted insults at them as they passed. The political tide was beginning to turn against the pell-mell radicalism of the Committee of Public Safety and the spate of executions which was its most terrifying expression. Some passers-by tried to stop the carts, take the horses from their traces and release the condemned prisoners. The armed guards, facing superior numbers in narrow streets, seemed about to give way when a member of the committee, Hanriot, rode up with a troop of soldiers and cowed the crowd. The carts proceeded on their way and the guillotine duly beheaded the 21 and their companions, within a half-mile of Picpus.

That day, 27 July (9 Thermidor of Year Two in the Revolutionary calendar) was the last day of the radical surge. Moderates in the

Convention broke the power of the Committee of Public Safety and, on 28 July, Robespierre, Couthon, Hanriot and 19 other radicals lost their lives under the guillotine. Sade, who had missed death on the penultimate day of the Terror by the bailiff's oversight, reported: "After that, the tension was much relaxed and, thanks to the good work of the inspiring companion with whom I have shared my heart and my life these last five years, I was released..." He left Picpus on 15 October, after petitions to the re-ordered Committee of Public Safety and to members of the Convention by himself and Marie Constance.

The committee had asked the opinion of the Pikes Section which, having swivelled again with the change in political direction, certified that it had "seen Citizen Sade fill various functions, as much in the said Section as in the hospitals, with keenness and understanding; and we testify that nowhere in our experience of him has arisen anything inconsistent with the principles of a true patriot..." To be fair to the Pikes, let's note that the group of signatories to this clean bill of political health appears to be entirely different to that which had put pen, back in March, to the description of the erstwhile ward chairman as a thoroughly counter-Revolutionary piece of work. It seems that, with the fall of Robespierre and his men, there was a similar collapse of factions loyal to them in the sections.

CHAPTER 27: PRICES, PUBLISHING AND PROVENCE

Once delivered from the queue for the guillotine, Sade returned to his more familiar difficulties. One of his first visits, having re-established himself at the household in the rue Neuve des Mathurins, was to the widow Girouard - her husband, Sade's printer and publisher, had gone under the blade in January - to see how publication of *Aline and Valcour* was progressing. Girouard had completed about half the type-setting for the four volumes and the complete first edition came out in the summer of the next year, 1795.

Meanwhile, a book in the press did not put bread on the table, or redeem silver from pawn, so Sade was quick to obtain a notarised copy of the Committee of Public Safety's order to release him, which also lifted a legal bar to his receiving income from his property, and sent it to the local administrations at Apt and the sites of all his other lands in Provence. He tried to re-open communications with Gaufridy - and obtain funds from him - but this was impossible for the time being because the notary was lying low in the south. His son Elzéar, and to a lesser extent the lawyer himself, had been involved in a southern uprising against the Revolutionary administration in Paris. Government troops put it down. Sade tried another tack to extract money from his estates, by writing directly, on 12 November, to Audibert, a tenant farmer, for his rent. He pointed out that the intervention on his income had been rescinded and added that failure to pay promptly would occasion a complaint against the tenant by Sade to the Committee of Public Safety, which would not fail to take up the case on behalf of such a tireless worker for "the people's cause". Sade added that a certain Payan, another resident of la Coste, should stop thinking he could continue to do as he pleased on the estate because, another Payan having lost his head alongside Robespierre during Thermidor, it would be simple to establish that anyone who shared "that notorious name was busy undermining the fatherland". After that bullying abuse of his greater knowledge of events in the capital, Sade told Audibert to locate Gaufridy, whom Sade would be able to help out.

Gaufridy surfaced of his own accord and a letter from him, at home at Apt, reached Sade within a week of the broadside to Audibert. Sade told the notary: "The death of the rogues [on the former Committee of Public Safety] has chased away all the clouds, and the calm we are going to enjoy will bind up our wounds," though he shadowed that optimistic flourish by adding, "my incarceration by the people with the guillotine before my eyes did me a hundred times more damage than could all the Bastilles in existence." Even so, his detention by the radicals had brought Sade some supportive attention from members of a reascendant Convention, he told Gaufridy, and "I would be only too pleased to approach them on your behalf." On 12 December, Sade secured a pardon from the republic for Gaufridy, in respect of the latter's dabble in separatist politics in Provence, pointing out to the lawyer that Marie Constance was the one to thank for this boon.

In the new year, 1795, Sade told Gaufridy on 21 January of the death of M de Montreuil, his father-in-law, about six months after the old man had been let out of jail, where he and Mme de Montreuil had spent some weeks, on suspicion of conspiracy against the Revolution, during the final stage of Robespierre's power. The judge may have succumbed to a very cold winter, made worse in effect by shortage of firewood and food - "you spend 25 francs a day yet you die of starvation," Sade complained, dipping his quill into an ink-pot standing in a bowl of warm water so that the ink should not freeze and stop his writing.

By the end of February, the combination of debts, vertiginous price inflation, hoarding of supplies, hunger and lack of funds from Provence forced even Sade, the life-long *rentier*, to seek a job. He asked a member of the Convention whether there might be something for him in the diplomatic service, as a director of a museum or library, or in writing to order "anything at all". Nothing seems to have come of this but, late in March, Sade heard from Gaufridy that the latter had managed to sell part of the Saumane estate, to the notary's father-in-law, for 60,000 francs through an elaborate deal whereby Sade received a further 13,000 francs, described as an advance on rents from his lands. This extra sum was thus disguised because any money Sade received for property sales was apt to be subject to a claim by his estranged wife, to whom he owed large sums under their separation terms (see below). The sale met a long-standing demand of Sade's, but he was soon fuming at Gaufridy for "damned negligence" in not having tried to coax a legacy out of a Provençal relative of the de Sades before the death of same five months earlier, about which Sade had just been informed.

The rapidly rising cost of living in Paris was harrying Sade into ever more pressing demands on Gaufridy for money from his estates. On 1 June 1795, Sade lamented to his agent:

"This year I will get through *thirty thousand francs* in assignats[1] ..., and for these thirty thousand francs, reduced to one maidservant and a lackey, I am dying of what is known as hunger, eating soup only once a *décade*[2] and beans the rest of the time... I have the same suit I had five years ago, and I am unable to offer so much as a glass of water to a friend. In the winter I'm in clogs, in summer in shoes made of selvage, and I'm getting through thirty thousand francs. What I'm telling you is the facts; it is true that I console myself for the destitution in which I live with the pleasant knowledge that my farmers are housed, they say, like princes, and buy every day country houses at my expense."

Sarcasm apart, he was having great difficulty coping with the high prices, so, like many other city-dwellers with rural links in hard times, he instructed his country agents to send, in large quantities, jams, cooking and lighting oil, candles, crystallised mandarins (a favourite of his), wine, anchovies and, "in old cases and under misleading labels, ... enough wheat to maintain four people". To have labelled the consignment "wheat" in those times of hunger would have been as good as sticking on a notice saying "steal this". Once it had arrived in Paris, Sade would have been able to take the wheat to a miller for it to be turned into flour, which he could then sell or have baked into bread. Even so, there were needs that distant estates could not supply. Sade grumbled to Gaufridy, in his letter of 1 June, that he was leading, "in a word, the most sober of lives, ... never to a show, no treats, my friend [Mme Quesnet], a cook and me, that's it! *sixty francs* a day gone west!"

Proceeds of the sale at Saumane had still not reached Sade by late-summer - Gaufridy was taking advantage of the high interest rates of the time to lend out the money at profit to himself.

Louis Marie, Sade's elder son, turned up out of the blue at his father's house in Paris at about this time, having avoided inclusion on the list of illegal emigrants. Sade - who knew that any of his letters might be intercepted by the authorities - reported Louis Marie as having told him that, "not knowing ... which side to cleave to, between my mother and you, I quit the army. I love the arts; I have made such

---

1 The distrusted paper money.

2 The Revolutionary calendar's 10-day week.

progress there that engraving and botany provide my living these days. I have travelled throughout France, the mountains, the plcturesque places; at last I set to work. I am back now ... equipped with all the papers and certificates to convince you of the truth of what I say. I'm staying in the Tuileries Section [in central Paris], I work at the museum every day, I do my civic duties in my section and I eat its bread[3]. Let anyone accuse me of having emigrated and they'll see how I'll answer..."

Louis Marie also told his father, so the latter reported, that the younger son, Donatien Claude Armand, had been on the Mediterranean island of Malta for five years, serving his Order of the Knights of Malta (in which his great-uncle, the Commander de Sade, had been a senior officer) and thus exempt from being declared an emigrant from France. This reunion should not be taken as establishing close relations by Sade with his elder son, who had seen very litle of his father all his life and had been raised as a Montreuil.

During the hard winter of 1794-95, while *Aline and Valcour* was still at the printer's, much of the ink Sade had to keep from freezing was going into the writing of *Philosophy in the Boudoir*. Neither work attracted more than a flicker of apparent attention at its publication - few people in France had the money or leisure for what were probably high-priced editions; besides, the general shortages also covered paper and ink. Even so, a small market for *de luxe* editions of licentious works remained - it takes very hard times indeed to wipe out that in a literate society - among the profiteers, lawyers and administrators who were thriving through barter, corruption and speculation amid the misery and shortages.

Philosophy in the Boudoir, published in 1795, includes a call on the French people for *One More Effort if You Want to be Republicans*. This interpolation outlines a protean republic in which murder - and revenge for murder - would be no crime, likewise theft and rape. In this last, nothing is taken away from women, who should be like "drinking fountains beside the road", available to all. This exhortation to create a society in which each person would need a high level of alertness and responsibility for self, in that the laws and public institutions would be minimal, ran counter to the political trend of the time. The argumentative, participatory radicalism of Paris was subsiding into a re-establishment of due process and hierarchical government under the

---

3 Basic rations were available at sectional headquarters to active citizens.

sort of property-owning lawyers who had come to the capital in 1789 to seek reform through the Estates-General, rather than the bloody upheaval that in fact ensued.

Philosophy in the Boudoir was published as "a posthumous work by the author of *Justine*", so as to fool any gullible authorities into thinking that the writer had passed beyond their reach, as well as to persuade those who had bought the "well-peppered" stuff of 1791 that here was more of the same. Another common camouflage of a pornographer's publisher was also used on the frontispiece, the origin of *Philosophy* being made out to be London, also beyond the scope of the French police, especially since Britain was at war with France.

Also between his release from Picpus, late in 1794, and the end of 1800, Sade brought out two enormous novels - *The New Justine or the Hardships of Virtue* (*La Nouvelle Justine ou les Malheurs de la Vertu*), the third and longest version of the tale of the put-upon virtuous girl perplexed by the debauchees who victimise her and others, and *The Story of Juliette or the Successes of Vice* (*L'Histoire de Juliette ou les Prospérités du Vice*). It is difficult to be sure, as Pauvert points out, of just when *The New Justine* and *Juliette* first appeared, not least because one is dealing with clandestine operations. It seems that Sade produced a large body of licentious works in the last six years of the 18th century, *The New Justine* and *Juliette* being the main ones, others having been lost to us. The tales of the two sisters, Justine and Juliette, did appear in 1800 and 1801, in a ten-volume book, running to some 3,600 pages in all and dated 1797. *Juliette*, its first edition ostensibly published "in Holland" but in fact prepared in Paris, runs to nearly 450,000 words, not far short of the length of *War and Peace.* One contemplates with awe Sade's wrist-aching labour of his mid-fifties.

Pauvert persuasively suggests that the 1797 date is another blind, intended to have the police at the turn of the century think the book was not the latest thing and so not worth putting at the top of their list of scurrilous publications to be pursued. Also, publication of anything like such a vast work in 1797 would have been most unlikely, with the French economy in a woeful condition, paper and customers being both very hard to come by. Further narrowing the probabilities, the two books, like *Philosophy in the Boudoir*, could hardly have been published before the end of 1794, Sade having been at full stretch at work on his plays, in his section and trying to get publication of *Aline and Valcour* finished, besides having been jailed for nearly 11 months in

1793-94. There is another pointer in the fact that Sade, in the spring of 1795, was often in the country, tackling "an essential work that I've been asked for..." Also, Pauvert has found bibliographies of 1796 which mention an edition of *Juliette*. Given the paucity of attention in 1795 to *Aline and Valcour* and *Philosophy in the Boudoir*, the small traces available to us of such an edition of *Juliette* should be no surprise. So it seems very likely that *The New Justine* and *Juliette* first went into print between late-1795 and late-1796.

Bear in mind that, in those days, an author sold a manuscript to a publisher for one fee, often in instalments, without royalties from sales. So there was a strong incentive for authors to re-vamp works and seek a new payment, especially in the case of those with word-of-mouth notoriety, such as was attached to *Justine* - especially also of those works which leant themselves to accompaniment by ever larger and more eye-popping sets of engravings. In this last regard, Sade's novels were very accommodating. One newspaper report of 1800, drawing on a police source, refers to nearly a third of the pages of *The New Justine* being devoted to engravings.

*　　　　　　　　*　　　　　　　　*

Sade and Marie Constance rented a small house at St Ouen, just outside Paris, in March 1796, taking it for 12 months.

His efforts, meanwhile, to bring in some money were not enough. In autumn 1796, he started to negotiate the sale of his "headquarters" in Provence - la Coste, lands and manorhouse, furniture and fittings - to Joseph Rovère, the equivalent of the area's Member of Parliament or Senator, for the buyer was representative for Vaucluse in the Revolutionary Directory's Council of Elders, part of the new national assembly in Paris. Rovère was much concerned with profiting by his position to amass wealth, in order to acquire properties in Provence. The special attraction of la Coste for him was the spring on the property, a reliable source of water being life to people and crops - and therefore profit to whoever controlled it - in that hot and dry part of south-eastern France.

The deal was to be done for 58,400 francs, plus a payment on the quiet by the purchaser to Sade of 16,000 which the former Marquise de Sade, being kept in ignorance, would be unable to claim under her separation contract. Rovère was to take possession on 22 September, first day of Year Five in the Revolutionary calendar. However, Renée Pélagie, from whom the sale of a property for which she was a mortgage holder could not be hidden, refused to relinquish her mortgage or to waive the rights of her children as prospective inheritors of this paper asset of hers. Despite this hiccough, Rovère's eagerness to have la Coste, and perhaps his confidence in his political clout when put into service of his acquisitiveness, overcame the encumbrance of the mortgage - to his satisfaction, at any rate - and the deal was completed on 13 October. It was marked by an unctuous politeness, especially by Sade, in the letters between the two parties, given the lie by a mutual contempt revealed in letters by each to outsiders. Sade was curling his blue-blood's lip at the *parvenu* politician, the latter sneering at the vendor as a hypocrite who never ceased to badger him for the money. Rovère had his work cut out finding the cash - in the sought-after old metal coins rather than the despised new paper notes - for Sade's payment on the side and to meet the fees to lawyers and land registry officials[4]. Rovère told his brother in December: "Hungry men do not await a meal with more impatience than this *fine fellow* awaits money."

There was a rumpus over whether Rovère should keep or hand over to Sade 1,800 francs as capital to provide annual alms of 90 francs, willed by one of the ex-marquis's ancestors, for the poor of la Coste. It may be that the purchaser saw himself as more of a land-owner than feudal lord with gracious obligations, or that he had little confidence Sade would indeed make the money available for relief of the indigent - or both. In any event, Sade got on his high horse and there was acrimony. The Elder told his brother on 24 March of the next year, 1797: "This M. de Sade is surely the most shameful rogue that lives and that France might contain."

Before long, Rovère's colleagues in politics were to deliver much the same opinion of him. A political upheaval on 4 September felled him. He was arrested and transported as a criminal to France's South American colony of Guyane where, being unable to withstand the tropical climate, he died at the end of 1798. His spring-borne domain in Provence collapsed.

---

4 We are before the days when, a government having decided to introduce a new currency, it could readily annul and withdraw the old one. There continued to be so little confidence in the economy of France under the Revolutionary administrations, when price inflation was often very high, that many people in business simply refused to accept the paper money and insisted on payment in gold or copper coins minted in the kings' time.

By then - in January 1797, in fact - Sade had applied the acknowledged proceeds from the sale of la Coste, plus perhaps money from the sale at Saumane, to down-payments on his purchase of two properties near Paris. As ever, he was looking for income from rents. The two new properties would bring in about 4,000 francs a year. His estranged wife, on learning about the change in sources of Sade's income from landed property, filed suit to establish that his obligation to turn over money to her was not relinquished by the sale of properties mentioned in the separation agreement and the acquisition of others.

When writing to Gaufridy in March 1797 about this, Renée Pélagie told him that her mother was well. Mme de Montreuil would have been at least 72 years old, and probably closer to 77, at that time, by when she had ceased to have any role in the life of her son-in-law. The date of her death is not certain, though 1799 seems likely.

His plays were still a source of frustration to Sade. His finances were usually precarious. He was still carrying the corpulence and some of the infirmities which had overtaken him in royal jails. In view of all this, it is no wonder his abiding irascibility flared when he was reminded that the libertinage of his prime had not been forgotten. In January 1797, he wrote to Charles Gaufridy, the notary's son who was taking over as Sade's agent in Provence:

"On account of your undisguised rudeness to me, sir, I owe you the most profound contempt. It is not done for a mere child of your stamp to speak of my misfortunes. These serve only to have decent people find me engaging and worthy of respect, and are to be none of your concern because, when I was undergoing them, you were having your backside spanked. Hence, be so good as to refrain from mentioning them...

"I ask that you no longer conduct my business and request your father to take it over again ... until the first of May... You, sir, are not at all to my liking... Do no more than send money due - I have not received a penny for a month."

It is not recorded whether Gaufridy *fils* appreciated the irony in Sade evoking the spanking of backsides - one source of his misfortunes - in seeking to quell mention of those same misfortunes.

On 20 April, Sade moved into another house at St Ouen, occupied in Marie Constance's name. Next month, with spring making travel easier and radical anger at ex-nobles having flagged, Sade set off for Provence at last, with his companion and her son Charles (probably a teenager by then), about his own business. He visited Gaufridy at Apt, looked in at la Coste, went to his estate at Mazan, where the local officials paid him a formal visit much as they might have done when he came by as lord of the manor in the old days. This time, though, they also posted a bailiff at the house where he was staying, to keep an eye on him lest he leave without paying his arrears of property taxes to the municipality. Sade was in the region to collect back rents in person but the Revolution had changed Provence and he found it difficult to get his way with old tenants and new officials. A wrangle with one of the latter, a tax collector called Noël Perrin, burst into litigation after Sade's choler had spilled into a letter to him on 18 June:

"Having come to this region, citizen, to collect revenues here which have not been paid to me in six years, I promise you that it is with unparalleled surprise that I have found, from the attached document, that you have let yourself rob me of a portion of my revenues, *yes, rob*, citizen, that's the word for it! Surely you have not dared to turn over to the nation's coffers the income of a man who has never emigrated in his life... So this income cannot have been deposited anywhere but in *your pocket*..."

Perrin, by contrast, kept his poise, and sued in a local court for 1,500 francs in damages, plus costs and an order that 500 copies of a judgement in his favour be distributed in the region so that his vindication be widely known. Sade, perhaps advised by Marie Constance and Gaufridy, seems to have understood that he had gone too far. On 13 July, he signed a notarised apology to Perrin, who was acknowledged therein as "enjoying the best of reputations, and rightly so." The penitent declared himself willing to have the retraction made public and to pay for it to be published. Perrin declared next day that, although this apology was quite unsatisfactory, he was concerned only to protect his reputation as a fiscal officer and so, out of respect for Sade's family (still numerous and prominent in Provence) and for those who had intervened to try to bring the matter to a conclusion, he would accept payment of his costs in having the retraction and his response printed and displayed in public places, Sade being also required to pay 24 francs in alms to the hospital at Carpentras.

The expedition to Provence continued to go badly. Long-dormant creditors noticed the return of the prodigal and presented old bills. Dr Terris, who had visited the château at la Coste often in the happy days of 1771-72 to treat Anne Prospère de Launay and other members of the household, claimed 72 francs. Lawyer Fage, who had tidied much of the mess left by the then-lord and master's summer weekend at Marseilles in 1772, emerged as another old professional lacking recompense - to the extent of 6,156 francs and small change. It seems that Sade, try as he might, was unable to deny 2,095 francs of this claim. Even creditors of his uncle, the Abbé, who had died 20 years before, slapped their bills under the visitor's nose.

As for further sales of property, which Sade was attempting at Arles, these were being frustrated by the fact that he was still registered by the Vaucluse departmental administration as an emigrant. This was becoming more widely known in Provence, as Sade circulated anew and drew attention to himself, there being in the south plenty of enemies, old and new, to spread the word of this impediment to buying and selling, and to receiving revenues. Besides, his wife seems to have been no longer disposed to accept sales of his properties on which she held mortgages - just about every square inch of his estates, that is. In March, she had told Gaufridy of her having filed with the authorities in Paris an objection to any such sales unless she were supplied thereby with funds due to her under the separation agreement, plus accrued interest. The national financial crises and price inflation since 1792 make it hard to calculate the sum owed, but it was far in excess of the combined value of Sade's properties.

A cart loaded with provisions scarce in Paris followed the coach when, come autumn, Sade and Marie Constance quit their futile campaign in Provence and travelled back to St Ouen, arriving on 22 October, by which time three politicians - Barras, Rewbell and La Revellière - had seized control of the Directory, the committee in charge of the country's administration since 1795. This change led to a resurgence of pressure for enemies of the Revolution to be jailed, and the new triumvirate revived laws against emigrants and priests. In November, Sade, still on the Vaucluse Department's list of emigrants, which meant he was liable to be arrested under the legislation, appealed to the chief of police and supported his plea with a dossier of a hundred or so documents to show he had not left France since 4 July 1789, when he had arrived at Charenton from the Bastille. None of this achieved the desired result - indeed, an agent of his at Mazan was warned by the local authority for having failed to respond to Sade's emigrant status by preventing any income leaving the estate for him.

On 5 July of the next year, 1798, the mistakes over the years regarding his full and correct name, starting by the font at St Sulpice on his second day of life, bore full fruit as the Police Ministry told Marie Constance that it was against recommending removal of the name from the Vaucluse list of emigrants. Look at the discrepancies of Christian names in various documents. Look at the number of Provençal Sades. How could the ministry be sure that the one taken off the Rhône Estuary list in May 1793 was the one for whom *citoyenne* Quesnet was seeking exemption? Many more such pleas were filed over the next three years, to no avail.

In December 1798, Sade was granted *surveillance* status, recognising that he was not abroad but reserving a decision on whether he had emigrated, and affording him no more scope for doing business in France than was allowed to French people who had really fled abroad since 1789. Thousands of individuals with a good case or enough influence were being taken off the lists of emigrants, as Revolutionary zeal faded in the late-1790s, but Sade, who had not set a foot outside the country since long before the fall of the Bastille, remained in limbo. Given the bad odour in which he was held by influential people in Provence who remembered him from before 1777, and by those whom he had offended much more recently, we should not wonder greatly at this. The chairman of the local administration at Mazan, in January 1798, privately informed a local notary representing Sade that "citizen Perrin, tax collector at Carpentras, is the prime mover in all this activity, and he is no friend of yours." *Justine*, too, would not have been forgotten.

This consideration that he had a long and malodorous record even gave Sade himself pause when, at the highest levels in Paris, he was pursuing his restoration to full rights and privileges as a Frenchman. Casting about for ways to approach Barras, one of the three Directors who were ruling France, entailed certain qualms. On 16 January 1798, Sade was writing - the full context is unclear - to a correspondent:

"They're giving us a letter for a friend of Barras and this friend, they say, will present my memorandum to this Director, who then, if he sees fit to oblige me, will set the minister [of police] into action, or not, if he doesn't want to please me. Another worry, another bout of despair for me to be thus made conspicuous. Barras, who's from Avignon, does he know me? And what will he make of the impressions he might have? Whatever might come of this, I have my innocence and my excellent revolutionary conduct in my favour, and that makes me keep my head held high... But the old adventures - put before a man from my region?"

There is no evidence of a response by Barras.

Sade's elder son, Louis Marie, had tried on various occasions since 1794 to bring about a truce between his father and the rest of the family, but the old man would not have it. (In January 1799, he was telling Gaufridy that his son was "a traitor" striving to upset efforts by Sade and Marie Constance to soften the heart of Renée Pélagie.) Any settlement which resolved the matter of the enormous sum owed by Sade to his wife would probably have cleared the way for his relatives and their influential connections to have him removed from the list of emigrants. However, such a pact could scarcely do other than take his properties out of his control and transfer them in some way to other members of the family, or their representatives, who would seek to reimburse Renée Pélagie, at least in part, through sales of those properties or through diversion of much of their revenues to her and her children.

Sade, afraid as ever of losing his one even half-reliable source of income, all the more so as old age lay in close prospect for him, maintained the quite contrary aim of selling his estates in the south in order to finance his life in Paris. The abiding bad faith in his failure to pay his wife her due under the terms of the separation accord did not help to bridge the gulf between the two factions.

Louis Marie, for his part, had cause for bitterness over the continuing recollection of his father's escapades. Pauvert quotes - placing it about 1799 - a passage from the memoirs of Victorine de Chastenay, intelligent frequenter of the salons of high society in Paris, who had among the acquaintances of her youth "M. de Sade, son of the all too famous madman - for what else can one call him? - in whom depravity extends to ferocity. His son was very different. Gentle, decent, sensible, and even amiable. I don't know how he attached himself to me and was very keen to become my husband... One fine spring afternoon had drawn mummy and me to the Tuileries [gardens in Paris], a shower of rain brought out all of a sudden the first fresh greenery of the leaves, producing an indefinable effect. M. de Sade gave me his arm; his declaration [of love] was made, and with an intensity to which I would not have believed him liable. I must confess, it touched me... But, not otherwise feeling for M. de Sade any sort of inclination, my deep gratitude did not prevent me from reflecting on the frightful risk of ever bringing into the world the grandson of the phenomenal man who had to be locked up at Charenton soon after this. I turned down M. de Sade..."

During 1798, Sade's creature comforts were crumbling, or so it seems. In January, the vendors of his new properties near Paris, not having received from him the balance of the purchase prices, were making noises about repossessing the estates. In June, a petition on Sade's behalf sought the protection of the public administration against his arrest for debt while proceedings over his properties were still under way and his request to be taken off the list of emigrants was active.

For lack of money, Sade and Marie Constance left the house at St Ouen on 10 September. She found lodging with friends and Sade stayed with one of the tenant farmers on his new properties, to which he was clinging by the skin of his teeth. This grip seems to have failed in October when the vendors of the properties, still not having received the rest of the price, won a court injunction against final transfer of ownership to Sade. The tenant, apparently no longer such, turned Sade out and he, according to his raging letters to Gaufridy, was reduced to cadging food and a bed for the night as and where he could. The eye trouble that had plagued him in jail returned in strength. He cursed Renée Pélagie, bemoaned his wretchedness and begged Gaufridy for money from the remainder of his Provençal estates.

Sade found shelter from the winter weather at Versailles, where "at the end of a barn, with my companion's son[5] and a maidservant, we eat carrots and beans, and we have a fire (not every day, just when we can) with sticks that we get on credit half the time. We are in such a bad way that, when Mme Quesnet comes to see us, she brings us some food, from her friends' place, in her pocket." In February 1799, Sade was working in the theatre at Versailles for a labourer's pay.

On 5 August, while Sade continued to scratch a living, the local administration of Clichy gave him a certificate of residence and citizenship, which strengthened his protection against arrest as an emigrant and meant that at least one municipality acknowledged his legitimate presence in France.

His hopes of his plays stayed alive. On 1 October, Sade wrote to a prominent politician to ask if he could read his tragedy *Jeanne Laisné* to him. There was no piece better fitted "to warm love for the

5 The boy Charles Quesnet.

fatherland in every heart..." and "this is just the time" to stage it. The politician was requested to use his clout to have the Théâtre Français in Paris "told unequivocally" to mount a production. On 13 December, Sade's play *Oxtiern*, in a re-written version, was produced at the Versailles theatre with the author in a minor role, but there was little reputation, or money, to be made out of such a small production.

There are always the provinces, for show people disappointed in the capital. In 1797 and 1798, Sade was sending a circular to directors of theatres in "the great and magnificent cities of France, so worthy, by their luxury and their riches, by their refined taste and the excellent intelligence of their inhabitants, to rival, and even often to surpass [Paris], that proud capital of the universe." And how might those splendid cities best employ their theatres? By staging 12 plays, listed with synopses, by Sade, "friend of the arts since [his] youth", whose services in person at a theatre could be secured from 22 October next (1798) by means of a prompt advance of 600 francs. He was prepared to stay for six months, directing a production of one of his dozen plays every fortnight for a fee of 500 francs, to be paid promptly on the first of each month, plus a final payment of 600 francs at the end of the season, the following 20 April. The playwright's pitch went on:

"Which means, citizen director, you shall acquire the full and entire ownership (though not the right to publish) of twelve new plays, adding up to thirty-five acts, and this for the meagre cost of six thousand six hundred [francs], which costs each one ... at no more than five hundred francs..." (These figures do not match the scale of fees because, I expect, Sade was reckoning in other costs of his which the management was to meet.) Truth to tell, some of the 12 plays dated from the author's time in the Bastille and one was the tried and derided *Oxtiern*.

France beyond the capital turned out to be no more burning for Sade's ageing portfolio of drama than was Paris itself. Lacking more than a few replies, he blamed this on his not having included reply-paid postage with his circulars. One response, from Nantes, revealed that the man he had remembered as the theatre director there was no longer in charge, the management having gone collective during the levelling Revolution. "If I was of any account in the running of the shows here, I would do everything in the world to put on some of your works this winter" - but, alas, my old friend ...

In October 1799, a money order had arrived from Gaufridy, but bearing a November date. It was negotiable at any time but, if cashed before its date, would realise only three quarters of its face value. In the meantime, Sade had to eat. He was even sinking to base theft, he moaned to his agent on 27 October: "Do anything to find funds for me, because I'm absolutely dying of hunger, I'm quite naked, obliged to resort to *vile deeds* in order to live... Yes, to *vile deeds*! Must I confess one to you?... Despair at having brought me to this pass by your tardiness!... Well, my friend, my dear lawyer ... I have been reduced to going and stripping the room and selling the effects of my son[6] because I was without bread!... *I stole them*!... Cruel friend, see where you have brought me..."

Taken to the end of his tether by chronic hunger and the winter cold, so he reported to Gaufridy, Sade was admitted to the unheated public hospital at Versailles near the end of 1799. Marie Constance had been selling items of her clothes to keep him fed but, by that stage, had to take a job so as to bring in enough money to look after herself and her son. Humiliated at having to accept charity alongside old beggars, so as to escape "dying at a street corner", Sade again found the price of sending a letter to Gaufridy and raged at him for letting the landlord reach such straits. How could Charles Gaufridy have gone to the property at Arles, knowing local officials had removed the sequester on income from it, and failed to get out to the tenant farms and collect rents, just "because of the cold weather"? "You can tell little Abbé Charles is a soldier of the pope - he won't go out when the weather's bad." Compare and contrast the diligence of Mme Quesnet, who was doing the rounds of officials in the capital on behalf of the erstwhile separatist soldier, Charles's brother Elzéar, whose political leanings had left him under a cloud. "We in Paris are not so lily-livered as you in Provence," Sade declared.

Sade waxed fiercer than ever with Gaufridy *père*. On 26 January 1800: "Everyone up here who witnesses my situation is revolted by your conduct ... if I let people read what Charles has written to me, they sympathise with me for being in the hands of a madman.

"To be brief, I cannot wait a moment more. Send my money or I will adopt any means necessary to prise it from your hands, as *grasping* as they are *barbaric*. I have been dying of cold and hunger in the Versailles public hospital for three months now.

6 Louis Marie.

"Today is Sunday. I hope that, when you heard Mass today, you prayed to God to forgive you for having *lacerated* me, *cut me into little bits* and for having *tortured* me, as you have over the last three years."

At least, in late-February 1800, his municipal protection against arrest kept him out of jail when a process-server arrived at Versailles to take him to prison on account of a court order, which he had not obeyed, to pay a creditor who had sued over unpaid bills. By then, Sade was out of the paupers' hospital and living with Marie Constance again. They were soon back at St Ouen and Cazade, a municipal official there, took up his case to the extent of writing to Gaufridy, on 5 April, to tick him off for slackness in attending to Sade's affairs. The notary replied at length and evasively.

By May, Sade was threatening Gaufridy with a civil suit and accusing him of accepting bribes from tenants in order to let them off portions of rent due. This was the last straw - Gaufridy resigned as his agent. Sade then acted on his promise to send a representative to Provence with "a measure of emetic strong enough to make you cough up". Marie Constance and Cazade set off from Paris with power of attorney to examine all the account books and visit the estates. This intervention seems to have brought some funds to Sade in Paris and, at the beginning of the next year, 1801, a lawyer at Carpentras, name of Courtois, took over as Sade's agent in Provence.

On the face of it, there is inconsistency here. Was Sade really in such a bad way, as he complained so ferociously to Gaufridy? Close to starvation? Reduced to living in a barn? Admitted to a wretched public hospital for months in order to survive? How could an owner and recent vendor of properties, educated beyond all but a handful of his fellow citizens, deft with his pen, have come to that?

In dealing with Sade, one must never lose sight of his tendency to exaggerate, never forget the standard of living he regarded as normal. His "dying of hunger" and "naked as a maggot" - appearing often in his letters at various stages of his life - are not to be taken literally. Notice, for instance, that he and Charles Quesnet, when lodged in "a barn", were attended by a maidservant. For Sade, even rock-bottom was staffed. He had been used, not least when in jail, to being very well fed, clothed and shod indeed - remember what a flamboyant figure he had cut when arriving for his rendez-vous with the quartet of prostitutes at Marseilles in 1772. Then the food shortages and price inflation of the

1790s overtook him and the rest of France. The contrast in the quality of his upkeep striking him hard, he was accordingly upset.

Besides, he admitted at least once that he had falsified medical certificates of his ill health in order to stave off trouble from creditors. He would not have stopped at a similar deception by way of bringing so-called ailments to bear in his ceaseless quest for funds from Provence. Gaufridy, hundreds of miles away, was in no position to check his master's claims in person. He might have reflected, though, looking at the handwriting in the choleric letters from St Ouen and Versailles, that it seemed as firm and neat as ever. Was the landlord really as troubled by hunger and failing eyes as he was making out?

Was he as hard up as he was making out? What happened to the money from the sale of la Coste? And the money from the sale to publishers of manuscripts - the acknowledged *Aline and Valcour* and the anonymous *Philosophy in the Boudoir*, *The New Justine* and *Juliette*, as well as others that may have been lost to posterity? Much of it was spent on the attempted purchase of the properties near Paris made possible by the sale of la Coste. (It seems Sade did retain ownership of properties acquired with proceeds of the sale of la Coste, though it is not clear how.) Another large sum may have been spent on acquiring the lease of the second house which Sade and Marie Constance occupied, in her name, at St Ouen. Then there was the constant drain of the high cost of living - in which sending, by the long-distance coaches, letters to Gaufridy and circulars to provincial theatres would have been no small item. Also, let's not forget Sade's abiding capacity to mismanage his affairs. The marquis - who had exasperated his father and then his mother-in-law by his impertinence to high society and his profligacy with his purse, and who had preferred to order picture frames rather than window frames when his wife was suffering cold and hard times at la Coste - was later the citizen who insisted on trying to keep himself afloat by turning out clandestine literature and peddling his yellowing portfolio of plays.

Sade might have argued in his defence that he had tried to secure a salaried job but that this possibility was most likely closed by prejudice against him in the public administration - a prejudice which also kept him, unjustly, on the list of emigrants and thus prevented him from turning his properties into a viable support for his establishment in Paris.

Those who wonder how Sade, if he was so poor and ill, was able to offer his services for a six-month season as director of a season of his plays, able to invite a prominent politician to visit him and Marie Constance at their house, able to stage *Oxtiern* and appear in it - they might find here, too, Sade's capacity for being careless with the truth. There is no guarantee that he could have fulfilled the demanding six-month programme of rehearsals if a provincial theatre had taken him up on the promise of his circular (though no doubt he would have pocketed any advances that arrived from the provinces). There is no guarantee that the politician whom Sade wanted to influence would have found comfort and good fare at the St Ouen house. There is no guarantee that the Versailles production of *Oxtiern* was good.

Yet I would guess that Sade, given a chance to tread the boards for the first time in nearly 30 years, and in one of his own plays, summoned enough of the old energy to cut a dash. Likewise, that old energy might have flowed again, if Sade had been given a chance to mount a season of his plays in some city where, as the new big fish in the small pond, he would dazzle the locals with many a tale, some of them true.

In this aspect of his life, as in others, the truth is elusive. Just one more thought: It might well be that Sade was not only a writer of manuscripts for the clandestine press, but also an investor in the complicated and expensive undertakings by which his words were turned into books. This would have multiplied his income from this illegal activity - give or take problems with police raids on printers, binders, engravers, distributors - and would have increased his need to disguise his involvement in it. With that in mind - and knowing that his letters to Gaufridy would probably serve as information for his wife and his other relatives, to whom he owed a great deal of money - Sade may well have felt moved to supply Provence with a stream of letters declaring himself to be indigent while, through most of the six years after his release from Picpus and despite various bad patches, he was not. (A police report in early 1801 described him as "enjoying quite considerable wealth".) Whether or not he was ploughing money, as well as time and labour, into clandestine book publishing, he had a strong interest in having his relatives and creditors believe he was on his uppers.

CHAPTER 28: LAST ARREST AND CHARENTON

On 6 March 1801, while Sade was in the office in Paris of Nicolas Massé, successor to the late Girouard as his publisher, police officers came in and arrested the two men. About the same date, the Paris police found - probably not at the publisher's office - what they called a cache of "obscene works, and of manuscripts of obscene works. These manuscripts are all in the handwriting of the ex-Marquis de Sade, who has always been regarded as the author of *Justine* ..., the most frightfully obscene work in this genre..." The manuscripts included that of *Juliette* and those of other such works by Sade, plus "twelve designs for licentious engravings". In the same series of raids, the police visited "de Sade's apartment" - a place he must have been using in Paris - and seized various papers, including most of the huge manuscript of the unpublished novel *The Conversations at Charmelle Castle*, since disappeared.

Three months before his 61st birthday, Sade had lost his liberty for the last time. Much later, the frustrated playwright noted: "Sentence to put in my Memoirs - *The intervals in my life have been too long*."

This turn of events had been in the making for some while. His *Justine* (especially), *Philosophy in the Boudoir* and *Juliette* had been available in Paris, and elsewhere in France, during the Directory's time, a period when the administration did not take a strong line on morality in public entertainments and the public prints, not least because of the corruption and inefficiency of the police and of the administration in general. There were many other such books in circulation and Sade was among thousands of people busy at the various tasks in the clandestine publishing world. However, the production of *The New Justine* and *Juliette* envisaged for the turn of the 18th century was a rare undertaking, for its size, running to 3,600 pages spread over ten volumes. The first novel was probably available in 1800, the second early in 1801. Noting that, in the period 1794-1801, Sade produced other long manuscripts, which were stifled before they could reach print and have been lost to us, he must have spent a prodigious amount of that time at his pen. This suggests, by the way, that he was not quite starving to death meanwhile. It suggests, too, that his activities in this field could not have gone entirely unnoticed by the authorities.

The books about the two fictional sisters were also outstanding because of the sum to be asked for them. Pauvert has it that the price per ten-volume set in 1800 was equivalent to 5,000 French francs in 1990 - let's say about £500 or $750. That estimate might be high by about 25 per cent, but a price equivalent to £375 ($560) would still have been very stiff. It seems that an edition of at least 3,000 copies was planned so, on that basis, a sell-out would have grossed the equivalent of £1,125,000 ($1,680,000). The consortium behind *The New Justine* and *Juliette* was aiming for a mighty commercial coup at the luxury end of obscene publishing and, even if Sade, as author and investor, were to have been in line for no more than five per cent, he was hoping for some fat payments.

However, in November 1799, the young general Napoléon Bonaparte forced the legislative assembly of the Directory to appoint three temporary consuls as the most senior level of government, with himself as First Consul. Under the new régime, the police, run by Joseph Fouché, was reorganised and given new backbone. The assembly was soon dissolved and Bonaparte began to consolidate his personal rule as a military dictator - his position as First Consul was made permanent in 1801 and he had himself crowned emperor of France in 1804.

At a different level, a straw in the wind of change had appeared on 29 August 1799 in the newspaper *The Friend of the Laws*: "We are assured that de Sades [*sic*] has died. The very name of that notorious writer breathes a deathly stench that kills virtue and inspires horror: he is the author of *Justine*... Even the most debauched heart, the most degenerate intelligence, the most bizarrely obscene imagination could create nothing so outrageous of reason, decency and humanity ... courage may set up republics but proper morality keeps them up..." Sade, to protect his anonymity, replied in other newspapers: "I cannot understand why Poultier wanted to kill me off and call me the author of *Justine*, both at once. He must be a regular murderer and slanderer to write such appalling lies. Be so good as to publish in your newspaper this proof of my survival and my complete repudiation of that notorious work *Justine*."

Then, on 24 September, *The Friend of the Laws* published his riposte at its columnist:

"No, I am not dead, and I would like to print evidence of my certain existence on your ... back with a very stout stick. I would do this indeed, were I not afraid of plague ooze from your reeky corpse. However, an honourable man needs only contempt to brush aside the prattle of a bonehead such as you. I am not the writer of *Justine*. I might go out of my way to prove this to anyone but such a dunce... A wise man spits at your sort of yapping cur and goes about his business. So yap on, whinny, howl, brew your poison; being incapable, like the toad, of spitting past the end of your tongue, so that the poison lands on yourself, you will besplatter only yourself rather than taint others."

This crude churlishness - reminiscent of the young de Sade's attitude to critics of his libertinage - did not stop the sniping. On 22 October 1800, the journalist Villeterque attacked Sade in print, referring to him as the author of *Justine*. Sade retorted with a pamphlet of much ill-measured haughtiness, protesting altogether too much.

After the arrest in 1801, the publisher Massé told the police where to find a large stock of newly printed copies of *Juliette*, stored ready for distribution, and he was released before the end of the year. During spring and summer of 1801, at least 11 premises - of bookshops, printers and bookbinders in and around Paris - were searched by police looking for copies of *Justine* and *Juliette*, or material for their preparation. The searches were usually in vain, for editions of the two works were multiplied and copies were always available, albeit at a high price. At one binder's successfully raided, girls aged 12 to 14 were employed in combining pages of text and obscene engravings for an edition of *The New Justine*.

The police having finished their search at the publisher's office on 6 March, some of them took the author to St Ouen and ferreted through Marie Constance's house. They found "a secret room with licentious plaster figurines" and pictures of "obscene content, mainly related to that notorious book *Justine*". Marie Constance promised to stand by him, as Sade was led away by the police, who also took various items from his room. During his detention by the police - Marie Constance was allowed to visit him three times in each *décade* - Sade insisted to them that the more objectionable manuscripts and notes found were in his handwriting because he was the publisher's copyist, not the author. This was not believed, not of a man who "was enjoying considerable wealth," according to the police.

On 2 April, Fouché and his Commissioner of Police decided that court proceedings were to be avoided because they would cause too much upset. The minister was aware of the contents of Sade's police files from pre-1789. It may be that the government was concerned to prevent him having the opportunity to mention from the dock various politicians who had associated with him since 1790, or to name prominent persons whom he knew to have had dealings with his publicly despised works. In any event, on 3 April, Sade was moved under an administrative order - the Consulate's equivalent of the old regime's *lettre de cachet* - to the Sainte Pélagie prison in Paris.

Sade suspected that he had been locked away because of another initiative by his relatives to put him where his writing would be supervised and its publication prevented. This time, such a move might well have come from the younger generation. Sade's elder son, Louis Marie, was becoming interested by then in returning to an army which, under Bonaparte, was rolling back France's royal enemies in Europe. The younger son, Donatien, was still abroad. The sooner people forgot about their father, the better their chances of advantageous marriages and good careers. The two sons, aged 33 and 31 when their father was arrested in March 1801, were Montreuils, as well as Sades, and so able to call on family funds and other help in any steps to curb their father.

In May 1802, after more than a year in jail, Sade petitioned the Justice Minister to be let out or brought before a court. He reiterated his denial of authorship of *Justine*, as he had been doing in his personal notebooks while in prison because everything he wrote could be read by the authorities. It was quite wrong that such muck as *Justine* was coming out in second and third editions while *his* works were not reaching the reading public, he noted.

It was decided to move him again. Sometime in February or early March 1803, he had tried, it seems, to obtain some sexual relief from youngsters who had been put on his corridor in Sainte Pélagie to cool their heels after they had caused a disturbance at a Paris theatre. The official record is not specific about just what Sade tried to have them do but the fellow prisoners complained and the authorities wrote of his "debased desires". They wrote also, having searched his room on that occasion, of having found there "an enormous instrument which he had made out of wax, and which he was using on himself, for the instrument had kept traces of its reprehensible insertion..." Not as pleasurable, perhaps, as the tailored dildoes his wife used to send him at Vincennes, but self-buggery had to be achieved somehow.

Early on 14 March, Sade was up and about because he had been told he was to be taken elsewhere that morning. The writer Charles Nodier was on hand and spotted him: "The first impression I had of him was of a gross obesity which restricted his movements so much that they lacked those vestiges of poise and elegance which were still apparent in the style and speech of the man. Even so, his tired eyes retained a certain something, a flash of intelligence and quality now and again, like a dying spark on a dead coal." Nodier also had the impression that Sade was being careful not to let what was left of his fire destroy what might be left of his chances of release: "... he was polite, almost obsequious, amiable, almost smarmy, and expressed respect for everything that is given respect."

The corpulent old prisoner was on his way to Bicêtre, a prison in Paris which had been something of a Bedlam until a few months before Sade arrived - a crowded, neglected madhouse where the inmates spent most of their time in chains and closely confined. It was still far from congenial accommodation, albeit improved, when he got there. He stayed for only six weeks.

His relatives prevailed upon the police to move him from Bicêtre - a noble family with a member held at such an ill-regarded jail was shamed thereby - to the asylum at Charenton, outside Paris, where he had gone from the Bastille in July 1789. During the Revolution, the establishment had passed from the control of a religious order to that of the Interior Ministry. Sade was not admitted until his family had undertaken to pay 3,000 francs a year for his board and lodging. The average for an inmate at Charenton was 700 francs. The police lectured the director of the asylum, François Simonet de Coulmier, as to how careful he must be not to let Sade escape and, for his part, the ex-marquis wrote to the director of his resolve to earn the official's approval and to dispel all the bad impressions which other people must have already planted in his head, as Sade put it. He arrived on 27 April 1803. Marie Constance was allowed to move in with him at the asylum, from August 1804 and at 1,000 francs a year, on the pretext that she was an illegitimate daughter of his who was caring for him. She was free to come and go, and spent some of her time in Paris.

Coulmier, a former monk, had attained some political prominence after 1789, as a member of the Estates-General and, later, of the

Consulate's legislative assembly. He may well have secured the job at Charenton through his contacts among senior figures in the Directory. He had no medical qualifications to take charge of what was intended to be a place of treatment for the insane, rather than a mere house of restraint. By 1797, the date of his appointment to Charenton as its first director under its secular régime, he was in his mid-fifties and concerned, like many politicians glad of public office in their later years, to keep his post by keeping his work in the public eye.

It is hard to decide how conditions were for inmates at Charenton, not least because the asylum was controversial in Sade's time, and his contemporaries have left conflicting reports of it. (The notion of holding the mentally ill in order to rehabilitate them rather than just keep them from doing mischief was radical, though gaining ground, early in the 19th century.) It is safe to say that no-one should conclude from the play by Peter Weiss - set in the asylum and numbering Sade among its characters, *The Persecution and Assassination of Marat as Performed by the Inmates of the Asylum of Charenton under the Direction of the Marquis de Sade* - that life for the inmates there was leavened by experimental, political drama enacted by themselves. Weiss, whose play was first published in 1964, was not concerned with historical accuracy as far as the conduct of the asylum was concerned.

However, plays were produced at Charenton during Sade's time there, starting in the second half of 1804 or the first quarter of 1805. The monthly theatricals gave Sade an opportunity to revive, in reduced circumstances, the function of actor-director-writer he had enjoyed at various periods of his life, most lavishly at la Coste with Beauvoisin nearly 40 years before. As had often been the way at the Provençal manorhouse, some roles at Charenton were taken by players from outside, including professionals from Paris this time, and many of those in the audience were visitors. Coulmier liked to create the impression that inmates of the asylum were benefiting by appearing in plays and joining the audience - this helped to publicise the work of the asylum - but there is a question as to who was allowed to appear in them and what value they had as therapy for the inmates. A certain Jean-Etienne Esquirol reported:

"The shows were a fraud - the mad people had no role whatsoever in the plays, [Coulmier] was cheating the public [when he maintained that they had]... The insane who watched these theatrical presentations were the object of the attention and the curiosity of a flippant, thoughtless and sometimes ill-intentioned public. The strange behaviour of these unfortunates ... provoked outsiders to mockery, to an insulting pity..." Father Esquirol further complained of "injury to the pride and sensibilities of these unfortunates", of "confusion sown in the minds of those few who still retained the faculty of awareness. Being assigned to watch the shows was a sign of favour, which aroused jealousies, quarrels and grudges - hence sudden explosions of frenzy, reversions to mania and rage..."

Esquirol was another pioneer in psychiatric treatment and might have had motives for envy of Coulmier's extensive establishment at Charenton. Even so, his remarks about certain attitudes among the outsiders in the audiences towards the inmates nearby ring true from a society where many people were used to regarding the insane as entertainment, as material for cruel mockery.

However, several other contemporary visitors to Charenton - favourable and otherwise towards Coulmier - reported that inmates did take roles in the plays, mentioning also Marie Constance, a professional actress until she took up with Sade in 1790, as having donned the greasepaint again. More than one outsider seems to have been impressed, and somewhat relieved, at the inmates in a cast having got to the final curtain without forgetting their lines or lapsing out of character and into lunacy. Experienced members of the professional stage found some inmate performers altogether up to standard.

As for Sade, after initial friction with him, Coulmier became glad of his theatrical expertise and the old thespian chose scripts from among unexceptionable comedies, dramas and operas of the time. He directed many of the productions, acted and sang in some, and wrote verse for insertion to established plays. Some of the verse was occasional, such as a piece in praise of Bonaparte and his family. The ever-aspiring playwright also brought out some of his own plays for the boards at Charenton. He flattered authority further with eulogies of Coulmier and a play dedicated to the asylum director. The irreducible atheist even wrote verses of welcome for the cardinal-archbishop of Paris (Bonaparte had long since made France's peace with the pope) when the latter visited the asylum in October 1812.

For all this unctuousness, any theatrical enterprise involving Sade could hardly proceed without a spat or two, especially when someone else was ultimate master of the revels. One day in October 1807, Coulmier announced that he did not want staged a production which had been in rehearsal for a month. Sade told his diary: "That sparked off a little bad temper. (I wanted to tear up the work.)" At a meeting in January 1808, Coulmier broke "his word of honour", according to Sade, by dropping a particular play from the repertoire. Sade confided to his journal that "this upset me greatly because of how much it cast down [Marie Constance], who cried about it all evening, and all this shows that the saga of vexations is never going to leave me." Indeed not - four months later, Sade was preparing to play a certain scene from a show "with the firm resolve not to sing in it any more no matter how much they applaud me." So there!

Coulmier himself was not the only source of annoyance for Sade the theatrical director. One resident - whether staff or inmate is unclear - complained to Coulmier: "He told me ... to do something needed for the décor and, as I was turning away to go and do what he was asking, he grabbed me roughly by the shoulders and said to me: 'Sir rascal, be so good as to listen to me.' I replied calmly...

"I must inform you that I had not gone near M. de Sade for several days because I was tired of his violence...

"As a result of this M. de Sade will give me no more parts in the plays..."

However, Sade was also useful to Coulmier in that he was able, through his contacts in literary and theatrical circles, to attract members of these to the diversions, on which the asylum director was able to spend public funds. (He also contributed from his own pocket.) Out of sight of the guests at the plays, firework displays and weekly balls, though, Coulmier's administration was by no means wholly attentive and even-handed towards the 400 or so inmates. One of various complainants to the authorities - not all of them anonymous like this one - wrote of:

"Buildings so run down that great expense will be required promptly to put them right... No more than 600 pairs of sheets for a house of 400 to 500 patients and only one blanket per bed. A great lack of clothing - to such a degree that two women have died of cold this winter and two men suffered frost-bitten feet ... meanwhile there is enormous expenditure on concerts and shows that do more harm than good. The attendants prepare and administer remedies according to their own whims... The medical supervision is next to non-existent... The insane are punished, rewarded, locked up, let out, even sent away as cured without the doctor being consulted... "

There were bizarre therapies for the mentally ill. It was an idea of the time that a disturbed patient ought to be jolted out of obsessional or anti-social behaviour by sudden immersion in water, the shock of this to be mitigated somewhat by encouraging words and tender attention. As administered by attendants at Charenton, however, the water treatment - in the form of sudden floods from overhead tanks or by forced immersion in a large bath to the point of drowning - often became a crude way to frighten inmates into submissiveness and for the staff to amuse themselves. There is no evidence that Sade was subjected to this kind of abuse, or to solitary confinement in the asylum's damp cellars or to beating.

Yet a certain Villiaume, a former inmate, described Charenton thus in his memoirs:

"Help available at all hours, a well-ordered disposition of people with various kinds of illness; corridors perfectly lit and ventilated, rooms kept clean and tidy; nourishing and abundant food; numerous nurses of both sexes, whom the administration keeps under close supervision; a huge raised garden in the form of an amphitheatre, from which one comes upon a charming site and a broad horizon; special heated rooms, a library, a nicely furnished salon; games of draughts, backgammon, cards or chess for recreation; that's what Charenton offers to its patients and which one doesn't find in the private sanatoriums, set up by money-grubbing speculators and managed, most of them, in a hard-handed way and with the most sordid penny-pinching..."

Explanation of the deep discrepancy between the different views of life at Charenton lies in the discrimination between patients according to their various mental conditions and - notwithstanding Villiaume's praise for public-sector medicine - according to how much they were worth to Coulmier by way of fees. The more deranged and the less lucrative were more apt to have their toes frozen and less apt to enjoy plentiful food.

Sade, a high-rate payer, was exceptionally favoured in that he was allowed the liberty of the buildings and the grounds. Throughout his last confinement, there was an intermittent conflict between two schools of thought as to how he should be dealt with. The familiar notion that he should be held in a massive fortress, as he had been at the Bastille, so as to have as little contact as possible with other humans, remained extant among certain officials and some of his relatives.

However, others were prepared to give him more scope to stay in touch with the world. Apart from Coulmier's sophisticated exploitation of his old charge's talents and contacts, there were those from beyond Charenton who got pleasure out of his company. Sade would entertain people from the Parisian theatre in his quarters at the asylum - as well as personal friends and acquaintances, even Coulmier himself on rare occasions - and there seems to have been something of a raffish cachet, for stage people and hangers-on, in visiting the shuffling old libertine, author of such stunning works as *Justine* and *Juliette*. Sade's public position, of course, remained a denial of authorship of these works.

There was certainly a line in outraged correspondence by visitors to shows at Charenton scandalised by the discovery that a certain "very fat, very forbidding, very ponderous actor," as one of them put it, was "the infamous scoundrel *de Sades!*" (This misspelling of his name was common.) Armand de Rochefort, a guest at a Charenton dinner to celebrate Coulmier's name day one year, found seated to his left "an old man with head bent, a fiery gaze. The white hair that crowned him gave him a venerable aspect which required respect; he spoke to me several times with such sparkling verve and lively intelligence that I found him very pleasant. When everyone was leaving the table, I asked my neighbour on my right the name of this amiable man; he told me that it was the Marquis de S---. On hearing that word, I distanced myself from him with as much terror as though I had been bitten by a venomous snake."

Mlle Flore, an actress of the day, kept her nerve better when confronted by the *loup-garou*: "I was regarding him like a kind of curiosity, like one of those monstrous beings, ... the all too famous Marquis de Sade... He had quite a handsome head, a little long, an aquiline nose, wide nostrils, narrow mouth, the lower lip protruding. The corners of his mouth were drawn down by a disdainful smile.

"His small, but bright, eyes were hidden under a strong brow [with] thick eyebrows; his creased eyelids covered the corners of his eyes ... ; his balding brow rose to an oval shape, his hair was swept upwards in the Louis XV style, lightly curled at the sides, all the hair perfectly powdered, and it was his own hair... He had kept fine manners and a great deal of intelligence..."

Sade's letters from the asylum suggest that, when in the vein, he could still strike a spark from his old tinder-box of choler and indomitability. It would be surprising if, when away from the constraint of having to suck up to Coulmier and the director's visitors, when wining and dining in the private company of unbuttoned theatricals who got a frisson out of being close to such a notorious figure, Sade had not loosed the beguiling call to licence and godlessness by which he had proselytised all his adult life. This is not to say that his room at Charenton was a miniature version of la Coste in the lord and master's prime, when Anne Prospère de Launay and half the quality of the region had been swayed by his presiding force. At the asylum, when off-stage, he was old, gross and - *pace* de Rochefort and Mlle Flore - often morose and scruffy, in an institution run by others and often made displeasing by dirt and derangement.

Sade's promise in advance to Coulmier, that he would seek to earn the director's approval, did not prevent him complaining about his detention. On 20 June 1804, he was writing to a committee on the liberty of the individual, set up in Bonaparte's new senate, that it was more than time for him to be put on trial. However, a few weeks before, the police had warned him to behave lest he be returned to the much greater discomfort of Bicêtre, and ordered an examination of what Sade had been writing at Charenton. Fouché, the Police Minister, whom the detainee was also petitioning, and his police chief decided, according to a minute of 8 September, that Sade could not be rehabilitated from his "constant licentious insanity" and that he must stay put. The police chief was none too pleased, probably in the spring of the next year, 1805, when he found out that Sade had taken Communion on Easter Sunday in the parish church at Charenton, outside the bounds of the asylum. He also handed around the collection plate. Coulmier received a written admonition to remind him that Sade could not be allowed out for any reason, unless there were police permission: "Did you not consider that the appearance of this man would be bound to cause revulsion and might occasion a public disturbance? Your excess of indulgence to Mr Desade [*sic*] is all the more amazing to me because you have complained strenuously more than once about his behaviour, especially about his surliness."

The surly one, almost certainly unaware of this telling-off, asked in 1806 for permission to leave Charenton twice a week (the Revolution's calendar, with its *décade*, was on the way out) to attend to his affairs, promising on his well-worn "word of honour" never to spend the night away from the asylum and not to take advantage of such permission except when absolutely necessary. Fouché was advised by one of his officials: "The former Marquis de Sade is too well-known, as are the execrable works which have come from his envenomed pen and which brought about his most recent arrest, for me to need to go into any detail about him. It is already quite enough that Mr Desade [*sic*] should enjoy a certain freedom inside the House, but if he was once spotted outside, that would be a public scandal. I judge therefore that his request must be rejected" - which it was.

Again, as at Vincennes, Sade resorted to numbers as he construed patterns and sequences to lend structure to his existence. The number of visitors he had received on a given day, the number of items on his dinner plate, the number of books borrowed and so forth were seen to constitute signs and signals. This time, though, little in the way of vertiginous, angry or hopeful conclusions about past wrongs done to him or about dates for his release was calculated out of these incidents. This time, at Charenton, he had people about him, especially Marie Constance, to distract him from obsessions. Also this time, there being no Renée Pélagie as buffer and provider, he could not keep himself aloof from concerns about his finances and properties, as we shall see.

He was moved by Mme de Staël's novel *Delphine*, which came out soon after his arrest in 1801, so far as to copy into his notebooks 42 extracts from it, these dealing mainly with various tribulations and especially the irksomeness of ageing. "It is horrible to find the encircling net of time drawing nearer without one's ever having known happiness," he noted from the novel.

His personal notes and diary from his life after his arrest in 1801 have been mainly lost. However, there is a record of his having written, most likely at Sainte Pélagie before 1804, two anti-*Justine* novels, since lost. His notes from late-1803 include this: "Stung by this charge [of having written *Justine*], I have just done two works ... in which I have overturned, destroyed, turned upside-down the insidious sophisms of *Justine*. But ... since literary people must be forever the victims of foolishness and stupidity, they're holding onto my works, publication is being held back (perhaps they'll even prevent their appearance) while *Justine* is spreading everywhere. Bravo, my friends! you'll cease to make any sense if you set yourselves against good and if you support evil..." There is no record of these works - whose titles were probably *Conrad* and *Marcel* - having been published.

The notes of 1803-04 also refer to Sade having in hand six unpublished works, including his collected plays, apt to occupy 16 volumes by his reckoning. His next bit of reckoning, based on a price of "30 francs per volume and editions of 2,000" copies, presumes a sum of 48,000 francs amassed thereby, "on [the prospect of] which I can confidently expect to ask for 20,000 so as to buy a country house." The arithmetic is as shaky as the notion that, the inflationary days of the Directory being past, anyone could charge 30 francs per volume (10 or 20 times the norm) for a book in 1804, and as the even more fantastical idea that Sade (this is Pauvert's point) could expect from a publisher more than a tenth of the gross - the 48,000-franc pie in the sky.

Perhaps he was thinking about the prices charged, and money to be made, from ventures in licentious publishing such as the ambitious scheme for *The New Justine* and *Juliette*, but the six works still on his hands at Sainte Pélagie were not of that kind. Perhaps he was longing too much in prison to be away to a country house. Perhaps it was just that his financial grasp was as unsound as ever. In any event, there were no takers among the publishers, any of whom would have done no other than puncture his dream.

Yet Sade sometimes repulsed self-pity and self-delusion, as it recurred during his last years, and opened the way for the generosity to others of which he was also capable. His will is dated 30 January 1806. Its first clause speaks of Marie Constance and of "my great gratitude for her care of me and for the genuine friendship she had for me from the twenty-fifth of August, seventeen hundred and ninety, till the day of my death; she having tendered these affections not solely with circumspection and selflessness, but also ... with the most courageous energy in that, during the terror, she saved me from the blade of the revolution which was all too surely poised over my head ..." Hence, Marie Constance was to receive 80,000 francs in cash, which the executor of the will, a notary at Charenton, was to place so as best to ensure for her "an income to secure her food and maintenance". This legacy was to pass, on Marie Constance's death, to her son Charles Quesnet, who was probably in his twenties by 1806. Sade also left to Marie Constance his furniture, clothes, books and papers, except for those handed down by his father, which were to go to his children.

Sade seems to have suspected that his will, in which his companion was the main legatee, might be contested by his children, who were urged, in the first clause, "to recall that they had promised the said Mme Quesnet a sum of this kind by way of acknowledgement of the care she gave their father and, in that this document does no more than agree with and presage their first intents, any doubt about their concurrence with my last wishes cannot occupy my thoughts for a moment, especially when I consider the filial qualities which have always been their mark and cause them to deserve my paternal affection."

It is not clear whether this wish was respected. There was enough property still belonging to Sade at his death for its sale to have realised enough cash to fund his legacy to Marie Constance. However, there is no trace of her for us after the last mention of her in Sade's diary just before his death. Personal effects of his, even down to a batch of empty bottles, were sold soon after his death at the behest of Donatien Claude Armand, the second son, rather than that of Marie Constance. From what we know of that son, whose tight-fistedness will become clear below, I would bet that Mme Quesnet, if she did see any of her late companion's money, had to struggle for every penny of it against his heirs.

(Donatien, by then the successor to his father's title, was still being complained of by the Charenton management, as owing arrears on his father's board and pocket money, three years after the old man had died. Donatien had dropped this first Christian name, shared as it was with his father, and preferred to sign himself "Armand de Sade-Mazan". After his father's death, he took care to be known as the Count de Sade, rather than take the alternative title of marquis made notorious by his father. Each successive head of the family did likewise until an inheritor in the mid-20th century decided that there was no shame in calling himself the Marquis de Sade.)

The most famous clause in Sade's will is the final one:

"I absolutely forbid that my corpse be opened, for whatever motive. I ask most insistently that it be kept for forty-eight hours in the room where I shall have died, placed in a wooden coffin, the lid of which shall not be nailed down until the above-required forty-eight hours have passed... During this period an urgent message shall be sent to Mr Le Normand, a woodseller of ... Versailles, asking him to come in person, with a cart, to take my body under his own supervision and in the said cart to the wood on my land at Malmaison ..., where I wish it to be placed, with no sort of ceremony, in the first thick copse on the right in the little wood as one enters it from the side of the old manorhouse along the broad track that divides it. The tenant farmer at Malmaison shall open [a] ditch in this copse, under the supervision of Mr Le Normand, who is not to leave my body until he has put it into the said ditch. He may take with him on this occasion, if he wishes, those of my relatives or friends who, albeit without pomp of any sort, might have been kind enough to give me this last proof of attachment. The ditch having been filled in, acorns are to be scattered on it so that the ground of the said ditch shall become green again and, the copse being as thick as it was before, the traces of my grave shall vanish from the surface of the Earth as, I hope, remembrance of me shall fade from the minds of men, except nevertheless the few who have been so good as to love me till the end and of whom I bear a very fond memory to the grave."

The final clause has been hailed, especially by French persons who regard their country as priest-ridden, as a fine valediction by an atheist who was as disdainful of any afterlife as of any posthumous glory among the living.

Perhaps, but consider the instructions that no-one should be allowed to conduct a post-mortem examination of his body as all of a piece with the wish for an unmarked grave and an irreligious interment without ceremony. I suggest that Sade, anxious as ever that no-one triumph over him by impinging on his person or prerogatives except at his own wish, was loath to be invaded or diminished even after death - especially in that he may have considered that the organs of such a notorious person might become objects of speculation and profit, or even of derision if put on show, as Inspector Marais had put the living marquis on show in Provence in 1778, to his great and abiding horror. What's more, a marked grave might be attacked by the ill-disposed. Covered by the greenwood, though, his remains would return to the great, regenerative mulch of nature, the ceaseless omnivorousness of which served to render virtue pointless and let vice be the true way for a human being, so Sade maintained. Thus lost, no-one would spit on them or turn a penny by them, just as no priest would invoke any Lord over them.

This spurning of reminders of himself for posterity was not a consistent element of his last years. Also in 1806, he wrote to Gaufridy, who had been his agent and his vexation, a long letter that seems to have been his first to the Provençal in nearly six years. The writer disguised his most recent vicissitudes by putting the long interval since his previous letter down to "the many moves" he and Marie Constance had made during the last five years, and gave his address as care of Coulmier, which covered the fact that he was detained in an asylum.

Sade's last bout of correspondence with Gaufridy had been all spleen and recrimination over the latter's handling of Sade's remaining southern properties and the supply of revenue from them. So the letter of 1806 started with a declaration that all the kerfuffle between them should be entirely put down to "events and circumstances", not least among which had been the old lawyer's son Charles, and there were no hard feelings as far as Sade was concerned. His heart had been against handing over his affairs to lawyer Courtois at Carpentras in 1801, "but there are so many occasions in life when one must go against the counsel of the heart." He had reckoned that, whether Gaufridy kept the management of the properties or not, "we would be able to remain friends." He had asked Courtois in the interim for news of Gaufridy, but there had been no reply on this score. (There is no telling whether Sade had done this in fact.)

All this bridge-mending and buttering-up suggests that Sade wanted something. Just so - he asked Gaufridy to send certain papers believed to have been saved from the sack of la Coste and "a manuscript of my memoirs ... which I have seen in the hands of your younger son and which he never wanted to give me. I repudiate this manuscript absolutely and I beg you to get it back to me..." (This remains a mystery, although the manuscript was to have been addressed care of woodseller Le Normand - he of the position of trust conferred in Sade's will - so that and the perfunctory repudiation suggest that the memoirs were not fit for the eyes of the authorities. I suggest Sade wanted to enliven his detention with reminders about his early exploits, perhaps also with a view to working some of them into a new scurrilous work of literature.)

Also, there were queries of Gaufridy about the best way to protect the financial interests of Marie Constance in view of her loans to him. Most important, there was advice wanted because of trouble brewing with the ex-marquise over property, with which we will get to grips in the next chapter.

Sade asked for "some information about la Coste, please, and about people I liked, the Paulets and others.

"... the manor... What condition is it in, I wonder? What about my poor park? Is there anything of me to be seen in it now?

"My relations at Apt, how are they faring?

"Maybe, now, would you be glad to have a word about me? So be it, *I am not happy*, but I am bearing up well. I can say no more to the inquiries which, I hope, still arise from friendship.

"Yours until death.

"Sade"

The Sade who stipulated in his will a farmer's ditch deep in the woods for his corpse wanted to know whether his erstwhile estate in Provence still told the world that de Sade had been there.

Armand, when the new Count de Sade, saw to it that his father's body avoided a post-mortem examination but put it through a Christian funeral and had it buried in a grave marked by a plain cross, without inscription, in the graveyard of the parish church at Charenton.

CHAPTER 29: REDUCTION AND DEMISE

Dr Antoine Royer-Collard, chief medical officer at the asylum at Charenton, told Fouché, on 2 August 1808, that Sade was not insane and so had no business being kept in a place where the sick were sent to be cured, not to be exposed to "the vile beliefs" of "the notorious author of *Justine*", which he was propagating by his conversation with inmates and by lending them examples of his writings. What's more, he was running the theatricals - of which Royer-Collard disapproved - at Charenton and sharing his accommodation with a woman who, despite what he claimed, was not his daughter. The doctor asked the minister to transfer this bad influence to a prison. There was friction between Royer-Collard and Coulmier, each of whom saw himself as the right man to run the asylum.

A senior official at the ministry noted that the doctor might be using the controversy over Sade to undermine Coulmier, "who has been taking advantage of M. de Sade's bright intelligence and inventiveness" to cheer up the inmates, but the official asked the police to investigate and report back. On 2 September, a police file told the minister that Coulmier "regards himself as lucky to have at the asylum a man who is able to give dramatic training to the mentally ill, whom he [Coulmier] wants to treat in this way." For all that, the report went on, it was scandalous that someone who had "corrupted public morals through his irreligious, scurrilous works and has committed many crimes" was to be found at Charenton, rather than in a prison. The same month, by way of counter, relatives of Sade intervened with the Police Ministry, and Deguise, the surgeon at the asylum, certified that, Sade's health being unsound, a transfer might be fatal. The ministry postponed any transfer. Then, on 11 November, it was fixed for 15 April of the next year, 1809, after winter. In late-March, however, the well-connected Lady Delphine de Talaru, a relative of Sade through his mother and widow of an associate of his during his dealings with constitutional monarchists about 1790, appealed with others to the police minister that the old ex-marquis be left where he was. The transfer notion was dropped.

Even so, misgivings about Sade's continued socialising and continued writing - both of which were easily noted, and readily contrasted with facilities available to less favoured inmates of the asylum - were soon moving along other official channels. The Count de Montalivet, the Interior Minister, under whose department Charenton operated, ordered on 18 October 1810 that, contact by Sade with the other inmates being dangerous, he was to be kept in isolated accommodation and allowed no writing material. (Fouché had lost his ministry through a political reverse three months earlier.) Coulmier, flourishing his dignity as an administrator much honoured by the state and a man dedicated to "the succour of the unfortunate" and to the "economising of public funds", replied that he was thus constrained to ask that Sade be taken away from Charenton, because he (Coulmier) was no jailor and no persecutor of fellow humans. He added that Sade had indicated, by improved behaviour over a considerable period of time, that he wanted to repudiate his former ways.

Furthermore, Coulmier argued, Sade was in a bad financial condition because his children had used his inability to control his affairs in order to strip him naked. This last point especially reads like pure Sade, whose favourite image of himself when bleating about his poverty was to present himself as "naked". Coulmier seems to have been susceptible to Sade's dramatics off-stage as well as on. The administrator was also worried, as he told the minister, by the fact that the asylum at the time was "owed about 9,000 francs for lodging, wood and lighting" in respect of Sade. The implication was that this was a more important consideration than hedging the old inmate about with closer restrictions.

In any event, Montalivet gave way somewhat. One of Sade's relatives, perhaps Mme de Talaru again, had visited the minister to assure him that Sade was not writing in order to have published outside France works which would be an offence to public morality. Sade was not put into solitary confinement but there were efforts to curb his contacts and activities. He complained to Coulmier, in December 1810, of not having access to the key of his room at all times, of being followed during his walks in the grounds and of having been deprived of pens and paper. For a time, he seems to have been forbidden visits to Marie Constance, whose rooms were only a few yards from his. Sade also tried to meet objections to his relations with inmates by offering a promise to speak to only three other named persons in the asylum - not including Marie Constance, who must have been understood to be exempt from these considerations.

His closest blood relatives, however, were the main instrument of Sade's comeuppance - slow and cumulative though it was. These were also in the camp of his closest enemies - Montreuils by half their escutcheons and all their upbringing - as well as being his own sons.

Louis Marie, Sade's elder son, was distinguishing himself in the armies of Bonaparte while his father was presiding over the theatrical diversions at Charenton. On 14 October 1806, Louis took part in the emperor's victory at Jena over the Prussians and, the following June, he was wounded in a battle at Friedland. By then, he held the rank of captain and his service had won him a mention in dispatches.

The other son, Armand, long since free of the distraction of military duties for France and taking care not to draw attention to his more recent service in exile with Russia, France's enemy, was the sharper edge of their father's nemesis. He had been back in France since 1803, based at the Montreuil château of Échauffour in Normandy, where his mother and sister were living. He was removed in March 1808 from the list of emigrants and, on 31 May, he visited Charenton to ask his father for formal permission to marry Louise Gabrielle Laure de Sade d'Eyguières, a distant cousin from Provence and daughter of the Count de Sade d'Eyguières who had acquired our delinquent marquis's Burgundian lieutenancy-general in 1778 **(see chapter 13)**. The count seems to have conspired in Provence against the Revolution in the early 1790s, then gone into exile, but he was swearing, to Fouché in 1802, his loyalty to the goverment of the day. In 1805, he was given official permission to re-establish himself on his southern estates and, early in 1807, he was back in Paris, full of wealth and influence. Thus, albeit a generation too late, the blood of the Montreuils, which Armand shared, was moving towards an alliance with that branch of the Sade dynasty which would suit the Montreuil view of society much better than the one with which it had mingled itself 45 years before.

The aged and somewhat mellowed Donatien Alphonse François Sade concurred with his son's request for paternal permission to marry and, at Charenton on 31 May 1808, the two began to draw up the appropriate document with a view to signing it before a notary public. All of a sudden, according to Sade's journal, Louis Marie arrived and asked his father for a word in private, during which the older son told his father, according to the latter, there was a "trap" in preparation and that, no sooner had the marriage been solemnised than "I would be taken from here to be put into a dreadful fortress..." With that, Sade went back to Armand, declared he would sign nothing and that the younger son should return next day. He left, followed by Louis Marie after the latter had assured his father that he would make sure nothing untoward happened to the old man.

Three weeks later, Sade told Armand there would be no permission for a marriage without the latter's firm undertaking to maintain his father's liberty and person. A family such as the Montreuils retains its contacts - revolutions may come and go, but a network of lawyers is always with us. Even before Sade had drawn up his formal expressions of opposition to the match, the family had secured a legal opinion that no emigrant from France, or even anyone so reputed, was in possession of his civil rights and so his children could marry as though he did not exist. Also, a senior appeal court judge was prevailed upon to ask Fouché, still the police minister in 1808, whether Sade was still on the list of emigrants. Three days after the request of 12 July, Fouché confirmed that the former marquis was on the list.

In high society, though, paternal permission for a marriage was good to have and Armand secured it, in a notarised declaration, on 20 July. Two days later, Louis Marie having visited his father again, this permission was withdrawn by the old man. The older son seems to have been concerned that his brother was conspiring, with the branch of the family into which he was trying to marry, so as to exclude Louis Marie from access to a share in family wealth. However, on 3 August, the permission to wed was reinstated as Armand and his father discussed it further, and notary Finot at Charenton, who must have been doing well out of all the documented mind-changing, sealed the accord on 1 September. Armand and Louise were married on 15 September. Their union produced four children, one of them the son who, in time, became Marquis, then Count, de Sade and passed the title to succeeding generations of the family.

Louis Marie had returned to active service on 15 August. Even his shining record in the French armies which were fighting a coalition of foreign forces in Europe proved of no use to his father when the latter tried to turn this to his advantage by petitioning Bonaparte for release from Charenton. He described himself to the emperor as "a father of a family, in the bosom of which he views as his consolation a son who is distinguishing himself in the armies, weighed down by the most unfortunate of lives for nearly nine years, in three different prisons... He is a septuagenarian, nearly blind, overwhelmed by gout and by rheumatisms in the chest and the stomach, which cause him to suffer horrible pains..." Once released, no-one would ever have cause to repent his having been given his liberty, the old petitioner added.

Sade's letter was dated 17 June 1809, by which date, although the news was yet to reach him, the distinguished military career he cited in his cause had been ended. Eight days earlier, Louis Marie had been in southern Italy on the way back to his regiment when his detachment was ambushed and he was killed, a victim of guerrillas who were resisting French occupation of Neapolitan territory.

His father might have shed a tear at the bereavement but he had regarded Louis Marie, so he put it when complaining to the authorities in 1804, as a member of "a dreadful coalition of relatives which I have never wanted to join, during the Revolution, neither in their actions nor in their opinions: furious at my abiding ... attachment, as much to the fatherland as to those who govern it, distraught at the order I was trying to bring to my affairs by satisfying all my creditors, by whose ruin these dishonest people were prospering, they have adroitly taken advantage of the fleeting moment of credit allowed [to them] by their return to France in order to bring down him among their own who never wanted to follow them [abroad]. There began my time of troubles. There began their deceitful accusations - and my chains..."

When he arrived at Charenton in 1803, Sade was already the object of his elder son's attempts to have him surrender his properties to his estranged wife and his children in return for a regular income sufficient to maintain him. More than once, he had seemed to accept, only to make that acceptance conditional on various demands - a greater payment for Marie Constance than the family had proposed, more money for his creditors than had been allowed (failing which, the relatives to bear the brunt of the creditors' ire), his insistence on keeping the property at Saumane, etc. All this, and his usual recalcitrance and unreliability in such negotiations, frustrated any accord with his family.

Hence the family's abandonment of hope of such a pact, especially once Armand was back in circulation and forging links with the de Sade d'Eyguières branch of the family. Sade's letter to Gaufridy, re-opening their correspondence in 1806 (or perhaps the previous year) after a long interruption **(see chapter 28)**, asked for advice on various matters, not least about an initiative by Mme Rovère, hard-up widow of the politician who had bought la Coste from Sade in 1796 **(see chapter 27)**, to sell the property as her only hope of solvency. "This sale," the inmate of Charenton fretted to his former agent, "is going to lead to a very big lawsuit between the stubborn Madame de Sade and this worthy lady, a suit in which they are talking of nothing less than expropriating from me the acquisitions that I made with the *Rovère money.* Can they do that? A word about that, I beg you..."

By all means: Sade's neglect and chicanery over his properties were rebounding on him at last. The needy Mme Rovère - once a marquise whom the late politician had saved from the guillotine during the Revolutionary Terror, at which she divorced her aristocratic husband and married the Provençal on the make - was trying to sell la Coste, her only asset of consequence. The ex-Marquise de Sade, her sons and their connections and advisers were trying to block the sale, or to make sure they got any proceeds thereof. Their grounds for intervening were not so much that the vendor had taken a big under-the-counter payment from the late Rovère to secure the sale, although this could be said to have tainted the transaction, but more that there were still mortgages of Renée Pélagie's on the property. This abiding encumbrance on the property might be no fault of Mme Rovère, the innocent inheritor of her husband's acquisition, but contracts were contracts and those which had established the mortgages of the then Marquise de Sade on the property were not to be set aside. Mme Rovère, not having the means to pay off the mortgages, was unable in law to sell the property without Renée Pélagie or her heirs having first claim to the proceeds. The property had much deteriorated over the years, while the arrears of interest on the mortgages had been growing, so the proceeds of any sale would have come nowhere near covering the sums owed on the mortgages, fresh spring on the land or no fresh spring on the land. The widow was "like a fury" at him, Sade reported. No wonder.

Besides, Sade's sale of la Coste had not been opposed by Renée Pélagie at the material time because it was meant to yield funds to buy other properties near Paris, income from which would fund Sade's payments to her under the terms of their separation of 1792. He had turned out to be just as lax in making these payments after the sale of la Coste as he was before. Here was another cause for the ex-marquise and her children to intervene in any further transactions where Sade had left his mark and they had a pecuniary interest. Whether or not Mme Rovère's effort to sell la Coste was the main trigger, the Sade-Montreuil-Eyguières alliance, as it stood in about 1807, went into action, not only to protect its rights as it saw them regarding la Coste but also to sweep the troublesome old inmate aside once and for all by getting their hands on his properties.

Why did it take the "dreadful coalition" so long to adopt this line? Having done so, why did the process take a long time? For one thing, the ex-marquise was old and declining into blindness, and perhaps not as assiduous as her younger son in pursuing a resolution of the problem. Louis Marie, her elder son, had to spend much of his time with the army. Armand was hobbled in his legal dealings by his emigrant status, not lifted until early-1808. Also, Sade's profligacy had left a mighty mound of documents which, for all the precise and legalistic Montreuils having done their best to keep track over the decades of great upheaval in France, required much study and ordering to the purpose in hand.

It was clear as could be, though, that Renée Pélagie, obese and failing at Échauffour, where she had begun nearly a half-century earlier to learn what sort of man she had married, was in possession of the first claims, stemming from rights first established in her marriage contract of 1763. Through those, an astute reading of the documents and a deft fingering of an abacus would establish, she was owed, by about 1808, some 546,000 francs in arrears of principal and interest on her dowry payments, husband and wife having separated. These rights - with the attendant sums which were growing incessantly - passed to Armand at her death in July 1810, she having outlived her elder son by 13 months.

Sade, anxious lest the initiative by Mme Rovère to sell la Coste lead to his being stripped of the properties he had acquired with the money he received from his sale of la Coste, moved to sell other properties of his which he reckoned not to be subject to legal proceedings, no doubt trying to go liquid and invest the cash elsewhere before these lands and buildings could also be placed *sub judice* and thus beyond his control. In this, as was his custom in these matters, he saw scope to pocket undeclared payments which his estranged wife or his children might not discover and so fail to seize from him in order to reduce his debts to her or to them. So Sade tried to sell his lands at Mazan to his long-standing tenant there, François Ripert, he who had taken in the damaged young maid fled from la Coste to Saumane in 1775. The old farmer, by 1808, had a son making a name for himself in Bonaparte's armies and was interested in acquiring an estate for him. Sade entrusted Ripert with the task of selling the remaining lands at Arles, a fifth of the proceeds to go to Sade on the quiet. The landlord's asking price for Arles of 130,000 francs was proving too steep but a deal was done with Ripert over Mazan, with 52,000 to the vendor declared in the notarised contract, plus 12,000 on the side.

The sale was dated 28 August 1810. By then, Louis Marie and his mother having died, Armand had inherited her rights, mortgages and properties; he had been restored to full French citizenship and was about to be allied by marriage to the de Sade d'Eyguières. He went into action. He exercised his legal right as the mortgage holder to intervene in the sale of a property which served as his guarantee, provided he was prepared to pay the difference between the sum outstanding on the mortgage and the price he proposed in out-bidding any would-be purchaser. In a case where the sum owed was in excess of the sale price, as was clearly so here, the mortgage holder had only to file a legal notice of his willingness to outbid the would-be purchaser. So, regarding the Sade property at Mazan, where a six-figure sum was due under the mortgages while Ripert was prepared to buy for only 52,000 francs, so the contract said, Armand filed his intervention documents and snapped up the property for no more than his legal costs.

In February that year, Sade had found his son's activities so irksome that he was raging at Armand over the latter's "infernal stubbornness, or better perhaps your determination against me to be vexatious, which you[1] have inherited from [the] execrable Montreuils - may you be one day torn apart, racked, by your children as you are mutilating me."

Sade brought down the asking price for the properties at Arles to 70,000 francs and sought much less for himself in secret payment - to no avail. Armand was able to take advantage of his position as his mother's heir - his sister Madeleine Laure, who never married, did no more than sign what she was told to sign - to acquire by November 1811 all his father's remaining properties, except that at Saumane for Sade had not sought a sale of the rest of the estate closest to his heart. The tenants there were every bit as slow and irregular about sending money to the landlord as Gaufridy had been before 1800.

On 16 January 1811, Sade had been removed at last from the list of emigrants on which he should never have been enrolled. By then, however, this was of no advantage to him for he had little scope to conduct business, his properties having mainly passed into the hands of his surviving son and that property he still held remaining under a cloud of mortgages.

1 The formal *vous*.

"My son Armand," Sade fumed to Ripert in September 1810, "is ferociously astute, litigious and irksome." However, the following June, to the same correspondent, Sade was writing that it was to preserve and ensure revenues for his father that Armand had intervened as he did - but it may well be that Sade had recalled, when taking up his pen that time, that Coulmier was apt to intercept and read all his letters, and that the old inmate had a strong interest in the director of the asylum, who was still owed a considerable sum in respect of Sade's arrears of fees at Charenton, continuing to believe there were funds to meet this debt and future charges.

Pending a definitive settlement, Armand agreed to let his father have an allowance of 150 francs a quarter over and above the cost of his lodging, firewood and lighting at the asylum. Also, Marie Constance found a paying job in or near the asylum, from sometime in 1812. There was an assurance from the Sade relatives that she would continue to receive 1,600 francs a year from the properties in respect of her money which she had turned over to Sade in 1790 soon after they met, on the strength of his promise of an income thereby. Marie Constance also held small mortgages on Sade properties arising from loans. Hence, she was able to maintain payments for her lodging at Charenton.

Even so, she and her companion were living with little cheer. Sade himself, over his properties as over his dreams, was a beaten man. "I am very much afraid," writes Pauvert towards the end of his book, "that this being whom nothing could reduce may have ended by finding himself in 1811, in many ways, *reduced*. I search in vain, through the three years which are going to bring his life to a close, for the dimension which he always used to show, by some facet or other, in the meanest of circumstances, for the fire which always ended up by erupting from one crack or other on the flanks of the volcano. I find neither the one nor the other ... in what is known of what he wrote then."

Indeed, many reverses, much frustration and old age had worn him down. He even - albeit only in confidence to his diary and on the late date of 17 November 1814 - admitted he had been in error. A note of a "discussion" with Marie Constance ends: "but it's I who was wrong."

As the arrears in his payment of fees at Charenton rose, Coulmier reduced his charges to Sade, which meant that the old man was allowed a lesser standard of service.

The Interior Ministry forbade plays and opera at Charenton from July 1811 and, though a few shows may have been given there after that date, Sade, writing bitterly in May that year, referred to the shows at the asylum as a thing of the past. The implication from his letter is that the ministry's prohibition arose from a mistaken belief that the theatre at the asylum was, as Sade put it, "a centre of horrors". Dances and concerts there were banned on 6 May 1813.

* * *

On 9 and 10 July 1811, Emperor Napoléon had resolved the debate over Sade's future by ruling that he was to remain at Charenton. This may have been in tandem with the ministerial decision to stop the shows - if Sade was to stay at the asylum, at least the activity where his influence was greatest would be extinguished. The imperial order was confirmed at the same level on 19 April and 3 May the next year. Various officials, whose names Sade did not always catch, visited him in the period 1811-13 to question him about his activities.

Napoléon, overwhelmed by a succession of defeats in battle against other European powers, after his main army had struggled back from Moscow through the Russian winter of 1812-13, abdicated on 11 April 1814. On 3 May, King Louis XVIII, brother of the Louis XVI who had gone to the guillotine 21 years before, entered Paris on his return from exile to occupy the throne of France. Coulmier, an appointee of the Revolutionary Directory who had been kept in office under Napoléon, was dismissed. He was succeeded as director at Charenton, on 31 May, by one Roulhac du Maupas, whose name had been recommended to the new royal Interior Ministry by Dr Royer-Collard, who had pressed in 1808 for Sade, the bad influence, to be sent away to jail.

With the return of the Bourbon royal house, and of many other aristocrats who had emigrated during the Revolution and the rule of Napoléon, noble titles of the old régime were restored. Our man was the Marquis de Sade again (Count de Sade, to be precise), not that he showed any interest in this.

He still regarded himself as a man of letters and pursued this calling at Charenton. His abiding interest in lasciviousness, although flagging somewhat, did not desert him in his last years but his scope for expressing this interest through literature was restricted by the continuing suspicion of him among the authorities. One of the manuscripts seized in the raid on his publisher's office in 1801 may have been that of a big novel for the armchair libertine market, *The Conversations at Charmelle Castle* (*Les Conversations du Château de Charmelle*), which has never reappeared since then - or so it seems, for this might have been, under an earlier name, in large part the work which Sade completed on 25 April 1807, *The Days of Florbelle or Nature Unveiled* (*Les Journées de Florbelle ou la Nature Dévoilée*). His notes for its composition show elements of earlier works, including *Philosophy in the Boudoir*, being included and developed in it. It had taken him "thirteen months and twenty days!" he exclaimed in his journal, and he had begun to write out the fair copy on 5 March 1806.

It is not clear whether Sade originated at Charenton any or all of what seems to have been a large work. His journal refers only to the writing of the fair copy and there are indications that *Florbelle* may well have been started in 1799 or even earlier, though after the Terror. The notes reveal the author reminding himself of greater and lesser amendments required to the text as the fair copy was under way, none of them fundamental, it seems.

The exact nature of *Florbelle* remains elusive because the fair copy stayed in its author's keeping for no more than six weeks. On 5 June 1807, three police officers, at least one a specialist in hunting down forbidden literature, arrived at Charenton and read to Sade an official order to seize all his papers. This had arisen from Fouché, still the police minister then, having ordered his men to find out whether Sade "was composing a licentious work in which persons in authority were treated with a criminal lewdness, and even whether there were a question of events linked to foreign politics."

The police took away all the papers they could find, for examination at their leisure, and the item which most exercised their attention - found not in Sade's quarters but in those of Marie Constance - was *Florbelle*, "a manuscript in ten volumes... This work is a revolting read. It seems that De Sade wanted to go beyond the horrors of *Justine* and of *Juliette*... It is impossible to read all at once these ... volumes of atrocities, of blasphemies, of wickedness. Throughout it all, there presides, amid the obscenity and the most sophisticated debauchery, a well-devised extravagance, a considered frenzy of which fortunately few men would be capable," said the report to Fouché. Nothing remains of the manuscript found in Mme Quesnet's rooms - we do not know whether she had been aware of its presence - and the only surviving pointer to its nature is 17 pages of Sade's notes for the work, with their promise of "eight dialogues, thirteen day-long episodes, a treatise on morals, one on religion, one on the soul, and one on God, one on the art of enjoyment, a plan for thirty-two brothels of men and of women for Paris, a treatise on antiphysics, and two novels..."

Also, besides the "manuscripts of plays, correspondence, scraps of libertine and sacrilegious writing, family documents, and above all handwritten diaries where he records minutely each day what he does and what is said to him about his domestic matters ...," there was found, "among the letters he has received since he has been at Charenton, ... some all in the same writing which show that he has disciples as vile as their master. They tell him of scenes of libertinage recently taken place where they boast of having used potions to induce a death-like state for several hours in women whom they have enjoyed in every way while torturing them, while having them shed three enormous bottles of blood." The district administrator, apparently taking these letters at face value, drew on a worn resort of the baffled police officer throughout the ages: "I hope to come to discover the author of this correspondence and of these crimes. I have reason to believe that he will not be able to escape the enquiries which I have set in train..." Whether the official did or not, there the trail goes cold for posterity.

The "scraps of libertine and sacrilegious writings", however, yielded "one where the author gives an account of the first bout of libertinage he undertook, he says, before embarking on the career in which he made such rapid progress. He tells that, after being sodomised from five until eight o'clock in the morning, always guided by the principle that makes him choose to mix impiety and libertinage, he went to confession and to take communion, thus leaving the rest of the day free for all the most frightful behaviour that debauchery has to offer. So one can see what was behind this very man, while he was working on these obscene and sacrilegious works, proffering the consecrated bread, at Easter in his parish church, and taking the collection, sword on his hip..." **(see chapter 28).**

The official had reserved a little extra outrage for his vision of Sade not only assisting at the Mass while vileness was brewing in his head, but also allowed out wearing the sword that marked him out as a gentleman, hence with the implication that he was no kind of detainee.

The authorities saw to it that Sade was put under a tighter regime at Charenton, but he was not transferred to a jail. After all, the examination of his papers had revealed nothing of the original object of the exercise - a search for lewd references to authorities of the day and links to events abroad, where France was still in conflict with many enemies. However, *Florbelle* was not returned to Sade and his consort. "My poor daughter[2] had been very much affected by this blow[3], and that caused me even more distress because I have no dearer friend in the world," Sade wrote in his diary.

While at Charenton, Sade may have written an anti-religious tract, *Refutation of Fénelon* (*Réfutation de Fénelon*), a rebuttal of a certain Christian theologian's thinking. Whether or not this was completed, it has not survived. However, a few sentences from Sade's notes for it, where he was haranguing yet again the God in which he still did not believe, may well offer the flavour of the piece: "Abominable abortion, here I ought to have left you to yourself, turned you over to the contempt which you[4] alone inspire, and to have ceased to combat you again through the dreams of Fénelon. But I have sworn to complete the job; I shall keep my word, happy if my efforts come to uproot you from the heart of your idiot devotees and, putting a little reason in place of your lies, can manage to shake your altars in order to plunge them back forever into the chasms of the void..."

Among the outlines of other novels, among yet more tinkering with revisions of his existing plays in yet more efforts to have them accepted by theatres, where Marie Constance was still delivering his scripts in 1814, his notes grumble about "boorish moralisers who would like to crush the strength that the writer gets from nature." He wrote at another point: "The fathers of the Church did not hesitate to paint vice in the brightest colours."

In his main works from Charenton that avoided confiscation, and have survived into modern times, Sade wrote cautiously. *Adélaïde of Brunswick* (*Adélaïde de Brunswick*), written in 1812, *The Marquise de Gange* (*La Marquise de Gange*), probably completed in 1812, and *Secret History of Isabelle of Bavaria* (*Histoire secrète d'Isabelle de Bavière*), completed in 1813, are based on various periods in French history. These three late novels - of which only *Gange* was published in his lifetime, anonymously in 1813 - deal with sanguinary conspiracies and revenges among the French nobility, all drawing on grimmer strains

---

2 Marie Constance's formal, false status at Charenton.

3 The search, after which she was ill for weeks.

4 *Tu* throughout this outburst.

of the erotic but all showing clear signs of the author's intention to satisfy the emperor's censorious police. *Adélaïde* contains an account of life in a monastery which the Vatican might accept, and a bandit with the heroine in his power does not proceed to the rape that seems imminent - quite unlike Sade's way with cloisters and helpless females in *Justine*. The eponymous protagonist of *Isabelle* undertakes crimes and conspiracies galore, but all within contemporary acceptability, Sade having tried in the preamble to the novel to wrap it in a cloak of historical accuracy by claiming that he had discovered documents about Queen Isabelle, who flourished about the end of the 14th century.

Sade was still trying to find a publisher for *Adélaïde* and *Isabelle* when, on 7 September 1814, Roulhac du Maupas, the new director of the asylum at Charenton, advised the new minister of the interior that the old reprobate would have to be moved from there because he could not be properly supervised. The ministry still had this under consideration on 5 November, the date of Sade's polite, written request of the director that the man who ran the local lottery office "may come, to rest the eyes of Madame Quesnet and myself by reading the newspaper [aloud to us]... I am far from the wish to infringe any rule. But this good man from the lottery office has done for me several copies of dramatic works accepted at various theatres and all passed by the police; I ask earnestly that he be allowed to carry on, for he and I will lose a lot by this interruption..."

Sade's handwriting at about this time was showing signs of his eyesight failing. This had troubled him on and off since he was locked up with the smoky flue in the dank Cell No. 6 at Vincennes. To judge by the request for a newspaper reader for them both, Marie Constance may also have been suffering with her eyes, albeit she was probably no more than about 55 years old in 1814. However, Sade may have calculated that the director would be more apt to allow the request if it were not on behalf of himself alone.

* * *

In his last months, Marie Constance was not his only female solace. There were visits by Mme de Talaru, but there was also a last-act *ingénue*. Magdeleine Leclerc was most likely the daughter of a woman employed at the asylum and was barely 16 years old on the date, near the end of 1812, when, it seems, she first visited Sade in his rooms. He kept track of her frequent visits in his diary but his figuring was not as reliable as it had been 30 years earlier at Vincennes when drawing up an account of his masturbatory episodes, so it is not easy to calculate from his numbered record of his encounters with her, which distinguishes carefully those that had taken place in a room, quite when the first of these occurred. No doubt, though, Magdeleine was "really young", younger than any of the prostitutes assembled by Latour at Marseilles in 1772. One of Sade's last diary entries remarks that she was to celebrate her 18th birthday on 19 December 1814 so, when he had made his marginal note in his journal that she had caught his eye for the first time, on 9 January 1808, she was three weeks past her 11th birthday.

This liaison across a wide generation gap may well have arisen from lessons in reading and writing which the old man of letters was giving the girl - a classic development - but it is clear that Mme Leclerc, Magdeleine's mother, was far from opposed to it, although there might have been a misunderstanding now and again. On 17 August 1814, according to Sade's diary, the mother "came at my behest. She demolished quite straightforwardly all that I had believed and written about her heretofore; she seemed still to have made up her mind to leave her daughter to me with no more conditions than those I had myself set..." On 26 August, Mme Leclerc came to warn Sade that someone had spotted the girl go into his rooms and shut the door - "but she didn't seem to me put out and promised to let me know if anything came of this."

Then, on 26 October, "the mother ... arrived at one o'clock and promised, with every appearance of honesty, ... that nothing would change our plans; she asked how I would do it; I explained to her..." There seems to have been a project for Magdeleine to live with Sade, once he had been let out of the asylum. Marie Constance, it appears, was no obstacle to this, in that she had long understood her platonic place in his life. Sade noted, on 19 August as his long-serving companion was about to leave for a few days in Paris: "Before leaving, and regarding M[a]g[de]l[eine], [she] speaks to me like an angel; she appeared to want to avoid being a great nuisance..."

Mme Leclerc, though, was insisting there be no formal arrangement before the old man had been released. It is not clear why, but she might have had an inkling that, while Sade was a detainee, his scope to control what remained of his wealth was circumscribed by his relatives and by the arrears on his fees to the asylum's management.

As of early September 1814, the arrears amounted to 8,934 francs, with little prospect of early settlement. Armand de Sade was arguing that he had by no means covered, through sales of his father's property, all that his father owed him as inheritor of the old man's debts to the late marquise, still outstanding at her demise. So, the surviving son maintained, he could not be held liable for debts incurred by his father in respect of a detainment which had been arranged *after* his parents' marriage contract, fount of his father's debts to himself. Even if all that were resolved, Armand was prepared to insist that the rates which had been set for his father's keep at Charenton were too high.

Whatever that stumbling block might have done to the plans of Leclerc, *mère et fille*, it was blocking the moves between Roulhac du Maupas and the interior ministry to transfer Sade from Charenton to somewhere more restrictive. For one thing, it would probably be even harder to impress on the connections of the infamous inmate, once he had left Charenton, that his bill there ought to be met; for another, it was likely to be cheaper to maintain him at Charenton, in an established asylum where he was one of many inmates supervised by staff who were no more numerous for his presence, than in a fortress where, as at Vincennes and the Bastille before the Revolution, few were watched by many, in a costly establishment. Besides, the new royal administration, successor to the defeated empire, had much more on its mind than one septuagenarian inmate of an asylum.

Sade himself, for that matter, was at least as much concerned with present pleasures derived from Magdeleine Leclerc as with a future ménage beyond the ample grounds of the asylum. What exactly did the wheezy, obese gentleman - who had claimed to have "thought of all that can be thought of in that line", even if he had not done it all - achieve by way of carnality with the girl some sixty years his junior? Sade, as he had been abruptly reminded by the police search of 1807, was apt to have all his papers scrutinised by the authorities without notice, and he was far from the resilience he had shown in the royal fortresses before 1789, so his diary jottings were more cautious than his letters from Vincennes had been. It seems certain that some sexual activity was meant by the symbol Ø in his diary. For instance, on 21 July 1814, Magdeleine was *chez* Sade, who reported: "I had arranged that Annette would bring the newspaper, having knocked once [on the door]; she came, and Mgl was quite overcome... She scarcely pulled herself together at all and in general was cold during all the Ø..."

Six weeks later, "it was easy to see that she had been ill... She had cut the p. of her c. ..." (In the original, *p. de son c.*; my abbreviations stand for "pubes of her cunt".)

Even when, as on 6 November, the girl "was very well, even showed some wit, [she] made me realise that, despite the obedience she had sworn to me, there were two things she would not carry out, and I saw that, as far as all that goes, she would only do what she wanted. She continues to be inactive and even cold during the session..."

Lessons in literacy were not neglected. On 9 October, "I was giving her a little lesson in writing and reading. She promised me to occupy herself with that during the long evenings." At this informal Collège Louis le Gros, the lone pupil's reading primer might not have been an orthodox one. On 17 September, she was "very amiable, and never was I better pleased with her; she brought *Le Portier des C[hartreux]*"[5], a book of erotic tales, not by Sade. Magdeleine gladdened her teacher by being "very attentive, ardent, etc."

Mlle Leclerc would mix pleasure of the moment with promise for the future. "She stayed two hours," on 30 October. "She was very amiable, promised to take wonderful care of me when we shall be together. She drank, wrote and sang ... she seemed wonderfully well, she brought me a pair of stockings" - for the fattest leg at Charenton.

A week earlier, Sade had recorded the girl as having been "still cold", and having explained that the ambience of the asylum was the trouble, that she "would be quite different outside." Still, Magdeleine had her period that day and there was no more than "a momentary thought of Ø".

On 20 November, her visit to Sade again coincided with her period - regular girl - but this time she was "very agreeable in conversation and carefree about the pleasures." She "talks about becoming a governess, says she wouldn't want to eat in the kitchen or with the cook..." - a budding snob below stairs, as her tutor had been over the almanachs of the nobility. "She had not worked on her writing at all, which annoyed me, but wasn't reading badly..."

No Sadeian erotic relationship would reach full flower without a sprig of jealousy and suspicion - so it was with his last one. In August 1814, a few days before Mme Leclerc visited him reassuringly, Sade was musing into his diary: "This unselfishness that Mgl affects shows

5 The title would translate as *The Gateman to the Carthusians* (an order of monks).

itself when she looks as though she's saying: *Oh, my god, don't go to so much expense for me, sir, for you'll never have me*; add to that the certainty ... that she comes to see you only as a *sign*[6] and you'll have proof positive that you are only the dupe in all this.

"As for her indulgences, this is what she has been told: consent to everything in order to gain his confidence, without that he wouldn't want to see you any more and our plan's a failure; in a word, they have made this girl into one of those spies that are put close to convicts to try to learn their secrets. Observe her coldness carefully, her lack of concern in pleasure and in conversation, and you'll see there constant evidence of what I'm suggesting, and it's since these visits[7] that she is acting in this way because, when she was a child, there was more truthfulness and openness in her."

So, like his wife 30 years earlier when Sade was imprisoned with his anger, Magdeleine Leclerc was seen not as a free agent but as an instrument of a mistrusted "them". Also, again evoking a recollection of the marquise and letters passing through the walls of Vincennes, there was a Lefebvre to get het up about, albeit in a spelling different to the name of Sade's erstwhile servant. On 21 July, Sade noted in his journal: "She says she knows Lefebvre by sight but not to speak to, and she assured me that she won't speak to him..."

Magdeleine was required to promise to have nothing to do with this man (of whom we have no other trace), to refrain from taking baths and to stay away from dances in the locality. Her mother was urged to support Sade in these strictures. This effort at control beyond the confines of the asylum and of his decrepitude was rather less effective, it seems, than his more spirited efforts in 1781 to circumscribe his wife's social life beyond fortress walls and his penned-in vigour. On 29 September, he was recording: "According to the reports made to me, it seemed altogether true that Mgl had been to all the balls and danced a great deal there" - bathed or not, we do not know.

The girl made amends on 23 October, when "she promised me clearly to stay faithful and very much attached to me, and that I could be sure of her." On 20 November, Sade's young visitor told him of two forthcoming dances in the Charenton area, which she would not attend "because she knew that would please me. I thanked her for that."

---

6 A sign of some pattern that applied to him, as with his numbers obsession at Vincennes.
7 To Sade.

Also on that date, as on many other of her visits, Magdeleine asked Sade for some chocolate. However, she did not gorge herself on it, remarking at one point that "she didn't want now to eat fine fare that later she would be without." She did not have the best of health, to judge by the number of times Sade described her as unwell or looking as though she had been ill, and she described herself, to Sade, as badly nourished. When the old man gave her three francs - the most cash she received from him for any one session - he was giving her the cost of her food for a whole week. Sometimes, Sade only handed over one franc to Magdeleine, as on 6 November, when "she made do with that and said some tactful things on the subject."

During the happy session of a week earlier, 30 October, when she had drunk, written and sang, and brought him a pair of stockings, "she said that she was going to be better fed and that she was very pleased with her mother, that at night she was taking eau de Cologne and sugar for her stomach and that this was doing her good..."

Sade's stomach, which was paining him increasingly, was in need of more than eau de Cologne and sugar. His best supporter among his relatives, Mme de Talaru, visited him on 21 November and "sympathised readily with what I was suffering and said in a very pleasant way that, if there was no fine wine being laid on for me, she would see to it herself, that the family was quite decided to bear the extra expense of this treatment..." Mme de Talaru persuaded the director to make some fine wine available to the old gourmet, but in the event there was less of it than he wanted.

Next Sunday, 27 November, Magdeleine "seemed very sensitive about my pains which I described to her. She had not been to any dances and promised not to go to any; she talked of the future, said that she would be 18 years old on the 19th of next month, went along with our little games as usual, promised to come back next Sunday or Monday, thanked me for what I was doing for her and made clear that she was not deceiving [me] nor wanted to deceive [me]... Mgl stayed for two hours and I was very pleased with that.

"Mgl. During her visit, all the libertinage of Rousseau's dances."

Whatever that recollection of a last arousing piece of education for his young pupil referred to exactly, Sade did not see her on the next Sunday or Monday, nor did she take a glass of his fine wine on her birthday.

By the day of their last session, Sade had long been an unkempt, aloof old party to most who encountered him. On 11 November, L.J. Ramon, a medical student, was attached to the asylum's staff. Many years later, he recalled his department's most famous patient: "I knew M. de Sade only because he had been pointed out to me. I often came across him walking alone, with a heavy and dragging step, dressed in a very careless way, in the corridor by the apartment where he lived; I never caught him chatting with anyone. Passing by him, I used to greet him and he would reply to my greeting with that cold politeness which banishes any idea of starting a conversation... Nothing could have made me suspect in him the author of *Justine* and *Juliette*; he impressed me as no more than a haughty and morose old gentleman..."

One of Sade's last letters, written in October 1814, concerned the 800 francs due to him from the sale of the timber when a coppice was felled on his remaining land at Saumane, where his uncle, the Abbé de Sade, had begun his education, formal and licentious, 70 years before. This sort of sum, which would have bought Magdeleine Leclerc's food for a year five times over, was useful mainly in paying the wages of his servant and Marie Constance's maid, as well as in helping to meet the costs of entertaining guests, Mlle Leclerc included.

His legs gave up supporting his obese trunk on 1 December 1814. He was moved from his gloomy, shabby, bookish rooms - where hung a portrait of Gaspard François de Sade, his grandfather, and stood miniatures of his mother, his dead son Louis Marie and his late sister-in-law Anne Prospère de Launay - to a different apartment with a servant to take care of him. It is not clear whether Marie Constance was on hand. Armand de Sade visited in the afternoon of the next day, 2 December, and asked Ramon to watch over his father through the night. The young man gave Sade some herbal tea and some prescribed medicine from time to time. He listened to Sade's noisy and laboured breathing becoming even more of a struggle then, towards midnight, the noise stopped. Ramon went to the bedside and found that the Marquis de Sade, just halfway into his 75th year, had died in his sleep.

SECTION C

CHAPTER 30: THE PICNIC OF FREE PLAY

"And now, dear reader, you are to open your heart and mind to the filthiest story told since the world began, a book unlike any found in Ancient or in Modern times. Imagine, now, that every pleasuring indicated by polite society or laid down by that Will-o'-the-wisp you talk about all the time but of which you know nothing while you call it nature - imagine, I say, that all those ways of pleasuring are to be explicitly left out of this anthology or that, wherever you might find them here, they will always occur along with a crime or tainted by some outrage.

"You will not like many of the extravagances about to be displayed for you, no doubt, and we know that all too well, but among them are a few that will stoke you up so much as to bring forth some spunk, and we ask no more of you, dear reader; if we have not shown everything, detailed everything, do not complain that we have been prejudiced because you cannot expect us to have figured out what you fancy. It's up to you to pick out what you like and ignore the rest; other readers will do likewise and, one by one, each of you will fulfil his want. It is like the story of a sumptuous banquet: six hundred different dishes set before your palate ...

"The diversity is genuine, that is guaranteed; examine carefully that passion which, at first sight, seems to be just like another, then you will notice that it is different, although but marginally so, and that it has the sort of refinement, the extra nuance, which differentiates and characterises the quality of libertinage that concerns us here."

Sade at work - intent to excite the libertine and debauch the susceptible; delighted, meanwhile, by the incidental prospect of scaring the timorous and shocking the prudish. As one of his voluptuaries of *Philosophy in the Boudoir* put it: "One must embellish these words with the most sumptuous of expressions; they must scandalise to the greatest extent possible, for it's very pleasant to scandalise: in that, there's a little victory for pride which is not at all to be sneezed at ..." Sade feeling on top and making things happen - in his element.

Even those who know little of him and have read none of his works might expect to find him thus - how could the arch-sadist, so perceived, be anything else? Yet a pall of fear and fascination has long obscured him, since before his name was taken into modern languages to signify an ill-understood urge to hurt in lust. I shall try to blow away that pall, to dispel both fear and fascination. In showing, as I hope to, that the trouble that dwelt in Sade lives in many of us, I shall try to avoid adding to the pessimism that can arise from contemplation of him and his like. The upshot is intended to be a better understanding of this trouble and of how to cope with it, how to prevent its formation and growth among us.

First, of course, know your beast, and his background.

The paragraphs quoted at the start of this section are from *The Hundred and Twenty Days of Sodom or The School of Libertinage* - if not "the filthiest story told since the world began" then quite sufficient until the filthiest comes along.[1] It is set in a remote castle of central Europe, cut off from the world by steep terrain and deep winter, where four libertine men of middle age and great wealth have assembled, by kidnap and hire, 36 people to delight them sexually for four months. The cellar and kitchen are sumptuously stocked and tended by six maids and cooks. Four *doyennes* of service to libertine men, steeped in prostitution and procuring, have the task of telling each day stories of various sexual encounters, so as to excite the four overlords to more exquisite exploitation of their prey - young and lithe, old and decrepit. The stories become more and more cruel, the depredations of the four masters become more and more bloody among the 36 as fire, knives, racks, pincers, ropes and more are told of and employed. Most of the staff pass through progressive dismemberment to slow deaths, beyond most imagining (one hopes).

On the first of March, at the end of the fourth month, the snows not having melted so as to allow travel from the castle, the four libertines step up their rate of massacre, having given a green ribbon to each of

---

1 Edmund Wilson, the US writer and critic, reported that, accustomed though he was to read at breakfast, he had to put *The Hundred and Twenty Days of Sodom* aside while he ate.

those who are to be spared on condition that they assist the four in the last of the mayhem. By the twenty-first of March, only 12 of the original 42 (sexual slaves plus kitchen help) have survived to return to France with the four men of wealth.

According to Sade and other writers of the 18th century, God was dead - but for this? To clear the way for *The Hundred and Twenty Days of Sodom*? Well, yes, for the pursuit of happiness is to take place in liberty and so may adopt any shape, however vile; yet no, the old world of imposed morality and hierarchy not having been challenged so as to facilitate orgy by force - for, in addition to liberty and the pursuit of happiness, the upheaval of the 18th century was also in the name of life. Here is a basic question: If your pursuit of happiness means danger to other people, should your liberty to pursue happiness be curbed by the rest of us?

* * *

By 1740, when Sade was born, the main disturbing ideas which gave rise to the movement known as the Enlightenment had erupted. Christian Europe in the Middle Ages was told from the pulpit that the Earth was the centre of God's universe, and believed it. To do otherwise was heresy, and heresy was dangerous, not least to those who uttered it. Then Copernicus, Galileo and other astronomers and mathematicians put this view of the significance of our planet into doubt by suggesting that the Earth was merely a satellite of the sun, which was merely one of millions of stars. So, although the Catholic Church in the mid-18th century was still reluctant to accept formally this line of thought, many informed people had come to accept it. From that, it followed that humanity was no more than a gathering of creatures on one of that multitude of objects.

Meanwhile, scientific inquiry in other areas was discovering similarities in the respective physical characteristics of humans and animals. Also, this line of inquiry had begun to point to phenomena in the human body as the cause of human behaviour, of mental illness, of good and bad temper, of benevolence and malevolence. The existence of a nervous system was becoming accepted and its actions were being investigated.

Sade, an inquiring reader, was aware of much contemporary scientific research.[2] In his prison notes, he referred polemically to "the feelings [of the body] being nothing but the different conditions or accidents of matter. Without the hand, without the sensation of touch, then none of the ideas acquired by that means; without the eye, without the sensation of sight ..." Pushing this line of thinking further, when writing to Marie Dorothée de Rousset, Sade asked rhetorically where lies the root of sexual crime if the one who commits it acts only at the prompting of "too much swelling in little vessels that suddenly transform a mind and turn the most honest of men into a villain."

This sort of thinking about the human organism tended to promote the view that men and women were no more than another species of animal, not special creatures with immortal souls, and that their actions were not willed by any god. The force that moved them - their conception, states of health and eventual death - was nature, which also directed the appetites of animals, the flow of waters, the strength of winds, the growth of plants, all that is. So it came to be thought. In this new light, the miracles and mysteries of Mother Church might be seen to shrivel into the discredited mumbo-jumbo of an ignorant past.

This sceptical attitude to God - if not a mere figment of superstition then no more than a Creator long since retired from directing the universe - remained a minority view and a cautiously expressed one in Sade's young days. Overt atheism was a crime throughout most of Christian Europe, punished not only by governments, especially where monarchs were Catholic, but also by the Inquisition of the Church, which was still zealous in hunting heretics and unbelievers. Diderot wrote of the need to keep a public mask, behind which one could continue to think one's own thoughts. Montaigne stated: "Truth must be upheld as far as the fire, but no further." Some holders of this minority view, however, were well-placed and influential. (Meanwhile, many beyond those who could read complicated, abstract texts - and had the leisure to discuss them - were able to pick up no more than an inkling of what was gnawing at the structures of the old scheme of things.)

---

2 While detained in royal fortresses, Sade would have been aware of scientific experiments with lightning conductors for prisons were used to mount such instruments, sometimes with upsetting results for parts of the structure. He may well have approved of the godly function of directing lightning bolts having been usurped by modern man.

Thinking along these sceptical lines led to questions such as: If all was moved or stilled by nature, which anyone might understand by observation and experiment, what value remained in the traditional belief that priests, hereditary monarchs and nobles were placed by God as rulers over the rest? If we are all animals, creatures of nature, should the cleverest of us not advance furthest in society, regardless of who our fathers were and of who heard our confessions - if any?

The undermining of traditional morality and hierarchical religion carries danger of there being no adequate successor to instruct and comfort humanity. Having erased God and the saints, to whom one might have prayed in adversity with hope of their aid, what trust can one put in nature and humanity, the uncertain quantities newly in the ascendant? Well, nature would remain a destructive force - of fire, flood, epidemic, earthquake and much besides - but not only could it yield its secrets to observation and experiment, it could also be harnessed and made more fruitful as scientific discoveries were applied to the environment. Likewise, humanity was full of violence and corruption, but could be improved by reason, by persuasive argument and good example, so as to enhance what was believed to be our natural inclination to benevolence, rather than to malevolence. Optimism was abroad.

So was aspiration to unbridled freedom, which is by no means always amenable to reason. Thinkers of the Enlightenment were bent on overcoming traditional ways which, though supports to many, were seen by the reformers as a straitjacket on everyone. Diderot wrote against "a morality contrary to Nature", imposed on the natural, uncivilised human in order to turn him or her into an "artificial" being. This imposition created and maintained a civil war within each individual as natural instincts came into conflict with rules laid down by others. "Mistrust anyone who comes to lay down order; to order is always to put oneself in command of others by restricting them." Diderot compared uncivilised people, unhampered by civil war in the head, to "a multitude of scattered and separate springs. No doubt some of these springs would collide from time to time; some of them would destroy each other. To prevent this nuisance, some individual of deep wisdom and sublime genius collected these springs and made a machine of them, and in this machine known as society they were made to act and react on each other, wearing themselves out unceasingly; so more were broken in one day under a state of law than would break each other in a year under the anarchy of Nature."

Released from regulation imposed by priests and judges, no longer intimidated by the prospects of hellfire and prison, humanity would blossom, realise its full potential, to the joy of all. This is a root of the liberal tree. Let everyone play freely; let there be nothing that cannot be said or done. It is up to the free players to cope with anything and everything, the argument goes. We would all be the better for this release - more diverse, more vivacious, more inquisitive; embracers of surprise, ready for change.

This potential would be for what exactly? Whatever humanity, individually and collectively, made of itself and its surroundings, always able to revise itself and the world as often as might be felt necessary or fun or worth trying - everything up for revision, apt to go into a melting pot. Does this seem too vague, too bewildering, too frightening? If so, that would be because we are wedded to the paths, the structures, that we know and find comforting. The core idea is to embrace the freedom to conceive of any change and seek to bring it about, via whatever co-operative effort is needed. The effort can entail a great deal of persuasion of other people, as in a movement for social or political change. Remembering that whatever takes place is to do so in liberty, then persuasion must not be abandoned in favour of force in order to achieve change.

Gently does it - for this would-be insurrection of ideas has to take place in the world as a whole, not just on the page or in conversation. However little caution you take over your own skin or reputation, as you break rules, remember to leave free the others with whom you would revolt, criticise dogma, frolic in the woods or whatever. Leave open the option of retreat back to the familiar, back to the foregoing rules. If liberty to pursue happiness turns out, for some people, to mean a return to hierarchical ways, the embrace of Mother Church, of king and country, so be it, while reasoned persuasion towards the other direction may yet continue. After all, liberty means the right to say "yes" to anything - and to say "no" to anything. Diderot kept this clearly in view: "Above all, be scrupulously honest and sincere with the destructible beings who cannot make us happy without their giving up the most valuable benefits of the world as it is."

This consideration for those who would like to face tomorrow - even in the all too probable case that they and the world have not been much altered by then, try as one might - is especially important when one is trying to load the furnace of argument and example with the shape and form of sexual relations, and to melt them down, ready for whatever new moulds people might want. Easier access to sexual pleasure - "the delightful rubbing together of two intestines," as Diderot put it - was large among the concerns of the Enlightenment (although you might have trouble deducing this from some of the books about it).

"Don't you see," argued Diderot against the notion of one's sexual partner being one's property (and so easier to have for one's pleasure), "that you have mixed up ... the thing which has neither sensibility, nor thought, nor desire, nor will of its own, which one leaves, takes, keeps, trades, without its feeling hurt or complaining - mixed up that with the thing which is not traded, which is not bought, which has freedom, will of its own, desire, which can give itself or hold itself back for a moment, give itself or hold itself back forever, which has grievances and which suffers, and which cannot be turned into something to be bought and sold unless its character is forgotten and violence is done to Nature?"

When sexual heat is in the air, loss of patience and resort to coercion are often close. The ideals of the Enlightenment have it that the protean embracers of freedom ought to choose unhindered among all the notions and bodies there are, engaging in debates and pleasures with any *willing* fellow-beings. One's smile may fade when one meets a refusal to join in - *m'sieur* would rather work alone in his laboratory than write poems with us in the meadow, the old sulk; *mamselle* would rather go on reading under the trees than copulate with us in the brook, the blue-stocking - but one may *not* drag them to the party, may *not* deny their right to stay aloof. Ask them again later, still politely and cheerfully.

What, though, if someone were moving among the happy, experimenting throng at the Enlightenment picnic with exploitation, not fair exchange of arguments and caresses, in his heart? With shackles at his belt and gold in his purse? He does not debate, he asserts - and scorns rebuttals. He does not make free love, he buys or seizes flesh and slakes his lust - a fatal lust at that sometimes.

Thinkers of the Enlightenment understood that the world in which they lived was one of force and crime - that was why they wanted to change it. Wilhelm von Humboldt extolled the necessity to maintain the "spiritual energy" of people by saddling them with the minimum of laws. He pinned hope for human progress on cultivated human minds controlling cultivated human sensualities, and believed that people were "by nature more disposed to beneficent acts than to selfish acts." However, Humboldt glimpsed the shadow over the picnic: let there be "no restraint [on people] except that necessary to prevent any infringement of rights."

At the sight of the spoiler of the fun, buying or compelling his satisfaction, the free players frown and feel obliged to give up their aspirations to debates, experiments and pleasures. They then have to dedicate much of their time to amassing wealth, so that some of it can be turned over to a treasury which hires persons away from what might be free play in order to become police. The police see to it that laws, made by ordered societies and intended to protect us from spoilers, are not infringed. All this apparatus of the state is erected under Humboldt's caveat that restraint is needed to prevent any infringement of rights. The experimenters might admit that this is a retreat from liberality, but one must protect one's life and health. If there are those whose pursuit of happiness runs to beating and murder, then, to preserve the liberty to live, one must have instruments by which to withdraw the liberty to kill. Now that one has wealth, that must be protected also.

This state of affairs makes it very difficult to persuade people even to believe in the picnic of free play as a desirable goal, let alone to pack hampers, put on straw hats, gather the children and set out merrily for the riverbank to frolic unprotected.

CHAPTER 31: ENLIGHTENED IN PARTS

For my purposes here, although there are many more to choose from, the arch-spoiler is the Marquis de Sade. I marvel that he has been embraced by some as a mighty demolisher of the old world of superstition, hierarchy and imposed morality, as one of the hardest hammers on behalf of the Enlightenment - albeit too hard for many, even now - clearing the ground for humanity's uninhibited freedom. Apollinaire called him "the freest spirit that may have yet existed." Swinburne wrote that he was an "illustrious and ill-requited benefactor of humanity". Sade, "fatalist or not, saw to the bottom of gods and men," Swinburne added. There is much more such tosh from other men, especially French researchers and publishers in this century who have given much of their time to bringing Sade's works to light, and become all too enamoured of them meanwhile.

By choosing carefully among his works, however, one can make out that Sade was in step with the main thrust of the Enlightenment. He was another who specifically maintained that, under tyrannical laws, people's spirits are dulled into lethargy. Any social pact by which people acknowledge certain behaviour as wrong was "a disgraceful yoke of error" if it inhibited people more than it satisfied them. Sade called on the French to turn themselves into citizens of high energy and constant alertness, rather than rely on regulations and police to protect themselves and their property. There was no fixed morality, such as the Catholic Church would have its faithful believe, but rather it was the education through which each generation passed that determined what it called virtue and vice. A great variety of activities regarded as sinful in the France of his time had been practised in different eras and different parts of the world, openly and with social acceptance. Sade had much evidence from world-wide research to support this view, so he claimed, and incorporated chunks of it into argumentative passages of his works.

Sade was impatient, like many other questioning thinkers of his time, with the censorious Church and governments which forbade even the discussion of the true nature of humanity and the universe - impatient also with the triviality into which this restriction tended to confine writing and conversation. This point from *Justine* is about variety in sexual behaviour but would be applicable to many areas of life which could not be openly examined: "People do not imagine how useful these pictures are in the development of one's soul. It may be that we are as ignorant of this science as we are only through the stupid reticence of those who seek to write on these topics. Chained by absurd fears, they only talk to us about puerile things that every fool knows, not daring, by putting a brave hand into the human heart, to bring out before our eyes its gigantic aberrations ... philosophy is our business here and ... let us no longer fear to bring forth vice in its nakedness."

When Sade, still seeming Enlightened and using a common device of would-be reformers of that era to give their ideas a framework on the page, created his utopia (in the novel *Aline and Valcour*), not only did he set it in the South Pacific, on which French writers of the Enlightenment were keen through their extensive second-hand knowledge of it, but he made his ideal island free of religion, private property, class distinctions and family life.

Also, Sade rejected "the barbarity of a god who can punish finite faults with infinite afflictions", and he spurned any idea of a life after that in the realm of Nature, where nothing left the physical universe but merely changed its form over time - "man today, worm tomorrow," as he put it in *Dialogue between a Priest and a Dying Man*.

Property, he wrote in *Juliette*, was "a crime by the rich against the poor," having its origin in a grab by the strongest of what they wanted. "When laws were laid down and the weak agreed to give up some of their freedom so as to keep the rest of it, their main aim in doing so was to go on enjoying their possessions in peace, thanks to the curbs introduced by law. The strong agreed to laws which they knew they could over-ride [and were glad of the restraints because these stopped the weak preying on each other, leaving the strong clear to prey on them at will]. So theft ... changed its form, became legal. Judges stole by being paid for doing justice that should be gratis. Priests stole by being paid for mediating between a man and his God. The trader stole by profiteering, by charging one third more than his goods were worth. Monarchs stole by arbitrary taxes and duties on their subjects. All these forms of robbery were allowed under the doubtful title of 'rights' and the law moved only against the most natural - that is, against the man who had no money and tried to take it from those whom he thought to be richer than he was, without knowing that the original thieves, against whom not a word was spoken, were the sole cause of the other man's crimes."

Sade the drawing-room dissolver of class distinctions saw in the Europe of his day "two classes ... one the rich slaves of their own pleasures, the other the miserable victims of fate." The rich were "forever adding to the chains of the poor, while multiplying their own luxury, while the poor, insulted and loathed by the rich, were given not so much as enough wherewithal to bear their burden... Those who ruled out any change [towards] equality were those who would lose if it came about."

As a progressive literary landlord, Sade showed understanding of the need to improve agriculture (another concern of the Enlightenment) by great reduction of taxation on peasant farmers and on the distribution of their produce. In his Pacific utopia of Tamoé, in *Aline and Valcour*, public granaries would store each harvest and ensure there was enough food for all, with any surplus being given away to needy neighbour countries. The citizens of Tamoé would enjoy equality of wealth while their children were raised in state schools, situated near asylums for the lonely, old and infirm. In these schools, children would be taught their duty to the whole community, rather than to a family, and learn the rudiments of agriculture and military training. There was to be no standing army (the soldier in Sade recalled how "there are surely few worse schools than those of the garrisons, few where a young man finds corruption sooner, in his style and in his morals"), no lawyers, no jails, no death penalty, no brothels, no professional artists, actors or musicians, and no money.

So our social and economic relations would be transformed in the world as reformed by the Enlightened Sade - sexual relations, too. In his didactic play *Philosophy in the Boudoir*, two libertines instruct a 15-year-old girl, Eugénie de Mistival, in certain ways of the world:

"*Mme de Saint-Ange*: A girl's chances of conceiving a child are related to how often she lets a man invade her cunt. She should carefully avoid this means of sampling pleasure; she should make available instead her hand, her mouth, her breasts or her arse. This last passage will provide her much delight - much more, in fact, than any other - and by the others she will give pleasure.

"As for the first means, the hand ..., Eugénie, one works at the organ of one's friend as though pumping it. After a bit of agitation, the sperm is emitted. While you are doing that, the man is kissing and caressing you. He wets with his fluid the part of your body he likes best. If the desire is for it to be spread over your breasts, you lie full-length on the bed, the erect member is placed between the two tits, which are squeezed together and after a few thrusts the man ejaculates and inundates you, sometimes as far up as your face. This is the least pleasurable method and is only any use with women whose breasts, due to repeated use, have become malleable and slack enough to provide a snug channel for the man's organ when it is held between them. The mouth is very much more delightful, just as much so for the man as for the woman. The best method here is for the woman to lie face-down on top of her fucker, her head towards his feet. He slips his cock into your mouth and, with his head between your thighs, he gives back in kind what you are giving him by putting his tongue into your cunt or by running it over your clitoris. In this position, you should use a bit of enterprise - grab the buttocks, finger and play with each other's arseholes, which is always essential to complete the pleasure. Lovers who really get into the swing of it, those with imagination, swallow the liquids that spurt into their mouths ...

"*Dolmancé*: ... To rob procreation of its due, and to go against what fools call the law of Nature, is indeed most diverting. Other harbours for the man's member are the thighs and the armpits, where his sperm may be spilled without danger of pregnancy.

"*Mme de Saint-Ange*: Some women push sponges inside their vaginas so that these prevent the sperm reaching the chamber where the generation takes place. Other women make their fuckers wear a little bag of Venetian skin, commonly known as a condom. This is filled by the semen, which can thus travel no further ..."

This lesson in copulation and contraception has dated little in the 200 years since it was written, not least in its disregard for the teachings of the Catholic Church, to which it runs quite counter. Sade's uneasy awareness of, and bottomless loathing for, the powerful and respected Church of the western Europe of his time mean that vituperation for this enemy is never far away as one reads his works. Even so, he sometimes managed to refrain from calling down secular fire on the obsolescent world, as he saw it, and concentrate on mapping the better future that he believed himself to be already helping to create. Much of

Eugénie de Mistival's day of wonders *chez* Mme de Saint-Ange passes as though the last confessional box were already on a pyre built by rationalist voluptuaries.

To clear the ground for untrammelled pleasure-taking, however, not only the fears of Hell and pregnancy have to be vanquished. One must also conquer a monster as old as they, if not older.

Here is Sade (via a male libertine in *Juliette*) taking his sword of reason to jealousy:

"It is not at all because one is very much in love with a woman that one is jealous of her, rather it is because one fears the humiliation that would arise from a change in her affection; the proof that there is nothing but sheer egoism in this passion lies in the fact that there is no lover who, if he is being honest, will not admit that he had rather see his mistress dead than unfaithful. So we are much more cast down by her inconstancy than by losing her, which means we are only thinking of ourselves in such an event. From this, I conclude that, after the unforgiveable extravagance of being in love with a woman, the greatest one can commit ... is to be jealous of her. This feeling is insulting to her because it shows her one's lack of esteem for her; it is an affliction on oneself and just as useless, being a sure way to make a woman want to let one down, just as it is to show her one's fear that she might do that very thing. Jealousy and the terror of being cuckolded both stem entirely from our prejudices about enjoying women; without that damned habit of stupidly wanting ... always to link the moral to the physical, we would easily rid ourselves of these prejudices. What! it isn't possible to go to bed with a woman without being in love with her, and it isn't possible to be in love with her without going to bed with her? Yet by what necessity has the heart a role in a matter where only the body takes part? There are two very different desires, two very different needs, it seems to me. Araminthe has the most beautiful body in the world, her face is sensuous, her big eyes are black and full of a fire that promises an ample release of her semen[1] as soon as the inside of her vagina or of her anus is sharply electrified by the friction of my penis... What need is there ... that the feelings of my heart be part of the act which puts that creature's body under my control! It seems to me ... that to love and to enjoy are two very different things ... For feelings of tenderness arise from rapport of temperament and of general

---

1 Sade meant vaginal fluid, the nature of which was not clearly understood in his time.

affinity, but are not at all due to the beauty of a bosom or the pretty curve of an arse, and these objects here[2] which, according to our tastes, may greatly excite our physical affections, have not, however, it seems to me, the same right to our mental affections. To complete my comparison: Bélise is ugly, aged forty, without a shred of grace in her person, not one regular feature, nothing attractive about her; but Bélise is intelligent, has a delightful personality and a host of things that bind themselves to my feelings and tastes. I would have no wish to go to bed with Bélise but would love her to distraction none the less for that; I would fervently want to have Araminthe, but I would detest her heartily as soon as the fever of desire had passed because I have found in her no more than a body and none of the mental qualities that can deserve the affections of my heart..."

The above quotation is consistent with some Enlightenment writers' semi-clandestine advocacy of fancy-free fucking, of the demolition of ideas of the body as property held in marriage or other forms of sworn sexual fidelity.

However, in that Sadeian quotation, one can also notice straight, inflexible lines being drawn across the shifts of the desired quicksilver society, by way of setting up compartments, divisions. The marquis was right - jealousy is a useless insult and we would be well rid of it - but he seems to regard it as only a hindrance to *pleasure*. There is not a hint of generosity - take intellectual stimulation with Bélise, sexual satisfaction with Araminthe, and never a reversal, even in the looseness of universal sexual and intellectual romp from which the monster jealousy is to be banished. Whether or not the two women understand and accept their allotted roles, which seems to be of no concern to Sade, he appears to have allowed no scope for patient, gentle exploration of whether Bélise might enjoy *le frottement voluptueux de deux intestins*, as Diderot put it, or of whether Araminthe might appreciate a discussion of counter-point in Rameau's music.

In this, the careful choosing among Sade's works so as to show him as an Enlightened writer begins to collapse under pressure of a strong hint of the spoiler of the sunny picnic of free play, with Sade as the sort of would-be infringer of other people's rights Humboldt warned about.

Yet Sade himself was not blind to the danger posed to other members of society by libertines whose pleasure lay in restricting and

---

2 The girls Juliette has supplied for a prospective orgy.

otherwise doing harm to others, albeit he did not, outside rare and qualified admissions in his letters, point to himself as such a perilous individual. So alert was Sade to the danger posed by the anti-social libertine that he offered ideas, consistent with the liberality of the Enlightenment, on how to cope with such a person. Jail was worse than useless: "The law is wrong when it only punishes, vile when its only aim is to crush the criminal without educating him, to scare him without improving him, to commit a crime as bad as the one that started the process but without any advantage coming from it..."

This from Sade is in harmony with his more vehement denunciations of prison on his own account when he was held in royal fortresses. "Jailers, idiots of every land and every government, when will you prefer the science of understanding humanity to that of locking them up and killing them?" he asked. In that science, Sade was abreast of the latest ideas, which pointed the way to modern knowledge of physiology and psychiatry: "The organs that determine our reactions to various tastes are formed in the mother's womb. This formation of ours is completed by the first objects we touch and the first words we hear..."

In *Justine*, he went further: "When the science of anatomy is fully developed, it will have no difficulty in demonstrating the relation between the physique of a man and the proclivities that rule his emotions. Pedants, hangmen, time-servers, law-makers, all you scum in the priesthood, what will become of you when we establish all this? What will your laws, your morals, your religion, your gallows, your heavens, your gods, your infernoes be worth when it is proved that one or other flow of juices, one or other kind of bodily tissue, one or other thickness of the blood, or of a different bodily fluid, can make people victims of your trials or of your rewards?"

In Sade's time, the notion was growing that certain liquids in the body governed temperament, but it was clear that thinking about the brain and the nervous system was in hand there. According to Sade, there was no place for God to work in those ways as they became less mysterious under the probe of rational science.

If the criminal is not to be locked up, how is he or she to be dealt with in society? Prisons were only excusable, he wrote in *Aline and Valcour*, if set up "in the hope of correction, but you must have a very thin understanding of humanity if you think that jail can achieve that. A criminal is not reformed by isolation but by [his] going back to the society he has wronged and receiving consistent punishment there, in the only reformatory that can put him straight. By contrast, clamped in a deadly solitude, ... his vices sprout, his blood curdles, his brain distils poison. He cannot satisfy his desires and that strengthens the criminal motives behind them". For Sade, still the Enlightened modern in his approach, the important thing was to reform society itself so that crimes, all but a few of which arise out of poverty or passion, disappear for lack of motivation: "Do away with the causes behind someone breaking the law and you will do away with the wish to break the law".

Redistribution of wealth to abolish poverty, and re-education of humanity to abolish jealousy and rage, might well wipe out crime by the poor and the passionate, but that would leave the criminal who breaks the law for his pleasure. From Italy in 1775, Sade referred in a letter to "that bizarre mania for doing something bad just for the pleasure of it ... one of the least understood, and so the least examined, of men's passions..." In *Aline and Valcour*, he declared: "There is no point in making laws to deal with these people - the stronger the walls erected to stop them, the greater their delight in knocking them down."

Sade went on to argue that, not least because these malefactors were few, they might be reformed in the community "by kindness and honours, or by trying to get them to change whatever it is in them that causes their behaviour." He did acknowledge that, "a criminal having been deemed dangerous," such a person had to be taken out of circulation to some extent, "by requiring him to work, by way of reparation, for those whom he has affronted, or by banishment."

While setting out his utopia of Tamoé, Sade went into more detail on the problem of the rare criminal who caused trouble for the hell of it. The emergence of vices in one's fellow citizens would be met neither by an embarrassed pretence not to notice, nor by silence out of fear of a beating at the hands of the criminal, but by clear and direct expressions of disgust and/or ridicule - that is, there would be a general, open concern to stop trouble before it became any worse. Sade did not envisage, in his ideal nation, that the miscreant could get away with telling do-gooders to mind their own business. This ready intervention by public opinion could be re-inforced, Sade elaborated, by making the criminals wear special clothes that marked them as anti-social.[3]

---

3 In the USA in October 1987, a judge at Portland, Oregon, ordered that, when a local child molester was let out of jail on parole, a notice (DANGEROUS SEX OFFENDER: NO CHILDREN ALLOWED) be fixed to his front door and his car. Sade, in his utopian vein, would have approved.

This advocacy of curative social pressure over a period of time matches Sade's prescription for his own libertine bent, as set out in a letter to his wife from his cell at Vincennes: "You cannot expect to have a man come away from the chasm in one leap... Settle for inculcating in him a desire for delights that are less violent than, but are in the same region as, those to which he was addicted. That way, you will bring him step by step away from the mire... A person's digestion has to take a diet gradually - an abrupt and total fast ruins it..."

However, in sketching his Tamoé, at least, Sade admitted that there might be those recidivists who remained impervious to parish-pump correction. It would be exile for them, and the islanders would cast murderers adrift in a boat with provisions for a month - which might be bad luck on communities less than 30 days down-current of utopia.

This is mostly rather fine, rather Enlightened, but the biographical first section of this book shows that, much of the time, Sade was not nearly so liberal, at his quill or away from it. So, despite the libertarian gloss, does this from *Juliette*:

"I allow the respectability of absolutely nothing among men, and this for the good and weighty reason that everything men have made has arisen from nothing but their self-interest and their prejudices... No being has the despotic right to submit me to what he has said or thought; and no matter how far I go in infringing these human dreams [of rules in religion, morality and politics], there is no individual on earth who can obtain the right to rebuke or punish me for doing so... By what unbelievable injustice will you call *moral* that which stems from you, *immoral* that which stems from me?...

"But, some object, there are things so clearly outrageous that it is impossible to doubt their danger or their horror... I know of no act of that kind, none which, recommended by nature, has not formed at some time the basis of some bygone customs, none ... which, being spiced by some attractions, has not become thereby legitimate and good...

"But, they stupidly go on telling you, since you were born in this clime, you must respect its ways. Not a bit of it: it is absurd of you to wish to persuade me that I must put up with [that]; I am as nature made me, and if there exists a contradiction between my tastes and those of the laws of my country, this fault, arising only from nature, ought never to be ascribed to me.

"But, they add further, you will harm society, if you are not removed from it. How boring! Abandon your stupid restrictions and give all beings the same right to avenge themselves for any wrong done to them: you will no longer need any written laws..."

There is the ominous sound of Sade whistling a tune different to that on the lips of the free players as they stroll to the consensual picnic. In place of laws, not reasoned argument but vendetta; any notion of immorality gone up in the smoke of an individual's right to unlimited pleasure and unlimited prey.

* * * * *

In trying to understand how far Sade was apt to proceed against the liberal grain of the Enlightenment, remember that the would-be reformers were far from achieving their aim. They were termites gnawing at the old structure, the old order - at economic relations where many feudal elements remained strong, at states where aristocrats still held great sway, at a Church which continued to inspire profound fear and respect. As is almost always the case in times of ferment for change, those who would demolish the old ways still followed those ways in their daily habits, their personal appetites, even as their reading and their thinking developed their understanding that change was necessary. Even someone ready to break moulds and leap into a life of unregulated improvisation had still to reckon with the power of the abiding structures. Diderot, for whom one taste of incarceration at Vincennes had been enough, cautioned the readers of his privately circulated writing:

"We will speak against senseless laws until they are changed and meanwhile we will submit to them. Whoever takes it into his own hands to break a bad law authorises everyone else to break good ones. It is less troublesome to be foolish among the fools than to be wise all alone. Let us say to ourselves that we will ceaselessly point to the fact that shame, chastisement and disgrace are being attached to acts that are essentially innocent, but let us not commit those acts ourselves because shame, chastisement and disgrace are the greatest of all misfortunes."

It might suit some to think that Sade diverged from Diderot and other cautious thinkers of the Enlightenment in that, while they were shying away from practising liberty under the old punitive order, the marquis was daring enough to risk punishment and disgrace, plunging beyond the established morality into a perilous, exciting freedom where existing expectations were made molten by his protean improvisations in pursuit of ever more exquisite happiness.

Is that right? Was Sade a man of freedom? We have it on the authority of Ronald Hayman that "Sade never understood how exceptional he was in not feeling frightened of freedom." Gilbert Lely wrote that Sade's "work acknowledges very few limits." He was, for Lely, "a great proponent of love."

I will look again at his life, his reading, and at his works, in presenting my view.

The if-only basis for history rarely bears much fruit but it might be useful here to wonder whether the marquis would have grown up differently if his elder sister had lived. Caroline Laure, come and gone before the boy was born - and Marie Françoise, his short-lived younger sister - appear not at all, or flit by, in other works on Sade, their brief existences seen as barely worth recording. However, their passage points to a lack which the older of them, at least, might have supplied. In what we know of the marquis's life before his wedding, there is no sign of girls whom he had to respect and with whom he spent enough time to discover that such respect was worth giving for the friendship it brought forth and fostered. There is no guarantee that, even if the older sister had survived, she and her brother would have been raised together, but she, or a female of like age and social status, could have required that the boy pay heed to her claims on his attention, pay heed also to her opinions and precedences.

From his early life at the Condé palace, we have a faint impression of his mother's attention divided between the Condé princeling and her son. Then, at the ménage in Provence of his uncle, the Abbé de Sade, who could not marry, the women were concubines and successive. School, the cadet establishment and the army were far from conducive to confronting the youngster with a female coeval free enough of worries about where the next meal was coming from for her respect and love to be won only through fearless give and take. By such steadfast girls do boys learn that the world - especially the women in it - is neither a great terror nor a great booty.

From the first, the females in his life seem at a remove. There were his Provençal grandmother and a governess, but he was with neither for long. If, like many rich boys in societies of cheap labour, he began his sexual experimentation with a servant, then he understood early that superior power - grown out of wealth and exercised through threat or promise - could extract sexual pleasure. A maid whose only other life had been in a labourer's tenement or on a sharecropper's plot of land, and whose prospects of another job were meagre, would find little scope for resisting a young master's demands, especially if supported by cash.

While the only son was growing up, finding everyone defined by a place in a pecking order, no woman was consistently present as his esteemed arbiter of behaviour or fount of love. Also, there is little sign of sustained friendship - no-one, of either sex, from his Parisian or

Provençal childhood homes, from school or military, or from the roistering, appears as friend to whom all could be said and from whom anything might be heard. (The relationship with Laure de Lauris was passionate, not friendly.) We are dealing with a figure whose history has been obscured by burners of documents and silencers of witnesses, but I suspect that the gaps hide no level-headed, sometimes justly blazing, girl who impressed Donatien Alphonse François into waiting his turn and not being beastly. Much pleasure, little amity; much heat, little warmth.

Nor, by the way, was there any influence that gave him a taste for work in co-operation with others.

* * *

The essential military alternatives are to kill or be killed, as Sade and his blue-blooded colleagues in the French army learned young, dividing the world into allies and enemies at an impressionable age. Also essential to the military life of hierarchical discipline are long stretches of boredom interrupted by short onrushes of mortal fear and wild excitement. Relief from the boredom, and relief at having survived the fear, came out in debauchery, young men daring each other on to wilder ways of spending their vigour - and the income of their fathers' estates. This recklessness, as old as aristocracy, was funded by old money amassed through ownership. It was regarded - and not only by those who practised it - as a rightful diversion, like the hunt, like war at the call of one's sovereign, fine wine and food, admission to the salons of the noblest and the brightest. As usual, there were plenty of poor young women (and men), as well as eager traders in various commodities, to provide the fences and furlongs for the gallops of the young rips.

"Poverty hands our victims over to us and makes them submissive," Sade wrote in *Juliette*, in his middle age when dreaming paper orgies that shortness of funds and shortness of breath were preventing him realising. In his younger days, he had had more of both.

* * *

Sade's adherence to libertinage without restraint did not stem entirely from his upbringing as an aristocrat and soldier. He was well read in texts of his times, well acquainted with the thinking of the Enlightenment, but by no means all of this was directed unequivocally towards persuasion, optimism and progress for all. In 1770, Baron d'Holbach brought out his book *System of Nature*. From prison, 13 years later, Sade called it "the foundation of my philosophy", although he did not take on board those aspects of Holbach's text which might have cramped his style.

Holbach argued against the modern notion of his time that the natural world consisted of sequences of causes and effects, which could be explained in full, once they had been sufficiently studied. He took the view that the universe was less susceptible to analysis and codification, in that it was always in unstable flux, the energy at work in it arising from the interaction of various parts. This idea, which in our era of scientific precision would be seen as vague, appealed to Sade, who was attached to the importance of energy and initiative in human relations. This fitted an individual who was thrilled by great forces in nature (Sade had seen the volcano Mount Vesuvius at Naples) and liked to regard himself as someone who had the drive to act upon others and hold them in thrall through his dynamism. He was less inclined to be moved by a view of the natural world as a wholly assessable process of causes and effects in which any release of energy would be dissipated by the resistance of matter, although some matter would be transformed.

This view of nature as capricious flux, forever destroying and creating, might seem like a rejection of what was in Sade's time the burgeoning scientific analysis and channelling of the universe, in favour of an older, mystical response to a harsh, rampaging deity of earth, air, fire and water. However, Sade and Holbach were firm in rejecting God and the afterlife. Sade probably took his frequent references to God as a "phantom" or a "chimera" from Holbach. From this spurning of God, it followed that priests were "the least useful people in society." (Another amen from Sade to that.) The soul was no more than a part of the body and died with it, so there was no point in thinking and acting so as to reap rewards in the next life. "It would be futile, even unjust, to demand that a person live virtuously if to do so were to cause that person unhappiness. If someone finds satisfaction in vice, then that is what he should embrace," wrote Holbach - a credo for the Sadeian way of life.

Even so, Holbach would not have warmed to the thought that he was offering a justification for libertinage, because "it obliterates all tenderness from the heart, all reflection from the intellect, once it has become a habit. The libertine's excesses choke any remorse that he might have felt after his early escapades."

Sade was also fond of citing Julien Offroy de La Mettrie, a contemporary physician who had specialised in venereal diseases before he became a doctor to an army regiment in battle. "Only good doctors should be judges," he wrote. La Mettrie followed the scientific line - and heresy for the Roman Catholic Church - that the true condition of the universe was to be determined by studying physical evidence and the results of experiments. Descartes had written that animals were machines; La Mettrie wrote that man was an animal and so might be considered a machine. The soul developed and decayed along with the body and, like the body, was subject to diseases, nervous disorders, madness - an extraordinary, forward-looking view in his day. He had been much impressed by the changes observed in himself during delirium while running a high fever. There was no soul without the senses. Motion was a property of matter, as one could observe from the movements of animals after death, rather than a property of a supernatural spirit dwelling in the body. La Mettrie also wrote of animal spirits or electric fluid that carried the body's perceptions to the brain.

The existence of God and a life beyond death could not be established scientifically and so were outside the scope of philosophy. Even if one supposed the existence of God, no-one could know which form of religion was to His liking; in any event, all such forms were deplorable because of the wars they spawned. Death was obliteration, the end, and so not worth bothering about. Nature was the main force in the universe, not God - a nature without purpose, without morality or equality, indifferent to its effects. Man was not responsible for his good or bad points so remorse over misdeeds was worthless and people were not in the wrong for following their instincts. They could be improved by education, but their tendency to evil was strong and instincts were stronger than education, La Mettrie believed.

He was greatly interested in sexual pleasure and variety, declaring: "There's woman in whatever you love" (*Tout est femme dans ce qu'on aime*). He also wrote: "From the worm to the eagle, we were born not to be wise but to be happy."

There was much material here for Sade to regard La Mettrie's work as new texts to support new scratching on an old itch to have one's way sexually. When access to the bodies of others was at issue, enlightened restraint and respect was apt to be cast aside, whatever the consequent harm to Diderot's "destructible beings".

Apart from his personal experiences and his reading of contemporary texts, Sade also drew fuel for his justification of vice from his researches into the customs, past and present, of distant lands. His letters and literary works sometimes digress into lurid and lengthy lists of sanguinary ceremonies and practices, quite counter to the attitudes of Catholic France towards incest, sodomy, infanticide, wife-murder or whatever penchant Sade, in his own right or via his ink-and-paper debauchees, might be promoting just then. The invocation of the rulers of Achem and Golconda, in a letter from jail **(see chapter 20)**, is typical.

This sort of anthropology should be taken with a pinch of salt. In the 18th century, many first encounters between European travellers and societies beyond their continent were of recent date. European readers had a great appetite for accounts of exotic peoples, as well as little scope for checking which were true and which were exaggerated. Sade, who never travelled outside western Europe, seized whatever stories of sexual and murderous mayhem came his way, and turned them to his purpose, which was to demonstrate that there was no absolute morality, that all notions about good and bad behaviour varied over time and from place to place. He and his network of fellow collectors of the bizarre and the bloody, from as far back as classical antiquity and as far afield as the ends of the Earth, were much more interested in adding exhibits to their bias for the evanescence of any morality than in verifying the sources of the items, many of which were probably coloured in the telling on their way into Sade's notebooks - and on their way out. His partiality is strongly suggested by his failure to cite any bizarre "respected practice" from strait-laced societies - England under the Commonwealth, say, or the colony of Massachusetts in the late-17th century - in his effort to make out that any behaviour one can conceive of had been a norm, sometime, somewhere. Nor did he mention Puritans forbidding the theatre - Sade the ever-aspiring playwright would have been hard put to find no "danger and repulsiveness" in that.

* * *

So far, then, Sade's life as boy aristocrat, army officer, budding rake and selective adherent to the thinking of his era does not look like an upbringing that would produce a free player who dared to live by Englightened principles. Let's look further.

Easy pleasure, available for money, creates or fosters in a young man an impatience and laziness towards women. He gets excited by the glamorous surface of one then, when she has palled, he seizes another, and so on. He does not wait to explore beyond the surface; meanwhile his capacity to tolerate and cherish through thick and thin does not bloom.

While this was the case with Sade, during his teens and twenties, there were so many female distractions that he might have been expected to take in his capering stride any off-handedness, any falling short of convincing attention to his pleasure, by courtesans and prostitutes, as long as they performed passably when with him.

However, he began to seek the best courtesans whom money could hire, such as Colet and Beauvoisin. The fact that other men about town rated them as such, and would have had them if they could, confirmed the desirability of these women. No man could hold on to such women when they decided to change patrons, or to withdraw themselves from the market, having made enough money to rest for a while or to retire.

Sade could not even have such a woman all to himself for long. We have the word of the well-informed Inspector Marais that the marquis was not wealthy enough to support a top-flight courtesan without at least one other patron also picking up her bills. In the case of Colet, he probably found out this by discovering that she had hidden from him the fact that she was entertaining another client. At the end of 1764, Colet was twinkling about with a pair of ear-rings that a duke had given her as a very expensive Christmas present, which signalled that, *chez* Colet, market forces had turned against Sade **(see chapter 6)**.

So these prime objects would be gone while he still wanted more from them - like his mother, busy with her attendance on her Condé patrons during her son's first four years and then out of reach altogether as she went abroad with his father and the boy was sent to Provence; like his remote and scolding father; also like his paternal grandmother, uncle and aunts in the south when he was sent back to Paris at the age of nine for schooling at Collège Louis le Grand; like his tutor the Abbé

Amblet when the schoolboy, just 14, was taken from his books to buckle on a sword and mount a charger for his king.

This elusiveness of hired women would be especially disturbing to a young man born "in the lap of luxury and plenty", brought up to be "haughty, domineering and quick-tempered", and to believe "that everything should give way to me, that the whole universe should accede to my whims and that, as soon as I wanted something, I should be able to have it", as Sade wrote in *Aline and Valcour*.

It has been suggested in other books that the stifling of Sade's main sexual affairs in his prime - those with Laure de Lauris and perhaps with his sister-in-law Anne Prospère de Launay - embittered him and that he had been a more open man, more apt to love and be loved, before these liaisons went wrong. The idea is that Laure was lost to Sade through his father and the Montreuils making marital merchandise of him for their own financial and dynastic purposes, and that Anne Prospère was snatched from him by his mother-in-law in her determination to break an affair that was blighting her daughter's chances of an advantageous marriage. After each of these reverses, Sade became more and more, to cite the title of one of his plays, *He Who Was Soured by Love*, so it is made out.

I have my doubts. Even if one allows that Sade was hurt by the collapse of the affair with Laure, he was far from being unharrowed pasture by that stage of his life. He had learned at an early age, probably under the wing of his libertine uncle, the Abbé de Sade, that women's bodies could be hired. He would have heard talk among his acquisitive relatives in Provence of calculations over money and status behind marriages among the nobility. His experience of prostitutes, probably begun in the army, was extensive by the time Laure took up with him, probably in 1761 or 1762. As for Anne Prospère, the end of that affair (if any) came in 1772, by which time Sade was even further steeped in disrespectful handling of women. One has to look both more closely and more widely at Sade's disappointments with women, so as to understand how he became set in his ways, rather than at his failed affairs with a few noblewomen.

Let's take it that Sade, in the first stage of his libertinage, would not have been disconcerted by less than total concentration in his women. A lad is so excited by his first encounters that he is unlikely to notice how humdrum the woman might regard the transaction as being. As time passes, though, and a man grows more experienced, what he used to accept as sufficient attentiveness may come to be seen as lukewarm perfunctoriness. The dull gaze is noticed; the pause to swig from the wine bottle annoys; the faked panting and squirming is recognised as such. The client loses the mood.

The most successful practitioners in various lines of endeavour that involve personal contact - advocacy, medicine, the stage, prostitution and others - are those who best convey complete engagement; that is, those who give the most convincing impression - sometimes true, sometimes not - that their whole concentration and their unreserved willingness to convince, help or delight are with you, for you. Among female sexual partners, the most successful in the eyes of a man is not she who is the most inventive and unflagging fucker - although that can be important - but she who is believed to be altogether his.

Total attention can be spontaneous, as with keen newcomers in many professions and crafts as they strive to perform well. Yet, with experience, one can develop the capacity to work effectively while letting the mind wander at times, even as one simulates complete engagement. Actors, applying techniques learned in class and rehearsal, can convince audiences eight times a week, after months in a long-running play, that every fibre of their being is committed to enthral the customers. Prostitutes develop a similar display for a succession of clients, each of whom can believe that his heat alone warms her into giving her best.[1] (The one heartfelt, unreserved and unfeigned engagement is that which comes from love - more of that later.)

The high attractiveness of such women as Colet and Beauvoisin lay mainly, I suggest, in their ability to convince each patron that *he* was the one for whom her heart beat and her body throbbed. If she had to admit to there being other patrons - well, *chéri*, they're just sugar-daddies I have to string along because, *hélas,* it costs such a lot to live. If there were a lapse of concentration, when she let the essential indifference show - well, I'm tired, feeling a little under the weather ... bored? with *you*, poppet!? Heavens, no!

Such a woman might even have been sincere in her affection and sexual attentiveness while a liaison was going well for her, but she had a

1 This will not necessarily be a seamless performance by the prostitute, sustained without allowing a glimpse of the indifference - or the calculation, contempt perhaps - behind it. Why make the effort to put across unwavering devotion to a man's pleasure when touches of what will pass as the real stuff will do? Especially when the client seems more excited about her body, or some part of it, or her fetishistic attire, than about what is showing in her eyes or sounding in her voice?

living - and a pile - to make while her charm and wits lasted. No wonder she and her kind put the beguilement on noblemen for their rents and tithes, and on farmers-general for their tax revenues.

The high-class courtesan's simulation with her patron could glamorise or cheer away his misgivings but, whenever this effect faded, he would return to his unease at her condition as a woman free to take or turn away any man. He would remember that he was, or could be, having to share the dazzling object, and could lose his access to her at any time.

In Sade's case, his attitude to boughten sexual encounters, however light and carefree it might have been at the best of times, turned leaden and recriminatory more than once. Beauvoisin was one courtesan with whom he quarrelled often and to whom he sent a snarling letter when she was breaking with him. "I have always been disgusted by the thought," he wrote to his wife from Vincennes in 1781, during a bout of jealousy towards her, "that a woman who is in my arms might have her mind on another man..." In *Philosophy in the Boudoir*, one of his characters asks: "What do you want when you are involved in the sexual act? You want everything near you to be giving you its total attention, be thinking only about you, concerned only about you." In one of his letters, Sade asserted: "He's no sort of man who doesn't want to be a despot when he has a hard on."

In trying to understand the Marquis de Sade, it is essential to grasp his need for the total attention of other people, which entailed a need to control them.

When the money - and the glamour of the lord of the manor and of the cavalry officer - was not enough to hold that attention in a sexual partner, what was apt to happen? I suggest that Sade's profound need for the sure and total engagement of the objects of his sexual desire had grown out of his disappointments earlier in life with emotional supporters, potential and actual. I suggest also that these disappointments led him to express his frustration in rage, and that rage in physical violence. We know he showed a propensity for this at various stages of his life, early and late, at liberty and in jail.

Given all this, it is unlikely that Sade, when young, *planned* to smack or beat any woman out of going through the motions and into giving him what he felt was his due in total concentration, when a sexual encounter was under way. The probability is that he threw a cuff in sudden anger at a face whose eyes were still sparkling at a compliment from someone else, or were dull with indifference at his presence and the prospect of yet another stretch of carnal hire by the hour. Then yelps and tears, signals of attention having been won - by force. A stirring in the young officer's loins would have meant to him then that tactics akin to simple childish bullying and the cavalry charge could be applied to sexual relations with similar success. That is, the off-hand woman, like the unbiddable infant playmate and the enemy soldier, could be galvanised by a blow, or the threat thereof, into a reaction of full engagement.

The fact that he might suffer a blow in return was beside the point, which was to cut through any capacity in the object person to ignore him. The light in the frightened or angry eyes of the prostitute as she fingers her newly tingling cheek, of the playmate as he clutches his newly bruised shin, of the enemy infantryman as he swears defiance and jerks up his pike at the charging horseman, all tell the attacker that he has hurled aside any detachment and that the object is with him exclusively. That part of the world at which he had set his aim is taking the fullest notice, confirming to the insecure, violent man that he exists. His concern is not to aspire to the "I think, therefore I am" of Descartes; he *impinges*, therefore he is.

* * *

What scope did Sade have for shocking women to attention by physical violence? It must have been limited among noblewomen and courtesans, at least, one would think. For instance, on the face of it, he could scarcely beat up Laure de Lauris without provoking reprisal in kind from the men of her family or arrest for assault. Also, there could have been scandal and he would have been thought a cad. From what we know of their liaison, he tried to keep her in line by mean menace, as in his letter to her **(see chapter 5)**, hinting he would wreck her chances elsewhere by revealing a venereal infection, but there is no evidence of physical assault.

Although courtesans were not written up in the almanachs of the nobility, it was not done for a gentleman to strike any such woman lest he be thought a fool. In the *demi-monde*, a chap who had lost his access to a particular courtesan was supposed to shrug his shoulders, wait for his finances to rebound somewhat (if necessary) and then tilt at the next young beauty tempted out of poverty to be introduced to the whirl. Again, we know that Sade loosed his spleen through his pen - letters to Parisian courtesans who had dropped him show the nastiness familiar to Mlle de Lauris - but the actresses and dancers who were available as courtesans would have been reluctant to risk injury, disfigurement or worse through assault by patrons or anyone else. They had their careers, on stage and off, to think about.

As for prostitutes, *chez* Brissault and at other brothels of the French capital in that era, they would have been much less well placed to object to a slap or a beating, especially if enough money changed hands to quell any resulting fuss before it reached the street. One can readily imagine Sade, after a blow landed in the heat of his frustration at feeling a prostitute to be lacking attention to him and to what his mother-in-law called his "I WANT", putting all to rights, in his view at least and without conceding one degree of his contempt for prostitutes, by handing a few more coins to the madame. She would pass some of them on to the woman as the latter pressed a cold cloth to her face or gasped to put some air back into her lungs and straighten up.

Let's remember, however, that although violence and threats of violence would not usually have been acceptable to noblewomen or courtesans, male violence can hold a woman, rather than repel her. There are women, throughout society, for whom beatings and threats are evidence of men's emotional commitment to them. While her man is punching and cursing his woman, he cannot be thinking of anyone else. Beauvoisin's many other options notwithstanding, she spent much time with Sade and it cannot be ruled out that something of what kept her interested - apart from the fun, the talk and the money - was a blow or two, as long as she saw they were thrown in the heat of a desire to have all of her, not in calculation so as to get pleasure from landing the blows, and as long as damage was slight.

Remember also that the women of Sade's time, with few exceptions, were more susceptible, through their upbringing and lack of choices in life, to men's behaviour than are many of their modern counterparts in western Europe and North America. Even a noblewoman such as Laure de Lauris might have felt constrained to do no more about a cuff from Louis de Sade, a male whom she did not outrank in society, than wince and put it down to experience - especially if they had a sexual relationship which she needed to hide from her relatives and the marriage market, and which she knew he could be vengeful enough to expose.

For all that, the likes of Colet and Beauvoisin were generally too successful in their trade - and the likes of Laure and Anne Prospère generally too high and mighty in society - to have to put up with much rough stuff, whether an unexpected punch in anger or an anticipated birching. The courtesans, though, might well have been prepared to offer, as an alternative safer for themselves, an exciting response to simulated violence - struck (but with silken cords), bound (but not too tightly), shrieking and writhing (but with forethought). Sade, man of the theatre and of its illusions, might well have fallen in with such a show, tickled at the control and scope for effect it appeared to be giving him. One can imagine such a resourceful operator as Beauvoisin leading Sade so deftly into and through a presentation of her private theatre of engagement that the young libertine's awareness of confection having displaced spontaneity would be minimal. The faked, hot-eyed botheration under assault has its place in the female sexual repertoire alongside the more common faked orgasm.

Be that as it may, Sade was an intelligent connoisseur of the theatre so the performances would have to be good in order to convince. If they were not - and remember that one becomes more difficult to enthral by simulation as one grows in experience - then Sade would have turned away from such *petits spectacles au boudoir*. If he had detected too much artifice in these, he would have become all the more apt thereafter to rage at such deceit in hired women and their boughten time. Notice his tendency, as he passed into his thirties, to seek "really young" prostitutes whose inexperience would leave them not only less well practised in disengaging their minds from their clients, but also less able to weave simulated responses to managed assaults.

Various of the women in Sade's young life - at all levels of society - might well have allowed him buggery. He extolled the practice in his writings and we know, from the episode with the Marseilles prostitutes **(see chapter 8)** and other events in his life, that he liked to indulge in it. Buggery usually gives less pleasure and more pain to a woman than vaginal intercourse, for all Sade's declamation of the contrary. The woman being taken anally was more likely to feel and show discomfort, call out in pain, beg for her partner to proceed more gently or stop altogether - all strong testimony to how greatly he was impinging on her and keeping her mind on his presence and actions. Even this delight would pall for Sade with a woman whose anus had become less tight as her tissues were slackened by repeated sodomy, which had also brought her to undergo the experience with less fuss. Hence another motive for his inclination towards "really young" prostitutes more apt to be pained and shocked by his buggery of them. Besides, the pleasure experienced by a woman being penetrated vaginally might well take away, through her ecstasy, her awareness of whoever was acting on her, thus dissolving her attention to him. "How contemptible in my eyes," Sade wrote during his travels in Italy in 1775, "is the woman who, concerning herself very little with her lover's [pleasures], values him only for the duration he can give to hers."

Sade's discovery of the magnetic effect of physical violence in sexual encounters - not least buggery of young women (and men) who were not used to it - made him even less disposed to patient exploration of a lover's qualities beyond the exciting surface and the attentive eye (seeming attentive, anyway). There is no evidence of any courtesan having stayed with him for long, no evidence of him having been a regular client of any one prostitute, no evidence of any long-lasting lover among the nobility.

When Sade was spending money on women who would allow, he hoped, blasphemy mixed with sexual release, what sort of attention did he receive? In the case of Jeanne Testard, kept on her feet throughout the night of 18-19 October 1763 while Sade spilled a pot pourri of blasphemies and coprophilia, she may have deserved congratulations for having seemed attentive enough meanwhile, though the notion of an enema being administered to her while poised over a crucifix would have been likely to dispel the indifference of many a practitioner of her trade **(see chapter 6)**. Also, on Easter Sunday 1768 in the little house at Arcueil, Rose Keller was very much *engagée*, convinced as she was of her mortal danger while the lashes fell on her back and her new employer threatened her with murder, without benefit of proper confession **(see chapter 7)**.

Sade may well have been cautious enough not to display his God-spurning to women in high society for his atheistic convictions, especially when combined with his sexual tastes, would be not only a prime topic for gossip but also liable to get him into trouble with the authorities. They did just that, even in a lower and more biddable social stratum, when he misjudged Testard's capacity to treat such an episode as all in a night's work and she complained to the police. Beauvoisin can scarcely have avoided, especially during the less festive days at la Coste in the summer of 1765 **(see chapter 6)**, hearing Sade hold forth on the certain non-existence of God, but he may well have refrained from revealing to her his anti-credo until he was sure she could take it in her stride and keep it to herself.

*

The individual worshipper might have constant, direct contact with God, who reciprocated with care and attention for every deed of every member of His flock; but the individual was also no more than one drop in the ocean of the faithful, and liable to the judgement of a God and of saints who were susceptible only to humble prayer, or not even to that, for all one knew for sure here below. Such a relationship does not sit well with a mortal concerned to have his share, and then some, of the attention of any being that he fastened onto - concerned also to have full scope to work on any such being, to make it accede to his arguments, fall for his glamour, absolve him from blame for his misdeeds, receive his penis in any orifice or fold of flesh, scream at his lashing - all according to which being was in view and which mode of impingement was under way.

Sade's desire to have and hold attention in his sexual encounters was consistent with his blasphemy, and with his disdain for going through the polite motions at gatherings of his peers, even for paying his respects to the king at court. His kind is irked at being expected to merge itself with a host of deferential nobles at a formal court of satellites around the might of a monarch.

*

Sade was not committed to the achievement of change by persuasion in freedom - an essential current of the Enlightenment. His wife adhered to him under his orders, as well as under her oath at the altar; Laure de Lauris was harangued and bullied; Anne Prospère de Launay was aggressively proselytised. Prostitutes, servants and creditors he exploited had little choice but to bend to his will. Sade might have called his approach - at least to those he regarded as his social equals - argumentative and assertive, rather than coercive. However, where does argument stop and coercion begin when the protagonist on one side is husband, lord of the manor, noble suitor, employer, cavalry officer, well-read debater or moneyed client? Besides, according to him, his social equals were few and certainly did not include such as prostitutes - who were to be used for relief, like the toilet - servants and the social-climbing Montreuils, who had bought him, from a higher echelon, in the marriage market.

Sade also had little regard for the belief, central in the Enlightenment, that the pursuit of happiness, through a society of minimal regulation, was open to all. He was a great believer in sweeping away imposed morality and laws so that one might fulfil one's potential for happiness, but had in mind, as his main literary works show, the pleasure of a libertine élite made up of those raised in it and those who managed to break into it later in life. In society according to Sade, you might fulfil your potential, if you could lift your head from the struggle for your daily bread. His attitude to those who could not shine and rise was as old as aristocracy and quite predatory. As for sweeping away laws that protected *his* property and *his* feudal enjoyment of revenues from it, that was out of the question. The Enlightenment pointed towards a society where all would be gainers. The only gainers in Sade's world were himself and the accomplices in libertinage whom he chose. I do not believe his radical activity during the French Revolution represented anything like a whole-hearted and abiding conversion to the contrary.

Sade diverged greatly from the ideal of the Enlightenment, of free play. He was a man who could not bear to live without circumscribing the freedom of others so as to control them and to seize their attention. His style was the old one of a rich seigneur, with a particularly immature bent. He could not abide being reduced to one fucker, one soul or one peer among many. He could not come to terms with being expelled from the centre of the universe - rather like the Pope and the rest of the Catholic hierarchs whom he despised.

CHAPTER 33: THE ONLY SAFE LIBERTINE

It is hard to tell whether Sade's dangerous urge was causing heavy damage. Young courtesans who experienced his overbearing need for their total engagement cannot have had their esteem for him, or for men in general, raised thereby. The fact that they might well have been used to that kind of behaviour from men does not excuse it, but underlines the belief in men that their power and wealth ought to enable them to buy any woman they want, body and soul. A young woman put into a milieu where such an attitude is being much exercised narrows her eyes and hardens her heart, and thus is the poison passed on as she too learns to regard the world as fruit to be sucked dry rather than an orchard to be shared and cherished. As well as doing that kind of damage to the morality and expectations of courtesans, their servants and agents, Sade was setting a sordid example for lads on their first outings in Paris, their fathers' money burning holes in their pockets.

Was he also doing heavy *physical* damage? In order to frustrate the fascination with this matter, Sade's relatives moved quickly and spent copiously to burn papers and to silence victims and witnesses. However, we know that, at one stage, Inspector Marais was advising certain procurers in the capital not to supply women to go with Sade to places where, unlike a room of a brothel, a prostitute would have no potential rescuer within call **(see chapter 6)**.

It may well be that Sade inflicted on various prostitutes worse beatings than the well-documented one suffered by Rose Keller **(see chapter 7)**, without their filing complaints to the authorities. They would have limped - or been carried - away to tend their wounds in private, their public silence secured by money, which had led them to risk their health in the first place. Others might have made as much fuss as Keller did, only for all traces of their grievances to have been lost through bribes and bullying at the time and/or by accidental destruction of archives during the last 200 years. Some of the gaps in Sade's story were caused by the upheaval of the Commune in Paris in 1870-71.

There are a few, but enough, indications from the France of Sade's time that murder by a nobleman of a commoner could be cleared up before any prosecution might be started, if enough money were spent and the appropriate arms were twisted. A prostitute suddenly cut from the scene in a Paris teeming with them might hardly be missed, especially if she were estranged from her family, perhaps through the very fact that she was whoring, or if her last and fatal client were known only to a procurer willing to write off the loss of goods in return for a lump sum from the client or his relatives. We cannot tell whether Sade, known as a violent man, ever carried out his threat, uttered to Keller if not others, to kill a hired sexual object and bury her himself. He declared from prison in writing, which he knew could be read by the police, that he had never done murder. Well, he would, would he not?

In *Juliette*, Sade wrote: "It is impossible that a man who has plenty of intelligence, plenty of power or plenty of money should go in for common amusements. Now, if he is refining his pleasures, he will come of necessity to murder, for murder is the ultimate excess of pleasure ..."

Plenty of intelligence he had. Plenty of power and money, though? That was a difficulty.

The weak financial acumen of his father, the Count de Sade, and the contrary quality in his mother-in-law, Mme de Montreuil, were the salvation, I suggest, of many prostitutes who would otherwise have felt the marquis's painful will to impinge. If Sade had been allowed more money by his father, while his son was single, and by his mother-in-law later, he would have had more to spend on sexual pleasure and to lay waste on a greater scale, as some of his better-provided and better-connected noble contemporaries did. Also, he would have had more funds of his own to buy silence about his crimes. He lacked the kind of money and influence required to silence Keller in Paris and to arrange for the overturning in Provence of his death sentence for sodomy and poisoning.

This seems to have been the crucial restraint on his mayhem, in that his debauches had to be of the cheaper kind - and in that he could never be sure that, if he were to have pushed his sexual assaults as far as maiming and murder, there would have been enough support elsewhere in high society, of which he was all too scornful, and enough money forthcoming from his relatives, to secure his continued liberty. The Marquise de Sade said: "My mother has always paid up and will pay up again, no doubt" - but she did not let her son-in-law reach nearly as far into the deep Montreuil purse, or draw nearly as heavily on the extensive Montreuil influence, as he wanted.

But a man can dream, and a dreamer needs to bend no knee at any court, needs no coin in his purse, to indulge himself under sure protection. "They don't conceive how pleasure is served by such assurances, don't conceive what one undertakes when one can say to oneself: 'I'm here alone, I'm here at the end of the world, concealed from all eyes and beyond the scope of any creature to reach me; no more curbs, no more barriers.' " Thus Sade in *The Hundred and Twenty Days of Sodom*, having one of his directing libertines anticipate the unlimited predation of the sealed orgy at Château Silling. Mme de Montreuil seemed to think that the reality at Château la Coste, in 1775, was similar: "In his château with her [the marquise], he thinks he has strength and to spare, and denies himself nothing."

One is drawn to think that Sade cannot have been anything like as destructive a predator in life, among those who came within his reach and were poor enough to need to stay there while he was having his way, as are the rich flayers and vivisectors of his literature among their herds of victims.

Yet the obscure trace that remains of the young maid taken hurt from la Coste to Saumane in 1775 **(see chapter 10)** cries that this opinion might be based on nothing more than a wish that it were so. One of Sade's fictional libertines - Saint-Fond in *Juliette* - laments victims dying because thus they slip away from his impingement on them: "When I immolate an object ..., I would like to prolong its woes beyond the immensity of the ages." The author might have known that feeling from personal experience with humans.

However, it might have stemmed from his observations of himself and others while hunting animals, or his imagination alone might have brought him such an insight.

The sure conclusion is that the only safe libertine of violence is a jailed one (as Mme de Montreuil came to believe), a reformed one (as Sade argued in his Enlightened vein), or a dead one.

CHAPTER 34: "NO PASSING JUDGEMENT ON ME"

Could Sade have been led away from the urge that made him dangerous in debauchery? If that were to have been tried by the sort of steadfast female whom he seems to have lacked, then she would have needed a remarkable combination of qualities. Even if there had crossed his path the unlikely one who understood what was needed, she might well have been in danger as she struggled to have him "take to a diet gradually", as Sade wrote in a letter from jail, indicating how he might have been reformed **(see chapter 20)**.

Marie Dorothée de Rousset, the resourceful housekeeper at la Coste, would not provide sexual service for Sade. "She can do anything with those five fingers of hers. At la Coste there was only one thing I wanted her to do with those very fingers, but she would not," Sade wrote from prison **(see chapter 18)**. However, perhaps because sexual contact was out of the question, he was able, sitting on "our bench" in the grounds of the manorhouse, to speak openly to her about himself, or so he claimed. Also, for a short period while he was behind bars ar Vincennes, Rousset managed, by letters, to persuade away some of Sade's pent-up rage with the sort of leg-pulling, often nicely turned and affectionate, that an attentive and alert family or community can apply to its termagant members and, by bringing them to laugh at themselves, have them understand what damage they do.

This effect of Rousset's did not last, though, for it was overwhelmed by Sade's bitter wrath. There was another good influence he did not keep for long enough, he wrote, probably of his childhood tutor the Abbé Amblet. There is no telling what period would have been long enough to steam the explosive wilfulness of the Marquis de Sade out of its touchy casing.

Anyone who took the task would have been risking - apart from any physical danger - moral subversion as Sade countered with his arguments, bullying and charm on behalf of his libertine way of life, arisen from a fierce conviction and assembled and voiced with the benefit of his training in rhetoric by the Jesuits **(see chapter 3)**. Rousset was sufficiently swayed to take his part against an entrenched and powerful body of revulsion in Paris at his behaviour, persisting in her efforts on his behalf even after she had read at least part of the secret ministerial file that detailed activities which, according to royal ministers, gave cause to keep him imprisoned. Anne Prospère de Launay, Sade's sister-in-law, seems to have been moved, by him, to some degree from her adherence to the Catholic Church as a canoness.

The Count de Sade and Mme de Montreuil, at different stages of the marquis's life, had some influence over him in that they held the strings of purses he wanted to dip into. From that position, they were able to restrain him somewhat, Mme de Montreuil directly and via Sade's Provençal agent Gaufridy. However, they never left the majority of his circle that never understood Sade well enough to find and keep sympathy for him. His father and his mother-in-law never had sufficient of his respect to alter him, not least because he believed - with some cause - that their essential interests were not his.

Renée Pélagie, his wife, seems to have been unable, by her sexuality or her intellect, to draw Sade into equal give and take, and to hold him there for long enough to help effect any more than passing alteration in him. Sade the young sexual adventurer found her "too cold and too pious", he told his uncle the Abbé de Sade **(see chapter 6)**. She almost certainly came to accept his arguments for behaving as he did during their marriage - a chief one having been that the alliance had not been his idea, rather that of their scheming relatives, so there was no reason for him to defer to the wishes of a partner he had not sought. Apart from that, there was his trumpeting about the necessity for men to live without restriction so as to reach their full extension in every way. Renée Pélagie, raised as a satellite, seems to have swallowed this line during many of the best years of her life.

How much did she understand of what was behind the glamour, rhetoric and philandering of her husband? During his bout of sexual jealousy towards her, virulently expressed by letters from jail in 1781 **(see chapter 19)**, she reported it to Rousset and asked the housekeeper: "Please let me know how he manages to think up all this stuff." After 18 years of that marriage, she had no idea?

To be fairer to the marquise, that is an easy sigh to utter with hindsight 200 years later, without her blinkers of an upbringing in unenlightened obedience. Also to give her more of her due, note that, although she probably spent more time with Sade than anyone else did between their marriage in 1763 and his removal from the Bastille in 1789, her access to him was far from regular and sustained. Renée

Pélagie and her "adored darling" were under the same roof for hardly a quarter of those 26 years. Even when they were together, how much still, receptive attention did he extend to her? Not much, I think, given his many distractions and his abiding urge to impinge on her and many others. When they met in jail as prisoner and visitor, the presence of an eavesdropping official was no more conducive to open and patient conversation than were Sade's outbursts of abuse on some of those occasions.

It is remarkable how little time - let alone receptive attention - Sade gave to anyone. Gaufridy, the useful yet obstructive agent in Provence, was in contact with Sade over decades yet they rarely met and the relationship, although marked by exchanges of confidences and intimate gossip, was always that of a lord of estates and his senior bailiff. Marie Constance Quesnet, who was with Sade for most of his life from 1790 until near the end in 1814, was a convenient housekeeper and literary sounding-board for Citizen Sade. We have his word that she was reading *Justine* "while it's hot", as Sade was penning it, and offered valuable comments and suggestions. Anyone, especially any woman, who read that stream of tortures of women by rich men in safe redoubts, and helped it on its way, was not fit for reforming the Marquis de Sade. In his corpulent later years, he was tender towards Marie Constance, it seems, in his wheezy, distracted way. However, Sade's querulous and cold-hearted calculation of how he would keep her near him through buying the poor woman another interest-bearing bond every five years carries the tone of his atttitude to their relationship **(see chapter 24)**.

Sade complained, about his stretches in jail, "the intervals in my life have been too long." Perhaps so, but it was he who provoked the stage managers to bring down the curtain so abruptly and the producers to keep the theatre dark for such long periods. Even while the show was running, Sade persisted in changing the supporting cast (especially the female members thereof). No friend, agent, servant, housekeeper, relative, wife, lover was allowed close enough for long enough to work a permanent alteration in him. People able to work such a change, and therefore equipped with discernment and independence, tend not to stay with those seized by a will to fuck and harangue while feeling no-one's impress.

There might have been periods of his adult life, before he went to prison in 1777 for an almost interrupted 13 years, when he refrained from libertinage. For instance, he probably had little scope for debauchery while restricted to the Montreuils' Norman estate of Échauffour in 1763-64 **(see chapter 6)**. However, gaps in current knowledge of his activities, many of them contrived by people who wanted to erase his bad reputation, cannot be safely distinguished from intervals in his roistering. Even if we allow all apparent breaks in the debauchery as real ones, they were only pauses in a tendency to which he always returned, while his flesh stayed willing.

Sade seems to have considered that something could be done to change him. Leaving aside certain departures in his letters from jail - as jokes, self-pity or longings to be out at any price - a wish for improvement in himself appears rarely, however. The most realistic, albeit fleeting, manifestation came from Vincennes in November 1781, when he regretted that he had not been sent "once a fortnight, an intelligent man, who would have worked on my heart and on my mind alternately, and would have put them both to rights." No such precursor of psychiatry visited Cell No. 6, nor did the inmate show any understanding, there or elsewhere, of how difficult improvement of himself would have been. A true reformation would have meant overcoming his profound desire to have and hold the attention of others, by violence if necessary, which Sade indeed found necessary.

Persecution by the authorities had no chance to bring about that change. Sade wrote: "Ten thousand years of imprisonment and five hundred pounds of chains would only fix my habits more securely" **(see chapter 20)**. In official persecution, there was no confirmation for Sade of an affecting total engagement to him, at least not once the reaction of the powers that were had congealed from a hue and cry for a fugitive libertine into a long confinement of one of many neutralised trouble-makers whose files were gathering dust in ministerial archives.

Sade wrote in *The Hundred and Twenty Days* that news of a nobleman having been executed in effigy provoked the man himself to orgasm: "There I am covered with opprobrium and scandal; stand back, stand back, I have to discharge on the strength of that!" Sade's own execution in effigy, at Aix in 1772 **(see chapter 8)**, and his reaction to it would have been the inspiration for that vignette, as well it might for the palaver at Aix was a splendid seal on his crime of sodomy and poisoning at Marseilles, the dummy execution having been conducted with much arcane ceremony before an intent crowd passing his name from one to another. What a hullabaloo - and all about him! Best of all, he was at liberty to enjoy the hearing about it.

As I say, though, the piquancy in being the focus of such official attention lost its savour whenever that focus was felt to be diffused. While on the run in Italy, away from people who would confirm, by referring to his escapades, what a devil of a fellow he was, Sade became bored and homesick. Back at la Coste, there would be immediate evidence of efforts by his wife on his behalf, in person or by letters from the north, and of machinations by his mother-in-law, as he saw them, to bring him down. The people of the estate and the village would testify, by their ordinary behaviour, to his place as a local kingpin, their lord of the manor, come execution in effigy, come sentence quashed on appeal. He complained by letter, while lying low away from Provence and in anonymity, that he was "not cut out to be an adventurer" **(see chapter 9)**. That is, he was not cut out to go about as anyone other than the Marquis de Sade, impinger extraordinary, proof against the effects of others.

He was profoundly disconcerted as the weeks turned into months and years at Vincennes after 1778, as he became a long-term prisoner. There was no pleasure in the squalor and the loneliness, in the scrabbling for numerical clues and structures among any hints of his own imagining, in the detached and time-serving staff flintily cancelling his exercise privileges if he raged at them - no sort of response to feed Sade's craving for the engagement of others, and so no scope to change his ways.

Pauvert writes perceptively that Sade avoided combat with authorities such as the royal court and legal tribunals, ignoring them in ordinary times, running away and hiding when pressed. He preferred to engage with Mme de Montreuil, an enemy *in person*.

I suggest that he felt the effect of his actions on her because, for a long time, he had plentiful evidence of the heat of her reactions to him as her main source of upset. When others pressed frustration upon him, he reviled them not only in their own right but also as his mother-in-law's "henchmen" and "satellites". Sade probably never met his mother-in-law after 1771, when he left Paris and its baying creditors for la Coste. However, although she became a remote opponent who could no longer be impressed face to face - as she acted through such agents as Gaufridy, policemen and officials - Sade kept flailing at her across the gulf. He could not forget the intensity of their relationship in the times when Mme de Montreuil still had hopes that he might become a credit to her family.

"Social combat demands the acceptance of a game in which he does not want to play. Against powerful combinations of interests which manifest themselves as enemies, one must range others, and thus cease to enjoy a solitude which carries as much in the way of social inconvenience as it does of personal advantage," Pauvert writes.

Yes, and Sade refused to associate with potential allies in order to combat his difficulties lest he lose his pre-eminence in the process. As cock of his lone walk, he was imperial, albeit with few and inconstant subjects; as an ally, in combat, he would have had to risk being constrained to kiss a sceptre held by another hand or by many - to risk being impinged on and altered.

Pauvert maintains that Sade refused "his own combat, the one for his freedom." Yes, except in intimate lists where the opponents were bound to react with heat, to show him that his blows, his very presence, were resounding. Here lies illumination of Sade as both he who was cast down by the fact and the prospect of being alone, and as he who was enraged by the fact and the prospect of company. "Solitude is lethal for me," he lamented from Vincennes. After he learned, on leaving the asylum at Charenton in 1790, that his wife was seeking a legal separation from him, he described himself thus, in a letter to one of his aunts: "I, who got married only so as to have some company in my house when I was getting old, here I am deserted, abandoned, isolated, and reduced to the sad fate in which my unfortunate father ended his days; of all the states of old age, the one I dreaded most of all." It all depended on what sort of person broke his solitude - if biddable, all well and good. On the other hand, when fuming from Vincennes in 1781 over the plan to transfer him to Montélimar **(see chapter 16)**, he declared that, if the project were maintained, "I will stay in a room there all the time and never come out, and therefore no-one will ever have the sweet pleasure *of passing judgement on me* ..." No assessors, no magistrates, no cold eyes proof against his charm, his tantrums, his fists, were ever to weigh up - or act upon - lonely Louis.

Besides, as regards his attitude to the authorities and their scope for having an effect on him, the marquis lived in a society where nobles were used to the idea that their influence and money could get them out of trouble. One could negotiate or bribe one's way out of being charged with an offence or, failing that, out of jail, just as one could be lobbied or bought into it in the first place. Someone as arrogant as Sade towards the powers of others was especially apt to view official punishment of crimes in this way. His father had had enough clout to get him out of jail after a notorious blasphemy (with Testard); his mother-in-law had managed to have his capital sentence set aside in favour of a mere admonition. None of this was apt to make Sade more open to any altering influence.

What's more, Sade had never drawn blood from any but the enemies of his sovereign and whores - both fair game for an officer and a gentleman, he believed - so there was no cause to keep him locked away, he also believed. He was accordingly unlikely to change in hiimself such old ways, accordingly surprised and upset whenever he was jailed, under the royal régime anyway, .

His belief in the likelihood of his connections springing him from jail did not begin to shrivel until some time after he had re-entered Vincennes in 1778. He came to understand then that his most powerful - because the richest and most diligent - connection had moved conclusively from being his potential liberator, for the sake of the dynasty into which he had married, into an implacable barrier against his return to circulation, also for the dynasty's sake. Once Mme de Montreuil had decided that the family name would be better served by his permanent imprisonment than by letting him out, there was no raising the curtain on Sade again - not until the theatre of France had been taken over by new management in 1789.

* * *

All this is not to deny that he enjoyed being whipped and buggered, in thus intensifying the engagement of other participants in sexual encounters and so increasing his own excitement. This is a different matter to punishment by dispassionate officials, by signatories whom one never sees and by their stony-faced employees. Here is a libertine man in *Justine*, revelling in a certain taste:

"... if only you knew the charms of this fantasy, if only you could understand what one experiences from the sweet illusion of being no more than a woman! Unbelievable distraction of the mind! One abhors this sex and one wants to imitate it! Oh! how sweet it is to achieve that, ... how delightful it is to be the trollop for all who want you, ... the frenzy and the prostitution, in being, all on the one day, successively the mistress of a burglar, of a marquis, of a valet, of a monk, to be by them in turn treasured, fondled, suspected, threatened, beaten, sometimes in their triumphant arms, and sometimes a victim at their feet, melting them with caresses, rekindling them with wildness..."

Always with their fierce and full attention - the motive for taking the lash, the penetration, the impingement in all deranged forms.

One might still argue that Sade must have got a thrill out of the arrest of August 1778, when a vengeful Inspector Marais and his men stormed into la Coste by night and carried him off **(see chapter 13)**. Plenty of engagement there - Marais and his team smashing through a door to nab their quarry, insulting him raucously with accusations about his sexual behaviour and calling him *tu*, what's more; then putting him on show, like a captured highwayman or a six-legged sheep, in the Provence of his birth and his esteem, on the way north. Yes, plenty of wild eyes, sweat and violence.

However, Sade seems to have found the episode very embarrassing and distasteful. From his cell at Vincennes, when refusing the proposed transfer to a jail in the south, he said he had had enough of being put on show in his father's region **(see chapter 16)**. The police raid on la Coste had not been sought by Sade and was always out of his control. He was unable to direct any engagement of the other participants in the affair, was unable to keep their minds on him. It was Marais's show and Sade was merely at the officer's disposal as his old chronicler of the vice squad dossiers exacted retribution for his escape from custody a few weeks before. Worst of all, it was no dream. Sade loathed being a trussed-up object, with no control over the proceedings. Remember how, even while the Marseilles prostitutes were beating him, he had charge of the structure of the event by ringing the changes among participants and activities, and by keeping score of the number of strokes through making marks on the mantelpiece **(see chapter 8)**. However much heat and excitement was in the air, Sade had to keep a grip. To change him, that grip would have had to be broken - but he was too fearful to let that happen.

CHAPTER 35: ALWAYS ON A TETHER AND ALWAYS ON A PRECIPICE

The Marquis de Sade went to jail in 1777, aged 36. He emerged in 1790, aged 49. Prison changed him, but not fundamentally. Sade called his time in Vincennes fortress *pressurage*, a pressing of grapes. The grapes had long been bitter and so the wine - the literature fermented in prison - was bound to make a bitter vintage. Jail was hard for an incorrigible impinger to take, as many officials who had to deal with him during his terms behind bars testified in their reports. When he behaved acceptably, he was usually either trying to lull the authorities into relaxing their vigilance while he prepared to escape (as at Miolans in the spring of 1773, **see chapter 9**, when he even performed his Easter duty as a Catholic), seeking to have his exercise periods or his wife's visits restored, or feeling so sorry for himself that his normal stroppiness was at a low ebb. His obsessions with numbers and lists, his contretemps with staff, his efforts to keep Renée Pélagie in his grip at long range, his letters - all these were not enough to meet his urge for engagement.

Sade had to spend a great deal of time alone. The trouble with people, Pascal thought, is that they are unable to stay quietly in their rooms. Sade could not stay within the bounds of his cell, although he had to remain there physically. He took up his quill to grasp the attention, via literature, of legions of his imaginary victims and, he hoped, that of many readers, shrivelling their hearts and criminalising their minds. The works that began to emerge at Vincennes and the Bastille were his wildest dreams of a criminal cornucopia pouring into his lap and into the laps of others. Having plunged into literature for fulfilment, his finances no longer governed the extent of the sexual swathe he could cut. Sartre wrote that one must risk one's life in order to feel alive; Sade needed to risk the lives of others in order to feel alive. Ink and paper became his proxy circus of fatal thrills. Sade reported to his wife that he was "caused to summon phantoms which I will have to give substance", but the phantoms had been taking shape, as the grapes had been turning sour, for years.

The substance that the phantoms took gave Sade his posthumous fame. The familiarity of the names of few authors can have as far outstripped the familiarity of their respective bodies of work as the name of Sade has resounded by comparison with the thin knowledge of what his writings contain and of what they mean. These days, readers may find his literary works published openly, nearly all of them available in French and many of them in English and other languages. I have not the space to deal with his works in great detail. I shall try to give an impression of what the five main surviving works indicate.

* * *

Justine remains the most familiar title. Its first reviewer, in 1792, advised his public: "It is both tiresome and repulsive to read... You young people whose sensibility has not been coarsened by dissolute living should steer clear of this book, which is a threat to the heart and mind! You adult men who have been placed out of danger by your experience and the quietening of your urges should read it to see how far the derangement of the human imagination can go, but put it on the fire as soon as you have finished it..."

The initial draft, called *The Misfortunes of Virtue* (*Les Infortunes de la Vertu*), of what became *Justine* was dashed off in a few weeks while Sade was still in the Bastille. Once he had been released by the Revolutionary government in 1790, this was expanded into *Justine or The Hardships of Virtue* (*Justine ou Les Malheurs de la Vertu*), dedicated to Marie Constance Quesnet. Sade had it published anonymously in 1791 by Girouard. (Various other editions, all probably unauthorised by Sade and one claimed to have been printed in Philadelphia, appeared from various French publishers in the next few years.)

Sade told the Provençal lawyer Reinaud **(see chapter 24)** that he had been "short of money and my publisher was asking for it to be well *peppered* and for him I have made it fit to stink out the devil..." However, this does not mean that Girouard was the sole hand behind *Justine* having turned out to be so scurrilous. In his letter to Reinaud, Sade was trying to shore up his reputation in Provence through a contact who was important in relaying the Parisian activities of the head of the Sade family to his relatives and retainers in the south of France. The 1791 version is clearly an extension of the draft written in the Bastille before Girouard and Sade had met and discussed terms. Any money the author received for his efforts was most welcome, and he already knew very well the profit to be won from well peppered literature.

Although Sade left his name off his 1791 version of *Justine*, wary of censorship, the vocabulary used in it would not seem obscene to most modern readers. Descriptions of sexual intercourse are veiled in elaborate circumlocutions - vaginas are "altars" and "shrines", erect penises are "very monstrous objects", "battering rams thundering at the gates". Such euphemisms were not only apt to make the book more acceptable to the authorities and those of his personal circle who might take offence, but also suited the character of the narrator and main protagonist, Justine herself. The last and longest version of the novel, by contrast, *The New Justine*, much revised and double the length of the 1791 edition, probably came out in 1800, having been prepared when the administration of France by the Directory was one of the least censorious of public morality in any European country before the end of World War I. This final edition abandoned first-person narration for a tale told by the author and cast aside euphemisms.

In the time between the first and last versions of the book, Sade had been through the Revolutionary Terror in Paris. I do not see this, however, as having caused him to re-write *Justine* as he did. His propensity for uninhibited accounts of sexual behaviour, including calculated destruction of victims, was exercised while he was still in royal prisons before 1790, via the text of *The Hundred and Twenty Days of Sodom*, for instance. The Terror would hardly have made anyone who had experienced it more likely to think well of human behaviour under pressure, but Sade was set in his ways, at his desk or away from it, by the time Louis XVI went to the guillotine. After 1794, when the Terror collapsed and Sade was released from the Committee of Public Safety's prisons, he was still winning no fortune or fame from his plays, prices were still very high in Paris, his agent in Provence was still erratic in sending revenue from the estates, and so his pen in its anonymous vein remained a necessary source of cash. Hence another, even hotter, version of *Justine*. Although the Directory was slow to censor, Sade left his name off the last version also.

All the versions of the novel are heavy with virtue beset, battered and bedraggled. Justine, a young woman of gentle birth and some education, falls on hard times and passes from one unscrupulous individual or band to another, all of these equipped to use and keep her and other women in well-appointed castles, monasteries, forest lairs.

As one misfortune succeeds another, and she passes from one secure exploitation chamber to another, Justine holds on to her belief that, no matter what abuse her body has to suffer, she remains virtuous as long as her faith and hope are not diminished by any sinful act of her own. She hopes that her immaculate conduct will earn her a reward in the form of some relief from the troubles that befall her, as Angela Carter pointed out. Men who exploit her want to have her heart go over to them, but she holds out against them, yielding only the flesh which she cannot defend against their wealth and strength. As such, she retains moral superiority, to which she is often the only witness, apart from her oppressors and God.

This stubborn morality of Justine is by no means inconsistent with her inertia and habitual obedience, her lack of capacity to learn and progress, to act decisively against an oppressor when a rare opportunity occurs. Carter wrote that Justine has "an egotistical heart" and "does not know how to do good". Remember that Sade was the creator of this limited female, he having been much averse to the idea of women who were free to ignore him or any other libertine man. No wonder, then, that Justine enjoys only brief respites from harassment, from such demands on her body and her whole attention that she has little time to do other than react to what is being forced on her and into her.

Yet the author allows her to keep her soul inviolate - no invader ever reaches her core during all the vicissitudes. One of the monks who takes her, in the final edition, identifies his sexual emissions at climax with lava erupting from a volcano, yet yearns for such copious ejaculations as to overwhelm whole towns. Justine's purity of spirit likewise eludes his will to impinge.

This irreducibility of Justine was drawn from life. She has no resilience, no ability to grow, only a dense little heart to which she admits only God. She is the stubborn, suffering, faithful, narrow, Roman Catholic woman of all the ages, unilluminated by education and encouragement to experiment and revise. Justine may acquiesce to - and even assist under threat - the libertinage that sweats and snarls around her, but she is incapable of being a true accomplice to the libertines. If Renée Pélagie, Marquise de Sade, was the model for any character in her husband's fiction, Justine is the one[1].

* * *

---

1 However, the member of the Sade circle given the nickname Justine was the cook from Montpellier, Catherine Trillet (see chapter 11).

The Hundred and Twenty Days of Sodom or the School of Libertinage is Sade's crude and oppressive fantasy of a winter spent in an orgy at a remote castle. Four middle-aged men, rich enough to sustain careers of constant depredation among all classes of human victim, arrange for Château Silling, in the mountains of central Europe, to be stocked with copious supplies of superb food and drink, as well as plenty of fuel for heating, before paths and bridges that link it to the outside world are destroyed behind the orgiasts on their arrival in late-October. The orgy of sexual exploitation proceeds according to rigid rules and set chronological sequences. The control by the four overlords is absolute; their safety against surprise or attack is total.

No wonder *The Hundred and Twenty Days of Sodom* was written in a clammy, dirty cell by a prisoner lacking the money to buy his way out, badly fed (by his own standards), bereft of company, liable to have his territory invaded by supervisors at any moment, with no knowledge of when he might be released, yearning for structure to define passing time and for outlets to satisfy his obsession with sexual impingement. Sade - lonely and masturbating - complained to his wife by letter that incarceration was bringing back to his thoughts "phantoms ... that had begun to fade away... When you overheat the pot, ... it's going to boil over." In the King of France's jails, he had a great deal of time for "these researches spurned by nature ..., these dangerous departures of an over-fiery imagination which, always running after happiness without ever finding it in anything, end by putting ghosts in place of reality and *unseemly deviations* in place of a straightforward enjoyment...

"This way of thinking ... is the only solace I know; it eases all my woes in prison, it makes up all my pleasure in this world and I hold on to it more fervently than to life itself" **(see chapter 20)**.

From another pen of the Enlightenment, the winter orgy might have been one of uninhibited play for all, of equal seekers after pleasure in an earthly paradise of sensuality, limited only by the flagging of the flesh and the satiety of the spirit, until the next experiment. The snow that isolates Silling could have been a beautiful boundary, a cool constant outside, as heightening contrast to the warmth, improvisation and surprise inside. Under Sade's quill, however, the snow is made another instrument of enclosure, like the walled-up gates and the will and wealth of the four masters. They seek their delights within a fixed formula whereby the other 42 participants serve them, concentrate on them, to the exclusion of any thought for God or other mortal.

The four - a duke, a bishop, a high court judge and a banker - made their fortunes by war profiteering, swindling, murder. Their experience of debauchery is profound and dedicated. They are apt, at orgasm, variously to "swooning", "lubricious rage [and] cruel deeds", "a spasm that throws him into a wanton fury dangerous to those who are serving his urges." Two of them have no interest in vaginal intercourse and all prefer to give or take sexual penetration at the anus. Among their retinue are their four young wives - plus four procuresses, four elderly, decrepit female servants and eight burly and well-endowed male prostitutes, all contracted to the orgy for pay. Kidnapped from their families or from their schools, at great expense in hiring gangs to waylay them, are eight young girls and eight young boys, aged 15 to 12 years.

During the two days before the orgy opens on the first of November, the four directors draw up a list of 35 rules, many of these concerned with the timetable of each day, which is built around a set of stories, each related to a sexual "passion", told by one of the procuresses in order to excite the four masters. The rules also lay down the subservient conduct of the girls and boys, who must kneel whenever they encounter one of the four "friends", and must use only the castle's chapel, converted for the purpose, as toilet. They may not do this as and when they want, but only as and when allowed by one or other of the four overlords, who are to inspect the lavatories for evidence of infringement, the penalty for which being death. During the four-month orgy, the masters vary, by order, the diets of certain of the retinue so as to tickle their own palates with different flavours as they eat shit from the various bodies. The lords occasionally try to outdo each other by showing who can eat turds from the decrepit, diseased old women, rather than sticking to those from young girls and boys on a régime of bland food.

This aspect of the impinging debauchee's urge for control is important. As Angela Carter pointed out, to lose free control of one's excremental faculty is to be deprived of the first, most elemental expression of autonomy. The four overlords emphasise that *they* retain this autonomy, by shitting when and where they please, wiping themselves afterwards or not according to their own whim. The four's troupe of objects does not even own other products of their bodies, including semen and vaginal fluids, for there are strict rules that they may only engage in sexual activity with the masters present and by permission of one or more of the four.

On the last day of October, the day before the orgy is to begin, the duke addresses the female captives: "Weak, chained creatures whose only fate is to please us, you are to expect nothing but humiliation ... the only virtue I recommend to you is obedience... Never forget that we will use you all and none of you should deceive herself by imagining that she can arouse in us any pity whatsoever. When inspired to rage at the altars which have been able to win from us a few granules of incense[2], our pride and our libertinage destroy [those altars] immediately that the illusion [which those have inspired] has satisfied our sensual desires; then the domination that our imagination has over us is dispelled in a moment by the return of contempt, almost invariably joined by loathing, to prime position in our minds. Besides, what could you offer that we do not already know to its last detail? What will you hold out to us that we shall not trample underfoot, often just as ecstasy seizes us? ...

"Think of your situation, and such a consideration should make you tremble... You are held in an irreducible fortress; nobody at all knows that you are here; your friends and relatives cannot find you; to the outside world, you are already dead; you still draw breath only at our pleasure, as well as for our pleasure... There will scarcely be any outrages into which we will not be plunged; ... offer yourselves to all of them without so much as a blink of an eye; demonstrate patience, submission and fortitude. The excesses of our passions might unfortunately bring about the end of some of you, in which case they should accept their destiny with courage; no-one is to live forever, and death before she grows old is the best luck a woman can have...

"What's more, you are not to wait for us to spell out our instructions as to what we want you to do; a gesture, a look, sometimes no more than our mood, will indicate our wish, and you will be punished as sharply for having failed to interpret that as you would be if you had ignored or gone contrary to a desire stated in detail... For instance, if the requirement were to see a certain part of your body and you were such a fumbler as to show a different part, you ought to understand how much that sort of disrespect would spoil our excitement and you ought to grasp how dangerous it is to dampen the ardent imagination of

2 That is, furious at the bodies which have excited the four to lose their self-possession in sexual ejaculation.

a libertine who, let us say, is wanting an arse to take his ejaculation, when a cunt is offered by some idiot...

"In general, you should reveal your fronts to us very rarely; bear in mind that this disgusting organ, which Nature must have made in a fit of absence of mind, is the one we always regard with greatest distaste...

"To sum up: cringe, tremble, anticipate, submit - if you do that you still might well not be entirely happy but you might not be utterly miserable. No scheming together, no little leagues, none of those mawkish sisterhoods that girls like such a lot. These tug the heart into fondness which makes it less ready to accept the only true surrender - the one for which we have marked you..."

To concentrate even further the minds of the object herd upon the masters, they also decree that there is to be no religious observance or any resemblance thereof - rather, "the name of God is not to be spoken, except when linked to invective or curses" - and, among the objects, not "the least show of mirth..."

With that, next day, the foursome's meticulously fenced free field of sexual fire is entered and the procuress Duclos begins the first story - not that her original name is Duclos for she was prostituted at the age of nine, as her stories soon reveal, and the madame followed the custom of the house by naming the novice after her first client. Sade's lesson in how to reach for control of women extended to robbery of names and imposition of those of men who could afford to buy.

The four libertines seize to themselves the definition of what is true, altering it at will, thus facilitating their retention of control by bewildering the captives, removing the structures of their lives as lived before they were kidnapped on behalf of the masters, then denying them all but the minimal certainties of their own suffering and death. The only solid framework is the power of the quartet, derived from their wealth, which also enables them to hire and keep the support of the strongest young men in the party.

"Money and a---, they're my country's gods," Sade wrote in one of his prison letters. In the original, *L'or et le c--*. Whether he meant *c* for *cul* or *con* (arse or cunt), we do not know, for he was writing with the police censors in mind, but the former is more likely, given his penchant for buggery. In any event, *The Hundred and Twenty Days* was a bitter fruit of the corruption and licentiousness among the rich of the France of his time. It was also a fruit of the personality of its author, he who enjoyed sexual use of servants - "these kinds of items of physical furniture" **(see chapter 10)** - and had one of his four masters at Silling declare: "There's nothing wicked in whatever gives you a hard-on, and the only crime on the face of the Earth is to refuse anything that does just that."

Sade claims in his preamble "six hundred different dishes" set before the reader. Yet the winter of mayhem at Silling - stories told by the four *doyennes* and deeds done by the four masters - fails to comprise the "sumptuous banquet" of "genuine diversity" that Sade advertised. The descriptions are thin, repetitive, unfurnished by telling detail. The victims are sketched no more than is necessary to establish that another item of temporarily diverting human flesh is pinned in place, for undisputed usage, perhaps to destruction, perhaps not, at the whim of the author. The flow of action is not only all one way, as the overlords batten onto the object herd without hindrance, but also that action is conveyed with haste and impatience, as though the author could not relax to his task, for all the time on his hands.

Sade did not mean the version of *The Hundred and Twenty Days* which has reached us to be the final one, as notes in the existing text make clear, and there is no knowing how elaborate or dense the story might have become. For all we know, a fully developed version - now lost - may have been written. However, none of his literary works indicates a capacity to offer characters, relations and descriptions of great depth and diversity. There are no grounds for thinking that the manuscript of *The Hundred and Twenty Days* is a fine flower of literature frozen in the half-bloom. It needs more than extra words to make it blossom.

The uneasy urge to press on to the next episode is an expression of desire to be imposing oneself ever more extensively. The four masters enter their captive objects and destroy them piece by piece. Lewd handling, buggery, vaginal intercourse, fellatio and corporal punishment are exceeded lest the objects become used to them and so able to have their minds on some other matter, even while their bodies are being abused. Pincers, hot irons, knives, scalpels ensure that the prey has its full attention on what is being done to it, for how can one achieve indifference to the pain of pulled teeth, severed fingers and toes, branded thighs, gouged eyes, sheared nipples, pierced scrotums, burned vaginal and anal passages... One of the wives of the masters is murdered by her pregnant womb being cut open by a man while he is buggering a young boy. Death is the only escape for those victims, in the last days of the winter, not given by the overlords the green ribbon that marks those who will assist the four in massacre of the rest, before a surviving 16 returns to Paris when the snows have melted.

There is no pretending that this piece of horror was written only to occupy Sade's time and hands in prison, and help him to sexual relief. He was specific in his intention to reach readers in the outside world - sometime, somehow - and seize their engagement by his "extravagances". Sade himself referred to authors whose "corruption is so dangerous, so seething, that their only purpose when they publish their vile books is that their crimes shall outlive themselves; these writers have to give up crimes but their damnable works will bring others to commit yet more crimes, and this knowledge consoles them as unavoidable death ends their lives."

Strange to tell, however, amid all the overbearing and exploitation of *The Hundred and Twenty Days*, Sade shows a rare and heartening insight as to how it might be resisted **(see chapter 10)**. During a description of one of the four overlords - the huge, muscular and sexually rampaging Duke de Blangis - comes this hint of a great lack: "Yet, for all that, ... a steadfast child might have thrown this monster into a panic; ... whenever Blangis found that he was unable to use his treachery or his trickery to overcome an enemy, he would come over fearful and cowardly; the least idea of any kind of fight on equal terms would have made him hide himself in the remotest region of the world."

*　　　*　　　*

The Hundred and Twenty Days, lost to Sade when the Bastille was invaded by the people of Paris on 14 July 1789, was not published until the 20th century. The much more acceptable novel *Aline and Valcour*, however, would have reached bookshops in France, as it did in 1795, even sooner but for the intervention of the Revolutionary Terror and the arrest of the author and of its publisher **(see chapter 26)**. It must be one of the very few novels which, while at the press, lost their publishers to decapitation by guillotine.

Aline and Valcour was drafted within sight of the censors at the Bastille, and was to be published under Sade's own name, so he avoided explicit sexual descriptions. However, he offered criticism of how the country had been faring under kings and priests, as well as pointers to how an ideal state might be conducted. He was cautious enough to wrap his satire of Bourbon France in a description of a fictional society in Africa. The novel is the best developed, most various, of Sade's surviving literary works and shows he could write serviceably for a wide range of readers, when he wanted, and offer some stimulating liberal ideas. Even so, it is an awkward parcel of various narrative elements, the main one being the thwarted love of two decent young people, Aline and Valcour, who are overcome by the cold manoeuvres of Aline's father, intent on having her marry a rich old banker so as to rescue the family fortunes. I will concentrate on two contrasted fictional societies visited in a journey by another character, Sainville.

In Butua, the African country that he visits and deplores, a feudal monarchy squeezes taxes and tribute from credulous, near-illiterate peasants who are subject to severe punishments for any breach of the law. Meanwhile, robbery and murder by the nobles are ignored by the authorities. Priests officiate on behalf of a deity - half-man, half-snake - and run all formal education, ensuring that women are taught nothing but complete submission to their husbands. A small and incompetent scattering of doctors practises no medicine unless paid. This is a Sadeian view of France under the royal administration.

However, Sainville sails on to the South Pacific Ocean, where he finds a much happier community, on the island of Tamoé **(see chapter 31)**, where the benign King Zamé tells of his disgust for the private property, social hierarchy, organised religion and authoritarian family life of western Europe, which he has visited. On warm and fertile Tamoé, society holds all property in common and runs all manufacturing, ensuring equality of wealth among the citizens and no class distinction. Children are brought up in state schools, with sexual segregation, spending some of their time tending gardens and fields, and learning duties as respectful citizens and marriage partners. The children may receive visits from their parents but may not leave the schools. At the age of 15, each boy is taken to a girls' school to choose a wife, unless he prefers to undertake work for the community instead of marriage. Any girl chosen has the right to refuse.

Each couple is given a plot of land and a house by the community. Most inhabitants are small farmers but others are in manufacturing, supplied by the community with the food they have not the land or time to grow. Public warehouses hold enough grain to maintain the island in case of two failed harvests. (Such a provision in the France of the late-1780s might have kept Louis XVI on his throne.)

Homes for the lonely and the handicapped are attached to the schools so that children shall learn to care for the less fortunate; citizens who neglect their land are moved to poorer ground; there are no jails, no death penalty and no brothels. Vices are quelled by the intervention of the community, expressing its disgust and ridicule uninhibitedly, tolerating the miscreant as far as possible but eventually sending recidivists into exile. The most worthy citizens are given titles with resounding names but no privileges.

There is no professional army; all boys and men have military training. There are no luxury arts and crafts; painting, theatre and music are strictly amateur and all art is directed to foster good citizenship. There are no priests, no organised religion and no lawyers, discussion of theology and jurisprudence being among the anti-social activities that could put a person in a wrong-doer's distinctive shirt. Tamoé has no money, just barter, and gives away surplus production to less fortunate islands nearby.

You can tell that Tamoé is very far from Silling Castle. It is evidence of what Sade could create when on his best, Enlightened behaviour. Even on Tamoé, though, a few restrictive lines are drawn. The schools teach the girls sewing and cookery, the boys military skills and sports, with no possibility of a boy taking up the needle or a girl taking to the running course. No-one is allowed more than two divorces.

Also dangerous for the general well-being in such a utopia is the scope for endless, small-minded blethering over who might be letting too many weeds sprout among his corn cobs or who might be trying to get shot of a spouse too many. Might the society be bland and tetchy through its lack of challenge to the individual and through a lack of scope to revise that society? It is a question for a theoretical paradise.

* * *

Tamoé is the utopia of Sade's Enlightened intellect. The imaginary society of his next main work, *Philosophy in the Boudoir*, is the utopia of his visceral desire for unresisted control. Both books appeared before the Parisian reading public in quick succession, in 1795, although *Aline and Valcour* had been mainly written in jail before 1788 and *Philosophy in the Boudoir* was penned with specially warmed ink during the cold winter before publication **(see chapter 27)**. The latter work was published anonymously.

Its structure is extraordinary, even by Sade's standards of crude stitching in one literary piece. A vehement, exhortatory pamphlet - *People of France, One More Effort if You Want to Be Republicans* - appears in the middle of an orgy of which the aim is said to be the sexual education of a 15-year-old girl, Eugénie de Mistival. She goes on an innocent afternoon visit to a married woman friend, Mme de Saint-Ange, then finds that Saint-Ange, her brother and his friend, a male lecher called Dolmancé, intend for her a lesson to change her life (**see chapter 31** for an extract from this part of *Philosophy in the Boudoir*). Mlle de Mistival turns out to be very quick and enthusiastic on the uptake as she is introduced, by argument and example, to abandonment of sexual inhibitions, religious scruples and filial respect. Towards the end of the proceedings, Eugénie exults: "Look at me: incestuous, adulterous, sodomitic all at once, and this in a girl who lost her virginity only today!... How is that for progress, my friends!... I'm damned for sure!"

Philosophy in the Boudoir[3] is set out as a play - for some highbrow theatre of the erotic unlikely to be permitted on any public stage, then as now, and made well-nigh impossible to perform anywhere by the demands on the sexual stamina of the performers, to say nothing of the length of the speeches that would have to be learned. In the main, the proceedings are acceptable as literature to the broad-minded reader nowadays, until they are poisoned towards the end by the treatment of the apprentice libertine's mother, who arrives to collect her daughter only to be insulted and fiercely tortured by the group. She is whipped, raped vaginally and anally by members of the group (including her daughter wielding a dildo), and made to have sexual intercourse with a syphilitic servant, after which Eugénie sews up her mother's vagina and anus with needle and thread.

Eugénie's lesson, even before the assault on Mme de Mistival, is all demolition of responsibility and seeking of pleasure, quite heartless. Even so, was she being given knowledge that would help her towards a life of free-ranging sexuality? I think not. Before the arrival of Mme de Mistival at the party, a letter from her husband, Eugénie's father, reaches the hostess, Mme de Saint-Ange. He writes that his wife

---

3 A recording, sound only, of the work is available in the original French, on a set of four cassettes, from the French company Livraphone (number LIV 154).

deserves punishment and he gives the libertines carte blanche as to their treatment of her. He adds: "Do not send Eugénie back to me until she has had some instruction ... I am quite content to allow you the first fruits, but be advised that your efforts will have been, to a degree, for my benefit." Between Sade and his female literary characters, there is always a directing or permitting male character. Dolmancé is the main instrument of Eugénie's education; her father is the unseen source of permission and the waiting beneficiary.

Mme de Saint-Ange, although one of Sade's less restricted female characters, tells in *Philosophy in the Boudoir* how her sexual rampage - "during my twelve years of marriage, I have been fucked by more than ten or twelve thousand individuals" - is allowed by a pact with her elderly husband: "On our wedding night, he told me of his penchant, also promising me that he would never stand in the way of mine; I swore I would obey him and we have lived since then in a delightful independence and consensus. My husband's pleasure is to be sucked and ..., while I straddle him, merrily sucking the spunk from his balls with my buttocks immediately above his face, I have to shit into his mouth! He swallows it!" Mme de Saint-Ange's many encounters are thus at the price of a deal with her husband. Wide-eyed Eugénie learns the lesson. Her hostess admits that, if a husband does not allow his wife sexual scope, she may enjoy it anyway, by deceit. However, she makes little of the point and the abiding impression is that her husband's wealth is the fulcrum on which the Earth moves so often for Mme de Saint-Ange.

In view of this reservation of control in rich male hands, the sudden digression of the call on the French people for another effort turns out to be appropriate, although it might seem on the face of it to run quite counter to the true theme of the didactic orgy. The hectoring pamphlet is expressed with a vim and fluency that shows there was still a spark in the obese 55-year-old, wrapped up against the bitter weather and fretting about the scandalous price of firewood, writing in the study at 20 rue Neuve des Mathurins.

Meanwhile, the upheaval of the royal régime's fall was subsiding. Paris and other French cities were tiring of revolutionary seethe and improvisatory politics. The wish to melt down society and reshape it was losing momentum. The better-educated and better-heeled movers of events, those commoners of ideas and property who had challenged the king's government in 1789 so as to advance themselves and their own kind, were consolidating their power in 1795 after the Terror.

Amid this congealment, and an ascendance of lawyers, from a former aristocrat, whom revolutionary zeal had nearly killed, came a wrought-up and uncompromising argument for a national embrace of a hotter ferment yet. Or so it seems. *One More Effort* starts by referring to the social and political context - "we are approaching our target [of becoming true republicans] but hesitatingly" - and adds: "I am worried by a feeling that we are about to fall short again. It is believed that we will have reached our goal when we have been given a set of laws. Throw out that idea, because what would we, who are without religion, want with laws?"

Then Sade rides his hobby-horse of militant atheism into a charge against priests and lay faithful who might be regaining influence among the French. Ridicule and hurled handfuls of mud were the proper greeting for such backsliders into the discredited superstition, the tract argued. King Zamé of Tamoé might have approved of that but, in his utopia without jails, he would have been aghast at the penalty, in *One More Effort*, for a second offence of trying to reintroduce religion - life imprisonment. When bent over the urgent task of remaking France, anonymously, rather than dreaming a Polynesian paradise under his own name, Sade's patience with theists proved thin.

Apart from allowing believers short shrift, the true republic would ensure liberty of conscience and of the press. What few laws there were would be mild, so that anyone, of any temperament, would be able to obey them easily. There should be no capital punishment because "the law, cold and abstract, is quite alien to the passions which can justify a person committing the cruel deed of murder." No law would forbid calumny (which does no harm to the virtuous person, whose goodness emerges enhanced), theft (which promotes "courage, strength, skill, cunning" and which "distributes wealth more equably"), lust or murder.

The permit for lust, Sade recommends, opens the way for prostitution, incest, rape and sodomy. His first justification of this declares: "The republic will be always under threat by tyrants around its territory, so the means to defend it cannot be moral because the republic will uphold itself only by war and there is nothing less moral than war... Legislators in [classical] Greece entirely appreciated the prime necessity of corrupting the citizens so that, as their moral delinquency clashed with foregoing values, there would arise the insurrection essential to a political system of sublime happiness which, like republican government, is bound to provoke the loathing and envy of neighbouring states. Insurrection ... has to be a republic's permanent condition. So it would be as absurd as it would be perilous to demand morality of those who were to maintain the constant immoral subversion of the established order. A moral man lives calmly and peacefully; an immoral man lives in constant seethe that drives him to, and makes him part of, the insurrection in which the republican has to keep the government he takes part in."

The language in Sade's justification of unorthodox expression of lust has more than a touch of the Chinese Cultural Revolution and of the notions, in that upheaval, of permanent conflict in order to uproot *hsiang-feng* (fragrant breeze, the Chinese euphemism for the bourgeois way of life). "Put daring above everything else, expose every kind of ghost and monster... Cast out fear. Don't be afraid of disorder ... revolution cannot be so very refined, so gentle, so temperate, kind, courteous, restrained and magnanimous," the Central Committee of the Chinese Communist Party exhorted in 1969. The committee and its Red Guards were concerned, like Sade, to prevent the society around them from slipping back into a previous hierarchical order, but they were not concerned to clear the way for the Chinese to bugger their brothers and sisters. Sade's sally, despite the high abstraction of the vocabulary, is more akin to street gang philosophy: "We're good because we're bad and, because we're bad, we can do anything we want - only wimps live any other way." That sort of attitude makes for hard luck on anyone seized by such a gang.

The justification for decriminalising rape - women should be like "drinking fountains beside the road," available to all - is suported by the contention that the damage done by rape would be done in love or marriage, sooner or later. As he put it in his prison notes, ten years earlier: "A man rapes a girl - he is lost. Yes, a bad thing for sure, but the consequence ... is no more than the girl being put into the class where she is bound to be sooner or later."

Further to that, *One More Effort* devotes much attention to a main Sadeian concern: "Now that we are back on our feet [politically speaking] and have shrugged off the load of prejudices that used to shackle us, ... we are convinced that lust ... is not to be trussed up or subject to the law, so our business is to establish the means for passion to be satisfied without interruption. We have to bring order into this area of activity and set up all the security required so that, when necessity pushes a citizen towards the objects of his lust, he can devote himself to performing with them all that his passions need, without the least let or hindrance because full liberty is never more important to a man than at such a time.

"Various houses - attractive, clean, spacious, well equipped and altogether safe - are to be built in each town; inside, people of all sexes and all ages, creatures of every possible kind, will be available to the desire of the libertines ... and every individual taking part will be subject to a rule of total subordination; the least refusal or reluctance shall be immediately and arbitrarily punished by the person thus thwarted."

Once the satisfaction of lust is the issue, laws and punishments return in force to the Sadeian republic of high seethe and necessary insurrection. It seems no-one is to be allowed insurrection against the rule of the republic's houses of forced sexual service. Sade saw the inconsistency and fumbled for an explanation:

In his lust "a man likes to rule, to be obeyed, to be surrounded with slaves obliged to satisfy him. When you deny a man the expression by which he rids himself of the clot of tyranny that nature has inserted at the centre of his heart, he will look for other ways to expel it and [the expression] will fall on any object available. It will disturb government. To avoid such a danger, allow full scope to those despotic desires that, despite himself, torment a man endlessly... Content at having been able to exercise his little sovereignty amid a harem of boys or sultanas whose submission your [the desired republic's] care and his money secure for him, he will go on his way satisfied and with no wish to trouble a government that ... supplies him ... with every means to satisfy his lust..."

With that, Sade declared sexual slavery in the dreamed-of republic, for reasons of state, so as to channel lust away from expression as insurrection against the government. Also, in passing, he laid down the crucial exclusion that access to these microcosmic sexual empires was to be available for money. What of the lust of those who could not pay? Would that not be a danger to government? Would there be a grant so that the poor could afford to enter the safe houses? Sade seems not to have considered that.

He further decreed in *One More Effort*: "No free being may ever be subjected to an act of possession; the exclusive ownership of a woman is as unjust as the ownership of slaves. All humans are born free and all have equal rights ... these principles establish that no sex can acquire a legitimate right to seize exclusive hold of the other, and no sex or class shall arbitrarily possess any other. Likewise, no woman living under the undiluted law of Nature can put forward, as justification for not making herself available to someone who desires her, her love for someone else, because that sort of adherence stems from exclusion and no man shall be denied having a woman once it is established that she shall belong to all men. Ownership can only be applied to a building or an animal, never to an individual who has our characteristics, and all the bonds that unite one woman to one man lack justification as they lack substance."

That "likewise" in the middle of the preceding paragraph is a very thin trapeze wire along which Sade steps from one platform, high in the big top of his circus of sexual liberation and sexual control, to another, much more shaky. The merest breath of rebuttal would surely have blown him off. He did not allow it into his tent, but wrote on: "So, if it becomes indisputable that Nature has given us the right to express our desires to any woman, it also becomes indisputable that we have the right to force [her] to submit." Then, in a footnote: "... this is only a matter of enjoyment, not of possession. I have no right to own that fountain I pass on the road, though I have a right to use it, I have the right to slake my thirst by the fresh water from it; likewise I have no true right to own some woman or other but I have the indisputable right to enjoy her. I have the right to compel her to allow me this enjoyment if she denies it to me, no matter what motive she has for doing so."

Back in the main text: "No-one can gainsay that we have the right to decree laws that force women to surrender to the ardour of whatever man wants to have her; in that violence may be necessary to support that right, we can use it within the law. In fact, has nature not demonstrated that we have the right to violence by giving us the strength to put women under our control?

"... The law that will require [women] to prostitute themselves, as frequently and in any way we want, in the houses of libertinage, ... and that will bring force to bear on them if they demur, will punish them if they are slow to comply or do not give full value - this law is one of the most equitable of statutes therefore, against which no sane person can rightfully argue."

So, Sade goes on, a man who wants "any woman or girl" could demand that she be "called right away to serve at one of the houses...

Supervised by the female orderlies there, she will be handed over to him in order to satisfy, with humility and submissiveness, all the diversions he might like to explore with her, no matter how odd and unusual they might be, because there is nothing so bizarre that it does not stem from nature...

"He who has the right to eat fruit must be allowed to pick it when ripe or when still green... However, it will be argued that girls of some ages would be damaged by a man acting upon them. This view is quite baseless for, having granted me the proprietary right of enjoyment, that right is not diminished by the consequences of that enjoyment... Did I not prove that it is lawful to bend the woman's will in this matter? Also that, as soon as she arouses the desire to take her, she must give herself over to this ..., abandoning her own feelings entirely? Any consideration of her well-being is irrelevant. Once this consideration threatens to reduce or dilute the pleasure of the man who wants her, and who has the right to appropriate her, then any thought for her age has to be set aside; whatever the object, sentenced by nature and the law to quench momentarily the thirst of the other person, might undergo is beside the point..."

Notice Sade the blame-shifter breaking surface for a moment, with "as soon as she arouses the desire to take her..." All their fault, the temptresses!

For women cast into gloom by the prospect of the sexual draft, Sade has a further plan to put everything right, according to his lights: "... we will redress the balance... We certainly should. Those women whom we have just enslaved so heinously - we must compensate them...

"If we agree, as we have, that all women are to be made available to our desires, then it follows that we may permit them full satisfaction of theirs. Our statutes must be amenable to their ardent characters. It makes no sense to regard women as honourable and virtuous when they are using their power to resist nature in quelling the desires which are far stronger in them than in us men; this topsy-turvy view of what is proper becomes even more absurd when we scheme to undermine their power through seduction, and then punish them for giving way to all our efforts to bring them low...

"So I maintain that women, having been endowed with a taste for carnal delight that is far more intense than ours, will be able to throw themselves into it unrestrainedly, clear of all hobbling marital ties, of all false ideas about modesty, opening themselves to as many men as they decide; I would allow them the enjoyment of all sexes and, as men may, the enjoyment of all parts of the body..."

Having made all well for womankind, Sade continued his precarious trapeze act on another length of wire. However, he had not made all well; he had cast down a basic human right - the right to say "no" to any request or demand. This was essential to the thinking of the Enlightenment, as it is essential to us now and will always be so. Diderot wrote of the right to give oneself or hold oneself back for a moment, give oneself or hold oneself back forever **(see chapter 30)**. Sade made out that he had outflanked Diderot's position by focusing on the *temporary* enjoyment of another person - the right to drink from the fountain without the right to own it. His reference to quenching a thirst, a lust, "momentarily" is his key point, but it does not raise his argument out of his casting-about for justification of untrammelled access to female flesh, all of it, whenever the itch is felt. How long would "momentarily" be? How would the most desired women and girls fare when "any consideration of [their] well-being is irrelevant"? Even if one allows Sade to apply a divided definition of possession to relations between men and women, he is still trying to legalise coercion, assault and rape, still using rules and money to shackle others to his sexual purpose.

By the way, if the Sadeian republic is to decree open season on the human body, be it never so young, why go to the trouble and expense of the cozy houses of libertinage and the supervisory orderlies? So that there be staff to mop up the blood and shit between bouts, and so as not to be doing it in the street and frightening the horses? So that every man can hold debauch in his own Silling Castle built at public expense, safe from attack by anyone who, exercising his or her right to unrestricted mayhem on flesh (or on the cash in a chap's trousers folded over the back of the chair), might fancy inflicting rape, theft or murder on a libertine or two?

Another point in *One More Effort* casts doubt on the licentious republic's equality for men and women. During his historical citations in justification of homosexual intercourse, Sade deals with lesbianism:

"Among the Greeks [of classical antiquity], this ... had political support. One consequence of it was that, women not looking beyond each other, they had less to do with men and so their detrimental effect on the running of the republic was much reduced." For a gentleman of the 18th century, steeped in classical literature, the models of republican democracy were pre-imperial Rome and the city states of ancient Greece. The voters in those republics were propertied men - small minorities of their populations - with women and slaves excluded from political decisions. The idea of a democracy in which all persons over the age of 18, except convicted criminals and the certified insane, may vote is a modern one that never occurred to Sade, or to all but a very few of his contemporaries.

The "children without fathers" who would result from the general libertinage would make for no difficulty "in a republic where each individual is to have no other mother but the nation... Don't think you are bringing up good republicans while children, who should belong only to the republic, remain trapped in their families..."

Rigorous triage would be applied as to who was fit to be a child of the Sadeian republic. Having cited, as usual, various classical and contemporary exotic examples of the practice, Sade advocates infanticide, the killing of those children "discovered not to measure up to the requirements for the defence of the republic", because "handsomely appointed and funded houses for the upkeep of humanity's dross" were "the least useful item of expenditure". Sade shared a belief, common among the literate of his day, that over-population was a pressing danger in western Europe. According to him, "a great rate of births has to be promoted in a monarchy, the despots amassing wealth by the number of their slaves, ... but guard against too much multiplication of a people made up of free individuals for you may be sure that revolutions always stem from an excess of population... There is no justice in curtailing the life of a sane and healthy individual, but there is nothing wrong with preventing the appearance in the world of a creature that is bound to be of no use to it."

The inconsistency is clear for Sade's republic of high seethe would be more likely to come into being where there was the ferment of a large number of individuals competing for whatever was available, apt to make "revolutions" and so keep everyone on the hop. This sounds like an old gentleman becoming rather annoyed at - perhaps even a little afraid of - the teeming, levelling crowds of late-18th century Paris, and distressed by that city's constant scramble for scarce commodities.

Also, the wish to cull humanity of the unfit speaks of the ancient impatience with the mentally deranged, who dwell in their own rapture and are hard to reach through the will to control and alter that Sade needed to exercise in order to feel secure and effective. Remember

Sade's loathing for the "madmen" around him when he was put into the asylum at Charenton in 1789. Besides, if the lame and the insane are not to live, how is the arch-criminal of the Sadeian imagination to find a full range of bizarre and repulsive sexual objects to have, thereby refining and extending his criminality to an excellence that sets him far above the common herd? Sade offered no answer in *One More Effort*.

He did argue, a few paragraphs later, that there was nothing criminal in despatching from this world a human who may already be of use to it, despite his assertion earlier in the same document that there was "no justice in curtailing the life of a sane and healthy individual". He described murder as "the most cruel offence a man may commit against another because it takes from him the one asset he has been given by nature, and this cannot be restored." The death of one individual, though, makes no difference to society as a whole. To nature, the death of a human animal matters no more than the death of any other animal, and there is no obliteration of any creature, rather a transformation of matter from one form to another through natural processes essential to nature's endless destruction and creation. "Small animals come into being as soon as a large animal has died... Will you dare to propose that one kind is more pleasing to nature than the other?" Nature would not heed the destruction of half - even all - the world, Sade added.

Murder is no political crime. "On the contrary, it is unfortunately one of the most important instruments of politics and administration." The "unfortunately" might well have been inserted to avoid annoying the post-Terror Committee of Public Safety, as was the next point. "It goes without saying, we are referring to the murders done in war, rather than to the outrages done by conspirators and rebels... What is war but the science of destruction? There is an odd short-sightedness in man, who teaches quite openly the art of murder, who exalts the most effective murderer, yet punishes the man who snuffs out his personal enemy! Has the time not come for such primitive anomalies to be resolved?"

However, the republic would need murder. "Republican morale demands a dash of ferocity; if the republican relaxes, if his energy falls off, he will be subjugated in an instant. An extraordinary notion arises just now, which might be daring but is correct even so... A nation already old and corrupt, which bravely throws aside the yoke of its monarchical government to adopt a republican one, will be maintained only by many crimes, because it is already rooted in crime and if it were to try to shift from criminality to virtue - that is, from a violent condition to a placid one - it would collapse into an inertia which would soon mean its sure demise...

"We should never impose any official punishment on a murderer, but let him run the risk of vengeance by the friends or family of his victim. 'I grant you a pardon,' said Louis XV to Charolais, who had just amused himself by killing a man, 'but I also grant pardon to whomsoever might kill you.'

"In short, murder is horrific, but often necessary and never a crime. A republican state must tolerate it."

Sade wound up his stirring pamphlet with a final exhortation to his readers: "Our courage has long been shrivelled by the habits of tyranny; despotism warped the way we live but we are being born again. The sublime achievements of the French mind and character, when at liberty, will soon be revealed; let us sustain, at the cost of our well-being and our lives, this freedom that has already cost many victims, not one of whom will be in vain if we reach our goal ... but unity, unity, lest we lose the harvest of all our efforts...

"Let us set up a few laws, good ones, ... that have as their aim only the citizen's peace of mind and happiness, as well as the glory of the republic. Also, people of France, having driven the enemy from your land, do not let your eagerness to spread your principles carry you any further, for their extension to all the world would require much shot and steel... Once the enemy has fled back across the Rhine, take notice of what I say, guard your borders and stand fast on our side of them. Revive your commerce, renew the vigour and markets of your manufactures, foster the arts and crafts anew, promote agriculture - all essential for a government ... whose intent must be to provide for every citizen without need to draw on outside help. Let the thrones of Europe collapse without your pushing them - your example, your success, will bring them tumbling down...

"If, out of the vainglory of seeking to set up your principles abroad, you fail to look after well-being at home, tyranny, which merely slumbers, will wake, you will be torn apart by internal unrest, your treasure and your soldiers will be spent - all that ... to kiss again the shackles that the tyrants ... will fasten on you... Let other nations witness your happiness and they will run to theirs by the path you have marked for them."

Napoléon Bonaparte saw the destiny of France differently, and so did much to make Sade's closing prophecy come true.

For all the well-turned rhetoric, the flaws in Sade's pamphlet are clear. The right to rob, rape and murder could well create the condition of high alertness and assertiveness that Sade claims to prize, but would soon tear apart the republic of seethe as private gangs and armies, run by acquisitive warlords, fought their way to a military aristocracy, headed after a time by a more or less acknowledged king - the very process and state of affairs that Sade was straining to prevent recurring in the France of the mid-1790s. The only way for an individual to advance would be through the patronage of a stronger individual or group; thugs and accomplices would flourish under the capricious protection of rich men. There is a hint of this in the play that occupies most of *Philosophy in the Boudoir*, even as Eugénie de Mistival and her instructors in libertinage take a breather from the debauchery *chez* Saint-Ange and prepare to hear *One More Effort* read by one of their number. The gardener Augustin - "delightful to look at, about 18 or 20 years old, ... whose member measures thirteen inches long and eight and a half around, [and who] comes ... like a waterspout" - has been brought from his hoe to add variety to the debauch and has acquitted himself satisfactorily.

However, the clarion call to the citizens of France is not to be uttered in front of the lower orders, it seems. "Away with you, Augustin; this is not for you. Don't be too far away, though; we will ring when we want you again," orders Mme de Saint-Ange. Then the upper crust settles down to hear of the utopia of unrestrained vendetta, unhindered theft, flesh on call and national economic self-sufficiency. It is the dream of an impatient aristocrat, unable to abide Church or state as he knew them, and driven to distraction by price inflation - not least at the brothels, perhaps.

* * *

Pauvert points to a difference between Sade's main works, written after his release from detention in late-1794 (*Philosophy in the Boudoir* and *Juliette*), and those he had conceived before that spell in prison (*Justine*, *The Hundred and Twenty Days of Sodom*, *Aline and Valcour*). The two works written immediately after his emergence from the Picpus sanatorium offer female protagonists of great assertiveness and sexual appetite - Eugénie de Mistival, Mme de Saint-Ange, Juliette and friends - by contrast with deferential and buffeted maidens in the earlier works - Justine, Aline, the kidnapped virgins of Silling Castle. Pauvert puts this down to the emergence in public during the Revolution of many women of mettle and independence, whom Sade could hardly have failed to notice, and to his time at Picpus, where there may well have been an atmosphere of licence and experiment, in word and deed, not least among the female detainees, under the unhingeing threat of the guillotine.

Too much should not be made of this difference, however. Note, in *The Hundred and Twenty Days*, which was written before the Revolution, Mmes Duclos, Champville, Martaine and Desgranges. They are the successful prostitutes hired to tell arousing tales for the winter at Silling Castle, during which they never lose their poise as inciters and abetters of exquisite mayhem, and never for a moment, therefore, appear in danger of being turned into victims by their four masters. Also, we might see in Juliette, for one, although she indeed seems to have sprung from Sade's pen after he had been at Picpus, more than a hint of the resourceful and acquisitive courtesans of Sade's youth some thirty years before the Revolution - Mlle Beauvoison perhaps **(see chapter 6).**

Be all that as it may, Pauvert is quite wrong to proceed to write that Picpus gave rise to a "tone of provocative happiness" in *Philosophy in the Boudoir*, and to say that it is "a happy book". This is no sort of tag to put on a book which advocates sexual slavery of any and all creatures a man might desire. Pauvert conjures up also "the new illumination which makes the feminine creatures in *Philosophy* appear radiant..." I do not imagine that Mme de Mistival - having undergone multiple rape, and forced penetratrion by a syphilitic, and with her vagina and anus roughly sewn shut - feels at all radiant at the end of her attempt to collect her daughter.

*　　　　*　　　　*

The zenith of Sade's career as a published author was marked by the apearance of the last version of *Justine* and of *The Story of Juliette or the Successes of Vice*. The latter created Justine's unalike sister, Juliette, who takes well to an early education in atheism and reverence for money, then revels in her exposure to debauchery and becomes an orgiast, thief and murderer on a grand scale, as well as a propagandist for her way of life.

While still a schoolgirl, Juliette finds her circumstances suddenly changed when her father is bankrupted and staff at her convent turn cold towards her. "Are Juliette rich and Juliette poor two different creatures?" the girl asks herself, decides that they are so regarded and that she will make her own way accordingly. Prostitution in a brothel leads to encounters with rich politicians and financiers, who lecture her on the necessity of total commitment to crime and advance her career.

A reader of this huge novel might think that, because the protagonist is a forceful young woman of mighty sexual appetite and quick intelligence, it tells of a new kind of female, one who expresses Sade's advocacy of sexual libertinage for women. Gilbert Lely wrote: "Through Juliette's total openness, we have all the women whom history and fiction put into our enthralled embrace... Beyond even Sodom and rising above time, she makes the attractions of any other woman laughable. Flexed and stridently demanding attention for her youthful energy, a bacchante drunk with desire, she offers her loins and opens the lips of her vulva with mother-of-pearl fingers to quench that ever-parched thirst to explore..." Apollinaire wrote: "Justine is woman as she was until now - enslaved, wretched and sub-human; her contrary, Juliette, represents the woman whose arrival [Sade] anticipated, a creature who cannot be understood at present, who is emerging from humanity, who shall have wings and shall renew the world."

Pauvert calls *Juliette* "almost constantly in flight, happy, inspired, *new*." He brackets it with *Philosophy in the Boudoir* in presenting "feminine freedom, absolute freedom personified by the women [in it]."

Angela Carter opined: "... [Sade's] great women, Juliette, Clairwil, the Princess Borghese, Catherine the Great of Russia, Charlotte of Naples [all characters in *Juliette*], are even more cruel still [than the great men in the novels of Sade] since, once they have tasted power, once they know how to use their sexuality as an instrument of aggression, they use it to extract vengeance for the humiliations they were forced to endure as the passive objects of the sexual energy of others...

"... Sade declares himself unequivocally for the right of women to fuck - as if the period in which women fuck aggressively, tyrannously and cruelly will be a necessary stage in the development of a general human consciousness of the nature of fucking; that if it is not egalitarian, it is unjust. Sade does not suggest this process as such; but he urges women to fuck as actively as they are able, so that powered by their enormous and hitherto untapped sexual energy they will then be able to fuck their way into history and, in doing so, to change it...

"... I would like to think that he put pornography in the service of women, or, perhaps, allowed it to be invaded by an ideology not inimical to women."

A beguiling notion has been allowed to mist the vision here. It is that of a potent female protagonist, precursor of women's liberation, a great criminal risen from poverty, spurning God, haranguing the Pope ("arrogant phantom," Juliette calls Pius VI to his face before denouncing the Catholic Church and joining him in an orgy on the altar of St Peter's Cathedral in Rome), fucking all manner of humans and even dogs and monkeys, coolly undergoing abortion to terminate a pregnancy begun by her father just before she shot him dead, debating theology, philosophy and public policy, thieving, swindling, murdering for profit and for the hell of it, and having wonderful orgasms galore. Juliette and one of her female accomplices take such a fancy to one young priest's big penis that they slice it off when erect and smartly have it embalmed for use as a dildo.

All this seems to have the stimulating makings of a piratical philosopher-queen of the Enlightenment fit to sweep superstition into oblivion, turn morality on its head, set phallocracy a-tremble and point the way for new women of nerve, verve and purpose.

Don't you believe it. Juliette operates always on a tether, albeit a long one, and on a dangerous precipice. She is always subject to men even more criminal and even richer than she, although there is only a few of them. There is always an overlord, reintroduced to the narrative after each spate of woman-directed rampaging, with whom the male reader can identify and who has all women, even the polymath-in-vice Juliette, within his reach. She may plot and perform many an outrage, make millions of money, but has to stop short of any tilt at one of the arch-criminal men who teach her and retain supervision of her.

"Outside," the 16-year-old Juliette is told by the government minister Saint-Fond, one of the richest and most powerful of her libertine mentors, as he shows her around one of his splendid houses, "you will be one of the greatest ladies of France; in here, you will be no more than a whore." On another occasion: "With me, in private, carry your submissiveness to servility; the more you grovel at my feet, the more I shall take pride in having you queen it over others." More than a decade later, the directing demon of the novel's last orgy is male, empowered by his having even more money than Juliette. His rage to destroy in lust is allowed to hurl aside her fear for the fate of her infant daughter, with whom she has just been reunited. The overlord, already in a rapture of slaughter, is allowed by Juliette to rape the little girl and cast her onto a burning brazier. "Your treacherous influence sweeps her away, it stifles in me all other feeling but that of crime and outrage," Juliette tells him, and helps him to keep the child from escaping before the fire has consumed her.

Juliette and other women libertines in the novel have to live an intensive seethe, as would the citizens in Sade's republic of *One More Effort*. They are under constant pressure to stay high, to flay with all their might, with not a moment of remorse lest their patron-accomplices, whose assessment of them is unblinking, demote them abruptly from the criminal élite to the only other class that exists for them, that of victims, potential and actual. Like her virtuous sister Justine, Juliette allows no options. Justine cannot emerge from the narrow virtuousness of her religious adherence; Juliette cannot move beyond the flinty-hearted pursuit of wealth and pleasure she has learned from rich criminals. When Sade composed, there were no key changes.

Noirceuil, one of the masters of mayhem who has chosen the young Juliette as a promising apprentice, concludes an orgy with a graduation address to her:

"The vivacity and impetuosity of a higher being's intelligence are so strong that it will stop at nothing; difficulties in the way are that many more pleasures and the conquest of them does not have to be regarded as evidence of depravity, as idiots suppose, but evidence of the intelligence becoming stronger. You, Juliette, have reached the age when your capabilities are at their height; you move into your prime prepared by diligent study, by poised reflection, by a sweeping rejection of all the boundaries and prejudices imposed and learned in childhood... that long and painstaking preparation will not be wasted, your career will be dazzling. A blazing and energetic character, rude health, great appetite in the loins, an icy heart, are all in place to support your resilient, enlightened mind. We can have every confidence, my friends, that Juliette will achieve all that lies within her scope; however, I advise her not to stop along the way, not even to pause for a moment; if she so much as glances behind her, she should criticise herself for the small progress she sees that she has made, rather than wonder at how far she has come."

Juliette has to withstand some heavy usage in long sessions of debauchery, with her intelligence, and her every orifice and limb, available to the whims of her patrons and partners. Her role is not that of a by-stander, steeling herself not to scream or go to the aid of the victims, as the mayhem thrusts on through flesh and blood, and the bodies are carted away. By-standers get hauled into the fray as further objects for fatal lust. Rather, she has to keep her wit ever-sharp and depraved as she designs, orchestrates and takes part in the pleasuring of others - a tonguing of this clitoris, a squeezing of that scrotum, a cutting of this throat, a well-timed word to that het-up client to help him withhold his ejaculation until the next, and more piquant, twist of the sanguinary revels. "I liked your style, whore, you got my cock up," is the sort of compliment she receives from her patrons.

There is no mixing mercy and massacre, according to the deserts of the victims. Thousands of them go to the fatal crucible, or are left maimed, or crazed with horror. Family life is trampled heavily. The libertines of this novel, even more than in other works by Sade, delight in telling, for instance, a father or brother that he must whip or bugger a daughter or sister because, if he refuses, she will be killed. Juliette is often the one who brings the distraught relative to erection, against his revulsion, so that he can perform the supposed life-saving act of penetration - "supposed" for the controlling libertine rarely keeps the bargain when the male relative has done the forced deed.

As Juliette learns, the life of high crime demands utter dedication. She can, and does, take breaks for physical recuperation but the mental concentration cannot waiver into thoughts of an occasional deed of charity or of how relieving it would be to retire and grow roses. Once committed to total criminality, it is a life's work at concert pitch. The "rude health" and "great appetite in the loins" attributed to her are not in themselves enough to sustain Juliette in her career. Here she is, giving an account of herself when newly arrived in Rome:

"... I was entering my twenty-fifth year. I had, however, still nothing to reproach nature for; far from having degraded any of my features, it had given them that air of maturity, of energy, usually withheld from those of a tender age, and I could say without arrogance that, if I was then regarded as pretty, I could now claim, with good reason, the peak of beauty. The fineness of my figure was perfectly maintained; my bust, always pert and well-rounded, was wonderfully firm. My arse, taut and of a pleasing whiteness, showed no effects of the excesses of lust to which I had exposed it; the hole was a little large, to tell the truth, but of a beautiful reddish brown, hairless, and never failing to attract tongues as soon as it was offered; my cunt was no longer very narrow but, with a bit of dalliance, some essential oils and some skill, all that took on again, at my bidding, the bloom of the roses of maidenhoood. As for the edge of my sexuality, what with it becoming sharper with age, it was all too keen, and always under my mind's direction - once in action, it was impossible to tire of it. But, the better to arouse it, I had begun to want wine and liqueurs, and once I was out of my head, there was no longer any excess I wouldn't commit; I was also using opium and the other stimulants of love-making... One must never have any fears about using such means to stir up one's appetite for lust - artifice always works better than nature, and the only drawback resulting from having tried them once is the necessity to carry on with them for life."

Some of her female fellow libertines do not last as long as Juliette does. Following the way of ever greater outrage, shown her by male arch-criminals, Juliette destroys some of these women herself, having become bored with them because their debauchery has become repetitive and lacking in flair, and having decided to steal their fortunes.

However, she enjoys a close, happy and profitable co-operation and sexual relationship with Durand[4] - a woman seer, poisoner, procuress and prostitute, even better equipped than Juliette to control her own destiny and impinge on that of others. Yet Durand is created as not wholly woman - her clitoris is so long and erectile that she is able to take a penetrative role in sexual intercourse, and her vagina is naturally blocked so she is unable to be penetrated by that passage and unable to conceive. Even those women whom Sade, dreaming enemy of motherhood and family life, does allow in his literature to conceive never bring a pregnancy to full untroubled term or give birth in

---

4 Sade, in his way, had a good word for lesbians, in a footnote during *Juliette*: "These charming creatures, which the opinion of fools condemns with so much stupidity, show in society the same quality they bring to pleasures - they are always more lively, more amiable, more witty than the others; nearly all of them have charm, talent, imagination; and so why hold against them a fault which is only due to nature? Dull men who follow ordinary pleasures, you turn against them because they refuse you, but an examination of those women who do love you always shows them to be almost as stupid as you are." Remember, though, Sade's point, in *Philosophy in the Boudoir*, that lesbian relationships helped to reduce the "detrimental effect" of women on politics.

tranquillity and joy. Sustained assaults on the pregnant until they miscarry, and murders of mothers with infants, are recurrent themes, especially in *Juliette*. One recalls not only Sade's fragmented relationship with his mother, but also his rage from Vincennes, via his wife, at his mother-in-law for having preferred to him "her daughter's vile and detestable embryos!"

Durand sustains high criminality, and great potency as a sorceress and malign physician, but she may not reproduce or, as soon as a faction of male politicians has decided to move against her for its own purposes, continue her life, it seems. "We have let you enjoy the fruit of your infamies during the three years you have been in Venice," three elders of the Venetian Republic tell Durand, having summoned her to their presence. "We require you to show evidence of your gratitude by ... committing crimes on our behalf... Do you have the double secret of spreading the plague in a city, and of saving those who would be pointed out to you?" Durand says she has not, although able to do both, and is allowed to leave the elders' presence, but shaking because the Venetians have not bothered to tell her to say nothing of their scheme. Having returned to the brothel she runs with Juliette, Durand says that she is marked for death because, having learned of the plan to spread the plague, she would be murdered whether she aided it or not. She leaves Juliette right away, lest the younger woman also be felled by the Venetians' concern to protect their conspiracy.

A few hours later, Juliette is taken to the politicians, who show her what they say is Durand's hanged body and expel her from Venice, having confiscated most of her wealth. The moment Durand shrank from committing a crime - however outrageous - that was within her capabilities, she was lost. The hangman of male wealth and power, on whose trap she had been standing all the while, moved to pull his lever, through a few strokes of Sade's pen.

Juliette herself nearly perishes through a similar lapse. At one point, she is told by Saint-Fond of his plan to starve to death two thirds of the people of France by buying food and keeping it off the market. Juliette, although well steeped in vice at the age of 21, gives an involuntary shudder before she can find the proper reaction of pitiless delight at the prospect of so monstrous a massacre. Saint-Fond spots the fall from disgrace at once and leaves without a word. Soon she is told, by a letter from Noirceuil, her other great instructor, to leave Paris with only the money she has to hand, abandoning all she has acquired through

Saint-Fond's patronage. "I would never have expected weakness in a woman whom I moulded and whose previous behaviour had been without blemish," Noirceuil admonishes the errant pupil.

Terrified in case Saint-Fond were to decide to have her killed, Juliette gathers the cash she has in her house and takes the first coach out of the city, resolving: "Buck up now, get a grip on yourself, we won't rely on anyone but ourselves... I'm still young... I will just have to start anew... O deadly virtue, you let me down once; don't you doubt that I will never fall under your vile influence again... Let's put out its flame in our heart for good ... because virtue is the mortal enemy of humanity... The biggest mistake one can make in a wholly corrupt world is to want to wage a lone battle against the general disease..."

She opens a gambling parlour in the city of Angers - which was where the first coach happened to be going - marries a rich count, in front of whom she feigns virtue until, learning that Saint-Fond is regretting he did not lock her up, she poisons her husband and heads for Italy, her heart more steely than ever. While playing the good wife of Angers, she has had a child - a daughter - so that the law shall recognise her as rightful inheritrix of her husband's wealth, which she duly takes.

During the long education of Juliette and of his readers, Sade rides his various hobby-horses: "Pity is no more than a selfish feeling that causes us to be sorry for others' misfortunes, which we are afraid might happen to us... Charity is bad for the poor ... and even worse for the rich, who think they have become virtuous when they have donated a few pence to the clergy or to layabouts - a fine way to hide your own vices as you promote those of other people." Then again: "If law and religion had not existed, there is no knowing what heights human understanding would have reached nowadays... Inventions and wonders of arts and sciences stem from strong passions ... Individuals who are not stirred by strong feelings are mere mediocrities... If laws recover their domination then a dangerous lassitude blunts the spirits of everyone...

"What does it matter to me that I might be oppressed [in the absence of laws], as long as I have the right to do likewise? I prefer to be oppressed by my neighbour, whom I can oppress in my turn, than to be so by the law, against which I have no power..."

Some neighbours have more power than others. Who would be poor and peaceful, and live next door to an arch-criminal out of Sade's pen? Or rich and innocent? Noirceuil suggests to Juliette that she should make for herself a long diversion out of a rich girl entrusted to her guardianship: "Steal her money and then put her in such a wretched state that you could readily add to your delight at any time by watching her decline; that is a more profound pleasure than killing her would be... Beyond the physical happiness from the pleasure, there will be the mental stimulation from comparing her condition and yours... It is a thousand times more delicious, while watching miserable creatures, to say to oneself: 'I am not as they are and so I am better than they are,' rather than to say only: 'I am delighted, but delighted among people who are as happy as I am.' It is the mishaps of others that make us feel our delights fully; amid people whose happiness is just like ours, we would never feel satisfied or relaxed ... in order to be happy one should never look up but always look down..."

Some of them, at least, should not become too miserable, it seems. Another libertine, less reflective than Noirceuil, delights *chez* Juliette and Durand in preying on a pregnant woman and her children. Their availability is due to their poverty - so far, so realistic - but Sade, on behalf of his readers, requires a certain desirability, so the libertine "is amazed that the wretchedness and privation of these unfortunate creatures has taken from them nothing of their freshness and their succulence."

An exciting health and vigour in members of the lower orders can be useful to women. Clairwil arranges for Juliette to join a secret society, the Fellowship of the Friends of Crime, number three of whose Instructions to Women Admitted to the Fellowship reads: "She must always take care to avoid what are known as dandies; that mob pays as badly as it fucks. Let her take up with serving men, burglars - that's the kind of trousers with a bit of go in them, and such bright lads can keep a secret! One can change them as often as one changes one's shift, and there's never any fear of indiscretion."

Noirceuil discourses a sight more coldly on usage and discard. Regarding himself as a man who has become bored with effects which cause "no more than a simple sensation", he turns his mind to taking pleasure from effects which cause an "agonising" sensation. He goes on:

"Isn't it so ... that a man's custom, in his pleasures, is to try to move the objects who serve his enjoyment, in the way that he himself is moved ...?" Then, focusing on the ways and means, once such an object is to hand and he is poised to inflict pain: "... it remains to be discovered whether I can make you take it or not. If I can't, go away and leave me be; if, on the other hand, my money or my connections or my status give me either some authority over you or some certainty of being able to overcome your complaints, then suffer ... all that it pleases me to inflict on you, because I must have my pleasure, and I could not have it without torturing you and without seeing your tears flow. In any event, don't be surprised, don't chide me, for I am the expresion of what nature has put into me ... ; by compelling you to serve my hard and brutal lusts, the only ones that succeed in bringing me to the height of pleasure, I am acting according to the same principles of taste as the soppy lover whose experience extends only to the roses of a feeling in which I recognise only the thorns; because, when torturing you, tearing you into pieces, I am enacting no more than the one deed that can move me, as that lover, dolefully taking his mistress's cunt, carries out the one deed that pleases him; however, he is welcome to his soppy delights, for it is impossible that they might move organs as strongly made as mine are.

"Yes, my friends, you may be sure that it is impossible for the being truly impassioned by the pleasures of lust to bring consideration into them, for that is fatal to pleasure and supposes a sharing that is impossible for those who want full enjoyment - any power shared is power weakened ... Try to bring pleasure to the object that serves your pleasures - you find right away that this is to your cost; there is no more selfish passion than that of lust, none more stringent in its requirements; there is absolutely no-one to be concerned with but yourself when you get a hard-on, and never give a thought to the object that serves us as a kind of victim whose fate lies with the rage of that passion.

"Don't all passions demand victims? Right! ... the worse the passive object is treated, the better one's aim is achieved; the more acute its pain, the greater its humiliation; its degradation is total, and so the more complete is our enjoyment. *One must not make the object feel pleasure, but make an impression on it; the impression produced by pain being far sharper than that produced by pleasure, there is no doubt whatsoever that the turbulence caused in one's nerves by witnessing the effect of pain is preferable to that caused by witnessing the effect of pleasure. There you have the explanation of the obsession of that crowd of libertines who, ... if they are to achieve erection and emit sperm, have to be carrying out deeds of the most atrocious cruelty, to be gorging on the blood of victims.*" (My emphasis.)

"There are some who do not experience the slightest erection unless they are looking at the forlorn object, in the agonies of its most violent pain, sold to their lubricious rage, and unless only they are the prime cause of those agonies. One wants to experience a strong turbulence in one's nerves; one feels clearly that the pain turbulence will be stronger than the pleasure turbulence, so one applies it and finds that it works well.

"But beauty, some idiot protests to me, softens a person, affects one, invites one to tenderness, to mercy; how can one resist the tears of a pretty girl who, her hands clasped, begs her executioner for mercy? Just so! This is what one is after, from this very condition the libertine in the case draws his most exquisite enjoyment - he would complain greatly if he were dealing with an inert being who felt nothing. That protest is as daft as that of the man who would assure me that one must never eat mutton because sheep are meek animals. The passion of lust wants to be served, it demands, it tyrannises; so it must be satisfied, all circumspection whatsoever set aside. Beauty, virtue, innocence, honesty, misfortune - none of all that therefore shall serve to protect the object we lust after. On the contrary, beauty excites us better; innocence, virtue and honesty adorn the object; misfortune hands it over to us, makes it pliable...

"What's more, there's another bit to bite through here - the kind of pleasure given by the sacrilege or the profanation of objects offered for our worship. Such and such a beautiful girl is an object for homage by fools; by rendering unto her my keenest and roughest passions, I experience the double enjoyment of sacrificing to that passion not only a beautiful object but also an object worthy of public worship...

"However, one does not always have such objects under one's hand; but one has accustomed oneself to enjoy through tyranny and one would like to do so every day. Well now, one has to know how to compensate oneself by other, minor pleasures - hardness of heart towards the wretched, refusal to relieve them, pushing them further into misery, if one can - these taking the place, after a fashion, of that sublime enjoyment of making an object of debauchery suffer..."

Juliette kept this sort of dangerous company and was such herself. Still, it was a rich life, if you did not weaken. Juliette, after two years of service to the arch-criminal Saint-Fond, soliloquises: "It is time, my friends, to tell you a bit about myself and especially to describe for you my opulence, fruit of the most terrible debauchery, so that you may compare that with the ... misfortune in which my sister [Justine] found herself meanwhile, through having been told to be a good girl...

"My household was on a mighty scale. You must have suspected as much, seeing all the expense I had to undertake for my lover. But, leaving out of account the multitude of items required for his pleasures, there remained for myself a splendid mansion in Paris, a charming property above Sceaux, a little house of the most delightful sort at Barrière-Blanche [near Paris], twelve lesbians, four chambermaids, a woman to read to me, two night attendants, three coaches, ten horses, four valets picked for their high quality of sexual organ, all the other appurtenances of a very grand house and, to be spent on my personal wants after the costs of my household had been met, there was more than two millions a year..."

"I rose every day at ten o'clock. Until eleven, I saw only my intimate friends; after that, until one o'clock, elaborate washing and dressing, attended by all my courtiers; at one precisely, I used to receive in private audience those who had favours to ask of me, or receive the minister [Saint-Fond] when he was in Paris. At two o'clock, I would fly to my little house, where excellent procuresses made sure that I would find each day four new men and four new women, with whom I would give the fullest scope to my whims. So that you may have an idea of the objects delivered to me there, it should be enough for you to know that there was no individual that had not cost me twenty-five louis at least - often twice as much. There is no imagining what I had among the delectable and rare in either sex... I would go back [to town] at four, and always have dinner with friends... No house in Paris could equal [my table] for splendour, for subtlety, for plenitude... One of my greatest pleasures lies in this minor vice [that of the gourmet] and I feel that, unless it is indulged to excess, one can never properly enjoy the others. Then I would go to a show, or entertain the minister if it was one of his days.

"As for my clothes, my jewellery, my savings, my furniture, ... I would value all that at more than four millions, of which half was in gold and in my casket, in front of which I would stand sometimes ... to wank my cunt and come over this wonderful thought: *I love crime, and here at my disposal are all the means I need to commit it ...*"

The gold is coolly earned. One debauchee in Italy, with Juliette and her associate Olympe Borghèse attending his pleasures, reminds them: "My tender feelings are quite apart from the bestowing of my cock; any indications of love from a woman I am fucking are enough for me to stop paying her in any currency but contempt and hate... I dislike a woman getting the idea that I am indebted to her in some way because I have befouled myself by a relationship with her; I require from her only submission and the same lack of affection as the convenience on which I squat every day when I open my bowels. I have never believed that the congress of two bodies has to, or even can, result in the congress of two hearts; this physical combination carries ... no scope for love..."

Quite so. *Juliette* is Sade's crowning work, where he shows that the key to fulfilment as a libertine is vast wealth, to buy flesh without limit and immunity from retribution. Untrammelled market forces run to brigandage and slaughter on a stupendous scale. Given the millions of money, given the cool concentration that these would have facilitated, this is how Sade might have been. As it was, he lacked both - for which mercy, much thanks.

CHAPTER 36: GREAT STRUCTURES AGAINST THE TIDES

Humboldt had seen the danger: Let there be "no restraint except that necessary to prevent any infringement of rights" **(see chapter 30)**. In twisting, so as to suit his desires, the argument for minimum regulation and maximum scope, Sade spat at Humboldt's careful exception to it. Yet his harping on liberty to impinge on victims, to commit crime without hindrance by a dispassionate apparatus of justice, to let individuals interact freely and restrain each other's depredations only by personal alertness and strength - all this runs quite contrary to his concurrent recourse to great structures and arrangements against change and surprise. The orgies occur in safe places, Silling Castle of *The Hundred and Twenty Days of Sodom* being the most gross example, created by wealth that has also bought or snared the victims.

In Sade's life, as Pauvert points out, there was "a remarkable rejection of hazard, of circumstances. It is always as though, as he went through life, he was refusing to respond any more than necessary to those grains of sand which cannot be avoided in the course of any human progress, and to the unexpected conditions which they bring about. The absurd ... has no rightful place in his universe, above all ... when that universe is practically enclosed, whether in a place of his and by himself, as at la Coste, or in prison and by others. In his mind, everything is in order, foreseen, for good or ill, as in a well-made play - all that remains is to get to know the lines, above all to be able to follow the production without becoming confused."

His writing demonstrated the importance he attached to a set of objects whose relation to him was fixed and reliable, a world of secure sequences, a universe of no surprises beyond a predictable range of possibilities. This dependence was also clear in his life. He was prone to bouts of distraction when his supports failed him - when no money was arriving from Provence, when the servants had walked out. He always depended on staff, of one kind or another; even when reduced to living in "a barn", in 1798, there was a maidservant to attend on him **(see chapter 27)**. Marie Constance Quesnet was his support in his old age, as he acknowledged. Such a man does not embrace liberty for all humanity.

Note another piece of evidence of Sade's unease at the prospect of the unpredictable. At Vincennes in 1780, he briefly and mistakenly believed that there was a plan to transfer him elsewhere by sea: "I have always feared and greatly detested the sea... Never mind a posting, never mind a command, even if I were made *king* of an island, I would refuse..." The mighty and unbiddable oceans upset his need for sureness.

Sade was able to see through his arch-criminals sufficiently to understand that they lacked the courage to prey openly in a republic of uninhibited vendetta. Yet, although he let the reader share his perception of the weakness behind their flaying and declaming, he did so no more than rarely. I have mentioned the passing insight **(see chapter 35)** that Blangis, the strongest sexual ogre at Silling, might have been panicked by the resistance of "a steadfast child".

Besides, in *Juliette*, during a rare excursion out of doors, Saint-Fond and the heroine are confronted by two masked men with guns. The arch-libertine is at once all of a tremor: "I am not one of those brave fools," he confesses. The men tie him to a tree - but, rather than take his purse or his life, they take down his breeches, for this is a playlet arranged by Juliette to give Saint-Fond a new *frisson*, with which he is eventually delighted. Later, safe indoors again, Saint-Fond is preparing his worst for a high-born family, arrested under royal warrant and then chained amid an orgy of depravity directed by Juliette, when the father of the family tells Saint-Fond what a rotter he is and demands a fair trial. "You coward - if I were to break free, you would flee in panic." "You are quite correct, but you will not break free; you are in my power," replies Saint-Fond, and proceeds to take horrendous advantage.

It is as though Sade could not prevent himself laying flaws into his over-bearing libertines, knowing that they did not attain the brave, protean, imperturbable self-reliance of the citizen of his ideal republic - and even that citizen would have relied on a municipal draft of sexual objects into publicly funded houses of libertinage. Sade seems to have known, without being able to accept the fact for long, that no-one would be up to living with no force but his or her own to rely on. Every creation of his scuttles about in the shelter of money - or under its threat.

Likewise, away from fantasies of his quill, Sade, lord of estates, put the new constitution of France between the battlements of his château and a would-be demolition squad in 1792, using his rhetoric to urge the notables down in Provence to remember that all citizens were required to respect private property **(see chapter 24)**. Also, there were the querulous conclusions he drew from weaver Trillet's pot-shot at him in 1777: "Today a stranger comes to ask for his daughter at the point of a pistol; tomorrow a labourer will come to ask for his day's pay at the point of a rifle" **(see chapter 11)**.

No tides - of the dreamed republic of seethe, of the real First Republic of France, or of the Bourbon era - were to be allowed to wash away money or the means to make and keep it. Throughout his writings, as throughout his life, one can hear the chink of coins. In the first letter of Sade's that I have quoted **(see chapter 4)**, he was telling of spending money on boughten sexual encounters; in one of the last **(see chapter 29)**, he was calling from Charenton for money, which helped to keep sweet Magdeleine Leclerc, his last object of sexual hire. Along the way, he used gold to recruit the young maids who were brought to la Coste in the winter of 1774-75, and to hold the useful Marie Constance Quesnet to him with interest-bearing bonds. As the glamour of his person declined and his liberty was shrunk, Sade was more and more apt to think of money as the way to satisfaction, and this showed under his pen.

The use of money, as ever, was to pin submissive bodies in such a way that their attention be altogether yours. Put their health in danger, their lives, the lives of their loved ones, the children in their wombs. During that and beyond that, make deep assaults on their individuality and autonomy - eat their shit, their nipples, their testicles, their new-born; burn, lash, flay, dismember. No-one is exempt, be they young and fresh or old and foul. Nothing that they can say, make, excrete, ejaculate, conceive, give birth to, decay into, own - nothing they can be or have any relationship with - can escape you or save them from you. You, the arch-criminal, act upon the victims presented - and upon others not present in that these latter are deprived of the chance to relate to those whom you have destroyed.

Nothing? In *Juliette*, one libertine says "the greatest pleasures stem from revulsions overcome." Indeed, Sade's libertines glory in their exploits as shit-eaters, womb-rippers, dismemberers, fuckers wearing abrasive shark-skin condoms, and other practitioners of the bizarre.

Even so, I wonder whether Sade was squeamish about a phenomenon much more common in sexual life - menstrual blood. Could the great breaker of icons and outrager of imposed morality have been susceptible to old taboos about coming into contact with women's monthly tide?

Menstruation is mentioned in his works: On 12 January, during the winter of mayhem by timetable at Silling Castle, the storyteller Martaine recounts to the four overlords how a menstruating girl is brought to a libertine's house, where he pushes her into a tank of very cold water and achieves orgasm thereby. The girl falls ill because, although she was pulled out of the tank promptly, the shock occurred while she had her period. However, the man in the story, this the 54th "criminal passion", has no contact with or sight of her menstrual blood. If she were bleeding from a wound, or befouled by shit, there would very likely be play with these excretions, given the pathology revealed through the *oeuvre*.

Also, in *Juliette*, a client of the heroine's brothel in Venice asks her "to have the goodness to advise me as to the day when your period will be at its most abundant", so that he might "kneel in front of you, lick your cunt and become drunk on those menses which I adore." He wants to "conclude the sacrifice at the same temple which I have just worshipped, while one of your servants ... has the kindness to thrash me with all her might." Juliette sets the date for "tomorrow - the thing you like starts today, and tomorrow, the storm." The client, Juliette reports, "satisfied his disgusting passion ... I received his disgusting homage, and was faker enough to make him believe that it was a great thing for me. I got out of him, apart from the five hundred sequins,[1] a diamond worth at least twice as much and which the old rogue gave me as a present to show me how much he was pleased with my good manners."

The client, whose language stands out as polite and elaborate to a fault, confesses at the first interview that he suffers from profound impotence and - this placing him even lower in Sade's scale of the contemptible - he is known to be a public prosecutor. Throughout the episode, Juliette is very much the detached professional on the make. She shows her distaste for the requirements of such a client, using the word "disgusting" twice - a very rare sentiment from this experienced maker of sexual mayhem who, by then, has coupled with animals,

1 A high price, even *chez* Juliette.

sought and undergone abortion, eaten human flesh, maimed and murdered children and pregnant women...

If Sade had been without the revulsion, widespread among men, for menstrual blood, the most imposing debauchees in his literature would be wallowing in it with the gusto and lurid language they bring to shit, semen, human flesh, and to blood shed by the whip and the blade. Noting the obsessive assaults on female reproductive organs - sewing up, sealing with fire, excising with scalpels and knives - I suggest Sade shied away from menstrual blood because it is evidence that the womb lives yet, and according to a rhythm not set by men.

Besides, still regarding Sade's adherence to arrangements against change and surprise, recall the preamble of *The Hundred and Twenty Days*, where he promises "a sumptuous banquet [of] six hundred different dishes, [from which,] one by one, each of you will fulfil his want" **(see chapter 30)**.

In effect, though, the obsession to control, to engage by violence and pain, leaves nothing for the reader who wants, in his closet literature, to read of mutual tenderness and shared orgasm amid free play. Sade's variations are on one theme only and his inventiveness therein, even by his own admission, has its limits. The narrator complains, during one orgy in *Juliette*, that words are not enough: "... it would have taken an engraver to convey to posterity this voluptuous and divine scene! But lust, too quickly exalting our actors, might not have given the artist the time to capture them. It is not easy for art, which has no movement, to make real an action of which movement is the whole essence..." A writer of more varied sexual concerns, more literary talent and less concern to fix the flux of events, would have neither left so many readers cold nor felt that unconscious yearning for a movie camera. (Sade, if born 200 years later, might well now be a maker of snuff videos.)

He extended, in his fiction, the protection against enemies that he wished for and the emotional release that the murders he dreamed of would have given him. Also, he was able to believe that, by his pen, he was a great criminal through spreading the good news of vice to countless people whom he would never meet.

*　　　　*　　　　*

One might argue, in a kind of mitigation, that a man moved by the will to impinge sought control of other people only so that he himself might be free. Having made others submit, he could then play freely among the obedient flesh, as a seducer might take and give enjoyment once he had caused the object of his desires to let him have his way. In the case of Sade, the urge was towards torture and murder, but in other men it might well not be taken to dangerous extent and their actions would be acceptable. The argument does not stand, though, because one cannot play freely among slaves, among the merely obedient. Even if the man acts the generous lover, compliments and caresses the object person before, during and after the deeds by which he achieves his sexual aim, even if he strives to give her orgasm, he remains master and she remains servant.

What is happening is the impingement by an owner or renter on a possession or hireling, not the expression of love between equals, because the object is not free to refuse or to leave when she wishes. Furthermore, even if the master stops when asked, lets the woman leave when asked, she is then a servant temporarily on leave, apt to be recalled, *unless* the man renounces his hold over her for all time and does not seek to restore it, thus changing the relationship definitively from that of controller and controlled to that of free and equal lovers, each of whom can give or withhold himself or herself for a moment or forever.

CHAPTER 37: JACK AND JOSÉ

Sade was not alone in using literature to express a lethal desire to impinge on women who would otherwise be free, or at least inattentive to a man. Even the women and girls who are not slaughtered in his writings, women who rampage without God and beyond the law, are subject to the patronage and the assessment of rich men. Also, they are liable to fall victims themselves unless they maintain a high seethe and collude with their patrons' desire to impinge ever more widely and outrageously. Juliette, the prime example, cannot break out of her role as imitatrix of male destruction because, if she were to do so, she might fall victim to that destruction.

At work in the thinking of the Enlightenment were notions which carried the implication - though rarely the explicit statement - that there was no just basis for male supremacy to continue in a society that aspired to equality, that it ought to fall along with all other hierarchies that stemmed from any estimation but that of talent. Sade understood this, to a degree, but tried, in some irreconcilable arguments as discussed above, to set women free to fuck while keeping them enslaved to be fucked. Other Enlightenment writers, while holding forth on the need to set man free, meant by that the liberation of the masculine half of humanity.

Economic changes in western Europe and North America after Sade's death further underlined the injustice and inconsistency of this line of thinking. During the 19th century, many more jobs were created in manufacturing, in service industries such as banking and insurance, in public administration, with the result that there were many more young women in the growing cities with a little money they had earned themselves - at the loom, on the production line, copying invoices and typing letters - and so with a degree of freedom. Their presence - out and about in the parks, cafés and dance halls - changed those cities.

The literature of the end of the 19th century and the beginning of the 20th includes Carmen, at first in a story by Prosper Merimée, and Lulu, in plays by Frank Wedekind. Both are projected to greater fame in the operas that bear their names, by Georges Bizet and Alban Berg respectively, and each dies at the end of her story. Carmen is stabbed near a Seville bullring by her lover José, Lulu in a London tenement by Jack the Ripper, neither having been allowed to survive as a destroyer of men's prospects through their unhinged reactions to her insistence on controlling her own sexual destiny. José throws over his military career in Spain and the prospect of marriage with a docile village girl for the excitement he feels with Carmen; Dr Schön spurns his respectable fiancée in Germany for the delight he experiences from Lulu; each man is destroyed by his inability to let a woman live freely.

Merimée and Wedekind, Bizet and Berg, were no more disposed there than was Sade to create a free female spirit who could deal with men on terms she laid down - could deal with them thus and survive.

CHAPTER 38: A BLUE FLAME, BURNING LOW

The greatest danger to one's success in seeking control of other people is not the others but oneself. The master must not only strive to lord it over his environment but also to keep a close grip on himself. In the intense experiences that he desires lies peril - of remorse at his predations, of diminished satisfaction through snatching at his pleasures too eagerly, and of becoming so excited that he loses his awareness of the attention he has from his victims, loses his perception of the effect of his crimes. This is a refined, Sadeian view.

Remorse is for the virtuous and the weak, the fools who make up the arch-criminal's prey. "What can there be in common between the man who can do anything and the man who dares to do nothing?" Sade asked contemptuously. Crime is to be embraced with no slacking, with not a flicker of mercy, and always with alertness for opportunities to commit more and greater outrages of robbery, corruption, rape, torture and murder. To hesitate or repent means you recognise that there are those who may judge you. All the while, one monitors oneself for signs of lassitude and remorse, and one is scrutinised by one's criminal associates for such signs. Juliette is kept up to the licentious mark by Noirceuil, Saint-Fond and others of her mentors, clients and playmates. When she seems to slip, their disapproval is fierce and she knows it might be fatal.

A rush at pleasure, when one is enjoying sexual predation, can mean not only premature ejaculation but also the victim expiring too soon, slipping away into a faint or death, and so beyond the reach of impingement. Sade wrote of the problem of "passion concentrated on one point resembling the rays focused through a magnifying glass and apt to set fire to the object" at the focal point. The discerning libertine reduces these risks through guided, managed orgies, such as the elaborately structured winter of *The Hundred and Twenty Days of Sodom* and many sessions in which Juliette and her associates extend the pleasure of various masters (and the agony of many captives) by their combined roles of participants and overseers. "Just a moment," says Delbène, abbess of the convent school where Juliette is brought up, interrupting a lesbian frolic with various of her pupils, "let's bring a bit of order to our pleasures; one doesn't enjoy them unless they're arranged."

Those of us who find no fear in *excitement that carries away detachment and considered perceptions* may well find strange the notion that great danger lies there. However, the Sadeian way is opposed to that of blithe rapture, which is full and sufficient pleasure to those who know it and embrace it. For the most refined of Sade's pen-and-ink libertines, it is necessary to strive for a composure that even the height of excitement cannot shake.

The libertine seeks excitement through crime. "What lack of movement! What frostiness!" Noirceuil scoffs at virtuous living. "What a difference in the other camp - what a stirring of my senses!" he extolls vice. The cardinal point, though, is to *know* that one's crimes are having an effect, otherwise they would disappear for the criminal and be crimes no longer, because only one's own impingements have value. So one must remain observant, a step away from one's own acts. Out of this arises a preference for plotting crimes rather than carrying them out. During the calm and concentrated preparation, there is plenty of time to savour the crime at the schemer's leisure, with no risk of his impingement being lost to his senses in the hurly-burly of the culmination. Completion is necessary - crimes left on the drawing-board break no hearts and stop no hearts - but the planning may be preferred for its sure composure.

In this connection, Sade's propensity for vice through literature may be better understood. With quill poised over paper rather than lash poised over bare flesh, he could *fix* his dreams. Even if what he was conceiving for the page distracted him to masturbate and so tumble into the delirium of orgasm, the written orgy remained as he had left it, in the aspic of his will as author. He alone could change, develop and bring to conclusion his literary plots.

The libertine also strives not to act in rage. The red mist of anger obscures one's effect. Rage is a fine inspiration for vice but an unreliable guide through it. The unbiddable aristocrat who had attacked the young Condé **(see chapter 2)** and the drawing of his supposed rival Lefèvre **(see chapter 19)** was well aware of the derangement that choler could cause.

Sade was also impressed by what he felt to be a close affinity of rage and sexual climax. During *Philosophy in the Boudoir*, the apprentice libertine Eugénie de Mistival is told by the experienced Dolmancé:

"Would the culmination of pleasure be a kind of frenzy if [nature] had not meant one's behaviour while copulating to be the same as one's behaviour while enraged?" Blangis, one of the overlords at the orgy of *The Hundred and Twenty Days*, when taking his sexual pleasure, was "no longer a man but a furious tiger... Wild yells, dreadful blasphemies ... he frothed at the mouth, he whinnied like a stallion..." Sade himself, so Rose Keller told the police soon after Easter 1768, uttered "loud and frightening cries" at the culmination of his flagellation of her **(see chapter 7)**. Also, we have it, by his *manille* letter of 1784 from prison, that he believed "nobody ... goes through what I go through in this crisis", "an epileptic fit", "convulsions, spasms and pain, *head-fled-to-hell*" **(see chapter 22)**.

Simone de Beauvoir suggested that Sade might have been afraid of his own orgasms, even while their immoderation gave him the illusion (a very common one) that in them lay sovereign pleasure. Their intensity, and his difficulty sometimes in achieving them, may well account, but only in part, for his concern to keep control during such episodes and their preliminaries.

The libertine who is bent on composure during his actions seeks to quell the dizzying excitement that might seize him because of the object or objects of his rage or of his desire. He tries to stay cool when the woman he wants appears naked before him or when he approaches some fetish that takes his fancy - a woman of a particular ethnic origin, say, or a man dressed in a certain way. If he can make his actions into a spectacle, observed from the distance of his detachment even while he performs them, then they keep the significance for him that derangement, loss of control, would wipe out. His sense of his own freedom to control, his sense of his own conscious existence, would be lost in the rapture of the plunge into the object that enrages or attracts him. He can stay in contact with the object only by a conscious performance on his part.

This cold, self-distanced impinger needs to be sure always of *his* responsibility for the object's enjoyment or pain or pleading or whatever effect he is having. He has no other way to be aware of his physical presence. That is, having protected himself from dissolving his consciousness of self in the delirium of the give and take of pleasuring, where his physicality would lead him to caper out of control, he has to act with calculation and observe his effects - this caress of the vagina produces a shudder of pleasure, that bite of the nipple produces a yelp of pain, this fall of the lash produces a scream, that thrust into the anus produces a gasp of delight...

In ecstasy, the awareness of the engagement that the criminal is drawing to himself from the other or others present escapes. The Sadeian literary protagonist studies so as not to lose himself in his animalness, so as to stay in the solitude of his consciousness, whatever may be happening around him. "All creatures are born separate and with no need of each other," Noirceuil tells Juliette. Sade repudiated the notion of equality expressed in mutual pleasing, and that of equality created by mutual pleasure.

Yet orgasm, like rage, does break the impinger's composure and observation. For the moment, he is mere flesh, lost. From this, avoidable only by those prepared to eschew orgasm altogether, arises another important value in the libertine having a great and disturbing effect on the objects on which he is focusing, whether by giving them pleasure or pain: While I am gone, while I have lost my detached observation as orgasm is overtaking me, you will remain affected by my actions, you will be unable to turn your attention to anyone or anything else. This is because I have caused you such delight or such agony that you have no choice but to continue to feel my effect on you and react accordingly, and that you will *still* be that way when I have recovered from the seizure and am ready to deal with you again.

This criminal, ever seeking impregnability against all enchantment, experiences orgasm as a frenzied crisis in his cold, tense body. As de Beauvoir wrote, his is a will intent on fulfilling the flesh without losing itself in the flesh. So he remains a being of the will and can never become a being of spontaneity, revelling in shared joy.

To help him keep a grip on his responses and maintain the required distance, the impinger uses accomplices and devices. In Sade's day, the former were the main aid; in our times of greater apartness and greater technical development, the latter are more favoured. The overlord who shares his actions in an orgy with others of his kind observes the others' activities and thus is helped in mastering his immediate impulses. (He is not merely multiplying his own effects by enjoying the fascination of the audience with his actions.) He can pause during his penetration of a body, withdraw his penis so as to postpone his orgasm, yet his excitement continues, under control, as he watches other libertines engaging the attention of object persons.

The voyeur, watching from the shrubbery through the gap in the curtains as a couple makes love, is similarly assisted; he is excited by the spectacle yet detached, protected against being overwhelmed into loss of control by direct embrace of another's flesh. His scope for orgasm, by masturbation, when *he* decides, is greater.

(Also, note that the undertaking of orgies and rapes with accomplices of proven reliability helps to secure the criminal against surprise by the authorities or by would-be victims who might fight back. We are dealing with a class of cowards, as Sade recognised, once in a while.)

Sade's propensity in life and literature for sexual accomplices - such as the valet Latour at Marseilles in 1772 **(see chapter 8)** and the hired help in the orgies at the little house at Arcueil in the 1760s **(see chapter 6)**, the masterful foursome at Silling Castle in *The Hundred and Twenty Days* and the libertines *chez* Mme de Saint-Ange in *Philosophy in the Boudoir* - may have arisen from sexual pleasures taken in company, or taken from company, early in his life. Perhaps he was excited by spying on his uncle, the Abbé de Sade, and the latter's hired women at Saumane, perhaps by experiences as a military cadet with rakish colleagues. In any event, in his younger days Sade could afford the repeated hire of accomplices; in his literature, he could create many co-operations and a multiplicity of victims.

The prime traditional device for aiding detachment in sexual action is the mirror, though it figures little in Sade's writings. The mirror, along the walls or fixed to the ceiling, is widely supposed to heighten sexual excitement, which it may well do but only in the way that caters to the cold manipulator who wants to keep his distance. A lover has no use for it. The mirror is unnecessary where there is mutual pleasure, where both or all are equal givers and takers. It is unnecessary wherever there is trust, for members of a community of much contact and total honesty will be told by other members whether they look well, their hats are on right or there is a piece of cabbage on their teeth - no need for the solitary check via the impersonal glass. The mirror is an instrument arisen from mistrust and a wish for solitude, put to use for personal detachment.[1]

---

1 Various accounts from around the world describe the reaction of communal tribespeople on encountering the mirror for the first time and being disturbed by its effect, shying away from its magical introduction of a self-consciousness they had not known, also disliking a new and solitary vanity sometimes occurring in tribal members who are drawn to the reflection. Victor Serge, in *Conquered City*, and Theocritus, in *The Idylls*, mention this.

To the honest, communal person, there is no difference between the quality of observed action and that of unobserved action. We of shame, solitude and exploitation know such a difference, however; we feel shock and shame when we discover that we are being observed, even if we are doing nothing of which we would be ashamed.

Since Sade's time, the photograph, sound recording, cine film and video-tape have joined the range of devices available to those who want to keep a grip on their responses and to be sure of the effect they are having through their sexual activity, to chill and preserve it as they multiply their observations though lenses and microphones. The Polaroid photograph and the video tape-recorder have reduced to seconds the wait for those wanting to see themselves and their objects as performers apart from themselves, to step away from love-making. The edit, re-wind and fast-forward facilities allow passages where the engagement of the object appears to waver - the stifled yawn as he unzipped his trousers, her scratching of an armpit while he was licking her thigh - to be wiped from the version prepared as electronic distanciation and confirmation of the events. Ready to be played back time and again, the edited version becomes the memory of the occasion.

Sade and his paper libertines used money and terror to achieve the engagement of their sexual objects; the modern equivalents of those libertines have new means to improve that engagement, after the fact. Sade was adept at altering his recollections of events to suit himself - this ancient editing mode remains as serviceable as ever - but he had to manage without electronic wipe, freeze-frame, splicing and slo-mo.

He who seeks to avoid losing his awareness in sexual excitement can not only have photographs and tapes of objects on whom he has acted; he can also use pictures and voices of people he has never met, never will meet. The man who telephones a specialised agency to order a sexual conversation is called back by a woman whose true name and location are kept from him. The women who have performed for the video-tapes and the magazines he stares at are given pseudonyms. They are hired performers who offer an illusion of engagement - this is the main attraction of pornography, not the nakedness - and the user can control his own excitement as he masturbates over however much stimulation he allows the packaged pseudo-engagement to arouse in him.

For many who live at a remove from sexual dissolution, from disappearance into ecstasy, except for their brief plunges during their carefully managed orgasms in carefully protected places, the physical presence and participation of human objects has become inadequate. The *dream* of gratification is far superior to any pleasure that real events can offer, although real acts and people may suggest the first threads of the dream that the distanced libertine weaves for his own delight. Here is Belmor, a rich client of Juliette, thinking aloud to that young arranger of his erotic entertainments:

"... letting our two minds have full scope, we conjure up lewd beings which unfortunately cannot exist. Oh, Juliette! how delightful are the pleasures of the imagination and how hedonistically one travels all the ways that its brilliant light shows us! Darling angel, admit that people have no idea what we invent, what we create, in those divine moments where our fiery spirits exist no longer except in the impure organ of lustfulness - what delights we enjoy when wanking each other as our phantoms become erect, how one caresses them in ecstasy! how one gathers them in! how one elaborates them through a thousand obscene episodes! The whole Earth belongs to us in those delightful moments; not one creature resists us; each one presents to our seething senses just the sort of delight that our boiling imagination believes most apt to it - we lay waste the world ... we repopulate it with new objects, which we destroy also; the means to every crime are in our hands and we use them all; ... all the episodes mounted by all the most hellish and most malign spirits did not reach, even in their most destructive effects, as far as we dare to carry our desires. *Fortunate, a hundred times fortunate,* said La Mettrie, *are those whose senses are always led by a lively and lewd imagination into the foretaste of pleasure!*

"Indeed, Juliette, I do not know whether reality measures up to the chimeras, whether the enjoyment of what we never have is not worth a hundred times more than the enjoyment of what we do possess: there's your arse, Juliette; it is before my eyes, I deem it beautiful; yet my imagination, always more inspired than is Nature, and more skilful I venture to say, creates from it other arses that are even more beautiful. And is the pleasure that this illusion gives me not preferable to the pleasure that reality is about to have me enjoy? What you offer me is nothing less than beautiful; what I conjure up is sublime. I am going to enact with you nothing that is beyond anyone else; yet it seems to me that, with this arse, work of my imagination, I will enact deeds beyond the invention of even the Gods."

Via Belmor, Sade presented this line of thought as a refinement of libertinage, an achievement, through the ever-reaching imagination, of delight beyond any that the mere physical environment, human and the rest, can offer. He could not have been expected to acknowledge that Belmor's preference for the "pleasures of the imagination" represents a device in the endless struggle to secure protection against rapture in love.

The struggle is a hard one, as Sade did acknowledge: "I have cited reasons to back my deviations; I did not stop when confronted by my doubts. I have conquered, I have uprooted, I have crushed everything in my heart that might have stood in the way of my pleasure." When not puffing himself up with pride as a self-made, self-sealed libertine, Sade was more inclined, however, to the whine he put in the mouth of Dolmancé, of *Philosophy in the Boudoir*: "It was men's ingratitude that shrivelled my heart."

* * *

The individual's effort to arm himself against surprise - by an enemy or by his own ecstasy or by remorse - can take him even further into immovable detachment. By iron-willed concentration, by vigilant observation of his own thoughts and feelings, the great criminal renders himself untouchable and irreducible. He embraces the belief, as de Beauvoir said, that the only free act is the act cleared of all feeling: that is, he is only his own man when everything he does proceeds from his sealed, composed, essential self, purged of any influence by emotion. He is all consideration and foresight, nothing of spontaneity. This concentrated, poised being is an implacable instrument for crime. Thus Sade dreamed the perfect libertine while trapped in his wavering character, his bloated body, his study and his indebtedness.

The ataraxic criminal has risen above petty vice and rash mayhem so as to transcend the natural violence of the volcano in eruption or that of the blood-maddened soldier in battle. He does not surrender to the destructiveness of the universe but consciously, calculatedly, imitates it, in open defiance. At this level, he knows no prejudice or shame, perceives no fear in himself. To him, everything is for his good. He cares only for the meaning of objects and events, and this meaning depends wholly on him. That which does not interest him does not exist for him. If he is whipped and penetrated, then this does not diminish his mastery in the least, whether he sought such an experience or not, because the only estimation that has any significance is his own. The refined criminal dominates any situation because his own attitude tells him so. In planning and committing a crime, he never gives a thought to remorse, for to do so would be to admit that others may assess him. He has rejected all morality so there is none by which to measure his actions.

This studied apathy - a tense, brooding viciousness rather than a bored lassitude - is so squeezed of emotion that it becomes akin to inertia, where the will has ceased to pulse. Here is another danger for the libertine who pursues detachment to such refinement. In seeking to protect his authenticity, his capacity to think and act by no other inspiration but his own will, does he destroy his freedom? Without feeling, can there be any action? Does hedonism, the delirious pleasure of his youth and immediacy, end in ataraxia? Does fear of failure to control others and impinge on them render down his spirit to a distillate of indifference? Does he die rich, safe and quite still? In that state, would he have come full, laborious circle to the sort of condition where he began, that of the being who receives no attention?

The child whose acts were impotent, because he was not heeded when he made them, is matched in young adulthood by the fucker whose effects disappoint him because he does not secure full attention from women, then matched in late years by the inert man who is not heeded because he has spurned all that is not of himself. If he does not act because nothing external to himself can touch him - the antithesis of the child's condition of all short-fused emotion and no reflectiveness - then he is as ineffective as the most ignored baby.

"This apathy that lets one smother passion, that preserves one's lucidity, is your defence against all dangers," Clairwil counsels Juliette, but she tells her pupil in crime, on another occasion, that she might have "rationalised my dreams too well. The indifference that my way of thinking gives me comes in the way of their moving me any longer."

However, Sade, the advocate of constant seethe, pointed the way to avoid decline from adamantine ataraxia into inertia. Clairwil, like his other arch-libertines, faces the need to cope with the consequences of self-transition from the violent emotions embraced in apprentice days, so as to feel alive and fulfilled in refined, composed criminality. The abiding requirement then is not only to avoid giving up vice but also to avoid repetition of crimes of a certain degree. With repetition, these become commonplace and a disappointment to the criminal, who thereby marks himself for his peers as a burnt-out case, all seething done. As such, he may become prey to other criminals, up-and-coming youngsters still robbing and killing for the quick thrill of it, or poised brooders and plotters who have not come to a halt; he might even give way to remorse and repentance. The way forward for the refined, cerebral criminal is to seek ever greater crimes, via mighty thefts and frauds, massacres galore, orgies that wring and destroy countless bodies.

The trouble with people, thought Pascal, is that they are not content to stay in their rooms - this inability to ignore the universe has to be managed by the sealed criminal to the extent that an irritation sufficient to provoke him into keeping the flame of action alive does reach him. This is to be a blue flame, burning low, steady and very intense. A prime fuel for that flame is the knowledge that the licence to desire and destroy without limit, which every embracer of vice grants to himself, must entail a licence to be desired and destroyed, as in Sade's republic of oppression unrestrained by law, so any way of life short of inertia requires a commitment to struggle and dominate.

Sade allows that anyone may aspire to this refinement of criminality, and accepts that it entails an aristocracy poised in malign energy and ruling over the herd of the doomed.

Camus wrote of "the extreme consequences of a logic in revolt - the sealed world view, universal crime, the aristocracy of cynicism and the desire for apocalypse." This last is impossible, for nature permits everything and absorbs everything with indifference. There is always a remainder and always a renewal, no matter how extensive and enduring the explosion and damage. The great mulch of the universe always functions. Sade admitted: "I abhor nature... I would like to upset its plans, block its march, stop the wheel of the stars, disrupt the globes that float in space, destroy what aids it, protect what harms it, ... insult it in its creation, and I could not do it." Also: "The greatest torment of mankind is the impossibility of offending nature."

For all the tension and struggle to avoid a plunge into careless rapture, for all the concentration to keep energy pouring into ever more effective crimes, the ideal act can never be achieved.

"We might perhaps attack the sun, deprive the universe of it or use it to set fire to the world - now there would be some crimes," sighs one of Sade's libertines. Another gazes at a volcano and yearns: "Mouth of every inferno, if only I could be like you, I could overwhelm all the villages around me, I could make many a tear fall!"

In Sade's works, men ejaculate over women's breasts and faces, exult in pregnancy as evidence of their effect on women, delight in the notion (as Andrea Dworkin puts it) of their sperm as agent of the death of women who expire during miscarriage or childbirth - but they cannot realise Clairwil's wish "to discover a crime which would continue to have an effect forever so that ... I would always be the source of a certain trouble, and that this trouble would expand to the extent that it caused a foulness so widespread or an upheaval so well established that, even after my life had ended, I would survive in the eternal endurance of my badness."

No-one can speak for the *eternal* endurance of Sade's badness - however, two hundred years on, it is still acknowledged.

CHAPTER 39: "EVERYTHING SCARES ME"

"I do not want to make vice acceptable; ... I do not want to make women adore the men who do them wrong - rather to hate them in fact... I have drawn my protagonists who live for vice as so repulsive that they cannot attract pity or love; so I venture to say I am a more moral [writer] than those who tread warily." Thus Sade, in defence of *Aline and Valcour*, which was published under his name. He would probably have said much the same of his anonymous published works if he had not been wary of trouble from the authorities for whoever admitted authorship of *Justine, Juliette* and *Philosophy in the Boudoir*. Was he really laying down a monstrous lesson in morality to warn readers off the horrors of extreme crime?

Swinburne went so far as to call Sade "that illustrious and ill-requited benefactor of humanity". Trying to lean towards that opinion, one can recall that Sade recognised much of the violence, corruption and hypocrisy of the France in which he grew up, that of the royal régime before the Revolution, and he belaboured it in his books. The four masters of the bloody revels at Silling Castle amassed their fortunes, the author makes clear, from the wars of King Louis XIV, rather as ancestors of Sade's in-laws, the Montreuils, probably did **(see chapter 5)**. Saint-Fond, royal minister and patron to Juliette, enriches himself through the opportunities that politics and public administration provide. The contrasted lands of Butua - weighed down by superstition, greed and ineptitude - and Tamoé - a utopia of sharing and good husbandry - are created in *Aline and Valcour* to make points about the shortcomings of Bourbon France.

Even so, Sade's informed contempt for delinquencies he saw around him was not enough to have him purge his most successful literary characters of them. If his "protagonists who live for vice" were meant to be repulsive, why do they prosper so mightily and have, by their own lights, such a wonderful time? Why are they never overcome by forces of virtue? Why do those criminal protagonists who are liquidated - such as Olympe Borghèse, Clairwil and Saint-Fond in *Juliette* - fall at the hands of villains as wicked as they? The four overlords of *The*

Hundred and Twenty Days of Sodom, Juliette and Noirceuil, Dolmancé and company of *Philosophy in the Boudoir*, all survive the rampages confected for them by their author and reach their respective last pages rich as ever and ready to do more mayhem.

The Marquise de Sade, sending comments on her husband's plays through prison walls, suggested: "... these sorts of characters are too strong and, in things done for the public, one must, for the general good, avoid too much disturbance of the fibres of heads which are not as firmly put together...

"... One must, you tell me, make [certain characters] known so as to protect people from them and to make them detested. That's true ... but there's a line one must not cross, so as to keep from a depraved mind the means to corrupt itself further..."

Her husband would have none of that: "It is not in the least necessary that, at the dénouement [of a play], vice is to be punished and virtue rewarded."

It has been argued by other authors that the Terror of the Revolution disappointed Sade, in that he had hoped a republic akin to that of his ideals would emerge from the collapse of the royal régime. The argument goes that this let-down soured Sade to the extent that his post-Terror works were more bitter and more sanguinary than those conceived before the excesses of the Revolution.

Such a view of Sade after 1794 takes too little account of the fact that, by then, he was in his mid-fifties and long since formed by his experiences under the old régime as aristocrat, officer, *rentier*, debaucher, prisoner and writer. The Sade who emerged from Charenton in 1790 and entered a career as a man of letters at liberty, with his pen and his rhetoric at work "now for one party, now in favour of another", his political opinions "shuttling" **(see chapter 24)**, does not impress as someone with high, clear expectations of his fellow humans, especially when they were politicking. He may well have been jolted by the voraciousness of the Terror, especially as he was seized by its administrators and brought close to the sort of death which many others had met in the city where he was incarcerated, but his first thought on release from Picpus in October 1794 was to return to his ménage with Marie Constance in the rue Neuve des Mathurins, and take up where he had been abruptly interrupted in his supervision of the printing of *Aline and Valcour* and in pressing his plays on theatre managements **(see**

chapter 27). This was hardly the manner of a man thrown out of his stride by recent events.

Note also that *The Hundred and Twenty Days of Sodom*, "the filthiest story told since the world began," was written in the royal régime's jail, shaped by memories in which the Committee of Public Safety had no hand.

Besides, there is weighty evidence from his personal life that Sade was no moralist, no egalitarian. His personal relations were manipulative - as Laure de Lauris, Renée Pélagie and Anne Prospère de Launay could testify - and seigneurial. He understood the aspiration to liberty, equality and fraternity, but could not embrace it. Simone de Beauvoir pointed out: "Sade had no experience of action. That a real communication among individuals might be allowed through an undertaking that would bring all people together in the joint aim to realise their humanity, if he suspected this, he was not seized by it; ... he dooms the individual to an insignificance that authorises violence against the individual ..."

Even in Sade's republic of high seethe and minimal laws, where everyone is supposed to be free to realise his or her potential whatever that turns out to be, the individual can be forced into sexual servitude.

What's more, one should not make out that *People of France, One More Effort if You Want to be Republicans* represents Sade's blueprint of the society he believed attainable from the cooling crucible of the Revolution, in 1794-95. The call to create the republic of high seethe appears to point to a transformation of France that is only one daring step away, but it stems much more from the author's abiding wish for a land stripped of God, priests and just about all laws except those which would conscript sexual victims. This wish was a Sadeian dream rather than an option which the Revolution was apt to embrace, in 1794-95 or at any other stage, as Sade understood, at least when he raised his head from his desk. Not so much one more effort, rather a few more masturbatory reveries.

As long before the Terror as the summer of 1782, from his cell at Vincennes, Sade had declared by letter that his heart was "hardened and closed against kind feelings." He also told his wife of his preference for "a universe of things and details, very delightful in my estimation, which know so well how to soothe my unhappiness when I let my imagination wander ... in all conscience, I am very glad that it all went as it did" **(see chapter 20)**.

There is valuable, forward-looking material in Sade's works, in that he was an early perceiver of the erotic as a mainspring of human behaviour. "The sexual passion is to the others what the nervous fluid is to life itself; it sustains them all and gives force to them all... Ambition, cruelty, greed and vengeance are all based on sexuality," says a libertine in *Juliette*.

Sade was also an early explorer - although some of his terms seem strange nowadays - of other modern ideas about human psychology and the nervous system, which suited very well his rejection of belief in divine direction of human behaviour.

In *Aline and Valcour*, he refers to an "electric fluid that circulates through the hollows of the nerves [and] is the carrier of pain and delight... This is the only soul that modern thinkers recognise." In the 1791 version of *Justine*, he punches harder: "When the science of anatomy is fully developed it will have no difficulty in demonstrating the relation between the physique of a man and the proclivities that rule his emotions. Pedants, hangmen, time-servers, law-makers, all you scum in the priesthood, what will become of you when we establish all this? What will your laws, your morals, your religion, your gallows, your heavens, your gods, your infernoes be worth when it is proved that one or other flow of juices, one or other kind of bodily tissue, one or other thickness of the blood, or of a different bodily fluid, can make people victims of your trials or of your rewards?"

It remains a good question **(see chapter 31)**.

However, as de Beauvoir noted, Sade also understood that one's preferences and tastes are formed by one's own attitude to an object - "the truth of a thing resides ... in the meaning which it has assumed for us during our particular experience," she wrote. This is a subversive notion to those who are brought up to believe in the intrinsic quality of each object, it having been made by God who alone may transform it and give it a different quality, albeit often through action by mortals. For instance, workers can make alloys of copper and iron, and shape those alloys into utensils, but this remains God's work. Likewise, a person may be altered by an injury or a change of hairstyle, but remains God's creature and keeps his or her intrinsic quality and value.

Yet, to believe that no object or person exists and has qualities unless perceived by a human being is a different view of the universe, a view which elevates the perceiver and allows the Sadeian belief that there exists only that which engages one's interest. A bolt of black silk cloth, say, may not be worth acknowledging by a certain man while it stays on the tailor's shelf, yet becomes interesting to the man, and so in existence, once it has been made into a tight dress and put on the body of a woman, thus forming an object that the man wants. Take away the dress and rip it to bits, put the woman into a jute sack, then they both rejoin the void which is a void because it does not interest the Sadeian man. Also, the object woman is of no interest to this man if she rolls into a ball when attacked and refuses to beg for mercy or cry, for the Sadeian man must have this object's sure and evident engagement if she is to be real for him. The Christian would say that the silk and the woman are facts to be considered according to their respective intrinsic qualities; the Sadeian would believe they are nothing unless significant to *him*.

Any woman who has been required by a man to dress or make herself up in a specified way - "because that's what turns me on" - will be familiar with this area of thought.

The hope of anyone who would maintain that Sade was creating a monstrous critique or satire of the life of vice flickers in the few indications that he saw through his protagonists. Blangis, raging overlord of *The Hundred and Twenty Days*, might have been thrown into a panic by resistance from a steadfast child; Saint-Fond, Juliette's ministerial patron, admits to being "probably the greatest coward in the world". Such glimpses of Sade's insight to an arch-criminal's susceptibility to cool resistance, by means of refusal to accept him on his own terms, suggest that Sade had insight into the brittleness in the tense personality that seeks eagerly for indomitability because, among other motives, it lacks that very quality. This is one reason why Sade himself dreamed so extensively about acquiring a power to control and impinge without limit. "I need to be consoled ... everything scares me," the 22-year-old Sade had confessed to Laure de Lauris in 1763 **(see chapter 5)**.

However, he was unable to proceed from his insight to a full understanding, and demolition, of the craving. This was beyond him, once he had reached for control, which is the tyrant's condition. From there, the road back to rapture, which is the child's condition, is very hard. He could only long for the opposite of rapture - a great concentration held in place by desperate tension, bracing oneself against all change and surprise, against the nightmare and impotence that can also possess the child, against the fear within.

CHAPTER 40: "I'LL READ A LITTLE, MY DEAR - DON'T WAIT UP"

It is difficult to plot Sade's influence on other writers and on human behaviour in general since his main works were published in the 1790s. The principal reason for this is that the immediate influence of his works on the public authorities has been to excite an urge to seize and burn them. While his name has entered modern languages across the world and become known to hundreds of millions of people, the horrific, albeit vague, reputation attached to that name has helped to make Sade's works taboo. For all the arrests of publishers, printers and booksellers, all the burning of volumes, however, most of the works that survived him have never been entirely out of reach.

A few literary figures have acknowledged his influence since his death. Saint-Beuve, writing in 1843, said: "Byron and Sade ... have been perhaps the two greatest inspirations to us moderns - the one published for all to read, the other clandestine, but not too clandestine." Indeed, Sade seemed to be an undergound avatar of literature with no holds barred, with sexuality frank and rampaging, man's expression unfettered by fear of gods or mortals. This impression was exciting and dangerous; it seemed to be needed to set literature and its readers free of superstition and of prejudice as to what could and could not be written and discussed, and could be acknowleged as felt within oneself. In coming to terms with the works of Sade, the world may believe that it has at hand instruments of change to be harnessed to its view of humanity.

The apparatus and atmosphere of prohibition, of course, have served to make the books even more sought after, even more apt to be regarded as the great secret truth about the world and its ways that *they* don't want you to get hold of.

The editions available have been by no means always accurate. The first publication of *The Hundred and Twenty Days*, early in this century after the manuscript had emerged from its long hibernation since July 1789, was riddled by errors. There is evidence, much of it from gentlemen travellers with an eye for the bizarre, of many editions of

Justine, *Philosophy in the Boudoir* and *Juliette* having been printed on the quiet around Europe, often in small print shops where a few trusted journeymen spent months at the stick on such a job. There might be errata galore in the resulting volumes but the reader would get the drift. French was more widely understood among the educated men of continental Europe, and even among those of Britain and the United States, in the 19th century and the first two decades of the 20th than it is now.

(It is probable that, until the 1950s, no near-accurate and complete edition of any of Sade's works existed in any language but French, unless such a translation were privately produced and circulated.)

Sade's works, in order to have widespread influence among the main formers of opinion in Europe and North America, needed to reach no more than that small minority of the population made up of literate men in possession of power - political, economic and social. In the town bookshop: "One hopes your worship will not take offence if you are invited for a moment into the back room of my emporium and with the suggestion that you might be so good as to find - yes, here it is - this extraordinary volume diverting. One has always been impressed by your worship's breadth of learning and taste, if one may say so. Rather expensive, I'm afraid, but quite an astounding..."

The influence of clandestine works - albeit "not too clandestine" - is by its nature hard to trace. A gentleman would not have Sade's works in plain view on his shelves, where their presence would provoke comment, gossip, prosecution - and perhaps lead to a mention in a visitor's memoirs which might come to inform historians. A gentleman would not usually record the possession or perusal of such works in his diaries and correspondence, except perhaps in code. The dangerous volumes would be in the locked bureau, discussed only with trusted fellow armchair subversives. A gentleman's wife, daughters and servants would not so much as hear of their existence. In the study, late of an evening: "I'll read a little, I think, my dear - don't wait up..."

The masonic movement may well have been a conduit through which Sade's works, and knowledge of them, were passed from man to man. The masons shared Sade's rejection of the Catholic Church and arose as a force opposed to royal governments in 18th-century Europe, as a network of secret masculine societies. This is not to say that Sade's books constituted any kind of text to which masons referred systematically for guidance and inspiration, rather that the iconoclasm of his thinking suited attitudes that drew many men to such brotherhoods and that, within such clandestine and closed networks, writings such as Sade's could circulate in some security.

Sade himself, by the way, was aware of the masons. In *Juliette*, a well-travelled male libertine seeks entry to such an order in Stockholm and interrogation of him by a grandee of the society goes thus:

"*Q*: What are your reasons for loathing the despotism of kings?

"*A*: Envy, jealousy, ambition, pride, anger at being ruled, my own wish to tyrannise others.

"*Q*: In your attitudes, do you give any thought to the well-being of entire nations?

"*A*: I concentrate on my own...

"*Q*: If you were to become powerful and rich, you would put these two endowments at the service of nothing but your pleasures and your whims?

"*A*: These are the only gods I acknowledge, the only delights of my spirit."

The applicant is found to be an A-1 candidate.

One can only assume - but safely, I think - that millions of male minds have been galvanised by the arousing salaciousness of Sade's works, then by their insistent attack on morality, finding in them a revelation, the reader's uneasy and formless urges given shape and expression in black-and-white certainties, arguing that *this* lays down the way to treat the world, especially the women in it.

One can safely assume, also, many widows and children staring in dismay at the contents of late master's private cabinet, the key having been taken from the watch fob of the newly deceased paterfamilias. One can assume also many kindly uncles: "Do not distress yourself. Sometimes a man finds it necessary to resort to diversions that a woman may not comprehend. Pray allow me to remove this disgusting material."

By one means or another, the poison is passed on, as Sade promised from jail he would not **(see chapter 20)**. The looked-for message travels: God is dead; nothing is forbidden; enjoy without limit. The fear and chains are forged anew.

CHAPTER 41: LIKE STEADFAST CHILDREN

Sadeian criminals still exist, in plenty. Sade was writing about an ancient and abiding urge, found in a multiplicity of relationships, although he was mainly concerned with the refined criminal. This figure, so far advanced in vice that he always keeps watch on his impingements and control of his reactions, might seem remote from the world familiar to most of us, that of anger and ecstasy, where the calculated impingement and the assault in cold blood are regarded as rare and abnormal, and are forgiven and understood less readily than is the crime of passion.

However, the rarity of cold-eyed orgiasts laying waste to victims in closed places is hard to determine for they are not likely to be spreading news of what they are doing. Now and again, though, there comes a glimpse that strongly suggests the malign spirit of Silling Castle is still at work - a report of South American prostitutes butchered in the making of a snuff movie for the hard-currency market, the arrest of a loner who turns out to have had three or four women chained in his basement, the trial of a group of men who have recruited children as sexual prey during a long and careful conspiracy, gossip about a batch of girls delivered to a hotel suite of an evening and collected next morning limping and bruised... Rich impingers can have their ways in secure mansions with shows produced to order by modern-day Juliettes, with hush money paid to anyone injured when the play gets rough.

One does not have to be as rich as Croesus, though, to set up an enclosed sexual tyranny on a small scale (compared with the wilder flights of *The Hundred and Twenty Days* and *Juliette*). Many a marriage is just that.

Sade insisted that the greatest criminals would be those who banked their rash youthful fire into a slow burn of brooding intensity that yields only considered actions, nothing spontaneous or rushed. This, he wrote, is the condition necessary for the most profound and enduring satisfaction, as well as the greatest safety against surprise. This state is lived by various amassers of wealth and influence now, as in all periods of history. The example that comes first to mind is that of a mighty organisation such as the mafia, where a young soldier or hit man who shows talent for stepping back from the fury of the fray can become, with time and practice, *capo dei tutti capi* - still hard and committed to crime, but now past rashness, a man of consideration, apart and deep.

Similar are business moguls who pass through the excitement of deals and coups with pulses racing in their early days, on to a steadier style and mode of thought - still breaking market regulations whenever they think they can get away with it, still giving no sucker an even break, still seizing every penny and every advantage, but now playing a longer game, living for a lasting glow of satisfaction - and a lasting fortune - rather than a yelp of delight and the price of a flashy car now and again.

Is detached, controlled criminality attained only at rarefied levels of society, of little relevance to most of us *gens moyens sensuels*? Simone de Beauvoir wrote: "... to inflict delight ... can be a despotic act of violence, and the torturer in the guise of a lover is delighted to see the credulous lover, enraptured with voluptuousness and gratitude, mistake maliciousness for tenderness." That is, you may not know that your lover is taking his or her pleasure from the fact that what he or she is doing to you is making you lose your mind in ecstasy, but you *are* being manipulated and the effect on you is being observed while your lover remains poised, does not join you in dissolving into rapture. The line between the loving gift of pleasure, into which both or all plunge, and calculated puppeteering can be difficult to spot.

Some men cultivate a certain detachment - turning the mind at inflaming moments to their insurance policies or whether they remembered to put out the dustbins - in order to delay their orgasms and so prolong their lover's pleasure. This sort of control is directed by a man at himself to ensure that his lover attains delight before he joins her in spontaneous and further enchantment, and not directed so as to observe more efficiently the range of effects he is having on her. As such, this temporary self-distancing is on the loving side of the line between love and manipulation.

A sure test of whether a man is a sharing lover or a puppet-master is supposed to be his orgasm (if any). What does he do and say as he lets go, lunges out of control? Juliette confirms that is where to inquire: "It's there, my friends, ... that you have to follow a man in order to know him well ...; it's having seen him in the embrace of lubricity ..., his character completely laid bare, ... that you can look for sure into the ... outpourings of his vile heart and of his fearsome passions." Some men call out the woman's name as they come, thus seeming to perform in their apparent derangement *the* act that proves they have melted into her, are truly with her. Truth requires report, though, that this can be achieved through concentrating extra-hard, so as to deceive a woman into believing a man broke free of his apartness.[1]

Let lovers be vigilant and they should spot any indications of detachment. Does it matter? Is ecstasy not ecstasy, whatever is going on in the head of whoever is helping you reach it? Perhaps, but any hint of your partner making you perform, rather than joining you in flights of fancy, should be noted. Detached manipulation by a sexual partner points to danger, which might not turn into horror for a long while but should be dealt with early. The distant lover might remain, for a long while, a manipulator whose effects are delightful, but the nature of his condition as such tends to lead him to want stronger and stronger evidence that he is impinging on the creature under his hands, taking his penis. The calculated caress of the clitoris and flick of the nipple now can become the bite and the twist later; the bite and the twist can become the lash and the bonds. The rehearsed murmur of endearments now can become the snarl of terrifying domination later.

The sooner a distant lover is persuaded to get close and forget himself in frolic, the better. Distant partners get set in their ways, as time passes, and stuck beyond reach. What's more, the loving woman who believes she could know no greater joy, so skilful is her man, though she suspects he is a chilly watcher at heart, might well find new and undreamed-of ecstasy with him once he has got lost in rapture. This does not mean turning herself into the fetish object he might want, but talking him and pleasing him into delighting in what she is and - as time passes - in what she feels happy becoming.

This is tricky ground. For instance, should she shave her legs or not? He wants her to, but is she of the shiny shins the natural woman or the fetish crafted in order to arouse rather than to be loved? If she doesn't shave her legs, what man will she be able to have and hold on to? Then again, these days, are depilated women the norm and so those

1 Libertine men of Sade's literature (and not only there) reach orgasm with terrible curses and blasphemies and insults - a sign of their fierce urge to continue to have an effect on the woman or the group with them, and on the universe in general, even in their moments of *head-fled-to-hell*.

who let their skin go hairy likely to be fetishistic? Well, this merging and dissolving into the Enlightened way to express love takes patience, which helps to make it interesting.

* * *

The impatience with other people, the disrespect for their rights, which leads to sexual crime, and crime of many other kinds, is a dazzling way of life. It can be difficult to remember, and convenient to forget, in face of temptation, that the victims are real and are done real harm. As de Beauvoir wrote of Sade, the arch-criminal desires our "misfortune, subjection and death".

What is to be done? Sade, in his more Enlightened moments, saw the way forward. "When will they choose the science of understanding people to that of locking them up?" he asked. In his fictional Tamoé, the busybody citizens of that warm island would see to it that public nuisances were persuaded, by kindness and concerned argument, to reform. Thus also should children be brought up, as adults rejoice in their rapture and guide them to understand their rage, helping them to courageousness, respect and a sufficient wariness. Much patience is needed.

In trying to diminish the criminality of the world, it is also of prime importance to educate boys and men to use no coercion in seeking to have girls and women. This could be taken to strange lengths. Should all men go about uniformly grey-clad, eyes downcast, like penitents in a story? Should they be allowed, by way of approach to a woman, no more than a standard printed card handed over by a wordless intermediary? No, for we must look for good conduct to stem readily, without need of formal regulation, from the real world, in which we try to create a universal understanding that any woman may give herself for a moment or forever, or never. Again, patience is needed.

There remains an irreducible right to ask for access to another's body, as well as an irreducible right to refuse. Acceptance and refusal are to be received with equal grace. Even so, this does not mean that one may pester any passer-by one fancies; one should use respect in picking the moment and in choosing one's words and gestures. Again, an alert community where there is mutual respect would deal with anyone who was too importunate, just as it would try to persuade users of pictures for sexual contact to drop that and relate to real bodies. Patience, still.

In the light of what is known of the outrages of Sade and other vicious men, should women declare most, or even all, men beyond redemption and shun them? There are separatist women, as well as those who do not go so far as to advocate a total break but who retain barely a flicker of hope for the transformation of men. Despite Sade, despite all the wrongs men have done and continue to do to women and to the universe in general, hope of their reform must remain. Women, like us all, should fight the sins, not the sinners. Men need women in order to learn how they go wrong and how to change for the better. Men, excluded from women's company and attention, would be apt to decline, in a deep and nasty sulk, further into vice in general and harm of women in particular.

Freedom is the goal - freedom from what ails men, freedom for all so that we may all play safely together. Also to that end, men must cease their violence against women, must cease to condone that violence in each other by failing to speak and work to expose and eliminate it.

How shall we enjoy each other, having recognised that much of what we do is harmful and that we are always in danger of causing damage?

Diderot stated that more separated and scattered springs, meaning people unaltered by civilisation, "were broken in one day under a state of law than would break each other in a year under the anarchy of Nature" **(see chapter 30)**.

Sade wrote: "The most perfect being we could imagine would be the one who distanced himself furthest from our conventions and deemed them most contemptible" - but this was belied by the rigid structure of his parasitism whereby the arch-criminal needs his rarity while the rest of the universe continues as object of his contempt and source of his prey.

With a nod to Diderot, we remember that anarchy - life without law because we love each other too well to need law - is indeed where we should be. Yet, while there are criminals, we cannot live without agreeing that certain acts are disallowed, and without protecting ourselves against such acts. Abandonment of all structure and rule will not do, not yet, though we should never forget that this is true freedom.

There remains much to improve - in oneself, in others and in the universe as a whole, before we can frolic at the picnic of free play. Our work is alertness against departures, in ourselves and everywhere, from true community in all relations - at home, at work, fucking, scolding, encouraging, teaching, building... Our work is to foster willingness to offer, and to accept, frank dialogue and selfless endeavour, rather than harangues and greed. There is plenty of grit to grind on, in raising people who are not like us, who are much better, and in maintaining a green and peaceful planet fit for them to inhabit.

Our work is to pursue happiness through love within reason, reason within love - and there can be no love without equality, as Jill Tweedie wrote. One should look at one's lover "carefully with *the world's eyes* as well as the eyes of love," she went on, adding that we should answer each other truthfully, comforting each other if that truth hurts.

That is, we need a love that dares to speak its blame - individual and communal - because we believe in progress pursued through reason, rather than a life reclined in pleasure, exclusion and dreams of apocalypse. That is the way to Keats's

... bower quiet for us, and a sleep
Full of sweet dreams, and health, and quiet breathing.

Without love in reason, reason in love, Sade's great howl of despair and loneliness - arisen from fear of losing himself in communion with a woman and with humanity - will go on.

Looking back on the Marquis de Sade, I see a distraught little boy, done with screaming in the dark to bring comforting attention - and thus bring evidence that he is not alone in the universe, that he exists; done with screaming in the dark to bring attention which has not come. Now he is fretfully pulling apart his toys so as to have *their* attention, at least, by way of substitute for his seeing eyes that gaze on him with a tenderness grown from a patience to explain, to guide, to share his joys, to love him.

Mme de Montreuil, his mother-in-law, doubted that he was capable of being happy **(see chapter 23)**. He was, however, despite it all. So are we, despite it all, if we become like steadfast children, strong and reassured because we are together, each with a hand to hold and so not scared of anything.

BIBLIOGRAPHY

Books by Sade

The complete works - those which are known to have survived - are available in French, from more than one publisher. The 15-volume collection published in Paris by Éditions Pauvert in the mid-1980s is recommended for its reasonable prices and good presentation.

English translations of some of the main works are available, from more than one publisher, but you are likely to find that none of these is other than the work of just two translators, Richard Seaver and Austryn Wainhouse, whose translations first appeared in the 1960s in the USA. Their work is competent in its way but they tend to flatten Sade's prose style, often over-writing and sometimes failing to match the neatness and brilliance of the best stuff. Given the economics of publishing these days, one cannot expect anyone to commission new translations into English of Sade's works, but they have not yet been properly served.

Still with English translations, there are three fat paperback volumes of works by, and commentaries on, Sade from Grove Press in New York. One contains, among other works, *Dialogue between a Priest and a Dying Man*, *Philosophy in the Boudoir*, *Justine* (1791 version), in Seaver/Wainhouse translations, published in 1965. Another volume has *The Hundred and Twenty Days of Sodom*, *Oxtiern*, *Ernestine*, and Simone de Beauvoir's essay *Must One Burn Sade?* from 1951-52 (see below). The essay is translated by Annette Michelson and the Sade items are translated by Seaver and Wainhouse, the whole published in 1966. The third volume is entirely taken up by *Juliette* in Wainhouse's translation, published in 1968.

As far as I know, there is no English version of *Aline and Valcour*. None should be expected, given the said state of publishing and the fact that this novel, which Sade published under his own name, does not carry the scurrilous reputation of his better-known works.

Books about Sade (* referred to in this book)

The main, and the best, biography in French is *Sade Vivant* by Jean-Jacques Pauvert*, in three volumes published by Robert Laffont in Paris, the first having appeared in 1986 and the last in December 1990. This offers first-class research and well-turned presentation of facts. I have drawn on it - as indicated in the text - and have done so gratefully. The book, running to some 1,700 pages, is available only in French. Readers of this book may discover what I think of some of Pauvert's conclusions.

Vie du Marquis de Sade, by Gilbert Lely*, was published in Paris, in two volumes, in the 1950s. As *The Marquis de Sade: A Biography*, in an English translation by Alec Brown, it is usually found these days as a big paperback from Grove Press in New York, published in 1961. Some of the information in this badly organised book has been shown by later research to be wrong. Also, Lely was far too fascinated by Sade to have been able to give a proper account of him. The translation is often clumsy and, in a few places, inaccurate.

The most profound work is Simone de Beauvoir's *Faut-il Brûler Sade?* (*Must One Burn Sade?*)*, an essay published in Paris in 1951-52 and still available in the original French from the publisher Éditions Gallimard in Paris. There is a good English translation in one of the Grove paperback collections of works by and about Sade (see above). The essay offers a summing-up of the meaning of Sade rather than an account of how he lived. Its rigorous abstractions can make it a daunting read. I have tried to draw some of its ideas into my book and to make them more accessible.

One of the best books on Sade before de Beauvoir came along was Geoffrey Gorer's *The Revolutionary Ideas of the Marquis de Sade* (Wishart, London, 1934), revised as *The Life and Ideas of the Marquis de Sade* (Peter Owen, 1953). These are thoughtul and fluent, especially good on the Sadeian urge to impinge on others and on Sade's political ideas. Even so, some of the historical information in them has been shown to be wrong, and they are hard to find nowadays.

Among the other biographies originally written in English - none of them recommended - there is *De Sade: A Critical Biography* by Ronald

Hayman*, which came out in 1978 from Constable in London and Thomas Y. Crowell in New York.

The chapter on Sade in Andrea Dworkin's *Pornography: Men Possessing Women** (The Women's Press in London, Perigee Books in New York, both 1981) gives short shrift to earlier, male authors in the field and shows total respect for women victims of Sade and of other male predators, which is all well and good, but there are factual errors in the small amount of biographical material that is provided.

My view of aspects of *The Sadeian Woman* by Angela Carter* (Virago in London, 1979) is set out in this book.

Other works (* referred to in this book)

The editions I have used of *System of Nature* (*Système de la Nature*) by Holbach*, *Supplement to the Voyage of Bougainville* (*Supplément au Voyage de Bougainville*) by Diderot*, and of works quoting Guillaume Apollinaire*, Charles Sainte-Beuve* and Julien Offroy de La Mettrie* are in French and long since out of print. Also out of print is the French commentary I have used on *The Limits of State Action* by Wilhelm von Humboldt*, who wrote in German. *The Rebel* (*L'Homme Révolté*) by Albert Camus* is available in the original French, published by Éditions Gallimard in Paris. The lines from Keats* are in book one of his poem *Endymion*. The quotation of Jill Tweedie* is from her book *In the Name of Love*, Jonathan Cape, London, 1979, there being also a revised and updated paperback edition, with the same title, from Pan, London, 1988.

MAIN INDEX

NAMES OF WORKS ACCOMPANY AUTHORS' NAMES WHERE APPROPRIATE

ALBARET (servant): 86, 87, 94, 196.

ALLÉE DE SONGY, François, Baron de l': 93-95.

AMBLET, Abbé Jacques François: 12, 16, 57, 59, 163-165, 227, 242, 259, 260, 272, 442, 454.

APOLLINAIRE, Guillaume: 488.

ARGENSON, René Louis, Marquis d': 4, 5.

AUDIBERT (farmer): 306, 362.

BACHAUMONT, Louis Petit de (*Secret Memoirs*): 83, 85.

BARBANTANE (diplomat): 252.

BARRAS, Paul: 371-373.

BARRY, Count du: 39.

The Bastille Revealed: 301.

BAVARIA, Elector of: 4, 5.

BEAUVOIR, Simone de (*Faut-il Brûler Sade?*): 134, 509, 510, 514, 520, 521, 527, 529.

BEAUVOISIN, Mlle: 38-40, 42-44, 45 and note, 46-50, 72, 89, 129, 132, 236, 240, 263, 385, 441, 443, 444, 446, 447, 449, 487.

BERG, Alban (*Lulu*): 505, 506.

BEZONS, Chevalier de: 183.

BIZET, Georges (*Carmen*): 505, 506.

BOISSY (playwright): 308.

BONAPARTE, Napoléon: 381, 383, 386, 390, 399, 400, 403, 406, 485.

BORELLY, Mariette: 78, 79, 81, 83.

BOUCHER (police officer): 204.

BOURDAIS (actor): 72, 82, 357.

BRETEUIL, Baron de: 193, 194, 202.

BRISSAULT (brothel-keeper): 37, 38, 446.

BYRON: 523.

CAMUS, Albert (*The Rebel*): 516.

CARTER, Angela (*The Sadeian Woman*): 465, 467, 488.

CASTÉRA, M de: 16.

CAZADE (public official): 377.

CHABRILLANT, Marquis de: 184, 241.

CHARDIN, Jean (*Travels*): 163.

CHARLES I, Duke of Anjou: 22.

CHAROLAIS, Count de: 484.

CHASTENAY, Victorine de: 373, 374.

CHENON, M (clerk): 285, 286.

CHOISEUL, Chevalier de: 48.

CICERO: 159.

COLET, Mlle: 36-38, 45, 89, 129, 236, 298, 441, 443, 447.

Collection of the List of Former Aristocrats: 301.

CONDÉ, Louis Henri de Bourbon, Prince de: 3-5.

CONDÉ, Louis Joseph de Bourbon, Prince de: 6, 9. 21, 436, 508.

CONDÉ, Princess de: 3-5.

CONTI, Prince de: 52.

COPERNICUS: 419.

CORBIN (tapestry-maker): 62.

CORDAY, Charlotte: 339.

CORDIER, Jacques René: 26, 27, 71.

COSSÉ-BISSAC, Louis Hercule Timoléon, Duke de: 351, 355, 356.

COSTE, Marguerite: 79, 81, 83, 85.

COSTE, Rose: 78, 81.

COULMIER, François Simonet de: 384-387, 389, 390, 394, 397, 398, 405, 406.

COURTOIS (lawyer): 377, 395.

COUTHON, Georges: 358, 359, 361.

CROËZER, Anne Thérèse: 27.

CROSNE, M de (police chief): 273.

DAMIENS, Robert François: 259.

DEGUISE (surgeon): 397.

DESCARTES, René: 197, 439, 445.

DESTOUCHES (playwright): 308.

DIDEROT, Denis (*Supplément au Voyage de Bougainville*): 420-423, 430, 435, 440, 481, 530.

DORVILLE, Mlle: 49.

DOUET DE LA BOULAYE, M: 38, 39, 47, 48.

DUCLOS, Lieutenant: 94.

DUFFÉ, Gothon: 97, 104, 116, 143, 144, 147, 153, 205, 216, 232, 270, 320.

DURAND, Father: 124, 125.

DWORKIN, Andrea (*Pornography: Men Possessing Women*): 517.

ESPRIT DE JÉSUS, Mother: 238.

ESQUIROL, Father Jean Étienne Dominique: 385, 386.

FAGE, Antoine: 69, 73, 82, 83, 87, 88, 96, 98, 371.

FINOT (notary): 400.

FLEURIEU, Présidente de: 305, 306.

FLORE, Mlle: 389, 390.

FOUCHÉ, Joseph: 381, 383, 390, 397-400, 407.

FOUQUIER-TINVILLE, Antoine Quentin: 360.

The Friend of the Laws: 381.

GALILEO: 419.

GAUFRIDY, Charles: 369, 376, 395.

GAUFRIDY, Elzéar: 362, 376.

GAUFRIDY, Gaspard François Xavier: 98-106, 109, 112-120, 123, 125, 126, 128-130, 134, 135, 140-144, 146, 147, 149, 150-152, 177, 179-182, 188, 191, 214-218, 239, 260, 268, 271, 273, 277, 279, 282, 283, 286-289, 291-295, 297, 300, 301, 303-307, 309, 312, 314, 316-319, 321, 323, 325, 327, 328, 332, 333, 335, 336, 340, 344, 357, 358, 362-364, 369-371, 373-378, 394-396, 401, 404, 455, 456, 458.

GIROUARD, Jean Joseph: 303, 353, 354, 362, 380, 463.

GIROUARD, the widow: 362.

GOUPIL, Inspector: 97. 98, 127.

GOURDAN (brothel-keeper): 234.

The Handsome Boy: 169.

HANRIOT (Revolutionary): 360, 361.

HAYMAN, Ronald (*De Sade: A Critical Biography*): 435.

HECQUET (brothel-keeper): 49.

HENRI II, King of France: 195.

History of the Troubadours: 163.

History of Vampires: 161.

HOLBACH, Paul Henri, Baron d' (*Système de la Nature*): 161, 199, 438, 439.

HUMBOLDT, Wilhelm von (*The Limits of State Action*): 423, 424, 499.

IBERTI, Doctor Giuseppe: 122, 220.

JOHN XXII, Pope: 2.

JUSPEL (police officer): 351, 354.

KEATS, John (*Endymion*): 531.

KELLER, Rose: 53-59, 61, 67, 74, 77, 82, 89, 115, 132, 265, 294, 448, 451, 452, 509.

LACLOS, Pierre Choderlos de (*Les Liaisons Dangereuses*): 278, 358.

LA JEUNESSE (alias Carteron, valet): 93, 104, 114, 127, 163, 215, 220, 225, 238, 245-247, 272, 348.

LALANDE, Joseph Jérôme Lefrançois de: 230.

LAMBALLE, Marie Thérèse de Savoie-Carignan, Princess de: 323.

LA METTRIE, Julien Offroy de: 439, 440, 513.

LANGEVIN, Mlle: 71, 72, 181.

LANGLOIS (valet): 53.

LA REVELLIÈRE-LÉPEAUX, Louis Marie de: 371.

LATOUR (valet): 77-79, 81, 84, 93, 94, 104, 142, 167, 232, 341, 411, 512.

LAUGIER, Mariannette: 78, 81.

LAUNAY, Anne Prospère de (sister-in-law of Marquis de S): 71-77, 81, 82, 85-89, 91, 92, 132, 141, 258 note, 271, 327, 370, 390, 416, 442, 447, 449, 455, 520.

LAUNAY, Françoise Pélagie de (later Marquise de Wavrin - sister-in-law of Marquis de S): 140, 180.

LAUNAY, Bernard René Jourdan, Marquis de (Governor of the Bastille): 258, 268, 269, 273, 280, 283-285, 348.

LAUNAY, Major de (Governor of Miolans jail): 93-95.

LAURIS, Laure Victoire Adeline de: 22-25, 28, 30, 31, 37, 236, 437, 442, 445-447, 449, 520, 522..

LAVERNE, Marianne: 77, 78, 81, 83, 85.

LEBLANC (*The Druids*): 221.

LECLERC, Magdeleine: 410-416, 501.

LECLERC, Mme: 410-413.

LEFEBVRE (acquaintance of Magdeleine Leclerc): 414.

LEFÈVRE (servant): 229-231, 348, 508.

LELY, Gilbert (*Vie du Marquis de Sade*): 176, 435.

LE NOIR, Jean Charles: 139, 164, 174, 175, 188-192, 194, 196, 197, 201, 226, 227, 245, 249 note, 269, 273, 285, 286.

LE NORMAND (woodseller): 393-395.

LE PELETIER DE SAINT FARGEAU, Louis Michel: 339.

LIGNERAC, Marquis de: 37.

LOSME-SALBRAY, Antoine Jérôme de: 258, 269, 273.

LOUIS XIV, King of France: 20, 26, 518.

LOUIS XV, King of France: 4, 14, 20, 30, 37, 55, 56, 65-67, 102, 269 note, 389, 484.

LOUIS XVI, King of France: 119, 142, 183, 199, 281, 283, 288-290, 309-312, 322, 324, 328, 333, 360, 406, 464, 473.

LOUIS XVIII, King of France: 406.

LOUVOIS, Marquis de: 39, 47, 48.

MARAIS, Antoine Thomas: 146.

MARAIS, Inspector Louis: 34, 37, 38, 44 note, 47, 48, 51, 58, 59, 127, 143, 145, 146, 153, 167, 170, 174, 177, 178, 194, 205, 206, 284, 394, 441, 451, 461.

MARAT, Jean Paul: 339, 359.

MARIE ANTOINETTE, Queen of France: 311.

MARIVAUX (playwright): 308.

MARTIN, Mlle: 238.

MASSÉ, Nicolas: 380.

MAUPAS, Roulhac du: 406, 410, 412.

MAUREPAS, Jean Frédéric Phelypeaux, Count de: 182, 239.

MÉNIL, Doctor: 122, 220, 252 and note, 253.

MERIMÉE, Prosper: 505, 506.

MIRABEAU, Honoré Gabriel de Riqueti, Count de: 157, 158, 194, 289.

MOLIÈRE (playwright): 308.

MOLINA, M: 197 note.

MOLÉ (actor): 298, 335.

The Monitor: 300.

MONTAIGNE, Michel de: 420.

MONTALIVET, Count de: 398.

MONTGOLFIER, brothers: 259.

MONTIGNY (brothel-keeper): 231.

MONTREUIL, Claude René Cordier de Launay, Président de (father-in-law of Marquis de S): 27, 29, 32, 36, 59, 83, 132, 137, 144, 196 note, 197 and note, 198, 235, 241, 275, 323, 324, 335, 338, 340, 341, 363.

MONTREUIL, Marie Madeleine, Présidente de (*née* Masson de Plissay - mother-in-law of Marquis de S): 27-30, 32, 34-36, 38, 40-48, 50, 57-68, 71, 73, 74, 77, 86, 87, 89, 91 and note, 93, 95-100, 102, 104-107, 109, 110, 112-120, 123, 124, 126, 128-131, 133, 135-138, 140-142, 145-150, 152, 161, 163,

172, 177-184, 186, 189, 191, 192, 196-201, 204, 217, 224, 233-235, 240-242, 247, 253, 254, 261, 267, 271, 273, 277, 289, 290, 293, 304, 305, 324, 340, 341, 363, 369, 378, 452, 453, 455, 458-460, 531.

NANON (alias Annette Sablonnière): 103, 113, 115-118, 123, 149, 175, 176.

NODIER, Charles: 384.

NOVES, Laure de: 10, 11, 162, 318.

OLIVIER, Chancellor François: 195.

OLONNE, Duke d': 183, 231.

OSMONT, Count d': 68.

PASCAL, Blaise: 462, 516.

PAUVERT, Jean Jacques (*Sade Vivant*): 47, 171, 197 and note, 202, 220, 258, 259, 267, 277, 285, 303, 347, 350, 367, 392, 405, 458, 486-488, 499.

PAYAN (farmer): 362.

PERRIN, Noël: 370.

PETRARCH, Francis: 10, 11, 162.

PIUS VI, Pope: 312, 488.

PLAN, Mlle du: 115, 175.

POITOU, William, Count of: 163.

Le Portier des Chartreux: 413.

POULTIER, François Martin: 381.

POYANNE, Marquis de: 7, 14.

PUGET, Pierre François de Rivière du: 270.

QUESNET, Charles: 306, 356, 369, 374 note, 377, 392.

QUESNET, Mme Marie Constance (*née* Renelle): 306-309, 317, 319, 336, 340, 344, 346, 354, 356, 361, 363, 364, 367, 369-374, 376, 377, 379, 382, 384, 386, 387, 391-393, 395, 398, 401, 405, 407, 409 note, 410, 411, 416, 456, 463, 499, 501, 519.

QUIDOR, Inspector: 284.

RAMEAU (composer): 430.

RAMEAU, du (procuress): 33.

RAMON, Doctor L J: 416.

RAOUSSET, Lady de (cousin of Marquis de S): 296, 297.

REGNARD (playwright): 308.

REINAUD (lawyer): 129, 290, 298, 303, 305, 307, 308, 333, 463.

RÉVEILLON, Jean Baptiste: 282, 283.

REWBELL, Jean François: 371.

RICHARDSON, Samuel (*Clarissa*): 210, 278.

RIPERT, François: 69, 70, 97-100, 118, 119, 123, 185, 275, 321, 403-405.

RIVIÈRE, Mlle: 51-52.

ROBESPIERRE, Maximilien de: 339, 352-355, 359, 361, 363.

ROCHEFORT, Armand de: 389, 390.

ROUGEMONT, Charles de: 156-158, 161, 174, 194, 198, 224, 227, 228, 256.

ROUSSEAU, Jean Jacques (*Confessions*): 161.

ROUSSET, Marie Dorothée de: 147, 151, 161, 163, 177-182, 187, 191, 194, 202-219, 222, 225, 229, 231, 232, 237, 239, 250, 270, 271, 346, 348, 420, 454, 455, 472.

ROVÈRE, Joseph Stanislas de: 367, 368.

ROVÈRE, the widow: 401-403.

ROYER-COLLARD, Doctor Antoine Athanase: 397, 406.

SABLONNIÈRE, Annet: 117, 118.

SADE, Caroline Laure de (sister of Marquis de S): 4, 436.

SADE, Donatien Claude Armand de (younger son of Marquis de S): 66, 71, 74, 78, 88, 137, 138, 180, 189, 190, 275, 290, 296, 297, 314, 322-325, 365, 383, 393, 396, 399-405, 412, 416.

SADE, Gabrielle Éléonore de (Abbess of St Benoît at Cavaillon - aunt of Marquis de S): 41, 179.

SADE, Gaspard François de (grandfather of Marquis de S): 3, 4, 8, 416.

SADE, Hugues de (ancestor of Marquis de S): 2, 10.

SADE, Jean Baptiste François, Count de (father of Marquis de S): 1, 3, 4, 5, 8, 9, 14-20, 22, 25, 27-30, 32, 34, 35, 39, 50, 51, 55, 56, 90, 378, 442, 452, 455, 460.

SADE, Abbé de (Jacques François Paul Aldonse - uncle of Marquis de S): 9, 10, 17, 19, 27-30, 32, 34, 35, 39-47, 50, 51, 58, 60-66, 69, 73, 76, 77, 88, 92, 98, 102, 104-106, 109-113, 115, 118, 162, 229, 275 note, 371, 416, 436, 441, 442, 455, 511.

SADE, Joachim de (ancestor of Marquis de S): 3.

SADE, Louis Marie de (elder son of Marquis de S): 51, 58, 60, 64, 65, 71, 74, 88, 137, 138, 180, 189, 190, 240, 241, 274, 290, 296, 297, 313, 322-325, 364, 365, 373, 376 note, 383, 399-404, 416.

SADE, Louise Aldonze de (*née* d'Astouaud de Murs - grandmother of Marquis de S): 8, 436, 441.

SADE, Madeleine Laure de (daughter of Marquis de S): 67, 71, 74, 88, 137, 138, 181, 189, 190, 272, 273, 287, 290 note, 296, 404.

SADE, Marie Éléonore, Countess de (*née* Maillé de Carman - mother of Marquis de S): 1, 3, 4, 5, 9, 12, 18, 29, 30, 59, 60, 61, 65, 90, 127, 128, 130, 436, 441.

SADE, Marie Françoise de (sister of Marquis de S): 4, 436.

SADE, Paul de (ancestor of Marquis de S): 1, 10.

SADE, Raimond de (ancestor of Marquis de S): 1.

SADE, Renée Pélagie, Marquise de (*née* de Montreuil - wife of Marquis de S): 25, 28, 30-32, 35, 36, 40-44, 47, 50, 58-74, 81, 82, 87, 88, 90, 91, 94-115, 117, 121-124, 128, 130-140, 142-144, 147, 148, 152, 153, 157, 158, 160, 164, 168-172, 177, 178, 180, 183, 185-187, 189-192, 194, 196, 197, 199, 200, 202, 203, 205, 208, 209, 212-217, 219-242, 244, 248-256, 258-260, 263, 267, 268, 270-277, 279, 280, 282, 283, 285-288, 290-296, 307, 320, 323, 325, 348, 364, 367-369, 371, 373, 374, 391, 402-404, 412, 414, 444, 452, 455, 456, 458, 462, 465, 520.

SADE, Richard Jean Louis, Commander de (uncle of Marquis de S): 9, 83, 105, 107, 145, 146, 177, 179, 275 note, 279, 293, 296, 365.

SADE D'EYGUIÈRES, Jean Baptiste Joseph David, Count de: 152, 399.

SADE D'EYGUIÈRES, Louise Gabrielle Laure de (daughter-in-law of Marquis de S): 399, 400.

SAIGNES, Lieutenant-Colonel de: 67.

SAINT-BEUVE, Charles: 523.

SAINT-FLORENTIN, Louis de (Duke de la Vrillière): 34, 59, 60, 65.

SAINT-LAURENT, Mme de: 179.

SANCHEZ, Father: 13, 197.

SARTINE, Antoine de: 34, 139, 176, 198 and note, 248.

SARTRE, Jean Paul: 462.

SERGE, Victor (*Conquered City*): 511 note.

SHAKESPEARE: 11, 261.

SIMIANE, Diane de: 3.

SORANS, Marie Louise Élisabeth Maillé de Carman, Marquise de: 183-186, 305, 348.

SOTON, Mlle: 319, 320.

STAËL, Mme de (*Delphine*): 391.

SWIFT, Jonathan (*Gulliver's Travels*): 279.

SWINBURNE, Walter: 425.

TALARU, Delphine, Countess de (*née* Rozière-Sorans; Countess de Clermont-Tonnerre through first marriage): 397, 398, 410, 415, 487, 488.

TEISSIER (valet): 16.

TERRIS, Doctor: 370, 372.

TESTARD, Jeanne (fan-maker and prostitute): 33-35, 42 note, 55, 67, 73, 77, 89, 166, 350, 448, 449, 460.

Theatre Journal: 300.

THEOCRITUS (*The Idylls*): 511 note.

TITIAN: 121.

TOLSTOY, Leo (*War and Peace*): 366.

TORQUEMADA: 198.

TOUR, Chevalier de la: 39.

TOUR, Count de la (of Savoy): 86-90.

TRILLET, Catherine: 124-127, 141, 175, 465 note.

TRILLET (weaver): 124-129, 141, 501.

TWEEDIE, Jill (*In the Name of Love*): 531.

VIDAL, Canon: 151.

VILLEDEUIL, M de: 280, 284.

VILLENEUVE-MARTIGNAN, Henriette Victoire, Marquise de (*née* de Sade - aunt of Marquis de S): 179, 296, 297.

VILLETERQUE, Alexandre Louis de: 382.

VILLETTE, Marquis de: 230, 238.

VILLETTE, Marquise de: 229, 230, 238, 312, 313, 333.

VIOLON, Joseph: 95.

VOLTAIRE: 9, 215, 222, 230, 312.

WEDEKIND, Frank: 505, 506.

WEISS, Peter (*The Persecution and Assassination of Marat as Performed by the Inmates of the Asylum of Charenton under the Direction of the Marquis de Sade*): 385.

WILSON, Edmund: 418 note.

INDEX OF WORKS BY THE MARQUIS DE SADE

Address of a Citizen of Paris to the King of the French: 310.

Adélaïde of Brunswick: 409, 410.

Aline and Valcour: 6, 7, 8, 12, 14, 277, 278, 283, 287, 292, 331, 354 note, 362, 365-367, 373, 378, 405, 426, 427, 431, 432, 442, 459, 471-474, 486, 518, 519, 521, 529.

The Bachelor: 222.

The Boudoir or The Credulous Husband: 298, 334.

Confessions: 278.

Conrad: 391.

The Conversations at Charmelle Castle: 380, 407.

Count Oxtiern: 300, 302, 375, 379.

The Days of Florbelle: 407, 409.

Dialogue between a Priest and a Dying Man: 166, 167, 277.

Ernestine: 300, 302.

He Who Was Soured by Love: 298, 299 note, 442.

The Hundred and Twenty Days of Sodom: 101, 108, 259-261, 268, 276 note, 277, 287, 291, 292, 302, 331, 418, 419, 453, 457, 464, 466-471, 486, 499, 500, 502, 503, 507, 509, 511, 518-520, 522, 523, 526.

Italian Journey: 220.

Jeanne Laisné or The Siege of Beauvais: 164, 374.

Juliette, The Story of: 267, 366, 367, 378, 380-382, 389, 392, 407, 416, 426, 429, 430, 434, 437, 452, 453, 486-498, 500-503, 505, 507, 508, 510, 513-515, 517-519, 521, 524-527.

Justine: 278, 303, 308, 331, 353, 366, 367, 372, 378, 380-383, 389, 391, 392, 397, 407, 410, 416, 426, 431, 456, 460, 463-465, 486, 490, 518, 521, 522, 524.

The Man of Whim: 163, 164.

Marcel: 391.

The Marquise de Gange: 409.

On the Way to Approve Laws: 328-331.

Philosophy in the Boudoir: 365-367, 378, 380, 407, 417, 427, 428, 444, 474-489, 492 note, 508, 509, 511, 514, 518-520, 524.

The Portfolio of a Man of Letters: 277, 278.

Refutation of Fénelon: 409.

Secret History of Isabelle of Bavaria: 409, 410.

The Seducer: 298, 300.

Tancrède: 260.

The Unequal Man: 301.

AN APPEAL

The author recommends to you the charity Womankind Worldwide, which provides funds for various projects throughout the world.

It helps to set up and run houses of refuge in big cities for homeless women and girls, to finance educational projects, as well as farming, manufacturing and marketing co-operatives run by and for women, and other such initiatives.

Women thus protected and empowered are less likely to become slaves or prey.

Womankind Worldwide is at: 122 Whitechapel High Street, London E1 7PT, England; telephone 071-247 6931; fax 071-247 3436.

The people there would be glad to send you further information.

Please help.

This appeal on behalf of Womankind Worldwide was unsolicited and the charity is in no way responsible for the content of this book.